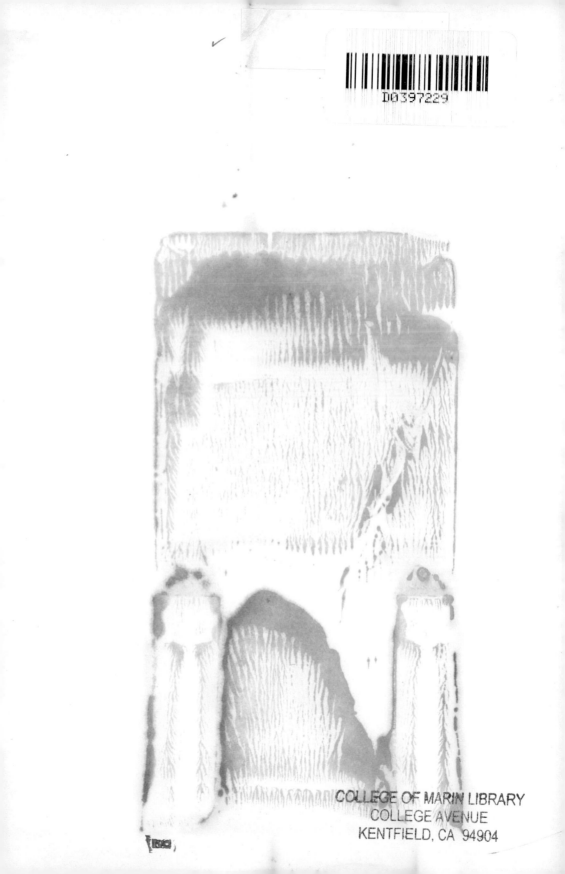

The History Makers

Leaders and Statesmen of the 20th Century
Edited by Lord Longford & Sir John Wheeler-Bennett

Chronologies and editorial assistance
by Christine Nicholls

The History
Makers

St. Martin's Press New York

Printed in Great Britain
Designed by Paul Watkins
Picture research by Anne-Marie Ehrlich

Library of Congress Catalog Card No. 73-79066
First published in the United States of America in 1973

Contents

The chapters have been placed in the order of their subjects' birth

Introduction

In the great convolutions of history it is true to say that events are either loosed or controlled by outstanding individuals, or that the events themselves produce eminent persons, who, in their turn, exercise notable influence on their times. It is not unusual to debate which of these influences is the more potent, or indeed whether only one of them exists at all. It will be remembered that at the inauguration of Jefferson Davis as the Provisional President of the Confederate States of America, it was said of him that, 'the Man and the Hour have met', and this would seem to strike a fair balance between the two. On the other hand, John Drinkwater has written of Oliver Cromwell and Abraham Lincoln that each in his day was 'the lord of his event', and certain it is that both of these attributes could be applied to a Winston Churchill or to a Franklin Roosevelt.

This, in effect, is what *The History Makers* is about. The twentieth century has seen more profound changes than any other period of history. In the course of its unfinished span man has passed from the horse-and-buggy stage to the possibility of lunar travel. Political upheavals and catastrophic wars have affected every person in every country. Great social, economic, and scientific revolutions have changed the daily lives of each of us.

These great events have coincided with the appearance of great personalities. Such men as Winston Churchill, Franklin Roosevelt, and Woodrow Wilson in the interests of freedom; such men as Hitler, Lenin, and Mussolini in the name of authoritarianism—all held the fate of the world in their hands. They moulded or rent it, built or destroyed, wrought constructively or destructively upon the wide panoramic stage of history. They were 'the lords of their events', the titanic artists who 'splashed at a ten league canvas with brushes of comet's hair'; they were the great doers of good or evil, who, born of the concatenation of the stars, clashed in the firmament of world affairs.

The History Makers is about some of these world leaders who presided over and, in many cases, brought about these momentous events of the twentieth century, and in each case the essays have been written by persons who are recognized experts in their fields. They tell the story of the history makers' lives and assess their places in the twentieth century. Many of the authors knew their subjects personally, and provide anecdotes from their own experiences.

6

In the compilation of this book there has been no attempt to present a standardized pattern; each author has been given freedom to write of his or her subject without regard to the views of each other, which, in some cases, may be seen to conflict in some degree. We laid down no hard and fast rules as to how the authors should approach their subject, other than that of adopting a broad chronological framework. Complete independence of thought has been assured, in that only the editors have read all of the contributions before publication.

At the outset it was decided to confine the scope of the book to the field of politics and statesmanship, thus intentionally excluding philosophy, science, economics, etc. Certain 'ground rules' were established, but were inevitably violated. For example, it had been our intention not to include any living persons, but exceptions have been made in the case of President de Valera and Mr Kenyatta, in the latter case because it seemed essential to us to include a representative of emergent Africa. Similarly, we had hoped to include a woman among our history makers, but for one reason or another we were compelled, most regretfully, to forgo this ambition. But we are happy to include two distinguished women historians among our contributors.

At first we hoped to standardize the length of the chapters. However, in the case of men like Roosevelt and Stalin whose careers dominated the century, or Adenauer whose career was exceptionally long, this did not prove possible.

We are conscious, too, of certain omissions. Readers may regret the absence of a number of names. We ourselves regret the absence of Aristide Briand, Venizelos, Mustapha Kemal Ataturk, Pilsudski, Chaim Weizman, and Thomas Masaryk, all of whom contributed substantially to the history making of the twentieth century. Others may have different candidates for inclusion. But despite the obvious limitations of space, the editors have included, with a few arguable exceptions, what in their opinion are the statesmen and leaders of 'the first league'. At any rate, we feel confident that the collection of essays here presented offers a remarkable cross-section of the outstanding history makers of the twentieth century and, moreover, a feast of fascinating reading.   *John Wheeler-Bennett & Frank Longford*

Clemenceau

by Lewis Douglas

LEWIS DOUGLAS was born in 1894 in Bisbee, Arizona, a State with which he has continued to be closely associated in mining, ranching, banking and general business. Having graduated from Amherst College and from the Massachusetts Institute of Technology in 1916, he taught history at Amherst for a short period before serving as a 1st Lieutenant in the Field Artillery during the First World War. In 1923 he embarked on a political career. He served in the Arizona House of Representatives from 1923 to 1925 and as Congressman-at-large from Arizona from 1927 to 1933 when he was appointed Director of the Budget by President Franklin D. Roosevelt. From this office he resigned in 1934. He returned briefly to academic life in 1938 as Principal and Vice-Chancellor of McGill University.

Throughout the Second World War Lewis Douglas was identified with the vital problem of logistics, first as Deputy Administrator of the War Shipping Administration and later as a member of the Combined Shipping Adjustment Board. After the Unconditional Surrender of the German Armed Forces, he was Special Adviser to General Lucius D. Clay on the Allied Control Council. In 1947 he was appointed United States Ambassador to the Court of St James's by President Harry S. Truman, a post which he held with great distinction until 1950.

Clemenceau

28 Sept. 1841	Born in Mouilleron-en-Pareds.
1860	Studied medicine in Nantes and Paris. Attracted to republican opposition to Napoleon III.
1865	Went to U.S. Remained in New England for three years, teaching French in a girls' school.
1869	Married Mary Plummer, who later had two daughters and a son. They separated after seven years.
1869	Returned to Paris.
1870	Elected mayor of Montmartre, Paris.
8 Feb. 1871	Elected as Radical in National Assembly at Bordeaux, where he voted against preliminaries of peace to end Franco-German war.
18 March 1871	Execution by mutinous soldiers of Generals Lécomte and Clément Thomas which he tried to prevent— brought him into collision with central committee of National Guard (illegal government in Paris).
23 July 1871	Elected to Paris municipal council.
1875	Became President of Paris municipal council.
1876	Was elected to Chamber of Deputies. Became leader of Radical section.
1879	Clemenceau demanded indictment of Duc de Broglie's Ministry.
1880	Clemenceau started newspaper *La Justice*, which became principal organ of Radicals in Paris. Built up reputation as political critic and

Previous page: Monument to greatness—French statue of Clemenceau

destroyer of ministries, but would not take office himself.

1885 Re-elected to old seat of the Var.

1892 Panama Scandal.

1893 Lost his seat and for nine years confined his activities to journalism.

1894 Captain Dreyfus convicted of treason.

1897 Founded *L'Aurore*. Supported Zola, whose exposé of the Dreyfus affair appeared in *L'Aurore*.

1900 Founded weekly review, *Le Bloc*.

6 April 1902 Was elected senator for the Var. Sat with Radicals and supported ministry of Emile Combes.

June 1903 Undertook direction of *L'Aurore*. Led campaign for revision of Dreyfus verdict.

March 1906 Fall of Rouvier Ministry at last brought Clemenceau to power as Minister of Interior in Ferdinand Sarrien's Cabinet.

1 May 1906 Strike of miners in Pas-de-Calais. Clemenceau resolved to use military, which alienated Socialist party.

Oct. 1906 Became Premier.

1907-8 New entente with Britain cemented.

1908 Franco-German rivalry for influence in Morocco.

20 July 1909 Defeated in Chamber during discussion on state of navy. Succeeded as Premier by Aristide Briand.

1911 Entered Senate again. Was convinced Germany meant war and did not want France to be unprepared.

May 1913 Founded daily paper *L'Homme Libre*, with himself as editor.

Aug. 1914 Beginning of World War I.

Sept. 1914 *L'Homme Libre* censored and suppressed. It reappeared two days later as *L'Homme Enchaîné*. Clemenceau strove to create a 'will to victory'.

Nov. 1917 President Poincaré asked Clemenceau to form government. He concentrated on war, making it clear that France wanted nothing but absolute victory.

March 1918 Germans launched great assault on Anglo-French line. Clemenceau joined in organising unity of command with Foch at the head.

11 Nov. 1918 Germany signed armistice.

1918-19 Preparation of Peace of Versailles. Clemenceau was president of the peace conference at Paris.

11 Nov. 1919 New Chamber elected.

20 Jan. 1920 Clemenceau's Cabinet fell. Alexandre Millerand became Premier.

1922 Clemenceau sailed for U.S. when it appeared that U.S. was seeking to dissociate itself from European affairs. Triumphant progress through U.S. towns.

1927 Published *Au Soir de la Pensée*.

24 Nov. 1929 Died at Paris while at work on his memoirs.

One of the most striking features in the history of the western world during the span of the last three-quarters of a century is that on the occasion of two great convulsions we have been saved by old men, well beyond the three score years and ten; men of wide experience; men of dedication to the public welfare; men of great cultivation and knowledge of history with a capacity to interpret their knowledge; men, dauntless and of unflinching courage and determination, with wide intellectual horizons; men who acknowledged no prospect of defeat, whose voices and personalities inspired their countrymen to reach the utmost heights of patriotism.

Both Sir Winston Churchill and Georges Eugene Benjamin Clemenceau were saviours of the western world, each in his own time—one during the latter part of the second decade of the twentieth century; the other only a quarter of a century later. Both came to the rescue of our civilization when the clouds of defeat hung heavily. Both were repudiated by the countries they saved—Churchill in the election of 1945 and Clemenceau when he failed to give his approval to a proposition contrary to his beliefs which, had he agreed, would have swept him into the most honoured office, the Presidency, of the Republic of France. But to him intellectual integrity was a greater and more enduring insignia of fame than high public office.

Georges Eugene Benjamin Clemenceau first opened his eyes on an uncertain world on 28 September 1841, in Mouilleron-en-Pareds in the Vendée. The world was to remain, for him at least, in a state of uncertainty throughout the span of his life. He grew up to be a person of very strong will and unflagging determination, with an inquisitive mind hungering for what he called 'realities'.

In books he found an escape from the dullness of adolescence. His reading was broad, covering everything in print that attracted his penetrating intelligence, in particular philosophy, science and history as they revealed the experiences and the emotions of the human race from its beginning.

For his father he had a deep affection and admiration. In him he found a consoling friendship and mental companionship. Dr Paul Benjamin Clemenceau was a person with compassion for those who possessed few of the amenities of life. His opposition to the Church, as firm as was his hostility to monarchy, inevitably brought him into open conflict with the regime of Napoleon III and caused him to be held in prison in Marseilles, pending transport to a penal colony in Algeria. Local indignation throughout the Vendée, however, was so intense at this miscarriage of justice that Clemenceau *père* was finally released.

The son vowed that he would revenge this act of injustice. To this sworn object of his life he remained always faithful. But his father, noting his anger and his determination, said to him, 'If you wish to avenge me—work!'

The portrait of Clemenceau when a very young man suggests that his appearance was serious but as engaging as it was handsome. Clemenceau's high cheekbones and his eyes that on occasion seemed to be somewhat slanted gave him a slightly Mongolian look which did not detract from his charm.[1] But in whatsoever stage of his career or in whatsoever circumstance, Clemenceau's appearance, with or without his drooping moustache, had a

12

magnetism which attracted wide attention and set him apart from other men.

The rugged nature of the country in which he was born, its own legendary mythology, his compatability with the peasants and the worship he had for his father moulded the general point of view and attitude toward society which was to make Clemenceau throughout his life an *enfant terrible* in French politics. Always a very simple man himself—in manner, in speech and in dress—he hated pomposity in all its forms with a characteristic violence. An independent man, he developed skills with his tongue, pen, pistol and sword which caused most men to shrink from challenging him on the field of honour or the public rostrum. Indeed, the fame of his talents with these weapons spread like 'the voice of the turtle' throughout the land.

His father's profession naturally appealed to him for he had inherited a deep sympathy for the less privileged. Accordingly, he went to school in Nantes and completed his medical education at the University of Paris.

England intrigued his inquisitive mind and induced him to take a voyage to London. There he met John Stuart Mill and made a reciprocal arrangement for translation with him. This was the beginning of a strong friendliness for Great Britain which remained with him throughout his life.

His curiosity was aroused by what he had heard and read about the new democracy on the far side of the Atlantic, this vast 'land of the free'. And so he set sail for the port of New York late in the year 1865. He travelled far and formed acquaintances with a wide variety of important figures, in and out of politics. He taught French and equitation at a girl's school, Miss Aiken's, near Stamford, Connecticut. There he met Miss Mary Plummer. The two young people were married on 23 June 1869 in New York in a civil ceremony, 'without benefit of clergy' for Clemenceau had early in life vowed to take no sacrament before an altar. They then sailed for France.

Not long afterwards, the Franco-Prussian War began and the defeat of France was rendered inevitable with the surrender of McMahon's army in Sedan, Bazaine's army in Metz and the capture of Napoleon.

Clemenceau, a few years before as the editor of *Le Travail*, had been imprisoned. The newspaper had been closed for being anti-monarchist. For this reason and because he had generated a large, friendly following among the people of Montmartre, Arago, on becoming Mayor of Paris, made Clemenceau the Mayor of that *arrondissement*.

The Napoleonic dynasty and the Third Empire received their final *coup de grâce* when Léon Gambetta introduced in the National Assembly a proclamation declaring them to be at an end. A period of change had dawned.

With the occupation of Paris by the Prussians, the National Assembly met at Bordeaux. To this Assembly, Clemenceau had been overwhelmingly elected as a Deputy for the city of Paris. His fame had begun to spread. The members of the Assembly, mostly of a reactionary cast, approved almost without debate the Prussian terms of peace which included the cession of the province of Alsace and a very large part of the province of Lorraine.

Clemenceau, bitterly opposed to the loss of any territory, advocated that France should fight on and that there should be no surrender. Throughout the remainder of his life one of his guiding passions was the recapture of those two provinces. A half a century later, when as President of the Peace

Conference at Versailles in 1919 and the sole surviving member of the Assembly that had met in Bordeaux in 1870, he saw his dream come to pass. The crepe that had been hung in sorrow upon the statue of Strasbourg in the Place de la Concorde was finally removed in a ceremony that was as dignified as it was gay.

Meanwhile, a Republic had been established with conservatives and reactionaries, many of them monarchists, under Thiers, who was temporarily in control of the machinery of government. Unable to control Paris, Thiers abandoned her and established the capital at Versailles.

It was during Clemenceau's time as Mayor of Montmartre that a significant event occurred which left an enduring mark upon his thinking. A number of pieces of artillery had been taken by the citizens of Montmartre from one of the parks of Paris and had been located on the Butte. Generals Le Compte and Clemont-Thomas were sent at the head of troops to recapture them. A gathering of Montmartrois met them, at first in a rather friendly and unobstructive mood, but when they resisted the taking of the artillery and Le Compte ordered the troops to fire on the mob—which they in complete insubordination refused to do—the crowd became angrier and angrier, seized the generals and took them off to the Chateau Rouge.

Clemenceau, who was in the Mairie, heard of the violence of the mob and, fearing for the generals' lives, started to elbow his way to the old dance hall through the ferocious crowd. The fury of the rabble was transferred from the generals to the Mayor who formerly had been held in such great affection. But before he could reach the Chateau Rouge, both prisoners had been lynched by the mob.

This was a very significant point in Clemenceau's life. It explains why, regardless of what the issue might be and irrespective of the intensity of his own convictions, he did everything possible within his powers of persuasion to avoid open civil war and all the acts of mob violence which he had recently experienced.

During the early years of their marriage, Clemenceau and Mary lived in almost complete harmony but, as he became more preoccupied with politics and, consequently, migrated more and more to Paris, a gap began to widen in their relations. Mary would accompany him to Paris for part of the time and then return to the parental home in the Vendée. At one stage Mary accused him of acquiring a mistress while he was away in Paris. In the study was a drawing of 'Marianne', the symbol of the Republic. 'There,' he said, 'is my mistress, my dear—La Belle France'. But after twelve years of a widening breach in their relations Mary informed her husband that she was leaving him to return forever to the United States with the children. The separation left a scar, deep and unhealable, on his emotions.

As the situation in Paris became more chaotic, Clemenceau became more involved in the political future of his country. Because of the brilliance of his public appearances and his opposition to the return of the monarchy, the shadow of which was hanging over Paris and the entire country, he became one of the leaders of the radical republican group.

In 1880 Clemenceau had started a newspaper called *La Justice*, which he edited especially to disseminate his political views. *La Justice* was accordingly always running on ice that was thinner than lace. He declined a generous offer from a friend with the remark that he who borrowed from a friend would often be the cause for the ruination of a friendship.

At a critical moment a wealthy financier, Cornelius Herz, purchased a minority interest in *La Justice* without as much as a suggestion regarding editorial policy or even a grumble. Clemenceau soon repurchased this interest, many years before the Panama Scandal broke over Paris.

That the power attendant upon social legislation could be misused by the State he was thoroughly aware. Among other things, Clemenceau's remarks about the possible abuse of power by organized labour sparked the famous debate between Jaurès, an able and wonderfully cultivated leader of the classical socialists, and himself.

From 1876 to 1893 Clemenceau was continuously a Deputy in the Chamber. During the interval between 1871 and 1876 he occupied a number of different political posts. His preoccupation with life became less with medicine and more with politics and the future of his country. It was during this period that he acquired the tag 'Tiger'. His own explanation of the tag is that there had been an extreme rightist journalist who disliked him very much indeed and who, after he (Clemenceau) had driven several people from office by the power of his tongue and the influence of his pen, dubbed him 'Tiger'. Later on, of course, the cartoonists took it up. It is possible that this caricature of Clemenceau—The Tiger Springing at the German Eagle—added much to his fame in France and beyond.

To his colleagues in the Chamber he was an enigma. He sought neither power nor monetary remuneration. Service of the public interest was his only motive. He destroyed where he disbelieved; created where he believed. Disliked and even hated by some, feared by all his colleagues, he was nevertheless one of the most beloved figures in France. Those who had achieved distinction in the arts and in the academic world were among his close friends. They included Victor Hugo's family and even the old man himself during the closing days of his life; Zola, Léon Daudet and a host of others distinguished in the field of sculpture, painting, literature and history. Claude Monet was one of his dearest friends; with him he would often visit at Giverny. And finally, when Monet died, he walked with his catafalque to the grave, remarking as an expression of his love and loss, 'I walk at my own funeral'.

There were a number of developments with which Clemenceau's name was linked. The Boulanger affair was one of these incidents. Clemenceau had known Boulanger as a young scholar at Nantes. In some measure Clemenceau had been responsible for General Boulanger's entrance into politics. But, when Boulanger's 'theatrical buffoonery' was shot to pieces by bits of evidence that indicated his design to restore the monarchy, Clemenceau shifted his position and was largely responsible for driving the General out of the country.

The Panama Scandal, as it was called, left its unmerited scar on the wholly innocent Clemenceau. Although he had no interest whatsoever in the project or in the financing of it, because of Herz's earlier association with *La Justice*, he fell, alas, a victim to one of the most skilfully organized and financed groups in the history of French politics.

When the initial capital of the project had been replenished, the financial directors in Paris established a large 'slush fund' in an effort to bury the truth behind an impenetrable wall of deceit. Baron Jacques de Reinach, a prominent and influential financier in Paris, had jurisdiction over the fund. When the lid of Pandora's box was blown off, Cornelius Herz, the paymaster for the 'slush fund', was accused of blackmailing de Reinach and of causing him to commit suicide.

This is one of the dark spots in French history. Many prominent persons were indicted; all were found not guilty because of their plea that they were acting 'for the honour of France'.

Because of Herz's former interest in *La Justice*, a dark shadow was cast upon Clemenceau's name. This implication, combined with additional charges, was brought before the Chamber. There were many who were relishing the opportunity to demolish the man who had so frequently demolished them. Deroulède spoke for some time. His indictment of Clemenceau was one of the most vicious and articulate charges of unproven treason in the annals of parliamentary records. This charge of Deroulède was supplemented by a different charge on a different score by a M. Milroy. Clemenceau during their accusations kept demanding that the evidence be produced. This neither Milroy nor Deroulède was able to do. So Clemenceau would often interrupt with the word 'liar'. Dejected and miserable, Milroy finally made his stumbling way out of the Chamber. Clemenceau, after Deroulède had finished his attack, delivered his defence in a logical, convincing manner, ending with the pungent remark, 'M. Paul Deroulède, you have lied'. Whereupon Deroulède announced his resignation from the Chamber.

But this was not the end of it. Clemenceau was soon to stand for re-election in the district of Arles. All the forces of the Senate and of the Chamber supplemented by other powerful interests were massed against him. The threats of hired ruffians—the circulation of scurrilous handbills by the thousands, every device aimed at causing his defeat—all were skilfully mustered and employed. Clemenceau, standing alone, fell before this massive attack.

Many thought that at last the Tiger had been brought to bay and killed for all time and that only his supine carcass would remain. But they had not reckoned with his dedication to the interests of France or with his indomitable character. He returned to his old home in the Vendée. There he lived for a time, reading, writing, studying, until at last his strong urge for activity brought him back, intermittently at first, to the scene in Paris, where, as one of his many biographers, Wythe Williams, so aptly said, 'There he rose from the dead'.

The people of his district soon unsuccessfully petitioned the Tiger to stand again for parliament. His reply was courteous: 'I require nothing of you except the encouragement of your friendship'.

The courts had acquitted Clemenceau of all complicity in the Panama

Scandal. They had held also that the documents which had been introduced in the case against him were forgeries. Whatever blemish there had been on his reputation was erased forever. Clemenceau concentrated on his work as a journalist, declining, on at least two occasions, invitations to form a government.

Towards the end of the century a startling event occurred in France. In 1894 Captain Dreyfus, a small, rather unimpressive officer, had been convicted of treason to his country before a Star Chamber Courtmartial and was sentenced to imprisonment on Devil's Island.

Clemenceau was at first convinced only that Dreyfus had been given an unfair trial. Ranc, who had been a prisoner with Clemenceau's father in Marseilles, and Bernard Lazare of *L'Aurore* with which Clemenceau had become associated, were certain that Dreyfus was innocent. 'In that case,' exclaimed Clemenceau, 'he is the victim of the greatest crime of the century.'

This perhaps was one of the turning points in Clemenceau's view, for immediately afterwards he was made privy to the documents and information possessed by Scheurer-Kestner which convinced him, not merely that Dreyfus had not received a fair trial but that he had been unjustly convicted. This was finally established during the trial of Zola. With Zola he had worked ceaselessly and untiringly on the preparation of Zola's great document which Clemenceau's genius entitled, *'J'accuse.'*

The final definitive acquittal of Dreyfus was one of the real landmarks in Clemenceau's life. His disclosure of the facts and his editorials—demanding at first a retrial, then a declaration of innocence, and ultimately producing Dreyfus' acquittal—had restored and enhanced his reputation in the eyes of the public. In 1902 he returned to public life as a senator from the province of Vaar. Soon thereafter he was appointed Minister of the Interior.

In 1907, five years later, he became for the first time Premier of France. His administration lasted until 1909 longer than any administration so far in the history of the Third Republic—when an unwarranted explosion of his temper produced a vote of No Confidence. 'Now,' he said, 'I can laugh and swear at the stupidities of others instead of perpetrating stupidities myself'.

During Clemenceau's administration legislation extending the period of military service from one to three years was introduced. This was not popular but Clemenceau felt that ultimately a confrontation between France and Germany was inevitable. German foreign policy, reflecting the temperament and personality of the Kaiser, was aimed directly at his beloved country.

While he was President of the Council the Casablanca incident occurred. Two German citizens, among others, had deserted from the Foreign Legion. The Kaiser demanded that they be returned to Germany. Clemenceau's attempt to compromise the matter by suggesting that the case go to arbitration was arrogantly declined. Prince von Radolin, the German Ambassador, informed Clemenceau personally that, if he failed to agree to the Kaiser's proposal, he was under instructions to demand his passport. The Tiger took his watch out of his pocket, looked at it, then promptly replied: 'Your Excellency, the Paris-Berlin Express leaves at nine o'clock. It is now seven.

You can catch it if you hurry.' The Ambassador did not ask for his passport; the German demands were withdrawn.

It was during this stretch of time between 1907-10 that a mutual and warm friendship between Edward VII and Clemenceau was formed. It was his fondness for Edward VII which persuaded him to concede that the British constitutional monarchy was not inappropriate.

During several conversations, some secret, between Clemenceau and King Edward, the latter intimated that he entertained a very low regard for his nephew, the Kaiser, and was distressed by Franz Joseph, the Emperor of the Austro-Hungarian Empire.

The Triple Entente was in part the result of the friendship between Clemenceau and Edward VII. The conversations between the two suggested that King Edward sympathized with Clemenceau regarding the Kaiser's designs; he was, however, unable to convince other contemporary British statesmen.

In international affairs a number of incidents were beginning to silhouette more clearly what was to come. In 1904 the French and the British had reached an agreement, the Entente Cordiale. In addition, the Kaiser had been progressively revealing ambitions to create a colonial empire extending over a vast part of the Middle East and parts of Africa.

In 1911 Clemenceau declared in a speech addressed to the substance of a proposed treaty made by Caillaux as Prime Minister in which he had yielded to the Kaiser: 'Five times since 1870 Germany has threatened war—in 1875 when Queen Victoria and Russia prevented her from finishing off the wounded of the battlefields of 1870; with the Schniebele crisis; and those of Tangiers, Casablanca and Agadir. Such is the preface to the work of peace submitted to us today . . . Germany believes,' Clemenceau concluded, 'that because we have been defeated we logically became vassals. The dead have given birth to the living and they will remain faithful to the dead.' This treaty, in which Caillaux had yielded to the Kaiser, so fired Clemenceau's vitriolic denunciation that Caillaux was forced out of office—prophetic of his fate five years later at Clemenceau's hands.

The period of growing tension in Europe finally culminated in the murder of the Archduke Franz Ferdinand at Sarajevo on 28 June 1914. 'This means war,' said Clemenceau. 'There is now, I believe, no escape.' And he turned upon the Senate as he had turned upon the Minister of War and accused it of having weakened the armament of France.

So the Great War began! The Schlieffen Plan, prepared in 1896, was substantially followed. The clouds opened; the thunder roared across Europe; lightning flashed in every capital; the deluge had commenced and it would not subside until the flood inundating Europe had obliterated parts of the foundation of western civilization. They were never to be repaired.

At first, Clemenceau responded magnificently. *L'Homme Libre*, a new daily paper which he edited, published one of the best editorials he ever wrote. It was a moving appeal to the people of France to come to the support of their beloved country, to cast aside all prejudices, party clichés and to dedicate their entire effort to the winning of the war and to the liberation of France for all time from the Germanic threat. He even called upon Poincaré in the

Elysée where they had, in effect, a rather touching reconciliation. Alas, it was a short period of calm before the Clemenceau storm. Gradually the Tiger returned to the jungle, wrecking and destroying ministries, from Briand's through Viviani's, some lasting for several months—one no longer than one day.

To capture the old, ferocious Tiger, some of the presidents of the Council offered him Cabinet positions. But to his Secretary, George Mandel, he said, 'No, I shall not accept because, far from seeking power like all the others, I am terribly afraid of it'.

Through the editorials of *L'Homme Libre* Clemenceau kept up his gunfire of attack on the administrations and the governments in office. He fell foul of the censor who erased his critical editorials. Clemenceau in retaliation changed the name to *L'Homme Enchainé*. The circulation of the paper increased enormously, together with the popularity of Clemenceau.

When the censor continued to eliminate his editorials Clemenceau then, on the floor of the Senate, ripped the administration to tatters and, pointing his finger at Louis Malvy, Minister of the Interior, and with utmost contempt in his voice, charged: 'You have betrayed the interests of France'. Two months later the government of Ribot fell.

The feeling between President Poincaré and Clemenceau made it increasingly difficult for him to suggest that Clemenceau form a ministry. But the hour was approaching when he would have no choice.

Early in the war, when the dangers were mounting and the prospect of defeat was becoming clearer, Poincaré made a note in his diary: 'I am always rather nervous . . . of Clemenceau's whims . . . It is certainly not for mere ambition that he wants office; it is because he is convinced that he can save his country and that he alone can do it . . . The day will come perhaps when I shall say—"Now that everything is lost, he alone is capable of saving everything".'

The clouds of impending catastrophe hung over western Europe and the British Isles. It may perhaps be fair to condemn Clemenceau on the score of creating the crisis by causing the downfall of previous governments. Whatever might have been, the hour had come when Poincaré had no choice but to invite Clemenceau on 13 November 1917, to meet with him at the Elysée. There Clemenceau was asked to become President of the Council and to form a government. In making the appointment Poincaré remarked that now *in extremis* it was his, Clemenceau's, task to pick up the reins of power. Thus, the Tiger, Georges Clemenceau, became ultimately the saviour of the western world.

He formed his cabinet generally of undistinguished but hardworking men, and completed his programme for the near future. This he laid before the parliament in a magnificent speech that was not unlike Churchill's some twenty-five years later when the western world once more was involved in a life and death struggle, facing the prospect of defeat. This is what Clemenceau said: '*Mais moi, messieurs, je fais la guerre*. In domestic policies I wage war; in foreign policies I wage war; always everywhere I wage war. Russia has betrayed us and I continue to wage war; unhappy Romania has been forced to capitulate but I still wage war; before Paris I wage war; in

Paris I wage war; behind Paris I wage war . . . And I wage war until the last quarter hour because the last quarter hour will be ours.'

A reluctant parliament was brought to its feet with rounds of applause for the Premier who had assumed authority and who it was hoped would carry the allies through to victory. Churchill, who was present in the Chamber when Clemenceau first appeared as Prime Minister, recalled that: '[The Tiger] ranged from one side of the tribune to the other, without a note or book of reference or scrap of paper, barking out sharp, staccato sentences as the thought broke upon his mind. He looked like a wild animal, pacing to and fro behind bars, growling and glaring; and all around him was an assembly which would have done anything to avoid having him there. But, having put him there, felt they must obey . . . The last desperate stake had to be played. France had resolved to unbar the cage and let her tiger loose upon all foes beyond the trenches or in her midst.'[2]

It is not frequent that a speech has aroused a nation and changed the course of history. Churchill aroused the determination of his own people and excited the admiration of the Western world. So Clemenceau, in his great speech, rose to the occasion; he struck the chords of resistance as few have struck them in the narrative of human events.

There were many things to be done, many matters to be corrected. He must, he thought, first destroy all semblance of treason, deceit, dishonesty and corruption. One of his problems, of course, was the immunity of a member of parliament. The elimination of this safe sanctuary was literally wrenched from a resistant parliament. Caillaux, Malvy and the *Bonnet Rouge* gang, together with others, were indicted, tried and found guilty. The trials were a relevation of the width and depth of the network of treasonable agents.

Having ousted and quashed the enemies within, Clemenceau then turned his face toward the enemy without. The army was his primary concern. He would make three trips every week to some portion of the front; almost always he would pick a very critical segment in order that the *poilus* might see him and he might talk with them. His presence at the front, in his baggy pants and turned-down hat, often under fire, boosted their morale, reenforced their determination and gave them an example of absolute confidence in victory and an exhibition of personal bravery. Clemenceau was becoming known as *Le Père La Victoire*. This was quite unlike the infrequent ceremonial visits to the front of Poincaré who was dubbed by the *poilus* 'our national chauffeur'.

These trips of Clemenceau's generally began at four or five o'clock in the morning and he would be back at his desk by the middle of the day or, when the front was distant, occasionally as late as midnight.

Once, when returning from an outpost through a communicating trench, he noticed a *poilu* in a field plucking wildflowers. It was one of those glorious, bright, clear French May mornings. The field was badly churned up with shell holes but there was a good deal of green foliage studded with hosts of poppies. Just as the Tiger saw the *poilu* the Boch laid down a barrage. The *poilu* fell, badly wounded. Before anybody could prevent him, the old man was out of the trench running across the field, shells bursting around him.

20

E PERE LA VICTOIR

EN HOMMAGE AMICAL
À
J.S. Douglas
1918
J.F. Bouchor

He reached the *poilu* who recognized him and handed him the bouquet of wildflowers with the words, 'I give you these as a token of the deep affection and love which we *poilus* have for you—*Le Père La Victoire*'.

The old man was deeply touched; he took the bouquet and replied, 'My child, I shall carry these with me to my grave'.[3] And he did.

One of Clemenceau's most important objectives after dealing peremptorily with treason and removing the taint of defeatism was the creation of a unified command on the Western Front. So long as there was no unity among the national military forces and so long as there was no compulsion to carry on an integrated general defense or offense in which all the allied forces in Western Europe would be without one Supreme Commander and one strategic and tactical plan, victory on the battlefield would be much more elusive. The British, recognizing the desirability of the unity of command but sceptical about the loyalty and competence of the French government, had put it off to some later date when trust would replace distrust.

In March 1918 came the beginning of Ludendorff's final gamble. The British Fifth Army front was shattered.

The time had come for Clemenceau to propose unified command. A conference was held in Doullens on 26 March in a very modest little tavern not far from the front. The tattered British Fifth Army kept marching by. Present at the conference were Lord Milner, who represented the British War Cabinet, Field Marshal Haig, Pétain, General Sir Henry Wilson, Clemenceau and others. Except for Clemenceau all were wrapped in gloom. Into this atmosphere suddenly marched Foch, full of confidence. His eyes flashed battle; he was determined to fight.

Clemenceau wasted little time in proposing that Ferdinand Foch, whom he, some years before, had appointed the Commandant of the Ecole de Guerre, become the Supreme Commander of all the Allied forces in the west. After a short private huddle among Milner, Wilson and Haig, this was only partly agreed to; Foch was named commanding officer merely to co-ordinate the Allied troops. This, however, was not quite enough.

Soon after the meeting at Doullens and the appointment of Foch, the Germans launched another powerful attack to break through the Allied lines in the direction of Paris. The German High Command was not to be frustrated. The Allies yielded ground but their line did not break. Again the Germans were compelled to bring their advance to a halt. Another Allied conference was held at Beauvais. Here all agreed that Foch should be the Commander-in-Chief of all the Allied forces in the west. Unified command had become a fact.

During these critical attacks Poincaré had insisted that Paris should be the primary object of defence, whereas Clemenceau believed that, if the British alliance were to be preserved, the Channel ports must be safeguarded. Clemenceau's view prevailed.

Meanwhile, the Germans with excellent concealment had been massing their forces for what was to be their last gigantic assault aimed at taking Paris. On 27 May a large scale attack between Rheims and Soissons was launched. It had pushed ruthlessly and irresistibly forward till it reached the Marne on the 14 July (Bastille Day) at almost the same spot on which the fierce thrust in August and September 1914 was successfully halted.

The exhausting, frightful trench warfare, broken by limited successes, had absorbed the intervening four years. The living can have no idea of the desolation and the complete devastation of 'no man's land'—stretching from north of Bar-le-Duc, through the Chemin des Dames and Cambrai into Belgium through the brick dust of Passchendaele and the ruins of Yprés to the coast. Churned up land pitted with great shell holes, some partially filled with stinking yellow greenish water—forests ripped to shreds, tattered stumps of trees and shattered villages battered into piles of dust and rubble— were the hallmarks of the four years through which the western Allies and Germany had passed.

The city of Paris was under constant artillery fire. Some were making arrangements for the movement of the government to Bordeaux. Clemenceau would not permit the Ministers to move. He would not be balked in his determination to remain close to the command post on the Western Front. Paris is where he would remain!

A deep depression fell upon France and esecially upon the capital. France had reached the nadir of her military fortunes. The Chemin des Dames was gone; the French line had been broken just as the British Fifth Army had been broken. The enemy was battering again on the gates of Paris. The atmosphere was thick with desperation. The Chamber was demanding that Foch and Pétain be thrown to the wolves. Would Clemenceau agree in order to save himself? His decision was typical—he would fight!

On 4 June he appeared before the Chamber of Deputies, resolute, poised, claws unsheathed, determined to fight it out without compromise. He spoke in glowing praise of the French *poilu* and the French military commanders, including Foch. He declared positively and with finality that he would not dismiss the generals: 'Condemn me, dismiss me from this post if you choose, I will not do what you ask of me'. His powerful speech carried the day. The vote of confidence was 337 to 110!

Every day was precious. The High Command in Germany felt that, if they could but cross the Marne in strength, they would bring about the collapse of the Clemenceau government which would be followed by the disintegration of the whole Allied complex in Western Europe.

The shattering of the German massive assault at the battle of Chateau-Thierry with American troops in action are matters of history. The Germans had staked their all on this throw of the dice—and had lost! The American army at St Mihiel and in the Argonne; the British moving without interruption from 8 August back to Mons where in August of 1914 they first met the Germans; and the French, though their forces were depleted, active and advancing on their portion of the front, made the end of the long, ghastly struggle inevitable.

At eleven o'clock on 11 November, silence fell upon the Western Front. Victory, only miraculously possible in November 1917, had come at last by 11 November 1918. Germany might have ruled the continent from the Vistula to the Pyrenees.

It is by no means an exaggeration to say that Georges Eugene Benjamin Clemenceau, *Le Père La Victoire, Le Tigre*, the demolisher of governments, was the one person who, holding on high the sword of Joan of Arc, preserved the Allied Forces intact until the day of victory on the battlefield.[4]

All this did not mean peace for Clemenceau or a relaxation. New issues were beginning to emerge.

In the middle of October, the influence of President Wilson began to appear in the diplomatic arena. This, with other developments—Colonel House had come to Paris—was prophetic in many ways of the difficulties of making a peace which Clemenceau said in the Chamber were 'much greater than the difficulties of winning the war'. It was a pity, Clemenceau thought, that a man like Colonel House could not be in a position of authority.

At Colonel House's suggestion, Clemenceau, Lloyd George, the Italian Prime Minister and himself, with the advice of the generals, put the terms of the Armistice into final form for presentation to the Germans by Foch. The American military and others favoured unconditional surrender and demilitarization. By many, Clemenceau was criticized for being too lenient. But they did not possess the full knowledge that was Clemenceau's, more especially the knowledge of Wilson's inflexible views about the Fourteen Points.

It was suggested that American forces might be withdrawn and that the United States might make a separate peace with Germany if the Fourteen Points were not agreed to.[5] This was merely one of the complications that might never have become reality but was a disturbing threat.

There were other complicating developments. The Russian Revolution was in full and successful swing. A demilitarized and very weak Germany might prove to be no barricade against the reconstructed military force of Communist Russia (fears of the West that were echoed twenty-five years later).

With all these matters in mind, the Fourteen Points with only two modifications—one in respect of reparations, the other the freedom of the seas—were finally accepted.

For Clemenceau, however, notwithstanding his own doubts and the attacks upon him, subsequently levelled with venom and force, there came an hour of extraordinary triumph before the very same French Chamber of Deputies which for months had wished to unhorse him but had not the courage to challenge the Tiger in his lair. *Le Père La Victoire* was the endearing title given to him in his hour of personal triumph. The old man was buried beneath a mass of telegrams, cables, letters, honours of all kinds.

'Now that I've read this text, it seems to me that this splendid, great and terrible moment marks the end of my task,' was the conclusion of his reading of the terms of the Armistice to the Chamber of Deputies.

Clemenceau's appearance before the Chamber after his meeting with Wilson was very impressive. He spoke approvingly of Wilson as a man. A vote of confidence—398 to 93—to conduct the peace negotiations was accorded him.

Colonel House has described Clemenceau as one of the great individuals of the world. 'He came at problems by direct attack . . . There he stood, almost alone among the old-time diplomats. His courage was too unyielding

24

to permit a dissimulation. He was afraid of nothing present or to come and least of all of mere man.'[6]

Clemenceau's absorbing object of concentration—the war—was behind him. The fires of sacrifice which he had lighted in France had begun to flicker, but there were no more fires for him to kindle. He felt drained of intellectual and physical vigour and so he retreated to his little cottage by the sea in the Vendée. Here the freshness and honesty of his mind, combined with the vigour of his body, were in full measure restored. And so to Paris he returned.

The Peace Conference which was convened on 18 January 1919, consisted of representatives of all the many nations which had been at war with the Central Powers. Many believed it should draft the peace convention. Clemenceau, however, took a wholly different view of the matter. He thought that the fewer there were, the more expeditiously and wisely peace could be achieved. Finally, after ten days, his point was carried. The 'Big Ten' were instructed to prepare the provisions of the Treaty.

Emerging from his apartment one morning during the course of the Versailles' negotiations Clemenceau was shot by a young assassin and was carried into his bedroom. Fortunately he was not fatally wounded. When the security officials came to seek an indictment he said, 'What charge can I make against him which is unimpeachably accurate? I think he should be indicted for bad marksmanship.' Within ten days, to the chagrin and dismay of his doctors, the old Tiger was back again in the midst of the struggle for a treaty.

The three principal figures among the ten were Clemenceau, Wilson (or in his absence, Colonel House) and Lloyd George. When Wilson was not present, there was always the shadow of the President of the United States falling across the conference table. Wilson was the idealist, with a profound knowledge of history, whose views, however, were untempered by experience and unmodified by personal observation of the way nation-states behave. Clemenceau was the realist, his idealism adjusted by a long life and a clinician's view of history and human nature; the one guided by vicarious experience, the other by the compulsion of fact. This was the basic reason for their difference of view regarding the League as a part of the Treaty and the Fourteen Points, all of which have since been shattered to fragments by practically every nation. Would ratification by the United States have avoided the post-war wave of nationalism and the cataclysm of 1939-45?

Between these two men was the wily, unreliable and highly mobile but very articulate master of intrigue, Lloyd George. Between him and Clemenceau little regard existed. The interchange of views between the Tiger and Lloyd George, with the 'Presbyterian Elder' as a spectator, often generated great heat. On one occasion, Lloyd George and Clemenceau almost engaged each other physically. However, the little Welshman, as Stephen Bonsal calls him, retreated into his corner of the platform with the remark: 'Well, I shall expect an apology for these outrageous words'. 'You shall wait for it

With Lloyd George (right) inspecting a guard of honour at Versailles

as long as you wait for the pacification of Ireland,' was Clemenceau's hot reply.[7]

There were three issues that separated Clemenceau from Wilson, with Lloyd George as a broker: the control of the left bank of the Rhine and the bridgeheads; the League of Nations as the core of the treaty (Clemenceau was wholly prepared to endorse it as a separate instrument); and finally, compensation for the vast destruction that France had suffered. (Clemenceau did not view this as the most important issue.) Lloyd George, playing the role of the broker, consistent with one of the tenets of British policy, was fearful of a treaty which would elevate France to a dominant position in Europe.

After repeated and protracted arguments, the first issue with Wilson was resolved by a reluctantly proposed guarantee of the United States to come to the defense of France if she were invaded. Britain was committed to join in the guarantee after it had been formally accepted by Washington. Reparations was a difficult one but not insoluble because, in Clemenceau's view, it was not the *sine qua non* issue. The central disagreement, however, was settled by a decision in Wilson's favour. Clemenceau's lack of faith in the League was in part abated by the guarantee regarding the left bank of the Rhine. There was a wide variety of ancillary issues important to Britain, Italy, Palestine, the Middle East, Turkey and others. For France, there was the question of her security.

To this issue Clemenceau, time after time, would come back. Speaking to both the Americans and the British he would say, in effect, 'your security is amply provided for'.

Week after week of unresolved issues passed. Even during the absence of Wilson, little progress was made. From the doubtful idealism of Wilson, as it seems today, and his assumed moral infallibility, no deviation seemed possible. Clemenceau had to choose between being adamantly stubborn, breaking up the peace conference or accepting at least with an appropriate promise of security some part of Wilson's doctrinaire views of the *form* of the treaty. Often he came back to the left bank of the Rhine for he could not believe that the German people were reconstructed; often he was repulsed.

On 31 March at the request of Clemenceau, Foch, in person, made his impassioned plea. Clemenceau thought that perhaps the allied Commander-in-Chief might carry some persuasiveness with his two opponents, Wilson and Lloyd George—all to no avail.

At any rate, Clemenceau was faced with a Hobson's choice. If he failed to agree, there might be the complete loss of American, and even perhaps, British support. If he agreed, he might get some concessions, notably, the guarantee of the left bank of the Rhine. Considerations of this character impelled him finally, doubtfully, with what great doubt—to accept the Wilson form and substance of the Treaty.

When the Treaty was presented to Count von Brackdorff-Rantzau for compliance his recalcitrant attitude, clearly authorized by the German government, should have been a flare of caution to all the powers of the western world. But they neither saw the blaze of danger nor heard the warning words!

The Treaty was completed in May and, after calling the German bluff, was signed on 28 June 1919. Clemenceau was acclaimed as the great saviour of France and worshipped almost as a demigod.

The election of the French parliament and of the President was next on the calendar. The new members elected were largely of Clemenceau's choosing. The person to succeed Poincaré as President was the most important issue. Many thought it should be Clemenceau.

The fight that he had fought had been finished; the old warrior was taking off his armour and putting on the soft comfortable clothes of an author. But if France wanted him, he would very reluctantly yield to her wish— France, 'Marianne', had always been his mistress.

When, however, he was told that unless he agreed to a certain proposition he might not be elected, he officially requested that his name be withdrawn. Deschanel, a pleasant nonentity, was elected.

In 8 rue Franklin and the Sables d'Olonne cottage he found his haven, and was at peace, if not with himself, at least with the world in which he lived. In the catholicism of his wide friendships, he always found diversion. He made certain that his grave would be properly cared for. There he hoped that he, accompanied by the bouquet of wildflowers, would finally come to rest by the side of his father—the man whom he loved most.

He returned to visit the United States slightly more than half a century after he, with his bride, had set sail from New York. He planned to interrupt his tour of the country by visiting a friend in Arizona where a town had been named for him. But an illness interrupted his stay and caused him to return to France.

After the war, he was in somewhat straitened circumstances. He had little income, for his whole life had been dedicated to the nation. His editorships and articles had produced little income during his period of power. In these circumstances, it came to him as a shock when his landlord proposed to increase the rent of his house in rue Franklin. The old gentleman was concerned. What should he do?

My father had been in charge of the American Red Cross warehouses on the Western Front since the spring of 1917. During the relatively short period of his stay in France, he had formed many friendships. One of them was an American, Henry Selden Bacon. Others introduced him to some of Clemenceau's friends—Senator Jeanneney, Madame Baldensperger and her husband, Fernand, a professor at the Sorbonne (later at Stanford University, California) and Madame Jacquemaire Clemenceau who was Clemenceau's daughter, and a wide range of Frenchmen in every walk of life. And so he was introduced to Clemenceau. The two were birds of a feather and became fast friends, uncompromising, simple, with a deep concern for the common person, and with a dedication to their basic principles of life.[8]

My father learned of the proposed increase in the rent of Clemenceau's apartment. Without saying a word to Le Père La Victoire, he forthwith bought the building. No action was taken in regard to the rent but undisclosed provisions were made for increasing Clemenceau's income. Of all this Clemenceau himself knew nothing until after the event when it was too late for the Old Warrior to undo what had been done.

After the great man's death a foundation was formed into which the title to the house passed. Certain of Clemenceau's friends, including Madame Boldensperger, a co-sponsor, were named as trustees and charged with preserving the building and its contents. Provision was also made for the selection of successor trustees. It was specified that the articles in that portion of the house in which the old man had lived were to be preserved exactly as they were at the hour of his death; a book open on a little table by his bed, books and papers on his great horseshoe desk, precisely as he had been using them when the end came. There the house stands today, identified by a simple plaque, at 8 rue Franklin, Paris, the 'Musée Clemenceau'. There, because of an endowment provided by my father, hopefully, it will remain for many generations to come—a memorial to one of the great men of modern history.

In August 1929, only three months before he died, Clemenceau invited my father and me to visit him at his lovely place on the shores of the Bay of Biscay. We spent the night at Nantes and the next morning drove to Bel-Ebat in Sables d'Olonne. The entrance gates had been thrown open and we found the old man in his wonderful little skullcap, grey gloves and all, waiting to greet us. As we got out of the automobile, he welcomed us with the remark, 'My dear friends, what do you think of my empire?' The reply had to be—for there was no other reply to be made—an affirmation of the old man's answer to his own question. 'This is the loveliest kingdom I have ever made.'

It was indeed a glorious empire. This simple, whitewashed fisherman's cottage with comfortable quarters for the great man, a dining-room with a kitchen in a bay lined with copper utensils, his old maid and the faithful Albert to watch over him. He took us to our simple but ample room.

We lunched together. Our host was most engaging, telling stories and recounting experiences. Albert was waiting on us with his usual careful attention, both to *Le Père La Victoire* and to his guests. Clemenceau had brought out what he considered to be the very best of his Burgundy white wines. He had been cherishing it, he said, for at least a decade and lately for our visit. He wanted us to enjoy it lovingly, like a sacrament. He, himself, had taken one glass; my father and I had taken several. He then called Albert, 'Albert, the doctors tell me I must not touch this glorious wine. Please pour me at once another glass!'

This is the way the luncheon hour and a half was spent, talking about America, about Europe and in general enjoying a very universal sort of conversation. He seemed to be very much interested because I was the only Congressman from the State of Arizona.

After lunch, he asked me whether I would like to walk about his empire with him. My father considerately disappeared while the old gentleman—short, stocky, vigorous even at the age of eighty-eight—took me through his glorious domain. The journey came to an end at one of those latticed, open-backed iron benches facing inland, on top of the breakwater, against which the waves of the Bay of Biscay pounded and broke. In the background was his whitewashed tiled cottage, beautiful because of its utter simplicity. Before us was a wild rampant mass of colour. The old man had taken flower seeds and had strewn them out—thousands of them. They had taken root wherever they chose to grow and made a massive slash of many colours as a foreground to the lovely fisherman's cottage in the background.

He began to talk. He talked about the men he had known. He talked about Wilson. Wilson, he confessed, was one of the most interesting men he had ever known as a companion. 'With Wilson,' he said, 'on purely intellectual grounds and in the fields of scholarship, I could have and did have a most enjoyable period of companionship . . . We had particular areas of common interests . . . But as to the political structure of Europe, however, we couldn't see as one. I hoped that I could generate the faith in the League of Nations that Wilson possessed. But I thought that the peace of Europe was too fragile to rest upon such weak foundations, untested by experience, untried against the battering of the nationalistic obstructionists.'

Then he talked about others—Lincoln whom he admired very much but had never met; all the figures he had known when he was in the United States—Conkling, Brownlow, Chase, Johnson, Greeley and the other great anti slavery editors of New York—all these people and a host of others; indeed, it was difficult to find somebody whom he had not known. During an interval in our conversation, I asked him why he had such admiration for Thaddeus Stevens, one of the least admirable characters who ever strode across the American political stage. There was a long silence, then the old man looked at me with that extraordinary, penetrating and quizzical gaze of his and said, 'My son, this is a very good question. I admired him for one reason. He could lash the House of Representatives into submission with his tongue.' To which I replied that that was a remarkable talent but not enough to admire him as an important American character.

Then the old warrior talked about other personalities. His dislike of Lloyd George was unconcealed; he thought, to use his phrase, that 'he was as empty as an empty eggshell', but with a great capacity to conceal his intellectual emptiness. Stresemann, he thought was a great man; he wished that France had had a person of his qualifications. To Foch as a general he gave full marks though he was at the time completing *The Grandeur and Misery of Victory* in which he seemed to be critical of Foch.

He talked about history and its importance in the intellectual inventory of any person, no matter in what occupation—politics, business, literature or science. After he had in his engaging way chatted about some of the great men he had known there was a pause. I broke it by saying to him, 'Mr President, you have lived almost the span of a century. You have made more governments and you have destroyed more governments than any other living man, even possibly than any other man in modern history. You yourself have exercised supreme power. You have been one of the most significant political figures in the western world over the course of the last century. What do you believe are the most important qualities that a person in public life can have?'

There was a long silence; then the old gentleman turned to me, placed his gloved hand upon my knee, looked at me with that whimsical but piercing eye and remarked, 'You are quite right, my son; I have lived almost the span of a century; I have destroyed more governments than any other living person and I have probably made more governments. I have seen kingdoms

31

formed; I have seen kingdoms demolished. I have seen thrones set up; I have seen thrones torn down. As I look back over the scene of my life I come to the conclusion that there are only two things in life that really matter. The first is to love and to be loved; the second is to be intellectually honest.' A pause, then, 'My son,' he added, 'nothing else in life really matters'.

We dined as we had lunched, just the three of us, Albert vigilantly watching over the table. Conversation flowed in much the same way as it had before— catholic, touching almost every subject: the politics of Europe, science, the United States, literature and the arts. After dinner was over and coffee had been served and a liqueur had been sipped, we bade farewell and left this last kingdom that Clemenceau had created.

This vignette has been concerned more particularly with Clemenceau's many engagements in politics. There was another side to him about which not a great deal has been written, certainly about which little has been noted in this short account of his life. People generally think of *Le Père La Victoire* as that destroyer of governments in France and as that Tiger who carried the Allies to victory in the 1914 war against Germany.

All his other accomplishments—and he had many—have fallen into that great pit of oblivion which swallows up so many of the lovely things of life. And so it has been with Clemenceau.

The accolade which he so overwhelmingly deserves must include his competence as a notable author. The books he wrote about his travels in Asia, among other things, his philosophical speculations, *In The Evening Of My Thought*, his one dramatic production which was given by the Académie Française and all of his periodical articles and editorials, sufficient to fill many folios, were written in a most engaging and attractive style.

His pen moved with grace, often with sarcasm, frequently with gaiety, pathos, kindliness and firmness but never, no matter the provocation, did it depart from the truth. At times there were extraordinary flashes like the flash of a 'Very' pistol at night in 'no man's land'—a scintillating command of language.

Science, medicine, distant lands, art—the whole spectrum of human knowledge—his pen elaborated. His own atheism was fascinating; he wished desperately that he could believe in some Divine Power but intellectually he could not bring himself to it. He had a clear conception of right and wrong; the standards which he applied were perhaps his own standards. Yet, to his conception of right and wrong he clung with tenacity, a faithfulness almost impossible to match in the philosophical complex and the dramatic behaviour of any other person prominent in public life, certainly in modern history.

It is impossible to document all of Clemenceau's sweeping talents and accomplishments; his abrasive infirmities, his explosive temper and his capacity for crushing rudeness. On balance, his claim to historical immortality is unimpeachable.

Even his detractors must accord greatness to him. Nor can those who examine his character carefully deny the hidden springs of unselfish emotion, the fearlessness, the reverence for the truth that were a part of this towering figure of the twentieth century—if not, indeed, of all time.

Winston Churchill swells the chorus: 'The fierceness, the pride, the poverty after great office, the grandeur when stripped of power, the unbreakable front offered to this world and to the next—all these belong to the ancients.'

'It is already certain that Clemenceau was one of the world's great men.'

[1] There is a legend that sometime after a group of Mongols had settled on the coast of France their strain of blood was insinuated into the veins of one of his ancestors and, like Lord Tweedsmuir's *Path of Kings*, remained dormant until Georges Eugene appeared upon the scene.

[2] Rt Hon. Winston S. Churchill, *Great Contemporaries* (London and New York, 1937) p. 272.

[3] There is another story, almost equally moving, of the way in which the bouquet of wildflowers was given to Clemenceau at the front. He himself referred to it in a speech made later before an audience of *poilus* at Rheims. The conclusion of both stories is identical. The bouquet went with him to his grave.

[4] It can be said also that without American intervention or the gallantry of the British forces, the outcome might have been quite different.

[5] What a tragic reverse of historic presumption! The Fourteen Points later were not agreed to by the United States; a separate United States treaty with Germany was made.

[6] George Bernard Noble, *Policies and Opinions at Paris, 1919*, pp. 90,91.

[7] Stephen Bonsal, *Unfinished Business*, p. 72. Bonsal was a distinguished journalist, knowledgeable about and a great admirer of *Le Père La Victoire* and an intimate of Colonel House.

[8] My father specifically asked that no reference be made to his friendship during his lifetime and to my knowledge this has been observed.

B

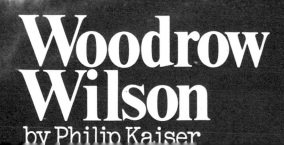

Woodrow
Wilson
by Philip Kaiser

PHILIP KAISER (b. 1913) graduated from the University of Wisconsin in 1935 and won a Rhodes Scholarship to Oxford where he was at Balliol College from 1936 to 1939. His war years were spent as an economist with the Federal Reserve Bank and later with the Board of Economic Warfare. He joined the State Department in 1946 with a special interest in problems of international organization. He was then transferred to the Office of International Labor Affairs in the Department of Labor and, in 1949, President Truman appointed him Assistant Secretary of Labor in charge of international affairs. He was one of the youngest members of President Truman's sub-Cabinet. In this post he served as chief U.S. delegate to the annual International Labor Conferences 1949-53 and was a member of the Inter-departmental Committees which developed the Greek-Turkish Aid Program and the Marshall Plan. There followed a period of non-diplomatic life which coincided with the Republican Administration of President Eisenhower, when he was a special assistant to the Governor of New York (Hon. Averell Harriman) and also Professor of International Relations at the American University, Washington D.C. He returned to the State Department in 1961, however, and was appointed by President Kennedy as U.S. Ambassador to the Republics of Senegal and Mauretania. He came to London as Minister under the Ambassadorship of the Hon. David Bruce in 1964 and remained there until 1969 when he retired to become the Chairman and Managing Director of Encyclopaedia Britannica in London.

Woodrow Wilson

28 Dec. 1856 Born. Educated at Davidson College, North Carolina, and Princeton.

1879 Entered University of Virginia Law School.

1882 Opened legal practice in Atlanta, Georgia, but soon abandoned this project.

1885 Published *Congressional Government*—analysis of organic functioning of the federal government.
Married Ellen Axson, who later had three daughters. Began teaching at Bryn Mawr women's college in Pennsylvania.

June 1886 Awarded Ph.D. at Johns Hopkins university.

1890 Appointed Professor of Jurisprudence and Political Economy at Princeton.

1902 Elected President of Princeton, in which position he brought students and faculty into closer contact and tried to reform educational framework.
Published his five-volume *A History of the American People*.

1910 Elected Governor of New Jersey, and pushed progressive programme through New Jersey legislature, which brought him into arena of national politics.

Previous page: Representative of might and morality. Wilson arrives in Paris, 1919. Now the 'New World' was redressing the balance of the 'Old'

36

2 July 1912 Nominated presidential candidate at Democratic national convention.

Nov. 1912 Presidential election. Republican party split when ex-president T. Roosevelt formed Progressive party—enabled Democrat Wilson to win election with his 'New Freedom' programme.

Feb. 1913 Revolt in Mexico. Huerta overthrew Mexican leader Madero.

April 1913 Approved formal introduction of racial segregation in several government departments.

Oct. 1913 Underwood Tariff Act reformed tariff laws by revising tariff rates downwards.
Tried to negotiate with Carranza constitutionalists in Mexico.

Dec. 1913 Federal Reserve Act which controlled private banking institutions by establishing a public board.

April 1914 U.S. naval force seized terminal facilities of Vera Cruz in Mexico.

1914 Clayton Anti-Trust Act prohibited injunctions in labour disputes.

Aug. 1914 Outbreak of First World War. Wilson proclaimed U.S. neutrality.

Sept. 1914 Federal Trade Commission which regulated commerce.

Feb. 1915 Rural credits system established.

7 May 1915 Sinking of British liner *Lusitania* by German submarine. Among drowned were 128 Americans.

Dec. 1915 Married his second wife.

1916 Won presidential election, campaigning on slogan 'He has kept us out of war'.

Dec. 1916 Tried to make peace through mediation.

2 April 1917 Following institution of unrestricted submarine warfare by Germans, Wilson asked Congress for declaration of war.

Nov. 1917 Bolshevik revolution in Russia forced Allies to be more specific about war aims.

Jan. 1918 'Fourteen Points' speech laid down peace aims. At first British and French unwilling to accept Wilson as arbiter of peace conditions, but later they yielded and agreed to fourteen points with certain modifications.

Nov. 1918 End of First World War. Congressional election won by Republicans—this weakened Wilson's position.

1919 Attended peace conference in Paris but was not always successful in negotiations. Nevertheless, his fourteenth point, the establishment of a League of Nations, was adopted.

Sept. 1919 Public opinion in U.S. turning against Wilson—dissatisfaction with treaty, inflation, industrial disputes, race riots.

Oct. 1919 Suffered thrombosis which impaired control of brain over left side of body. Unable to carry out official responsibilities for nine months.

March 1920 U.S. Senate voted against ratification of peace treaty with Germany. U.S. was thus kept out of League of Nations.

1920 Presidential election won by Republicans. Harding became President.

3 Feb. 1924 Died.

Although very much a man of his time and a product of his religious and social background, Woodrow Wilson left a legacy of ideas and presidential style that has greatly influenced succeeding presidents. Hoover admired him[1]; Franklin Roosevelt was 'haunted by Wilson's ghost'; Truman conceived of the Presidency in Wilsonian terms; Kennedy's inaugural speech was squarely within the Wilsonian tradition and Wilson is one of two chief executives whose portraits hang in the White House office of President Nixon[2]. Wilson has been so influential mainly because he was the first president to confront the great foreign and domestic problems facing the American chief executive in the twentieth century: the role of the government in industrial society, and the role of the United States as a world power. In the fifty years since Wilson's death, American presidents have had to cope with the same basic issues that preoccupied him and they have acted largely within the framework set by Wilson's successes and failures.

Thomas Woodrow Wilson was born in Staunton, Virginia on 28 December 1856, into a Presbyterian minister's family whose forbears had filled Scottish pulpits for six generations. His father combined the direction of the Augusta Female Seminary of Staunton with the pastorate of the Presbyterian Church. A compelling preacher who relished words, he also cut a figure in a drawing room. He was idolized by his son whom he in turn adored. In Wilson's early, awkward years, his father, a proud and concerned parent, spent many hours with his sickly son who did not fit easily into school or even childhood.

Although the grandson of an abolitionist, Woodrow none the less inherited a respectable Southern gentleman's prejudices and code of behaviour and a strong Calvinist puritan conscience, but not his father's good constitution. Too sickly to attend school before he was eleven, Wilson was tutored at home by his father, who especially emphasized the arts of speaking and writing. As a result, Woodrow studied primarily in order to be able to speak or to write books. Early in life, he decided on a political career and chose Gladstone as his hero which led Herbert Agar to comment that 'The choice of Gladstone . . . is appropriate—the two men being much alike in character, in quality of mind, and in their intimate knowledge of God's hopes and plans'[3].

When Wilson was fourteen, his family moved to Columbia, South Carolina, a town devastated by the Civil War and still suffering under 'carpet-bag' rule. He often listened to his father lecture at the theological seminary and joined a prayer group. For the rest of his life he would get comfort from praying on his knees twice a day.

The infuence of his 'incomparable'[4] father cannot be exaggerated. Joseph Wilson early decided that his son would be a great man. As long as his father lived, Wilson consulted him before every major decision of his life. They shared the same strong faith in the teachings of the Presbyterian Church and in God's purposes, one of which was to make Wilson a great man. Woodrow's poor health, chronic digestive trouble, headaches, weak eyes, and his unprepossessing appearance all presented him with severe handicaps. But his sense of mission grew strong enough to overcome them all.

In 1873, Wilson made a painful break with home and went to Davidson College where he lived in austere discomfort. His introspective bent became more pronounced, and he confessed to his mother that he regretted having spent too little time fearing God and too much serving the devil. By spring he was suffering from a nervous breakdown, the first of several, and had returned home to recover his emotional balance and physical strength. After a year and a half, he went back to college, this time to Princeton[5] where he made a few close friends, primarily through the Liberal Debating Society he founded. Wilson's friends admired him for knowing what he wanted from life, but they found him inclined to talk like a preacher even in private conversation. Speech was his great joy and he dearly relished applause. He became a student of the British political system, wrote two prize essays (on Bismarck and on Pitt) and formed a conviction that the most effective government resulted from a strong chief executive.

Wilson chose the law as a route to politics. He entered the University of Virginia Law School in the fall of 1879. Once more the nervous strain of life proved too much and in the middle of his second year, he returned home where he completed his work alone, passing brilliantly the examination for the Bar in June 1882. In September, he and a classmate opened a practice in Atlanta, Georgia. But the law was not to Wilson's taste. No good at attracting clients and too moralistic to accept those who did not have right obviously on their side, after a year he gave up the law to return to graduate school.

The study of political science at John Hopkins now became the path to a political career. His first book, *Congressional Government*, won the John Marshall prize and became something of a classic. It was accepted as a thesis for his Ph.D. He stuck out the two-year course at the insistence of the sensible, loving and lovely Ellen Axson, a daughter of a minister, whom he married as soon as he received his Ph.D. in June 1886.

In a revealing letter to his fiancée, he had written, 'I have the uncomfortable feeling that I am carrying a volcano about with me. My salvation is in being loved   There surely never lived a man with whom love was a more critical matter than it is with me.' He realized his need for complete respect, approval and affection, and found in Ellen an adoring wife in whom he could confide.

To earn money while he was at Hopkins, Wilson took to lecturing. On one occasion, he characterized socialist reformers as 'long-haired and wild-eyed'[6] and, when challenged, explained that 'by saying such things, one could make people believe one was a conservative and then go ahead and do progressive things'. His moral armour was showing chinks. Other chinks would appear throughout his career as he carried out God's purpose, sometimes with a disregard for the truth or for other people's rights and feelings.

After teaching at Bryn Mawr, a women's college in Pennsylvania, and at Wesleyan in Connecticut, in 1890 he was appointed Professor of Jurisprudence and Political Economy at Princeton, an appointment he had eagerly sought. Here his eloquent lectures on public law drew hundreds of students. He also continued to give public lectures. In an America dismayed by the power of money and the increasing concern with making it, his emphasis on righteousness, on individual responsibility and a simpler Jeffersonian society, all gave his listeners new hope for the future.

Wilson was elected President of Princeton in 1902, chiefly because of his popularity as a professor and orator, and because the retiring President

Patton thought of him as a safe choice who would be content to preach a new gospel without making upsetting changes. Little did he know his man. Before long, Wilson was redesigning the curriculum and, through the innovative preceptor system, brought students and faculty into closer contact. However, when he attempted to change the traditional private eating clubs into democratic residence halls under the direction of the University, he encountered strong resistance. The entire Princeton community lined up for or against the quadrangle proposition which Wilson saw as 'the salvation' of Princeton and of the democratic spirit in education. His own commitment took on the colouring of a religious crusade. His emotions warped his judgement and made it impossible for him to separate issues from men. When his one great friend and confidant, John Hibben, tried to get him to compromise, Wilson treated him with cold contempt and never again sought Hibben's friendship.

Throughout his life, Wilson's friendships followed this pattern. Almost daily, he would seek the comfort and advice of the friend of the moment. When the friend disagreed with Wilson's uncompromising pursuit of an objective, and offered an alternative course, Wilson thought him traitorous and would summarily drop him forever. This syndrome recurred at critical moments in his life; at Princeton, as Governor of New Jersey, and tragically at the end of his Presidency.

Wilson turned defeat from the dormitory project to his advantage when he received national publicity for a stirring speech to alumni in Pittsburgh in which he stressed the importance of education serving 'the needs of the common man' and not merely the children of the rich. It was a blood and thunder speech against special privilege, and was welcomed as such by progressives across the country. However, Wilson's position as President was further underminded by the way he dealt with the trustees over the site for a new graduate school. He insisted on having his own way, refusing compromise solutions. The trustees felt Wilson was motivated primarily by jealous resentment of Dean West of the Graduate School and backed the Dean against the University President.

By the end of 1909, after four years of battle with West and the trustees over the new Graduate School, Wilson's standing in the University had reached a low point. The governorship of New Jersey appeared as a welcome way out from the impasse at Princeton as well as a means of fulfilling his now heightened political ambitions. Wilson's election as Governor was the first of an extraordinary series of events that led to the presidency.

Ironically, he owed his launching into national politics to a conservative, George Harvey, the editor of *Harper's Weekly* and a man of considerable influence on Wall Street. It was he who recognized Woodrow Wilson as a possible conservative alternative to a third term for Roosevelt or a fourth nomination of Bryan, and who saw the governorship of New Jersey as a necessary step to the White House. Harvey had known Wilson since 1902 when he published Wilson's five-volume *A History of the American People,* and in 1905 had given him a dinner in New York's Lotus Club, proposing him as a candidate for the presidency. He followed this up by printing Wilson's thirteen qualifications for the office in *Harper's Weekly*.

By 1910, corruption in New Jersey politics had been prevalent for so long that Harvey was able to convince the Democratic boss, Jim Smith, that to win the gubernatorial election that year, he had to nominate a 'reform' candidate, and that Wilson was an ideal choice. Though many of the delegates had never heard of Wilson, Smith forced the State Convention to nominate him.

Smith, who, like President Patton of Princeton before him, made the mistake of regarding Wilson as 'safe', soon realized the enormity of his error. As Governor, Wilson demonstrated a genius for sensing public opinion, and manipulating it for his political objectives. He broke with Smith, destroying his Democratic organization and blocking his return to the United States Senate. He forced a progressive programme through the New Jersey legislature, and his success during his first year in office won Wilson the support of progressive elements throughout the country. By 1912, the progressive movement was reaching its apex, and helped propel Wilson into the White House. It took double political luck, however, to make Wilson the beneficiary of this progressive momentum: Wilson's nomination against all the precedents as the Democratic candidate; and a suicidal split in the Republican Party.

Wilson was a long shot in the Democratic Party's convention in 1912. The leading candidate, Champ Clark, Speaker of the House of Representatives, received a majority of the delegates' votes on the first ballot. Until that convention, any candidate who received a simple majority always went on to win the two-thirds vote required for nomination. Wilson's victory on the forty-sixth ballot was due in part to the support of William Jennings Bryan, leader of the Party's western progressives and the Democratic candidate for President in three previous elections.[7] Bryan preferred the progressive Wilson to the conservative Clark. Ironically, before becoming Governor, Wilson, considering himself a Jeffersonian Democrat, had consistently opposed Bryan in his bids for the presidency. In 1907 he had written, 'Would that we could do something at once dignified and effective to knock Mr Bryan once and for all into a cocked hat.'

The Democratic nomination would have been a dubious prize but for the split in the Republican Party. The election of 1912 marked a dramatic protest against the effects of the extremely rapid industrialization of the previous fifty years, and the increasing concentration of economic power in the hands of trusts. The progressive viewpoint dominated the election. Not only did the Democrats turn to Wilson; but ex-president Teddy Roosevelt split the Republicans by forming the Progressive Party after the conservative Old Guard forced President Taft's re-nomination. The Republican split enabled Wilson to win with the smallest popular vote since Lincoln's triumph over three other candidates in 1860. It was only the third time since 1856 that a Democrat had been elected President.

The campaign was dominated by the debate between Wilson and Roosevelt on the proper role of the government in the economy. Roosevelt, who as President had gained a reputation as a trust-buster, argued now that the government should regulate monopoly rather than abolish it. Wilson, however, insisted that monopoly would eventually destroy both economic and political freedom, and his 'New Freedom' programme sought to destroy monopoly and retore free competition which he—like so many other Americans—saw as the epitome of the American system. More a call to a return to an earlier past than a programme for innovation, 'The New Freedom', as Richard Hofstader has written, 'was an attempt of the middle class with agrarian labour support to arrest the exploitation of the community, the concentration of wealth and the growing control of politics by insiders, and to restore as far as possible competitive opportunity in business'. Of the two approaches, Roosevelt's New Nationalism was the more realistic, as Wilson's own experience was to show, but both shared an underlying principle: that the government must be used as an instrument to achieve greater human welfare in the economic sphere. The election results proved that Wilson and Roosevelt had caught the temper of the times. Between them they received 70 per cent of the popular vote, Wilson 42·5 per cent and Roosevelt 27·5 per cent. Taft trailed both with only 23·5 per cent.[8]

Even before his entry into politics, Wilson had had strong views on the importance of the presidency in American government. In *Congressional Government* he had written, 'The President is at liberty both in law and conscience to be as big a man as he can', and that the centre of power in the American system must rest in the presidency. Wilson was vigorous and resourceful in putting his theories into practice. For the first time since John Adams, a president delivered his messages to Congress in person; he lobbied at the Capitol for action on his bills; legislation was drafted in the executive branch; and Wilson developed to a fine art the use of patronage for the purpose of influencing Congressmen and Senators. Theodore Roosevelt had been the first president since Lincoln to assert any of the latent powers of the Presidency; Wilson went far beyond Roosevelt in his attempts to make the executive the supreme branch of the government.

Nor did Wilson hesitate to appeal to public opinion over Congressional heads. In 1913, when his first piece of major legislation, the reform of the tariff laws, was in danger of being mutilated by pressures from special interests, Wilson publicly attacked the tariff lobby. 'There is evidence that money without limit is being spent to sustain this lobby and to create an appearance of a pressure of public opinion . . . It is of serious interest to the country that the people at large should have no lobby and be voiceless in these matters while great bodies of astute men seek to create an artificial opinion and to overcome the interests of the public for their private profit . . .' The public responded to Wilson and the Senate passed the first tariff reductions in decades[9]. Wilson thus became the architect of the modern American free trade tradition[10].

There followed in rapid succession the Federal Reserve Act of 1913 establishing concentrated control of the country's banking and currency system; the Clayton Anti-Trust Act; the creation of the Federal Trade Commission; and a law providing for an eight-hour work day on inter-state railways. All of this and more he accomplished during his first eighteen months in office. Never before had the country seen so much social and

economic legislation pass through Congress so rapidly; only twice since—
under the administrations of Franklin Roosevelt and Lyndon Johnson—
has anything comparable been achieved.

Paradoxically, most of Wilson's legislation had the effect of regulating
the economy rather than restructuring it as Wilson had proposed during
his campaign. Wilson's failure to effect any fundamental changes in the
structure of society signalled the progressive failure to reduce concentration
in the economy, but his regulating reforms established important precedents, later expanded by the New Deal. The regulatory approach, however,
had its limitations. A business recession struck America in 1914, and
Wilson—sharing the general ignorance of macro-economics then prevailing
—was forced to call a halt to reform. The halt, however, was not permanent.
Early in the election year of 1916, with an eye on the large progressive vote
of 1912, Wilson again shifted his course. Signalling his new bent with the
appointment of the progressive Louis Brandeis to the Supreme Court,
Wilson then pushed through Congress a Rural Credits Act, a Workmen's
Compensation Act and a Child Labor law, measures for which he had
previously shown little enthusaism. They may have been politically inspired
but they still added significantly to Wilson's domestic achievements. The
latter were the first real attempts to use the government as an instrument for
economic welfare, and their institutional legacy is at least equal to that of
any other president.

After the outbreak of war in August 1914, Wilson turned his attention
increasingly to world affairs. Domestically, the essence of American
progressivism, particularly in the hands of Wilson as its foremost
exponent, was moralism[11]; Wilson brought the same cast of mind to
foreign policy. He felt strongly that it was America's duty to use her moral
influence to promote liberty, justice, and a righteous peace. When he became
President, he seemed to believe that America could make her destined impact
on the world through example rather than direct involvement. He appreciated, however, that in the modern world it was no longer realistic to assume
that the non-interventionist precepts of Washington and Jefferson were
necessarily adequate guides for American behaviour.

The Mexican crisis, precipitated by the cruel murder of the revolutionary
leader, Madero, by the reactionary Huerta, posed Wilson's first major test
in foreign affairs. While Theodore Roosevelt had pursued intervention in
the Caribbean with barely concealed cynicism, Wilson's Mexican policy
was characterized from the outset by idealistic aspirations. 'Morality and
not expediency is the thing that must guide us,' he stated. 'The influence of
the United States must be used in support of constitutionalism.'

This commitment to constitutionalism led Wilson into a more tortuous
involvement than Roosevelt had ever contemplated. The establishment and
maintenance of a democratic regime in Mexico worthy of support proved
more complicated than he had foreseen. Wilson demanded elections from
Huerta but questioned their results after Huerta cleverly rigged them to his
advantage. Wilson, unable to appreciate the unsavoury facts of Mexican
political life, was then drawn more deeply into Mexican internal affairs by

43

his decision to support the Carranza constitutionalists. When Huerta countered by ordering guns from Germany, Wilson landed marines at Vera Cruz to prevent the import of arms he felt might be used against America. 'There can in what we do be no thought of aggression or selfish aggrandizement,' he told Congress. 'We seek to maintain the dignity and authority of the United States only because we wish always to keep our great influence unimpaired for the use of liberty both in the United States and wherever else it may be employed for the benefit of mankind.'

It is not difficult to think of parallel policies that have been pursued by some of Wilson's successors in other parts of the world. It would be a mistake, however, to follow the error of contemporary revisionist historians[12] who have questioned Wilson's sincerity. If anything, his errors stemmed from an excess of sincerity and moralism. The effects of his policy, however, were no less disastrous. He was eventually forced to abandon his intervention after leaving a legacy of animosity that took a generation to overcome[13].

With the outbreak of war in Europe, the problems of Mexico receded into the background. America's posture towards the First World War became a subject of controversy as soon as it became apparent that the conflict would not end quickly. Americans remained divided on the issue at least until the actual entry into the war in 1917. Many were sympathetic to the Allies; others, particularly those of German or Irish descent, had favoured the Central Powers. The American economy was already deeply intertwined with those of the Allies. As the war continued, American interests acquired an increasing economic stake in an Allied victory. U.S. exports to Allied countries rose from $824,000 in 1914 to $3,214,000 in 1916, while trade with the Central Powers virtually ceased. If commerce with the Allies had been severed, they would have been unable to carry on the war while the denial of Americans' access to Allied markets would have had serious effects on the American economy. Most of this trade, moreover, was made possible by the large credits provided to the Allies.

Wilson's immediate reaction to the outbreak of war was to call it a conflict 'with which we have nothing to do and whose causes cannot touch us'. He believed that by remaining neutral, America could act as 'the mediating nation' and exercise 'the force of moral principle'. At the same time, he insisted that America's rights as a neutral must be fully respected by all belligerents. Because German violations of these rights—through submarine warfare—involved loss of life while British violations did not, and because of personal sympathy for the cause of the Allies, which reflected the predominant view in America, Wilson's advocacy of 'neutral rights' bore more heavily on Germany than on Britain.

The first serious confrontation with Germany came after the sinking of the British liner *Lusitania* on 7 May 1915, when 128 Americans were among the 1,198 lives lost. American protests led to a German decision to spare large liners and to take precautions to ensure the safety of passengers[14]. After further sinkings in the following year, however, the United States' threat to break off diplomatic relations caused the German government to abandon unrestricted submarine warfare—partly because the German Chancellor, Bethmann-Hollweg, still hoped for a compromise peace and wished to avoid

44

Wilson addresses a joint-session of Congress urging declaration of war against Germany

American entry. In the meantime, Wilson faced a united Republican Party in the election of 1916, campaigned on the slogan, 'He has kept us out of war' and won a razor-thin victory in his bid for re-election[15].

In December 1916, after his re-election, Wilson tried to make peace through mediation. Success in this effort would have precluded direct American involvement in the war. He appealed to both sides to state their peace aims. When no satisfactory replies were received, he proceeded to specify the settlement they should seek. He called upon the belligerents to help create a new world order that would incorporate the principles of self-government, freedom of the seas, and limitation of armaments rather than a peace based on the balance of power or entangling alliances. Neither the Allies nor the Central Powers were willing to make peace on these terms and an opportunity for a moderate peace settlement was lost.

The final victory of the militarists within the German government in early 1917 led to the resumption of unrestricted submarine warfare on 31 January and made U.S. entry into the war practically inevitable. In the wake of further German sinkings, on 2 April 1917, Wilson asked Congress for a declaration of war. Wilson had been reluctant to become involved but when the pressure of events, public sentiment, and his own sense of mission impelled him to do so, he was determined that the war should be fought to achieve the highest ideals rather than to satisfy selfish national interests.

There was a responsible body of American opinion, including Secretary

of State Lansing and Colonel House, Wilson's closest adviser, which supported the Allies and called for intervention because they believed that a German victory would endanger American security[16]. As the embodiment of progressivism, however, Wilson had to justify his intervention in moral terms[17], and in the main the American people, still in the grip of the progressive impulse, responded in the same spirit.

In his speech before Congress on 2 April, Wilson emphasized that the United States was prepared to fight for those things that were even more precious than peace—'for democracy . . . for the rights and liberties of small nations and for a universal dominion of right by such a concert of free people as shall bring peace and safety to all nations and make the world itself at last free'.

The Bolshevik Revolution in November 1917 ensured that the war would indeed become an ideological struggle, and forced the Allies to become a great deal more specific about their war aims. As soon as they seized power, Lenin and Trotsky called for a just peace based on the renunciation of territorial annexations and self-determination for subject peoples. It was no accident that Wilson's famous Fourteen Points speech followed very shortly in January 1918[18]. The Fourteen Points which laid down Wilson's peace aims embodied his idealistic foreign policy programme; they were also his opening salvo in a campaign against Lenin for the allegiance of European peoples, as well as a brilliant stroke of psychological warfare against the Germans. Wilson called for open diplomacy, freedom of the seas, frontiers based on national self-determination, freedom for the subject peoples of the Austrian, German, Turkish and Russian Empires, the establishment of a world organization of nations, and—significantly—a German withdrawal from Russia. The great struggle to determine the shape of post-war Europe had begun.

Wilson's programme related his own vision of the post-war world to that of the non-revolutionary liberal and socialist forces of Europe[19]. Wilson had become the spokesman of progressive liberalism at home; he was now projecting this doctrine on the world scene so that he could act simultaneously as a spokesman for internationalism and anti-imperialism as well as for his kind of American nationalism. He identified his American values with universal liberal values: America had a mission to lead mankind toward the orderly international society of the future.

The publication of Wilson's Fourteen Points intensified party divisions inside Germany and helped bring about an earlier armistice. Wilson's liberal anti-imperialism also coincided with the aims and aspirations of the liberals and social democrats in Western Europe. Their identification with Wilson's idea of making a more rational and orderly world system out of independent nation states helped them to resist the violent solution of socialist revolution advocated by Lenin. It also provided the liberal left with an essential weapon in their domestic struggle against the right-wing forces which were committed to the maintenance of the *status quo* internally, and to the traditional values of European imperialism.

The conservative forces—controlling the government of France, and holding positions of great importance in England—were not happy with

Wilson's Fourteen Points. They favoured a punitive peace against Germany and intervention to overthrow the Bolsheviks in Russia. While the weakness of their own position and the strength of public opinion forced the conservatives to accept the Fourteen Points with minor reservations involving freedom of seas and reparations, they succeeded in persuading Wilson, whose attitude toward the Bolsheviks was a mixture of horror and understanding, to assist in armed intervention in north Russia and Siberia. The Bolsheviks themselves maintained a strong distrust of Wilson but quickly began to use the Fourteen Points as propaganda for their own ends.

Events in the autumn of 1918 set the stage for the difficult, frustrating negotiations at Versailles. The German Revolution that Wilson had hoped for occurred; eventually, an armistice was negotiated, largely on the basis of the Fourteen Points. At the same time, however, conservative forces in the allied nations improved their position. The 1918 'Khaki Election' in Great Britain strengthened the Tories enormously, and in America, the Republicans, running largely on a platform for a punitive peace, won control of the Congress in the off-year elections of 1918. Wilson had blundered during the campaign by making the peace treaty a partisan issue; later he compounded his mistake by failing to include a Republican of stature in the American delegation at Versailles. Thus both Wilson and Lloyd George's freedom of action was severely curtailed in the coming deliberations. The conservative forces were increasingly anxious not only to impose a punitive settlement on Germany, but to prevent the threatened spread of Bolshevism to Eastern and Central Europe[20].

Essentially there were three competing visions of the post-war world during the period when the Versailles Treaty was negotiated. The first— that of the Bolsheviks envisioned a spreading workers' revolution throughout Europe, and a victory for international communism. The second—the Wilsonian view—foresaw the spread of parliamentary democracy and reformist capitalism, and a new diplomacy based on the Fourteen Points to preserve the peace. The third, advocated most forcefully and effectively by French Premier George Clemenceau, favoured a punitive peace involving vast reparations and loss of territory for Germany, the defeat of democratic socialism, and the overthrow or containment of the Russian Revolution. None of these visions was sufficiently realistic to produce a lasting European settlement. Ultimately, by following the third, the Allies made another great war almost inevitable.

Weakened politically by his defeat in the Congressional elections of 1918, Wilson was unable to overcome the resistance of his Allies, particularly Clemenceau and Orlando of Italy, on questions of frontiers, notably Fiume and the Saar, reparations, and the disposition of the German colonies. Lloyd George, who shared Wilson's attitudes on some of these points, was equally handicapped by domestic difficulties, while Wilson's real allies— the democratic socialists of Western Europe—were unable to exert much pressure on the peace conference. The victory of those who favoured a punitive peace for Germany ensured that the German Revolution—which Wilson had done so much to promote—would be largely discredited by the peace settlement its leaders would have to sign.

Wilson, now hampered by illness as well as by political weakness, reacted to his compromises and failures on many specific points by pinnings his hopes on the Fourteenth Point: the League of Nations. Since, like most Americans, he still rejected the balance of power as a peace-keeping mechanism, he failed to appreciate that leaving Russia out of the post-war order would create a substantially unbalanced situation and looked to the League to resolve any future international disputes. With regard to the Soviet Union, he was at least able to prevent any large-scale intervention. While hardly sympathizing with the Bolsheviks, he understood some of the reasons for their success, and agreed with his advisers that the American people would not support any sustained intervention. On the other hand, he was induced to participate in some of the measures taken against the Soviets, thereby contributing to their belief that there was little to choose among the bourgeois states.

Thus Wilson's hopes for a just and humane peace based on a new world order were doomed by political division at home, by the conflicting aspirations of the victors, by the impossibility of integrating the Soviets into the post-war European system, and ultimately, by the very complexity of the situation with which he had to deal. At the same time, however, Clemenceau's victory was a hollow one. The punitive Versailles territorial and reparation provisions made German bitterness inevitable, while conservative hostility towards Russia precluded the restoration of a real balance of power. The French contented themselves with the illusion that the new Eastern European states would contain both Germany and Russia—a concept whose bankruptcy was dramatically realized in the Nazi-Soviet Pact of 1939. The peace of Versailles was based on the extraordinary circumstance of both Germany and Russia having been defeated. And such a peace was not destined to endure[21].

Wilson had accepted many compromises at Versailles in order to gain adherence to his Fourteenth Point, the establishment of the League of Nations. Never admitting publicly that the terms of the treaty had fallen short of expectations, he argued that the creation of the League would justify the sacrifices of the war. His obsessive rejection of amendments to the League Covenant[22] was self-defeating in the light of conditions he was facing by the fall of 1919. The idealism engendered by the war had begun to dissipate and public opinion was turning against him. American groups with ties to the old world criticized Wilson for failing to satisfy the demands of Ireland, Poland and Italy. Liberals who had been among Wilson's staunchest supporters were bitter about a settlement which perpetuated the evils of the pre-war world and provided little hope of realizing Wilson's Fourteen Points. They also found that Article 10 of the League Covenant obliging the signatory powers to respect and preserve the territorial integrity and existing political independence of all members would be used to sustain the *status quo*. And traditional isolationists, like Senator Borah, who had been silent during the war, now vigorously attacked Article 10 because it meant permanent involvement in world affairs, including a commitment to go to war to defend member states against aggression.

Nor did domestic developments help Wilson. Inflation sky-rocketed in

1919; there were violent industrial disputes, race riots in several cities, and a Red scare that provoked Attorney General Palmer's disgraceful anti-communist raids. With the war over, the American people were growing weary of Wilson's idealism and turning their attention to more mundane domestic problems.

The Republicans, smelling victory in 1920 and spurred on by Senator Lodge, Wilson's arch enemy, were doing everything possible to turn Wilson's deteriorating position to their political advantage. In face of a situation that demanded resourcefulness, imagination and flexibility, Wilson failed lamentably. He insisted that the Senate accept the text of the League Covenant without changes. He even broke off personal relations with Colonel House, his most intimate adviser, when House suggested Wilson permit moderate amendments[23] to facilitate the treaty's approval. With the Senate refusing to comply with his demands, Wilson went to the country, against the advice of his doctors, in a frantic attempt to rally public opinion behind his position. Before completing his tour, his health broke and he returned to Washington, a desperately ill man. For nine months he was unable to carry out the responsibilities of his office. In one of the most extraordinary episodes in American history, the country was kept ignorant of the fact that Mrs Wilson[24], with the assistance of the President's doctor, had assumed the Government's executive functions.

Within a year after Wilson was stricken, in two separate votes, the Senate rejected the treaty. In the presidential election of 1920, which became a plebiscite on Wilson's internationalism, the Republicans won by a landslide. The victory of Harding's isolationism and 'normalcy' was bitter proof that America was not yet ready for Wilson's 'noble experiment'.

Wilson was a sad, frustrated invalid during the four years of life that remained to him, but he never lost faith in the validity of his ideas and policies. He died in February 1924.

The twenties was a decade of great American prosperity based on an expanding national market which buttressed post-war isolationist sentiment. There was a return to passive administrations led by passive presidents. Wilson seemed throughly discredited. The crash of 1929 brought on the greatest depression in American history, and unhinged the world's economy posing new threats to the fragile inter-war peace. It revived the need for affirmative government and the Wilson experience as a guide for presidential action and style.

Beginning with Franklin Roosevelt, all presidents have been influenced by Wilson's conception of the Presidency and the way he used the office to deal with both the country's economic and social problems, and the issues of war and peace. When F.D.R. assumed office in 1932, he had to deal with economic and social problems more complex and more pressing than any previous president. His temperament and personality, his appreciation of the institutional legacy of the Wilson administration, in which he had served as Assistant Secretary of the Navy, and his commitment to the Wilsonian conception of the presidency, enabled Roosevelt to meet the demands of the American people for immediate remedial action.

Through constant personal contact with members of Congress, effective use of patronage, executive formulation of bills, and direct appeals to the public against special interests[25], Roosevelt pushed through a programme which greatly increased government involvement in the economic life of the nation. In strengthening executive power and leadership to combat the depression, F.D.R. also relied heavily on the experience of Wilson's war-mobilization in 1917-18, and on some of the men who had carried it out.

Roosevelt went beyond Wilson in reviving the tradition of attempting to achieve economic and social justice within the framework of a regulated capitalism. F.D.R. made government responsible for social security, wages and hours, housing and unemployment insurance. He was also the first president who attempted to use the new techniques of macro-economics[26] to improve the performance of the nation's economy.

This trend has continued. The Employment Act of 1946 passed under President Truman declared full employment an objective of national policy and established a Council of Economic Advisers in the Office of the President to help the government chart a course of steady economic growth. Though a relatively passive President, Eisenhower accepted in principle the commitment to manage the economy, while President Kennedy vigorously implemented it. Kennedy's guide-lines for wage settlements, his attack on U.S. Steel for announcing price increases without first consulting the government, and his innovative tax policies added new dimensions to presidential involvement in managing the nation's economy. President Nixon's belated conversion to Keynesian economics and his subsequent imposition of wage and price controls indicate that the Wilsonian legacy of government's active economic engagement is now accepted by both parties.

In dealing with international affairs, particularly the Second World War and its aftermath, Roosevelt, Truman and their successors also profited from Wilson's achievements and failures. F.D.R. had supported the League when he ran for Vice President in 1920. He was not unresponsive, however, to isolationist sentiments which persisted into the 1930s[27]. He was discouraged by the unfavourable public reaction to his 'Quarantine the Aggressors' speech in 1937, and until the fall of France, he moved cautiously on foreign affairs.

F.D.R.'s sympathies, however, lay with the Allies for practical balance of power as well as ideological reasons. A masterful tactician, he anticipated American involvement and took steps early to avoid Wilson's errors. Even before Pearl Harbour, he appointed two distinguished Republicans to his Cabinet as Secretaries of War and Navy. He saw to it that Republican Congressional leaders were associated with the peacemaking process at its earliest stages and he was able to commit the United States to membership in the United Nations prior to the end of hostilities.

Thus Roosevelt was more successful than Wilson in securing a broad concensus in favour of his policies. In his attitude towards American war aims, he showed a desire to combine Wilsonian idealism with enlightened realism. In his early definitions of these aims, and particularly in the Atlantic Charter, he resorted to flights of Wilsonian idealism in an effort to arouse support for the war. On the other hand, however, his belief in the possibility of coexistence with Stalinism, his attempts late in the war to prepare the American people for a less-than-perfect peace settlement, and his scepticism about the efficacy of the United Nations reflected an attempt to avoid excessive idealism. His death foreclosed the possibility of his trying to put his mixture of idealism and realism into practice.

Within two years of Roosevelt's death, Harry S. Truman, with a somewhat different perception of the state of the world, had produced an activist foreign policy in many ways reminiscent of Wilsonian idealism. By 1947, it was clear that Western Europe was economically prostrate and that the Soviet Union represented a major ideological threat to Western democracy and a military threat to world power balance. Truman, therefore, decided that the situation called for an American commitment on a world-wide, Wilsonian scale; and the more specific goal of this commitment—the containment of communism and Soviet power—made it easier for him to break through the barriers of isolationism than it had been for Wilson.

Through his Greek/Turkish policy, Marshall Aid and membership of NATO, Truman allied the United States to Western Europe and made it possible for her to revive economically and politically and to resist Stalin's pressures[28]. Significantly, it was a Labour Government in Britain which took the lead in organizing the European side of the new Euro-American alliance. The success of Truman's policies was largely due to the close collaboration between his administration and the non-Communist left in Western Europe.

Truman also committed the United States to opposing Communist aggression in other areas of the world, where possible using the United Nations for that purpose. He successfully resisted Moscow's challenges in Iran and Korea as well as in Berlin and Western Europe.

Truman's foreign policy combined balance of power considerations with some of Wilson's moral fervour and sense of mission to spread American ideals throughout the world. While Truman himself avoided a potentially disastrous American involvement in the civil war in China, the moral crusade against communism which he helped to inspire created a climate in which extremist critics of his policy could make political capital out of any Communist success. The idealistic heritage of Wilson proved a double-edged sword: moralism and idealism were perhaps essential for the creation of a foreign policy concensus in the United States, but at the same time they induced an over-simplified view of a changing world. This view, untempered by a rigorous refinement of American interests and assessment of American power, ultimately led to American commitments beyond her capabilities and, many Americans now argue, beyond her interests.

Mutatis mutandis Truman's successors have managed foreign policy in the Wilsonian tradition. A sense of moral obligation to defend freedom anywhere in the world and a continuing, open-ended political, economic and military commitment to that objective have been the basic ingredients of the policy. The spirit of this policy reached its apogee in John F. Kennedy's inaugural address in 1961[29]. By 1963, however, Kennedy had realized the nature of the Communist world had altered to the extent that accommodations with Soviet Russia were both possible and desirable, particularly after the nuclear missile crisis; and by the late sixties, the Vietnam war had raised fundamental questions about the basis of American policy in the decades ahead.

The gradual realization that the cost of Vietnam is unjustifiable has co-incided with the realization that communism has lost its monolithic character and that the United States is no longer the predominant power in shaping contemporary international relations. Grave doubts have arisen about the extent of American commitments—doubts reinforced by the fact that the country is beset by pressing social and economic problems that raise basic questions about her own values. Indeed, it is the Wilsonian moral strain in American overseas policy that has been most called into question at the very moment when the Wilsonian moral strain in terms of the American domestic social order is being so strongly aroused.

This heightened introspection should not distract the American people from learning to live with the part of the Wilsonian legacy which makes a major international role commensurate with her capabilities an enduring component of American life. Such a role is an essential ingredient of a peacefully ordered world. Americans, however, are more likely to accept it in the post-Vietnam era if the other part of the Wilsonian legacy is abandoned— that part which has led the United States to aspire to shape the world in the image of American ideals and has caused her to over-react and to over-extend herself.

[1] Herbert Hoover, *The Ordeal of Woodrow Wilson* (London, 1958) Preface VII-IX, *et passim.*

[2] For Nixon's attitude toward Wilson, see Gary Wills, *Nixon Agonistes* (Boston, 1970) p. 20, *et passim.*

[3] Herbert Agar, *The American Presidents* (London, 1936) p. 291.

[4] Wilson's own word.

[5] Then called the College of New Jersey.

[6] Ely, *Ground Under Our Feet*, quoted in Arthur Walworth, *Woodrow Wilson, American Prophet* (New York, 1958) vol. 1, p. 43.

[7] Even after Bryan threw his support to Wilson, it was necessary for the latter's managers to win over the city bosses and the delegates backing Congressman Underwood in order to nominate Wilson. See Arthur Link, *Woodrow Wilson and the Progressive Era 1910-1917* (London, 1954) p. 13.

[8] Eugene V. Debs, the Socialist candidate, received 6·2 per cent.

[9] The law also provides for a federal tax on incomes over $3,000. The sixteenth amendment which made such taxes constitutional had been approved earlier in the year.

[10] Cordell Hull, F.D.R.'s Secretary of State and the father of reciprocal trade agreements, was a Wilson apostle.

[11] It has often been overlooked that Wilson's morality and progressivism did not encompass the American Negroes. After successfully soliciting their support in the election of 1912, he rejected a request to establish a National Race Commission and angered Negro and White liberal leaders by approving the formal introduction of segregation in several government departments. For further details, see Arthur Link, op. cit. pp. 62-66.

[12] *Wilson* by William A. Williams in *New York Review of Books*, 2 December 1971. The article is a review of eight books on Woodrow Wilson.

[13] Samuel Flagg Bemis, *Woodrow Wilson and Latin America*, from Edward Beuhrig, *Wilson's Foreign Policy in Perspective* (Bloomington, Indiana, 1957).

[14] They also led to the resignation of Secretary of State William Jennings Bryan, who did not share Wilson's desire for America to play an active though non-belligerent role in the world crisis and favoured peace at any price.

[15] Wilson went to bed thinking he had lost, but California, New Mexico and North Dakota narrowly went Democratic—the returns from the West were late because of the time difference —and Wilson squeaked through.

[16] Soon after the outbreak of war, House wrote to Wilson. 'If Germany should win, we will have to abandon the path which you are blazing for future generations . . . and build up a military machine of vast proportions.' In his diary, House stated that Wilson agreed.

[17] The two positions were not mutually contradictory. In fact, in this case, they sustained one another.

[18] John Wheeler-Bennett, *Brest-Litovsk* (London, 1938) p. 146.

[19] For fuller treatment of this point see Norman G. Levin, *Woodrow Wilson and World Politics* (London, 1968).

[20] For a full treatment of the influence of domestic politics on the Versailles negotiations see Arno J. Mayor, *Politics and Diplomacy of Peacemaking* (New York, 1967).

[21] A. J. P. Taylor, *Origins of the Second World War* (London, 1963) p. 41.

[22] Wilson had introduced some changes in the Covenant in response to Republican proposals made before his return to Paris in April 1919—domestic issues were excluded from the League's province, and regional arrangements like the Monroe doctrine were specifically safeguarded— but refused to accept any further changes after he brought the treaty home.

[23] It was generally accepted that a two-thirds majority was willing to approve the treaty with moderate reservations.

[24] This was the second Mrs Wilson. The President's first wife had died in August 1914 and sixteen months later he married Edith Bolling Galt, a Washington widow.

[25] Radio provided F.D.R. with a powerful new instrument for communicating with the people, and he used the presidential press conference more extensively and effectively than any predecessor.

[26] Despite the fact that he never really understood Keynes.

[27] Just as Wilson had campaigned in 1916 on the slogan 'He kept us out of the war', F.D.R. promised in the 1940 election 'Your boys are not going to be sent to any foreign wars.'

[28] Truman had obviously learned from Wilson how *not* to handle Congress. He got his key international legislation through the Republican controlled 80th Congress and then won the 1948 election by campaigning against the 'do-nothing, good-for-nothing 80th Congress'!

[29] We shall pay any price, bear any burden, meet any hardship, support any friend, oppose any foe to assure the survival and the success of liberty.'

Wilhelm II
by Sir John Wheeler-Bennett

SIR JOHN WHEELER-BENNETT (b. 1902) was educated at Malvern College but owing to ill-health was unable to go up to Oxford. In 1924 he founded the Information Service on International Affairs, which subsequently became the Information Department of the Royal Institute of International Affairs, of which he was a member of the Council for sixteen years. His activities took him throughout Europe, the Commonwealth, Asia and the United States while specializing in American, German and Irish affairs. During the War he served in Britain, the U.S.A. and Europe with the Ministry of Information, the Foreign Office and SHAEF and was later attached to the British Prosecution Team at the Nuremberg Trials. In 1946 he became first British Editor-in-Chief of the captured German Foreign Ministry Archives.

He was a founding Fellow of St Antony's College, Oxford, in 1950 and has been a visiting Professor and Scholar-in-Residence at various American Universities. In 1958 he published the official *Life of King George VI*, was knighted the following year and also appointed Historical Adviser, Royal Archives. He is a Trustee of the Imperial War Museum.

His numerous works of history and biography include *Hindenburg, the Wooden Titan* (1936); *Brest-Litovsk, the Forgotten Peace* (1938); *Munich, Prologue to Tragedy* (1948); *The Nemesis of Power: the German Army in Politics* (1953); *John Anderson, Viscount Waverley* (1962); and, in co-authorship with Anthony Nicholls, *The Semblance of Peace: the Political Settlement after the Second World War* (1972).

Wilhelm II

27 Jan. 1859 Born. Educated by a tutor, Hinzpeter, and at Kassel gymnasium and Bonn university.

1866 Prussian victory over Austria and the lesser German states.

1871 Prussian defeat of France. William headed victory parade with his father and grandfather.

1877 Undertook military training, chiefly in Potsdam.

Feb. 1881 Married Princess Augusta Victoria of Schleswig Holstein-Augustenberg, who later had six sons and a daughter.

1886 Attached to Foreign Ministry by Bismarck.

16 March 1888 William I died and was succeeded as Kaiser by his son Frederick.

15 June 1888 Frederick died and was succeeded by his son, William II. His henchmen were Eulenberg, Waldersee, and Holstein.

18 March 1890 Forced Chancellor Bismarck to resign. Caprivi became Chancellor, Marschall Secretary of State for Foreign Affairs, and Holstein chief of political department in Foreign Office.

1890 Heligoland treaty—a rapprochment with Britain. William wanted to counteract incipient Franco-Russian rapprochement by improving

Previous page: formal portrait in the uniform of a Field Marshal. The Kaiser's left arm was withered

relations between Triple Alliance and Britain.

1894 Hohenlohe became Chancellor.

Jan. 1896 Angered Britain by sending President Kruger of Transvaal congratulatory telegram on suppression of Jameson raid.

1897 Von Tirpitz became Secretary of State for naval affairs—heralded an expansionist naval policy aimed at challenging Britain's naval supremacy. Von Bülow given control of foreign affairs—he believed in policy of overseas expansion to enhance Kaiser's prestige.

Oct. 1897 Germany seized Kiao-Chow in China. Failure of attempts by British ministers to enlist German support against Russia in Far East.

1900 Von Bülow became Chancellor. Boxer rising in China. William sent German contingent to help suppress rising and urged them to behave like 'Huns' towards their foes.

1904 Anglo-French understanding affecting colonial claims, especially in Egypt and Morocco. William urged foreign office to defend German interests.

Feb. 1904 Russo-Japanese war in which Japanese victories weakened Russia.

1905 Ostentatiously visited Tangiers and challenged French supremacy in Morocco. Delcassé, French Foreign Minister, fell from power. German pressures achieved international conference on Morocco.

July 1905 Secret treaty of Björkö whereby German and Russian emperors swore eternal friendship.

Jan. 1906 Algeciras conference on Morocco disappointing for Germany. Britain and France driven into closer co-operation by German pressure.

1907 Anglo-Russian agreements removed sources of conflict between the two countries.

1906-10 Growing naval rivalry between Germany and Britain.

1908 *Daily Telegraph* affair in Germany. William's indiscreet interview weakened his domestic position and estranged him from Bülow.

1909 Bethmann-Hollweg replaced Bülow as Chancellor.

1911 Crisis over German pressure on France about Morocco. Resolved by compromise, but only after Britain had declared its support for France.

1912-13 Wars in Balkans weakened Turkey and strengthened Serbia. Hence German/Austrian influence in Balkans diminished.

1914 Murder of Archduke Francis Ferdinand of Austria at Sarajevo. German government encouraged Austrians to send harsh ultimatum to Serbia and promised support— 'blank cheque'. General war followed. Schlieffen plan to knock out France before Russia could intervene effectively in the war failed on the Marne. Russian forces defeated at Tannenberg and the Masurian Lakes by Hindenburg and Ludendorff.

1916 Battle of Verdun lost by Germans. Hindenburg and Ludendorff took over command of German armies and thenceforth dominated conduct of war and diplomacy.

1917 Unrestricted U-boat warfare brought U.S. into war against Germany. Bethmann-Hollweg dismissed and succeeded by Prince Max von Baden.

11 Nov. 1918 Armistice ended First World War. William went into exile in the Netherlands.

4 June 1941 Died.

illiam II of Hohenzollern—ninth and last King of Prussia; third and last German Emperor[1]—dominated the political stage of Europe for the thirty years of his reign and left upon the twentieth century as indelible an impact as it is possible to imagine. His place in history, high on the debit side of the ledger, is indisputable. The question of absorbing interest is how, despite his many gifts and undeniable intelligence, he achieved this eminence. Whence sprang this man of 'infinite variety' who coined such household phrases as 'a place in the sun', 'shining armour', 'the rattling sabre' and 'Attila and his Huns'; who believed—and quite genuinely—that he ruled by Divine Right; who was the first man in modern times to be internationally indicted as a War Criminal; who was capable of both dignity and vulgarity to an amazing degree; whom a former Russian ambassador to the Imperial German Court described to me as 'the rudest man I have ever met' and whom many of his English contemporaries did not hesitate to designate a 'howling cad'; the man, incidentally, in whose arms Queen Victoria died.[2]

Though it is tempting to rely too greatly upon psychological explanations for these phenomena, there would seem to be no doubt that therein lies some part of the elucidation. Had William II been born a physically normal child the chances are that his character would have developed along normal lines; but this was not so. Within a month of his birth it was discovered that his left arm was paralysed, the shoulder socket injured and the elbow joint dislocated. The muscular condition was considered so bad that, in the then elementary state of orthopaedics, no doctor dared to attempt a readjustment of the limb. The result was a prevalent and increasing weakness.

William, in whose mind and character it must be admitted there appears a certain similarity to those of his great uncle, Frederick William IV,[3] entered upon life therefore with a severe handicap which was to cause him physical suffering and mental frustration and, while it is both easy and dangerous to over-emphasize the psychological effects of these difficulties, it must be accepted that at least a part of the eccentricity which later manifested itself in his disposition, was attributable to the untoward circumstances of his birth.

The incurable disability of his left arm proved the greatest hindrance to his physical and psychological development and the utmost skill and care would have been powerless to assist him had not the child himself co-operated with an unusual energy and resolution. Confronted with a sense of bodily helplessness and the awkward diffidence inseparable from it, William displayed a fortitude and a perseverance which must evoke our admiration and sympathy. He submitted to electrical treatments which caused him extreme pain and to gymnastic exercises which racked his frail young body in sweating torture. When all proved fruitless he set himself with patient determination to hide his affliction beneath a cloak of simulated use. The left hand would rest with apparent ease in his belt or pocket and, later, on the hilt of his sword; and so accomplished did he become in these deceptions that the infirmity would pass almost unnoticed even at the dinner-table.

But pretence did not satisfy the boy. A Prince must not only be equal, he must excel, even though the process cost him endless suffering and humiliation. William learned with infinite pains to become a strong swimmer, an excellent shot and a fearless horseman. It also became possible for him to use his left hand when playing the piano, a relaxation which he enjoyed, though he was no concert performer.[3]

Physical disability and the overcoming of it is never without its repercussions. The process itself is traumatic, the after-effects varying but always significant. In some cases it stengthens the character beneficially, emphasizing a kindly attitude to others similarly incapacitated and a general sense of compassionate understanding; sometimes it evokes an aggressive assertiveness; sometimes past frustration seeks to find compensation in great gusts of rage. Certain it is that no sufferer of this nature emerges unchanged from his ordeal.

It was impossible therefore that a sensitive and delicate nature such as Prince William's should escape the scars of his suffering, even though his efforts were eventually crowned with success and achievement. From his earliest boyhood he felt impelled to take the lead and to outdo his companions in sports and pastimes. The will to excel in spite of his affliction urged him to behaviour which otherwise might well have been alien to him. He drove himself forward against his weakness, shielding his natural timidity with a self-protective and compensating covering of aggressive self-assertion, which later developed into a certain boorish brutality.[5]

With every effort directed towards attaining the outward and physical attributes of a future monarch, it was inevitable that the spiritual and inward side should suffer. Despite the considerable—even brilliant— intellect which he soon revealed, young William failed to develop any power of concentration. It soon became evident that any mental discipline, even the gentlest, any sort of pressure at all, any attempt to formulate his deeper nature, was resisted to the utmost. That spirit of reckless irresponsibility, brooking neither criticism nor correction which became so marked a characteristic—and which reached its apogee in the dismissal of Bismarck— was already making its appearance.

The relation of young William with his parents was also undoubtedly one of the strongest influences in his psychological development. There was a tradition of harshness and conflict in the Hohenzollern family, which had already provided its famous example, in the relationship between Frederick the Great and his father. Carlyle's passionately worded picture of the young prince beaten, burned, frozen and manacled at the orders of the King reads like a nightmare of lunatic savagery. But from the day of the Great Elector each successive generation sulked and rebelled against parental restrictions, and in its turn abused and terrorized its sons.[6]

This absence of understanding and affection was notable in the childhood and adolescence of William vis-à-vis his parents. The Crown Princess Victoria, very much Queen Victoria's daughter and perhaps even more so the Prince Consort's, herself brought up in a strict regime, was not inclined to relax the rigid code of her own upbringing in regard to her own children. Maternal compassion was replaced by a sense of dynastic responsibility and perhaps in her innermost soul there was something repellent to her in this crippled first-born. She had longed for a son—'My whole heart was set upon a boy and therefore I did not expect one' she had written to her mother—but the longing had been for one who should inherit her husband's blond handsomeness and not this pale, diffident, mis-shapen child who—as she wrote to Queen Victoria—'would be a very pretty boy were it not for that wretched unhappy arm which shows more and more, spoils his face (for it is on one side), his carriage, walk and figure, makes him awkward in all his movements and gives him a feeling of shyness, as he feels his complete dependence not being able to do a thing for himself'.

With an intuition unduly developed by suffering, the young Prince sensed the disappointment of his parents at his physical shortcomings and their unexpressed preference for his younger brother and his sisters. He resented this believed injustice with the bitterness of which only a precocious child is capable and in his craving for the affection which was not forthcoming at home he turned to the one individual who had never failed him in devoted attachment, his grandfather the veteran monarch William I.

The friendship between the Emperor and his eldest grandson ripened with the years, not at all to the approval of the boy's parents who feared that such attention would put ideas into his head which, as the Crown Princess wrote to Queen Victoria 'was neither wholesome nor good'. More especially did they resent, in later years, the fact that the grandfather persisted in bringing the young Prince into relations with their inveterate enemy, Bismarck. The adulation of the aged Emperor and the subtle influence of the Iron Chancellor did indeed leave their imprint on young William who had inherited both his grandfather's rigid devotion to Prussian monarchical principles and his father's fantasies of German imperial mysticism. He adored the Emperor and admired the Chancellor; but with most others he was boorish, self-assertive and reckless, traits that were all too apparent to his father, the Crown Prince Frederick. In commenting to Bismarck in 1886 on a suggestion that the twenty-seven-year-old Prince William should be initiated into the secrets of German foreign policy, the father wrote, 'In view of the unripeness and inexperience of my eldest son, combined with his tendency to bragging and conceit, I consider it positively dangerous to allow him to come into contact with foreign affairs'.

Already in Prince William's unchecked headstrong youth there was apparent that weltering in self-pity, later to develop into wild hysteria, which every now and then distracted his judgement and—as for instance after the Eulenberg-Moltke scandals of 1907[7] and the *Daily Telegraph* affair of 1908[8]—plunged him into such acute despair that he considered the possibility of abdication.

Present too were the early prognostics of that almost pathological hatred of Socialists and Socialism and his fears of a repetition of the popular revolutionary events of 1848 which had driven his grandfather, the Regent—then known for repressive reasons as the 'Cartridge Prince'—in temporary flight from Berlin. 'I have no doubt,' William II told the Emperor Alexander Regiment of Guards in March 1901, 'that, if ever again the city should presume to rise up against its master, the regiment will repress with the bayonet the impertinence (*Frechheit*) of the people towards their King',[9] and some few years later, in his famous New Year's letter of 1906 to Prince von Bülow, he exhorted his Chancellor to 'shoot down, behead and eliminate the Socialists, if need be by a blood bath'.[10]

Nor were there lacking the symptoms of that irresponsible impulsiveness which evoked the notorious congratulatory telegram to President Kruger in January 1896 on the ignominious failure of the Jameson Raid and also, most tragic of all, the reckless 'brinkmanship' of the 'blank cheque' given to Austria-Hungary in July 1914.[11]

Such were the strangely conflicting elements in the background and mentality of the man who, at the age of twenty-nine, inherited the German and Prussian crowns on 15 June, 1888 — the 'Year of the Three Emperors'. Disliked and distrusted by his too rigid parents, well loved and overly indulged by his doting grandfather, subtly flattered and cajoled by the astute Prince Bismarck who essayed to use him as a weapon in his bitter battle with the Crown Prince and Princess, it would have been strangely improbable if William II had been anything but what he was. The circumstances and influence of his upbringing, his adolescence and his young manhood were such that it would have required a more balanced psyche and a stronger character to surmount them and to control their recoil.

Nevertheless one must admit the verdict of a Russian diplomat and courtier in considering this very subject: *Ça explique mais ça n'excuse pas.*[12]

The foreign policy which William II inherited from his grandfather was that of Bismarck in his latter years. Having destroyed the military potential of France and therefore temporarily eliminated her as a serious political rival, the Iron Chancellor had also, by founding the German Empire, erased the powerful influence which the Tsars of Russia had exercised in the German courts since the days of Alexander I. Bismarck's aim therefore was to insure against the revival of French political reactionary spirit which might culminate in a war of *revanche*. To do this he pursued a policy based on a balance of power. He achieved a partnership between Germany, Russia and Austria-Hungary in the *Dreikaiserbund* of 1881, while concluding the Triple Alliance with Austria-Hungary and Italy in the following year, to which Rumania adhered a year later. With fantastic agility the Imperial Chancellor performed miracles of political jugglery but always he conceived of Germany as a *continental* power content with her position as a dominant force in Europe.

There were those, however, among the Prince's enemies who held that Germany had outgrown his policy of 'limited objectives' and had reached the stage of national and international development which entitled her to become a world power in the sense of expansionist activities. Germany was a 'Johnny-come-lately' among the great colonial nations such as Britain and France and this, they thought, should be remedied; moreover it was necessary that Germany should be recognized as exercising a spiritual and nationalistic leadership over all Germans, whether within her boundaries or without.

Of these potential policies Bismarck was intolerant. He was convinced that an adoption of the doctrines of Pan-Germanism would alienate Russia who would feel herself menaced, and he set great store by Russia's friendship.

Similarly, the pursuit of colonial ambitions would bring Germany inevitably into competition and ultimate conflict with Britain because colonies implied a fleet and a great German naval programme would be regarded by Britain as a challenge to her supremacy in sea-power. The existing rivalry between Britain and France might well be composed in the face of such naval competition and Bismarck counted upon keeping France isolated.

The honeymoon between the young Emperor and his aged Chancellor did not last long. Bismarck was frankly apprehensive of his sovereign's approach to policy, William was intolerant of the Old Man's warnings and disapproval. The Kaiser was strengthened in his desire to be rid of Bismarck by the knowledge that the Chancellor's boorish and dictatorial attitude had alienated many political groups in Germany, and his threats of a *Staatsstreich* against the *Reichstag* were creating serious tension. On 17 March 1890, the Emperor 'dropped the pilot', who had navigated the German ship of state for thirty years. Although perhaps justified by the critical situation which faced him, the Kaiser's action initiated a train of events which culminated in the decline and fall of the German Empire.

William II was essentially, in many respects, a typical product of his age, desiring to be a 'modern' King, seeking contact with savants, merchants and technicians. At the same time however, he was completely and sincerely imbued with the concept that monarchs derived from Divine Grace. 'Modern' he might desire to be but he was, beyond question, reactionary at heart and it was from this moment of his separation from Bismarck that the forces of conservative dynasticism were given their heads. Those who urged pushful expansion abroad found support and encouragement from their Imperial master, and the prevailing insistence that Germany must under no circumstances yield priority of place to Britain emanated from William himself and was to influence the political thoughts and credos of his chief advisers.

These men were pygmies in stature beside the Iron Chancellor who, though he could be brutal and ruthless, on occasion unprincipled and mendacious, yet had a grasp of statecraft to which none of his successors could attain. They were, for the most part, meagre men, lacking the vision, the imagination and the caution of Bismarck. Of the pre-war Chancellors, General Count von Caprivi-Montecucoli was a man of integrity but possessed of only limited imagination, whose attempts to create an orderly and coherent administrative system in the Reich broke down in the face of departmental feuding and court intrigues.[13] He was followed by an aged non-entity, Prince zu Hohenlohe-Schillingfürst, and although their successors, Prince von Bülow and Herr von Bethmann Hollweg were men of greater intelligence, there was a fatal tendency, particularly in Bethmann, to mistake 'brinkmanship' for statesmanship.[14]

The outstanding figures of the pre-war period of William II's reign were in the armed services. Field Marshal Count von Waldersee and his greater successor, Count von Schlieffen, together with Grand Admiral von Tirpitz, exercised a major influence in both domestic and foreign policy which though resounding to the immediate glory of Germany, was in the long run to bring about her downfall.

Nearly all these figures were, for one reason or another—either genuine admiration or self-advancing sycophancy—vehement in their exaggerated flummery towards the Emperor. They served him the heady brew of excessive blandiloquence, praising his leadership in his demands for 'a place in the sun' and applauding his outbursts of bombast and *braggadocio*, his support for the building of a German High Seas Fleet and his claims to equality with Britain in every sphere of policy; even condoning his play-acting farce of whitening his face when he preached to the crew of the *Hohenzollern*! Flattery rose like incense at some medieval shrine, it ascended unchecked imperially and obviously enjoyed.[15]

Yet none of the counsellors appears to have understood the curious ambivalence of attitude which William II entertained for England. His was a love-hate complex embodied primarily in his personal relations. Next to his adored grandfather, William I, he held his grandmother, Queen Victoria, in profound affection and esteem—and even awe, but his relations with 'Uncle Bertie' (King Edward VII) partook of mutual antipathy.[16] While galled by the superiority of Britain and the failure of his English relations to take him seriously, he envied the free and easy manner of King Edward and the effective manner in which the British Royal Family identified themselves with all strata of the general public, from the aristocracy, with whom they shot and dined, to costermongers who shouted 'good old Bertie' as the King drove by.

Within twenty years of the dismissal of Bismarck all the old Prince's prognostications had been fulfilled and the 'new men' of Germany, headed by their Emperor, had achieved every one of his forbodings. By 1893 Russo-German relations, on the amicability of which Bismarck had laid so great an emphasis, had become so exacerbated that Russia had concluded a treaty of alliance with France which remained secret until four years later, and although William II sought to off-set this alignment by the bizarre episode of the secret Treaty of Björkö in July 1905, whereby the German and Russian Emperors swore eternal friendship, neither was able to gain the acquiescence of his constitutional advisers and the whole transaction became *quelque chose pour rire*![17]

Similarly, Germany had become a colonial power of some standing with imperial possessions in China, insular possessions in the Pacific and colonial holdings in East and South West Africa. She had, moreover, embarked on a 'Greater German Navy' programme. Attempts by Joseph Chamberlain and Lord Haldane to arrive at an Anglo-German understanding had been rebuffed and relations between the two countries reached an hitherto all time 'low' when in 1906 the German navy added the construction of 'Dreadnoughts' to its building programme. As Bismarck had foreseen, Britain and France had composed their differences over Egypt and Morocco and had eliminated the memory of Fashoda in the halcyon conclusion of the *Entente Cordiale* in April 1904, which placed Britain on the periphery of the Franco-Russian alliance and of which the solidarity against Germany was demonstrated in the course of the Moroccan crises of 1905 and 1911.

In the course of each of these two last diplomatic episodes Germany suffered a rebuff which merely aggravated her ego, her sense of 'encirclement' and her political ambitions. The Kaiser's entourage, and especially the military and naval leadership, demanded a policy of toughness in international affairs, and did everything they could to strengthen William's resolve in times of crisis. Talk of war was commonplace, although great inconsistency was shown in choosing the objectives of German policy. Sometimes Britain was seen as the enemy, sometimes Russia. But the tone of belligerence was unmistakeable.[18] As a result the peace of Europe became the more disastrously menaced. The lid of the powder-keg had been unsealed, the trail was in process of being laid, only the striking of a match was needed.

On Sunday, 28 June 1914, the match was applied. The Emperor was taking his ease under the awning on the deck of the imperial yacht *Hohenzollern* on the afternoon of that day, contemplating with relish and relaxation the pleasures of the Kiel regatta in which he always took a strong interest and a prominent part. Suddenly there appeared alongside a steam pinnace, in the stern sheets of which stood a young naval officer in an obvious state of excitement. He waved a green paper, then folding it up he placed it in his cigarette case and threw it on deck. Opening it the Emperor learned of the murder that morning of his friend and recent host, the heir to the Austro-Hungarian throne, Archduke Franz Ferdinand, and his morganatic wife Sophie, Duchess of Hohenburg in Sarajevo at the hands of a Serbian nationalist gunman.

The Emperor at once called off the regatta and returned to Berlin, where on 5 July he received the Austrian Ambassador, Count Lazlo Szögyeny-Marich, in two long audiences, separated by luncheon, to which the Ambassador was invited to stay. The upshot of this meeting was the famous 'blank cheque' which formed the major responsibility of William II for the First World War.

The Emperor informed Szögyeny that Germany would give 'full support' to Austria-Hungary in her action against Serbia, even in the case of 'grave European complications' even should these lead to war between Austria and Russia. Moreover, he added, if Austria decided upon military action she ought to march at once. He also told the Ambassador, who so reported to Vienna, that 'We [the Austrians] would regret it if we let the present crisis, which was so favourable for us, go by without utilizing it'.[19]

This was indeed playing with fire in two respects. It gave the Austrians a free hand in dealing with Serbia, even if Russia supported her small Slavic ally, and it played into the hands of the Imperial Chancellor, Bethmann-Hollweg, whose proclivity for 'brinkmanship' led him to grasp the opportunity of the calculated risk of a diplomatic coup for Germany and Austria-Hungary, even at the risk of a limited war.[20] Here is the clue to the basic assumption of German policy. For three fateful weeks after the assassination at Sarajevo, both the Emperor and his Chancellor were operating in a world of illusion. The dangers of a general war were, in their belief, very limited. Austrian military action against Serbia, if it happened at all, would be over and done with before anyone could do anything about it and Europe would be faced with a *fait accompli* similar to that of the annexation of Bosnia and Herzegovina in 1908. Both Russia and France were still too militarily weak to do more than protest and in any case the Franco-Russian alliance was believed to be of no great value. Britain would certainly remain neutral. All in all Germany was well placed to weather the crisis whichever way it developed.

Yet, though the Emperor did not want or expect a general war, he did not wholly exclude its possibility and he deliberately ignored one vital factor which, had he considered it, should have given him pause for reflection. He was fully cognisant of the Schlieffen Plan which provided for the invasion of France and for a sweep through Belgium. He knew that Britain—and indeed Germany—was a guarantor of Belgian neutrality. Even though Britain's loyalty to the *Entente Cordiale* might waver, her pledged word to Belgium would certainly be honoured.[21]

Having given his fateful advice to Austria, William II joined his fleet in Norwegian waters where, according to his own account, he only learned of the Austrian ultimatum to Belgrade of 23 July from the Norwegian press and not from Berlin.[22] The abject submission of the Serbian Government (25 July) convinced him of the wisdom of his original judgement. The whole matter was settled. He had maintained the peace of Europe, while at the same time scoring an outstanding success for Germany and displaying his own mastery of statecraft. 'A brilliant diplomatic triumph' he declared, 'no excuse for war; no need to mobilize'.

But it was too late. History had moved too fast and too far for so satis-factory an outcome. In Vienna and Berlin the soldiers had taken over. Conrad von Hötzendorff and von Moltke had moved with unlooked for celerity and now Bethmann stood aghast at the results as it became daily more evident that both he and his Emperor had made a hideous miscalcu-lation.[23] William II's reactions to the European complications, which were now multiplying almost hourly, were neither those of a politician, a states-man, nor even a realist, but of a dynast. In his fond and fundamental faith in the Divine Right of Kings he believed that his fellow monarchs, Tsar Nicholas II, King George V, the Emperor Franz Joseph, King Victor Emmanuel, together with King Carol I of Rumania and Tsar Ferdinand of Bulgaria, would respond to a word in season from himself and by their royal power prevent the European catastrophe. Nothing of the sort, however, happened; his fury and his consternation mounted, and when the British attitude finally became clear his disordered mind expressed itself in what was probably one of the most hysterical marginal notes in history.[24]

No Roman Emperor exercised greater martial authority than nominally did William II when he went to war at the head of his armies in August 1914,[25] but little by little the War Lord became the prisoner of his paladins and the control of German destinies passed even more completely into the hands of those enigmatic and anonymous figures who wore the coveted wine-red trouser stripe of the General Staff. The fiction of the Emperor as Supreme War Lord did not long survive the failures of the German armies on the Western Front at the Marne and the Aisne. New popular idols had appeared on the Eastern Front with Hindenburg's and Ludendorff's victories at Tannenberg and the Masurian Lakes and before the brilliances of these luminaries even the star of the Hohenzollerns waned and paled. By 1915, whispers were cir-

Overleaf- centre: with his cousin Britain's King Edward VII. Left and right: British suspicion turned to hatred symbolized by these two wartime cartoons in Punch

culating that the Supreme War Lord should if not adbicate, at least relin-
quish the conduct of the war to Field Marshal von Hindenburg as Chief of
the Armed Forces and Dictator of the Reich, a course of which the principal
advocate was none other than Grand Admiral von Tirpitz. [26]

Though this drastic solution for Germany's war-time political problems
was never put into operation the fact that it was bruited and canvassed in
the highest circles indicated clearly that around William II 'the divinity
that doth hedge a King' had lost much of its mystic qualities, and when
William II was compelled to appoint Hindenburg and Ludendorff to the
Supreme Command in the following year, his position thenceforward rapidly
deteriorated into that of an item of excess and unwanted impedimenta at
Imperial Headquarters.

For the next two years Hindenburg and Ludendorff dominated not only
the conduct of the war but the whole domestic and diplomatic policy of the
Reich—including the diminishing influence of the Emperor. With his
authority they insisted on the introduction of unrestricted U-boat warfare
and therefore made America's entry into the war inevitable. They demanded
the establishment of a Kingdom of Poland and thereby destroyed all hopes of
a separate peace with Tsarist Russia. The predatory nature of their demands
upon France and Belgium ruined whatever chances of success may have
attended the Papal peace proposals of 1917. It was they who were responsible
for the return of Lenin and his colleagues from Switzerland to Russia in the
famous 'sealed train', and the rapacity of the terms which they subsequently
enforced upon the Bolsheviks at Brest-Litovsk not only defeated their

UNCONQUERABLE.

The Kaiser. "SO, YOU SEE—YOU'VE LOST EVERYTHING."
The King of the Belgians. "NOT MY SOUL."

own ends but outraged the civilized world as an example of naked annexation.

When final defeat came in November 1918 the pale shadow of the Emperor, deserted by all save a handful of loyal courtiers and retainers, crossed the Netherlands frontier, a refugee from mutiny and revolution. Even in this he was too late to save his royal house. Had he abdicated at any moment during the ten days preceding the afternoon of 9 November, he might well have saved the crown and the dynasty. Only the followers of Liebknecht and Haase were genuinely republican and they formed a minority—if a vociferous one—of the Socialist movement. The Majority Socialists, led by Fritz Ebert, realized their own unpreparedness for assuming the burden of office and government and when their time came they crossed their Rubicon with profound reluctance.[27] Before this moment arrived they moved heaven and earth to secure the establishment of a constitutional monarchy with a regent—preferably Prince Max of Baden—acting in the name of one of the sons of the Crown Prince. The only insurmountable obstacle to this sole source of salvation for the Hohenzollern dynasty, and indeed for German Social Democracy itself, lay in the adamant refusal of William II to sacrifice himself for the continued welfare and existence of his throne, an inflexibility which he maintained until, in desperation, Prince Max himself announced his renunciation of the crown. William II had performed his last disservice to the Prussian monarchy. As one who had publicly advertised his dynastic belief, in the final analysis, he failed to sacrifice personal arrogance for the cause of dynasty.[28]

THE WORLD'S ENEMY.
THE KAISER. "WHO GOES THERE?"
SPIRIT OF CARNAGE. "A FRIEND—YOU'R ONLY ONE."

The Warlord. The Kaiser inspects his troops on the eastern front

Exile is always a traumatic experience; however it affects its victims in different ways. All are apologists, all rationalize, but some become rancorous and embittered; some cynical and even frivolous; some mellow and mature in dignity. William II fell into the last of the categories. In the peaceful political climate of the Netherlands, championed and protected by the indomitable Queen Wilhelmina against the demands of the Allied Powers for his extradition to face his indictment as a War Criminal under the Treaty of Versailles, the ex-Emperor—first at Amerongen and then at Doorn—became milder, more humorous and more sauve during the last twenty-three years of his life.

It was at Doorn that I stayed as his guest during the third week of August 1939. He was a charming and considerate host. We spoke of many things and he replied very frankly in the majority of cases; there were few figures in his past who escaped the back-lash of his reminiscent tongue; but one's chief interest was to discover whether, in the contemplation of his life and times, he had any regrets. Greatly daring, I asked him if he had ever regretted dismissing Bismarck and to this he made the indirect and Delphic response; 'I might not do it today'.

We discussed the events of the summer of 1914 but he added little to what he had already written in his memoirs—that it was all the fault of Russia, that Britain had betrayed him, etc.[29] He made no mention of the 'blank cheque' to Austria and dismissed it curtly when I brought it up. Yet just at the end there was a reversal of this attitude, though again an indirect one. I was summoned to say goodbye to him and he was good enough to ask me to return the following summer. (This, I repeat, was in August 1939!) Then a look of infinite sadness came into his face and he said in a lower voice, 'No, you won't be able to, because the machine is running away with *him* as it ran away with *me*'.[30]

William II died on 5 June 1941 and his passing caused scarcely a ripple of public interest. The agonized attention of the world was centred at that moment on the failure of the gallant and tragic issue of the Battle of Crete and the Emperor's death passed almost unnoticed.

How then shall one assess, some thirty years after his death and over half a century after his downfall, this strange historic personage whom one of his biographers has aptly designated 'A Fabulous Monster'?

He was not, I think, an evil man in the sense that Hitler and Stalin were evil men. He did not conspire and cabal against the peace of Europe. His misdeeds were those of a blunderer and an amateur rather than a villain; a poseur rather than a plotter. But yet it was his impulsive and irresponsible gesture of the 'blank cheque' to Austria of 5 July 1914 and his absenting himself thereafter for a three weeks holiday in foreign waters that made virtually inevitable that which he genuinely desired to avoid—a general European war.

Sir Winston Churchill, with his characteristic magnanimity and shrewd historic judgement, has written that:

No one should judge the career of the Emperor William II without asking the question, 'What should I have done in his position?' Imagine yourself brought up from childhood to believe that you were appointed by God to be the ruler of a mighty nation, and that the inherent virtue of your blood raised you far above ordinary mortals. Imagine succeeding in the twenties to the garnered prizes, in provinces, in power and in pride, of Bismarck's three successive victorious wars. Imagine feeling the magnificent German race bounding beneath you in ever-swelling numbers, strength, wealth and ambition; and imagine on every side the thunderous tributes of crowd-loyalty and skilled unceasing flattery of courtierly adulation.[31]

There could be no better diagnosis of the psychological background of William II, but his real tragedy was that he should ever have been Emperor at all. Nature had designed him for a life of intellectual and artistic activity; fate destined him for a soldier and a sovereign. As a private individual his quick intelligence and brilliant, if unstable, intellect might well have outweighed his capriciousness and lack of judgement. As a public figure his every defect became magnified, his every waywardness a common topic. Upon this Prussian youth, with his withered arm, the floodlight of publicity beat relentlessly almost from his birth until he found his only comforting warmth within its blaze.

Few men in the history of our times have cast so great a spell over the world as William II with so small a foundation of personal merit. For thirty years he was the leading figure of Europe; but he owed his position of influence almost entirely to the chance that he became German Emperor at the moment when, having successively defeated Austria and France in war, the Second Reich was in the full tide of a development in population, industrial wealth and military power more rapid than any of its European rivals. Yet he possessed certain superficially brilliant qualities of mind which enabled him to play the part of a sovereign with great effect. Supported by the loyalty and power—not to say sycophancy—of a great industrial and military hierarchy, he appeared to many to be himself endowed with greatness. But in truth, though he himself never realized it, he was but a small man who, 'with the confidence of Phaethon' had been born to a task far too great for him. On a lesser stage such a tragedy might have passed unnoticed; but on the great stage of world politics he remains a tragic example of a man whose creditable qualities were betrayed by his own defects. His personality and his character, ever brittle and erratic, collapsed under the ordeal of combat, and the ignominy of his flight into Holland was only partially redeemed by the dignity with which—saving one lapse[32]—he comported himself during the long years of his exile.

[1] Frederick I, Imperial Elector and Duke of Prussia—the great-great-great-grandfather of William II—declared himself King in 1701. William's grandfather, William I, was proclaimed German Emperor by Bismarck at Versailles in 1871.

[2] 'She was so little and so light,' the Kaiser said to me of this occasion.

[3] King Frederick William IV of Prussia (1795-1861) suffered a paralytic stroke in 1858, as a result of which his mind became completely occluded, and the functions of the crown were discharged by a Regent, his brother Prince William, the future German Emperor.

[4] The Emperor William II touches but briefly and lightly on his youthful sufferings in his book of memoirs *My Early Life* (London, 1926) but in the course of a visit which I paid him at Doorn in August 1939 he elaborated on them in some detail. I have given some account of this visit in *A Wreath to Clio* (London, 1967) and in the *Virginia Magazine of History and Biography* (Richmond, Va., April 1972).

[5]There was that habit, for example, of which his Chancellor, Prince Chlodwig zu Hohenlohe-Schillingfürst, writes so feelingly, of turning inwards the gems and seals of the many rings which he wore on his right hand and thereby crushing in a grip of agony the fingers of the person whom he might be greeting. I have undergone this experience; it is exceedingly painful. There was also his other and even less attractive habit of administering a sharp slap on the buttocks of some unsuspecting victim. When this happened to Tsar Ferdinand of Bulgaria it not unnaturally led to grave political consequences.

[6]Nor was this harshness confined to royal *fathers*. The Margravine of Bayreuth (Frederick the Great's sister) records that at the age of six she was so much surprised at the unusual experience of being fondled and caressed by her mother, on the latter's return from a long journey, that she broke a blood-vessel!

[7]In 1907 a succession of homosexual scandals occurred in Berlin, engineered by Holstein and Maximilian Harden to implicate certain friends of the Emperor, including Prince Philip zu Eulenberg und Hertefeld and Count Cuno von Moltke, both of whom were convicted. Shortly thereafter an elderly military adjutant who was dancing a *pas seul* dressed in a ballet skirt for the delectation of his sovereign, collapsed and died of heart-failure. This also did little to enhance the imperial image.

[8]On the 28 October 1908, the *Daily Telegraph* carried an interview given by the Emperor to one of his English hosts in which he declared that despite his heart-felt friendship for England, his patience was becoming worn by the constant and deliberate misrepresentation of his policies on Britain. This caused a storm in the Reichstag which was not alleviated by Prince von Bülow's frivolous and inept handling of the affair. When he had recovered his equilibrium the Emperor dismissed his Chancellor.

[9]Christian Gauss, *The German Emperor as shown in his Public Utterances* (New York, 1915) p. 172.

[10]Quoted by Fritz Fischer in *Germany's Aims in the First World War* (New York, 1967), with introductions by Hajo Holborn and James Joll, p.22.

[11]See below, p.64.

[12]Quoted by Michael Balfour in his admirable and penetrating analysis, *The Kaiser and His Times* (London, 1964).

[13]An excellent account of this period is given by J. C. G. Röhl in his *Germany Without Bismarck, the Crisis of Government in the Second Reich 1890-1900* (London, 1967).

[14]An exception should be made in the case of Baron Freidrich von Holstein, the head of the German Foreign Ministry, whose ability was outstanding, if his personality was unattractive. As Harold Kurtz has commented, 'Before his papers were published in the 1950s, more nonsense had been written on this grim and withdrawn civil servant than perhaps any other figure of the nineteenth century'. *The Second Reich, Kaiser Wilhelm II and his Germany* (London, 1970). Many of the myths surrounding Holstein have been exploded by Professor Norman Rich in his definitive biography: *Friedrich von Holstein, Politics and Diplomacy in the Era of Bismarck and Wilhelm II.* 2 vols. (Cambridge, 1965).

[15]Apropos of the personal adulation of the Emperor by the German aristocracy, more particularly the newly created industrial nobility, the 'Ruhr Barons', Frankfurt bankers, Hanseatic shipping magnates and others, who grovelled before him, Count Ottokar Czernin, the former Austro-Hungarian Foreign Minister, sharply criticized to me the custom of kissing the Emperor's hands on entering or leaving his presence which he (Czernin) characterized as 'something quite extraordinary', comparing it most unfavourably with the etiquette of the Austrian Court which was fundamentally more strict and protocolaire. 'At Vienna,' he had written in his memoirs, 'one would never have seen high officials kissing the Emperor's hand. Even the most servile would never have stooped to it.' *In the World War* (London, 1919) p. 184.

[16]E. F. Benson, *The Kaiser and English Relations* (London, 1936) pp. 67-68; 235-237.

[17]It was at the close of his visit to the Tsar that William II, as his Baltic squadron steamed out of Russian waters, sent a farewell telegram addressed to 'The Admiral of the Pacific from the

Admiral of the Atlantic', a conjunction of designations which left an unfavourable impression in London, Washington and Tokyo.

[18] This is well illustrated in an excellent article by J. C. G. Röhl, 'Admiral von Müller and the Approach of War, 1911-1914'. *The Historical Journal* (London, 1969) pp. 651-673.

[19] cf. Fischer, pp. 53-54.

[20] Konrad H. Jarausch, 'The Illusion of Limited War: Chancellor Bethmann-Hollweg's Calculated risk, July 1914', *Central European History* (March 1969), pp. 48-76.

[21] There is here a curious similarity with Adolf Hitler's misreading of the sincerity of British policy in August 1939.

[22] Ex-Kaiser William II, *My Memoirs, 1878-1918* (London, 1922) p. 242.

[23] 'By God, we did not want this war', Bethmann wrote to Weizsäcker on 30 August 1914. (Jarausch, p. 76).

[24] cf. Kurtz, p. 113.

[25] The relationship of the Emperor to his army rested on the basis of a unique personal bond. Through his Military Cabinet he exercised his rights of nominations, appointments, pensions, promotions and all military favours. The Chief of the Great General Staff, together with all corps commanders and inspectors-general, had right of direct access to him, and the reports of the military and naval attachés from diplomatic posts abroad went directly to him and not to his Ministers.

[26] Grand Admiral Alfred von Tirpitz, *My Memoirs* (London and New York, 1919), vo. II, pp. 314-16, 317, 320, 322, 343-4.

[27] Theodore Wolff later wrote of Fritz Ebert, 'There might be something of exaltation in waking up famous like Byron, but it was less pleasant to find oneself in the morning the Supreme Commander of the Revolution after going to bed a member of the respectable middle class.'

[28] There had been those, among them General Wilhelm Groener, who had succeeded Ludendorff as First Quarter-Master General in October 1918, who felt that the Emperor should place himself at the head of a forlorn hope. 'If he were killed' Groener told me he had said to Hindenburg, 'it would be the finest death possible. If he were wounded, the feelings of the German people would completely change towards him.' *Hindenburg, the Wooden Titan* (London, 1935) p. 187.) The Emperor has given as his reason for refusing to consider this advice that he would not sacrifice the lives of more brave men to make a setting for his own exit. (*My Memoirs*, p. 200.) Of this decision Sir Winston Churchill has written, 'No one can doubt that he was right.' *Great Contemporaries* (London, 1938) p. 44.

[29] *My Memoirs*, pp. 242-257.

[30] This was the Emperor's sole reference to Hitler, direct or indirect, during the several days of our conversations.

[31] *Great Contemporaries*, p. 33.

[32] When Hitler entered Paris in June 1940, a telegram of congratulation was sent to him from Doorn bearing the Emperor's name. It has never been established whether this was done with the cognizance of the Emperor or owed its dispatch to the excessive zeal of his *Umgebung*.

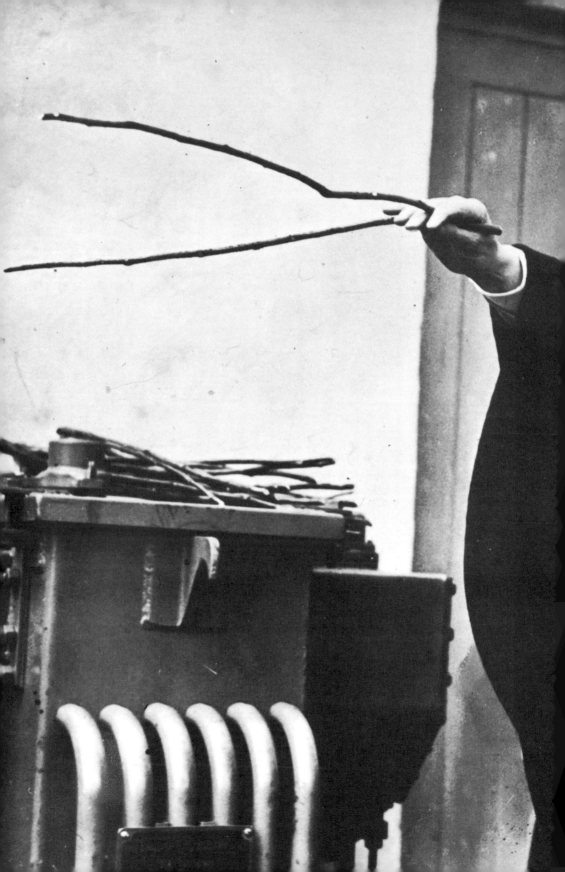

Lloyd George
by AJP Taylor

A.J.P. TAYLOR (b. 1906), a Lancastrian by birth, was educated at Bootham School, York, and Oriel College, Oxford. He early distinguished himself as a lecturer in Modern History first at Manchester University and later at Oxford, being elected a Fellow of Magdalen College. He delivered the Ford Lectures in English History at Oxford in 1956 on the subject of 'The Trouble Makers' and the Leslie Stephen Lecture at Cambridge in 1961 on 'Lloyd George', on which same subject he edited a volume of twelve essays by younger historians in 1971. A.J.P. Taylor was appointed Honorary Director of the Beaverbrook Library on its foundation in 1967 and his biography, *Beaverbrook*, was published in 1972.

Among his other works of distinction are *The Habsburg Monarchy, 1815-1918* (1941); *The Course of German History* (1945); *The Struggle for Mastery in Europe, 1848-1918* (1954); *English History, 1914-1945* (1965), and *The Origins of the Second World War*, in 1961.

David Lloyd George

17 Jan. 1863	Born. Educated at National Church school in Llanystumdwy.
1884	Set up lawyer's office in Criccieth after qualifying as a solicitor.
1888	Married Margaret Owen, who later had two sons and three daughters.
1890	Stood as Liberal candidate at by-election at Caernarvon Boroughs. Held this seat until year of his death.
1899	South African war, the culmination of years of tension between British and Boers. Lloyd George made himself a national figure by championing Boer cause.
1902	Led nonconformists against education act of Balfour, the Prime Minister, because it continued to help Church of England schools.
1903	When Chamberlain adopted tariff reform, Liberals were reunited under banner of free trade.
Dec. 1905	Balfour resigned and Campbell-Bannerman formed Liberal government. General election in which Liberals gained a strong majority. Lloyd George appointed President of the Board of Trade.
1908	Asquith succeeded Campbell-Bannerman as Prime Minister on latter's retirement. Lloyd George became Chancellor of the Exchequer.
April 1909	Lloyd George introduced the People's Budget which increased direct taxation of the wealthy— rejected by House of Lords.
Jan. 1910	General election—Liberal ministry formed. Parliament bill introduced and resisted by House of Lords.
Dec. 1910	General election—Liberal government formed.

Previous page: the political wizard was also a water diviner

Aug. 1911 Parliament Act became law. It removed the Lords' power to interfere with financial bills and substituted for its veto of other bills the power to delay them for two years.

1911 National Insurance Act—Lloyd George's great achievement. This attacked poverty caused by illness and unemployment by a system of compulsory insurance.

1914 Lloyd George fought against Churchill's proposed increases in naval estimates.

Aug. 1914 Germany's invasion of Belgium persuaded Lloyd George to support war.

Sept. 1914 Battle of the Marne, then deadlock on the Western Front. Asquith's government seemed to have no war policy.

April 1915 Lloyd George supported Churchill in pleading for diversion from Western Front—suggested an attack on Dardanelles which would open front in Balkans from which Germany could be attacked from rear.

May 1915 Unsuccessful campaign in Dardanelles. Conservative leader Bonar Law, supported by Lloyd George, pressed for a coalition, which Asquith formed. Lloyd George appointed Minister of Munitions

March 1916 Mesopotamia campaign failed.

June 1916 Kitchener, Secretary of State for War, was drowned on way to U.S.S.R. and Lloyd George succeeded to his post. He concluded that there must be new leadership.

Nov. 1916 In order to evade authority of chief of general staff, Lloyd George proposed a Cabinet committee of three which would be in effect a war dictatorship. Asquith disagreed. Lloyd George and Bonar Law resigned. Asquith's coalition fell.

7 Dec. 1916 Became Prime Minister, supported by most Conservatives and Labour and about half the Liberals. Consented unwillingly to Haig's offensive in Flanders.

March 1917 Created Imperial war cabinet, so that Prime Ministers of Dominions could be consulted. Russian Revolution began.

April 1917 Entry of U.S. into war on side of Allies.

Dec. 1917 Capture of Jerusalem by British forces.

Feb. 1918 Established civilian control of strategy.

March/ April 1918 Last German offensive. Lloyd George appealed to President Wilson for American troops to be sent into front line.

July 1918 Second battle of the Marne which saved Paris and doomed Germany.

Aug. 1918 British forces began offensive.

11 Nov. 1918 Armistice.

Dec. 1918 General election. Victory for Lloyd George. But with Labour in opposition, and Liberals divided, he was dependent for support on Conservatives, who were out of sympathy with his radical views.

1919 Treaty of Versailles making peace between Allies and Germany. League of Nations created. Guerilla war in Ireland with intention of ending British rule.

1920 Government of Ireland Act which partitioned Ireland.

April/ May 1920 Genoa conference at which Lloyd George tried, but failed, to bring Germany and U.S.S.R. back into community of nations.

April 1920 Unemployment Insurance Act extended 1911 scheme to virtually all workers.

1921 Depression with two million unemployed.

Oct. 1921 Anglo-Irish treaty, offering Ireland dominion status.

Sept. 1922 Lloyd George prepared for war against Turkey, thus forcing Turks to moderate demands against Greeks. His stand alarmed Conservatives, as had Anglo-Irish treaty.

19 Oct. 1922 Conservatives repudiated coalition. Lloyd George resigned and Bonar Law formed government.

1926 Lloyd George refused to join his fellow-Liberal, Asquith, in condemning General Strike.

End 1926 Asquith retired and Lloyd George became leader of Liberals.

1929 General election. Liberals won only 29 seats.

1935 Lloyd George produced plans for a British New Deal, but they had no effect on general election.

1939 Lloyd George advocated alliance with U.S.S.R.

May 1940 His last great speech contributed to fall of Chamberlain. He repeatedly refused to join Churchill's government.

Jan. 1941 Lloyd George's wife, Dame Margaret died.

1943 He married Frances Stevenson, who had been his secretary.

Jan. 1945 He became Earl Lloyd George of Dwyfor.

26 March 1945 Died.

On 19 October 1922 the Conservative members of Parliament met at the Carlton Club. For the past six years they had supported a Coalition Government led by Lloyd George. Now a general election was approaching. Should the Conservatives continue to support the Coalition? Or should they fight the general election as an independent party? Stanley Baldwin led the movement for independence. He said of Lloyd George: 'He is a dynamic force, and it is from that very fact that our troubles, in our opinion, arise. A dynamic force is a very terrible thing; it may crush you, but it is not necessarily right.' By 185 votes to 88 the Conservatives resolved on independence. Lloyd George resigned as Prime Minister the same day. He never held office again. Baldwin went on to be three times Prime Minister and to become the outstanding figure of the inter-war years.

Baldwin brought Lloyd George down, an achievement about which he often boasted. But, for good or ill, he saw Lloyd George the most clearly. 'Dynamic force' was the deep truth about Lloyd George, the explanation of his character and career. A gift for action was his only consistency. He cannot be tied down to any single policy or outlook. He began as a radical and democrat, maker of the People's Budget. Later he saved capitalism from the Socialist discontents after the First World War. In his early days he was a pro-Boer and next door to a pacifist. Then he became the Man Who Won the War and advocate of a united Empire. In the First World War he spoke out for the Knock-out Blow; in the Second he wanted a negotiated peace. He called himself a 'ranker'—the only one ever raised to the premiership. He became the friend of millionaires if not of kings. He conducted a war of terror against the Irish and then gave them virtual independence. Out of office he was a demagogue. In office he was a tyrant, the Big Beast of the Forest. Essentially the pattern was always the same: a dynamic force driving towards new action. Lloyd George was the nearest to a Napoleon that British politics have known.

His humble origins were no legend. David Lloyd George was born in Manchester on 17 January 1863. William George, his father, was a struggling school teacher, who moved to a farm in Pembrokeshire soon after David was born. In 1864 William George died. The family were taken over by David's maternal uncle, Richard Lloyd the shoemaker of Llanystumdwy. In this remote village of North Wales Lloyd George grew up. He attended the local Church school, the only school in the neighbourhood. Faithful to his uncle's Baptist teachings, he rebelled against the doctrines of the Established Church. With his uncle's backing he qualified as a solicitor. In 1884 he set up his laywer's office in Criccieth. He became the spokesman of the oppressed and unprivileged—quarrymen against their masters, tenants against their landlords, Dissenters against the Established Church.

These early years in Wales helped to shape Lloyd George's political outlook, providing as it were the luggage he fell back on when he had no other stock. He rated highly the Nonconformist element in British life. As the twentieth century wore on he overrated it. Almost his last campaign, the Councils of Action in 1935 and 1936, were designed to mobilize a Nonconformist conscience which no longer existed. He had experience of poverty and understood the problems of the poor at first hand. But it was agrarian poverty, the poverty of the tenant farmer and agricultural labourer. More than once, when seeking a radical cause, he turned to the Land question. He had no experience of industry and understood neither the trade union movement nor the socialism which often went with it. Political Labour was a blank spot in his career and the most vulnerable one. Finally Lloyd George always presented himself as the little Welshman. But he soon moved away from Welsh nationalism. The Welsh stage was too small for him. Lloyd George was British as well as Welsh, determined to play a great part in the affairs of Great Britain and the British Empire. When he fell back on Wales, this was usually a sign that things were going wrong with him elsewhere. Symbolically he only came fully home to Wales when he was approaching death.

In 1890 Lloyd George stood as Liberal candidate at a by-election for Caernarvon Boroughs. He won by eighteen votes and held the seat without a break until the year of his death. In the House of Commons Lloyd George was another David, defying the giants of the day. He set himself against Joseph Chamberlain, the erstwhile Radical who was now the mainstay of Unionism. He was ready to go against Gladstone himself in the cause of Nonconformity. Political speeches were for Lloyd George not literary compositions. They were a form of action, expressing every mood from aggression to sweet conciliation. He could provoke dukes to apoplectic rage. At the same time, as Tom Jones put it, 'He could charm a bird off a branch but was himself always unmoved.' Though Lloyd George was a skilled parliamentary debater, he did not rate Parliament highly. His great successes came at public meetings. He said, 'My audience is the country.'

This was the age when all leading statesmen addressed public meetings. Most of them spoke solemnly and with an air of responsibility even when they aroused enthusiasm. Lloyd George was from the first an entertainer. He soon became the most famous Radical speaker in the country. His opportunity increased with the Boer War when he could champion an unpopular cause. Lloyd George was the most notorious pro-Boer. His meetings were often broken up. At Birmingham he had to escape from the hall disguised as a policeman, and Joseph Chamberlain regretted that he had been allowed to escape alive. As the war dragged on, Chamberlain was discredited and Lloyd George vindicated. In 1902 Lloyd George led the Nonconformists against Balfour's Education Act. In 1903, when Chamberlain took up tariff reform, the Liberals were reunited under the banner of Free Trade. Here Lloyd George was one champion among many. Moreover he never cared greatly about Free Trade—in his eyes a negative and even an antiquated cause: 'You cannot feed the hungry with statistics of national prosperity.'

In 1905 the Unionists left office. Campbell-Bannerman formed a Liberal Government, and the Liberals triumphed at the general election. Lloyd George became President of the Board of Trade. This was a striking tribute to his achievement. He had broken into politics from outside. He had no training in economics or administration. Yet he was at once brought into the Cabinet with a senior post of great responsibility. He reflected: 'Here am I with no business training, and I shall have to deal with all these great business men.' He added sardonically: 'I found them children.' A further step forward came in 1908. Asquith succeeded Campbell-Bannerman as Prime Minister. Lloyd George became Chancellor of the Exchequer—the second place in the government with prescriptive right of succession to the premiership. The partnership between Asquith and Lloyd George was perfect while it lasted. Asquith was firm and serene in the supreme position. Lloyd George cared nothing for rank in itself and was content to act as Asquith's loyal second.

He did so now and to great effect. The political situation seemed desperate. The Liberals, despite their great majority, could not carry their measures against the opposition of the House of Lords. Lloyd George always operated on the principle: 'I was never in favour of costly frontal attacks, either in politics or in war, if there was a way round.' In 1909 he brought in the People's Budget. He translated social reform into fiscal terms, levelled against the rich and the landlords. Either the House of Lords must accept the budget, as it had always done in the past, or, by rejecting it, provoke a constitutional crisis. The Lords fell into the trap. They rejected the budget. A general election left the Liberals in power. The budget was belatedly passed. The government followed this with a Parliament Bill, limiting the powers of the House of Lords. Once more the lords resisted. Once more a general election left the Liberals in power. In August 1911 the Parliament Act became law. Radicalism had triumphed, and Lloyd George was the principal architect of victory.

Characteristically Lloyd George was not deeply interested in the constitutional conflict. He wanted to get things done, not to achieve victories of principle. In 1911, while others contended over the Parliament Bill, Lloyd George was busy with a task of greater significance for the future: the introduction of National Insurance. This was the origin of the Welfare State. All advances in welfare from that day to this stem from it. Any other statesman would have developed such a far-reaching scheme after prolonged inquiry and elaborate reports by a commission. Lloyd George sent a single civil servant to study Bismarckian social insurance in Germany and then improvised his proposals on the basis of a verbal report. When Lloyd George presented the bill to the House of Commons most of the clauses were blank, and he made them up as he went along. His treatment of the Opposition was also unusual. Instead of presenting National Insurance as a party measure, Lloyd George listened to suggestions from all sides and carried the Bill without serious difficulty.

Behind the aggressive speaker on the public platform there was concealed a conciliator who wanted to reach results by compromise. At the height of the constitutional battle, Lloyd George proposed a Coalition which would resolve all the great problems of the day. This initiative proved barren, but Lloyd George had shown the way he would go—a man of measures, not of party, a dynamic force who threatened traditional loyalties. In a more personal way, too, Lloyd George stood outside party. He had few political friends. Only Winston Churchill—another outsider so far as the Liberals were concerned—called him 'David'. Lloyd George found his friends among newspaper editors and self-made business men. Despite his political hostility to the rich, he admired captains of industry, in whom he saw the triumph of the Radical spirit. He wanted to become rich himself and speculated unwisely, buying shares in American Marconi when the British Government were negotiating a plump contract with the English Marconi company. Though Lloyd George was exonerated after a somewhat unsatisfactory parliamentary inquiry, he did not free himself entirely from the taint of corruption.

Despite this setback, Lloyd George continued to enhance his political standing. He developed striking gifts as an industrial conciliator, and the trade unions had more confidence in him than in any other Liberal minister. He tried to find a way round in the bitter contests over Ireland, seeking— though in vain—to appease Ulster without estranging the Home Rulers. He pinned his own hopes and those of the Liberal party on a Land campaign, reviving the prosperity of the smallholders. There were great meetings, but in the industrial areas which made up most of England little response. When 1914 opened Lloyd George was back on an apparently pacifist track. He fought hard and ingeniously against the increases in the naval estimates that Churchill proposed. He declared that the two great empires, Great Britain and Germany, were drawing closer together. Some observers credited him with the idea of splitting the Liberal party and leading a Coalition of Radicals and Socialists.

These speculations were silenced by the outbreak of the First World War. There were many who expected Lloyd George to oppose British entry and to take the line which Charles James Fox had done during the wars against revolutionary France. Instead he waited on events. Germany's invasion of Belgium resolved his doubts as it did those of others. Once committed Lloyd George was as strenuous for war as he had previously been against it. He was admired, whether deservedly or not, for his firm handling of the financial crisis which the outbreak of war provoked. He provided the guarantee that the Nonconformist conscience, still an essential element to a Liberal government, would support the war and not turn to pacifism. He excelled on the public platform, now as fierce against the Germans as he had once been against the dukes.

To outward appearance and no doubt in his own mind also Lloyd George remained loyal to Asquith. Without premeditation events were pushing him on to an independent course. The Liberal Government had no war policy. The leading ministers, though admirable talkers, lacked executive capacity. Asquith was supine on principle as well as by nature. In his opinion, the only duty of ministers was to stand aside while the generals and admirals won the war for them. Kitchener, who had been hastily botched into the office of Secretary for War, was expected to provide all the initiative necessary. Then nothing happened. There was deadlock on the western front after the battle of the Marne and no great engagement at sea. The newspapers began to say that Lloyd George was the one man who would get things done, and the public began to believe the newspapers. This was not a planned campaign. It was the process, impossible to trace, by which the nation made up its mind.

In May 1915 there was a political upheaval. Lord Fisher, the First Sea Lord, resigned in protest against the campaign at the Dardanelles. Bonar Law, the Unionist leader, insisted on a Coalition to cloak the general discontent, and Lloyd George seconded him. The last Liberal Government left office. There was much shuffling of appointments, Asquith being more concerned to keep the Unionists out of key posts than to devise an effective government. The one vital innovation was the appointment of Lloyd George as Minister of Munitions. This was perfectly in tune with his character. Here was a newly created ministry: no staff, no tradition, at first not even any office furniture. No one knew how it was to work or what precisely it would do. Lloyd George had no doubts. Shortage of shells had been the great scandal of the war. Lloyd George meant to end it. The Ministry of Munitions was one vast improvisation throughout the time that Lloyd George ran it. It produced far more munitions than the War Office asked for, though never more than the armies needed. It disregarded all considerations of expense and all vested rights. Lloyd George even persuaded the trade unions to renounce their restrictive practices for the duration. The Ministry of Munitions demonstrated perhaps better than any other single achievement Lloyd George's ability to get results.

Having solved the problem of munitions, Lloyd George was ready to move on. He could say with Chatham: 'I know that I can save this country and that no one else can.' His chance seemed to have come in June 1916 when Kitchener was drowned on the way to Russia. Lloyd George became Secretary of State for War, believing that with this the supreme direction was in his hands. He was mistaken. Sir William Robertson, Chief of the Imperial General Staff, had secured the sole direction of strategy. Lloyd George

Total War: British troops on the devastated Western Front, 1917

was confined to the production of greatcoats and uniforms for the soldiers. As usual he sought a way round.

In November 1916 he proposed a Cabinet Committee of three which would be in effect a war dictatorship. In origin this was a move against Robertson, not against Asquith who would have remained as Prime Minister. Some of those who backed Lloyd George were anxious to get rid of Asquith altogether. Asquith equivocated, accepting Lloyd George's proposals at one moment and rejecting them at the next. Finally Lloyd George resigned and Law, the Unionist leader, went with him. Asquith resigned in his turn. His Coalition Government fell. After prolonged negotiations, with Asquith refusing anything other than the first place, Lloyd George became Prime Minister on 7 December 1916. He said: 'I did not want this' and 'I wonder whether I can do it'.

Lloyd George came to power as an individual, not as the leader of a party. Most Unionists and Labour men and about half the Liberals supported him as the man who could win the war. But he had no organization behind him. As Sorel said of Napoleon III, his origins condemned him to success. He broke all the received rules. He abolished the traditional Cabinet and substituted a War Cabinet of five which was a barely disguised dictatorship. He created half a dozen new ministries and put at their head businessmen, not politicians. At his direction, these new ministries introduced a haphazard system of war socialism—food rationing, direction of labour, control of prices. Thanks to Lloyd George, the war at home was run efficiently, and social discontent was allayed until after the war ended.

Lloyd George had also to contend with those who had the military direction. With the admirals he succeeded. He imposed convoys for merchant shipping when the admiralty declared that this was impossible. Convoys beat the U-boats. Without convoys Great Britain could not have remained in the war. This was Lloyd George's greatest contribution to victory, and a decisive one.

Against the generals Lloyd George made less head-way. Sir William Robertson remained inflexible. Lloyd George feared to go against the generals when he was locked in combat with the admirals. He consented unwillingly to Haig's offensive in Flanders, popularly known as Passchendaele or the 'battle of the mud'. Lloyd George explored many ways of circumventing Robertson and Haig. The Imperial War Cabinet which he summoned in March 1917 was one such manoeuvre. The Supreme War Council of the Allies was another. Neither achieved the desired result. It was a weakness of Lloyd George's position that, though he regarded the strategy of the generals as wrong, he could not himself devise one that was right. His own favourite was an offensive in Palestine, and this led to the capture of Jerusalem by British forces—a Christmas present of useful publicity for Lloyd George, but not a stroke of much effect against the Germans.

1918 was Lloyd George's year of terror and triumph. In February he got rid of Robertson and established civilian control of strategy. In April 1918, battered by the last German offensive, the Allies at last set up the unified command that Lloyd George had always wanted. In this time of high peril he rose to the challenge of events. He remained cheerful and confident.

He appealed personally to President Wilson for American troops to be sent at once into the front line. In August 1918 British forces went over to the offensive. The Germans began a retreat which ended only with the armistice of 11 November. Lloyd George was truly the man who had won the war. No other British statesman except perhaps Winston Churchill has commanded such a measure of popular acclaim.

Lloyd George turned his popularity to good account. The general election of December 1918 was a plebiscite in his favour. Bonar Law said: 'He can be prime minister for life if he wants to'. Yet, at this moment of supreme triumph, Lloyd George's position changed. His one asset was success. During the war the test of success was simple. It was victory. He made many promises during the electoral campaign. Homes fit for heroes; the world safe for democracy; make Germany pay. Which of these promises should be fulfilled? Lloyd George was committed to contradictions: a peace of revenge which would be also a peace of reconciliation; a great role for the British Empire and at the same time a withdrawal from world affairs; an end to poverty without any fundamental change in the social system, thus satisfying both rich and poor. Lloyd George's position also changed in more practical terms. During the war he had been at the head of a real Coalition supported by all three parties. Now Labour was in open opposition. The Liberal remnant was torn asunder, with even Lloyd George's strongest supporters looking wistfully over their shoulders at the Asquithians. Lloyd George was at the mercy of the Unionist majority in the House of Commons—a majority totally out of sympathy with his Radical spirit and policies.

Success went to his head. He became tyrannical as he had not been before, truly the Big Beast of the Forest. He grew impatient with criticism, overruled his colleagues, jumped from one expedient to another. His record of success remained remarkable. He made the Treaty of Versailles more conciliatory than it would have been otherwise. Thanks to him, the Rhineland was not separated from Germany; Danzig did not go to Poland; the Saar did not go to France; reparations were put on a basis which would have been sensible if the Germans had tried to work it. After the Paris Peace Conference and until his fall in 1922 Lloyd George dominated international affairs, moving with endless ingenuity from one conference to the next. He ended the wars of intervention with Russia and reached agreement with the Bolshevik Government. At home he restored social peace after a period of general discontent. He circumvented the challenge from the railwaymen and the miners until they ceased to be dangerous. In Ireland he fought a bitter struggle against Sinn Fein. Then, turning round, he made a treaty with them, which brought peace to three-quarters of Ireland. It was not his fault that Northern Ireland has continued to haunt British politics to the present day. Such a record of achievement would have satisfied any other statesman for a lifetime. Lloyd George accomplished it all in under four years.

It was of no avail. The support for him dwindled. Mutterings of opposition grew louder. After the turmoils of war men no longer wanted to be at the mercy of a dynamic force. They wanted a quiet life—tranquility as Bonar Law called it. Lloyd George's own nature worked against him. He had never followed a consistent line or held consistent principles. Achievement was his guiding star; crisis was the air he breathed. He continued to insist that a Coalition under his leadership was needed to ward off the imminent perils of the time. Many were coming to think that the perils were themselves caused by Lloyd George's ceaseless activity. The principal peril he invoked was social discontent. He wanted a union of moderate men or even a centre party in order to combat the 'extremists'. This was a dangerous topic for Lloyd George to raise. Immediately after the war he had faced the threat of social upheaval and had overcome it. In seeking to raise it again, he was condemning his own work. In practice the social peril meant the Labour party—hardly a revolutionary body—and, by aligning himself with the Conservatives against Labour, Lloyd George was in fact going with the rich against the poor, a thing he had often declared he would never do.

More fundamentally Lloyd George was the victim of events. He had assumed that Great Britain was still a rich and prosperous country. If she could pay for the war, as she had done, then she could pay for social reform in peacetime. British prosperity lasted only until the autumn of 1920. Then there was a depression with over a million unemployed. Lloyd George was as much at a loss as everyone else. Later, when out of office, he tried to devise remedies, where nearly all others remained helpless until the Second World War provided an answer of itself. He took no effective action while he was Prime Minister. He had promised success. He reaped failure, not through his own fault. The dynamic force had lost its justification.

By 1922 the Conservatives were turning against Lloyd George. The breaking point came in the autumn when Lloyd George, in a last burst of dynamism, prepared for war against Turkey. His stand was successful: the Turks moderated their demands. This did not help him. The Conservatives did not want any more successes of this kind. On 19 October 1922 they repudiated the Coalition. Lloyd George's reign was ended.

Any other man would have been cast down by a reversal of this magnitude: dictatorial Prime Minister at one moment, disregarded individual at the next. Lloyd George was unperturbed. In his eyes, though perhaps not in those of anyone else, success was still round the next corner. He never grasped the extent of the distrust which he had aroused during his years of power. Still worse, he could never adapt himself to the party system. Nominally he returned to the Liberal Party, even presenting himself once more as Asquith's lieutenant. On any great issue he took his own line. During the General Strike of 1926 he advocated conciliation when official Liberal policy was to support the government. After it he faced unemployment—the problem that had ruined him. This was a characteristic Lloyd George enterprise. In theory he was now leading the Liberal Party. In practice he devised an economic policy all alone: committees of experts directed by himself, plans for coal, industry and the land improvised in a creative spirit. Just before the general election of 1929 he produced a pamphlet with the challenging title: 'We Can Conquer Unemployment'. Here was the old dynamism and the old daring: not measures of amelioration but the Knock-out Blow. Officially Lloyd George's policy became the policy of the Liberal Party. Most Liberals did not understand it, and those who did disliked it. A Liberal Government in 1929 would have been again a one-man show.

The Liberals did not do well at the general election. There was a minority Labour Government, kept in power by Liberal votes. Lloyd George tried to drive the government into action. Labour drifted helplessly, overcome by the great Depression. By the summer of 1931 there was again talk of a Coalition: Ramsay MacDonald nominally in power as Prime Minister, Lloyd George providing the real inspiration and leadership. It was not to be. Lloyd George had an operation for the removal of his prostate gland. While he was out of action, there was a financial crisis. A National Government was formed without him. A general election gave its supporters an overwhelming majority. The Conservatives at their most helpless were back in power. Lloyd George would have nothing of this. He declared from his sick-bed: 'If I am to die, I would rather die fighting on the Left.'

Lloyd George was now completely isolated. He had broken with the Liberals. The Left was now the Labour Party, and Labour would not touch him. He retreated into the writing of his War Memoirs, battering against the generals whom he had failed to defeat at the time. There was a last burst of the old energy. In 1935, with another general election approaching, Lloyd George produced plans for a British New Deal. The National Government trembled. A Cabinet sub-committee was set up to investigate Lloyd George's plans. He laboured with the committee but in vain. Nothing would stir the Government into action. Lloyd George then launched a public campaign: an appeal to the people against the parties. Nothing came of it. The dynamic force spluttered ineffectively in the air.

Lloyd George continued to raise his voice on great issues. In 1939 he advocated alliance with Soviet Russia. In May 1940 his last great speech contributed powerfully to the fall of Chamberlain. Some thought that Lloyd George should become Prime Minister. His physical powers were failing. He repeatedly refused to join Churchill's Government. He was accused of being a defeatist. This accusation was false. Lloyd George doubted whether Great Britain on her own could achieve a total victory over Germany. What he wanted was that Great Britain should show that she could not be defeated and that then a negotiated peace would follow. He even imagined that he would be the man to negotiate it. The calculation was not altogether mistaken. Only the entry of Soviet Russia and the United States into the war made total victory possible.

In 1943 Lloyd George married Frances Stevenson, who had been for more than thirty years his devoted secretary and mistress. In 1944 he left his Surrey home for Llanystumdwy. He had returned to his Welsh origins. He still walked defiantly in the stormy winds. His favourite quotation was from *Kidnapped*: 'Am I no a bonny fechter, Davy?' He could not face the turmoil of a general election and yet wanted to make his voice heard on the peace settlement. On 1 January 1945 he became Earl Lloyd-George of Dwyfor. On 26 March 1945 he died peacefully. The dynamic force was stilled.

Baldwin
by R A Butler

LORD BUTLER (b. 1902), son of a distinguished Indian proconsul, was educated at Marlborough and Pembroke College, Cambridge where he achieved a 'double-first' in Modern Languages and History. An early interest in politics led him to the House of Commons in 1929 as Conservative member for Saffron Walden, a seat which he retained until his retirement in 1965, when he was created a Life Peer. During this period he held a variety of Cabinet offices, including those of Chancellor of the Exchequer and Foreign Secretary, and also served as deputy Prime Minister. In addition he was Chairman of the Conservative Party and of the Conservative Research Department.

On his retirement from politics in 1965 he was elected Master of Trinity College, Cambridge, with which his family had been associated for a number of generations. He was sworn of the Privy Council on entering the Cabinet in 1939, created a Companion of Honour in 1954 and appointed a Knight of the Garter in 1971. In the same year he published a volume of memoirs entitled *The Art of the Possible*.

Stanley Baldwin

3 Aug. 1867	Born. Educated at Harrow and Trinity College, Cambridge.
1892	Married Lucy Ridsdale, who later had two sons and four daughters.
1908	Conservative M.P. for Bewdley, Worcestershire. He held this seat until his resignation in 1937.
Dec. 1916	Parliamentary Private Secretary to Bonar Law who was leader of the Conservative party and a member of Lloyd George's coalition war cabinet.
Jan. 1917	Junior Lord of the Treasury.
June 1917-21	Joint Financial Secretary to the Treasury in the Lloyd George cabinet.
1918	Allied victory in First World War, followed by 'khaki election' in which Lloyd George's coalition won a large majority.
1921-22	President of the Board of Trade.
Sept. 1922	Lloyd George resigned.
Oct. 1922	Conservative victory in general election. Became Chancellor of the Exchequer in Bonar Law's ministry.
May 1923	Bonar Law resigned because of illness and the king asked Baldwin to form a government.
Nov. 1923	Baldwin dissolved parliament on the issue of protective tariffs, which he favoured. General election. Baldwin failed to get overall majority, so resigned. First Labour government formed.
Nov. 1924	General election because minority Labour government defeated in Commons. Conservative victory, and Baldwin Prime Minister.
Oct. 1925	Locarno agreement between Britain and Italy guaranteed the frontiers between France and Belgium and Germany. This seemed to bring the

Previous page: after his retirement, Stanley Baldwin delivers a radio broadcast

era of post-war hostility between Germany and her western neighbours to an end.

May 1926 General strike. Baldwin's calm leadership helped to overcome the strike without serious civil conflict.

1927 Trade Disputes Act outlawing general strikes and political levies in trade unions.

July 1928 Franchise extended to women over twenty-one.

May 1929 General election which Baldwin lost.

Oct. 1929 Contrary to the wishes of many Conservative colleagues, Baldwin in favour of Irwin declaration proposing dominion status for India.

1930 Chancellor of Cambridge University.

Aug. 1931 International trade depression caused economic and financial crisis in Britain. Labour government divided over measures to deal with crisis. Macdonald formed National government with Conservatives, leaving most of his own party in opposition. Baldwin appointed Lord President of the Council.

1932 Baldwin leading spirit behind 10 per cent ad valorem tariff and Ottawa agreements which established protectionism.

June 1935 League of Nations Union in Britain held 'peace ballot' which resulted in strong public expression of distaste for armaments but acceptance of international sanctions against aggressors.

June 1935 Macdonald retired from public life and Baldwin succeeded to leadership of National government.

Nov. 1935 General election in which Baldwin retained Conservative majority in National government.

Nov. 1935 Hoare-Laval agreement for a proposed settlement of Abyssinian war by cession of Ethiopian territory to Italy. Baldwin at first acquiesced, then bowed to public indignation and rejected the pact.

Jan. 1936 Death of King George V.

1936 Worsening international situation: German occupation of Rhineland; Italian conquest of Ethiopia; Arab-Jewish rioting in Palestine; civil war in Spain.

March 1936 Expansion of British armaments in response to growing menace of German rearmament programme since Hitler's accession to power in 1933.

Oct. 1936 Crisis over Edward VIII's desire to marry Mrs Simpson. Baldwin thought the Empire would not withstand a 'morganatic' marriage.

Dec. 1936 Edward VIII abdicated.

May 1937 Resigned Prime Ministership to Neville Chamberlain and accepted peerage—first Earl Baldwin of Bewdley.

14 Dec. 1947 Died.

Stanley Baldwin was at once the most interesting and effective Prime Minister with whom I have served. His special success was on the home front. He has been widely criticized for his conduct of foreign affairs but at home, by a mixture of languor and cunning, he was a better party leader than A. J. Balfour and Bonar Law. It is difficult to class him against Asquith who, like Baldwin, preferred the home front to the foreign. Asquith may have been a greater scholar but Baldwin achieved his own end in a more subtle way and retired at his own chosen time.

Churchill stands pre-eminent as a war leader but had to confess defeat at Baldwin's hands over India and the abdication. Lord Salisbury concentrated largely on foreign affairs and insinuated his nephew A. J. Balfour as Leader of the Party and Prime Minister. I agree with Robert Rhodes James in his life of Lord Randolph Churchill, that the party was 'too long shut up in the Hotel Cecil'.

Baldwin succeeded to a régime of hard-faced businessmen under Bonar Law. They enjoyed watching their leader 'throwing gravel in the faces of their opponents' during debate. Baldwin transformed this builders' yard atmosphere into that of a well humoured Conservative and Labour opposition, contrived to buttress the constitution, and to achieve the maximum of good will.

To be a good Prime Minister demands a certain amount of background. A. J. Balfour was a philosopher. Starting with his book, *A Defence of Philosophic Doubt*, he pursued his studies all his long life. At times, especially when he was Secretary for Ireland, he showed great determination. At others, the title of his first book seemed reflected in his vacillations. Asquith had a fine classical background. The Younger Pitt was from his earliest days versed in the art of rhetoric. Robert Peel, and, to a greater extent, George Canning, profited by the Oxford School of training for politics and by their sojourn at Christ Church.

At Trinity, Cambridge, Baldwin was indolent and this we shall examine later. But throughout his life he was deeply versed in English literature. As a boy he lay on the floor on his stomach reading book after book propped up before him. He enjoyed the family relationship with the men and their wives who worked for his father's firm and he later made moving references to this relationship. He wondered as a young man whether to enter the Church. This pre-occupation meant not so much that he was captured by religion, but that he felt dedicated to the happiness and indeed social improvement of his fellow beings. Baldwin set himself to create ideals of good behaviour and harmony between the classes.

Baldwin was 'interesting' largely because of his family background. His father was 'half grandee and half Hebrew prophet'; his mother, Louisa, came of the Macdonald family which made a bridge between the medievalism of William Morris and the modern stories of Rudyard Kipling. Georgiana, one of the Macdonald sisters, married Burne-Jones. Alice married Lockwood Kipling and Agnes, Edward Poynter, later President of the Royal Academy.

It was the background of these families which enlivened much of the lonely Stanley's youth. When he could not get company, he read. His greatest joy was Walter Scott. *Tales of a Grandfather* introduced him to history. He said, 'The best and most readable history is that written with the strongest bias'. He pictured medieval history in the illustrations of Froissart's *Chronicles*. Speaking later to the English Association he remembered the *Morte d'Arthur, Pilgrim's Progress*, Blake, Kingsley, Dickens, *The Adventures of Tom Sawyer* and *The Adventures of Huckleberry Finn*. Later in life he always repaired to a library if he wanted 'to cheer strained hours and illuminate dark places'. He became more and more in the habit of sniffing and fingering the books before reading. In passing it should be said that a catalogue of his childhood and adolescent reading gives no idea of the extent or range of his browsing or noting of every variety of book in his later age. In a discussion on unemployment in the thirties he would more than likely reach out for and sniff a volume of Charles Kingsley.

It is small wonder that Baldwin could write and speak English. I never tire of 'To me England is the country and the country is England'. One can hear,

'The sounds of England, the tinkle of the hammer on the anvil in the country smithy, the corncrake on a dewy morning, and the sight of a ploughman coming over the brow of a hill, the sight that has been in England since England was a land . . . and above all most subtle, most penetrating and most moving, the smell of wood smoke coming up in an autumn evening, or the smell of scutch fires; that wood smoke that our ancestors tens of thousands of years ago must have caught on the air when they were coming home with the result of the day's forage . . . These things strike down into the very depths of our nature, and touch chords that go back to the beginning of time and the human race, but they are chords that with every year of our life sound a deeper note in our innermost being.'

Baldwin visited me in our country house in Essex in 1935, towards the end of his time as Prime Minister. He asked to be left alone in my library all the day before his speech at 6.30 in the evening. I asked him to speak on Lloyd George and the tithe problem but he replied that these were just the subjects which his critics would enjoy the most. He would therefore speak only of the countryside. He asked me if I had any novels by Mary Webb. I obliged him and he settled down peacefully. He was surprised at my recommending *Joseph and His Brethren* by Freeman, which occupied him till 6.20. He said he would discuss *Ciceron et ses amis* by Boissier later in the evening. Meanwhile he said that the view of the elms and the rising corn reminded him of Constable. When the speech was over he reminisced again in the library saying, 'if you want to be Leader of the Party you should steer between Harold Macmillan and Henry Page Croft. I do so and that is why I am still there'.

While the fête was still in progress I received a message from Winston Churchill, 'Thank you for asking me to your residence. Mr Baldwin is the most outstanding political leader of our time.'

Let us look back on the reasons why his alternations of indolence and action were so effective. We will pass over his first period as a Victorian businessman and his time as a 'Quiet Backbencher'. By the time he was forty-two, the Coalition Government had been dismissed, largely owing to speeches by Bonar Law and Baldwin at the Carlton Club. He had pondered deeply on this at Aix-en-Provence, where he had decided to get rid of 'the goat' Lloyd George. In the ensuing Government, Baldwin became Chancellor of the Exchequer and made the surprising American debt settlement which his colleagues had great difficulty in endorsing. When Bonar Law's health deteriorated Baldwin was summoned by the King to be Prime Minister. George Curzon, as A.J.B. said, was disappointed. The rapid accession to office from comparative obscurity reminds one in some respects of the Younger Pitt, except that Baldwin was twenty years older than his exceptional predecessor when he achieved this success.

When Baldwin was made a Privy Councillor as Financial Secretary to the Treasury, the officials credited him with a certain lack of 'pushfulness'. This in fact was one of his great attributes and would have prevented him from writing memoirs. He always seemed to get everywhere by surprise and yet at critical moments, such as the fall of the coalition, he acted ruthlessly.

His English was limpid and would have embellished any book of memoirs. This came from his mother's side, the Macdonalds and their relationship with Burne-Jones, Kipling and Poynton. Baldwin decided in his later years, as indeed was typical of his earlier life, that he would not answer back. 'Old Sealed Lips,' as we used to call him, retained this characteristic right through his life. This indolence was a great attraction to many and would have pleased Talleyrand, *'surtout pas trop de zêle'*.

Lord Francis Williams in *A Pattern of Rulers* tries to make out that an incident at Harrow was traumatic for the young boy's future career. The boy was caught sending a mildly pornographic book to his cousin at Eton, and was so roundly turned on by Dr Butler, the Headmaster, that he was never made a monitor or communed with his Master again. No doubt Baldwin was somewhat thrust into himself when he went to Trinity and found Dr Butler translated there as Master. The fact is that both during his latter time at Harrow and his last year at Trinity, the young Stanley learned certain habits of indolence, and adopted a muffled reserve that were features of his later life. This man who could captivate and hold the House of Commons was fined by the Trinity Debating Society, the 'Magpie and Stump', for not speaking. His father was distressed when he got a third in history having changed over from classics.

I met Baldwin when I was President of the Union at Cambridge. He came to speak in favour of a motion that 'Rhetoric is the Harlot of the Arts'. His speech followed his own particular line which he adopted with such success against Rothermere and Beaverbrook. But the final voting was equal and I had to give the casting vote, which I did against Baldwin in favour of rhetoric. Next morning when I saw him off at the station he bought me a shocker at the bookstall saying, 'Intellectualism is a sin worse than death'. To this belief he held during his whole career. But it did lead to misapprehensions and in certain cases positive distrust. His friends were Edward Wood (Lord Halifax), Lord Bridgeman, F.E. Smith, even Curzon to whom Baldwin paid so elegant a tribute on his death. His friendship with Edward Wood influenced Baldwin and led him to take his courageous line over India—'and then there's Edward', he used to say. When S.B. made friendships they were so fast and firm, and he was himself fundamentally so poetic

94

August, 1931. Partners in coalition: Baldwin with Ramsay MacDonald

a character, that something is missed if one relies solely on the Davidson diaries' references to Baldwin. Also a wrong impression is given that he depended too much on his immediate official advisers. He was devoted to John and Joan Davidson who told him all the news. We miss part of the essence of Baldwin by not being able to talk to Halifax and Bridgeman, but Joan Davidson's accounts are ever faithful.

I went down to see Baldwin when he was staying with the Davidsons in June of 1941.

'It was June and the summer was vainly trying to emerge. S.B. was sitting in the porch rather like an old villager outside his cottage. He stood up for a while when we arrived, but then said he felt his arthritis too much and we all sat down and talked before dinner. His first agonized question was, "Did any of you foresee the collapse of France?" I had been told that he had been suffering from very serious depression, and so I took as optimistic a view of the situation as I could. During dinner I noted that S.B. had lost none of his old habits. He sniffed the knives and forks and curled up his eyes and clicked his fingers in exactly the way he used to do. But his conversation had declined in vigour, point and quality. At 9 p.m., this being a typical British household, there was a rush to hear the news. S.B. pulled out an old turnip watch and asked if he really need participate in this ritual. Joan Davidson gave way and the women went off to hear the BBC. We then talked for more than an hour, and the theme to which S.B. continually returned was that his military advisers had told him Germany would not be fully prepared until 1942; he had therefore felt that by starting rearmament when he did, in 1935, he was just in time.'[1]

Before I take further the controversial question of Baldwin and rearmament which is partially answered in his statement to me at Berkhamstead, I would like to discuss his much underrated contributions to foreign policy. His latest biographers[2] face up to his difficulties over foreign policy as follows:

'Unlike Lloyd George, Baldwin did not believe in trying to be his own Foreign Secretary. The answer to perhaps the most disputed question of all his political life, the extent to which he understood and shaped British policy abroad, can be found only in the full story of the inter-war years, but from the beginning he showed a humility, not to say a diffidence about the interventions which historians have repaid by ignoring their frequency and their effect.'[3]

I may say in passing that I think historians in general, especially G. M. Young and the Churchill school, show up very meanly in delineating Baldwin. S.B., perhaps wisely, showed a diffidence with Curzon. He said to Austen Chamberlain, 'But you are Foreign Secretary'. Yet his help in bringing about the Locarno settlement is on record. One of Baldwin's rare mistakes was when he and Hoare were 'broken on the wheel of public opinion' over the Hoare-Laval pact. First the Prime Minister should have insisted on Hoare coming home to explain why he, accompanied by the fiery non-appeasing Vansittart, had agreed to sign 'in a hot room'—as Sam Hoare explained to me—the document they did. Only a short time previously Hoare had made a forceful and successful speech on the ideals and practice of the League of Nations; all this was thrown away and it was the contrast between these ideals and the *real politik* of the Abyssinian pact which led to a flood of troubles in the country. Hoare resigned, while Vansittart remained in the most gracious room in the Foreign Office to bombard his superiors with notes on the importance of not negotiating with the Dictators. Baldwin remained and his position was never quite the same again.

But it is perhaps in the field of re-armament that Baldwin's reputation suffered most. Mr Churchill's index remark that Baldwin had 'put party before country' combines in its brevity, bitterness, inaccuracy and injustice. *The Times*'s obituary did not leave the ex-Prime Minister to lie in peace. Their obituary notice—a medium not commonly employed to stir up the flames of living party controversy—read as follows:

'Democratic leadership demanded that he should go to the country with a frank acknowledgement of the dangers, challenging its illusion with inconvenient truth and risking defeat. But he hesitated to take a course that might place the control of national policy in the hands of a man who, in his view, was more likely to accelerate than retard the onset of war. He made the worst of two worlds. What he sacrificed to political expedience obscured the real issue, delayed the education of the public opinion and impeded the process of rearmament, on the speed of which the success of any conceivable foreign policy then depended.'

It is clear if we read what Mr Baldwin said in 1936 that he was not alluding to the 1935 election at all. In the 1935 election Baldwin advocated strong re-armament and I supported this in Saffron Walden. As I have said above, Baldwin informed me at Berkhamstead that his advisers told him that Hitler would not be in a position to use his striking power before 1942. He therefore was wrongly advised in thinking that he had started to re-arm in time in 1935.

Baldwin's own question referring in particular to the Fulham by-election was, 'Does anyone think that this pacific democracy would have rallied to the call of re-armament at that moment?' He went on, 'I cannot think of anything that would have made the loss of the Election from my point of view more certain.' Young indictment of Baldwin has been answered by Reginald Bassett in the *Cambridge Journal* of November 1948. I do not believe that anyone *at the time* thought Baldwin meant the 1935 election. Nobody who has not lived through that time can appreciate what a prisoner the Cabinet as a whole was of the Peace Ballot atmosphere of 1934 and 1935. This can easily be criticized, but the Government was to a large extent wrongly influenced by the very wide degree of public opinion in the country which it governed. Nearly eleven million signatures to the Peace Ballot were obtained by the most strenuous band of investigators and the results were announced by Lord Robert Cecil in the Albert Hall. The first question asked whether the country should remain a member of the League. The next asked whether the voter was in favour of all round reduction of armaments. The third questioned whether people were in favour of an all round abolition of naval and military aircraft. All these, including the third, attracted the answer 'Yes', although for a year and more international agreement on such re-armament had been beyond the bounds of possibility. The last question was more complicated and asked whether if one nation were to attack another the rest should combine to stop it by economic and non-military measures or, if necessary, military measures. How the compilers of the question imagined that after answering 'Yes' to the first three questions, there could be sufficient military equipment to

D

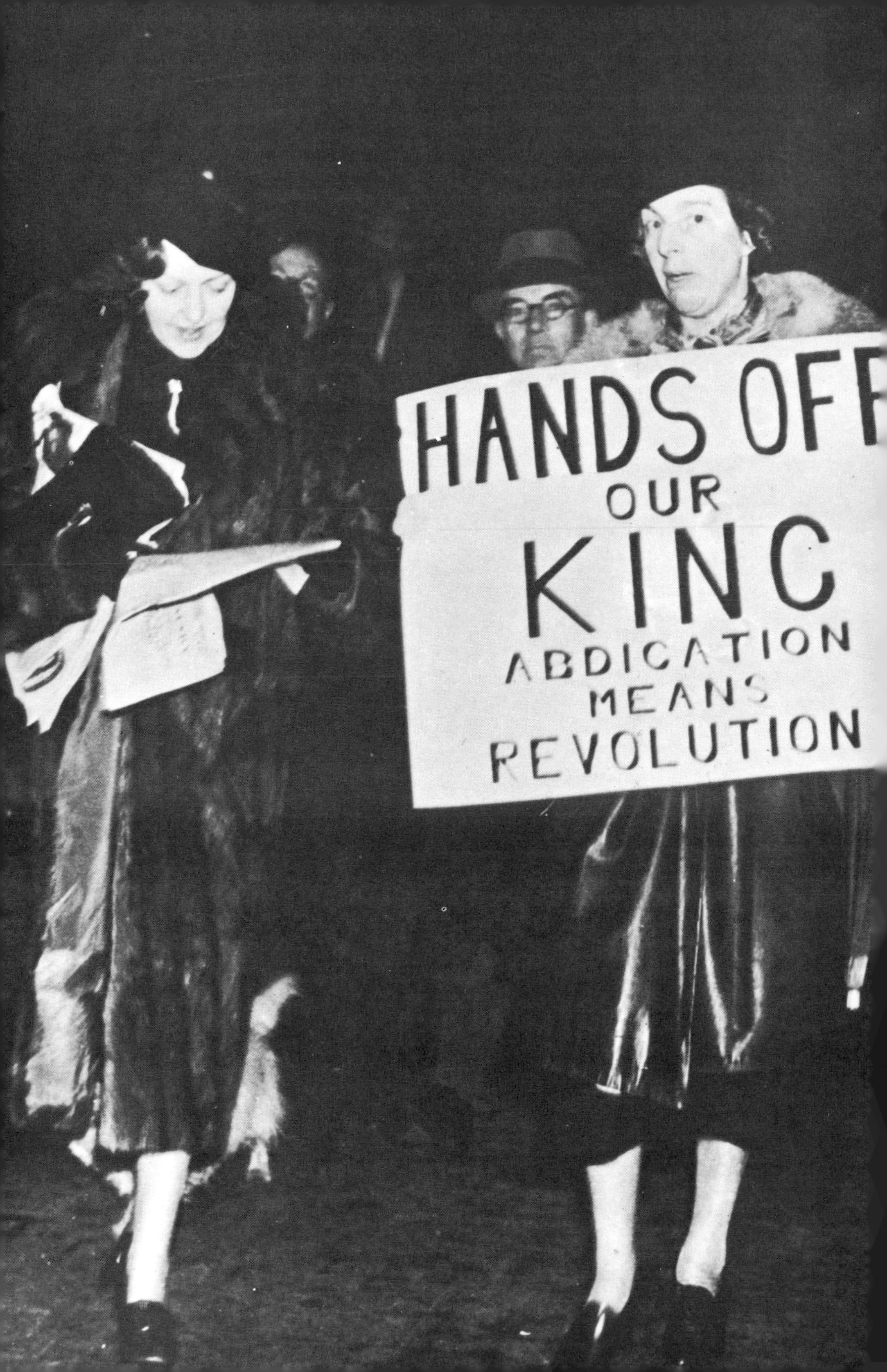
HANDS OFF
OUR
KING
ABDICATION
MEANS
REVOLUTION

answer this last question in the affirmative, it is hard to say, yet seven million voters answered 'Yes' to military sanctions.

Baldwin spoke at Glasgow on 23 November 1934, explaining that such complicated questions could not be answered by a simple 'Yes' or 'No'. The result was that the very ballot instituted to ensure peace became dynamite for use in party politics, and itself made war more certain by delaying re-armament.

There are two important episodes in Baldwin's career which cannot possibly be omitted. One is his struggle over India in the early thirties and the other, his finale, the sad story of the abdication. Had Baldwin not taken his stand over India, the state of the vast sub-continent might, by 1939, have resembled that of Ireland in 1921, a country torn by civil commotion open to the armies of Japan and perhaps afterwards to the impact of Communist China.

For Baldwin, and in fact for us all, at the time, the Indian issue was opened up by the Irwin declaration of 1929 in favour of Dominion Status for India. Baldwin's speech of 7 November 1929, following on the Declaration, can be described as follows: 'For half an hour he wandered loftily among his own thoughts revealing a profound and imaginative insight into the whole historic problem of our connection with India past and future.' He talked of the 'split migration of the Aryan peoples', and wondered at the chance which had brought the hard bitten Aryan of the North to labour with and for the meditative Aryan of the tropic zone. This sort of speech explains why Baldwin held his party on India and kept Churchill at bay.

But this task lasted several years. It is difficult now to imagine a minority of eighty Conservative M.P.s opposing their own Government in votes, nightly in the Commons and every few months in the Conservative organiza-tion in the country. This herd was led by a noble but ill-informed 'Bull' who bellowed his most powerful and picturesque oratory over a variety of audiences. Clearly Winston was out to win, not only on the Indian issue but of the Party organization in the country, for it was at provincial meetings I think Churchill had learned from his father, Lord Randolph, the importance of the Party organization in the country, for it was at provincial meetings that some of the closest divisions took place. Wherever the clashes occured Stanley Baldwin's quiet oratory prevailed and won the day.

Winston Churchill refused to serve on the Joint Select Committee of both Houses of Parliament to which the problem was remitted; but his particular henchman, Lord Salisbury, worked for him. Lord Wolmer (later Selborne) and Sir Henry (later Lord) Page Croft, also assisted Churchill. Page Croft roused the Conservative lieges by referring to the legions coming back to Rome (i.e. England) to go 'on the dole'.

India has in her history brought much pageant and colour into our parliamentary life, witness the India Bill in the time of Pitt and Fox, the trial of Warren Hastings and the like. The voice of Burke may not have been heard in my time but I can still hear Churchill describing the Indian peasants 'rising with the dawn to bow to implacable gods' and Eustace Percy's lucid persuasion in favour of the Government. Stanley Baldwin

Not everyone agreed with Baldwin's firm line in the Abdication Crisis

may not have decided the Indian issue, that was postponed till 1947, but he showed India that, animated by Dicey and Anson, we had produced a print on which their independence under Nehru and his daughter has finally been based.

My reference to the legions coming home to the dole enables me to say that the thousand-page life by Middlemas and Barnes does not say enough about Baldwin as a controller of the economy. Churchill's five years as Chancellor were disappointing, ending up with the departure from the Gold Standard and its stark social consequences. The truth is that Victorian and early Edwardian Prime Ministers were not primarily economists, with the exception of Gladstone and Peel. In the Baldwin era it seemed to be normal for the Bank of England to have a superimposed influence on social affairs, rendering a high level of unemployment a feature of our economic life for too long. Young reformers, such as Harold Macmillan, did not have as much influence on the policy towards the unemployed as they should. The crisis of 1931 opened mens' eyes to the need for stern financial measures, but there is no doubt that unemployment disgraced the thirties and was not adequately dealt with.

By December 1937, another great crisis was noted by Lucy Baldwin in her diary. This derived from the relationship between the young King and Mrs Simpson. In handling this affair Stanley Baldwin showed the highest qualities of wisdom and statesmanship. The whole affair has been amply recorded in Lord Birkenhead's *Life of Walter Monckton*, the King's intimate friend and adviser.

Since his death a welling of sympathy has gone out to the Duke of Windsor. But what Baldwin saw clearly was that the Dominions would not stand for a morganatic marriage and that the Head of the Church could not well contemplate marrying a twice-divorced woman.

The situation was a poignant one, the delicacy of which was enhanced by the sincere partnership of Churchill with the King and the undisguised attempt by Beaverbrook to overthrow Baldwin. The issue was really decided by Baldwin's final moving speech in the Commons. I can remember him ferreting in his left hand pocket for an envelope and pieces of paper on which he had made some notes. The prose that emerged from this medley was pure and conclusive.

It now remains for me to justify Baldwin's place among the leaders of the twentieth century. I think by his action and demeanour Baldwin avoided a social revolution in Britain. He helped to establish within the constitution the modern Labour Party and he brought to industrial disputes an atmosphere which is lacking today.

The General Strike of 1926 and the Coal Strike are today very apt subjects for discussion. On 6 March 1925, Baldwin made his most famous speech, 'Peace in our time and land.' It was the epitome of that allusive, indefinable but ever present phenomenon—Tory Democracy. The Prime Minister said, 'We stand for peace, we stand for the removal of suspicion in the country. We want to create an atmosphere, a new atmosphere in a new Parliament in which the people can come together.' The spiritual fervour of his appeal was echoed throughout the chapels and churches of the country.

Baldwin had great personal courage. Any ruthless action, such as his speech at the Carlton Club meeting overthrowing Lloyd George, was preceded by months of thought, in this particular case during long walks at Aix. He acted with similar courage before and during the General Strike. He was ready to go out of politics rather than to resile on India. Throughout his political life he was the target of attack and intrigue. He flouted and beat the Press Lords and won the famous Westminster by-election.

He was inspired not only by the wood smoke and scutch fires of rural England, but by the whole history of our land. In an age of unrest abroad and turmoil at home, he stood for the preservation of 'ordered liberty', a phrase he borrowed from his beloved Burke. His belief in constitutional propriety and the reign of law embellishes endless of his speeches, whether to learned societies or political audiences.

Baldwin's retirement to Astley was indeed a sad thing. After his wife's death he handled alone or left unopened a flood of recriminatory correspondence accusing him of neglect in preparing his country for war. I have described how he calculated that he had started re-armament in time. His lapses were cruelly exploited by Winston Churchill. But after Winston had assumed power he behaved magnanimously towards Stanley Baldwin, so indeed he should, by putting his memory and achievement in proper perspective. In particular we should remember Baldwin's intensely valuable contribution in avoiding a social revolution in his country, in saving the monarchy from a mistaken position and, within his means, doing his best to avoid chaos and confusion in India and to set her on the path to independence.

[1] *The Art of the Possible*, pp. 87-88.

[2] Keith Middlemas and John Barnes, *Baldwin*.

[3] Keith Middlemas and John Barnes, *Baldwin*.

I am indebted to the *Times Literary Supplement* for permission to use certain phrases and paragraphs from a previous review which I wrote of Stanley Baldwin's biography by Messrs Middlemas and Barnes. What I now wrote is of necessity much longer and more expanded, but this does not reduce my obligation for permission to repeat certain passages of a previous article.

101

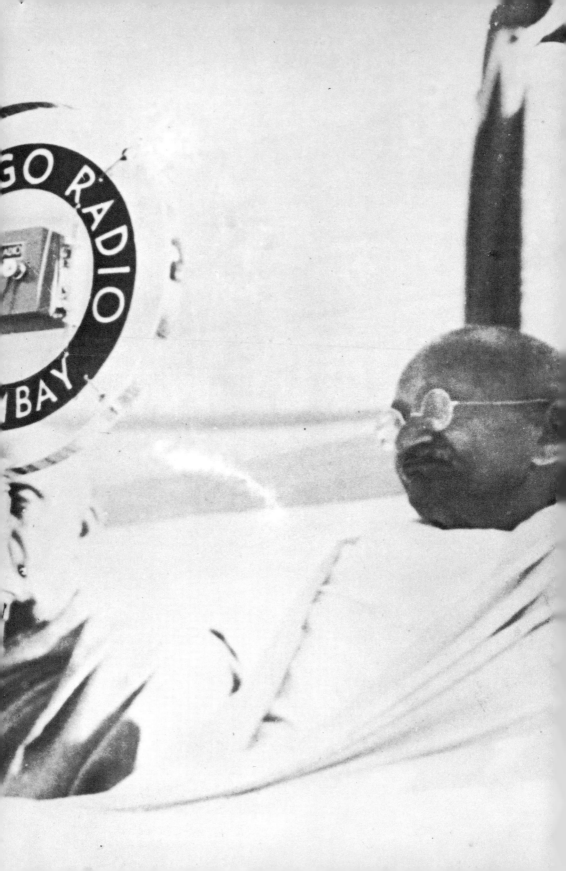

Gandhi
by HV Hodson

H. V. HODSON (b. 1906) went from Gresham's School, Holt, to Balliol College, Oxford, being elected a Fellow of All Souls in 1928, and from 1931 until the outbreak of the Second World War he directed the *Round Table*, first as Assistant Editor and then as Editor, during which time he became intimately acquainted with the countries of the Commonwealth and the United States. His war service included Head of the Empire Division of the Ministry of Information, Constitutional Adviser to the Viceroy of India and a divisional head in the Ministry of Production. At the close of hostilities he joined the staff of the *Sunday Times*, of which he became Editor in 1950. In 1961 he resigned to become Provost of the Ditchley Foundation, in which post he continued for the next ten years. Among his published studies are *The Great Divide; Britain-India-Pakistan* (1969), and *The Diseconomics of Growth* (1972).

Mahatma Gandhi

2 Oct. 1869	Born in Porbandar. Educated at Alfred High School in Rajkot.
1881	Married Kasturbai, who later had four sons.
1887	Matriculated, then spent three years in London studying law.
1891	Was called to the bar at the Inner Temple.
1891-93	Practised law in Bombay and Rajkot for two years.
May 1893	Went to South Africa. Adopted personal regime of self-denial *(brahmacharya)*.
1894	Founded Natal Indian Congress party. His reputation as a lawyer was rising.
1904	Took over weekly *Indian Opinion*, to fight Indian settlers' cause.
1906	Transvaal government passed bill which required every Indian to register fingerprints. Led by Gandhi, they refused, adopting campaign of non-violent resistance *(satyagraha)*.
1909	Wrote *Hind Swaraj* or *Indian Home Rule*. Corresponded with Tolstoy.
1910	Started his Tolstoy farm (on principle that life of labourer is life worth living).
1914	Passage of Indian Relief Act in South Africa.
Jan. 1915	Returned to India and Rabindranath Tagore hailed him as 'Mahatma' (great soul).
May 1915	Founded a *satyagraha ashram* at Ahmedabad with 25 inmates.
April 1917	Gandhi's enquiry into plight of peasants in Bihar led to improvements.
April 1918	Helped in recruiting for Indian army.
March 1919	Widespread discontent. Government enacted Rowlatt bills to empower authorities to

Previous page: in his later years, Gandhi addresses a public meeting

imprison without trial those suspected of sedition. Gandhi launched *satyagraha* campaign, but violence broke out—Jallianwalabagh massacre near Amritsar. Gandhi called off campaign.

1920 Death of Tilak, leader of Indian national movement. Gandhi supported Khilafat agitation for preservation of Ottoman caliphate.

Sept. 1921 Gandhi adopted loincloth as his dress, as symbol to promote spinning-wheel (the means of freeing India from its dependence on Lancashire mills).

Feb. 1922 Led mass campaign of civil disobedience in Bardoli district (Gujerat). After an attack on police, he suspended it.

13 March 1922 Arrested and tried for sedition. Pleaded guilty and was sentenced to six years' imprisonment.

Feb. 1924 Operation for appendicitis and was released from jail.

Dec. 1924 Became President of Indian National Congress.

1927 Simon Commission on constitutional reform boycotted by Congress.

Oct. 1929 Congress declared its goal was complete independence.

12 March 1930 Salt march, to protest against tax on salt, organized by Gandhi. He was arrested in May.

26 Jan. 1931 Released.

12 Sept. 1931 Reached London to represent Congress at Round Table conference.

1 Jun. 1932 Re-arrested.

Feb. 1933 Identified himself with untouchables, whom he called 'harijan' (children of God) and started *Harijan* weekly.

1934 Resigned from Congress. Devoted himself to touring on behalf of harijans and to promoting spinning wheel.

1935 Congress decided to take provincial office under new constitution which gave democratic autonomy to provinces under ultimate British control.

1937 Congress swept polls because of Gandhi's constructive programme.

1939 S.C. Bose, militant left-wing Bengali leader, elected President of Congress. Gandhi obliged him to resign.

Sept. 1939 British Viceroy took India into Second World War without consulting Indian leaders, so Congress ministers resigned.

Jan. 1940 Gandhi corresponded with M. A. Jinnah, leader of Muslim League and later founder of Pakistan. Gandhi hoped for unity.

Oct. 1940 Launched individual civil disobedience to win freedom of speech against war.

March 1942 Sir Stafford Cripps came to India with offer for settlement which Gandhi thought worthless. He influenced Congress to reject it and initiated 'Quit India' campaign.

Aug. 1942 Arrested and detained at Poona.

Feb. 1944 Death of wife.

May 1944 Released on grounds of health.

March 1946 After end of war and advent of Labour government in Britain, British mission under Lord Pethwick-Lawrence arrived in Delhi with plan for three-tier federation. But Gandhi wanted Hindu-Muslim reconciliation and a united India.

June 1947 Britain announced plan to partition India—accepted by Congress and Muslim League.

15 Aug. 1947 Independence Day. Shortly afterwards communal riots in Calcutta provoked Gandhi to fast. His appeal calmed the riots.

Jan. 1948 Communal riots in Punjab—200,000 died. Gandhi fasted for reconciliation.

30 Jan. 1948 On way to prayer meeting, Gandhi shot dead by Hindu fanatic.

D*

We British are apt to make heroes of our former imperial foes. A statue of the rebel George Washington stands in Trafalgar Square. In our own time, Archbishop Makarios, Eamon de Valera and Jomo Kenyatta have been translated from obloquy to honour. Mahatma Gandhi scarcely needed such elevation. Even in his most anti-British days he was never quite the hated opponent, and during his lifetime respect always softened enmity. He was a symbol of universal ideals as well as Indian nationalism. He thus needed the less a reassessment of his merits or an erasure of his faults.

In his lifetime, many British people found Gandhi enigmatic, self-contradictory and, by implication, hypocritical. This may be because they judged him as they would an Englishman, not as an Indian and a Hindu, though even his closest friends of his own faith also found him enigmatic: 'I have known Gandhiji for thirty-two years', said Jawaharlal Nehru to Lord Mountbatten, 'and I can still never guarantee that I can fathom his mind'. Hindu philosophy stresses 'the many-sidedness of truth'. Its caste-bound social system and its multifarious deities perplex those brought up in a monotheistic and individualist tradition. Gandhi saw no incompatibility in the many contrasts observable in his philosophy and conduct, contrasts which make it impossible to encapsule his personality in a catalogue of traits. Nehru called him 'An extraordinary paradox'. If he was naive, he was also cunning; if high-principled, opportunist; if transparent, enigmatic; if tolerant, fanatical; if always ready to negotiate, impossible to pin down; if for long periods quietist, on occasion the spearhead of revolt; if dedicated to non-violence, the leader of campaigns inevitably incurring violence; if ascetic, pleased by the best and loving the company of women; if catholic in his view of religions, profoundly Hindu in feeling; if obsessed by Hindu-Muslim unity, opposed to any big constitutional concession to the Muslims; if ready to assume leadership, equally ready to avoid responsibility. To attempt a Hegelian synthesis of these antitheses is an abuse of ingenuity. It is simpler and closer to truth to say that they were different aspects of one man whose thoughts were more profound than his decisions in action, in whom the native practicality of the *bania* often warred with the native mysticism of the Vedic philosopher; one who propounded a system of thought so difficult to apply to hard political problems that any immediate practical action they indicated would almost certainly be wrong.

The closer India came to self-government, the more unacceptable or confusing became the Gandhian prescriptions. The fatal moment was the decision of the Congress to take provincial office under the Constitution of 1935, which gave democratic autonomy to the provinces under ultimate British control. Thenceforward political principles, whether Gandhian or other, became subject to the political tyranny of the possible. It was the resignation (under Gandhi's influence) of the Congress provincial ministries in protest against India's being 'dragged into the war' that gave the Mahatma his renewed chance to dictate its fundamental policy. This influence turned the scales against the Cripps offer of 1942 which might possibly have diverted Muslim aspirations from separatism to an all-India role. Only with great skill did Lord Mountbatten stop him from denouncing the settlement of

June 1947 and thus plunging political India into chaos. Gandhi's own words show, indeed, that chaos held no terror for him when matched against adherence to his principles. Though one of the most powerful political figures of his time, he was not a political animal. If he had a *political* philosophy, it was anarchy, nostalgia for a golden age of primitive self-sufficiency.

In person Gandhi was slight, awkward and unprepossessing; a bony, bald, plain little man in steel-rimmed spectacles and a *dhoti*. But his appearance was affectionately familiar to millions throughout the world. He had great charm, which impressed his opponents as much as his friends. His voice was mellow, his sense of humour strong; he was a most agreeable man with whom to talk. Jawaharlal Nehru wrote of him:

'This little man of poor physique had something of steel in him . . . In spite of his unimpressive features, his loin cloth and bare body, there was a royalty and kingliness in him which compelled a willing obeisance from others. Consciously and deliberately meek and humble, yet he was full of power and authority, and he knew it, and at times he was imperious enough, issuing commands which had to be obeyed. His calm, deep eyes could hold one and gently probe into the depths: his voice, clear and limpid, would purr its way into the heart, and evoke an emotional response. Whether his audience consisted of one person or a thousand, the charm and magnetism of the man passed on to it.'

Viceroys were pleased to be called his friend: not only the liberal, religious Irwin, or Mountbatten, the out-going man of action, but even the stern conservative Linlithgow, with whom his correspondence is on the same plane of mutual respect as the exchanges, quoted below, at his 1922 trial. Leaders of the Congress, like Jawaharlal Nehru or Vallabhbhai Patel, were faithful to him more in affection for himself than in admiration of his policies. They called him 'Bapu', a word more intimate than Father, more respectful than Daddy. Thousands who had never met him knew him by the diminutive Gandhiji, a tribute of familiarity not awarded to British Prime Ministers since the days of 'Dizzy'. If to Winston Churchill, in a famous phrase, he was a 'half naked fakir', by the same token he had for his countrymen the holiness of poverty self-imposed.

Mohandas Karamchand Gandhi, known in the latter part of his life as the Mahatma (or Great Soul, a title exuberantly conferred by Rabindranath Tagore in 1915), made his first venture in political leadership in South Africa in 1895, two years before Queen Victoria's Diamond Jubilee saluted the apogee of the British Empire, and died at the hand of an assassin in 1948, less than a year after India's independence had marked the beginning of its end. Although that combination of dates was no coincidence, neither was it a manifestation of cause and effect. All Gandhi's life was spent in the shadow of imperial domination, much of his effort in striving for its end; but his basic philosophy was no more anti-imperialist than it was anti-capitalist, or anti-state-socialist for that matter; for more than twenty creative years the object of his agitations remained social rather than nationalist; and Indian independence might have come more or less when it did, some say even sooner, had there been no Gandhi, no *satyagraha* movement, no Salt March nor other display of the Gandhian

ethic in India. Certainly the manner of its coming was to him not a climactic triumph but a devastating defeat.

What is true is that his ethic flourished in the peculiar atmosphere of British imperialism in its prime, and among Indians subject to British rule. At other times, among other people, it might have spluttered like a squib and been extinguished either by a harsh governmental heel or by the damp of apathy or the dowsing of power politics. Because the time was ripe, because the Indian people were fertile soil and the British the tolerant and suggestible people that they were, Gandhi became the unrivalled prophet and symbol of Indian nationalism, and his methods gained successes which other circumstances would have denied them. Just because he was a man of his time, when the time changed, as it did with the impending achievement of self-rule, his mark upon the policies of India and the Indian political masses was soon all but obliterated. His posthumous impact upon history is being made, above all, upon the hearts and minds of generations and lands which knew him not.

To recall the main events of his life is to display a pattern totally unlike that of any contemporary political leader or social seer. Born in 1869, the son of a chief minister of a Princely State in Kathiawar, a *bania* (merchant) by caste and a Vaishnavite (follower of Vishnu) by religious upbringing, he was an indifferent scholar and came to England to read for the Bar as the easiest way of gaining a professional qualification. It was as a lawyer for a Muslim trading firm that he went to South Africa in 1893. There he was inspired to champion the cause of the Indian community against the degradation and discrimination that they suffered, and chose, from increasingly deep faith, the method of non-violent activism, which he dubbed *satyagraha*, truth-force. At this time, too, he was converted to a personal regime of all-embracing self-denial, or continence—no meat, no alcohol, no tobacco, no stimulants, no sex, no worldly possessions—known as *brahmacharya*, which thenceforward mingles inextricably with his methodology of *satyagraha* in his total philosophy. In Natal he founded his first model rural community, animated by such social and personal ideals.

His successes in South Africa were limited, though in 1914 he seemed momentarily to have conquered with the passage of the Indian Relief Act; and after the triumph of Afrikaner nationalism in the year of Gandhi's death all that had been gained on the road to equality of status for Asians was eventually lost. Gandhi, however, returned to India in 1914 a hero among his countrymen. His first two *satyagraha* campaigns there were characteristically socio-economic—against a rack-renting system of exploitation of poor indigo-farmers in Bihar, and on behalf of striking cotton-mill workers in Ahmedabad, when he rallied a failing cause by a threat to fast. Both campaigns achieved their goals. Gandhi's anti-imperialism was still hypothetical. 'If I should find it necessary for the salvation of India that the English should retire,' he said in 1916, 'I would not hesitate to declare that they would have to go'. Even his anti-imperialism was not anti-British. His genuine affection for Britain was shown by his first reaction to the outbreak of Hitler's war; or again by his charming gesture upon the engagement of the future Queen Elizabeth II and Prince Philip. He told Lord Mountbatten

Gandhi in the early years of the century—then an attorney in South Africa

that he wanted to give them a wedding present but could not because he owned nothing. The Viceroy suggested that he spin a thread which his 'honorary granddaughters' could weave into a table-cover. This he did, and the Queen has kept his gift among her most treasured possessions.

Back in the First World War, in 1918 he even agreed to help in recruiting for the Indian Army—in which operation, needless to say, he was not a success. In that same year, however, a tough measure for the protection of law and order against a rising tide of violence, known as the Rowlatt Act, aroused his anger and tipped the scales against his acceptance of British rule. Under his impulse the first national *satyagraha* campaign was launched. In a sense it succeeded: millions of Indians responded, and in the end the Rowlatt Act was quietly shelved. But in another, Gandhian sense it was a disaster. Violence broke out on all hands, culminating in the horror of the Jallian-walabagh massacre near Amritsar. Gandhi called off the campaign, fasted in penance, and confessed, in a famous phrase, to a 'Himalayan blunder' in allowing the masses to take part in action which if it was to remain non-violent required iron training in self-control. Although there followed other civil disobedience movements, of a more discriminating and specific kind, with varying results, the same lesson was repeated four years later, when on the eve of a tax-strike in Bardoli a score of policemen were horribly destroyed by a mob which set fire to their station. Gandhi at once suspended his carefully-prepared and advertised campaign. A few weeks afterwards he was sentenced to six years' imprisonment for 'bringing or attempting to bring into hatred or contempt or exciting or attempting to excite disaffection towards His Majesty's Government established by law in British India'. Gandhi pleaded guilty.

The beautifully-mannered exchange between him and the Judge, Mr C. N. Broomsfield, I.C.S., is one of the most revealing passages in the vast Gandhi archive, for the light that it throws both on the Mahatma's attitude towards the British and the British attitude towards him; both were ambivalent.

Mr Gandhi: Before I read this statement, I would like to state that I entirely endorse the learned Advocate-General's remarks in connection with my humble self. I think that he was entirely fair to me in all the statements that he has made, because . . . to preach disaffection towards the existing system of government has become almost a passion with me . . . He is quite right when he says that as a man of responsibility, a man having received a fair share of education, having had a fair share of experience of this world, I should have known the consequences of every one of my acts. I knew that I was playing with fire. I ran the risk, and if I was set free, I would still do the same . . .

I wanted to avoid violence. Non-violence is the first article of my faith. It is also the last article of my creed. But I had to make my choice. I had either to submit to a system which I considered had done irreparable harm to my country, or incur the risk of the mad fury of my people bursting forth, when they understood the truth from my lips. I know that my people have sometimes gone mad. I am deeply sorry for it and I am therefore here to submit not to a light penalty but to the highest penalty. I do not ask for mercy. I do not plead any extenuating act.

The defendant's statement begins with an explanation of 'why from a staunch loyalist and co-operator I have become an uncompromising dis-affectionist and non-co-operator'. After referring to his experiences in South Africa, to the Rowlatt Act, and to the Khilafat agitation (in which he had made common cause with the Indian Muslims) for the preservation of the Ottoman Caliphate, it continues:

I came reluctantly to the conclusion that the British connection had made India more helpless than she ever was before, politically and economically . . . Before the British advent, India spun and wove in her millions of cottages just the supplement she needed for adding to her meagre agricultural resources. This cottage industry, so vital for India's existence, has been ruined by incredibly heartless and inhuman processes . . . I have no doubt whatsoever that both England and the town dwellers of India will have to answer, if there is a God above, for this crime against humanity which is perhaps unequalled in history . . .

The greatest misfortune is that Englishmen and their Indian associates in the administration of the country do not know that they are engaged in the crime I have attempted to describe . . . that a subtle but effective system of terrorism and an organized display of force on the one hand, and the deprivation of all powers of retaliation or self-defence on the other, have emasculated the people and induced in them the habit of simulation. This awful habit has added to the ignorance and the self-deception of the administrators . . . I hold it to be a virtue to be disaffected towards a government which in its totality has done more harm to India than any previous system. India is less manly under the British rule than she ever was before. Holding such a belief, I consider it to be a sin to have affection for the system . . . In fact, I believe that I have rendered a service to India and England by showing in non-cooperation the way out of the unnatural state in which both are living. In my humble opinion, non-cooperation with evil is as much a duty as is cooperation with good. But in the past, non-cooperation has been deliberately expressed in violence to the evil-doer. I am endeavouring to show to my countrymen that violent non-cooperation only multiplies evil . . . Non-violence implies voluntary submission to the penalty for non-cooperation with evil. I am here, therefore, to invite and submit cheerfully to the highest penalty that can be inflicted upon me for what in law is a deliberate crime and what appears to me to be the highest duty of a citizen.

The Judge: Mr Gandhi, you have made my task easy in one way by pleading guilty to the charge. Nevertheless, what remains, namely, the determination of a just sentence, is perhaps as difficult a proposition as a judge in this country could have to face. The law is no respecter of persons. Nevertheless, it will be impossible to ignore the fact that you are in a different category from any person I have ever tried or am likely to have to try . . . In the eyes of millions of your countrymen, you are a great patriot and a great leader. Even those who differ from you in politics look upon you as a man of high ideals and of noble and of even saintly life . . . It is my duty to judge you as a man subject to the law, who by his own admission has broken the law and committed what to an ordinary man must appear to be grave offence against the State. I do not forget that you have consistently preached against violence and that you have on many occasions, as I am willing to believe, done much to prevent violence. But having regard to the nature of your political teaching and the nature of those to whom it was addressed, how you could have continued to believe that violence would not be the inevitable consequence it passes my capacity to understand . . .

I propose in passing sentence to follow the precedent of a case in many respects similar to this case that was decided some twelve years ago, I mean the case against Bal Gangadhar Tilak under the same section. The sentence that was passed upon him as it finally stood was a sentence of simple imprisonment for six years . . . which I feel it my duty to pass upon you, and I should like to say in doing so that, if the course of events in India should make it possible for the Government to reduce the period and release you, no one will be better pleased than I.

Mr Gandhi: Since you have done me the honour of recalling the trial of the late Lokamanya Bal Gangadhar Tilak, I just want to say that I consider it to be the proudest privilege and honour to be associated with his name. So far as the sentence itself is concerned, I certainly consider that it is as light as any judge would inflict on me, and so far as the whole proceedings are concerned, I must say that I could not have expected greater courtesy.

Tilak was the activist, Hindu-traditionalist, Mahratta leader of the Indian national movement, who had died in 1920. Gandhi's hero-worship of this defender of child marriages and the caste system, who was far from hostile to violence, is as remarkable as is his ranking of the decay of the peasant industry (which was the fault of industrialism as much as imperialism), not India's political subjection, as a crime against humanity unequalled in history.

Only two years later Gandhi was released from prison on medical grounds. In December 1924 he became, reluctantly and as a symbol of solidarity at a time of internal dissension, President of the Indian National Congress. It was an honour which he never again accepted; after 1934 he held no office whatever in the Congress, and often spoke of himself as 'not even a four-anna member'. He was content, and with practical reason, to exercise his great authority over its members high and low from a position of detachment, a combination of prophet, oracle, confessor and court of appeal. Through the years this authority was continuously wielded through his personal influence over the Congress leaders; in part that influence was due to their personal love and loyalty, in part to their knowledge that his hold over the Indian masses was far stronger and more enduring than their own. But from time to time it was decisively exerted to achieve particular ends.

Two characteristic episodes will suffice as examples. In 1939 Subhas Chandra Bose, the militant Left-wing Bengali leader who eventually in World War II defected to Germany and then to Japan, was elected President of the Congress. Had his sway lasted, the history of India's struggle for independence might well have been very different: guerilla or destructive methods might have replaced those of non-violence; alternatively the Congress might have finally split. The Mahatma emerged from his monastic seclusion, and so successfully browbeat the All-India Congress Committee that Subhas was obliged to resign. The second example was the fate of the Cripps Mission in 1942. Sir Stafford Cripps brought out an offer of independence, after the end of the war, under a constitution to be framed by Indians themselves. He negotiated with representatives of all Indian parties, including the Congress Working Committee led by Jawaharlal Nehru. Gandhi was neither a negotiator nor a member of that Committee, yet it was his influence, virtually his veto, which caused the Congress finally to reject the offer. When in 1946 the Cabinet Mission offered a plan for a three-tier federation, Cripps was again the most active British negotiator: from the lesson of 1942 he felt that to win over the Mahatma was vital to success, but he found 'the Old Man', as he called him in his diary, so impossible to pin down that he finally gave up in despair. Cripps's judgement of the need was wrong; for by 1946, with independence clearly on the horizon, and national power within the Congress leaders' grasp, Gandhi's influence was already on the wane.

Between 1924 and 1942 the Mahatma led a characteristic series of intermittent non-violent actions. In 1928 he called the tax strike at Bardoli which he had planned and abandoned six years previously, with remarkable success both in the avoidance of violence and in the eventual response by government. A year later he made his most dramatic gesture, designed to promote his demand for complete Indian independence— the famous Salt March. At the head of a swelling procession he walked two hundred and forty miles from his *ashram* (retreat) to the sea coast, where he symbolically violated the salt monopoly. This demonstration was followed by nation-wide civil disobedience, with some violent episodes; and by the arrest of some hundred thousand people, including the Congress leaders and Gandhi himself. In 1931 he was released and invited to talks with the Viceroy, Lord Irwin. *Satyagraha* was halted, and Gandhi attended, as single representative of the Congress, the Round Table Conference in London called to consider a new constitution for India. In that milieu he was in-effective, though his personality impressed itself upon many British people for whom he had previously been only a legend. Back in India, disappointed and frustrated, he was again imprisoned in the course of a continuing con-frontation between the government and successive disobedience campaigns, but his impulse for action seemed to have slackened.

His reaction to the outbreak of war with Hitler's Germany in 1939 was far from that of a man of destiny. 'I was sorry to find myself alone among the Congress leaders,' he wrote in his weekly journal *Harijan*, 'in seeking that whatever support was to be given to the British should be given uncon-ditionally', though in accordance with his principles such support could only be moral. But he later forsook this characteristically ambiguous attitude, and he backed the Working Committee's call for the resignation of the provincial Congress ministries later in 1939; after rejection of the Cripps offer in 1942 he initiated the 'Quit India' campaign which led to his incarceration and that of all the active Congress leaders, and proved one of the most miscalculated moves ever made by the Congress. In February 1943 he began a fast in the Aga Khan's palace at Poona, in which he was imprisoned: the government refused his demands, which were somewhat obscure, and he eventually broke fast without changing anything. Later he was released on medical grounds. In the negotiations for a constitutional settlement conducted by the Viceroy, Lord Wavell, in 1945 and by the Cabinet Mission under Lord Pethick-Lawrence in 1946 his part was complex and tantalizing, but the key was his insistence that the Congress, as an all-community body, should never accept the claim of Mr Jinnah and the Muslim League that they alone could represent the Indian Muslims.

In this stance, whatever its tactical consequences (which may well have been the final acknowledgement that partition into Pakistan and India was the only way out), Gandhi was exhibiting the concern for relations between the communities and castes of India which preoccupied him during his last years, a time when his direct impact on the main course of events—inde-pendence and partition—was less than his unique status as the embodiment of Indian national feeling suggested. (His long conversations with Lord Mountbatten, when the Viceroy was making up his mind what constitutional

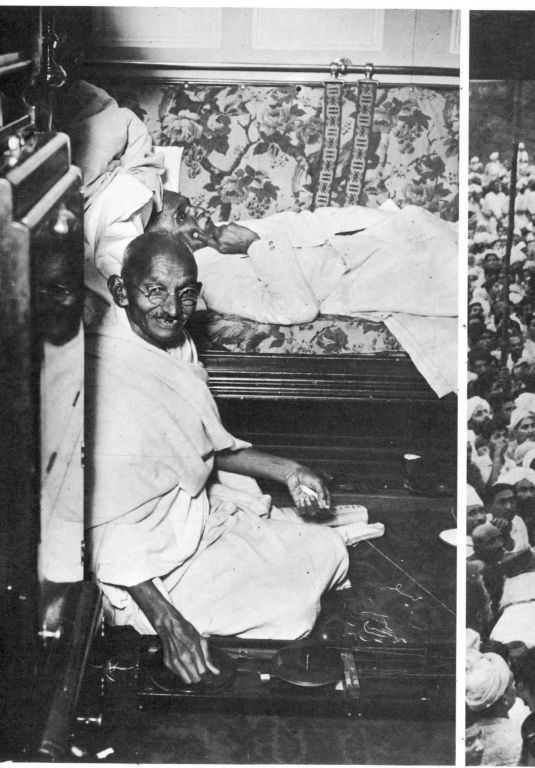

Gandhi weaving in his cabin in 1931 on voyage to Round Table, and (right) at a prayer meeting in Madras

plan to propose, were peculiarly enigmatic and futile, in that the solutions he propounded seemed to ignore altogether the realities of the political situation and the struggle for power.) He devoted himself to championship of the Untouchables, the Harijans or 'people of god' as he called them, against the social oppression of the upper Hindu castes, to the point of living among them in a Harijan 'ghetto'. This was no new cause for the Mahatma, and to him more than any other man the lowest castes of India owe such liberation as they now enjoy.

His action for Hindu-Muslim reconciliation was no less characteristic. When Independence Day came on 15 August 1947, Gandhi was absent from the celebrations, striving by his example and the force of his personality to show the way of peace in divided and distracted Bengal. When the communal slaughter in the Punjab threatened to spread to Bengal, Gandhi entered upon a fast unto death. Within four days the threat of inter-communal violence had faded. 'My dear Gandhiji,' wrote Lord Mountbatten to the Mahatma, 'In the Punjab we have fifty-five thousand soldiers and large-scale rioting on our hands. In Bengal our forces consist of one man, and there is no rioting. As a serving officer, as well as an administrator, may I be allowed to pay my tribute to the One Man Boundary Force.' In the North-West, among the Muslims and Sikhs and Hindu *jats* of the Punjab, the Gandhian influence, so far as it ever had a hold, was utterly overwhelmed by inter-communal hatred and destruction. As many as two hundred thousand men, women and children, perhaps more, lost their lives, and some five million lost their homes. Flooded with refugees, Delhi itself, the capital of the Moguls and the British raj and newly independent India, was threatened with uncontrollable inter-communal slaughter. On 12 January 1948 Gandhi announced that he would fast, even at the cost of his life, for the sake of Hindu-Muslim peace, especially in Delhi. The specific conditions that he laid down all concerned the rights and safety of Muslims. After six days, satisfied by the pledges of an all-party peace committee, which did indeed do much good in Delhi, he broke his fast, but not before he had also caused the Indian Cabinet reluctantly to reverse its decision to withhold, until Pakistan gave way in Kashmir, a sum of Rs. 55 *crores* (£41 million), owing to Pakistan under the partition settlement.

Both the method and the objects of these last Gandhian interventions reflect alike the outward coherence and the inner contradictions of the Mahatma's philosophy. It was not a political creed but essentially a Rule of Life which the circumstances of his time drew into the political field, where it encountered difficulties no less than those to be found in applying to politics the Sermon on the Mount. To understand it we must go to its roots.

Satyagraha, or truth-force, Gandhi's term for the mode of peaceful action to change a situation deemed evil, is not in his ethic a doctrine or ideal standing by itself. It is a derivative of *ahimsa* (truth), and when *ahimsa* is forgotten, he taught, *satyagraha* rots. 'The word "Satya" (Truth),' wrote Gandhi, 'is derived from "Sat" which means being. And nothing is or exists in reality except Truth. That is why "Sat" or Truth is perhaps the most important name of God. In fact it is more correct to say that Truth is God, than to say that God is Truth.' Christians cannot but recall the first verse of

116

Right: with the Mountbattens in 1947

St John's Gospel: 'In the beginning was the Word (*Logos*), and the Word was with God, and the Word was God.' Nor is *satyagraha* to be thought of as just a means to an end. On the contrary, 'renunciation of the fruits of action', says Gandhi in his commentary on the *Bhagavad Gita*, is 'the matchless remedy'. *Satyagraha*, though directed to particular occasions, incorporates an end in itself. It is positive: '*satyagraha* differs from passive resistance as the North Pole from the South'. 'Truth transcends history,' Gandhi once said in explaining why the Mahabharata had taught him more than Gibbon's *Decline and Fall*; and the phrase tells us much. History, he is saying, is not truth, nor are contemporary facts: they are only part of truth, which stands above them. Truth is to be found in thought, in mystical communion, in myth as much as record, in eternal verities. It is the transition from transcendent truth to current action that provides the difficulties, the contradictions and the Himalayan blunders. Not by chance is *ahisma*, truth, which Gandhi preached as the fundamental lesson, itself a negative and derivative notion, the opposite of *himsa*, untruth. Untruth is simple and easy to comprehend; truth is complex and needs a lifetime of learning. The transition from thought to action, from the perfect to the possible, can be a personal agony as well as a political conundrum. 'My conception of *ahimsa* impels me always to dissociate myself from almost every one of the activities I am engaged in . . . The spirit in me pulls one way, the flesh in me pulls in the opposite direction . . . I can attain freedom not by a mechanical refusal to act, but only by intelligent action in a detached manner. This struggle resolves itself into an incessant crucifixion of the flesh so that the spirit may become entirely free.' (What echoes of St Paul!)

So the next stage in the evolution of the Gandhian philosophy was *brahmacharya*, total continence. Reverence for truth must not be distracted by worldly pleasures or ambitions. Asceticism, however, is a practice as hard to define as to conduct. Where indulgence of the flesh begins is a disputed frontier. Gandhi was often criticized by his opponents for such mitigations of self-denial as preferring dates brought from the Army and Navy Stores to those offered in the fly-blown bazaar. The fact remains that he lived simply, eschewed all stimulants and luxury, and left very few physical possessions.

His philosophy obviously owes much to Western as well as Eastern thought. The impressionable young Gandhi was deeply affected, while studying law in London, by Tolstoy, Ruskin, Thoreau, Mathew Arnold, by the theosophists and vegetarians who were the *avant-garde* of post-Victorian revolt, and most obviously by the New Testament in English. His utterances to the end of his days are peppered with phrases from the Christian Bible, liturgy and hymnal: 'thought, word and deed', 'a humble and a contrite heart', 'mortifying the flesh', 'our bodies are the real temples rather than buildings of stone', 'powers of darkness', 'in the twinkling of an eye', 'the letter killeth, the spirit giveth life'. And he customarily led Christian hymns at his latter-day prayer meetings, his favourites being significantly 'Rock of Ages' and 'Abide with Me'. Here is his portrait of his true devotee of the Gita:

He is the devotee who is jealous of none, who is a fount of mercy, who is without egotism, who is selfless, who treats alike cold and heat, happiness and misery, who is ever forgiving, who is always contented, whose resolutions are firm, who has dedicated mind and soul to God, who causes no dread, who is not afraid of others, who is free from exultation, sorrow and fear, who is pure, who is versed in action and yet remains unaffected by it, who renounces all fruit, good or bad, who treats friend and foe alike, who is untouched by respect or disrespect, who is not puffed up by praise, who does not go under when people speak ill of him, who loves silence and solitude, who has a disciplined reason.

It is as plain as day how much that owes (even the phrase 'is not puffed up') to I Corinthians XIII, 5-7.

None the less there is a difference. Gandhiism has its deepest roots in Hindu belief and tradition. 'My life would be a burden to me,' wrote Gandhi to Nehru in 1933, 'if Hinduism failed me. I love Christianity, Islam and many other faiths through Hinduism. Take it away and nothing remains for me'. Gandhi's creed went beyond Tolstoy in pacifism, or Ruskin in discarding the values of a business world, or indeed the Holy Gospel in its teaching of humility and renunciation. Christian writ is full of the imagery of competitions and reward: races and prizes and vanquishings and crowns. Gandhian doctrine in its pure form abhors even pride in the achievement of good. It is neither works nor faith that justifies, but the purity of the inner spirit. Virtue is literally its own reward.

Despite manifest failures—which he penitentially acknowledged—Gandhi's public actions can be best understood by reference to this difficult system of doctrine and action. No aspect of them is more perplexing—or more revealing—than the instrument of the fast. Gandhi's first demonstrative fast was performed close to the start of his active career in India: his last was ended only a dozen days before his death. Those occasions were separated by thirty years, but by only a few, if famous, public fasts. These seem, in review, to express the opportunism—sometimes brilliant, sometimes inept—with which his spiritual philosophy was transmuted into mundane political action. Gandhi ascribed such decisions as entering upon a fast to an Inner Voice, which others might call intuition or native shrewdness. Were the fasts a form of blackmail? In effect they were, though Gandhi hotly repudiated such intention. He would say that his fasting was meant to quicken men's consciences, not to coerce them against their will. The occasions were significant: the consciences he sought to prick were those of his fellow-countrymen. On the only occasion on which a fast directly challenged the British *raj* his motives were hard to discern and acceptance of the challenge left him impotent.

Satyagraha, mass peaceful action, was different, a deliberate confrontation with authority. So long as the authority was alien and undemocratic, the issue was simple enough. But as Gandhi's life neared its end the old order changed. He had painfully foreseen the debasement of the instrument that he had forged into an agency of political power when the major objective of Indian self-rule had been attained. As independence approached in 1947 he pleaded for the Congress to detach itself from government and party politics and become the conscience of the people, striving not for power but for non-violence, for the betterment of the poor, for the defeat of untouch-

119

ability, for the rejuvenation of village life, for all the enduring causes which were even dearer to him than had been the overthrow of imperial rule. His pleas fell on deaf ears. Congress became the governing party, with its immediate past President, Jawaharlal Nehru, as Prime Minister, a year before the transfer of power. Vallabhbhai Patel, the 'strong man of the Congress', whom Gandhi had characteristically cast as leader of the detached, watch-dog Congress that he wanted, became Home Minister of States and began the immense task of re-drawing the map of India to absorb the Princely States.

Disillusioned, Gandhi again retired to the wings of the political stage. The horrors of the massacres in the North-West persuaded him that, as he wrote in his diary, he 'had to be in Delhi and "do or die".' He did, and he died. The outcome of his last fast, regarded by many in India as ignoble appeasement of Pakistan and the Muslims, may be counted the proximate cause of his assassination by a fanatical Hindu.

Of this doom Gandhi seems to have had a strong foreboding. There is a hint in his last writings and utterances of the Agony in the Garden, of awareness of impending martyrdom. 'No man,' he wrote in his diary, 'if he is pure, has anything more precious to give than his life'. On 30 January 1948, as he approached his evening prayer meeting, he was shot dead with the name of Rama on his lips.

For the Mahatma's true disciples the prospect was indeed as dark as the morrow of Calvary, without a Resurrection. The motherland had been rent into two hostile nations. Within each, though mass slaughter had slackened, Hindus and Sikhs and Muslims oppressed and feuded with the opposite community. The creed of non-violence had suffered its gravest wound at the very moment when millions might have celebrated its victory over imperialism. The Indian National Congress had become a ruling party, committed to the industrialism and modernization which he detested; the corruption of power was beginning to eat its heart. Nothing that has happened since in independent India has lightened the Gandhian gloom. Hyderabad and Goa were taken by force. Two wars against Pakistan and one against the invading Chinese have left India a state as military-minded as any of the successors to European empire. A radical split in the Congress followed inevitably (though after a long delay due mainly to the personal authority of Jawaharlal Nehru) the bequest of a one-party ideology to a multi-party, parliamentary democracy. Even the Green Revolution, which has staved off India's hunger, has brought its prime benefits to the richer farmers rather than the mass of poor *ryots* and landless workers who predominate in India's villages and whom the Mahatma championed. The drift from the country to the cities, which Gandhi sought to reverse, has been accelerated. It is true that devoted apostles of the Gandhian faith, like Vinoba Bhave and Jaya Prakash Narayan, have laboured without stint to reclaim the dignity and well-being of the peasant: but their achievements are small oases in a desert land.

All this might tempt us to dub the Mahatma the most eminent failure of the twentieth century. But that is a view too narrow in space, too short in time. Though most of his work and teaching was done in India, he was a world-wide influence in his life-time and he remains a world-wide portent now. The centenary of his birth was publicly celebrated, not only in India and in Britain (where the Archbishop of Canterbury preached in St Paul's Cathedral, and the Prince of Wales, the Prime Minister and the last Viceroy of India, Earl Mountbatten of Burma, spoke in the Albert Hall), but also in innumerable countries in every continent. Since Gandhi's days, outside the Communist world two ideologies of radical action have been manifest. One is violent. It starts from the premise that the system to be overthrown is imposed by force and will respond only to force. Its exponents include the Black Panthers, the 'provisional' I.R.A., the Naxalites of Bengal and the *tupamaros* of Latin America. The other ideology is non-violent. Its premise is that force escalates force, and that revolt by violence begets only chaos or a new tyranny. Its exponents include the followers of Martin Luther King in the United States and peaceable civil rights movements throughout the Western world. If our complex, vulnerable modern societies are not to be plagued to death by urban guerrillas, it is the restraint and indeed the success of these non-violent protesters that will save it as much as the established mechanism of law and order. Though they may not know it, Mahatma Gandhi was their great forefather and prophet, their Abraham. Many of their methods of action were learned from him—the rent strike, the sit-down, the symbolic march. Much of their philosophy is his (though personal asceticism is not their rule). Many of their experiences and setbacks are those he suffered, not least the constant risk that non-violent action may ignite violence: it was running this risk too close that Gandhi called his 'Himalayan blunder'. If they seek a bible, they could do worse than study the testament of his life and writings. Like Cranmer at the stake, he lit a candle which will not be put out.

Lenin
by Harrison Salisbury

HARRISON SALISBURY (b. 1908) graduated from the University of Minnesota in 1930 and then embarked on a career of journalism with the United Press, of which he became successively London Manager, Moscow correspondent, and Foreign News Editor. In 1949 he joined the staff of the *New York Times*, serving as correspondent in Moscow until 1954 when he returned to the New York offce, ultimately becoming Associate Editor. He was a Pulitzer Prize winner in 1955 and is the author of a number of authoritative works on Soviet Russia, among which is his Homeric account of the siege of Leningrad, *The 900 Days* (1969).

Lenin

23 April 1870	Born. Educated at school in Simbirsk and university of Kazan.
8 May 1887	Execution of Lenin's older brother, Alexander, for plotting assassination of Tsar Alexander III. This turned Lenin's thoughts towards politics.
Dec. 1887	Expelled from university of Kazan for participating in student demonstration.
1891	Gained law degree as external student.
1893	Moved to Petersburg. Became member of revolutionary socialist group run by Radchenko.
1895	Went abroad to visit exiled exponents of Marxist theory.
Dec. 1895	Arrested.
1897-1900	Exiled in Siberia. Wrote treatise on history of Russian industrialization—*The Development of Capitalism in Russia.*
March 1898	Social Democratic party tried to unify itself, but failed. However, it established a party structure.
July 1900	Went abroad.
Sept. 1900	Settled in München. Started a revolutionary newspaper, *Iskra.*
1902	Socialist Revolutionary Party formed—to become Lenin's opponent.
March 1902	Lenin's book *What is to be done?* made him famous among socialists.
May 1903	Moved to Geneva.
July 1903	Congress of Russian Social Democratic party held in Brussels and London. Attended by Lenin, who succeeded in getting a central committee composed of three of his own supporters. His faction became known as 'bolshevik', whereas an opposition faction, led by Martov, became known as 'menshevik'
Jan. 1904	Japan began war against Russia. Socialist attitude to this war was that it was a crime perpetrated by Tsarist government against Russian people.

Previous page: May 1917—Lenin, the new ruler of revolutionary Russia, with military leaders in Red Square

124

Jan. 1905 Revolution, in which leading figure was Gapon in Petersburg. Ended after concessions by Tsar.

April 1906 Social Democratic party meeting in Stockholm.

May 1906 New legislature—elections boycotted by bolsheviks.

July 1906 Dissolution of first Duma (lower legislative house) because of its inflammatory programme.

1906-10 Agrarian measures passed which were intended to create class of independent farmers.

5 March 1907 Second Duma opened. Social Democrats and Socialist Revolutionaries took active part in elections.

April-May 1907 Fifth Congress of Social Democratic party held in London. Lenin failed to gain outright control of new central committee.

10 June 1907 Second Duma dissolved because it was openly revolutionary.

May 1909 Lenin published *Materialism and Empiriocriticism*.

1912 Bolsheviks broke with mensheviks and created separate party. Lenin appointed Stalin member of new central committee.

March 1917 Outbreak of revolution. Tsar abdicated.

April 1917 Lenin returned to Russia, to Petrograd. He opposed Provisional Government led by Kerensky of Socialist Revolutionary party.

July 1917 At height of anti-bolshevik campaign by mensheviks, Stalin organized Lenin's escape from Petrograd.

Sept./Oct. 1917 Lenin wanted armed uprising—conflicted with views of Zinoviev and Kamenev.

6-7 Nov. 1917 Provisional Government overthrown by bolshevik detachments. Kerensky escaped from Petrograd. Lenin took power.

1917-21 Civil war.

Early 1919 Communist parties multiplying in Europe.

2 March 1919 First congress of Communist International held in Moscow.

25 April 1919 Poles attacked U.S.S.R., probably because of news that bolshevik attack on Poland was impending—Lenin's idea of revolution from the outside.

March 1921 Lenin introduced New Economic Policy to stimulate commerce and trade—small peasants were allowed to return to capitalism.

1921 Famine.

27 March 1922 Eleventh Party Congress—Lenin's last major appearance, for he had become ill.

20 Nov. 1922 Lenin's last public appearance—

at a speech to Moscow soviet. Kamenev assumed public control.

6 March 1923 Lenin suffered debilitating stroke.

21 Jan. 1924 Lenin died. In his will he advised followers to remove Stalin from party's general secretariat.

Vladimir Ilyich Ulyanov, or Vladimir Lenin as the world knows him, once said of the nineteenth-century Russian writer and philosopher, Nikolai Chernyshevsky, that he possessed 'perfect revolutionary pitch' in the sense that some artists have perfect musical pitch. It was the kind of a remark which perhaps told more about Lenin's hero-worship than it did about Chernyshevsky but it is worth recalling because, as the years provide us with a better perspective from which to evaluate Lenin, it seems more and more appropriate to say of the Russian Bolshevik leader that he himself possessed 'perfect revolutionary pitch'.

Half a century, more or less, has passed since Lenin's death—long enough for history and the historians to begin to draw up a balance sheet. Clearly, it is impossible to compile a list of the geniuses of the twentieth century without including Lenin's name. In fact, many would put Lenin at or close to the top along with Einstein, Freud, and, possibly, Henry Ford. No other man has so placed his personal stamp upon the politics of the twentieth century, no other twentieth-century name has moved more people, shaken more societies, so changed the political and economic surface of the globe. The name of Lenin does not echo down the corridors of the century. It thunders.

And yet, and yet—just what is the legacy of Lenin? Did he, and his Bolsheviks after all, *make* the Russian Revolution? Is today's Soviet Union the society of which Lenin dreamed? Is it Lenin's word which still stirs the revolutionary hurricanes of the far places of the earth—China, for instance, the sullen societies of Asia, Africa and Latin America, and the embattled ghettoes of Europe and America?

The answers to these questions are not easy. While it may not have been obvious fifty years ago, it is perfectly evident today that neither Lenin nor his Bolshevik comrades had any hand in the making of the Russian Revolution of March 1917. Nor, for that matter, had they a perceptible role in the first Russian Revolution, that of 1905. The torrent of passion, hatred and fear which followed the events of 1917 effectively confused the minds of distant observers as well as those of the Russian participants themselves. This turmoil had far from died away before the legend-makers began their jubilant task of rewriting history in accordance with doctrine, an amiable occupation in which Right and Left collaborated on a simplistic tale in which Lenin emerges as the 'Hero-Villain' of the 'Revolutionary Epic'. It is still believed today and the task of extricating the man from the myth is difficult, even with the benefit of perspective.

Lenin gave no visible signs of genius in his early years. He was a good student and a good son in a comfortable, rather old-fashioned schoolmaster's family in a sleepy Volga river town where the conventional virtues were highly prized. But the 'five's' which he customarily won in his lessons gave him no special distinction. All the Ulyanov children won 'five's' and so did the children of a thousand similar families of serious, honest, hardworking, patriotic sentiments. Lenin did not grow up in a revolutionary milieu, unless you want to say that all of Russia in the seventies and eighties of the last century provided such a milieu. In fact, the only unusual entry in the Ulyanov family history relates not to Lenin but to his older brother, Alexander, an even more promising, more serious, more diligent student than Vladimir.

To his family's dismay, Alexander was arrested on 1 March 1887 for plotting the assassination of Tsar Alexander III and eight weeks later died on the gallows at Schlisselburg. It was a lightning stroke which changed the fate and fortune of the Ulyanov family and although there were those later on, like Angelica Balabanoff, who insisted that it was not his brother's death which fixed the course of Lenin's life, it is, none the less, a fact that until the moment of Alexander's arrest there is no evidence that Vladimir (then almost seventeen) had displayed even the slightest interest in politics, let alone revolutionary politics.

In other words, Lenin's politicization, to use the contemporary term, occurred suddenly and certainly it was his brother's death which gave the event not only traumatic impact but emotional depth. From the spring of 1887 onwards, many things were to happen in Lenin's life; but almost all of them related intimately to his revolutionary course.

Not, it should be quickly said, that instant politicization was unusual in the Russia of those days. It had happened to Lenin's brother and it happened to one generation of young people after another.

Once politicized, Lenin soon stood out among the hundreds if not thousands who were prepared to lay down their lives to create on the ruins of decadent Tsarism a new society, one based on truth and equity and justice for all.

Lenin stood out because he coupled his passion for destruction of the evil society (as he perceived it) with a pedantic, meticulous and disciplined programme for achieving this aim. He ruthlessly put behind him the tactics of his martyred older brother. Assassination, individual feats of heroism, terror—all this he categorized as revolutionary romanticism. He embraced a different programme—the creation of a military (and militant) revolutionary elite. Priests and nuns of the Red Banner, professionals dedicating their whole lives and entire beings to the cause, who by precise organization, skillful tactics and comprehensive strategy would overthrow the lumbering goliath that was Tsarist Russia and erect a new Jerusalem in its place.

He took his model from the very Chernyshevsky whom he idealized for 'perfect revolutionary pitch' and patterned his life upon Chernyshevsky's fictional revolutionary, Rakhmetov, a man who slept on a bed of nails to toughen his body, who put sex behind him and whose only indulgence was a good Havana cigar. Lenin even omitted the cigars. He ate revolution, slept revolution, lived revolution. Nothing else mattered. He gave up his favourite passion—chess—for the minutiae of organizing an underground movement. He condemned himself to live without music—Schubert moved him too much, melted the steel fibres of his soul.

There was no one among the revolutionaries like Lenin, no one so puritanical in his life, so maximalist in his personal demands. This put him ahead of all the others, so that Trotsky later was to say in full honesty that by the time Lenin went abroad into exile in August 1900, he was not only fully developed as a revolutionary leader but so recognized by his fellows. He had by this time assimilated the ideas of Marx and Engels and begun the task of adapting and applying them (as he understood them) to Russian conditions.

By this time another characteristic of Lenin had fully matured—his conviction that the end justified the means. Whatever the means. Perhaps there was some slight qualification there, but it is difficult to specify. His ruthlessness against any political opponent, the virulence of his rhetoric, the savagery of his tactics, the stealth, slyness, and even deceit which he employed (and publicly sought to justify) was notorious in the intrigue-ridden, faction-torn, paranoid world of the revolutionary exiles.

Angelica Balabanoff could never understand this trait in Lenin—why he employed every possible weapon against his political opponents, even members of his own party who disagreed with him. It was commonplace for Lenin to call an honest man dishonest, a principled man guilty of bribery, or a loyal revolutionary a traitor.

To Balabanoff Lenin explained that to seize power every means must be used. 'Even dishonest ones?' she asked. Lenin replied, 'Everything that is done in the interest of the proletarian cause is honest'. He once told a young acolyte that he followed the following principle in arguing with an opponent, 'First, stick the convict's badge on him, and then after that we'll examine the case'.

Lenin's genius was seen by his contemporaries as his ability to create a secret disciplined underground organization within Russia, skilfully directed from abroad, capable of carrying on propaganda and agitation for the revolutionary cause and of organizing a revolution relatively immune to penetration and disintegration by the omnipotent agents of the Tsar's Third Section.

There was some truth in this. Yet 1905 occurred spontaneously. The instigating force was a strange man, half police agent, half messiah, called Father Gapon. He and his cause were fought tooth-and-nail by the less-than-corporal's guard of Leninist revolutionaries in St Petersburg. The event was neither planned nor forseen by Lenin and, worse, he himself did not even return to Russia until the revolutionary force had spent itself and the Tsar's Premier, Count Witte, was beginning to get the country back in hand. Had Lenin died after 1905 his name would have been a minor footnote in the turbulent turn-of-the-century history of Russia.

Perhaps Lenin drew a lesson from 1905 which enabled him to succeed later on? Perhaps, but the literal truth is that his organization was so savagely wracked by Tsarist police infiltration that it could hardly be kept alive in the years leading up to 1914. It was financed by a few radical millionaires and by bank robberies. The end, as Lenin had said, was justifying some remarkable means. Nor was this all. Lenin split and split again with his revolutionary comrades. He trusted no one's judgement but his own. His handful of followers dwindled. He became known within Russia as a 'splitter' and in Russian exile circles as an eccentric used-up man. As for success in conspiratorial underground organization, Lenin's praetorian revolutionary ranks were penetrated with ease by the Tsar's police—several of his most valued associates, it transpired, were police agents, including the leader of

128

the Bolshevik faction of the Duma. (Not that the other revolutionary organizations had a better record. All of them were riddled with agents and provocateurs.) Nor could it be said that Lenin's tactics had been so successful that he had won the allegiance of the workers and peasants. Bolshevik strength among the workers was greater than before 1905 but still minimal, and the peasants followed not the Bolsheviks (of whom they had hardly heard), but Lenin's most bitter revolutionary rivals: the S.R.'s, the famous Socialist Revolutionaries.

So Lenin entered the First World War isolated in his Swiss exile and disheartened by the conduct of the international socialist movement, the failure of socialists to follow their principles of solidarity, and by their readiness instead, to support their national causes in the European conflict.

Nothing could have been more discouraging than the course of the war. The movement in Russia hit a new ebb. Finances were so bad that Lenin barely managed to support himself by eking out articles for the encyclopaedia. In February 1917, his situation was particularly parlous. Revolution looked light years away. Lenin hardly knew where his next meal was coming from. Maxim Litvinov, the future foreign minister, not infrequently paid for dinner for Lenin and Lenin's wife, Nadezhda Krupskaya. Lenin did not even have enough money to print or distribute his leaflets. On the anniversary of Bloody Sunday (22 January 1917, the date of the 1905 revolution) he gave a sad speech before a tiny group in Zurich declaring that 'we of the older generation may not live to see the decisive battles of this coming revolution'.

When revolution finally came, Lenin was more out of touch than he had been at the outbreak of 1905. Not until 14 March 1917, the day before the Tsar's abdication, did he even become aware of what was happening in Petrograd. His initial reaction was that this did not concern him too much. It was a bourgeois revolution in which his Bolsheviks would play little or no role. In fact, 'his Bolsheviks' were scattered to the four ends of the earth—Lenin, Zinoviev, Lunacharsky, Litvinov, Chicherin, Radek and others had lived for years in Switzerland; Bukharin and Trotsky (still an opponent, not a Bolshevik) were in New York; Stalin, Kamenev and Sverdlov were in Siberian exile. The top Bolshevik in Petrograd was the twenty-six-year-old Vyacheslav Molotov, and Molotov's associates could be numbered on the fingers of two hands. They played no role in the overturn of the Government (nor did any revolutionary movement). It was a spontaneous uprising of the people, unled, undirected, unplanned, unplotted, unprogrammed, yet succesful beyond the dream of any revolutionary—Bolshevik, Menshevik, Anarchist or S.R.

However, Lenin quickly changed his mind about the Revolution and he was swifter in returning to Russia in 1917 than he had been in 1905. With the help of the Germans he managed to get to Petrograd by early April. Did he find that his lean, disciplined military organization, united around the principle of democratic centralism had the situation in hand? Hardly. The Bolsheviks were only a piping squeak in the revolutionary chorus, their voices (for they were not united) drowned out by the chorus of others—the vaulting Kerensky, the Cadets, the multi-Party trustees of the bankrupt Tsarist regime. The Mensheviks, Lenin's deadly enemies, had been faster

129

Overleaf: Moscow, October 1917, during the revolution that shook the world. Barricades and Bolshevik orator addressing a street meeting

off the mark. The S.R.'s had moved triumphantly into the countryside. And Lenin himself, on his return, first had to win his own party over to what his colleagues—and anyone else in the country who was listening—thought were tactics of insanity. For Lenin returned to Russia breathing fire. His programme was: Down with the Provisional Government! All Power to the Soviets! (which he did not control but was confident he would control).

He won the day with the Bolsheviks as he had won it many times before— by willpower, by utter confidence in the rightness of his views, by giving no quarter to anyone, by invoking to the full his leadership status, by the energy, vindictiveness and passion of his insistence that his programme and his programme alone was the right programme, the inevitable programme, the sole programme which made sense and which would bring victory.

He carried the day. He carried it by overturning logic and reason and common sense and, indeed, all of the precepts of Marx and Engels who had scholastically but authoritatively insisted that the overthrow of a feudal state (Russia) *must* lead to the establishment of a bourgeois society. Lenin cast that aside. Russia, he said (only slightly equivocating so that his words would not present so harsh a contrast to those of the Master) would pass straight through into Socialism (i.e. Communism).

130

Here is where Lenin demonstrated his 'perfect revolutionary pitch'—perhaps not entirely perfect at first, for he did misjudge during the 'July Days' of 1917 and fail in a preliminary bid for power, but perfect in the sense that in a time of turmoil, he had a precise goal and an undeviating strategy for attaining that goal. The goal was seizure of power from the faltering Provisional Government and the raucous congeries of competing forces and the establishment of his own small clique as Russia's ruler. In a time when Russia was a sink of doubt Lenin had no doubts and he was able to cut through the confusion with the cold blade of his powerful logic.

He demonstrated to the full his utter confidence in the tactic of any means to an end. He put the precepts of Marx and Engels aside and went for broke. He callously stole the agrarian programme of the S.R.'s without so much as a by-your-leave, certain that the peasants were a tidal force and they would sweep him into power with his (borrowed) slogan: Peace, Bread and Land.

In the end it was not a revolution which put Lenin in power. It was a coup d'état carried out with no remarkable skill, over the open opposition of some of his supporters (Kamenev and Zinoviev) and distinguished neither in execution or tactics from the commonplace coup by which one South American general replaces another in the presidential palace. As in all

131

coups, it was the military (the army and the sailors) which tipped the balance. Lenin and his lieutenants had won the support of the Petrograd garrison (for the most part). The resistance put up by the Provisional Government and Kerensky was so passive that there was virtually no bloodshed. In Petrograd only two or three persons were killed, probably by accident.

The coup was hardly a tribute to Lenin's conspiratorial skill. The Bolshevik plans had been broadcast in the newspapers. The day and date of the proposed uprising was known to the Provisional Government and every well-informed person in Petrograd. It succeeded because Lenin struck against a hollow shell—the Kerensky government was *in extremis*. The stage was almost vacant. Only Lenin was ready, willing and eager to fill it.

T his was Lenin's genius. He dared to take what the others hardly dared to hold—the power to lead a great country. He did this, to be sure, in the name of the proletariat. His Bolshevik Party would act as the surrogate of the proletariat and carry out a dictatorship in its name. But this, as Trotsky had already pointed out, was an exercise in substitution. The Party was the surrogate of the proletariat. The Party's Central Committee was the surrogate of the Party. The Politburo was the surrogate of the Central Committee and the surrogate-in-chief was Lenin himself (or whoever might come to head the Party).

Did Lenin foresee this with the unerring vision of a master strategist? Hardly. He was convinced of his ability to seize control of the state, but he was by no means confident of his ability to rule the state or to hold power on a permanent basis. For that, he was frank to admit, it would be necessary for the advanced states of Europe, and particularly for Germany, to rise in revolt and establish Marxist regimes. For while Lenin had been willing to strike for Communist power in an emerging feudal state, he was still enough of a classical Marxist to assume that the Master was basically right, that is, that the overthrow of the bourgeoisie must occur first in the advanced western industrial states and specifically in Germany. Even Lenin was prepared to concede that the Communist success in Russia was a historical anomaly and that if Germany failed to go Red, the Bolshevik regime in Russia was doomed.

Yet, here again, Lenin was proved wrong (as was Marx). Revolution came to Germany but it was fleeting. Long before his untimely death Lenin had to face the reality that for a long time to come, Russia must go it alone on the socialist path. He transferred his hopes to the East—revolution, he felt, was just around the corner in China and India. But this was whistling in the dark. After all a man had to believe in something.

Thus, it could well be said, that Lenin was no better at understanding Russia's revolutionary course than he had been in sensing the moment when revolution itself would strike Russia. Wherein, then, did his genius lie? Quite clearly in the realm of practical politics. He went for the jugular in November 1917. Once in power his instincts for practical politics never left him. He solidified peasant support of his regime with utter carelessness for legality or equity, destroying all of the other parties of the Left and particularly the S.R.'s who held the majority position in the country. He won the

Civil War against the Whites and defeated the Anglo-French intervention because he headed a disciplined centralized regime which had a single aim and a single dictator (himself). But he won it, too, because he persuaded the peasants that their interests, that is their ability to win the land and hold it, were best served by himself and the Bolsheviks. He did not hesitate to adopt the motto of the hated General Trepov whose order for suppression of 1905 was, 'Don't spare the cartridges'. Lenin spared neither cartridges for his enemies nor the lives of his own cadres. It was life-or-death for the Bolsheviks, and it came so close to death that no one who fought in those battles ever erased it from his mind.

So Lenin brought Communism to Russia. Or did he? His country lay exhausted and bleeding at the end of the Civil War. Industry had ground to a halt. The trains did not run. The land lay fallow. Lenin had decreed what he called 'war communism' to survive during the Civil War—that is, all business and industry was confiscated by the government, the little food that was available was rationed. The rifle ruled. The peasants possessed the land but they produced little. Now, in extremity, Lenin brought back Capitalism. He called it the 'New Economic Policy'. But the name did not make it smell the sweeter in Marxist nostrils. Foreign concessionaires were begged to come in and take over mines and factories. Private businessmen were implored to produce. The peasant was cozzened. It slowly made the wheels move again. It saved Russia and saved the Bolsheviks, but not even Lenin pretended it was Communism. He called it 'State Capitalism' but he did not try to hide the fact that it was a regression which had nothing in common with Marxism.

The Revolution had been made to overthrow tyranny—the rule of the autocrat, the Tsar's secret police, the exile-and-prison system, the censorship, the suppression of free thought and expression, the heavy hand of oppression, the ritual and superstition of the Church, the poverty of the working man, the degradation of the peasant. Its goals—Lenin's goals—were the noblest of man's aspirations.

But what had Lenin achieved? He reimposed the censorship on the second day of the new regime. The *Cheka* under Felix Dzershinsky had replaced the Tsar's Third Section. It was more terrible, more efficient, more pervasive than anything the Romanovs dreamed of. The prisons had never been so full. Exile resumed. Every other party had been suppressed and in Lenin's own party the old freedom of debate and violent exchange of opinion was beginning to vanish. The Church was oppressed—many high Church officials were shot and churches closed. Had the plight of the working man improved? No, in honesty, he lived even closer to subsistence than before. The owners were gone in many places, but the State had changed places with them.

One class and one class alone had benefitted—the peasants, whom Marx notoriously distrusted and whom Lenin, himself, admitted were probably Russia's most retrogressive class with an unerring instinct for private gain and personal selfishness.

This was the legacy which Lenin was compelled to contemplate in 1922, the first year in which all of his energies had not been exhausted—and more than exhausted—in revolution, war, civil war, foreign intervention, national crisis, famine and catastrophe.

The greatest irony, as Lenin looked about, was that he saw on every side signs and symptoms not of change, but of the triumphant survival of the old Russia—the old Russia which he and his comrades so sincerely hated. He looked to his government and found it immersed in bureaucratic red tape which had not changed since the days of Radischev; and why, indeed, should it? The civil servants in large part were the very civil servants who had doffed their caps to the Tsar, the *chinovniki*, with the thinnest layer of Communist cadres overseeing them. Long since Lenin's dream that any cook could run a bank or factory had been proved the flimsiest of oratory. Russia, as Lenin could only too clearly see, was lumbering back into the well-worn tracks of the past. To be sure the landlords were gone. To be sure the capitalists were gone (except for those welcomed back under N.E.P.). To be sure the Church was, he thought, fatally wounded. To be sure the bourgeoisie was fighting only a rearguard action (he hoped) in the ranks of the N.E.P. But the great state apparatus, like a juggernaut, held to the same basic direction. The old sins of Russia still ruled her—greed, incompetence, shiftlessness, corruption, inefficiency, ignorance and cultural backwardness.

Nor was the situation much better when he surveyed the ranks of his own elite. For, truth to tell, there was so little of the elite left after five years of terror and toil. Among his new Bolsheviki he saw the same resurgence of the traits of the old Russia—the national chauvinism, the arbitrary bureaucracy, the insensitivity to personal concerns. All of the obnoxious traits of the old Tsarist style coming to the fore in the new Soviet administrators. The Party did not function as it had in the past. No longer was it a small, flexible, disciplined group of bourgeois intellectuals (Lenin would never have used those words, but they describe most of his cadres). Now it was filled with ambitious time-servers, men-on-the-make, clodhoppers, men who had made things go by iron will and iron discipline in the desperate days of the war.

The year 1922 was Lenin's last. He did not die until January 1924; but 1922 was the year in which began the succession of strokes which ultimately took his life. Despite them—and in part, because of them—he had time to contemplate what he had wrought. His mind was not impaired (nor would he be fatefully paralyzed until the final debilitating stroke on 6 March 1923).

To look back through Lenin's writings of that year is to walk with a man in agony. Lenin knew now that his Revolution, his ideal of the new Russia had gone wrong. Optimist that he was, he still thought he could make it come right; but he was desperately concerned because the state of his health told him that he had so little time in which to act. The essays, the directives, the articles, the memoranda flowed from his pen and later, when he was unable to write, from his lips as he dictated to his corps of faithful secretaries.

It would be wrong to suggest that Lenin sensed the ultimate tragedy of his Revolution. He was far too sinewy, far too confident of his powers to put things right. But he knew. He knew that the Revolution was not what he had dreamed, not what he had planned, not what he had hoped, not what Russia needed. He could make excuses—the failure of western Europe to revolt as predicted, the terrible toll of war and intervention, the incredible cultural lag of Russia, the inevitable reliance upon the backward peasants. He could and did cite all of these factors in extenuation. But even then he was too much of a realist not to face up to the basic problems: the government was not working as it should, it was too much like the government which had been overthrown and, worst of all, most serious of all, his own comrades, his own Bolsheviks, were not proving to be men of the quality and skill which was necessary, first, if the work was to be carried on in a manner which might guarantee success and, particularly, which would guarantee that Lenin's own goals would remain the Bolshevik goals if and when he had to lay down the baton which he had so insistently wielded.

Much of the body of Lenin's work in his last months was unknown or little known until Nikita Khrushchev opened the archives in 1956 and caused it to be printed. Almost certainly there is more which still reposes under Russian lock and seal. Perhaps some of it has been irretrievably lost—destroyed in Stalin's egregious effort to make himself over in the distorted image of his predecessor. But enough remains to catch the flavour of Lenin as he struggled with his terrible creation. His anger almost screams from the pages: 'I declare war to the death on dominant nation chauvinism. I shall eat it with all my healthy teeth as soon as I get rid of this accursed bad tooth . . . *Absolutely!* . . . Our state apparatus is so deplorable, not to say wretched that we must think very carefully how to combat its defects . . . We have been bustling for five years trying to improve our state apparatus but it has been mere bustle . . . etc.

The frustration boils from Lenin's pages and finally culminates in his famous 'testament' dictated with great determination, in the midst of pain and constant threat of another arterial stroke on 23, 24, 26, 27, 28, 29, 30, 31 December and 4 January 1923. A final addendum in the form of three brief notes was dictated 5 and 6 March 1923.

By now Lenin understood the heart of the problem. It lay not only in the legacy of the state apparatus and society which had been inherited, like it or not, from the Tsars. It lay within his own cherished Bolshevik ranks, in the personality, methods, policy and men who would have to carry on after his death.

Here too the anger, bitterness and even outrage flamed up, nowhere more violently than in the next to last communication (so far as is publicly known) which Lenin left behind him—a brief personal note in which he told Stalin (with copies to Kamenev and Zinoviev) that he knew of his rudeness to his wife and 'have no intention of forgetting so easily what has been done against me'. He offered Stalin the choice of an apology or the breaking off of personal relations. Four days later Lenin suffered the fateful stroke which deprived him of the power of speech and writing.

Of what ideas was Lenin dreaming in the weeks before his body finally collapsed? He was talking and writing of the co-operative movement—as a solution to Russia's agricultural problems. He was facing up to the reality of 'State Capitalism' and hoping eventually to resume the interrupted course toward his chosen goal of Socialism and Communism. He was trying to figure out a system which would enable the government to free itself of the terrible sloth and inefficiency which riddled it. He hoped somehow by creating a force of State Inspectors (shades of Gogol's Inspector-General!) to make the ramshackle system work and he hoped, in the long range, that education would raise Russia's cultural level to the point at which it could create a decent and reliable civil service. He was fighting strongly the chauvinistic traits of his comrades and trying to keep the country on an even keel so far as foreign trade and foreign relations were concerned.

Most of all, he was worried about his own party, the Bolsheviks. It was not only a question of leadership—there were leaders but they quarrelled, they were rivals, they had opposing programmes. He could see only too clearly (and he was *so* right) the split which loomed ahead between the two best men, Stalin and Trotsky. How was he to fight it? First, by warning the Party that the situation existed and would grow worse. Next, by warning them to remove Stalin from office (if they could—and even then he was not entirely confident that this could be done). And thirdly, and this was a measure of his desperation, by proposing to enlarge the Central Committee and bring in new blood which, he insisted, should moderate inner party tensions. He could not really have believed this. He was too old a Party man, too skilled a cliquist himself; but he was at the end of his wits. He had no other legacy to leave his party. It was the best he could think of suggesting.

It is enough to run lightly over Lenin's legacy of ideas, his testament to his party, to realize that the state which eventually emerged after Lenin's death in 1924 was not the state which he had envisaged, nor was the Party the Party which he had hoped he was creating. The post-1924 Party was not entirely different, of course, and many of the things Stalin did Lenin might have come to, given time. Perhaps, he would have abandoned his thoughts of agricultural co-operatives and launched a bloody collectivation drive in the countryside as Stalin did—but it does not seem likely. He would undoubtedly have embarked on the five-year plans for industrialization. He toyed with this kind of planning in his last months and proposed an independent status for a State Planning Agency. But if he had not been prepared to sweat the capital for construction costs out of the peasants, the pace would not have been so turbulent. Would he have split the Party as Stalin did? Perhaps, but not in that way. He had no great faith in the redemption of sinners but he was not known for ruthless treatment of Party comrades (as differentiated from non-Party men who he relentlessly pursued, notably in the case of the S.R.'s whose execution he ordered). But Stalin's maniacal purges were not Lenin's way; nor was Stalin's cult to Lenin's taste—least of all the pseudo-Lenin cult which Stalin invented.

The contrast between the Russia which was shaped and moulded under Stalin's pitiless hands and that of Lenin's last aspirations runs too endlessly for even a quick summary.

So, we ask ourselves, what measure of reality is there in the concept of Soviet Russia as a 'Leninist' state; what relationship is there between Lenin the real man and the Leninist legend now barnacled to the keel of all great Communist movements?

Today's image is not in reality Lenin the man; not Lenin the theoretical

Marxist (who never built Marxism in his own land); nor even Lenin the programmatic guide, the philosopher and continuator of Marx and Engels. In the first place, he was not much of a theoritician and in the second place, the state he created had little Marxism in it.

No, the real legacy of Lenin, the one which his followers perpetuated in his own land and many others is his pragmatism—his mastery of practical politics, his willingness to go to any extreme to achieve his ends; his utter lack of programmatic formalism or structural vision. This essential Leninism is epitomized in one of the very last of Lenin's memoranda, written in that bitter winter of 1922-23 when he was struggling for existence, struggling to make clear his thoughts, struggling to lay down guidelines for his party and his country after he was gone. He had been reading N. S. Sukhanov's *Notes on the 1917 Revolution*. Sukhanov was a bystander—something more than a bystander but not quite a participant in the events of 1917—and he had been close to Lenin, even lending his apartment for a conspiratorial meeting in the autumn of 1917. Yet he was not a Bolshevik (Stalin, of course, eventually shot him) and Lenin read his account of 1917 with passionate interest but also with scorn and disdain. Finally he exploded to Sukhanov:

'Where have you read that variations of the customary historical sequence of events are impermissable or impossible?

'Napoleon, I think, wrote: "On s'engage et puis . . . on voit." Rendered freely this means "First engage in a serious battle and then see what happens." Well, we did first engage in a serious battle in October, 1917 and then saw such details of development (from the standpoint of world history they were certainly details) as the Brest peace, the new Economic Policy and so forth.

'And now there can be no doubt that in the main we have been victorious.'

This was the most precise analysis Lenin could have made of his overview. First, he made the Revolution, that is, the coup d'état which put him in power. Then—and only then— did he cast his eyes about and try to decide what to do with the mighty state which had so unexpectedly fallen into his hands. He died with the question unresolved, the direction of the state unperceived by himself and only dimly by his comrades.

What was his legacy? To be sure he became a symbol of the Revolution which he did not in fact make, and a symbol of the revolutions to come which would be made in his image, but not in his reality as a man. Also, he left to his own party the fatal apparatus of its own destruction—the structure of the inverted pyramid, the doctrine of 'democratic centralism' which forbade Party factions and open Party quarrels, and the ritual of military obedience which imposed on each Communist the duty of implicit fulfilment of Party orders.

The Leninist concept of a dedicated brotherhood with himself as the wielder of the baton proved the perfect instrument for Stalin and his heirs.

Only one slight addition was needed to Lenin's structure. He had applied terror to the enemies *of* the Party, not to members *of* the Party. Stalin and his successors subtly blurred this distinction and applied terror to their enemies (real and imaginary) *within* the Party. With this critical emendation, the Leninist legacy was completed and the final distortion of Leninism was achieved.

E*

Smuts

by Sir Philip Magnus

SIR PHILIP MAGNUS (b. 1906), on leaving Oxford, entered the Home Civil Service. He wrote a biography of *Edmund Burke* based on a mass of papers which he unearthed at Wentworth Woodhouse in Yorkshire. He served from 1939-45 in the Royal Artillery (Major) in Iceland and Italy. Living since the war at Stokesay Court in Shropshire, he has concentrated upon public work and writing. He has served for many years as Chairman of the County Planning Committee, is Chairman of the Governors of Attingham College, and has been Chairman of a Juvenile Court. He is a Trustee of the National Portrait Gallery, and has written biographies of *Raleigh* (1968), *Gladstone* (1954), *Kitchener* (1958) and *King Edward the Seventh* (1964).

Jan Christian Smuts

24 May 1870	Educated at Riebeeck West School, Victoria College (Stellenbosch) and Christ's College, Cambridge, where he studied law.
June 1895	Returned to South Africa to practise law at Cape Town bar.
Dec. 1895	Jameson raid, which destroyed Smuts' confidence in Cecil Rhodes, Prime Minister of Cape.
1897	Moved to Johannesburg and renounced British nationality. Married Sybella Margaretha Krige.
June 1898	Became State Attorney of the South African Republic (the Transvaal, which had had its independent existence as an Afrikaner republic confirmed by the British at the Pretoria Convention in 1881).
June 1899	Bloemfontein conference to discuss conciliation between British interests in South Africa (Milner, High Commissioner, wanted to assert British supremacy throughout the land) and Boer aims (to prevent the *uitlanders* in the Republic, who were mostly British, from getting the vote and thus possibly destroying the Republic's independence of the British).
Aug. 1899	Smuts worked for appeasement by offering five years' franchise under certain conditions.
12 Oct. 1899	Outbreak of South African war.
June 1900	After fall of Pretoria Smuts became a guerrilla fighter.
April 1902	Joined Boer leaders at Vereeniging in negotiations with Lords Milner and Kitchener. Both Boer republics (Transvaal and Orange Free State) were transformed into crown colonies.
Feb. 1906	Went to London to urge Campbell-Bannerman, who had become Liberal Prime Minister in Dec. 1905, to give Transvaal immediate self-government. He succeeded.
March 1907	Transvaal became self-governing colony with Botha Prime Minister and Smuts Colonial Secretary. Both worked to put an end to

Previous page: now an ally of Britain. Smuts arrives at Pretoria during First World War

feud between Boer and Briton in South Africa.

1907 Smuts framed education act which permitted Afrikaner children to be taught to some extent in Afrikaans.

Oct. 1908 Smuts arranged national convention of the four self-governing British South African colonies— Transvaal, Cape, Natal, and Orange River—to consider some form of political union.

31 May 1910 Union of South Africa came into being. Botha was Prime Minister and Smuts his right-hand man.

1911 Laws passed to preserve racial hierarchy in mines.

1912 Herzog founded Nationalist party to preserve identity of Afrikaners as a nation within dualistic white South African nation.

1913 Natives' Land Act to limit areas in which Africans could buy land.

1914 After Gandhi's agitation Indian £3 tax was removed. Gandhi left South Africa.

Jan. 1914 Industrial unrest in mines and general strike proclaimed. Smuts ended strike by declaring martial law and deporting nine strike leaders.

Sept. 1914 South Africa entered First World War, planning to conquer German South-West Africa.

Oct. 1914 Some Boers objected to this and rebelled.

July 1915 Smuts took part in South-West African expedition which forced Germans to capitulate.

1915 General election. Botha and Smuts' party (South Africa party) lost its absolute majority and became dependent on support of Unionist party (British South Africans).

1916 Smuts became Commander-in-Chief of Imperial forces attempting to conquer German East Africa.

March 1917 Smuts transferred to London as South African representative at Imperial war conference. He advocated foundation of a league of nations.

1917 Became a Privy Councillor.

June 1919 Treaty of Versailles made post-war settlement. Smuts was involved in negotiations.

Aug. 1919 Botha died. Smuts became Prime Minister.

Sept. 1920 General election left Smuts dependent on Unionist support.

1921 Attended Imperial Conference in London and tried to solve Irish problem.

1922 White miners struck because Africans were being employed for semi-skilled work, and seized control of wide areas.

10 March 1922 Smuts proclaimed martial law and suppressed insurrection with military force.

1923 Imperial Conference in London at which Smuts was isolated on issue of South Africa's Indian minority.

June 1924 General election at which colour issue was central. Smuts' own constituency rejected him. Herzog became Prime Minister. Smuts found another seat and led opposition.

1926 Published Holism and Evolution.

1931 Statute of Westminster—the British government would not exert authority over dominions.

Feb. 1933 Coalition government. Smuts joined Herzog's government as Deputy Prime Minister and Minister of Justice.

1934 Herzog and Smuts fused their parties, but many of Herzog's Nationalists seceded under D. F. Malan.

Sept. 1939 Outbreak of Second World War. Herzog wanted neutrality, Smuts war. Smuts prevailed and Herzog resigned. Smuts became Prime Minister.

1941 Smuts received the honour of British Field Marshal. He visited England four times during war to be consulted by Churchill.

July 1943 General election. Smuts triumphed over Malan's divided opposition.

1945 Smuts attended signing at San Francisco of United Nations charter.

1948 General election. Smuts defeated by Malan fighting on an apartheid slogan. Smuts led opposition. Became Chancellor of Cambridge University.

11 Sept 1950 Died at his farm near Pretoria.

At the end of the First World War Smuts wrote with relish, 'the tents have been struck and the great caravan of humanity is once more on the march'. That metaphor is characteristic of a nature which attained full stature whenever men and nations were convulsed. Absorbed by foreign affairs, scientific study and philosophical speculation, Smuts felt diminished by the racial and other domestic issues which focused the interest of his fellow Boers. While they narrowed their sights and constructed mental laagers, he made the world his stage and spent his life perpetually on trek.

Born on 24 May 1870, on a farm near Cape Town, Smuts graduated with first class honours in science and arts at Stellenbosch, before arriving at Christ's College, Cambridge, with a law scholarship in October 1891. Serious to the point of priggishness and oppressed by poverty, he cursed the leaden skies, displayed intense reserve and took exercise in long solitary walks.

After passing 'brilliantly first' in all examinations, Smuts refused a law fellowship. He was at pains to clear his mind of what he later termed a fog of conventional prejudice. He composed in his lodgings at night a study of the personality of Walt Whitman, but the manuscript of that therapeutic exercise was rejected by every publisher to whom he sent it.

Returning home in June 1895, Smuts practised law at the Cape Town bar. He hero-worshipped Cecil Rhodes, Prime Minister of the Cape, who advocated a union of hearts between Britons and Boers. Dreaming with boyish ardour of a sub-continental federation, Smuts publicly attacked the selfish Boer nationalism of Paul Kruger, President of the Transvaal. He urged the two ruling white races to form one South African nation and to expand together into Rhodesia and the north.

Sickened by the Jameson Raid, Smuts migrated to the Transvaal and renounced his British nationality. As briefs rolled in he made a spirited raid himself upon Stellenbosch, where he married and carried off to Pretoria a schoolteacher and former sweetheart, Isie Krige, with whom he lived happily ever after. Having the luck to perform a legal service for Kruger, which engaged the aged President's affection, Smuts was appointed, aged only twenty-eight, State Attorney of the republic.

Although convinced that the glitter of gold and diamonds was driving British imperialism beserk, Smuts worked for appeasement until the outbreak of war in October 1899. He then published a fulminating pamphlet, *A Century of Wrong*, which he would have liked to suppress in later years, and became a daring guerilla leader after both Boer republics had been overrun. Carrying Kant's *Critique of Pure Reason* and a Greek *Testament* in his knapsack, he returned to the veld, earning a hero's reputation. He was raiding Cape Colony as a commando general in April 1902, when he obeyed a summons to join other Boer leaders at Vereeniging in negotiations with Lords Milner and Kitchener.

Convinced by Kitchener that the Liberal Party would probably win the next British general election and subsequently concede self-government, Smuts argued strongly for acceptance of the stark surrender terms. Continued resistance appeared suicidal and, after an agonized debate, both

Boer republics were transformed into crown colonies.

In rebuilding his life Smuts sought security. He invested shrewdly in the purchase of farms the money which he earned by legal practice; and he started to formulate an optimistic and highly personal system of philosophy which he called 'holism', and which provided him with the comfort of an inner light. This suggested, amongst much else, that 'the day of the small independent sovereign state has passed away', and that 'we are unmistakably in for larger human groupings in that holistic process which fundamentally moulds all life and all history'.

Envisaging a federated South Africa as the earliest of those larger human groupings, Smuts descried a means of reversing the war's ostensible verdict. It was evident that in a self-governing dominion the Boer element must swamp the British. Reverting therefore to the politics of his boyhood, he asked Britons and Boers to appreciate that they had fought for a common ideal. That ideal, obscured temporarily by passion, was a united South Africa according equal rights to all white men.

Arriving in London within a month of the formation of the British Liberal Government, Smuts had a critical talk on 7 February 1906, with the Prime Minister, Sir Henry Campbell-Bannerman. Relying on Smuts's promise that republican agitation would be suppressed, Campbell-Bannerman contrived to overcome his colleagues' doubts. Self-government was granted accordingly, and the four former colonies were federated into a self-governing dominion by the Union of South Africa Act, 1910.

Smuts provided the dynamism needed to effect that result. He delivered countless speeches, conducted tortuous negotiations about race, language, tariffs and other delicate complex issues and earned, perhaps inevitably in that process, the reproach of being 'slim'. He was happy to serve as number two (Minister of Defence, the Interior and Mines) to General Louis Botha, the Union's first Prime Minister, who was universally trusted and loved; and Mrs Smuts used to say that the friendship between Botha and her husband was the strongest which she had ever known.

Resolved not to wreck the Union on the rock of his country's colour problem, Smuts acknowledged its fundamental importance while confessing that he saw no solution. He trusted and argued that a future generation would contrive to handle it successfully, and much preferred, in the meantime, like most people until the 1920s, to envisage the racial issue in terms of the relationship between Britons and Boers. Because Milner had fought to establish British dominance, Smuts concentrated primarily upon preventing a resurgent Boer nationalism from tearing the Union apart.

Smuts endorsed, in those circumstances, a law which barred non-whites absolutely from sitting in the Union Parliament. Existing laws, which denied voting rights to all non-whites in the Transvaal and the Orange Free State, to almost all of them in Natal, and to Africans, but not to coloureds (persons of mixed white and non-white descent) in the Cape, remained undisturbed. The coloured franchise in the Cape was specifically protected in the Union Constitutution by entrenched clauses, which were abrogated with difficulty in 1936.

By pushing the problem of colour under the carpet, Smuts forfeited the

143

Overleaf: Boers besiege Mafeking (left); and (right) burning farm, part of Britain's reprisal for guerilla warfare

initiative. Many liberal-minded Britons would have liked to open a safety-valve by permitting a few educated and propertied Cape coloureds to make their voices heard in the national Parliament. Traditional Boer attitudes were left instead to indoctrinate the Cape and Natal, and to provide Smuts's opponents with most of their political capital. By formulating in theory and implementing in detail an increasingly comprehensive programme of separate development, or apartheid, those opponents siezed the initiative, dragged colour into the forefront of politics and used it to oust Smuts from power.

While shelving the main problem, Smuts was involved early in a quarrel with the government of India about the status of some 300,000 Indian immigrants, settled mostly in Natal. M. K. Gandhi had been grossly humili-ated when he came to South Africa as a young lawyer to represent an Indian firm, and he returned to plead his people's cause against discriminatory laws. After advocating passive resistance he was flung into gaol, but was released at the urgent request of the government of India which obtained some sub-stantial, if impermanent concessions.

'The saint has left our shores,' Smuts exclaimed in 1914, 'I sincerely hope for ever'; but he governed as he must and not as he might have wished. He assured Gandhi that he felt no prejudice and that in happier circumstances he would have valued his friendship, but 'your civilization is different from ours. Ours must not be overwhelmed by yours. That is why we have to go in for legislation which must, in effect, put disabilities upon you.'

Smuts often appeared harsh, and sometimes arrogant, because he neglected the arts of insinuation and address. He was too detached and impatient to court popularity, to tolerate slow-wittedness, or even to conciliate critics. Having been appointed directly to high political office after experience of high command in the field, he lacked training on the back benches or in opposition in the normal give and take of public life. But his authoritarian attributes were displayed to advantage during a period of menacing industrial unrest in 1913-14.

A mob of white miners, striking for higher wages and the recognition of their unions, siezed control of Johannesburg. The police and the Union defence force failed to restore order, the British Government withheld imperial aid, and Botha and Smuts had to swallow their pride. At the risk of their lives they rode into Johannesburg and conceded most of the strikers' demands.

Bills were drafted to implement that settlement, but the trouble deepened and spread. New and preposterous demands were formulated, the railways ground to a halt and the coalminers struck in Natal. In January 1914, when Botha was prostrated by illness, a general strike was proclaimed and Smuts faced a revolutionary situation.

Having reorganized the defence force on a commando basis, Smuts dispatched it to key points after proclaiming martial law. Cannon were trained on the strikers' headquarters, and the movement collapsed like a pricked bubble. Without an instant's hesitation Smuts deported, illegally and

secretly, the country's nine most prominent Labour leaders in a troopship.

Defending that action in an inordinately long speech in Parliament, Smuts admitted that he would not have trusted the courts to convict the exiled militants, and argued that a nation's safety constituted the highest law. The house divided in his favour amid violent Labour protests, and he displayed comparable spirit when some Boer War comrades rose in revolt in October 1914, after the proclamation in August of war with Germany.

That anti-British rebellion was crushed by Botha and Smuts who subsequently undertook together the conquest of German South-West Africa. Returning refreshed and triumphant, they were disappointed by the result of a bitterly contested general election, in the course of which an attempt was made on Smuts's life. The South Africa party (mostly Boer), which had sustained them in office, lost its absolute majority and became dependent upon Unionist (British) support. General J.B.M. Hertzog's Nationalists, who had seceded two years earlier from Botha and Smuts, joined Labour in opposition.

Accepting a lieutenant-general's commission in the British Army, Smuts undertook the congenial task of conquering German East Africa (Tanganyka). But the enemy fought like tigers under General von Letto-Vorbeck, who subsequently became one of Smuts's most cherished friends. The Germans were still in the field, although very severely mauled, when Smuts was recalled in January 1917, and translated to London as his country's representative at an imperial war conference.

While remaining a member of the South African Cabinet and Parliament, Smuts stayed in England for two and a half critical years; and his presence boosted morale. Acclaimed a romantic hero, formed in Kitchener's image, the ex-enemy turned friend was made a privy councillor and invited to attend regularly meetings not merely of the Imperial War Cabinet, but of the British War Cabinet as well. Smuts was tempted to round off that apotheosis by accepting Lloyd George's offer of a vacant safe seat in the House of Commons, but after consulting Botha he prudently declined in order to avert ciriticism at home.

Avoiding great houses and political hostesses, Smuts much preferred a simple background, and people who shared his serious but heterodox philosophical interests. He craved above all a measure of the sympathetic understanding which made his family life in South Africa ideally happy, and he was extremely lucky to find exactly what he wanted in a Quaker household in Oxford.

In England in 1906 he had met and greatly liked two grand-daughters of John Bright, Alice Clark, and her sister, Margaret, who married a banker, Arthur Gillett. All three possessed an unlimited capacity for drawing him out, and they became intimate friends of the Smuts family in consequence. The Gilletts often visited the Smutses in South Africa, and Smuts left his impersonal London hotel suite to enjoy their hospitality in Oxford whenever he could. Their house in Banbury Road provided him with that relaxed experience of English home life for the lack of which while at Cambridge he had been miserably homesick; and their unaffected goodness and kindness touched his heart.

At the imperial conference Smuts opposed all federal schemes. He argued that the empire should be encouraged to evolve into a commonwealth of nations, within the wider context of a league, on what he privately described to the Gilletts as 'holistic' lines. He advocated the foundation of a league of nations, and published in a pamphlet many practical suggestions which President Wilson adopted and which helped to mould world opinion.

I n handling urgent concrete issues Smuts's contribution was particularly valuable. He became, for example, chairman of the war priorities committee, and he was mainly responsible for the creation of the Royal Air Force and of an air ministry. Ignoring methods which had served in South Africa, he settled a Welsh coal strike by appealing personally to the miners in a whirlwind speaking tour; and in secret conversations with Count Mensdorff, the Austro-Hungarian Foreign Minister, in Geneva, he proved that the doomed Hapsburg empire lacked the means if not the will to make peace.

After visiting the battle fronts and refusing the Palestine command, Smuts perpetrated an indiscretion which helps to illuminate his character. A passion for action made him discount human factors, and he astonished Lloyd George by offering to lead into battle the American armies which were being assembled in France. Believing that their commander, Pershing, was manifestly second-rate, Smuts hoped that a South African might be acceptable, in preference to a Frenchman or Englishman, as the United States' principal combat general under Pershing's overall command and with his consent and goodwill. But Lloyd George was at pains not to outrage American sentiment by allowing the least hint of that ingenuous proposition to become known.

When Germany collapsed Smuts recalled Vereeniging and pleaded for magnanimity. He warned fellow-statesmen in Paris that a future war would be the inevitable consequence of the many gross financial and territorial injustices of the Treaty of Versailles, which he did not decide to sign until the last moment. In farewell messages to the British nation he caused anger by advocating the treaty's drastic and early revision, in order to secure a genuine reconciliation and enduring peace.

Smuts's mind was too ice-cool to appreciate the intensity of the hatreds which war had aroused, and which statesmen had stoked in order to squeeze from their peoples the extreme and immeasurable sacrifices needed to attain victory. Botha, who signed the treaty with equal misgiving, died in August 1919, and Smuts found himself installed as Prime Minister less than three weeks after returning to South Africa.

He became not merely Prime Minister, but Minister also of Native Affairs and Defence; and he could not help now regarding himself as primarily a world statesman. He asked the Gilletts to say frankly what Ulysses could really be expected to find to do in his remote twentieth-century Ithaca. They begged him to display public concern about his country's principal internal problems, including the colour problem and falling gold and wool prices. But because almost all his speeches continued, nevertheless, to revolve around the prospects of the League of Nations, the opposition accused Smuts of being totally alienated from his own people. Complaining privately that politics provided 'no life for a Christian', he publicly expressed surprise and concern that 'this nationalist wave' in South Africa and elsewhere 'should be reaching its climax just as we are entering on the great international order of the world'.

A general election in September 1920, left Smuts dependent upon Unionist (British) support; and he did not hesitate to secure his position by effecting a total fusion between his own South Africa party and the Unionists. Dubbed a 'British stooge' and an 'imperialist lackey' by the Nationalists, he attended an imperial conference in London in 1921, and plunged cheerfully into a strenuous attempt to solve the Irish problem. He conducted useful secret talks in Dublin with de Valera and others, before returning home to face a deteriorating industrial situation.

Falling gold and coal prices had prompted the chamber of mines to cut wages, and to employ Africans for semi-skilled work. Both measures infuriated the Labour party, and the white miners struck. Smuts ordered them back, subject to redundancies, at reduced wage rates, but the men defied him, adopted commando tactics and siezed control of wide areas. Crouching silently like a tiger awaiting the moment to spring upon its prey, Smuts suddenly proclaimed martial law (10 March 1922), marched north with adequate military force and suppressed the insurrection after three days' fighting at the cost of heavy casualties on both sides.

When the Nationalists joined Labour in denouncing him as a man of blood, Smuts sought to buttress his tottering government by redressing the political balance. He invited Southern Rhodesia to enter the Union of South Africa on extremely favourable terms, but a referendum held in Southern Rhodesia rejected that offer. Nothing now seemed to go right for Smuts, and at another imperial conference in London in 1923 he was completely isolated on the issue of South Africa's Indian minority. Driven into a corner, he dismayed many admirers by refusing to accept interference in his country's internal affairs, or to tolerate criticism of any kind.

Accused in London of practising one standard of morality while preaching another, Smuts was equally mortified at home. The Nationalist and Labour parties complained that he was at best a negative, lukewarm segregationist, instead of a positive, convinced upholder of the cardinal doctrine upon which South Africa's economy and civilization were founded. At a general election in June 1924, the colour issue was central, and Smuts's own constituency rejected him. His government was ousted, and a Nationalist-Labour coalition took office under General Hertzog.

Smuts found another seat and led the opposition, while seeking consolation in philosophy. Holism and Evolution, published in 1926, exhibited his intellectual Odyssey. Filled with unresolved contradictions, it was damned with faint praise in academic circles, but it expressed the sanguine creed by which he lived. Estranged from the Dutch Reformed Church, and ignoring christian dogma, he insisted that the innermost nature and trend of the entire evolutionary process was divinely inspired. It was good, purposeful and capable of being intelligently analysed—'Our deepest thoughts and emotions are but responses to stimuli which come to us not from an alien, but from an essentially friendly and kindred universe.'

Relishing the correspondence in which that book involved him, Smuts embarked on a lecture tour of the United States. He plunged into a study of African palaeontology and pre-history, delivered the Rhodes memorial lectures in Oxford, and the presidential address to the British Association for the Advancement of Science in its centenary year, 1931. But he ached to return to power and siezed his chance in 1932, when the crippling effects of the world slump on South Africa's economy prompted a demand for a more broadly based government.

Pocketing his pride, Smuts successfully approached Hertzog, and joined his government in February, 1933, as Deputy Prime Minister and Minister of Justice. But an even more startling event occurred in 1934. Hertzog and Smuts agreed to fuse the parties which they respectively led into one United (South African National) party which swept the country in a general election. That expedient deal, however, proved unacceptable to a substantial body of their former supporters. Many of Hertzog's Nationalists seceded under Dr D.F. Malan to form a 'purified' Nationalist party with vague and temporary Nazi overtones, while a smaller section of Smuts's South Africa party seceded under Colonel C.F. Stallard to form a British-oriented Dominion party.

After failing to restrain Hertzog from initiating fresh apartheid measures, Smuts considered resignation. But he soldiered on as Minister of Justice, hoping for a chance to avert the lowering threat of a new world war which he had long foreseen. In Britain and elsewhere he delivered impressive speeches against Hitler, Mussolini and Japan, while approving in 1938 of the Munich settlement.

The outbreak of war in September 1939, tore the Government and the United party asunder. Hertzog asked Parliament for a declaration of neutrality; his deputy, Smuts, demanded war; and, after a dramatic debate, Smuts's amending motion that war should be declared on Germany was carried by eighty votes to sixty-seven. Hertzog resigned when the Governor-General, Sir Patrick Duncan, refused his request for a dissolution; and Smuts, who succeeded him as Prime Minister, became Minister also of Defence and of External Affairs.

Exhilarated by the challenge of tremendous events, Smuts told the armies which he dispatched to Ethiopia and North Africa that he would not exchange his own battle experience 'for all the gold of the Rand'. When Hertzog and Malan argued after France's collapse that the war was hopelessly lost, Smuts countered their plea for a negotiated peace by proclaiming himself commander-in-chief. He infuriated the Nationalists by accepting the rank and habitually wearing the uniform of a British field marshal, and by flying north to confer with Churchill in London or Cairo whenever his presence was requested urgently.

Lean, tight-lipped and fresh-complexioned, with pointed beard and haunting grey-blue eyes, Smuts ate and drank sparingly. He enjoyed testing his physical stamina by occasionally climbing Table Mountain until he was aged seventy-six; and 'bountiful Jehovah' was one of his most frequent and characteristic expressions. Wasting no time on small talk, he was an extremely quick worker, aided by a phenomenal memory which had in early life been almost photographic. Known to their few intimates as Oubaas and Ouma, he and Mrs Smuts lived an old-fashioned patriarchal life surrounded by their children, grandchildren and servants. Both loved and understood children and were loved by them in return. Mrs Smuts, who managed all her husband's finances, hated the Prime Minister's pompous residences in Cape Town and Pretoria. Universally respected, and a strong, positive, lovable personality in her own right, she remained a bustling Boer farmer's lady uncompromisingly until the end.

Smuts visited England four times during the Second World War; and if, in some British ears, his great set speeches had begun to sound repetitive, and even platitudinous, his dauntless courage, imperturbable serenity and giant stature extorted admiration. He crowed with merriment and happiness when, after Hertzog's death, he triumphed over Malan's 'purified' but divided opposition in a well-timed general election in July 1943.

In his grandly simple way Smuts caused much gossip at the time by an innocent but indiscreet friendship with Princess (later Queen) Frederika of Greece, who was aged twenty-four and beautiful, and who had four brothers fighting on the German side. With her husband, Prince Paul, and their children, the Princess had fled to South Africa when German armies overran Greece, and she conquered the septuagenarian Prime Minister by proclaiming herself a convert to holism which no-one else ever pretended to understand. Because Mrs Smuts understood her husband, and because, it must be assumed, King Paul understood his wife, neither attempted to interfere. But the unconcealed warmth of that friendship invited ridicule which hurt Smuts's reputation.

Opposing the Normandy invasion plan, which he attributed to Russian and American pressure, Smuts would have preferred to strike from Italy at Germany's soft under-belly, and to advance East with the object of saving as much as possible of central and southern Europe from communism. He described the British Commonwealth's eclipse as catastrophic, and the British withdrawals from India and Egypt as acts of unparalleled folly. Appalled by the British electorate's dismissal of Winston Churchill, Smuts

flew almost as a spectator to the conference at San Francisco which established the United Nations. But a reference to fundamental human rights, which he drafted in the preamble to the charter, was used at the first meeting of the General Assembly in New York as a weapon against his country and himself.

The quarrel with India about the status of Indians in South Africa flared again into a blaze in New York; and, on returning home early in 1947, Smuts complained in a broadcast that he had encountered 'unbelievable misunderstandings . . . a solid mass of prejudice'. He wrote to his confidante, Mrs Gillett, 'I am going to do whatever is politically possible, and may even exceed the limits of political expediency. But I dare not do anything which will outpace public opinion too much on the eve of an election which may be the most important ever held in this country . . . What will it profit this country if justice is done to the underdog, and the whole caboodle then, including that underdog, is handed over to the wreckers?'

Smuts's Cabinet had vetoed unanimously during the war a plan which he had formed to train and arm non whites as soldiers. Whereas he was always seeking hopefully for ways of enabling whites and non whites to live together, his opponents invariably fared best when they concentrated upon inventing new ways of compelling whites and non-whites to live apart. The general election of 1948 was a contest between those opposite concepts. Malan's slogan was apartheid, pushed to its extreme limit in theory and practice on all fronts; and Smuts's government was defeated by a narrow margin. Smuts lost his seat, but another, which he fought and won, was handed over to him by a supporter.

Smuts led the opposition but now found that task intensely uncongenial. 'I almost,' he wrote, 'look upon it as a degradation, and cannot understand how the English came to look upon opposition as an honourable role.' But he could not rest. He planned, for example, a sequel to his book on holism, did his utmost to help Dr Weizmann and the state of Israel, and derived more intense satisfaction from his election to the chancellorship of his old university, Cambridge, than he did from any other of the immense number of honours which he received.

In a speech at Cambridge on 10 June 1948, when he was installed as Chancellor, Smuts described European civilization as humanity's supreme achievement. Crabbed South African Nationalists charged him promptly with having always been much more at home in Europe than in his own country; but, two years later, 300,000 people lined the streets of Johannesburg to acclaim the greatest man whom his country had ever bred when he received that city's freedom on the eve of his eightieth birthday. Happy but exhausted after that and other ceremonies, Smuts suffered a massive coronary thrombosis on 29 May 1950, at his 2,000-acre farm, Dornkloof, superbly sited on the high veld near Pretoria.

He lingered for weeks in that beloved rambling house. It contained a large working library, but few comfortable chairs, and there was no formal garden. On 11 September, accompanied by Mrs Smuts, he enjoyed a drive into the surrounding countryside; and, that evening, as he prepared to go early to bed, sank unconscious to the floor and died without pain.

October 1942: with Churchill inspecting defences in south-east England

Churchill
Elizabeth & Frank Longford

LORD LONGFORD (b. 1905 as Frank Pakenham) went to Eton and from there to New College, Oxford, where he achieved a First in Modern Greats. He joined the staff of the Conservative Party Economic Research Department in 1930 and in 1932 became first a Lecturer and then a Student in Politics at Christ Church, Oxford. In 1936 he joined the Labour Party and, during the Second World War, served as Personal Assistant to Sir William Beveridge, then engaged on his great plan for social reform and the Welfare State. With the advent of the Labour Party to power in 1945 he was created a peer with the title of Lord Pakenham and appointed a Lord-in-Waiting, subsequently becoming Chancellor of the Duchy of Lancaster, Minister of Civil Aviation, and First Lord of the Admiralty. In 1961 he succeeded his brother as seventh Earl of Longford. In 1964 he became Leader of the Labour Party in the House of Lords, and served in Mr Wilson's Cabinet as Lord Privy Seal and Secretary of State for the Colonies (1964-66). He was appointed a Knight of the Garter in 1971. He is the author of, *inter alia*, two works on Irish history: *Peace by Ordeal, the Anglo-Irish Treaty of 1921* (1935 and 1972) and (with Thomas P. O'Neill) *Eamon de Valera* (1970).

LADY LONGFORD (b. 1906, *née* Elizabeth Harman), whose mother was a member of the Chamberlain family and therefore related to Joseph, the architect of Empire, Austen, the artificer of the Locarno Pact, and Neville, the signatory of the Munich Agreement, attended Headington School and Lady Margaret Hall, Oxford. She married Frank Pakenham in 1931. Between 1935 and 1950 she unsuccessfully contested various seats in the Labour interest. In 1960 she began a highly successful literary career with a historical study on *The Jameson Raid*, to be followed by *Victoria R.I.* (1964) and a magnificent biography of the Duke of Wellington, of which the first volume, *Wellington, Years of the Sword* was published in 1969 and the second, *Wellington, Pillar of State* in 1972.

Winston Churchill

30 Nov. 1874	Born. Educated at Harrow and Sandhurst.
1895-99	Soldier and journalist in Cuba, India, and Sudan.
1899	Defeated as Conservative candidate in by-election in Oldham. Reported South African war for *Morning Post*.
1900	General election. Won Oldham as Conservative candidate.
1904	Joined Liberal party and won fame for attacks on Chamberlain and Balfour.
1906	General election. Won North-West Manchester as Liberal candidate. Appointed Under-Secretary of State for Colonies in the new Liberal government under Campbell-Bannerman.
1908	Appointed President of the Board of Trade in Asquith's ministry. Married Clementine Hozier, who later had one son and four daughters.

Previous page: Churchill in 1911, then Home Secretary. In full dress uniform of Privy Councillor he takes a cab to Buckingham Palace

154

1910 Appointed Home Secretary. Laid foundations for unemployment insurance. Gained notoriety for decision to send troops to Tonypandy to quell labour disturbances.

Oct. 1911 Appointed First Lord of the Admiralty. Strengthened fleet, against Cabinet opposition.

March/ After outbreak of First World War,
April 1915 he initiated ill-fated expedition to Gallipoli.

May 1915 Resigned after failure of Gallipoli campaign. Appointed Chancellor of the Duchy of Lancaster.

Nov. 1915 Began active service in France.

June 1916 Returned to parliament as private member.

July 1917 Appointed Minister of Munitions in Lloyd George's coalition government. Stimulated production of tank, which he had originally fostered in Admiralty.

Jan. 1919 Appointed Secretary of War

1921 Appointed Secretary for the Colonies.

1922 General election following fall of Lloyd George's coalition government. Churchill lost his seat at Dundee, having stood as a National Liberal. Baldwin became Prime Minister.

Dec. 1923 General election. Churchill lost as Liberal candidate at Leicester. Ramsay Macdonald led Britain's first Labour ministry.

Sept. 1924 General election after Liberals withdrew support for Macdonald's government. Churchill won as Conservative candidate for Epping and Baldwin appointed him Chancellor of the Exchequer.

1925 Britain returned to the Gold Standard.

1926 Churchill adopted militant attitude to General Strike.

May 1929 Conservatives lost general election. Macdonald formed second Labour administration, dependent on Liberal votes.

1930 Churchill resigned from Shadow cabinet because of acceptance of plan for Indian self-government. He henceforth campaigned for retention of Imperial rule in India.

Aug. 1931 Formation of National government under Macdonald. Churchill not included.

Dec. 1936 Churchill supported Edward VIII at time of abdication. This hindered his campaign to drive government into more rapid re-armament.

1938 Churchill warned against danger of German aggression and opposed Munich agreement Baldwin's

March 1939 Churchill pressed for formation of National government.

3 Sept. 1939 Britain declared war on Germany after Germany's invasion of Poland. Chamberlain appointed Churchill First Lord of the Admiralty.

10 May 1940 Hitler invaded Low Countries and France. Chamberlain forced to resign. Churchill Prime Minister Coalition Government.

June 1940 France was overrun. British troops retreated from Dunkirk. Churchill's famous 'We shall never surrender' speech.

June 1941 Hitler attacked U.S.S.R. Churchill declared support for Soviet war

Aug. 1941 Churchill met President Roosevelt at Placenta Bay. The Atlantic Charter was signed, setting out principles upon which future world peace could be established.

Dec. 1941 Japanese attack on Pearl Harbor. Hitler declared war on U.S.A. Churchill visited Washington and the Grand Alliance was forged. *Prince of Wales* and *Repulse* sunk by Japanese.

Feb. 1942 British loss of Singapore.

June 1942 Fall of Tobruk during Churchill's second visit to Washington.

Jan. 1943 Meeting between Churchill and Roosevelt at Casablanca. 'Unconditional surrender' formula evolved.

Feb. 1943 Battle of Stalingrad. German 6th Army surrendered to Russians.

Feb. 1943 Beveridge Report on social insurance.

Nov./ Meeting at Tehran between
Dec. 1943 Churchill, Stalin, and Roosevelt. Churchill unable to achieve guarantees for Polish independence. Discussion on future of Germany.

June 1944 The Second Front. Anglo-American invasion of France.

Sept. 1944 Quebec conference between Roosevelt and Churchill.

Feb. 1945 Yalta conference between Churchill, Stalin, and Roosevelt. U.S.S.R. was committed to support Allies in Far East.

July 1945 Potsdam conference.

July 1945 General election. Defeated by Attlee's Labour party, Churchill became leader of opposition.

Aug. 1945 Atomic bombs dropped on Japan.

Feb. 1950 General election. Again the Conservatives lost.

Oct. 1951 General election. Conservatives gained majority of 26. Churchill became Prime Minister.

1953 Awarded Nobel prize for literature and Order of the Garter.

5 April 1955 Resigned as Prime Minister but remained in House of Commons.

1959 Retained seat in general election

24 Jan. 1965 Died.

Wellington was once asked whether he did not think that disturbed times called forth great men. Napoleon, for instance? 'I think not,' replied the Duke. 'Bonaparte is a man apart; you must not put him into the common scale; he might have started up at any time.' The Duke's remarks are curiously relevant to a later great man, Winston Churchill. Was he a hero for all seasons? Or was he that phenomenon in which the Duke of Wellington did not believe; a genius who arose in response to the needs of the time?

Winston Churchill's career opened under auspices that were at once the best and the worst. Born on 30 November 1874 at Blenheim Palace, he was a direct descendent of the great Duke of Marlborough. His father, Lord Randolph Churchill, was a scintillating Conservative leader who, through error and fatal illness, crashed in early middle age. The resolve to fulfill his father became a powerful driving-force in the young Churchill. So did the urge to satisfy his American mother, the dazzling Jennie Jerome.

On the other hand, Winston's youth, far from being warmed by family radiance almost withered from neglect. The bullying he endured at school and the backwardness and boredom he displayed there, were all by-products of parental indifference. His need to toughen himself until he was as strong as the bullies probably helped to produce the egoism and aggressive will-to-be-first which antagonized so many of his later colleagues. Continually deflated by his father's harping on his crass stupidity, he crawled into Sandhurst Military College at the third attempt. Suddenly his intellectual curiosity spurted into flame and he passed out twentieth out of 130.

From then on he felt that his military progress depended on three things: concentrated work, the reckless courage of a gambler and the frequent intervention of some higher power, by which at critical moments he would always throw a six. Once, on an impulse, he joined the scouts for a day's excitement during the Boer War, and escaped death through sheer luck. He commented: 'I had thrown double sixes again'. Churchill had faith in his star. When he left the military for the political arena, he took his faith with him. In due course he came to believe that destiny had saved him up for leadership in the greatest war of history. Of America's entry into the Second World War after Pearl Harbour he was to write, 'It certainly was odd that it should all work out this way; and once again I had the feeling . . . of being used, however unworthy, in some appointed plan'. It is said that every man needs luck, to be great. Perhaps this is another way of saying that he must have a more than rational confidence in his future.

Churchill never visualized his real future as being in the army. He was commissioned in the 4th Hussars in 1895, but he first came under fire not with his regiment but with the Spanish Army fighting Cuban rebels. This was not his eccentric idea of how to climb the military ladder. It was an expression of his will to be at the centre of excitement. He willed excitement because he loved it. 'I like things to happen, and if they don't happen I like to make them happen.' He also willed it because people would pay him to write about great events, but not about the plodding life of a subaltern. The young Churchill was conscious of straitened means. The army was no gold-mine. But he soon found that he could spin gold with his pen. From Cuba he sent home his first war articles to the *Daily Graphic*. Thereafter the prospects of sensational and lucrative journalism played a substantial part in directing him to this or that battlefield. Soon after Cuba he got permission to serve as war correspondant in India with the Malakand Field Force. Here was the material for his first book. Next he popped up at Omdurman, charging valiantly with the 21st Lancers—and also sending thrilling dispatches to the *Morning Post*. He was a free-lance in both senses. During the intervals he had spent with his regiment, he had played enterprising polo and read for hours while others took a siesta. Again, however, his reading showed him less concerned to train himself for his profession by studying all the military authorities, as did the young Napoleon and Wellington, than to make up for the university education which he had never had and always regretted.

He soaked himself in Macaulay and Gibbon, read Darwin and Schopenhauer and took a sympathetic look at *The Martyrdom of Man*, that masterpiece of nineteenth-century religious scepticism by Wynwood Reade. Meanwhile he was continually bombarding his lovely socialite mother with requests for books about politics—'Debates, Divisions, parties, cliques and caves'. Badly as Lady Randolph had performed her maternal duties while he was a boy, she became an industrious dispatcher of reading matter for her absent son.

In writing *My Early Life* over thirty years later, he announced that his military career had been entirely due to a nursery passion for toy soldiers—not a high recommendation. By the age of twenty-five he had decided to resign from the army. His first stab at politics was unsuccessful; he stood as a Tory for Oldham and was beaten. Earlier that same year, 1899, he had written to his mother: 'What an awful thing it will be if I don't come off'. But if he did not come off in Oldham he might do so in South Africa, where the Boer War was raging. He went out as the *Morning Post*'s special correspondent—and was promptly taken prisoner. His spectacular escape from captivity had its importance for his development. People mistakenly thought he had broken his parole, a legend which contributed to future impressions of his unreliability. His escapade was quite legitimate but incredibly lucky. With his faith in his star confirmed, the gloom he had felt while behind bars deepened his conviction that he was made for a life of action not contemplation. 'It is a pushing age,' he had said, 'and we must shove with the best'. So he pushed his way out of prison and shoved himself back into the army, where he assisted at the relief of Ladysmith with an *éclat* not diminished by the telling. His youthful virtues, he remembered afterwards, had been push, persuasiveness and perseverance; while he had signally failed to achieve punctuality or reserve. His ideal was to be 'generous, true and fierce'. Equipped also with vibrant imagination, he plunged into the twentieth century. The splash he made was well up to expectations. Not only did he become M.P. for Oldham in the 'Khaki Election' of 1900, but he earned himself £10,000 on an extensive lecture tour which took him as far as America. At twenty-six he was a national figure—a rotter to some, a hero to many more—and might almost be called an international phenomenon.

Right up to the First World War Churchill continued to fulfill his extraordinary promise, the imperfections of genius not yet retarding his progress.

He flew higher and higher into the empyrean, carrying, as it proved, one and even two time-bombs in his luggage. Deserting the Conservatives to join the Liberals in 1904, he entered the Cabinet as President of the Board of Trade in 1908; two years later he was Home Secretary and by 1911 First Lord of the Admiralty. In each post he made a permanent mark. He was personally responsible for initiating trade boards to help the worst paid workers, and for a national system of labour exchanges; he laid the foundations of unemployment insurance. He showed a more explicitly humane attitude to prisoners than any Home Secretary until R. A. Butler half a century later. The Fleet he strengthened in the face of Cabinet opposition. On the eve of war he took a strong personal responsibility for making the crucial move. As Lord Kitchener was to say to him in his darkest hour: 'Well, there is one thing at any rate they cannot take from you. The Fleet was ready.'

Then there was his massive biography of his father. 'It was acclaimed,' says Professor Plumb, 'as one of the great political biographies of the age'. Plumb describes this justifiably as 'a gross over-statement'. Still, it was an astonishing production for a young man of thirty-one without much formal education and no historical training. If his life had ended in 1914, in his fortieth year, 'we can surely say', writes his son with truth, 'he would not have been denied a page in history'.

He would also have established his family. In 1908 he married Clementine Hozier, and by 1914 his only son and two of his three daughters had been born. The marriage was remarkable. Clemmie's entire devotion to Winston helped her to understand and interpret rather than to ignore his temperamental difficulties. For his part, he never wasted a moment or an ounce of energy in glancing at another woman.

He was now the most significant member of the Cabinet, after Asquith, Grey and Lloyd George. Yet to quote Lord Beaverbrook who was well placed to know, he was hated, feared and mistrusted by the Tories. His change of party was to some extent responsible, but equally so was the vehemence of his attacks on his former companions. 'Of course,' he wrote to Lord Salisbury, 'politics is a form of tournament in which much mud-slinging and invectives are recognized weapons. But taking part in such an ugly brawl does not in my mind prejudice personal relations.' Unfortunately his victims were seldom able to engage him on equal terms and nourished a growing resentment. He was still a Tory when he referred to his party as consisting of 'peers, property, publicans, parsons, and turnips'. Later on he had this to say of the House of Lords, 'If the struggle comes it will be between a representative assembly and a miserable minority of titled persons who represent nobody, who are responsible to nobody and who only scurry up to London to vote in their party interests, their class interests and in their own interests'. He stirred up still deeper antagonisms when he transferred his rhetoric to the Irish question. His father, Lord Randolph, had aroused Unionist ecstasies by proclaiming that 'Ulster will fight and Ulster will be right'. Winston, while at times ambivalent, struck harsh notes on the opposite side of the argument. Here forgiveness was not to be accorded easily.

Damage to his reputation in Labour eyes was more lasting. Even if misunderstood and frequently misrepresented, his attitude to strikers left him a permanent legacy of hostility. 'By 1912,' as A.J.P. Taylor points out, 'Churchill's earlier radical reputation was dispelled so far as the industrial workers were concerned and it was never fully restored later'.

The time-bombs were thus Tory and Labour antagonism.

When the war came Churchill was poised for greatness or disaster. The visible success of their operations determines more or less the fate of all politicians. With Churchill, who had risen so high and so fast and given so many hostages to fortune, it seemed bound to make the difference between supremacy and extinction.

Winston Churchill's part in the First World War falls into five sections of unequal significance. From October 1911 to May 1915 he was First Lord of the Admiralty and one of the innermost circle directing the War. In May 1915 he was drummed out of his key position through the eccentric resignation of the First Sea Lord (Fisher) and the deep-rooted hostility of the Tories who were necessary for the new Coalition. Till November 1915 he occupied the sinecure post of Chancellor of the Duchy, sharing a paper responsibility for the remainder of the Dardanelles campaign, which he ardently championed, but stripped of all influence on its conduct.

From November 1915 until May 1916 he served in France, finishing in command of a battalion. An interlude followed in which he was once more a civilian at Westminster but passed over for office when a new Coalition was formed under Lloyd George. In July 1917 he was brought back into the Government by Lloyd George as Minister of Munitions, and rendered effective departmental service till the Armistice of 1918. In after years he was judged almost entirely on one aspect of all this—his connection with the Gallipoli campaign.

Other elements in his record, however, have aroused their share of controversy. Few would now blame him for minor naval reverses at the beginning of the war. Critics have been less kind to his personal attempt at the head of a naval force to rescue Antwerp at the end of September 1914. He telegraphed Asquith offering to resign his office and 'undertake command of the relieving and defensive forces assigned to Antwerp'. The offer produced Homeric laughter when retailed by Asquith to the Cabinet. Even so, Sir Basil Liddell Hart argues that the strange sortie paid off. The same historian, far from idolatrous towards Churchill, gives him full marks for being one of the two independent originators of the tank.

It would be churlish not to mention the gallantry and physical stamina he showed in his front-line service. The formidable Colonel 'Ma' Jeffreys had begun by breaking an hour's silence as they rode together with this frigid welcome: 'I think I ought to tell you that we were not at all consulted in the matter of your coming to join us!' Not much later he was inviting Churchill to be second in command. Churchill, however, had higher military expectations and in any case his heart still lay in politics. Meanwhile he made a genuine impression on serving soldiers.

The Gallipoli controversy will continue to divide retrospective strategists. Robert Rhodes James, in his definitive work, if any work on Gallipoli is

definitive, points out how the battle of words has ebbed and flowed for half a century. Was Gallipoli the one large imaginative idea to come from the Western powers? Was it on the contrary doomed from the start? In the event it proved to be a major Allied failure and Churchill, who had deliberately identified himself with it, paid the penalty which is the lot of the losing leader in war.

From his point of view the story was utterly tragic, so that we are not surprised to learn from Lady Churchill that she thought he would die of grief. It haunted him all his life. In his own classical apologia, *The World Crisis*, he argued with indomitable, if selective eloquence, that the enterprise in spite of everything could have succeeded if he had not been thwarted by the feebleness or disloyalty of others. Among them Asquith, Kitchener and Fisher were the obvious culprits, with additional fatuity on the spot. But as his biographer, Martin Gilbert, points out, once a military invasion was agreed on, the real control passed out of his hands. Even if he had remained at the Admiralty he could never have determined the outcome. His own comment years later comes close to the mark. His real unwisdom lay in trying to promote a major enterprise of his personal conception from a subordinate position. With luck he could have won a great triumph, but he would have needed to throw double sixes more than once.

In terms of reputation he lost ground which he never recovered in the lifetime of the Gallipoli families. He was growing strong in the House of Commons a year later when suddenly the cry was raised, 'What about the Dardanelles?' It echoed round the Chamber, in Gilbert's words, like a widow's curse. Nor is this only metaphor. Fifteen years later Frank Longford, whose father had been killed at Gallipoli, was offered a post by Mr Churchill which he respectfully declined. When he told his mother, the most charitable of women, her eyes blazed with horror: 'Of course you knew that if you had accepted you could never have looked me in the face again'. It took Churchill twenty-five years to regain the nation's confidence.

Of the twenty-five years between the wars, Churchill spent eight and a half in office: 1918-22 in Lloyd George's coalition, 1924-29 as Chancellor of the Exchequer in Baldwin's Conservative administration. In neither case was his achievement worthy of him. The earlier period has, it is true, been immortalized in *The Aftermath* by some of his most vivid writing. But in the world of deeds he will be remembered chiefly for the extremity of his anti-Bolshevism and futile interventionism in Russia. 'Meanwhile Russia,' he concluded on reflection in *The Aftermath*, 'sharpens her bayonets in her Arctic forests and mechanically breathes forth through half-closed lips her doctrine of hatred and death'. These words, a clue to his own attitude for many years to come, were not likely to be forgotten by the Communists.

He looked back with satisfaction, almost sentimentality, on his part in the creation of the Irish Free State. In reality he did not have much influence on the Treaty settlement itself, but in the crucial months that followed he was the British minister most directly involved. Not unnaturally he pressed the Irish signatories hard and sometimes brutally to honour their side of the bargain. He was proud to recall a message from the Irish leader Michael Collins: 'Tell Winston we could have done nothing without him'. But Collins

Churchill's finest hour. Shortly after Dunkirk he gazes over the Channel

said other things about Churchill in other moods. The relationship between Churchill and Collins, the man whose hands, as Churchill wrote, 'had touched the springs of terrible deeds', was never warm and close like that between Collins and Birkenhead.

The years 1922 to 1924 were occupied in a party sense with his return to the Conservative fold. A man can rat but not re-rat, was one of his own flavoured sayings. But with the fall of Lloyd George and the rise of Socialism there was no alternative. From 1924-29 he was Chancellor of the Exchequer, through the generous act of Baldwin. Even his devout admirers play down this period. His rumbustious militancy in the General Strike finds no latter-day defenders. His return to the Gold Standard, an admitted disaster, is blamed on his advisers. As a social reformer he was not by this time in the same class as Neville Chamberlain, and his responsibility for the considerable social reforms of these years tends to be overlooked.

What cannot be gainsaid is that up to 1929 Churchill was a vigorous exponent of economy in the armed forces. As Chancellor, he was all too well placed for this purpose. A few years later—and later still in his War Memoirs—he lambasted most vehemently the failure of MacDonald and Baldwin to secure Britain's defences.

Yet when all is said, his speeches as Chancellor were so powerful, his books and other writings so stirring and popular that in 1929 he was in no sense whatsoever a fallen star. With the death of Birkenhead in 1930 he was (with the doubtful exception of the ageing Lloyd George) by far the most brilliant figure in British politics. If a national crisis arose he might well be the one man who could cope with it. Almost at once, however, he seemed to put himself out of the running.

In 1931 Churchill formally withdrew from Baldwin's Shadow Cabinet. It was a momentous step both for Churchill himself and for the course of history. The specific reason given was 'divergence on Indian policy'. Baldwin was supporting the Labour Government who were pressing forward with plans for Indian independence. Churchill resolutely opposed them. For the rest of his life he maintained a diehard attitude towards India, incidentally a point of sharp difference between himself and President Roosevelt. He had described Gandhi and Nehru as 'evil and malignant Brahmins'. As was his way, he congratulated Nehru at a later Commonwealth Conference on his courage in dealing with mob violence. But his epigram about Ghandi—trying to conciliate him was like feeding cat's meat to a tiger—was not even an appropriate simile, considering Gandhi's diet of goat's milk.

This separation over India, which widened later, kept Churchill out of government until 1939, on more than one occasion to his clear disappointment. It is tempting to calculate, as he himself seems to in his memoirs, that this was all for the best, leaving him uncontaminated when war broke out. One should note the actual reasons that he gives in *The Gathering Storm* for his breach with Baldwin. 'My idea,' he wrote, 'was that the Conservative opposition should strongly confront the Labour government on all great imperial and national issues . . . Mr Baldwin felt that the times were too far gone for any robust assertion of *British Imperial greatness* . . .' (our italics). Not surprisingly Roosevelt was to regard Churchill as an imperialist. That was certainly how he was looked upon in British progressive circles before the war. The label cannot be disposed of easily. Rhodes James, however, puts the point correctly: 'Churchill's imperialism was essentially nationalistic. The empire was an instrument that gave to Britain a world position thát she would not otherwise have had.' Churchill was not an acquisitive imperialist or one who delighted in lording it over other races. But in his own words, 'Integral communities like human beings are dominated by the instinct of self-preservation'. He was obsessed with the self-preservation of Britain and deeply concerned about the empire as necessary for that purpose.

As the thirties wore on the immediate survival of Britain blotted out all else in his mind. He himself considered that he had given his first formal notice of approaching war in 1932. From then till the war he banged away indomitably, wonderfully well informed for a private person, amidst much incomprehension, hostility and boredom. Historians have not failed to notice that in October 1937 he declared his belief that 'there was a good chance of no major war taking place in our lifetime', but this relatively optimistic utterance must be treated as an exception. His attitude to collective security was at first equivocal. At the time of the Abyssinian War he was still clinging to the hope of detaching Mussolini from Hitler. One of the present authors, meeting him for the first time in his home at that moment, came away entranced but confused. A little later, under the grand heading 'Arms and the Covenant', he seemed likely to provide a rallying point alike for right-wing and progressive patriots. At this juncture, his lonely, quixotic support of Edward VIII at the time of the abdication ruined his position in the House of Commons. In the Spanish Civil War he was, as he later put it, 'on both sides'—an unconvincing stance.

From the rape of Austria (March 1938) through the destruction of Czechoslovakia to the outbreak of war (September 1939) he can hardly be faulted in his tremendous one-man crusade for a policy of rearmament, alliances, and uncompromising resistance to Hitler. This seemed far beyond the capacity or desire of Neville Chamberlain and his colleagues. At the time of the Munich by-election in Oxford he sent good wishes through his son Randolph to some of those, like the present authors, who were promoting opposition to the Government candidate. While peace lasted, Churchill was too hot a proposition for Chamberlain to handle No one doubted that he would be indispensable to any British government that found itself at war.

Winston Churchill will be regarded for many years, perhaps always, as the greatest Englishman of the twentieth century. It is often said that if he had died just before the Second World War, at the age of sixty-four, he would have gone down in history as a brilliant failure. A genius manqué would be a better description. His supreme place in British and world history rests, then, on his war leadership. On this point the overall verdict is almost unanimous.

Lord Attlee, Churchill's deputy for five years, is emphatic. 'Churchill I consider was the greatest leader in war this country has ever known. Lloyd George had an instinct that told him when the Generals were doing anything

Overleaf: Time of trial: the view from the dome of St. Paul's as London burns in the Blitz; German bombers over London (inset)

wrong, but he did not have the military knowledge to tell the Generals what was right. Winston knew his stuff and the Generals knew it.' An Admiral highly distinguished in the war, and subsequently in industry, told F.L. that Churchill's strategic conceptions 'cost thousands of lives'. But 'without him we should have lost the war.' Thousands and even millions found themselves mysteriously strengthened by him. In an analytical study of his time at the Admiralty (September 1939 - May 1940) Professor Marder concludes as follows: 'Churchill had a unique capacity to inspire others well beyond the limits of what they supposed to be their own capacity'.

Churchill took over from Neville Chamberlain on 10 May 1940, the very day that Hitler's forces poured into Belgium and Holland. No one who heard his opening broadcast can fail to recall the thrill of those early sentences: 'My policy is to wage war. War without stint: war to the uttermost'. No prospect was entertained then or later except that of total victory. Here at last was someone who found and communicated an exhilaration and a nobility in a just war for the independent existence of Britain.

By 4 June, following the miraculous escape from Dunkirk, he was making in the House of Commons what Harold Nicolson, M.P., described in a letter to his wife as the 'most magnificent speech' he had ever heard. Its theme was, 'we shall never surrender'. But after the miracle of Dunkirk there was no second miracle. France was not saved; despite Churchill's telling Pétain what he would do to the Germans: *'Nous les frapperons sur la tête'*—an echo of Wellington's famous answer to the question what *he* would do if cornered: 'Give them the biggest thrashing of their lives'. By June 1940 Britain was left alone to face a Hitler dominating the Continent. Few outsiders gave much for British chances. But the heroic tones rang out more confidently than ever and the British people responded fiercely and gaily. The Home Guard with a few rounds apiece positively longed for a crack at the enemy. Roosevelt, now convinced beyond argument that Britain would literally fight to the death, made his first great decision to provide material aid. There followed the Battle of Britain, the Blitz, the Battle of the Atlantic. When Churchill was told that Britain's neck would be wrung like a chicken's, he joked, 'some chicken, some neck'.

Better than any man Churchill knew that in the long run Europe's survival depended on American military intervention. Yet he could never quite say so in terms. All he could do was somehow to bring the magic words 'New World' or 'United States' into all his greatest speeches. In January 1941 Harry Hopkins, the President's closest adviser, came to Britain on a crucial visit. He sent word back to the President: 'Churchill is the government in every sense of the word—he controls the grand strategy and often the details—labour trusts him—the army, navy, air force are behind him to a man. The politicians and upper crust pretend to like him. I cannot emphasize too strongly that he is the one and only person over here with whom you need to have a full meeting of minds.' Later Hopkins could not find adequate words to express 'the determination of the British to defend this island and finally to win this war'.

Nevertheless it took another year, and the Japanese attack on Pearl Harbour, to bring in his country as an ally. By that time Russia had been invaded and Churchill, setting aside his inveterate antipathy, had promised every assistance that Britain could give. 'If the devil,' he remarked privately, 'were attacked by Hitler I would try to say a few favourable words about him in the House of Commons'.

It can be said in retrospect that the Allies were now bound to win the War. But for Churchill some of the bitterest blows were still to come: the loss of the *Prince of Wales* and *Repulse*, of Singapore and Tobruk among them. Recalling his relief at being alone when he heard about the first of these disasters, he said he felt a 'direct shock'—as if one of the Japanese's bombs had scored a direct hit on him personally. Britain would, however, play her full part in ultimate victories. Germany was broken at last and, with the help of the atom bomb, Japan not long afterwards. Churchill's comment on Labour's landslide victory in the General Election that followed was one of his happiest: 'I have won the race—and now they have warned me off the turf'. As he once said of Curzon, 'his invincible humour came to his aid,' though he was deeply hurt.

How could one ever evaluate Churchill's personal contribution in the field of strategy? Many things went wrong, the Norwegian and Greek campaigns, for example, in addition to the incidents just mentioned. The concentration on the African and later the Italian theatres will remain controversial, as will the delay, largely his doing, in postponing a Second Front until 1944. In all these matters he had a far bigger say than anyone else, though he never remotely resembled Hitler as a war dictator or took decisions off his own bat. If he had had his way he would have made a major assault on the soft under-belly of the Axis. Control of strategy in the last year of the war, however, virtually passed out of British and into American hands.

Even if he had still been in his prime when the war ended and had continued as Premier, his post-war years must have smacked of anti-climax. As it was, he was seventy in 1945, and seventy-six when he returned to office. His claim to immortality was already established by the end of the war and not perceptibly added to thereafter.

The British struggle for survival and the world cause of freedom from tyranny remained his righteous obsessions. At the beginning of *The Gathering Storm* (1948) he records his grim assessment: 'After all that we have suffered and achieved we find ourselves still confronted with problems and perils not less but far more formidable than those through which we have so narrowly made our way'. He called the last volume of his war memoirs *Triumph and Tragedy*. He said of the Labour leader, Ernest Bevin, after the General Election: 'I am glad that my friend Ernest Bevin is going to the Foreign Office. He'll roll all over the map of Europe but at least he's against the Communists.' The Communist spectre, in his eyes, had fully replaced that of the Nazis.

It is facile to say that he could have understood all this earlier and that he was taken for a ride by Stalin at Yalta and elsewhere. There was in fact little that he could have done about it until, after Roosevelt's death and the subjugation of Poland, American eyes were opened. 'The P.M. came away from Teheran,' reported Lord Moran, 'appalled by his impotence'. After

Yalta he was 'conscious of his own impotence far more than at Teheran'. Churchill's insight was not lacking but the force available was all too weak.

F.L. was minister for the British zone of Germany in summer 1947. Churchill lumbered up to him at a Buckingham Palace garden party. 'I am glad,' he spelt out slowly, 'that one English mind is suffering for the miseries of Germany'. The minister, Irishman though he is, felt profoundly honoured. He became aware that Churchill was the only politician on either front bench at that time who openly visualized Germany as a friend in the near future; partly from humanity and compassion, partly as a counterweight to the Russian advance.

Much of this was no doubt in his mind at Fulton. It was visible in his famous speech at Zurich when he called on France to take Germany by the hand. His whole championship of European unity sprang from the same source, as well as from a more positive vision. The European ideal operated somewhat fitfully when he became Prime Minister again (1951-55). Before the end of his premiership he strove desperately to find new ways of reaching a settlement with Russia.

In old age he had become very benign towards younger politicians and human beings generally. 'You in the Labour Party,' he told us at a small dinner, 'represent the same *slice* of England that I represented in Mr Asquith's cabinet'. He seemed well disposed to all parties but to owe no special allegiance to any, although he was, at the time, leader of the Tories. When he died on 24 January 1965 the whole world mourned him. Representatives of the highest rank gathered at a unique funeral. The six candalabra which had last stood round Wellington's coffin were brought up from the crypt of St Paul's to stand round his. The British people, having once given him their trust, loved him increasingly. It was hardly credible that it should ever have taken him so many years to win their hearts.

The time has come to measure Churchill's impact as a world figure. How the Americans reacted to him is obviously one touchstone. If we take the public tributes paid to him in Congress when he was made an honorary American citizen, and again after his death, it is clear that one ray of his genius dazzled them above all others. He stood for the right to be free. 'In all the countless words to be written about Churchill in years to come,' said a Congressman quoting Eisenhower, 'one incontestable refrain would ring out, "He was a champion of freedom".' John F. Kennedy called him 'the most honored and honorable man to walk the stage of human history in the time in which we live. Whenever and wherever tyranny threatened, he has always championed liberty.' In the torrent of praise there is something very like monotony—the monotony of absolute concensus.

It was John F. Kennedy who also found inimitable words to express the secondary but scarcely less vital aspect of Churchill's genius: the war-winning musketry of his speeches. 'He mobilized the English language,' said the American President, 'and sent it into battle'. There was not one of Churchill's great purple, or rather crimson passages which did not echo round the United States. 'Their finest hour'—'We shall fight them on the beaches'—'Give us the tools and we will finish the job'—'Never in the field of human conflict'—the lot. As the molten words dropped into millions of minds, like metal from the top of an ancient shot-tower, the United States proclaimed him as 'truly *one of us*'. Not just because, through his mother, he was half American; but because, in the words of an American newspaper, 'he helped us to fight for our freedom'. Never had so many owed so much to a single man.

At home, the editor of *The Times* found it good to see in 1941 Churchill's 'cheerful, challenging—not to say truculent—look'. The diaries of Harold Nicolson vividly convey the magical effect of his voice. Again and again he would harangue an anxious, despondent or critical House of Commons and each time you could *feel* their spirits rising. What was his secret? He explained himself during the presentation of the Sutherland portrait in 1955. He had always spoken direct to the lion which he believed existed under every British skin. 'It was the nation and the race dwelling all round the globe that had the lion's heart,' he wound up, 'I had the luck to be called upon to give the roar'. His audience, among whom were these authors, revelled in the twinkling scowl on the pink face, and the familiar growl in the voice that became a crow of merriment.

There was one sphere in which overseas' opinion was more pleased with him than the people at home. Churchill's charisma in the presence of foreigners enabled him to paint Utopias of far-reaching grandeur. In Zurich as already mentioned, he spoke of 'The United States of Europe'. To Adlai Stevenson he called himself whimsically, 'an English-speaking Union'. An American journalist heard him say he could see the arm of destiny outstretched to bring about common British and American citizenship. In striking contrast was his antipathy to 'the brave-new-world business' of domestic reform. It was the same Churchill who trumpetted at thirty-three, 'I refuse to be shut up in a soup kitchen with Mrs Sidney Webb', and at seventy declined to meet Sir William Beveridge. He evaded all plots of Beveridge's personal assistant (F. L.) to bring them together, and when they met accidentally on board ship, Lord Moran described the rendezvous as a 'bleak little function'. Churchill told Moran in 1944 that he had no post-war message. 'I had a message. Now I only say, "fight the damned socialists".' That was a moan not a message, as he well knew.

Without being a party-man, he shared the traditional enthusiasm of romantic Conservatives. Like Wellington, he was the servant of Crown, Constitution and Empire. He thrived on romance, owing many of his verbal felicities to an aversion to the commonplace. It was he who changed the name of Local Defence Volunteers to Home Guard, and of Communal Feeding Centres to British Restaurants. Britain herself he preferred to call 'The Island'. Few modern historians will allow him the power of getting inside the real past. What he could do, and do magnificently, was to bring a romantic vision of the past right into his own present, and use it with matchless effect for the task in hand—victory over Hitler. His image of 'The Island' was perhaps more compatible with Napoleon's invasion fleet than the German Air Force. Through this image he none the less evoked a thousand years of dauntless British history and the gallant fulfillment of standing alone.

F*

Churchill's humour and geniality—his comic tubby boiler-suit, his mischievous grin, his confidential V-sign and fat cigar—cheered people round the world, while his tenacity and boundless vigour won their astonished admiration. At eighty-eight he found himself sitting by Elizabeth Longford at dinner. Benightedly, she thought to make things easy for the old gentleman by talking about the British generals in the Boer War. Sweeping them away he pronounced himself interested in the problems of contemporary Canada. Similarly, Nicolson remembered his latter-day delight in uproarious Question Times at the House of Commons and horror of becoming an elder statesman.

Much has been written, and rightly, about his attacks of depression, called by him 'Black Dog'. See-sawing moods assailed him particularly in youth, in old age, and when he had nothing to do. After Gallipoli, for instance, he described his alternate flights of buoyancy and 'chewing black charcoal'. His painting was partly therapeutic. 'Happy are the painters,' he wrote, 'for they shall not be lonely'. When he reached heaven he planned to spend much of his first million years painting, 'to get to the bottom of the subject'. No doubt his second million will be devoted to learning the 'cello, which at eleven he had longed in vain to be taught.

Still in the context of heaven, we approach one of his most revealing remarks. 'Is it to be the cherub or the tiger?' he asked Graham Sutherland, when about to sit for the portrait which, as is well known, he finally rejected. As well as showing that Churchill, like the great actor he was, perfectly understood his different 'parts', the question answered itself. It was not the cherub in him ('All babies are like me', he pointed out when a new grandchild was said to resemble him) but the tiger which won for him his place in history. He was a man for one season: the terrible season of war. 'They could get more out of me in two years of war,' he wrote in 1916, 'than in a hundred afterwards'. Not that he accepted this distinction with callous satisfaction. There were times when he seemed shocked by his own relish for war-making. 'My God! This, this is living history,' he exclaimed to Margot Asquith in 1915. 'Why, I would not be out of this glorious delicious war for anything the world could give me.' Then the glowing eyes clouded with anxiety lest the word *delicious* should jar on her. 'I say,' he added, 'don't repeat that I said the word "delicious"—you know what I mean'. Was it a coincidence or a literary echo? The same word had been used by Churchill's hero, Stonewall Jackson, during the American Civil War. 'Delicious excitement!' Jackson muttered to General Lee at dawn just before battle. 'It is well that war is so horrible—we would grow too fond of it.'

To Churchill war was 'vile and wicked folly and barbarism'. At the same time it was a happening, the supreme event; and events were the breath of his life. Events were his friends, his boon companions, more so than most human beings. The few contemporaries he loved deeply had to be events in themselves, like Birkenhead, Beaverbrook and Lloyd George. (In his last years, to adapt words he himself used about Scrimgeour, the Prohibitionist who defeated him at Dundee in 1922, 'He was surrounded and supported by a devoted band of followers', his youngest daughter and her husband never far from his side.) His writings throb with 'the march of events', 'the whole moving throng of events', 'the stroke of world events'. What, he asked, was Lord Curzon's failure? That he did not try to dominate events, murmuring instead, 'Events must take their course'. War, with its chances to be taken or rejected, was Winston Churchill's *métier*. Apart from Wellington, a special case, he was the first British Prime Minister who had had a military training. He waged war day and night, it was said; one war was hardly enough for him, certainly not one department of state. Someone told him that Roosevelt accused him of having a hundred ideas a day—four of them good. 'It comes badly,' snapped back Winston, 'from a man who hadn't any ideas at all' Obsessional Churchill might be, but no one could say that he did not, in his own favourite words, 'rise to the level of events'. A nation and half a world rose with him.

Adenauer
by Anthony Nicholls

ANTHONY NICHOLLS, born in Carshalton, Surrey, in 1934, was educated at Sutton County Grammar School and in 1953 won an Open Exhibition to Merton College, Oxford. After National Service in the Royal Air Force he read history at Oxford, graduating in 1958. He decided to specialize in recent German History and spent two years at St Antony's College, Oxford, and at the University of Munich. In 1960 he obtained a B.Phil. degree in Modern European History and, after a year at Merton College as a Lecturer, he was elected to a Research Fellowship at St Antony's College. Since then he has been working in the field of European history. He is now an Official Fellow of St Antony's and a University Lecturer. He published *Weimar and the Rise of Hitler* (1968), and is co-author with Sir John Wheeler-Bennett of *The Semblance of Peace* (1972). He was co-editor of *German Democracy and the Triumph of Hitler* (1971, St Antony's Publications No. 3) and contributed a chapter on Germany to *European Fascism* (1968).

Konrad Adenauer

15 Jan. 1876	Born in Cologne. Son of a minor Prussian official. Educated at a secondary school in Cologne and then read law at Freiburg and Bonn Universities.
1904	Married Emma Weyer, daughter of a good Cologne family.
1906	Adenauer elected to Cologne City Council.
1916	Emma, Adenauer's first wife, died.
18 Oct. 1917	Elected Mayor of Cologne.
Nov. 1918	Collapse of Imperial Germany. Western Allies occupied the Rhineland, including Cologne.
1919	Versailles Peace Treaty. Cologne remained occupied. Adenauer revived Cologne University, closed since 1798.
1926	British occupying force evacuated Cologne.
1930	Allies evacuated the Rhineland. Nazis made gains in German *Reichstag* elections.
1932	Nazis became the largest party in German *Reichstag*.
1933	Hitler appointed Chancellor. All political parties banned except Nazis. Adenauer dismissed from his post as mayor and forced into hiding.
1935	Having established his right to a pension he settled in Rhöndorf near Cologne.
1939	Hitler attacked Poland and World War II began.
July 1944	Plot against Hitler's life. Adenauer arrested in general round-up of suspected opponents. Released after two months.
March 1945	Cologne occupied by the Americans who appointed Adenauer mayor.
May 1945	Germany surrendered unconditionally and was divided into four zones of occupation. Cologne was in the British Zone.

Previous page: Born before Hitler, the 'old man' of German politics is still thoroughly in command of the situation in 1953. Here he arrives at an election meeting

Oct. 1945 Adenauer dismissed for 'incompetence'. Began active career in the Christian Democratic Party (C.D.U.).

Feb. 1946 Adenauer became Chairman of C.D.U. in British Zone of occupation.

March 1946 Zonal Advisory Council set up in British Zone. Adenauer headed C.D.U. delegation.

Oct. 1946 *Landtag* of North Rhine-Westphalia met with nominated membership. Adenauer leader of C.D.U. delegation.

April 1947 C.D.U. won first elections to *Landtag* in North Rhine Westphalia.

May 1947 U.S. and British Zones of occupation united economically in 'Bizonia'.

June 1947 First announcement of Marshall Plan for American aid to Europe.

June 1948 Three western powers announced their intention to create governmental bodies in their zones and to administer them in a unified way. German mark revalued by western powers. Soviet authorities blockade Berlin. Airlift begins.

Aug. 1948 'Parliamentary Council' elected by *Lander* parliaments in the western zones to draw up constitution for West Germany. Adenauer became its President.

May 1949 Berlin Blockade ended. Constitution of West German Federal Republic accepted by West German *Länder*.

Aug. 1949 Federal German elections. C.D.U. largest party.

Sept. 1949 Adenauer elected Federal Chancellor by the *Bundestag* in Bonn.

1951 West Germany agreed to join 'Schuman Plan' coal and steel common market.

May 1952 German Contractual Convention signed between West Germany and the western occupying powers, restoring German sovereignty over domestic and foreign relations whilst retaining Allied rights of a defensive character.

April 1953 Visited U.S.A. and created good relationship with Dulles.

Sept. 1953 *Bundestag* elections. Adenauer won an absolute majority in the Federal German Parliament.

Oct. 1954 West Germany invited to join NATO. Remaining restrictions on West German sovereignty abolished.

Sept. 1955 Adenauer visited Moscow. Diplomatic relations established with Russia and agreement that German prisoners of war in the Soviet Union should be returned.

1957 Adenauer won the third *Bundestag* elections.

Sept. 1958 Adenauer met President de Gaulle at Colombey les Deux Eglises. Beginning of close relationship with Gaullist France.

Aug. 1961 East Germans sealed off East Berlin.

Sept. 1961 Bundestag elections won by Adenauer, but C.D.U. dependent on liberal Free Democrats to form a government.

Oct. 1962 '*Spiegel* Affair' which led to cabinet crisis and a weakening of Adenauer's position.

Jan. 1963 Franco-German treaty of Friendship and Co-operation.

Oct. 1963 Adenauer resigned as Federal German Chancellor.

19 April 1967 Died

Of all the statesmen who shaped the destinies of Europe in the twentieth century, Konrad Adenauer was one of the least colourful. Unlike Hitler or Mussolini, he was no demagogue. Unlike Lenin or Trotsky, he was no romantic revolutionary. His face will never adorn the T-shirts or the wall posters of the younger generation, and their elders have not enshrined him with the same reverence shown to Churchill, de Gaulle or—in an earlier era—to Bismarck. Yet in his own way he was more effective than any other German leader since the founding of the Wilhelmine Empire—not excluding Bismarck himself.

To begin with, the very length of Adenauer's Chancellorship was a remarkable achievement. Under the Weimar Republic there had been thirteen Chancellors in fourteen years and even more changes of government. Hitler, creator of the thousand-year Reich, had tried to secure uninterrupted enjoyment of power by ruthlessly eliminating his opponents. Yet by April 1945 he was dead, and his Reich had died with him. Adenauer, having been elected Chancellor in 1949 by only one vote—and that, as he was fond of boasting, his own—remained at his post until October 1963, a span of fourteen years. Among his predecessors as Chancellor only Bismarck could claim a longer innings. Even that particular comparison would be unfair to Adenauer.

The 'Iron Chancellor' established his position with the help of glorious victories won by the Prussian Army. Sadowa and Sedan created an aura of invincibility which helped him over-ride domestic opposition. The German people whom he led were ill-equipped to question the expertise of their rulers, especially in the field of foreign policy. By 1949, the situation was very different. Germany had been utterly defeated; her people were totally disillusioned. Bitterness and scepticism were widespread; heroism was at a discount.

Of course nobody expected that Adenauer would turn out to be a hero. For one thing he was far too old. When, on 20 September 1949, he mounted the rostrum in the *Bundestag* to outline his government programme, he was already seventy-three years of age. At that time his Chancellorship appeared to be of a provisional character. Few of those present could have imagined that, ten years later, Adenauer's leadership would have developed into such an institution that it had become a national joke[1]. This was not simply attributable to Adenauer's longevity, although that was remarkable enough. It was also the result of single-minded determination and sheer physical energy which enabled him to outstrip rivals only half his age.

Adenauer was born in Cologne in January 1876. As is often pointed out, this means that he was older than Gustav Stresemann or Adolf Hitler, and only five years younger than Friedrich Ebert, the first President of the Weimar Republic. Perhaps of greater importance was the fact that Adenauer's home background made him something of an outsider in the Prussian-dominated Reich of Bismarck and Wilhelm II. It was true that his father had served as a ranker in the Prussian campaign against Austria and had achieved the unusual distinction of being made an officer in the field. Even after marriage to a woman of modest means forced him to resign his commission, Adenauer's father continued to serve the Prussian state as an official in a law court. There can be no suggestion that he or his family were disloyal to the Hohenzollerns. Yet socially, geographically and spiritually they were set apart from the type of society which dominated Berlin at that time.

Most Rhinelanders regarded themselves not only as Germans but as Western Europeans whose cultural level was superior to that of the boorish Prussians. Perhaps even more important than this intangible regional loyalty was the very clear conflict between Roman Catholicism and Protestantism which affected the Rhineland provinces of Prussia during Adenauer's childhood years, and which never really disappeared until the foundation of the united Christian Democratic Party after 1945. Adenauer, like most Rhinelanders, was a Roman Catholic. The Centre Party which he joined as a young man had come into existence to protect Roman Catholic interests against the pressures exerted by a strongly Protestant Prussian state. In the 1870s, Rhinelanders had suffered under the *Kulturkampf* legislation enacted by Bismarck. The Chancellor's accusation that the Centre Party was an organization of *Reichsfeinde* (enemies of the German Empire) lingered in the minds of the Prussian-German establishment even after the *Kulturkampf* itself was dead. This religious alienation seems to have had its effect on Adenauer's attitude towards Prussia. He was always a good German, but scarcely a loyal Prussian subject. Whereas many ambitious men went to Berlin to further their careers, Adenauer stayed firmly in the Rhineland and was eventually rewarded by seeing Germany's capital established almost literally on his own door-step. This was a piece of good fortune which—like others in his career—did not occur without some assistance from Adenauer himself.

Adenauer, then, came from an unpretentious home. He was not an outstanding scholar, and financial difficulties almost prevented him from going to university. After completing his legal studies without great distinction, he served for a time in the office of a Cologne solicitor who was also a leading member of the local Catholic Centre Party. Through his good offices Adenauer obtained a post on the Cologne city administration, where his diligence and attention to detail enabled him to gain rapid promotion. He was a member of the Centre Party and married into one of Cologne's best Roman Catholic families. In 1917 he reached what seemed to be a remarkable pinnacle of achievement for a young man without the benefits of inherited fortune or social position. At the age of forty one, he was elected Mayor of Cologne by the City Council.

The mayor of a great German city was, and still is, a figure of far greater power and influence than his British counterpart. The *Oberbuergermeister* is not a short-term *primus inter pares*, but a man wielding executive authority whose term of office may last for many years. In a country where civic pride often outweighed public interest in national politics, the post of mayor was more prestigious than a seat in the *Reichstag*. To hold down his office, Adenauer had to combine political astuteness with executive efficiency. He was called upon to do so a year after his wife had died at the age of thirty-six, and after he himself had suffered a frightening motor accident which had left his face permanently disfigured. For a long time afterwards he suffered from recurrent headaches and insomnia. Even without these personal problems his task was daunting enough. Cologne, like other German cities, faced increasing hardships during the war as the result of food and housing shortages. In November 1918 the defeat of the German Empire brought it up against new and quite unexpected problems. Revolutionary disturbances threatened to subvert law and order. Enemy occupation followed the collapse of German military might. Adenauer found himself having to act to preserve his homeland against French-sponsored separatism.

Adenauer himself was never a separatist, despite accusations to this effect by his political enemies. His particular regional viewpoint did, however, enable him to realize earlier than many other German leaders that French demands for security would somehow have to be met if Germany also was to enjoy stability and peace. Only by working to uncover the common interest of Frenchmen and Germans in their mutual prosperity could the danger posed by French chauvinism be overcome. After the Second World War, the relationship with France was just as crucial to Germany's future, and the chances of assuaging French hostility seemed even less promising. Adenauer had not forgotten the lessons of the Weimar period; he managed to appease France in the process of re-establishing German independence.

Most of Adenauer's energies during the Weimar period were devoted to the development and expansion of Cologne. He ruled his urban fiefdom with absolute authority. An obstinate man who possessed no great rhetorical gifts, he wore down opposition by relentless argument and meticulously marshalled arrays of fact. He was a master of committee-work, taking endless pains to buttonhole potential friends or wavering opponents, tailoring his arguments to suit his listener and never being discouraged by temporary setbacks.

The new political climate—with the Centre Party sharing power in both the Reich and Prussia—meant more opportunities for civic enterprise. The shabby treatment accorded to Cologne under the Hohenzollerns could now be rectified[2]. Adenauer presided over the re-establishment of its university and the creation of a vast green belt around the city. Civic buildings and civic enterprises were on a grand scale. When the depression hit Germany in 1930, Adenauer showed no great enthusiasm to sacrifice his city's interests for the common good, and his attitude outraged the austere Reich Chancellor, Heinrich Bruening. For his part, Adenauer was never impressed by the political leadership in Berlin. He disliked Stresemann, whom he suspected of being ready to sacrifice the Rhineland for the sake of stabilizing the mark in 1923, and he regarded Bruening as incompetent. More than once there was a possibility that Adenauer might form a ministry in Berlin, but he would not commit himself to lead a minority cabinet.

He was wise to stay in Cologne. In the Weimar period the Centre Party—of which he was not even the leader—had no chance of becoming large enough to dominate German politics. Adenauer himself lacked the support of the Army and the President, upon which Bruening or Papen were to build their authority. The time for his appearance on the national stage had not yet come.

In 1933 Adenauer's career apparently collapsed. The Nazis removed him from his post and conducted a campaign of harassment against him. He was arrested for short periods and at other times forced to live in seclusion. After several nerve-wracking years of uncertainty he was allowed to retire to Rhoendorf, a village near the Rhine between Cologne and Bonn. There he built a house overlooking the river and devoted himself to his lifelong passion for gardening. He was in his sixties; political activity seemed out of the question. So far as is known, he did not take part in any oppositional activity under the Third Reich, although he made no move to collaborate with the Nazis. Nevertheless, after the attempt on Hitler's life in July 1944, Adenauer was held with other political prisoners at a detention centre in Cologne and was lucky to be released alive. In March 1945 American forces crossed the Rhine near his home. He and his family emerged, after a week of sheltering against intermittent bombardment, to find that the Americans wanted him to resume his post as mayor of Cologne. Although in his seventieth year Adenauer agreed, stipulating only that his appointment should be kept secret to protect his three sons who were still serving in the German Army.

Adenauer faced a heart-breaking situation. Cologne had been a major and early target for Allied strategic bombing raids and the city was in ruins. Its communications were destroyed, food and fuel were either scarce or non existent and the problems of the city were exacerbated by a large refugee population. It was typical of the mayor that he did not simply immerse himself in the business of keeping Cologne alive, but at once began to plan and scheme for a new Cologne which should rise out of the wreckage to future splendours. Such far-sightedness did not endear him to his conquerors. After the fighting was over, Cologne passed under the control of the British, and on 6 October, they summarily dismissed Adenauer from his post on the grounds of his 'incompetence'. The immediate cause of his removal was his objection to a British demand that he cut down trees in the green belt of Cologne for fuel. Adenauer himself preferred to think that the predeliction of a British Labour government for Social Democrats made him politically unattractive to them. This is almost certainly untrue, since the decision to dismiss him was taken by a local commander and does not seem to have been discussed at high level.[3]

There were, however, more general reasons why the British did not find Adenauer an easy collaborator. He was far too powerful a personality to confine himself to questions of day-to-day provisioning and communications, which were the only matters the British wanted to see him tackling. They were also very suspicious of any attempt to set the occupying powers against one another. On the day before his dismissal in 1945 he gave an interview to newsmen in which—after criticizing Allied niggardliness about fuel supplies—he urged the Western Powers to unite their occupation zones into a federal state to prevent the Soviet Zone presenting itself as the 'true German Reich'. Such a view was anathema to the British at this time; it was disloyal to their Soviet Allies and smacked of devious German politicking. It was hardly surprising that Adenauer was replaced.

The manner of his dismissal was, however, unnecessarily harsh, especially as it involved banishment from Cologne, where his second wife was seriously ill in hospital. Too much can be made of incidents like this; Adenauer's policy towards Britain was not simply based on personal whim. The British diplomats and soldiers with whom he had to deal in later years were men of sophistication and goodwill and he valued their collaboration. Nevertheless, there is evidence that his experiences in 1945 rankled and helped to prevent the development of any very warm association with British leaders to match those Adenauer later enjoyed with John Foster Dulles or Charles de Gaulle.

Adenauer's personal experience of British displeasure was not the only reason why he should have doubts about the attitude adopted by Britain in the years after 1945. The British, like the Americans and—in a rather different way—the Russians, wanted to transmogrify Germany so that German militarism and National Socialism could never again threaten her neighbours. This involved stringent control over, and reduction of, German industrial production; the arrest and punishment of Nazis considered to have participated in criminal activities; the exclusion of former Nazis from public office and the 're-education' of the German population to eradicate nationalist and militarist inclinations. The lines of policy laid down at Potsdam for the Allied occupation of Germany meant that measures which Germans could only interpret as punitive would have to be taken by the Allies. The most obvious example of this policy was the dismantling of German industrial plant and its transference to Russia as part of German reparations to the Soviet Union. Since the British occupied the most important—albeit the most severely damaged—industrial area of Germany in the Ruhr, German hostility to dismantling, which Adenauer shared, was concentrated especially on them.

Underlying the friction over individual issues of occupation policy was a fundamental conflict about the manner in which Germany should be re-habilitated. This conflict did not only divide the Germans from their con-querors; it also raged within Germany, and was at the root of the bitter division between German Social Democracy and the parties of the Right. It was felt by many that, if the country was to be permanently liberated from national chauvinism, there must be a fundamental change in society, which would eliminate the power of those classes upon which the Imperial and Nationalist Socialist regimes had been based. This view was, of course, inherent in Soviet attitudes towards the German problem, even if it was temporarily masked by the drive to establish a communist-dominated 'anti-Fascist' front in Germany. In the West too, there was a great deal of sympa-thy for the view that Germany needed radical social changes if she was to be accepted back into the comity of nations. For their part the German Social Democrats, led by the fiery and physically indomitable Kurt Schu-macher, also demanded the socialization of German industry as a means of creating a just society. It was not unnatural, especially in view of Britain's Labour Government, for the Anglo-Saxon powers to look to the German Social Democrats when seeking collaborators among the German people. Their record both before and after Hitler's rise to power made them seem the most obvious choice of partners in an attempt to create a new German democracy.

180

The Social Democrats (S.P.D.) had never bowed the knee to Hitler, and their supporters had shown a remarkable degree of solidarity even during the darkest days of Nazi tyranny. When the Weimar Republic had collapsed in 1933, only the German Social Democrats had the resolution to stand up in the *Reichstag* to oppose the Enabling Law which gave Hitler plenary powers and signified the end of German parliamentary democracy.[4] On the other hand the Centre Party, to which Konrad Adenauer belonged, had caved in under the dual pressure of the Nazis and the Vatican. In a largely vain attempt to secure Roman Catholic rights under the Third Reich it had agreed to Hitler's Enabling Act and then to its own dissolution.[5]

It was not, therefore, surprising that the Western Allies should have regarded Social Democrats with favour when selecting Germans for administrative tasks or quasi-political functions after the end of the war. Furthermore, the German Social Democrats themselves had maintained their activities during the war in a number of exile organizations. After Hitler's defeat many of their former supporters were eager to re-establish the Party on German soil. Despite the Western Allies' ban on political activity, they were among the first to mobilize their followers. A strong organization had always been a feature of German Social Democracy, party functionaries from the Weimar era provided the necessary administrative expertise, while younger, more militant members, who had often shared the comradeship of suffering in Nazi concentration camps, sought to give the party a new drive and moral force which would attract the disillusioned masses of the German people. Both these elements in Social Democratic experience were embodied in the Party's West German leader, Kurt Schumacher, a respected figure from the Weimar period who had been incarcerated for ten years in Dachau concentration camp.[6] By May 1946, when he was elected party chairman by the first post-war congress of the S.P.D., the Social Democratic Party could boast 600,000 members. If anyone seemed likely to lead a future civilian German Government, it was Kurt Schumacher. The Allied authorities—especially the British—could not ignore this fact in their relations with German politicians. Many Social Democrats were appointed to positions at lower levels of administration and were especially prominent in the press and radio licensed by the military authority. By the spring of 1946, German Social Democracy had built up a head start over its political rivals, an advantage which at first looked impossible to overcome.

Yet Adenauer did overcome it. His success was due partly to the extraordinary vigour with which he threw himself into the task of organizing his chosen party—the Christian Democratic Union, and partly to the shrewdness with which he shaped the appeal of that party to Germany's defeated population.

Unlike their Socialist rivals, the Christian Democrats had to create a new political movement. The middle-class parties of Imperial and Weimar Germany had proved incapable of withstanding competition from the Nazis and had disappeared unhonoured and unsung in 1933. The only German party of a socially heterogenous character—the Roman Catholic Centre—had, as we have seen, also tried to make its peace with Hitler. In any case a sectarian party could not hope to attract the mass support necessary to provide a real counterweight to the Social Democrats and the Communists. Although the Centre was revived in some parts of Germany it had little success. Adenauer and his friends plumped for a new inter-denominational Christian Party which would unite Protestants and Roman Catholics. This had been a dream of some Centre Party politicians, including Adenauer, for many years, but only after the catastrophe of the Third Reich had conditions become favourable for its realization.

Before Hitler's accession to power in Germany, the Protestant majority in the country had seen no reason to unite in a Christian Party based on the Roman Catholic Centre. The complete eclipse of the old German middle-class parties in 1933 had created a new situation. Then many millions of German people had rallied to Hitler's 'National Revolution' as a means of regenerating Germany without actually damaging the basic structure of society. For them the Nazis had represented the triumph of 'idealism' over the 'materialism' of an outmoded system of parliamentary democracy, with its self-seeking political parties and trade unions. In 1945 these illusions had been shattered; in their place there was a political and spiritual vacuum. German conservatism had been both compromised and humiliated by the Nazis. On the other hand, the Weimar Republic remained a most repellent model for the majority of Germans. It was associated with *Parteihader* (Party squabbles) and sectional interests. Even those middle-class Germans who had been brave enough to plot resistance against Hitler, had generally thought in terms of a corporate state in which such divisive institutions as trade unions and political parties of the old type would play no part. As for the Marxist solutions put forward by the Social Democrats and Communists, they were no more attractive than they had been in the 1930s. The very fact that, under Russian pressure, there seemed a serious danger of Germany being Sovietized, added to the urgent need felt by many people for a viable alternative to Marxism. Under these circumstances many Germans—especially of the younger generation—turned to Christianity as the one element in their cultural heritage which had not been compromised by the Third Reich and defeat in the war, and which seemed to offer both a spiritual message for the individual and a formula for social harmony.[7] It seemed that the Christian approach could create a new society without jettisoning traditional values or plunging Germany into a class war.

This Christian movement was of enormous significance for the Germans because for the first time in their history it enabled them to create an effective, moderate, broadly based, conservative party which ranged over a wide spectrum of regional, social and professional interests. It was certainly loosely knit and heterogenous in its composition; Christian labour organizations, industrialists, small business and handicraft groups, and agricultural interests all playing their part in it. It also had to preserve an uneasy balance between the two main Christian denominations; Protestant and Roman Catholic. But its survival and success meant that the anti-democratic, nationalist elements which had played such a powerful role in German politics since the time of Bismarck were stifled and could no longer make an effective appeal to the propertied classes.

The architect of this success was Konrad Adenauer. He was the man who seized on the essential elements in Christian Democracy's appeal and winnowed out the dangerous illusions harboured by many of its founders. These illusions were not unnatural in the atmosphere of post-war Germany, and they were shared in some degree—and with more disastrous results— by the Social Democrats. The first was that Germany had to create a new form of social order to replace Western capitalism. To be sure, this was not to come about as the result of a Marxist class struggle, but should take the form of 'Christian socialism'. The exact nature of the Christian Socialist programme was vague, but it certainly involved state control of major industries and some kind of planned economy. Adenauer would have none of this. For one thing, he himself distrusted monopolies and power concentrations, and believed that competition and private enterprise would enable the German people to develop its talents more effectively if it were held within the confines of socialist planning. This was particularly true in a country whose industrial plant had been ravaged by war. For another thing he realized that the Christian Democrats could not successfully be conservative and revolutionary at the same time. Although the zeal of the Christian Socialists was a source of energy to the new movement, the mass of German people, and particularly those who had at any time fallen under the spell of National Socialism, were suspicious of idealism and wanted peace and security above all else.

Hence when, in the winter of 1945-46, Adenauer applied himself to tailoring the Christian Democratic programme, he played down the socialist elements in it.[5] This did not mean, however, that the C.D.U. would simply be a laissez-faire party dedicated to serve the interests of big business. Adenauer carefully avoided association with any one interest, nor did he subscribe rigidly to any watertight economic theory. His attitude in such matters was pragmatic. His party retained a powerful group of Christian trade unionists and others whose chief concern was social welfare, and Adenauer was quite ready to give them encouragement so long as they did not seem to be undermining the principle of private ownership.

The second illusion to which numerous German politicians were prone was the belief that Germany could in some way retain her independence of both the Western Democracies and the Eastern Soviet power and create a 'middle way'. They hoped that a united Germany could even act as a bridge between the two conflicting ideologies. This belief seems partly to have been a hang-over from wartime attitudes; Germans did not want to feel that they had to accept the values of their conquerors. It was also part of a natural attempt to maintain German unity and independence. The founders of the Christian Democratic movement in Berlin, Jacob Kaiser and Andreas Hermes, were inclined towards this viewpoint. Not surprisingly, they thought the Party ought to be directed from the capital of the Reich. They were therefore opposed to any anti-Soviet alignment, since their own base was under Soviet control and they depended on the goodwill of the Soviet authorities.

Adenauer was clear that such ambitions could lead nowhere, quite apart from the fact that his own position in the party would be weakened if the

183

Berlin group gained control of it. For Adenauer, the Western orientation of the C.D.U. was self-evident; it had to build up its power in the Western occupation zones and it needed to look to the Western Allies for support. He himself took great care to build up the C.D.U. organization in the British Zone and to establish himself at its head. At one crucial meeting, held in Herford in January 1946, Adenauer turned his age to good account when he coolly took the chair by right of seniority. He never relinquished it. Kaiser and the Berlin C.D.U. quickly found themselves hamstrung by Soviet obstructiveness, and the Western sections of the Party refused to recognize their authority.

There is one other aspect of Adenauer's Christian Democratic policy which was to bear electoral fruit as time went on, and this was his attitude towards former Nazis. Schumacher was passionately concerned about this problem. He rejected the right of foreign powers to condemn Germans collectively for the evils of the Third Reich, but he was correspondingly determined that the Germans themselves should put their own house in order, and eliminate Nazi elements from positions of responsibility. Adenauer disliked Nazis but did not launch a crusade against them. De-nazification was an Allied affair, and widely unpopular. He preferred to let sleeping dogs lie. As a result his C.D.U. later won the votes of many old Nazi supporters for whom a 'Christian' party might not otherwise have proved particularly attractive.

The trend of international events also started to work in Adenauer's favour in 1946. Relations between the Soviet Union and the Western Powers began to deteriorate very sharply. The development of the Cold War demonstrated Adenauer's far-sightedness in plumping for integration with the West. It also strengthened his own position within his Party. The Marshall Plan of 1947 effectively set the seal on the economic division of Germany, since the Soviet Zone—like other Soviet-controlled countries—refused to benefit from it. The Berlin Blockade of the following year saw Germans and Western Allies draw together in an anti-Soviet stance, and for the first time the German public began to evince real enthusiasm for the Western camp. Already in July 1946, Russian obstructiveness in the field of Four-Power administration had caused the British to establish a new German state, or *Land*, covering the Ruhr and the Rhineland. This was the state of North-Rhine-Westphalia, and it became the most important administrative area in the British Zone. It meant that one of Adenauer's long-standing objectives— the break-up of Prussia and the establishment of a powerful West German political entity—had been achieved.[9] Adenauer became chairman of the Christian Democratic delegation in the Parliament of the new *Land*. By 1947 the Christian Democrats were established as the strongest single party there. Once again they owed a good deal of their advantage to Adenauer, who had refused to accept Schumacher's offer of a common front against the Allies so long as the—then apparently weaker—C.D.U. accepted Social Democratic leadership.

Nevertheless, in 1948 Adenauer was still only a regional politician in Germany and—unlike Schumacher—was not at all widely known in the country as a whole. The German equivalent of *Who's Who* for that year did not even list him.[10] His chance to impose his leadership on the whole of Western Germany came with the establishment by the Western allies of a Parliamentary Council to create a federal constitution for all three Western Zones. Adenauer was elected President of this body—largely because of his age and experience. It seems that a number of Social Democrats were quite happy to have an 'awkward old niggler' like Adenauer kicked upstairs into this post, since it was imagined that the real work of constitution-building would be done in the main sub-committee of the Council, whose chairman was a Social Democrat, Carlo Schmidt.[11] Adenauer, however, had no intention of being a figure-head.

Those who thought they had side-tracked him had overlooked the fact that Germany was still an occupied country. Not for the last time, Adenauer used his relationship with the occupying powers to strengthen his own position. He became the channel of communication between the Council and the Allied commanders, and in their eyes he was the chief spokesman of the nascent West German state. Furthermore he used his status as President of the Council to impress his leadership on the Christian Democratic Party, which was still fragmented on a zonal basis. While the Social Democrats were locked in fierce argument with the Allied authorities about the nature of the new constitution, Adenauer was busy organizing his party for the West German elections which would take place when the negotiations were over. He calmly ignored criticism of his absences from the Parliamentary Council, and toured the country rallying Christian supporters in readiness for the impending fight. The upshot of his energetic   if partisan—activities was that by the time the Allies and the Parliamentary Council had agreed to the fundamental law which was to establish a West German Federation, the Christian Democrats were better prepared for the elections than would have seemed possible a few years earlier. Furthermore, it was Adenauer who controlled the electoral machine.

It was not only in the field of organization that he made his presence felt. Adenauer realized that the most pressing matters which concerned the German electorate in 1949 were bread-and-butter issues such as unemployment—aggravated by masses of refugees from the East—food shortages and an appalling lack of living accommodation. The Social Democratic answer to these problems lay in nationalization and state planning, a policy which clearly worried many Germans, but which could at least make an appeal to those who felt themselves to be under-privileged and unfairly treated Adenauer saw that the C.D.U. must have an effective answer to this Socialist programme. He found it in Bavaria in the ample shape of Professor Ludwig Erhard. Until 1949, Erhard had avoided joining the Christian Party, largely because he did not find its Bavarian version to his taste. He had produced a scheme for a so-called 'social market economy' which would give the maximum elbow-room to private enterprise whilst maintaining the right of government interference in the public interest. In February 1949, Adenauer persuaded his somewhat reluctant colleagues to adopt the 'social market economy' policy as their own. It became a major domestic political issue. The Social Democrats were contemptuous. Erhard's programme was furiously attacked by Schumacher as 'the fat propaganda balloon of private

185

enterprise filled with putrid gases of decaying Liberalism'.[12] These putrid gases proved powerful enough to lift the C.D.U. balloon very successfully in the first West German elections, held on 14 August 1949. The combined C.D.U./C.S.U. vote was 7·36 million as against 6·93 million for Schumacher's party. It had been a close-run thing, but Adenauer had won.

Nevertheless, there were plenty of shoals ahead. Adenauer himself was still not recognized as his party's candidate for Chancellor. The C.D.U. could not rule without coalition partners, and there were many who thought that the country's weak position required a national government, in which both the C.D.U. and the Social Democrats should play a part. It was one of Adenauer's most significant contributions to the stability of the Federal Republic that he rejected this demand. He insisted that—since the main conflict in the elections had been between the two concepts of economic policy advocated by the C.D.U. and the S.P.D.—the two leading parties must oppose one another in the *Bundestag*. He therefore persuaded his colleagues to seek association with the liberal Free Democratic Party (F.D.P.), and other small parties of the Right. By taking this step, Adenauer ensured that opposition to the Federal government was represented by a large, prestigious party which was entirely committed to upholding the democratic constitution established under the Basic Law. At the same time he associated most of the conservative forces in Germany with the government of the new Republic. The situation was thus very different from that which had pertained in Germany after 1919, when the coalition parties in the Weimar Republic had faced right-wing opposition fundamentally opposed to the Republican system itself.

On 20 September 1949, Adenauer formed his first government. As Chancellor, his most pressing task was to consolidate his relatively good relations with the Western occupying powers and to impose his own conception of German development on them and on his own followers. He was, paradoxically enough, aided by the fact that, under the Occupation Statute, which governed the Republic's relations with its occupiers, the Germans were not allowed to run their own foreign policy. There was no Foreign Minister in the Bonn cabinet. This meant that Adenauer could shape foreign policy in his negotiations with the Allied Control Commissioners whilst pointing out to his parliamentary critics that such matters were beyond their competence as the result of Allied restrictions imposed upon Germany.

Adenauer also possessed considerable advantages over his predecessors in the 1920s who had constantly tried to renegotiate the terms of the Versailles Treaty. In 1949, the facts of total defeat and occupation had left the Germans with fewer illusions about their position than had been the case in 1919. The threat of Soviet domination was far more real and frightening to them. On the other hand the prosperity of Allied countries, as well as of Germany, depended on the good will and material aid of the United States. This aid was forthcoming, but only at a political price. Part of that price was a willingness on the part of Britain and France to accept a rehabilitated Germany into the Allied camp.

Adenauer was well fitted to exploit this situation. Whilst declaring with great unction that reunification was his ultimate goal, the Chancellor set about creating a new Germany, which should form an independent sovereign state in Western Europe. His easy relations with Allied officials did not imply any softness towards them in negotiations. He realized that, precisely because West Germany was becoming essential to Western security, she could exert a good deal of pressure on her occupiers. This pressure could only be applied effectively, however, if the Germans showed that they had something to offer to the West, and that they were no longer to be feared as potential aggressors. One of Adenauer's earliest—and most fiercely criticized—diplomatic moves as Chancellor was to accept German membership of the International Ruhr Authority, which would administer Germany's most important industrial complex. He was accused of surrendering German rights by doing this. In fact he gained for Germany a voice in policies which affected the whole of Europe, and was also able to prevent the threatened dismantling of much industrial equipment in the Ruhr area.

During the next three years, there followed a series of hard, if civilly conducted, wrangles between Adenauer and the Allied High Commissioners over the future of the Federal Republic. In the early days of these discussions the Chancellor would be summoned from Bonn up a steep and wooded hill to the eyrie-like fastness of the *Petersberg*, a palatial hotel which had been taken over by the High Commissioners as their headquarters.[13]

There, Adenauer struggled to put an end to Allied dismantling policies and to eliminate Germany's inferior status as an occupied country. His most inflexible opponent was—not surprisingly—the French High Commissioner, M. François-Poncet. The rate of progress was not always rapid, but bit by bit Adenauer gained ground. On 6 March 1951, the Occupation Statute was revised so that the Federal Republic could control its own foreign policy. Domestically this made little difference; as far as the Germans were concerned, Adenauer went on shaping their foreign policy for them. No separate minister for foreign affairs was appointed until 1955, when the loyal and pliable Heinrich von Brentano was given the post. Nevertheless, it was a step towards German rehabilitation; others followed. In April 1951, Adenauer went to Paris to sign the Treaty committing Germany to the Schuman plan for European co-operation over coal and steel. The following month the Federal Republic joined the Council of Europe, and in May 1952, agreements were signed which envisaged the end of Germany's subordinate position as an occupied power and enrolled her in the ill-conceived European Defence Community. When the latter proved abortive in 1954, Germany became instead a member of NATO, and later of the Western European Union. By this time the Federal Republic was regarded by many Americans—and in particular by Secretary of State, John Foster Dulles—as a 'model child' (*Musterkind*) among their European Allies.

On 5 May 1955, Adenauer had his diplomatic reward for this determined adhesion to the Western camp. German sovereignty was fully restored to the Federal Republic. Yet his policies had certainly not gone uncriticized. The Social Democrats accused him of sacrificing German unity, and there was much apparent truth in their arguments. The Soviet Union could not be expected to accept a unified Germany aligned to Britain and America. The logical outcome of Adenauer's policy was the permanent loss of the Soviet occupation Zone—since 1949 described as the German Democratic Republic—and the territories east of the Oder-Neisse boundary.

In fact it is doubtful whether any more favourable arrangement could have been secured for the Germans. Certainly their situation was vastly superior to that envisaged for them during the war by Allied planners, who had talked of German dismemberment and stressed the need to reduce Germany's industrial capacity. It is true that various schemes were bruited abroad for the unification of a neutralized Germany, but these were totally impracticable and would only have served to retard the restoration of sovereignty to the Western parts of the country. It was absurd to imagine that such a large and potentially powerful European state could expect to be left in a vacuum like Austria or Finland. Furthermore, the removal of Germany from NATO would have undermined confidence in the future of Western Europe and might thus have had enormous economic as well as political consequences. One should not forget that in 1949 the prospects for European security and economic growth looked far from attractive. It was only during the following decade that many objectively well-founded fears for the future were dispelled.

Indeed, the 1950s were years of constructive endeavour and burgeoning optimism in the Western hemisphere; it was a decade which we now look back on with nostalgia as a brief respite in a troubled century. Numerous historical, economic and social factors contributed to this, but the part played by political wisdom should not be overlooked, and Konrad Adenauer deserved his share of the credit for enlarging human happiness.

He certainly received full credit from the Germans. Adenauer's rise in popularity was meteoric. In November 1951, one public opinion poll found that in answer to the question, 'Who do you think is currently the most competent German politician?' only 19 per cent chose Adenauer with 45 per cent 'don't knows'. Two years later, 62 per cent chose Adenauer.[14] In the field of foreign policy, the dangerous experiments suggested by his Social Democratic critics did not recommend themselves to a public which lived too close to the Iron Curtain to want to risk sampling the unpalatable delights of a 'people's democracy'. Rearmament was naturally unpopular, but in the last resort the security afforded by NATO outweighed all other factors. By 1959 the Social Democrats themselves came to recognize this in their new and carefully moderate Godesberg Programme which jettisoned both the nationalistic and the socially revolutionary elements in their party's platform.

On a personal level, Adenauer's success in negotiating with the Allies established his authority in the eyes of most Germans. He became *Der Alte* whose judgement had to be respected and in whose capable hands the fate of Germany could be allowed to rest unchallenged. Even more important from the point of view of Adenauer's domestic position was the development of the German economy. Marshall Aid and a plentiful supply of skilled—or at least highly adaptable—labour, made possible the so-called 'economic miracle' which was the central feature of post-war German life. Nevertheless, it also owed a great deal to the pragmatic policies of restrained laissez-faire contained in Professor Ludwig Erhard's 'social market economy'. After the 1953 election, Adenauer's Party enjoyed an absolute majority in the German *Bundestag*. Even Hitler had never been able to obtain such a vote of confidence from the Germans in an open election.

Although Adenauer himself did not interfere very much in economic affairs—being caught up in the rarified atmosphere of international relations—his influence was exercised decisively against dogmatic and inflexible policies. Early in 1951, for example, he acted to avert a threatened coal strike by coming to an arrangement with the leader of the German trades union organization, the D.G.B. (*Deutscher Gerwerkschaftsbund*), according to which the right of *Mitbestimmung*, or co-partnership, should be extended to workers in the iron and coal industries. This arrangement was bitterly unpopular with Adenauer's coalition partners, the Free Democrats and the German Party, whose support was partly drawn from industrial interests. Nevertheless, the co-partnership law was carried through the Federal Parliament with the combined votes of the C.D.U. and the Social Democrats. It marked a blow against unlimited capitalist authority in industry, but in practice it also helped to undermine ideological assaults on capitalism from the Left. Co-partnership worked in practice as an aid to good management, and the stake given to the trades unions in industrial efficiency reduced their desire for state ownership. 'Socialization' had been an element in even the Christian Democratic Party's policies after the war; now it was quietly buried, and by the end of the decade the Social Democrats, too, had turned their backs on it. Adenauer's government had chosen the middle way, and it had worked. A nation supposedly renowned for its attachment to dogmas and extreme solutions had shown real genius for compromise. It was a demonstration of the way shrewd political leadership can help create an environment in which constructive forces can operate effectively. The contrast with the inter-war era was very marked.

It should not be imagined, however, that Adenauer's regime was one of unfailing paternal benevolence. It had unsavoury characteristics which tended to become more noticeable as time went on. Adenauer had never been a man to show much consideration to those who opposed his will, especially if they were to be found in the ranks of his own colleagues. The West German constitution had been deliberately framed to give the executive more stability vis-à-vis Parliament than had been the case with the Wiemar Republic. Adenauer's style of government enabled him to establish the authority of the Federal Chancellor even more firmly than had at first been envisaged. Although by no means monologues, his cabinet meetings were not usually the scene of long-winded arguments on matters of principle, nor did he encourage the taking of votes in them. An early attempt by President Heuss to participate in cabinet was repulsed, and the political influence of the President never approached that exercised by Friedrich Ebert or Paul von Hindenburg during the Weimar era.

The Federal Chancellor's Office, presided over from 1953 by the industrious, if controversial, figure of Dr Hans Globke, became a powerful administrative organ which strengthened Adenauer's hand vis-à-vis possible opposition from subordinate ministers. The intelligence services, too, reported directly to the Chancellor, who apparently did not shrink from investigating the private lives of his own colleagues and discreetly hinting that failure to comply with his wishes might lead to embarrassing disclosures. Indeed, Adenauer demanded complete loyalty from his ministers. He insisted on being kept informed about all departmental affairs, even if he remained aloof from them in practice. This determination to maintain control of policy was most marked in the field of foreign relations, where the unhappy Herr von Brentano—whose loyalty to Adenauer was beyond question—received several reprimands, and was finally forced to resign amidst an atmosphere of intrigue and ill-will. Adenauer never hesitated to dispense with those who were no longer useful to him, and in such cases his methods were rarely marked by sensitivity to the feelings of others. A minister might discover his loss of office from the newspapers, or even the doorman at his own ministry.[15]

So far as more conventional opposition was concerned, Adenauer was none too fastidious about his methods of repelling it. The old Bismarckian refrain, that opposition to the government weakened Germany's international position, was often to be heard emanating from the *Umgebung* of the Chancellor. He was quite ready to use smear tactics when it suited him; in the 1953 *Bundestag* elections his campaign included accusations—later proved false —that two Social Democratic politicians were involved in treason with the East Germans, and in the 1957 elections he launched an extraordinary propaganda onslaught against the S.P.D. leader, Erich Ollenhauer, suggesting that his party would pave the way for the Soviet domination of Germany. By the same token, Adenauer never took kindly to criticism from the press, although he was adept at utilizing journalists for his own purposes. The press developed into one of the most vigorous elements in post-war German political life, and Adenauer's relations with it were never entirely smooth. His political style irritated journalists because, when faced with serious criticism, he would often prefer a joke or a gratuitous insult to a closely-reasoned reply. 'Adenauer,' wrote one of his bitterest critics, 'was neither willing nor able to argue the advantages and drawbacks of a given policy in debate. Instead he smothered his audience in Druidic incantations and exhorted it to have patience and faith in the Federal Government . . .'[16] Certainly Adenauer was better at the arts of persuasion when practised in private; his performances on the electoral platform were not always edifying.

The most notorious example of high-handedness towards the press in the history of the Federal Republic occurred in October 1962, when the editor and a number of journalists on the *Spiegel* news magazine were arrested and accused of violating national security by publishing military secrets. The action against the *Spiegel* was accompanied by nocturnal raids on staff and editorial offices, and the dubious use of diplomatic pressure to obtain the arrest of the chief accused, who happened to be on holiday in Spain. Matters were made worse by the fact that the affair involved the controversial figure of Franz-Josef Strauss, the West German Defence Minister. He had been the target of a campaign by the *Spiegel* accusing him of arrogant misuse of ministerial powers. Strauss was highly regarded by Adenauer, and it appeared

190

January, 1956. Adenauer inspects West Germany's new army

not unlikely that his actions had enjoyed at least the tacit consent of the Chancellor.

For many Germans—especially the young—the whole affair seemed to reflect some of the most sinister aspects of their country's recent history. A wave of indignation swept the country and a ministerial crisis ensued. After a good deal of prodding from below, the leadership of the Free Democratic (Liberal) Party, at that time in coalition with Adenauer's C.D.U., refused to continue in office without at least obtaining the resignation of Herr Strauss. Indeed, at one stage Adenauer's own survival seemed very much in the balance. *Der Alte's* iron nerve—together with the indecision and moral cowardice of his opponents—carried him through, but not without severely denting his reputation. Although he had not himself initiated the *Spiegel* action he had evidently condoned it and afterwards sought to brazen it out by a disgraceful speech in the *Bundestag* accusing the *Spiegel* of committing treason for money.

As one historian of the incident remarked, 'in assessing the style of the Bonn political system, the Chancellor's insensitivity to the policy aspects of the *Spiegel* investigation is at least equal in importance to the poor judgement of one of his ministers'. [17] Adenauer's moral stature had crumbled perceptibly as the result of the affair; accusations by his critics that he was a 'democratic dictator' rather than a constitutional Chancellor seemed to be confirmed. [18] Furthermore, the resignation of Strauss showed that Adenauer

was no longer the invincible figure he had seemed in the previous decade. From then on his days in office were obviously numbered.

Indeed, in common with many other historical figures, Adenauer had begun to lose his political momentum at the time when his power seemed most assured. By 1958 his prestige was enormous. He had won another convincing victory in the 1957 *Bundestag* elections. His stature as a statesman was recognized at home and abroad. When Germans were asked in October 1958 which great man in their history had done most for his Fatherland, Adenauer was chosen—ahead even of Bismarck and well clear of Hitler in third place.[19] Germany's industrial expansion continued apace, and by the end of the decade Germany's 'economic miracle' was arousing the admiration of the world. A new generation of Germans was growing up unscarred by the memory of the Third Reich and secure in its enjoyment of material prosperity.

Yet in the field of international relations—a preserve Adenauer regarded as his own—new difficulties were appearing. No sooner had the Chancellor managed to integrate Western Germany into N A T O and persuade his countrymen to recruit an unpopular new army, than his Anglo-Saxon allies began to lose their enthusiasm for large-scale conventional forces. At the Four-Power Geneva Conference in 1955, Anthony Eden produced a scheme for arms inspection and force reductions in Central Europe. The following year the Chancellor was even more shaken when the Americans themselves began discussing the so-called Radford plan to slim down the numbers of Western conventional forces and to rely more heavily on atomic weapons. Although he still trusted Mr Dulles, Adenauer was suspicious of proposals—championed in public by men such as George F. Kennan and Hugh Gaitskell—to thaw out the atmosphere of Cold War which existed between the Soviet Union and the West. He reacted by harping on the permanent threat from Russia and Germany's right to reunification, themes which became less and less fashionable as time went on.

There is, indeed, some doubt about the extent to which Adenauer took the issue of reunification seriously. It is possible that he may have come to believe his own rhetoric about it, but it is difficult to imagine that he shared Dulles's naive conception of a Soviet Russia so weak and perplexed after Stalin's death that she would surrender the German Democratic Republic without some massive counter-concession.[20] Adenauer claims in his memoirs that he did not think the Russians could afford to leave Eastern Germany, and there is little reason to doubt the truth of this remark.[21] His own attempt to negotiate face-to-face with the Russians, when he visited Moscow in September 1955, had done nothing to improve his estimate of Soviet policy. After several days of very hard bargaining, he had achieved nothing except the return of some ten thousand German prisoners of war. In return, the Russians were able to establish diplomatic relations with Bonn.

In general, Adenauer's policy seems to have reflected a desire to prevent the old 'Potsdam coalition' of victor powers re-establishing itself at the expense of Germany, and a rather more realistic concern over the impact of East-West conciliation on the domestic politics of the Federal Republic.

His fear was that Allied concessions to Russia would reveal to the German people that their integration into Western Europe implied the continuing division of Germany. This was a fact which Adenauer himself had accepted at a very early stage, but which German public opinion was not yet ready to digest. At the time, many Western—particularly British—observers were impatient with Adenauer's refusal to contemplate recognition of the German Democratic Republic or the Oder-Neisse frontier with Poland. The fact that his position became less and less defensible in logic and his arguments more and more oracular did nothing to mollify his critics. Yet rational justifications for his policy could be found, even if they were difficult to articulate publicly. The first was that, however obvious the division of Germany had become, and however much Adenauer's own policies had contributed to it, an open admission of that situation would have precipitated a serious political crisis in Germany. In particular it would have split those essentially conservative forces which the C.D.U. had succeeded in welding together so laboriously since 1945. At least another decade of prosperity and social consolidation was needed in the Federal Republic before recognition of the status quo could be contemplated without risking serious domestic repercussion. Although Adenauer was a party politician, his policy did not just benefit the Christian Democrats, since Germany's Western neighbours would have been the chief targets of recrimination if a nationalist uproar had burst forth in Bonn.

By nature a cautious man, Adenauer began to appear as the chief dog-in-the-manger so far as East-West *détente* was concerned. His suspicious attitude grew more marked as the centre of interest shifted from disarmament to the status of Berlin, where German interests were most obviously threatened, and over which the British, at least, seemed not disinclined to make concessions. Mr Macmillan's strenuous, and ultimately successful, efforts to obtain an atomic test-ban treaty were another straw in the wind to Adenauer, who seems to have regarded it as a sign of Soviet–Anglo-Saxon rapprochement. Many of his fears were certainly imaginary; in any event the Potsdam coalition did not reappear. Yet his anxiety over German security remained, and was strengthened by the death of Dulles in 1959. Adenauer had always mistrusted the British; after 1960, he reacted cautiously to the new Democratic administration under John F. Kennedy, which took over in the United States.

It was in this situation that there began a curious and largely infelicitous relationship with the new ruler of France, Charles de Gaulle. Adenauer had been concerned from the very outset of his Chancellorship to improve feelings between Germany and France. This was a diplomatic principle of long standing for a Rhinelander like himself. Furthermore, good Franco-German relations were essential if Adenauer was to achieve the objective which had been implicit in all his dealings with the occupying powers—the integration of Germany into a closely-knit Western European community. It was in pursuit of this objective that he had welcomed the Schuman Plan and joined the abortive European Defence Community. Yet thereafter, the European cause did not flourish in the way the Chancellor had expected. Further progress towards political integration did not occur. Once again, the culprits seemed to be in London, where successive British governments had refused to participate in either the Schuman Plan or the European Economic Community. Furthermore, British politicians did not make very much effort to cultivate close ties with the Federal Republic, but preferred to stress their 'special relationship' with the United States. On the other hand, de Gaulle's new Fifth French Republic represented both a danger and an opportunity for Adenauer. The danger lay in resurgent French nationalism, which de Gaulle seemed to personify and which might in turn arouse a nationalist reaction among the Germans. Adenauer had always feared that the old enmities of the nineteen twenties and thirties could reappear in Germany if the progress of European integration was thwarted.[22] The opportunity was to associate Germany with a historic figure whose prestige might help to raise the stock of Western Europe at a time when world politics were apparently dominated by the super-powers of the United States and the Soviet Union. Hence it came about that Adenauer's last years as Chancellor were marked by an ostentatious *rapprochement* with Gaullist France. This began with the visit to Colombey-des-deux-Églises in September 1958, continued with a series of informal conversations and state visits, and culminated in the signing of the Franco-German Treaty of 22 January 1963. Adenauer seems to have hoped that this would form the basis for an effective association of West European continental states, especially in the fields of defence and foreign policy. Certainly it was the failure of discussions about proposals for such a union which led de Gaulle and Adenauer to pledge their troth in what the latter insisted on describing as an historic treaty.[23] This obsession with continental security was a reflection of Adenauer's disillusionment with the United States, whose government he feared to be too fickle in purpose to defend Europe effectively, and his distrust of Britain as an American client. Indeed when, in 1962, the British themselves changed their tune about the Common Market and decided to apply for membership, Adenauer did nothing to ease their passage.[24]

There was certainly some merit in the demonstrative burying of hatchets between France and Germany. The ceremonial visits and public rhetoric which accompanied this reconciliation also had a domestic political value which was not lost on either the French President or the German Chancellor. But all in all, it was a period of frustration in which Adenauer's basic designs could not be said to have prospered. The fact was that de Gaulle was less a good European than a nationalistic Frenchman. His objectives did not admit any genuine European integration. His policies towards NATO were positively mischievous if European security really was in danger, and he showed an embarrassing lack of concern for German sensibilities about such matters as the Oder-Neisse frontier. German 'Gaullism' was always a contradiction in terms: it really reflected attempts by the less scrupulous elements in German politics to play upon national resentments for domestic purposes. Adenauer's motives were undoubtedly more defensible than this, but the Franco-German Treaty can hardly be regarded as the crowning glory of his Chancellorship. In any case, by the time it was signed, Adenauer's career had nearly reached its end. The *Spiegel* crisis and its aftermath had made it clear that his tenacious grip on power was at last being loosened.

Most of his party followers felt that Ludwig Erhard, the symbol of German prosperity, would achieve more in a new election campaign, and their calculations proved correct. Adenauer did not, however, bow out gracefully. He openly despised Erhard and did everything he could to obstruct his being elected Chancellor. It was not an edifying spectacle, especially since Adenauer, like Bismarck before him, had done nothing to prepare any well-qualified successor, and was therefore at least partly responsible for the resulting confusion and despondency in the ranks of the C.D.U. Progressively more isolated in his own party, and under pressure from his Free Democratic coalition partners, Adenauer was finally forced into retirement. His period in office ended on 15 October 1963. He had outstayed his welcome, but he left his country in a far better shape than had seemed feasible in 1949.

After his retirement as Chancellor, Adenauer still retained his post as Chairman of the C.D.U., and occasionally made carping comments on the work of his successor, Ludwig Erhard. Nevertheless, his political influence was no longer significant. He devoted himself to writing his memoirs, which eventually filled four monumental volumes of remarkable opacity.[25]

He died at home amongst his family on 19 April 1967. His state funeral was attended by leaders from all over the Western world, including President Johnson of the U.S.A., who had not been well enough to accord a similar honour to Winston Churchill, two years earlier. It symbolized the extent to which Adenauer had helped rehabilitate Germany in the eyes of her Western neighbours, and testified to the unique position which he had carved out for himself in the history of twentieth-century Europe.

To sum up, Adenauer presents us with an instructive example of how little attention should be paid to the wide-spread journalistic obsession with the advantages of youth in politics 'Gerontocracy' is a meaningless jargon word: what counts is not the date on a statesman's birth certificate, but the freshness of his mind. Adenauer brought a new realism to German politics an attitude far removed from the ill-fated *realpolitik* of his predecessors. In many ways he was an unattractive figure, but he responded to the needs of his age, and for this he deserves to be remembered.

[1] To take two examples: Adenauer was supposed to have asked one of his great-grandchildren what he wanted to be when he grew up. The child answered that he would like to be Federal Chancellor. 'But that is impossible,' came the reply, 'I already have that job.' Another cabaret quip was the claim that the initials of Adenauer's party —the C.D.U. —stood for *'Conrad Der Unsterbliche'* (Conrad the Immortal).

[2] The Rhineland provinces had been added to Prussia only after the defeat of Napoleon in 1815. Cologne itself had been downgraded from a cultural and commercial centre to a frontier garrison town. Its ancient university—closed by the French in 1798—had not been reopened by the Prussian authorities.

[3] Terence Prittie, *Adenauer, A Study in Fortitude* (London, 1972) p. 109.

[4] The other predominantly working-class party, the Communists, would have opposed the Bill, but their Reichstag members were under arrest or banishment.

[5] For the somewhat unhappy role played by both the Centre Party and the Vatican in 1933, see: Guenter Lewy, *The Catholic Church and Nazi Germany* (London, 1964), Chapters 1-3; Heinrich Bruening, *Memoiren, 1918-1934* (Stuttgart, 1970) pp. 639-674; and K.O. von Aretin, 'Prälat Kaas, Franz von Papen und das Reichskonkordat von 1933', in *Vierteljahrshefte für Zeitgeschichte* (July, 1966).

[6] For a sympathetic but by no means uncritical picture of Schumacher, see Lewis J. Edinger, *Kurt Schumacher, A Study in Personality and Political Behaviour* (London, 1965).

[7] A moving account of one young German intellectual's introduction to politics during this period is given by the late Waldemar Besson in his article:*'Wie ich mich geändert habe'* in *Vierteljahreshefte für Zeitgeschichte*, vol. 19, nr. 4 (October, 1971) pp. 398-403.

[8] Though he did accept nationalization of the coal industry.

[9] Prussia was formally abolished by order of the occupying powers on 25 February 1947.

[10] R. Morsey, *'Der politische Aufstieg Konrad Adenauers* 1945-1949' in *Adenauer Studien*, vol. I. Ed. R. Morsey and K. Repgen (Mainz, 1971) p. 30.

[11] R. Morsey, *Adenauer Studien*, vol. I, p. 32.

[12] Paul Weymar, *Konrad Adenauer. The Authorized Biography* (London, 1957) p. 250.

[13] In September 1938 it had housed Mr Neville Chamberlain's delegation to see Hitler at Bod Godesberg. Later it was to be put at the disposal of Queen Elizabeth II on her visit to the German Federal Republic in May 1965.

[14] E. P. Neumann and E. Noelle, *Umfragen über Adenauer Ein Porträt in Zahlen* (Allensbach and Bonn, 1961) pp. 131 and 136.

[15] R. Morsey, *Bruening und Adenauer. Zwei deutsche Staatsmaenner* (Duesseldorf, 1972) p. 34.

[16] Rudolf Augstein, *Konrad Adenauer* (London, 1964) pp. 87-8.

[17] R. F. Bunn, *German Politics and the Spiegel Affair* (Baton Rouge, 1968) p. 184.

[18] To cite the title of the critical biography of Adenauer by Charles Wighton (London, 1963).

[19] Neumann and Noelle, *Umfragen ueber Adenauer*, p. 153.

[20] On 15 August 1955, Dulles wrote to Adenauer commenting on the achievements of the Four-Power Geneva Conference. He claimed that the policy pursued by the Russians at the conference was born out of weakness, that the reunification of Germany was 'in the air' and that the Russians needed a breathing space for which they might be willing 'within a few years' to pay the price of reunification. How far this reflected Dulles's true feelings and how far it was designed to mollify Adenauer is not capable of proof; Adenauer himself was far from sanguine about the prospect. See Konrad Adenauer, *Erinnerungen, 1953-1955* (Stuttgart, 1966) pp. 483-4.

[21] Ibid., pp. 483-4.

[22] He had held forth about this with particular passion to the Prime Ministers of Belgium and Luxembourg, M. Paul-Henri Spaak and M. Joseph Bech on the occasion of the London Conference in September 1954. See Rudolf Augstein, *Konrad Adenauer* (London, 1965) p. 32.

[23] Konrad Adenauer, *Erinnerungen, 1959-63 fragmente* (Stuttgart, 1968) p. 212.

[24] Ibid., pp. 177-8.

[25] In fairness it should be remarked that the fourth volume consists only of fragments assembled after his death.

Stresemann
by Agnes Headlam-Morley

AGNES HEADLAM-MORLEY (b. 1902) is the daughter of that distinguished diplomatic historian Sir James Headlam-Morley, C.B., who was Historical Adviser to the Foreign Office for many years. After attending Wimbledon High School and Somerville College, Oxford, Professor Headlam-Morley began an academic career of distinction on her appointment as Fellow and Tutor of St Hugh's College, Oxford in 1932. She contemplated abandoning this career for politics in 1936 when she was adopted as prospective Conservative candidate for the Barnard Castle Division of Durham. Wiser counsels prevailed however and Professor Headlam-Morley became recognized as one of the most popular and accomplished teachers in the field of European history. In 1948 she was appointed Montagu Burton Professor of International Relations at Oxford, a chair which she retained until her retirement in 1970.

Gustav Stresemann

10 May 1878	Born. Educated at Andreas Gymnasium in Berlin and at Berlin and Leipzig universities.
1900	Obtained doctorate for thesis on Berlin's beer industry. Joined industrial association in Saxony.
1907	Elected to German Reichstag as representative of National Liberal party, which had close links with industry.
1912	Election. Stresemann lost seat but returned to Reichstag through by-election in 1914.
1914	Outbreak of First World War. Stresemann supported war effort and annexationist war aims. At same time he became dissatisfied with governmental system and favoured giving more authority to Reichstag.
1917	Fall of Bethmann-Hollweg, which Stresemann helped to bring about. Stresemann became National Liberal leader in Reichstag.
Nov. 1918	German defeat and revolution. Stresemann remained loyal to monarchy. He refused to join new Democratic party which appealed to left-wing liberals, and he founded German People's party (D.V.P.).
1919	Strongly opposed acceptance of Versailles peace treaty, and his party voted against constitution of Weimar Republic.
March 1920	Kapp Putsch: unsuccessful attempt by disgruntled military units and nationalist extremists to overthrow republic. Stresemann adopted ambiguous attitude to the *putsch*.
June 1920	Reichstag elections brought gains for D.V.P.
May 1921	London Ultimatum to make Germany accept Allied schedule for for reparation payments.
July 1922	Supported law to protect republic passed after Foreign Minister, Rathenau, was assassinated.

Previous page: 'the Good German'— photographed in Italy

Jan. 1923	French occupied Ruhr after German default on reparations payments. Germans adopted passive resistance. Their currency was destroyed by inflation and social chaos threatened
Aug. 1923	Became Chancellor in 'Great Coalition' which included Social Democrats. He abandoned passive resistance and paved way for stabilization of German mark. But conflict with Social Democrats weakened his position.
29 Oct. 1923	Socialist/Communist government was suppressed in Saxony.
23 Nov. 1923	Resigned.
Nov. 1923–Oct. 1929	Was Foreign Minister in a series of coalition governments.
Aug. 1924	Dawes Plan accepted at conference in London, settling immediate problem of reparations payments.
25 Jan. 1925	German note to London suggesting western security pact.
9 Feb. 1925	German formal proposal to France for western security pact.
27 April 1925	Hindenburg elected President.
5 Oct. 1925	Security pact proposals resulted in Locarno treaties—opposed by General von Seekt, head of Reichswehr.
24 April 1926	German-Soviet non-aggression pact. Stresemann did not want gulf between U.S.S.R. and rest of Europe.
8 Sept. 1926	Germany elected to League of Nations with seat in League council.
1926	Met French Foreign Minister Briand at Thoiry and discussed plans for Rhineland evacuation and return of the Saar to Germany. No immediate result.
Dec. 1926	Awarded Nobel Peace Prize.
Jan. 1927	Allied Control Commission withdrawn from Germany.
Aug. 1928	Germany signed Briand-Kellog pact in Paris—a comprehensive agreement between the great powers renouncing war as an instrument of policy.
June 1929	Young Plan drawn up to settle future reparations payments.
Aug. 1929	Hague conference. Young Plan accepted by Germany's creditors and French agreed to evacuate Rhineland in 1930. Schacht, the German expert on the Young committee, resigned on grounds that Germany had won only meagre concessions.
11 Sept. 1929	Stresemann's last speech at League of Nations in Geneva, in which he pressed his hopes for European economic union.
3 Oct. 1929	Died.

Gustav Stresemann was born in Berlin on 10 September 1878. He was the youngest son of Ernst Stresemann who ran a small retail business in bottled beer. Later he did well in White Beer, a Berlin speciality which, according to Stresemann, was vastly superior to any other brand. His mother, to whom he remained devoted, did all she could to encourage 'the dreamer' to get on with his work and his reading. They lived in a cold, grey house in a north-eastern suburb. It was a happy home.

Gustav attended the Andreas Gymnasium. He did excellent work in history and literature. As was not uncommon among young Germans he made a hero of Napoleon. He did not regret this later in life—only the mean spirited would deny greatness in their enemies—but his real and abiding love was for Goethe and all his works. In mathematics he was a hopeless non-starter. At examinations he usually handed in a blank paper. Once the master rejoiced to see him busily writing away—but there were no sums. He had been testing his memory by putting down as many lines of Goethe as he could in the time.

At the University of Berlin and afterwards at Leipzig he studied political economy. Mathematical ability it seems was not required. He joined a liberal *Burschenschaft*. He and his companions had a harmless brush with the police when, on the fiftieth anniversary of 1848, they demonstrated with black, red and gold banners in commemoration of those who died in the revolution. Family loyalty was strong. He wrote his doctoral thesis on the retail trade in bottled beer.

His appearance was deceptive. He looked robust—almost like a caricature of a German, square, thick-set, with receding fair hair and rather piercing pale blue eyes. In fact his health was always precarious. He was unfit for military service. As time went on he suffered to an increasing extent from recurring physical illness, but he never lost his capacity for mental concentration. He had a powerful intellect combined with a subtle sensitive disposition. A lover of art, especially music and poetry, he was realistic in his assessment of political possibilities. He had been brought up a Lutheran. In his last year at school he had studied the critical work of Harnack. In spite of his interest in modernism and his preoccupation with the things of this world he never rejected the simple piety of the Lutheran Church.

Stresemann entered the Reichstag in 1907 as a National Liberal under the leadership of Basserman, whom he succeeded in 1917. The German liberals had little in common with what Stresemann call the 'Manchestertum' of English individualists and free traders. The party had been forged in the struggle for unification, the establishment of a strong central government.

When war came he supported the *Burgfrieden* or party truce, and welcomed the loyal response of the Social Democrats. He never doubted the rightness of the German cause and joined in the demand for annexations which would include Belgium, the French iron mining districts of Longwy and Briey, and large areas in Poland and the Baltic provinces. He had been much influenced by Friedrich Naumann's ideas of *Mitteleuropa*. The greater Germany, an economically self-supporting industrial and agricultural complex, would attract the allegiance of neighbouring states—including France. The victory of Germany would give peace to the world. He gave full support to the unlimited submarine war and developed a short-lived admiration for Ludendorff.

Stresemann differed from the Nationalists and from the right wing of his own party in urging the need for constitutional reform even in time of war. The Chancellor and the Secretaries of State should be made responsible to the Reichstag. The government would be strengthened not weakened if leaders of the great political parties were called to office. Universal suffrage should be introduced in Prussia as in the Reich. The abolition of the weighted franchise (*Dreiklassenwahlrecht*) which gave an artificial majority in the Landtag to big business and landowning interests, was no longer a Prussian but a German issue. In this he agreed with the Chancellor, Herr von Bethmann-Hollweg. None the less he allowed himself to be entangled in the manoeuvres of Erzberger and the High Command which led to the fall of Bethmann-Hollweg in the summer of 1917. It was a clash of temperament and personality. 'Bethmann' he said, 'was a born pessimist. By his whole attitude and manner of speaking he transferred unto others his own depression, doubts and hesitations.' No country could win a war with such a man to lead it.

The defeat of Germany came to Stresemann as a shattering blow. Till the end he had remained confident of victory and had dismissed as treason every murmur of defeatism. On 2 October at a meeting of party leaders an emissary of the High Command announced that the military situation made an immediate armistice necessary. Ebert, it is recounted, went white as death. Stresemann looked as if he had been struck. The next day Stresemann summoned to Berlin the constituency leaders of the National Liberal Party. He told them fair and square that the politicians had been given false information about the submarine war, it was the High Command not the Parliamentarians who had lost their nerve. He was prepared to serve with the Social Democrats under the new Chancellor, Prince Max von Baden, who formed a Cabinet responsible to the Reichstag, but Prince Max said that he needed the 'nationalist' parties in opposition.

There followed a time of strain and difficulty in which Stresemann came to accept the new Germany that had emerged from war and revolution. He opposed the signature of the Treaty of Versailles, but he did not turn to intransigence or bitterness. Never then or later did he question the loyalty and patriotism of those who thought it necessary to submit to a dictated peace. He would have preferred a constitutional monarchy but found it possible to work constructively within the framework of the Republican Weimar Constitution. He failed to achieve union with the Progressives and entered the new Reichstag as leader of the Peoples Party—it numbered only twenty-five, a depleted remnant of the old National Liberals.

The early years of the Weimar Republic were distracted by endless controversies over reparations and monetary inflation. It was a time of economic distress which in 1920 and again in 1923 led to a revolutionary situation which was a graver threat to the fabric of society than the political upheaval of 1918. The Treaty of Versailles, Stresemann held, was an infringement of the pre-armistice agreement by which Germany was bound to pay only for damage done to civilians. Now she was subject to a financial burden which vastly exceeded this amount and was quite beyond her capacity to pay. From time to time the Allies sought to enforce interim demands by the application of sanctions. The London Ultimatum in 1921 led to the occupation of Dusseldorf, Ruhrhort and Duisburg—according to the Treaty a default in reparations could be met by a prolongation, not an extension of the occupation. In January 1923 Poincaré ordered French troops to march into the Ruhr. The Belgians joined in this further breach of the Treaty which the British representative on the Reparations Commission had opposed. The whole population of the richest German industrial area immediately downed tools. The government of the Reich bore the cost of strike pay for the unemployed, since the Reich budget was running at a deficit the money was raised by printing bills of exchange.

Stresemann had not opposed previous attempts at a settlement. He threw scorn on what he called the 'policy of catastrophe'—you refuse to concede unjust demands; the Allies resort to force; the result is chaos and disaster; you survey the ruin and say 'I told you so'. But now, in common with the other party leaders he held that there could be no negotiation until the invading troops were withdrawn. He had come to realize that Poincaré's overriding purpose was political, the separation of all occupied territories, and the setting up of a buffer state under French control. In August 1923 Stresemann became Chancellor at the head of the 'Great Coalition'—from Social Democrats to People's Party. It was expected that he would unite the nation in firm resistance to French aggression.

Dr Adenauer, who was two years younger than Stresemann, was already Mayor of Cologne. He and his colleagues were summoned to Berlin to discuss conditions in the Rhineland (the Ruhr was cut off from the rest of Germany and French *poilus* stood guard at the barbed wire entanglements). Years afterwards Adenauer recalled how on a bleak autumn evening in Berlin he experienced a moment of despondency verging on despair, when there seemed no hope of bringing succour to a suffering people—in that darkest hour it came into his mind that the way to recovery must be found by reconciliation with France.

By November Stresemann realized that they were at the end of their strength. Faced with the danger of anarchy—the disintegration of the Reich—he called off the passive resistance without even the minimum concessions on which he had insisted. To the so-called patriots who had turned against their own government he appealed in the words of the poet:

> You fought in the murk and the darkness
> You struck your enemy down
> But when in the daylight you saw him plain
> It was your own dear country slain.

There was a moment of doubt about the loyalty of the Reichwehr but when General von Seekt was given executive powers he acted rapidly. The Communists were suppressed in Saxony, the Bavarian revolt collapsed. Stresemann was utterly repelled by Ludendorff's disloyalty in supporting Hitler, whom he dismissed as a rabble-rousing bogus revolutionary.

Surrender was made necessary by the complete collapse of the mark.

The printing presses were working overtime; the currency had lost its value as a medium of exchange, the consequent confusion caused a rapid fall in production. Stresemann, who had a naturally sound judgement in the choice of experts, secured the services of Luther as Minister of Finance and Schacht as Governor of the Reichsbank. A new currency, the Rentenmark, was issued on 15 November. (On that day the value of the old currency was ninety-two billion paper marks to one gold mark.) Schacht was adamant in insisting on a strict limitation of issue and stuck to this through all the difficulties of the ensuing deflationary crisis.

Stresemann's last act as Chancellor was to arrange for the return of the former Crown Prince. This led to an Allied note of protest. Stresemann answered that only the German Government could decide whether or not a German citizen could return to his country. He had met the Crown Prince on a visit abroad and had confidence in his good sense and integrity.

Those hundred days as Chancellor must, one may suppose, have left an indelible impression. During the succeeding years as Foreign Minister Stresemann pursued high aims and won great renown. But always, I think, he kept in mind the essential need: to secure the unity of the Reich and freedom from military occupation. At this time he formed a lasting friendship with Lord D'Abernon, the British Ambassador. D'Abernon had recognized his quality when he was still in opposition; when the British Government havered and hesitated he gave him unfailing moral support and it may be supposed a good deal of sound advice on currency affairs.

It was evident that the value of the new currency could not be maintained unless there were a reasonable reparations settlement and some kind of international loan. Within a year this was made possible by the fall of Poincaré, and the willingness of the Americans to give expert advice and guidance. The Dawes Plan was acceptable to the French since it was an interim arrangement and did not infringe anybody's rights under the Treaty of Versailles. The annuities were calculated in accordance with Germany's presumed capacity to pay and could be adjusted in the event of fluctuations in gold prices. The sums paid into the reparations account could be transferred across the exchange only at the discretion of the Agent General for Reparations, an impartial American expert. There was an immediate revival of confidence and the Dawes Loan was over subscribed.

It was Lord D'Abernon who suggested that the reparations agreement should be followed by a political settlement. Stresemann had always recognized that insecurity was the root cause of French intransigence. None the less he was cautious. Germany was still subject to distrust and he did not wish to expose his government to contempt and humiliation. His meeting with allied Ministers in London for the signature of the Dawes Plan had not been altogether happy—'and the tone in which they speak to us'. D'Abernon would have none of it. He pointed out that if Stresemann did nothing Great Britain would in all probability commit herself to France and Germany would be isolated. The first German note suggesting a western security pact was addressed to London on 25 January 1925. It was followed by a formal proposal to France on 9 February. The German initiative embodied Lord D'Abernon's conception of an 'iron curtain': the inviolability of the western

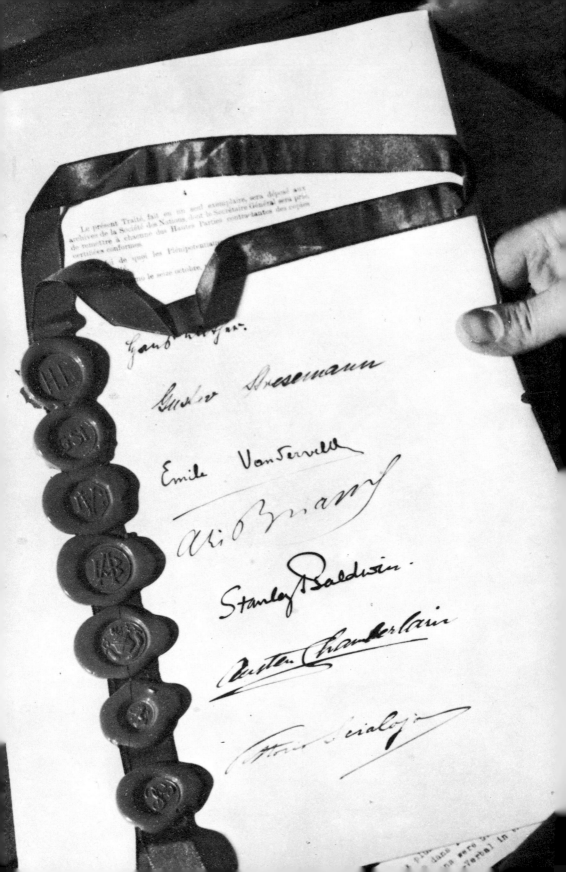

frontier of Germany and the permanent demilitarization of the Rhineland. All the states concerned were to settle differences by peaceful means.

This first step which led to the signature of the Locarno Treaties in October was followed by a period of doubt and hesitation. Strict diplomatic secrecy was preserved until the French answer was received in June. It included a demand for a guarantee of the German-Polish frontier.

Stresemann's immediate purpose had been to secure the withdrawal of enemy troops. Having embarked on the new policy his horizon widened and his determination grew. He spared no effort to convince the German people that they would be the first to gain by a firm system of security. He welcomed the Anglo-Italian guarantee of the western frontier. The French insisted that treaties should be signed at the same time with Poland and Czechoslovakia. France would give military support in the event of German aggression. This was entirely alien to his original intention but he accepted it on the understanding that Germany would not be bound to approve the eastern frontier but only to submit disputes to peaceful settlement. At the Locarno Conference Stresemann stuck to his original point that Germany could enter the League of Nations only as a great power with a permanent seat on the Council.

In overcoming opposition at home he had been greatly assisted by the withdrawal of French troops from the Ruhr and the sanctions towns in August; the evacuation of the Cologne Zone followed at the end of the year. These were the first fruits of the new policy. He came to respect Austen Chamberlain and paid tribute to his integrity, candour, and devotion to the cause of peace—though he grumbled sometimes at the schoolmasterly manner. Briand and Stresemann responded to each other with a genuine warmth of feeling. It was a stormy friendship, rich in possibilities.

To Stresemann Locarno was not an end but a beginning. He spoke not of 'fulfillment' but of 'understanding', and 'reconciliation' which should lead on to an agreed revision of the Treaty of Versailles. He hoped for a colonial mandate and for the renunciation of the War Guilt Clause which had done untold harm in alienating from the Republic not only the reactionaries but many young idealists. Union with Austria would, he thought, be inevitable in the long run. But French opposition was unrelenting and for Germany the bankrupt remnant of the Habsburg Monarchy would be a liability rather than an asset. Desiring friendship with Italy he refused to raise the issue of the South Tyrol. German policy he held should concentrate on revision of the eastern frontier, especially in regard to Danzig and the Corridor. He discussed this freely with Lord D'Abernon who was inclined to be sceptical. Later, in 1926, Herr Sthamer, the Ambassador in London, reported that Sir Montague Norman, had predicted a financial collapse in Poland, he had suggested that Germany might take part in economic reconstruction in return for treaty revision. Writing privately to the Ambassador, Stresemann expressed his gratification that influential people in England were beginning to show an understanding of the most important issue of German— perhaps of European—policy. 'The collaboration of England is a necessary condition for a peaceful solution of this problem, and for us only a peaceful solution comes into consideration.'

The Locarno Pact was a sincere attempt at international settlement. Stresemann's was the second signature

It is not I think necessary to look for any spectacular conversion or change of heart in Stresemann. As is usual when we study the lives of great men we find qualities of mind and character that are inherent, but they grow and develop with time, experience, and opportunity. It is limited and shallow people who stay the same. Stresemann was always an ardent patriot. He was generous, optimistic, resilient, he grew in insight and understanding, and in his capacity to recognize and do justice to the motives of his opponents. His opinions changed, but at each stage he was intent to convert others to his way of thinking. He hoped above all to win over the youth of Germany to his own aspirations. Addressing the members of a right wing student corps he talked to them of Stein and Hargenberg, the heroes of the wars of liberation. He told them that they must work together with other classes for the rebuilding of Germany, he condemned those who sought to denigrate the Germany of the past, the old Reich, the old army, but he also condemned those who would not serve the new Reich. He paid tribute to the soldiers and officials who had stood loyal in the hour of defeat and ended 'our task is to strive with all our powers to ensure that peace is kept in Europe and that within this area of peace Germany shall be given the opportunity to heal the wounds which the war has dealt her. All countries suffered from war, even the victors. But Germany more than any other has an interest in peace. We must strengthen our national life by furthering peaceful understanding.'

He was an accomplished parliamentary leader and remained Foreign Minister in a series of shifting Coalitions. The splitting up of parties was a grave defect in the Weimar constitutional system. He regretted the limitation of his own People's Party to the representatives of bourgeois and business interests but hoped that it might serve as a link between classes and parties on the left and on the right. He feared that Hindenburg's nomination and election as President would have an adverse effect on foreign opinion, but was fully reconciled when he found him loyal and reliable.

Stresemann was from his student days radically opposed to every form of anti-semitism. He had many Jewish friends and his wife was partly Jewish. Addressing the merchant community at Hamburg he spoke of free enterprise, free commercial activity as a condition of material prosperity. But the Germans must beware lest in the pursuit of wealth they neglect their heritage in literature, art, and philosophy. He concluded that the outstanding part played by the small number of their Jewish fellow-citizens was perhaps due to the fact that they excelled not only in business efficiency but in gifts of the spirit and intellect. The politician he held was a servant who must somehow keep things going and make it possible for the writers and artists, the actors and musicians, to pursue their calling. And yet it grieved him that Goethe, the greatest of all, had been indifferent to the struggles and aspirations of a people in search of unity and freedom. He took comfort in the thought that Goethe himself was speaking in the words of Epimides.

> Doch schäm ich mich der Ruhestunden
> Mit euch zu leiden ward Gewinn
> Und um den Schmertz den ihr empfunden
> Seid irh doch grösser als ich bin.

(Shameful are these hours of leisure; to share your sorrow were my gain; and for the grief that you have suffered; you are greater than I am.)

Some historians have held that Stresemann was playing for time, that he was party to secret plans for rearmament and intended in alliance with Russia to turn against Poland and the Western Allies.

Such indeed was the purpose of General von Seekt. A dedicated soldier and brilliant organizer, Seekt succeeded in retaining the nucleus of a general staff. The small long-service army of 100,000 men allowed under the Treaty of Versailles became a highly trained corps of potential officers and N.C.O.s. The clandestine foreign connections of the Reichwehr and former armaments firms insured up-to-date technical knowledge. Air force pilots were trained in Russia. As a would-be maker of policy Seekt has been over-rated. At the crucial Cabinet meeting in June 1925 he vehemently opposed the proposed security pact—'what we have lost we will take back'. Stresemann won the support of his colleagues—including the nationalist ministers—and in future rojected all attempts at interference by the military. Seekt still talked as though his opinion counted, but in fact it did not. His approaches to Hindenburg had no effect.

Stresemann certainly knew that something was going on between the Reichwehr and the Red Army, he probably knew that there were plans for building prototype tanks and submarines in Holland and other neutral countries. He thought it better not to interfere. My own view is that he did not think it important—not sufficiently important to risk political upheavals and recriminations. This is not as absurd as it may seem. Material rearmament in Germany was insignificant, as Hitler discovered in 1934 when he started pretty well from scratch. France and her eastern allies were fully, and it was assumed efficiently, armed. In the Stresemann papers there is a report on the manoeuvres in 1927. In the event of war Germany's position would be hopeless—*trostlos*. She could not fight even a defensive war against Poland alone.

In December 1926 the matter came into the open as a result of revelations in the *Manchester Guardian* which led to a heated debate in the Reichstag At Geneva it had been decided that the Allied Control Commission should come to an end. Stresemann now urged that there should be a general limitation of armaments under League supervision, the unilateral disarmament of Germany was unjust and unrealistic. Even so he went cautiously. He realized that to get the French to give up their military preponderance would be a long and difficult task. In 1928 Hermann Muller, the socialist leader, returned from a meeting of the League Council indignant at some bellicose utterances by Briand. Stresemann calmed him down; Briand talked like that when carried away by his own rhetoric and one must remember the pressure of opinion in France. On another occasion he remarked that hard though his own lot might be in dealing with 'unreasonable personages' it was nothing compared with that of Briand who had to work in the same Cabinet as Messrs Poincaré, Tardieu and Barthou.

Negotiations with Russia began at the end of 1924 when it was first proposed that Germany should join the League of Nations. The Russians were, it seems genuinely, convinced that the League of Nations was a capitalist organization directed specifically against the Soviet Union; to them Germany, friendless and isolated in defeat, was a potential ally against the West. Maltzan, the Secretary of State at the Foreign Ministry, and Brockdorff-Rantzau, the Ambassador in Moscow, were both anti-French. They hoped to win Russian support and play off one side against the other. They did not hold with Seekt's extreme views and Brockdorff-Rantzau grumbled a good deal about the meddlesome interference of the military missions in Russia. When Stresemann became aware of the issue he sent Maltzan off to Washington and insisted that he alone should determine policy.

On 7 April 1925 Brockdorff-Rantzau gave a full explanation of German intentions to Litvinov, the Commissar for Foreign Affairs, and this was confirmed by a written statement handed to Kretinski, the Ambassador in Berlin, on 25 April. According to this document the immediate purpose of German policy was to secure the evacuation of the Cologne Zone in accordance with the Treaty of Versailles. The present French government seemed inclined to give up 'the military solution' but it was essential to satisfy the need for security. The Guarantee Treaties prepared at the Peace Conference had not been ratified and should now be replaced by a Security Pact in which Germany would take part as an equal. For Germany the renunciation of Alsace-Loraine was no more than a theoretic, sentimental sacrifice since she could not get it back in any case. Germany would never accept the eastern frontiers, she would undertake only to settle disputes by peaceful means. This also was a 'theoretic sacrifice' since she was not in a position to force Poland back within her ethnographic frontiers and would not attempt to do so.

In this statement and in later conversations with Kretinski, Stresemann emphasized that in joining the League of Nations Germany, the only unarmed power, would make it clear that she was not in a position to impose sanctions against Russia. (At Locarno the Secretary General of the League of Nations did in fact give an assurance that in the application of sanctions the geographic and military circumstances of member states would be taken into account.) He tried to allay Russian fears by pointing out that as a member of the League Council Germany would be able to veto aggressive action against the Soviet Union.

The Russians were suspicious by temperament; their procedure was endlessly tortuous. If the military contacts between the Reichwehr and the Red Army were broken that would be the end of the trade agreements that had been confirmed after the signature of the Treaty of Rapallo. Stresemann for his part protested strongly against the double policy by which the Soviet Union sought friendship with a democratic government whilst instigating the subversive activities of the Comintern.

Stresemann had not intended to reach any conclusion with Russia until after Germany had joined the League of Nations. In fact her admission was postponed from March until September 1926. The German-Soviet Treaty was signed on 24 April. It was a neutrality agreement pure and simple. There were no secret clauses. The Treaty is in no way comparable with the Nazi-Soviet Pact of 1939. The obligation to preserve neutrality would apply only if the other party were engaged in a defensive war—it did not run counter to the League Covenant.

Stresemann said once that Germany—given her geographic position—could not ignore Russia. 'If we have relations with Russia and the West this means a double-sided policy but never (*nie und nimmer*) a policy of duplicity.' Like many other western statesmen he hoped, I think, for a change in the Soviet System. 'It is in the interest not only of Germany but of Europe that there should be no unbridgeable gulf between the Soviet Union and the rest of Europe. Somehow, by some means, Russia too must take part in the great community of peace.'

In fact Stresemann concentrated increasingly on a western rather than an eastern policy. After Germany's admission to the League of Nations in 1926 he and Briand met in private at Thoiry on Lake Geneva. They had a good lunch, drank a bottle of wine—some say more than one—and settled between them the affairs of Europe. (There had been a good deal of diplomatic preparation and Austen Chamberlain had approved of their meeting.) Germany it seemed had achieved financial stability, but the French franc was now under pressure; there had been a sharp fall in July (235 to the pound). Briand suggested that Germany should pay a capital sum to France by raising a loan on railway bonds ear-marked for reparations, in return France would agree to the evacuation of all occupied territory. The Saar plebiscite would be held immediately and Germany would pay for the re-purchase of the mines. It came to nothing. Poincaré, who was now Prime Minister, proved himself a sound and skilful financier. He succeeded in stabilizing the franc without German assistance and funded the foreign debt on favourable terms.

Stresemann maintained until the end that the Thoiry policy was right. For France prosperity would come not by the humiliation of Germany but by 'the friendly co-operation of the two countries which in so many respects, and especially in trade and commerce supply each others deficiencies'. The German people for their part must be prepared to accept economic burdens in order to win unity and freedom.

In 1928 he went to Paris for the signature of the Kellog-Briand Pact and had his only meeting with Poincaré. He came away convinced that there could be no political agreement without a final settlement of reparations. In subsequent negotiations Poincaré insisted that Germany must pay the cost of France's foreign debt—and in addition an *indemnité nette*.

This led on to the Young Plan. Stresemann consulted Parker Gilbert, the Agent General for reparations. It might, he thought, be better to wait till a time of depression, lest in a period of comparative boom Germany's capacity be over-estimated. But Gilbert urged him to go ahead. He set great store by the confidence that would result from a final settlement. This American emphasis on confidence and credit—though well meant—seems strange to us now. Germany had punctually fulfilled her obligations under the Dawes Agreement. This, as Stresemann pointed out, had been done entirely on borrowed money. The rate of taxation was high but for the whole period there was a passive balance of trade. The foreign loans vastly exceeded the reparations payments, they were taken up not only by industrial firms for capital development but by public authorities for expenditure on amenities which would lead to no increase in production. None the less, encouraged by the Americans he decided to push ahead.

The Young Plan was approved by the political leaders at the Hague Conference in August 1929. Stresemann had hoped for a final ending of the legacy of war. He achieved an undertaking that the occupation of the Rhineland should end in 1930, five years before the appointed time. Nothing was done about the Saar Valley.

At the Hague Philip Snowden demanded a larger share on behalf of the British Government. This meant a small increase in the German liability. Schacht had been critical of the whole procedure but agreed to the original proposal because the immediate annuities would be less than under the Dawes Plan. After the Hague Conference he resigned and threw in his lot with Hugenberg who had launched a violent attack on Stresemann's policy. Hitler, the demagogue, joined up with the right-wing newspaper magnate. After Stresemann's death the Young Plan was carried by a large majority in the Reichstag. Hugenberg's attempt to defeat it by referendum secured but meagre support.

During these last years Stresemann's aims became not more but less ambitious. At the League Sessions in 1929 he took up the question of minorities. He had some sharp exchanges with Zaleski, the Polish Foreign Minister, about German language schools in Upper Silesia. Later he supported the Canadian delegate in proposing a permanent commission to supervise the enforcement of existing minority rights and suggested the possibility of a new charter—not to encourage assimilation but to secure the peaceful co-existence of different ethnic groups in all member states. Stresemann's German critics condemned it as a propaganda move to cover up his evident failure to achieve any revision of frontiers. The cynics at Geneva, and there were plenty about, saw in it a devious method of causing trouble and raising the issue by the back door. Stresemann, I think, had come to believe that the true interests of Europe would be served by reducing the importance of political boundaries. The New States with mixed nationalities would gain influence and win esteem if, by following the example of Switzerland, they proved that it was possible for people of different race, language, and cultural tradition to live together in harmony.

In his last speech at Geneva (11 September 1929) he spoke once more of his hopes for European economic union which would be the basis for closer political co-operation. The League of Nations would be strengthened not weakened by the breaking down of barriers between its European members. Was it mere fantasy to look forward to a planned economy, a common currency, a common postal system? Earlier at the University of Heidelberg he had spoken of politics as the art of the possible directed to the future. In the pursuit of immediate limited aims the politician must never lose sight of the ultimate goal, the reconciliation of conflicting interests in freedom and equality.

Stresemann did not live to see either the evacuation of the Rhineland or the breakdown of the Young Plan. The collapse of credit came not in

Germany, as the experts had expected, but in the United States. The consequent depression was more widespread and more devastating than anything that had been predicted. In Germany short-term loans were called in, production fell, and by 1932 there were six million unemployed.

During his last year in office Stresemann was grievously ill. He died on 3 October 1929. He was succeeded by men of courage and good will. They lacked his political skill, his stature, his insight. Would he have realized that in time of depression the government must stimulate, not check expenditure? Could he have made an end of reparations and won international support for a rational economic policy? Could he by so doing have defeated the revolutionary forces of communism and national socialism? We cannot tell. In writing to Lord D'Abernon he had called for a revival of the spirit of Locarno and urged the need for active British help in the building of the New Europe. These indeed were the years of lost opportunity.

ΛE

Stalin
by Edward Crankshaw

EDWARD CRANKSHAW (b. 1909) is recognized as one of the most outstanding authorities on both Soviet Russia and the Austro-Hungarian Monarchy. His pre-occupation with Russia dates from his experiences with the British Military Mission in Moscow during the Second World War. He served as Correspondent on Soviet Affairs for *The Observer* from 1947 to 1968 and is the author of many works on those countries on which he has made himself a recognized authority.

Apart from his two brilliant Habsburg studies, *The Fall of the House of Habsburg* (1963) and *Maria Theresa* (1969), his Soviet studies include *Russia without Stalin* (1956), and *Khrushchev: a Biography* (1966). He also edited Khrushchev's own memoirs in 1970.

Joseph Stalin

21 Dec. 1879	Born. Educated at parish school at Gori and theological seminary at Tiflis.
1898	Came under influence of Marxism.
1899	Was expelled from seminary because of views.
1901	Was elected a member of clandestine Social Democratic committee at Tiflis.
April 1902	Was arrested and imprisoned. Meanwhile elected a member of the Social Democratic committee guiding the movement in the Caucasus.
1904	Escaped from Siberia. Social Democratic party split into bolsheviks and mensheviks. Stalin joined bolsheviks, who were not popular in his homeland, Georgia. He translated Lenin's writings from Russian into Georgian.
Jan. 1905	Revolution. Stalin was in background organizing bolshevik fighting squads.
1905	Stalin first met Lenin, in Finland.
1906	Attended party conference in Stockholm.
1907	Attended party conference in London. Became bolshevik leader of Baku, and was many times arrested and deported.
1912	Bolsheviks broke with mensheviks and created separate party. Lenin appointed Stalin member of new central committee.
5 May 1912	Stalin became first editor of *Pravda*.
End 1912	Attended bolshevik conference in Cracow.
1913	Went to Vienna to write *Marxism and the National Problem*, but was regarded as a man of action rather than a theoretician. Arrested and deported to Siberia.
March 1917	Outbreak of revolution. Stalin returned from exile and became editor of *Pravda* again.
July 1917	At height of anti-bolshevik campaign by mensheviks Stalin organized Lenin's escape from Petrograd.

Previous pages: More powerful than the Tsars; unsurpassed by any of them in ruthlessness. Stalin at May Day Parade, 1950. On his right: Bulganin; to his left: Malenkov, Beria, Mikoyan, Molotov, Kaganovich, Andreev, Krushchev . . .

Sept./Oct. 1917 Stalin supported Lenin in controversy which arose when his desire for armed rising conflicted with views of Zinoviev and Kamenev who were opposed to insurrectionary tactics.

Oct. 1917 Joined Military Revolutionary Committee headed by Trotsky. Insurrection in which Stalin played no active part.

26 Oct. 1917 After bolshevik victory, Stalin appointed commissar of nationalities to effect the party's programme for 'self-determination' for oppressed nationalities.

1917-21 Civil war.

June 1918 Stalin in charge of defence of Stalingrad (Tsaritsyn). Rivalry developed between him and Trotsky, the commissar of war.

May 1919 Organized defence of Petersburg.

April 1922 Appointed secretary-general of the party

1923 Lenin ill. Stalin, Zinoviev, and Kamenev planned to debar from power Trotsky, who was generally regarded as Lenin's successor.

21 Jan. 1924 Lenin died. In his will he advised followers to remove Stalin from party's general secretariat.

May 1924 But Stalin retained his office.

Autumn 1924 Propounded views of 'socialism in one country', which was a departure from Leninist internationalism.

April 1925 Defeated Trotsky and broke with Zinoviev and Kamenev.

1928-29 Turned against Bukharin, Rykov, and Tomsky. Began speedily and drastically to industrialize U.S.S.R. and to collectivize agriculture.

Jan. 1929 Expelled Trotsky from U.S.S.R.

1930s U.S.S.R. transformed into great industrial power. This often led to scarcity of consumer goods and popular discontent, which was ruthlessly suppressed. In order to free labour for industry and to increase food production, farming was collectivized.

Nov. 1932 Suicide of Nadezhda Alliluyeva, Stalin's wife.

Nov. 1936 Stalin introduced quasi-liberal constitution.

1936-38 Great purge trials in which most of old bolsheviks and some military leaders were charged with treason.

March 1931 Stalin appeared willing to come to terms with Hitler, his plans for anti-Hitler coalition with West having come to nothing.

Aug. 1939 Stalin made bargain with Hitler under which U.S.S.R. and Germany divided spheres of influence in eastern Europe.

Aug. 1940 Trotsky assassinated in Mexico.

6 May 1941 Stalin assumed premiership.

22 June 1941 German attack on U.S.S.R. surprised Stalin.

Aug. 1942 Stalin met Churchill in Moscow. Stalin wanted second front opened in eastern Europe, but Churchill would not agree.

1943 Battle of Stalingrad. Russian army broke German military strength.

Dec. 1943 Tehran conference, attended by Stalin, Churchill and Roosevelt. Stalin opposed Churchill's scheme for Mediterranean campaigns and asked for landings in France. He persuaded Roosevelt.

Feb. 1945 Yalta conference attended by Stalin, Churchill, and Roosevelt.

July/ Potsdam conference to make
Aug. 1945 post-war settlement. Stalin committed U.S.S.R. to join U.S. and Britain in war against Japan.

March 1946 Stalin Five Year Plan, which continued to stress heavy industry at expense of consumer goods

1946 Growing coolness between U.S.S.R. and west.

End 1948 U.S.S.R. tried to squeeze western powers out of Berlin. The west broke blockade with airlift.

5 March 1953 Died.

Here is Stalin as seen in an extremity of disillusionment by the Yugoslav Communist, Milovan Djilas:

'An ungainly dwarf of a man passed through gilded and marbled halls, and a path opened before him: radiant, admiring glances followed him, while the ears of courtiers strained to catch his every word. And he, sure of himself and his works, obviously paid no attention to all this. His country was in ruins, hungry and exhausted. But his armies and his marshals, heavy with fat and medals and drunk with vodka and victory, had already trampled half Europe underfoot, and he was convinced that they would trample over the other half in the next round. He knew that he was one of the most cruel and despotic figures in history. But this did not worry him a bit, for he was convinced that he was carrying out the will of history.'

Stalin was then at the summit of his glory. It was the man who in his victory speech had recently announced to the Soviet people that there was to be no respite after their terrible struggle with Hitler, itself the culmination of nearly thirty years of revolution, civil war, famine, forced labour and terror: they were to tighten their belts against the next war and prepare to be driven and whipped through at least fifteen more years of privation until their production of steel, coal and oil was sufficient to turn the Soviet Union into an impregnable fortress, 'proof', in Stalin's words, 'against all accidents'. He was set on a course which positively invited 'accidents'. There was no need for this.

It was also the Stalin who knew how to present himself to the Russian people, crushed beneath his terror, as a stern but loving father; to Churchill as a warrior with nerves of steel and a statesman's grasp of detail; to Roosevelt as a shrewd and understanding national leader who would be a natural ally against British imperialism; to the successors of these two men as an almost infinitely far-seeing, evil genius presiding over a vast and monolithic Communist empire which was soon to include China. All this at a time when the Soviet Union was on its last legs, devastated, ruined, exhausted, its vitality drained by the killing or slow death in labour-camps of millions of its most able citizens, crowned by the war-time loss of twenty million more.

Djilas, with his fascinating descriptions of Stalin relaxed in the midst of his entourage, was the first man to give a picture of him as he was behind closed doors. Since then, others—notably Khrushchev and Stalin's own daughter, Svetlana, have amplified and elaborated the image of a gangster chieftain. For most of the time he ruled not through the formal paraphernalia of Politburo sessions and organized consultations with expert advisers but, rather, with casual, off-hand, arbitrary, often contradictory commands as he swung from one mood to another—vindictive, terrible, matter-of-fact, self-pitying—in the course of interminable midnight feasting and carousing surrounded by his inner circle of henchmen. They had to put up with being teased, tormented, shouted at, bullied—terrorized in a word—while trying to divine their master's real wishes. Sometimes too sleepy to keep their eyes open or too drunk to understand, they would go away and do as they were told—or, desperately daring, postpone action in the hope that the boss would forget. They themselves were the men who appeared in public, boot-faced, as Stalin's closest colleagues, taking their manners from Stalin himself, and holding in his name the power of life and death over millions:

Molotov, Kaganovich, Voroshilov, Zhdanov, Khrushchev, Beria. All went in fear of their own lives. All bowed low. All submitted to gross humiliations. Molotov, even while he was showing his iron face to the outside world, had to stand by without protest and see his wife imprisoned. Kaganovich accepted without a murmur the suicide of his brother, himself a member of the Government, to escape arrest and torture. Even the wife of the venerable Kalinin, President of the U.S.S.R. and nominal Head of State, was arrested, tortured, held in prison for seven years, and not released until her wretched old husband was dead, smothered in honours.

All these men, and more besides, had stood by their master during the great purge years, profiting from the extermination of superiors and rivals. Themselves corrupt and terrorized, they went out from the Presence to spread corruption and terror through the length and breadth of the land.

It had not always been like that. For nearly twenty years, until he was thirty-eight, Stalin had led the life of a revolutionary in and out of prison. For years after that, in a position of great power, he had lived frugally and worked very hard. But his way of reaching decisions and of communicating them to his own inner circle of followers, once so shabby and obscure, seems to have been always essentially the same. He must also from the beginning have been a latent hysteric; but until he was fifty, in 1929, he kept his hysteria under fairly rigorous control, only occasionally lashing out viciously at the risk of damaging his own contrived image. After that it no longer mattered and the image changed. With Trotsky exiled and the opposition groups recanting their heresies and making submission, he was Peter the Great for a time. At the beginning of this incarnation, seized by a frenzy, he took on the vast peasant population of Russia single-handed and beat them and beat them again, destroying them in millions, reducing great tracts of the land to starvation, and permanently crippling agricultural production. Then he was Ivan the Terrible, intent on avenging himself on those who had ever opposed him or Lenin (which meant practically every surviving Bolshevik) and going on to destroy not only the survivors of the men and women who had made the Revolution, but also hundreds of thousands, millions, of their fellow countrymen, including practically all those Party members who retained a shred of idealism. In so doing he shattered the laboriously constructed fabric of the new Soviet society and, on top of that, the Red Army itself, the guardian of that society and the god to which it had sacrificed itself.

Then came the war, and soon he was Alexander I, recovering astonishingly from a mental and nervous collapse in the first weeks of the German invasion to transform himself into the great patriotic Tsar, finishing up as the latter-day arbiter of Europe. Afterwards he contrived to be Peter, Ivan and Alexander all rolled into one, extending his Russian imperium beyond the dreams of any previous Tsar. Even while he was behaving among his cronies like an inferior Roman emperor and like a gangster towards his own and subject peoples, he could still bring forth the quality of extreme and calculating caution which had marked his rise. He could retreat in Berlin and head his country out of danger in the Korean war. He had even begun to feel his way in 1952, clumsily and tentatively, towards a reorientation of foreign policy in belated recognition of the facts of atomic warfare—until he was seized by that last murderous fit of paranoia, heralded by the so-called 'Doctor's Plot', which threatened the lives of many of the men who for so long had been running the country in his name. They were saved only because Stalin died first, miraculously and melodramatically, in March 1953.

This was the man who had started off as a penniless student revolutionary, to become so quickly Lenin's 'wonderful Georgian'; who was, indeed, for long a member of Lenin's innermost circle, trusted and highly valued by Lenin and appointed to positions of formidable power—until, on his death-bed, Lenin suddenly had his eyes opened to the sort of man he was and, too late, urged the comrades to reduce him quickly.

Until then Stalin's progress had been caution itself, punctuated by curious outbreaks of violent recklessness—manifestations of character which pleased Lenin, who could be exasperated by too much talk and not enough action on the part of his followers. Until Stalin, quite unnecessarily, allowed himself to get out of control and pushed his luck—first by vicious and independent bullying in Georgia, the reports of which Lenin for some time refused to believe, then by, of all things, repeatedly going out of his way to humiliate and insult the untouchable Krupskaya, the dying hero's wife.

This was the faint foreshadowing of a pattern that was to be repeated time and time again: cautious, elaborately calculated progress towards a long series of particular and limited goals, interrupted by convulsions of destructive hysteria. But the pattern was complicated by another element, an almost feline capacity for lazy relaxation which would manifest itself in what can only be called a policy of drift in face of all matters, up to and including the security of the State, not strictly relevant to the conspiracy of the moment.

For above all, of course, he was a born conspirator. From 1899 to 1917 he had plotted and intrigued for the overthrow of established authority—and for his own hand; then for another ten years he continued to plot, but now against his Bolshevik comrades, until he had reached the point at which he could turn on them and destroy them. He continued to plot, now against the society and the army which he had helped to create and which sustained him—until he could tear them to pieces and replace them with a horde of cowed and obedient slaves. By the time he emerged to deal face to face with the leaders of the Western world he was so set in his ways that, regardless of his views about the world revolutionary process and the nature of his long-term aims, he could only continue to operate as a one-man conspiracy, using the techniques he had perfected, some of them learnt from Lenin himself, in his years of obscurity. But as a one-man conspiracy he was forced to rely too much upon the promptings of his own intellect which, when constructive ideas were called for, was not up to the job. Not to put too fine a point on it, this man whose talents for devious self-advancement were such that they came to hypnotize the world, was, outside this highly specialized activity, stupid. He was also ignorant to a degree.

It is difficult to consider Stalin in a short space because it is impossible to

With Lenin in 1922. Too late, Lenin came to distrust his powerful subordinate

sum him up. He was something outside common experience. So was Hitler. But Hitler at least made clear the motives that impelled him and the goals he sought. We know what he wanted to do and roughly why. We can see how close he came to success and how far he fell from it. His successes and his failures can be measured like the successes and failures of other powerful figures. But nobody knows what Stalin wanted to do, or indeed, if he wanted to do anything at all except achieve power for its own sake. He never declared himself or gave any credible hint of his motives in his writings and speeches. In his last twenty-five years he clearly saw himself as a great historical figure. But what was his role? His actions were contradictory and frequently muddled. He never seems to have made up his mind whether he wished to be regarded as the great patriotic leader or the master of an international revolutionary movement—or as Genghiz Khan. All these aspirations, if in fact he had them, and others too, got in each other's way. There was no subtlety about the way he kept the world guessing; there was only confusion arising from impulse and short-sighted pragmatic responses to changing situations. His life-work, whatever it was, found itself devoured and rotted by muddle. The only certain thing is that he failed in everything he appeared to undertake except the attainment of personal power on a scale unprecedented in the modern world. Perhaps this was all he wanted. If so his success was complete. He died in his bed, at seventy-four, his power undiminished.

Tactically he was a genius, strategically he was inferior. Almost everything he did with an eye to the long term (with the solitary exception of his own advancement; and even this was more of a hand to mouth process than it looked) was wrong.

In his early days this did not matter. He was not required to think, only to plot. Unlike his politically minded contemporaries at Oxford, Harvard, the Sorbonne, he was not then visited by dreams of high office. He was the lowest of the low, an outcast on the run, and likely to remain so. The most he could aspire to was personal survival in order to play his part in the disruption of a detested society into which he had been born—as the son of a drunken cobbler in Gori, near Tiflis, the capital of a quasi-colonial province of the Russian imperium: Jossip Vissarionovich Djugashvili. He had one of those devoted mothers, who was determined to make him a priest: she got him into a Church school, and he did well enough to earn a place in a theological seminary at Tiflis. There, like so many students, he was soon caught up in subversive activity and, at twenty, expelled.

That was in 1899, and for eighteen years to come Stalin was committed to the career of professional revolutionary, and an unusually determined one at that. There is nothing to suggest that he was moved by compassion for the lot of the downtrodden and oppressed. Indeed, the fact that in after life he never made up a story to account for his conversion suggests that he had no feelings at all beyond that envy and hatred of the prosperous and established which, in the light of subsequent developments, would have seemed to him self-evident and the most natural thing in the world, calling for no comment. In a Georgian of hot, vindictive temper with centuries of tribal vendettas behind him and a contempt for the stolid Russians into the bargain, his hatred and envy took on a savage edge. On top of this, the sort of calculating, cautious approach which is so often the intellectual expression of stupidity went uneasily together with an inborn compulsion to live dangerously.

All this appealed to Lenin, who was not as pleasant a character as is commonly supposed. And in understanding the nature of Stalin's rise, which on the showing of his enemies is inexplicable, making no sense at all, it is essential to realize that he was very close to Lenin—not exclusively close, as he was afterwards to claim with such a blatant array of falsified history and forged photographs that he discredited himself completely, but a great deal closer than Trotsky ever allowed—or, indeed, could bring himself to understand.

He joined the recently created Social Democratic Workers' Party in 1899. With his eye for the concrete he liked their programme, as opposed to the vaguer and more erratic aspirations of the much larger Social Revolutionary Party, which reposed its trust in the peasants for whom Stalin would have had nothing but contempt. The theoretical certitudes of Marxism, as interpreted by Plekhanov and Lenin, would have made an immediate appeal to his seminarist's training. When Lenin split the Party into the Bolshevik and Menshevik wings in 1903, Stalin was away in Siberia serving his first term of exile (he was to be imprisoned and exiled four times, three times escaping, the fourth time returning in triumph to Petrograd when the prisons were opened after the fall of the dynasty), but he at once recognized in Lenin's exclusive, centralized, disciplined, hectoring approach a spirit to which he naturally responded.

He aligned himself with the Bolsheviks forthwith and remained with them through thick and thin. In the light of hindsight it is permissible to discern another reason for this choice of allegiance. The Caucasus and Transcaucasia formed very much a Menshevik stronghold. As a Menshevik, young Djugashvili would have been one among many; but as a Bolshevik, he was able to form his own small but compact power base which he soon came to dominate. Throughout his whole career from then on he was never to move outside an area which he could personally and physically dominate—a fact which was never understood by those in later years who believed that he was intent on encouraging revolution on a global scale: what interested him after 1945 was the subjugation of lands adjacent to Russia which he could control with Russian arms, and he overreached himself only in the cases of Yugoslavia and Berlin. What interested him in the first decade of the century was building up a party organization, first in Batum, then in Baku, which was his own. He worked very well with a handful of like-minded toughs, Ordzhonididze and others, who were to help him to supreme power before he turned on them.

He was extremely active and very bold and soon caught the eye of Lenin, tirelessly agitating, polemicizing, pronouncing anathema on all who differed from him (including his dearest friends) far away from Russia. He was assiduous in keeping up with Lenin's arguments and transmitting them to the faithful in Baku and elsewhere. Since a great part of Lenin's teaching at that time was anti-democratic and dictatorial and, as such, badly received by all Mensheviks and some Bolsheviks, the great man was naturally attracted to the unknown promoter of his views. Soon he had more practical reasons for his interest. For after the collapse of the 1905 Revolution, in which Trotsky, Stalin's exact contemporary, made his name as a supreme agitator and demagogue (and a bitter opponent of Lenin), the heart went out of the revolutionary movement and Russia seemed once more sunk in apathy. But not Stalin (he was not Stalin then, but Koba, calling himself after a legendary Georgian outlaw, a revealing choice). The Party needed money, and Koba helped to organize the notorious 'fighting squads' which undertook successful raids on banks and bullion trains.

Good Social Democrats—all the Mensheviks and the soberer Bolsheviks—regarded this sort of banditry with distaste, even horror: it was not Marxist cricket. Lenin alone, who made up his rules as he went along, found it a good idea, and was condemned by the comrades for saying so. Never a man to be ruled by principle, but very clever indeed at elevating expediency into principle, he found in Koba a man after his own heart and watched from afar with extreme attention the way in which by ceaseless driving and manoeuvring this rather shy, sly, unobtrusive, seemingly diffident recruit with his slight build, the heavy Georgian accent, was contriving to turn Baku into the most active centre of Bolshevism inside the Russian empire. The two men met only fleetingly on Koba's brief trips away from his home ground at Tammerfors in Russian Finland in 1905, in Stockholm in 1905, in London in 1907, in Cracow in 1912. But their meetings were enough to convince Stalin, once he had got over his slightly shocked surprise at the misleadingly casual modesty of Lenin's bearing, that he was backing the right horse. And, to cut a long story short, in 1912, at Lenin's insistence, he was co-opted a member of the five-man Central Committee which assumed leadership of the Bolshevik Party after its final and formal split with the Mensheviks—and was soon bringing out as editor the first issue of *Pravda*. He was now very firmly a senior member of the national leadership of the Party, and although for by far the greater part of the next five years he was to be sequestered in prison and in Siberia, when the prisons opened in March 1917, he came back to Petrograd to assume leadership of the Petrograd Bolsheviks as his natural right (taking it over from the young Molotov, who had been holding the fort), pending Lenin's return from Switzerland a month later after the legendary journey across Germany in the famous sealed train.

Few people noticed Stalin in those chaotic days. The March Revolution had been an affair not of professional revolutionaries but of a mass uprising, a spontaneous outbreak of strikes and troop mutinies sparked off by a bread shortage in Petrograd. In the very moment of his triumphant return Lenin shocked all the Bolsheviks and outraged the Mensheviks by his flat refusal to celebrate the revolution as a triumph and by his obsessional and bitter determination to sabotage and destroy the Provisional Government and all its works. The interesting thing about Stalin at this time was the way in which he lay low while contriving to keep Lenin's confidence. Sometimes he hedged, sometimes at critical moments he said nothing; but close to Lenin he stayed, through the abortive

July rising which ended with the Bolsheviks proscribed and Lenin in hiding, and then on through the final decision to strike and destroy in October. Trotsky had formally joined forces with the Bolsheviks in July and, with his brilliance, dynamism, boldness and flamboyance was stealing everybody's thunder. But Stalin was very much on the spot, and, seeing which way the wind lay, overcame the almost physical jealousy, loathing and contempt which he felt for Trotsky and backed him in the call to action. In doing so he stole a most decisive march on Zinoviev and Kamenev, who disgraced themselves in Lenin's eyes for actively and persistently (in fact far from unreasonably) opposing the great October gamble.

When Lenin came forward to assume charge of Russia's destiny Stalin was at his side, his copybook unblotted, a member of the Politburo and the government minister, or commissar, responsible for all the minority nationalities of the old empire, which, together, accounted for nearly half the total population. His claim to this office had been established by the laborious production of a paper on the nationalities question written in 1913 at Lenin's behest. Stalin had in fact done nothing since then, and he was not to produce another idea of his own, and that a not very recondite one, until in 1924, immediately after Lenin's death, he adopted and pushed the anti-internationalist slogan: 'Socialism in One Country'. For the rest he was content to operate in the shadows, which were very deep and almost infinitely extensive in the period of civil war, intervention, chaos and famine which followed. He retained Lenin's confidence by his shrewdness and practicality and by the way in which he tackled the dull organizational work which others despised; at the same time he used his opportunities to place in key positions throughout the provinces men who thought as he did, the rough, tough, anti-intellectual revolutionaries who had made their way inside Russia by organizing study groups, party cells and strikes—men who had borne the heat of the day and now scorned the returned emigrés and were attracted as to a magnet by Stalin as the man of few words who got things done and kept a clear head on his shoulders. To these, increasingly, were added ambitious adventurers with an eye to the main chance.

In March 1922 he was made General Secretary of the Bolshevik Party, which not only gave him effective control of the whole Party machine with its ramifications everywhere but also enabled him to manipulate in his own interest the agenda of the Politburo of which he had been a founder member. It is clear that by the time Lenin suffered his first stroke in May of that year Stalin must have had his eye firmly on the succession, knowing very well that the only man he need fear was Trotsky. It is interesting that during this whole period of the slow accumulation of power, Stalin carefully refrained from exposing himself or making enemies—apart from Trotsky, whose position he continuously sought to undermine. Indeed, he presented himself very much as a middle-of-the-road man, a moderate and a reconciler—so much so that when Lenin turned in savage fury on Zinoviev and Kamenev after their opposition to the October coup, Stalin, while making it clear that he supported the rising, nevertheless went out of his way to plead for the lenient treatment of the two men he was a few years later to humiliate, and afterwards to kill.

By the time Lenin died, in January 1924, Stalin had all the necessary threads in his hands. It must have been a blow of a quite sickening kind when he discovered that at the very end Lenin had turned against him. There was nothing he could do to protect himself. From the moment of Lenin's death he had stepped forward as the most devoted son of the lost leader, for his own purposes inaugurating a cult of Lenin's infallibility. Now, four months later, he had to sit miserably through a Central Committee meeting listening to the reading of Lenin's testament, this condemnation from the grave. It should have been the end. A simple vote against him would have ruined him. He was saved by, precisely, Zinoviev and Kamenev—not because they loved him but because they thought they could manage him and needed him in their coming struggle with Trotsky. Like so many others who thought they could use Stalin for their own ends, in that moment they were doomed.

Stalin was forty-five and on the verge of his ultimate triumph. What did he believe? What moved him other than the desire for personal power, first secret, then increasingly open power? His words and his actions until this point give no clue. He seems to have operated in a sort of void, aloof from the comrades, pursuing his own path, valued by Lenin for his courage, ruthlessness, cool-headedness and organizational powers, qualifying as a Bolshevik because he knew, more or less, how to say the right things— which were the things that Lenin said. He continued on his almost sleepwalking rise, using the comrades to destroy each other, sitting back and expressing himself moderately while leaving it to his followers to shriek for strong action against those who opposed him—until he thought the moment had come to reveal himself and started to lash his opponents with a brutality which shocked everybody. Even when he was doing this at the 15th Party Congress in December 1927, with Trotsky safely exiled, his attitude towards the Russian situation as a whole was one of studied moderation. He had already come out scornfully against those who demanded forced and rapid industrialization, against those who wanted to collectivize the peasants. Everything was going well enough as it was, he declared. There was no need for dramatics. Under the slogan 'Socialism in One Country', the Soviet Union would forge steadily ahead, putting first things first and moving into an era of unexampled prosperity.

Then, suddenly, the earthquake. In the summer of 1928 the country was threatened by a shortfall of grain—only two million tons, but enough to cause famine and disrupt the industrial economy. For once Stalin was faced with the necessity of positive and unequivocal action. The policy of drift had put Russia on the rocks. It was, it is not too much to say, the first constructive decision that this extraordinary man had been called upon to make, and he responded with a convulsion. He now held all Russia in his hands, and he could do to the Russia of illiterate peasants and workers what he had done to the tempered Party of Lenin: he could transform it. All moderation was swept aside. With no preparation, with no attempt to think the consequences through, a crash programme of collectivization by the most brutal and wasteful means was conjoined with a crash programme of industrialization which took no account at all of the realities of the economy or of the limitations of the men who would have to sustain it. Something had snapped in Stalin's brain, and all the pent-up fury and vindictiveness, so carefully restrained for so long, came pouring out: a panic reaction overnight into a manic frenzy. In no time at all he was Peter the Great, declaring that the Soviet Union had ten years in which to overcome her traditional backwardness—the backwardness which had led to all the humiliations of Tsarist Russia—and stand armoured against the world.

This was not calculation, and it was not rational. Perhaps not, people say, but it was magnificent. It was not magnificent; it was lunatic. In 1928 the country had painfully pulled itself out of chaos, and agricultural production had recovered its pre-war level—though certainly something had to be done to make it worth the peasants' while to deliver food to the towns. Industry was being built up, and with foreign help could have been made to grow steadily and fast. Provided 'Socialism in One Country' really meant that Stalin would abandon, or at least thoughtfully shelve, the export of revolution there was nothing to stop the most extensive exploitation of foreign technical and material help. But he could not think straight. The Comintern remained active, producing very little in the way of practical results but creating the maximum of distrust and suspicion in the outside world. Desperately needed foreign technicians and engineers were subjected to constant harassment and on several occasions charged with sabotage and made the victims of demonstration trials: even German engineers were subjected to this treatment at a time when, under the Treaty of Rapallo, Russia and Germany as the two outcast nations had drawn close together with an eye, above all, to mutual help in the building up of their armed forces.

It has frequently been claimed that Stalin showed extreme subtlety and skill in riding two horses at once. He himself may have believed this: like Lenin before him he had a simple faith in the superior efficacy of the lie, almost any lie, to the truth. In fact all too often he got the worst of both worlds. He was not a far-sighted man: skill in seeing round corners is not the same as vision. Brilliant at calculating his own immediate advantage, he showed time and time again an inability to think through a given policy to its logical consequences. His supreme strength lay in the perfect ruthlessness with which, when faced with consequences of his own ill-considered actions which would have brought a lesser man to suicide, he did not change course but drove on, smashing down all obstacles at whatever cost in human suffering and lives. He was sure that the Russian people would put up with the sort of treatment that nobody else would have dared inflict on them; and he was right.

When he launched his forced industrialization programme he had not the faintest conception of what was involved. When he smashed through with the collectivization he did not foresee that he was destroying the very basis of Soviet agriculture. When he set out to revenge himself in 1935 on all who had ever opposed him and to eliminate anyone who might oppose him in future, he did not see that the hysteria thus engendered would not end until all the most useful members of society had been shot or consigned to living death in the camps, or that his great army, to which so much had been sacrificed, would be broken and demoralized.

Propaganda painting Overleaf: An uncharacteristically benevolent Stalin receives bouquet from conference of wives of Soviet engineers in 1936.

It has seemed desirable to dwell in a certain amount of detail on Stalin's rise to power and the early manifestations of his supremacy within the Soviet Union because when the time came for him to address himself to the world at large, to play the statesman, the same pattern of elaborate deception and intrigue, followed by terror and intimidation, was to be repeated this time on an international scale. Indeed, it may be said that from 1934 onwards the skills which he had employed to achieve domestic mastery were mainly directed towards the extension and consolidation of Soviet influence abroad. At home there was no further scope for the complex, devious obsessive preoccupation with aggrandizement through intrigue in which his nature found its truest expression. He needed more worlds to conquer.

The course within the Soviet Union was set: it was a case of driving on, flattening by brute force all resistance real or imagined, actual or potential; of reducing a great people to mindless obedience. The excesses of the terror arose from two separate causes: vengefulness manifesting itself in the vindictive determination to punish; fear arising from an exaggerated idea of the power of the exiled Trotsky to organize a successful conspiracy against the ruling junta. Stalin did not believe that Trotsky and those he accused of conspiring with him had in fact committed the specific treasonable acts with which they were charged; but there can be no doubt that he was ridden by the fear of what they might be able to achieve: their capacity for mischief, it must have seemed, was limitless. It should not be forgotten that in December 1934 when the murder of Kirov in Leningrad (almost certainly at Stalin's own instigation) set the stage for the blood-purge of

the next four years, 1917 was still only yesterday to Stalin, who could obviously never forget the ease with which Lenin and his minority party of Bolsheviks had accomplished their historic coup. None knew better than Stalin the latent power of a determined, disciplined, secret body of men with clear-cut destructive aims. None knew better than Stalin that he and his lieutenants ruling through the secret police were not, as the outside world believed, the natural leaders of an all-powerful revolutionary party commanding popular loyalty, but, rather, no more than a brutally victorious faction which had established its dominance by force and guile. The spectre of Trotsky allying himself with a hostile power and promising half the Ukraine or Siberia in return for military intervention against the Stalin regime must have seemed very real.

This was one sort of built-in distortion of vision. A distortion of a different kind was Stalin's initial misreading of the causes of Hitler's triumph in Germany. Fascism he regarded as an unexceptional example of capitalism in decay. So the German Communists must welcome the destruction of liberals and reforming socialists. The Social Democrats were by definition inveterate reformists, thus traitors to the working class in their revolutionary struggle. The sooner and more completely they were crushed the better: the Communists could then work and wait for the final upheaval. Stalin was not, of course, alone in this fatuous conviction; Trotsky in his position would certainly have shared it. For one of the remarkable things about these unprincipled men was the way in which they were blinkered by dogma—dogma which, in certain aspects, achieved almost the stature of principle. Only a Lenin could appear to be principled while remaining

effectively untramelled, the inspired opportunist who knew how to dress up his grossest deviations to look like holy writ. But Lenin was no longer there to explain the differences between Russia and Germany, between Germany of 1918 and Germany of 1931. And Stalin was busily engaged in isolating and preparing to kill all those survivors of Lenin's party who had the least understanding of any country other than Russia.

When, belatedly, Stalin began to be alarmed by Hitler and imperiously called for popular fronts and collective security, it clearly never crossed his mind that by unleashing his reign of terror at home while conducting a campaign of slander against the very governments Litvinov was so assiduously wooing, he was, to put it mildly, inviting a certain scepticism about the honesty of his intentions and his reliability as an ally.

He was also obsessed (another inheritance from Lenin) with Britain and the British Empire as the supreme and most dangerous enemy. This persistent and extravagant overrating of British strength and cunning is still very hard for any Englishman who was politically conscious in the 1930s to grasp as a fact. But a fact it was, Bonar Law, Ramsay MacDonald, Baldwin, Neville Chamberlain notwithstanding. The conviction was partly emotional (England had been the main instigator of the Intervention, the main villain of the Civil War), partly received tradition (perfidious Albion), partly uncomprehending (how could a small off-shore island hold sway with such effortless ease over the most far-flung empire in history?). From his earliest days as Lenin's successor—and Lenin himself had seen in British imperialism both a most potent foe and also, as it were, the soft under-belly of the capitalist system—Stalin had plotted devotedly against England, even while his main energies were absorbed by problems nearer home. His first major excursion into foreign policy had been directed above all at destroying British influence in China. To this end he was ready to flirt with America, France, Japan, and to mount a major and complicated exercise in China itself, which, incidentally, offered a first-class example of Stalin's brilliance as a tactician and weakness as a strategist. At one moment, before the final emergence of Chiang Kai-shek and the Kuomintang as *de facto* masters of China, Stalin was pursuing no fewer than four mutually contradictory policies simultaneously. While maintaining correct relations with what was left of the official Peking regime, he entered into amicable arrangements with several opposed war-lords, actively assisted Chiang in his military struggle, and at the same time backed the Left Kuomintang, seeking to infiltrate it with Communists in its efforts to destroy Chiang.

The skill and finesse that went into this complex operation was worthy of a better cause. Stalin may or may not have assisted in the development of a situation inimical to Western, above all British, interests in China. But he quite failed to gain a special place for Russia. And all the subsequent turns and twists of Soviet Far Eastern policy, the betrayal of the Communists to Chiang Kai-shek, the post-war occupation and looting of Manchuria, the heavy snub administered to Mao Tse-tung on the very eve of his triumph in 1948, his leaving China to carry the burden and the perils of the Korean War—all these expedients and manoeuvres could only end as they did—with severely strained relations between the two great Communist powers in

Stalin's life-time and the spectacular breach after his death.

This pursuit of an immediate advantage, real or imagined, without regard to the consequences in the longer run, was Stalin's trademark. His accommodation with Hitler in 1939 was clever enough as a tactical exercise, but its possible consequences were not thought through. When Stalin made a pact with his declared arch-enemy he was sure that he had brought off the coup of the century. He thought he understood Hitler. Here was a realist like himself, concerned exclusively with his own advantage and personal aggrandizement. Two neo-imperialists were conducting a deal of the kind their predecessors had so happily concluded in days gone by: Catherine and Frederick dividing up Poland; Alexander and Napoleon plotting together on the raft at Tilsit. Stalin, who suspected everybody and trusted nobody, really convinced himself that he could rely on Hitler's word. It never crossed his mind that he was dealing with a lunatic messiah. It was characteristic that he did not clearly perceive his vulnerability should Germany triumph in the West. Even at the eleventh hour, in June 1941, he refused to believe the overwhelming evidence of Hitler's malign intentions and ordered his front-line troops to hold their fire in the first hours of the invasion.

Very well, it may be countered, Stalin made mistakes. Who does not? Consider the mistakes, some very similar to Stalin's, made by his opposite numbers in England and France. In fact Stalin had no opposite numbers in England and France. The governments of Chamberlain and Daladier would be hard to rival in incompetence. But neither of these paladins were entered for the Bismarck stakes. Stalin's claims to greatness as a national leader and world statesman must be measured not against run of-the-mill politicians who made no such claims, not against the achievements of democratic prime ministers intent on a quiet life and peace at almost any price, but against the great nation-builders, against Frederick, Bismarck, Peter the Great himself. He put himself forward as a strong man, a supreme leader with a dynamic policy, working, if not to overturn the world, at least for the security of the Soviet Union and for Russian aggrandizement, even if by aggrandizement he understood no more than the recovery of all the lands ruled over by Nicholas II. In fact, in his appeasement of Hitler he combined the morals of Frederick of Prussia with the ineffectiveness of Neville Chamberlain.

Of course he had every reason to suspect the intentions of England and France. At the same time, as already observed, he was incapable of seeing that his own behaviour was a prime cause of their distrust and hostility. He also overrated, almost fatally, their military strength and preparedness. When it came to an understanding of Hitler he missed the master-key: the publicly expressed intention of carving out of the Soviet Union a vast area of *Lebensraum* for Germany. The man who made no bones about absorbing half of European Russia into the *Reich* was to be bought off with half Poland, which in any case was not in Stalin's gift. This is the sort of mistake no serious statesman could have made. Chamberlain, who made a precisely similar mistake, at least had to pay his personal share of the price paid by the people who elected him. Stalin was able to shift the whole cost on to the backs of his unfortunate subjects.

Admittedly he had a bad quarter of an hour. For a brief period his confidence was shattered by the failure of his supreme exercise in *Realpolitik*. When the Germans invaded he suffered what appears to have been a form of nervous collapse. Not without cause. It is at least questionable whether Hitler would have attacked in 1941, or even gone to war in 1939, had he not been impressed by the state of confusion and weakness revealed by the fears so publicly advertised by Stalin and his lieutenants during the show trials of the middle thirties. So-called 'enemies of the people' were being discovered on every side. Hitler knew very well, if nobody else did, that there was no truth in the wild charges of plotting with Germany flung out against the 'Trotskyites', to say nothing of the Red Army higher command. Of what, then, was Stalin afraid that made him go to such extremes of violence and mayhem? Surely he must believe, and have reason to believe, that treachery encompassed him as a threat to his very existence? There was also the evidently very shaky state of the Red Army itself, which even by 1941 had by no means recovered from the massacre of its officers in 1937.

Even as things turned out, had Stalin properly utilized the breathing space, nearly two years, between the Pact and the invasion, had he given orders for full mobilization and the intelligent deployment and alerting of his still formidable army, outnumbering the Germans in manpower, tanks and aircraft, had he taken key commands out of the hands of corrupt and incompetent police generals and time-servers, the calamitous impact of the Nazi assault would have been greatly reduced.

So Stalin had reason to lose his nerve. It is not too much to say that his own actions from 1934 onwards, crowned by the ineptitudes of the Winter War with Finland and his almost abject exercise of appeasement towards Hitler, amounted to an open invitation to attack.

As we know, after a few weeks during which he disappeared from view and signed no orders or instructions, Stalin recovered his nerve and emerged from the shadows as the great Generalissimo. Once more he was in his element. There was nothing to be done but fight through, regardless of the cost. The qualities which had carried him through the bitter struggle for the collectivization and the slaughter of the purge years were now to bear him on to ultimate victory in war. Now, as then, he simply put his head down and drove on. The brutality of his driving at the cost of unnecessary losses on a monstrous scale must be held against him; but to his credit must go the patience, fortitude and almost superhuman nerve called for in the reconstruction, training and equipping of the new armies which were to sweep the Germans back from the Caucasus and the Volga to Berlin. Stalin was indeed the victor. But it was a victory costing far more than he should, or need, have paid. That it cost no more than it did was very much due to the contribution made by Western material help, above all in the form of American trucks coming up through Persia, which transformed a horse-drawn army into a motorized one in time for the great sweeping movements of encirclement and pursuit which marked the progress of the Russian war from the final stages of the Stalingrad battle early in 1943. Stalin, of course, never acknowledged the importance of Lend-Lease, or even publicly gave thanks for it.

He was now the great statesman battling with adversity to whom all things must be forgiven. It is strange to reflect that until the signing of the pact with Hitler Stalin had never presented himself in person as the master of the Soviet Union. Now, in war, he was to meet on equal terms the leaders of the West. The qualities with which he impressed Churchill were precisely the qualities which had impressed Lenin in days gone by: his eye for the immediate and the concrete, his powers of instant organization, his contempt for generalities and his grasp of relevant detail, his mixture of boldness and caution, his bluntness (he was foul-mouthed only among his foul-mouthed henchmen, before subordinates, or with visiting Communist worthies). That quality of relaxation which had distinguished the years of his manoeuvring for supreme power after Lenin's death here again stood him in good stead. Churchill was affronted by the hectoring rudeness with which, on occasion, he impugned allied motives; but Stalin saw quickly enough when he had gone too far, and knew—superb actor as he was—how to turn on that rough, twinkling-eyed, bullying good humour which took in so many victims. Roosevelt was deceived by the sly, man-to-man charm of this stalwart man of the people who knew how to act the part of a ward politician of the most reassuring kind, concerning himself with an easy, cynical shrewdness with his own parish, his own voters, as it were, in such comforting contrast to Churchill's romantic vision, unregenerate imperialism and bulldog histrionics. Stalin was the greatest actor of them all: he did not let his acting show. It was a virtuoso performance on the part of a gangster chieftain who enjoyed dissembling even more than he enjoyed killing: not even a Stalin could kill a man more than once; he could deceive him times without number.

But what was the object of Stalin's virtuosity? What beyond the magnification of his own power through the enhancement of Soviet power did he hope to achieve? The accepted function of a national leader is to hold his country together, to equip it for its own defence in war, to prosper it in peace. The conventional foreign policy of a national state is designed to serve these ends, whenever possible at the expense of other nations. Even the outstanding predators of modern times, Frederick, Napoleon, Bismarck, Hitler, even Mussolini, were all possessed by a dream which embraced a concept larger than themselves and was bound up with the well-being of their chosen people. Their dreams may have been absurd, misguided, evil. But all saw themselves, even while pursuing personal glory, as serving others and contributing to the prosperity of millions—even though the goal must be reached by blood and fire; even though, as in the case of Hitler, millions of human beings regarded in one way or another as sub-human must be destroyed to make room for the chosen ones. But what was Stalin's dream other than the pursuit of personal power? What people did he serve? What qualities did he perceive and understand in any human being beyond gullibility, self-deception, selfishness, cruelty, greed?

He won supreme power in his own land. He extended the frontiers of that land. He appeared on the international stage as one of the grandest of the grand. All this brought no good but only injury to the Soviet people. While this great actor presented himself to the Western allies as a crusader and to

231

Overleaf: Stalingrad—the turning point. Russian soldier raises the red flag after German surrender; (inset) Russian defenders in action

the Russians at war as the father of his people; while he soft-pedalled the role of the Communist Party and appealed to patriotic feeling, inviting the Orthodox Church, which he had all but driven from the earth, to stand up and bear witness that God was on his side, he delivered the effective government of the Soviet Union into the hands of Beria and the N.K.V.D. He had the chance to get and keep the people on his side: but he preferred to break them. The massacre of the Polish officers in Katyn Forest; the brutal deportation to Siberia of hundreds of thousands of Poles, Esthonians, Lithuanians—men, women and children—when the Red Army moved into their countries—these atrocities were understandable: Stalin could have said with Hitler that he was killing foreigners, or sending them to slow death in the camps, to make life better for honest Soviet citizens. But, alas, as we have seen, for more than a decade before the war honest Soviet citizens had been treated very much as the Poles and the Balts were now treated. And so it was to continue. Entire populations of certain ethnic groups and minor nationalities, citizens of the Soviet Union whom Stalin considered unreliable or who had incurred his personal displeasure were rounded up—from the Volga Germans to the Crimean Tatars and the Chechens and others of the Caucasus—and marched off to the terrible trains en route for Siberia, their homes abandoned, the names of their homelands erased from the map.

Stalin, as Lenin's heir, had a clearly definable interest: it was to work for the world revolution in order to establish an international socialist order based upon equity and concord. If, for whatever reason, Lenin's heir decided to abandon this dream and devote himself to the advancement of the Soviet Union, his duty, the sole excuse and justification for his being, was to secure the prosperity of his own peoples at the expense of the rest of the world.

He could, of course, postpone the drive to world revolution until he had built up the Soviet Union into a model irresistible in its attraction. But what he did in fact was to subdue his own peoples through terror, starving the peasants in the interest of the towns, but seeing the towns not as shining armatures of a new society, rather, as barracks serving the factories for the production of heavy industry, which meant guns before butter. What it came to in the end was that it did not matter what Stalin believed or felt, either about world revolution or Soviet power or Russian glory. Everything he did was directed to one end: the subjugation of the largest possible area and the greatest possible number of people to his will. In his later years his will, his personal power, was perfectly identified with Soviet power. And Soviet power for him did not and could not exist beyond the line that could be held by the Soviet presence—his own presence that is, operating through the armed forces—or the immediate threat of it. Just as in his early days of mastery his power did not exist for him beyond the line within which he and his creatures could corrupt or destroy all life. At first he had been content to deliver the Soviet Union into the hands of the Yagodas, Yezhovs, Berias, Molotovs, Zhdanovs, slave-drivers who themselves were slaves. He would put a Khrushchev in charge of all the wealth and riches of the Ukraine, viceroy over forty million souls, himself going in fear of his master's frown. So, in the years after the war, he installed his puppets in Poland, East Germany, Hungary, Rumania, Bulgaria, Czechoslovakia. And the spirit which had produced the Katyn massacre, the betrayal of the Warsaw rising, the great purges, and the collectivization, now presided over the *Gleichschaltung* of eastern and central Europe.

No doubt Stalin was successful in outmanoeuvring Churchill and hoodwinking Roosevelt at Teheran and Yalta. Certainly he showed persistence and skill in winning for the Soviet Union, for himself, not only all the lands ruled over by the last Tsars, but also, for all practical purposes, and as an effortless sequel to the expulsion of Hitler from half Europe, all the territories up to the Elbe. But to what purpose, and at what cost?

For the man who after 1945 turned Europe into a graveyard, corrupted it morally and ruined it materially by looting what the Germans had left, was at the same time engaged in spreading over all the Soviet Union a blight more total than ever before.

If ever a national leader had a chance to recover from past excesses and rally his country round him in constructive, patriotic effort that leader was Stalin in 1945. After their colossal sacrifices and in the profound relief of victory the Russians were in no mood to remember, even those who understood, that these sacrifices in large part were due to Stalin's failures. In the end he had led them to victory. Their country was devastated beyond the imagination of those who were not there to see it. But the devastation had been perpetrated by the Germans. It could be made good. The Soviet people had proved their patriotism, their personal loyalty to the great leader and teacher: he would now lead them into the promised land.

Instead he took them straight off into the wilderness. Returned prisoners of war, returned civilians from forced labour all over Europe, instead of being welcomed were led off under guard and either shot as deserters or sent off in droves to Stalin's own labour camps or to remote banishment. The labour camps multiplied on a monstrous scale. Russia, starving and in ruins, was told that there was only one task ahead—not the steady, hopeful rebuilding and transformation of their society, but toil with no reward for at least another fifteen years—toil not to make the Soviet Union a country fit to live in, but to build up a military complex strong enough to face any conceivable threat from outside—and this at a time, after Hiroshima, after Potsdam, when America had the atom bomb and Russia did not. Instead of seeking cooperation and assistance in rebuilding, he brought the curtain down, and everything he did until his death was a direct challenge to his late allies who wanted only to live in peace.

It may be agreed that the late allies made innumerable mistakes. They failed to understand Stalin's mentality as they had failed to understand Hitler's. They did not, for example, understand his absolute determination to be master of Poland and secure himself in eastern Europe generally. They did not understand that in exchange for complete domination over Rumania, Bulgaria, Hungary, Czechoslovakia and East Germany, he was ready to desert the Communists of Greece and, at least for a time, to double-cross Tito in Yugoslavia. They did not understand that the wise old, wily old bird of Teheran and Yalta was behaving off stage as he appeared to Djilas, as depicted at the opening of this essay, in the days when he took it for granted that he had Tito under his thumb.

Truman with his abrupt ending of Lend-Lease, with his dramatic assertion of the celebrated 'Doctrine' in the middle of the Moscow Conference of 1947, only increased Stalin's crass suspicions of an actively hostile West preparing to act in concert with a resurrected Germany. But the provocation to the Western Allies had already been extreme.

In 1945 Stalin had the chance of a new deal which would have cost him nothing, brought only good to Russia, and secured him a place in history as a gangster transformed by high responsibility into a great statesman (Khrushchev was later to achieve all this: it could be done). He feared America by all means; he feared the swift recovery of a revanchist Germany. The Soviet Union was weak to the point of exhaustion after all the ruin and the killing—how weak Stalin alone knew. But he lacked the imagination and the vision to perceive the immense advantages that could accrue from an open confession of weakness at that time. He was a man who knew how to operate only through strength—the negation of statesmanship. He had to recover strength. A man capable of a grand strategic vision, a man capable of pursuing a long-term course and thinking in broad, bold categories, whether for good or evil, a man who could detach himself from the compulsive deviousness in which he gloried—a Peter the Great, for example —would have moved heaven and earth to achieve a period of detente, lulling the West, soothing America with sweet reason, profiting from her great wealth to build up his own. By all means, if he was sure there must one day be a clash, he should have set to work to construct his own nuclear weapons. But he knew, or should have known, that for the time being there was nothing whatever he could do to protect Moscow and Leningrad from nuclear attack if America was determined on a pre-emptive strike. Knowing this, he set out on a line of policy most calculated to invite this reaction.

At the cost of unlimited trouble and expense he built up a glacis of satellite states which would have been a useful protection in 1930 but were utterly useless as long as America alone held the bomb and largely irrelevant after 1949 when Russia had her own. In so doing he raised a world in arms against him. By the time the breaking of the Berlin Blockade in 1948 had proved even to Stalin that if he pushed too far he would be faced with very determined resistance, but that America would go to great lengths to avoid a shooting war, the division of the world into two armed camps was irreversible. It is sometimes said that far from being a defeat for Soviet policy Stalin's action in Berlin and in East Germany generally provided him with a much needed assurance that the Americans were not spoiling to attack. He would have looked silly if things had turned out otherwise. What in fact he achieved was the inauguration of NATO in the spring of 1949 and the rapid rearmament of the West. By autumn Stalin had his own atom bomb and Russia was now irrevocably launched on an unnecessary programme of arms manufacture which was to act as a crippling drag on the economy.

Admittedly the West was slow to experiment with serious gestures. But with the inauguration of the Marshall Plan in the autumn of 1947 America had made a serious effort to recover from past errors, giving Stalin a chance to think again before deliberately severing all constructive relations with the western world and condemning his country to stultifying isolation.

And it was clear that at this point there had been serious discussion in the Kremlin as to the correct course to pursue. Czechoslovakia and Poland were at first allowed to respond to the American initiative. Molotov himself arrived for the Paris conference with a mind to all appearances by no means closed. But almost at once, on orders from Moscow, he hardened, denouncing the Marshall Plan as a blatant attempt on the part of America to achieve economic domination over Europe. The Czechs and the Poles were called to order and told to change course. The Cold War from this moment was finally joined. Stalin preferred to go it alone, cost what it might. This man so supremely confident in so many ways, was a paranoic. He was the war leader and national hero who could not feel secure until he had driven into obscurity the man who above all others had helped him to victory, Marshal Zhukov. He was the statesman and self-proclaimed leader of the Communist world who lacked confidence in his capacity to maintain his personal ascendancy over anything but a closed and heavily insulated society. From 1947 until the end of his days he turned his back on diplomacy, speaking to the governments of the outer world only in terms of military threat. A true statesman would have revelled in the challenge of the Marshall Plan, accepted aid wherever available, used it to build up the great society and turned the tables on the givers. Stalin was not a true statesman, he was a gangster out of his depth. His mind was so devious and vile that he saw only deviousness and vileness in others; and when he could not fathom the workings of that supposed deviousness he went to ground.

There were so many things he did not understand. He did not understand China. He did not even understand the Balkans. His misjudgement of Tito and the Yugoslavs, like his misjudgement of the Finns in 1939, was the clearest indication, if any was then needed, that he lacked the least sense of the imponderables governing or complicating human behaviour. 'How many divisions has the Pope?' That seemed to Churchill a good, earthy joke, apposite in its context. But to Stalin it was not a joke at all. It was essentially a serious question, and the only question he knew how to ask. For him such qualities as pride, faith, honour, even a bloody-minded determination not to be pushed about, did not exist. The least sign of dissent or opposition in any individual meant only one thing to him: namely that that individual was dedicated to his downfall. It never occurred to him that a man might fight simply to be left alone.

At times the unlimited foolishness, venality and self-deception of mankind seemed almost to justify him in the total contempt in which he held it. But never quite. Even inside the Soviet Union, which for a time appeared to be reduced to a level of corruption, abjectness and imbecility from which no society could conceivably recover, the human spirit survived.

It may be, as many insist, that without Stalin to hold it together the new Soviet Union could never have survived, that the peasants would have starved the towns, that industry would have collapsed in anarchy, that the many nationalities forming the republics of the Union would have fallen away. It is impossible to tell. Lenin may already have reduced the country to the state in which it could be sustained only by the bloodiest of tyrannies. No other way was tried.

Roosevelt
by Samuel Rosenman

SAMUEL ROSENMAN (1896-1973) began his political career shortly after graduation from Columbia University Law School in 1919. He was elected in 1921 to the New York State Legislature where he served five terms. He first met Mr Franklin D. Roosevelt in October, 1928, when, at Mr Roosevelt's request, Rosenman joined him as an adviser in his successful campaign for the New York Governorship. Governor Roosevelt, when he took office on 1 January, 1929, appointed him to the Office of Counsel to the Governor.

He was closely associated with Roosevelt from then until the death of the President in April 1945.

In 1932, he organized the group of university professors, who came to be known as the famous 'Brains Trust', to advise the Governor on national problems in his campaign for the Presidency. Governor Roosevelt appointed him later that year a Justice of the New York Supreme Court, where he served ten years. In 1943, Roosevelt asked him to resign from the Bench to serve in Washington full-time, and appointed him to the new office which he created for Rosenman, called Special Counsel to the President.

On Roosevelt's death, President Truman asked him to continue as Special Counsel until the conclusion of the War. Rosenman finally resigned in February 1946 to return to private practice.

He is the author of an illuminating book *Working With Roosevelt* (1952) and was the editor of the thirteen volumes of the *Public Papers and Addresses of Franklin D. Roosevelt*, which cover the Governorship and the Presidency.

Franklin D. Roosevelt

30 Jan. 1882	Born. Educated at Groton School, Harvard, and Columbia University School of Law.
1905	Married President Theodore Roosevelt's niece, Anna Eleanor, who later had four sons and a daughter.
1910	Became state senator in New York state.
March 1913	Appointed Assistant Secretary to the Navy, a post he held for seven years. Learned to negotiate with labour unions.
1914	After World War I broke out, Roosevelt became advocate of preparedness.
1920	Nominated for vice-presidency at Democratic Convention. Campaigned on behalf of U.S. entrance to League of Nations. Defeated in Republican landslide.
10 Aug. 1921	Struck by poliomyelitis and lost use of legs.
1928	Elected governor of New York. His programme was to give tax relief to farmers, to develop water power,

Previous page: Inaugural address, March 1933. To millions of Americans suffering in the depression Roosevelt's idealism and confidence brought new hope

cheap electricity and old age pensions.

29 Oct. 1929 Wall Street collapsed and Great Depression began.

1930 Re-elected governor of New York. Depression had had catastrophic effects.

1931 He established Temporary Emergency Relief administration, the first of the state relief agencies.

Nov. 1932 Presidential election. Roosevelt campaigned on 'New Deal' programme of recovery and reform, and won election. Democrats also won majorities in both houses of congress.

4 March 1933 Inaugurated as president.

9 March 1933 Roosevelt ended depositors' runs on banks by closing all banks until Congress allowed those in sound condition to re-open.

March 1933 Programme of drastic government economy and legislation to legalize beer.

1933 New Deal legislation:
Congress established Federal Emergency Relief administration—federal funds appropriated for relief of human suffering.
Tennessee Valley Authority created to provide flood control and regional planning for an impoverished region. Civilian Conservation Corps for reafforestation and flood-control work.
Existing farm credit agencies consolidated into Farm Credit Administration.
Home Owners' Loan Corporation helped home owners threatened with mortgage foreclosure.
Agricultural Adjustment administration helped restore farm prosperity.
'Truth in Securities' Act to protect investors.
National Industrial Recovery Act. Labour received guarantees on wages and hours.

Jan. 1934 Roosevelt stabilized gold content of dollar.

1935 Social Security Act—unemployment and old age insurance. Works' Progress administration gave work to unemployed.

Aug. 1935 Neutrality Act—U.S. would not intervene in wars.

1936 Re-elected president.

Feb. 1937 Roosevelt proposed re-organization of Supreme Court because it might invalidate his key measures. This failed.

1938 Started to build up U.S. defences.

Nov. 1938 In Congressional election Republican seats greatly increased.

Sept. 1939 Outbreak of World War II.

Nov. 1939 Congress repealed arms embargo provision of Neutrality Act and Roosevelt sent arms aid to Britain.

April 1940 Hitler invaded neutral countries of Denmark and Norway.

May 1940 Hitler invaded neutral countries of Holland, Belgium and Luxembourg.

June 1940 France fell and Britain stood alone.

Nov. 1940 Roosevelt re-elected to an unprecedented third term as president.

1941 Roosevelt occupied Iceland and Greenland.

March 1941 Lend Lease Act, by which U.S. financed aid to Britain and Allies.

June 1941 Hitler launched attack against U.S.S.R.

Aug. 1941 Roosevelt and Churchill met off Newfoundland and proclaimed Atlantic Charter.

Sept. 1941 Roosevelt extended Lend Lease to U.S.S.R.

7 Dec 1941 Japan attacked Americans at Pearl Harbor, Hawaii. This brought U.S. into war.

Nov. 1942 U.S. invaded North Africa.

Jan. 1943 Roosevelt and Churchill met at Casablanca and proclaimed doctrine of unconditional surrender.

July 1943 Allied troops invaded Sicily.

Sept. 1943 Allied troops invaded Italy.

Nov. 1943 Roosevelt, Churchill and Stalin met at Tehran and discussed D-Day offensive.

6 June 1944 D-Day. Allied invasion of Normandy.

Aug. 1944 Meeting at Dumbarton Oaks to discuss formation of U.N.

Dec. 1944 Roosevelt re-elected President.

Feb. 1945 Roosevelt, Churchill and Stalin met at Yalta. Agreement that U.S.S.R should enter war against Japan after defeat of Germany. Agreement on establishment of U.N. organisation.

12 April 1945 Roosevelt died.

March 4 1933, the day of the first inauguration of Franklin D. Roosevelt, was cold, cloudy and cheerless. It was as cheerless as the nation's economy; for by that day the lowest depths of the Great Depression of 1929 had been reached. It was the deepest point to which the United States economy had sunk in all its history.

Roosevelt had just recently finished campaigning for the Presidency in all parts of the United States. He had seen hundreds of thousands of people in the streets of a score of cities, and from the back platform of his campaign train in a hundred railroad stations—all crowding around to catch a quick glimpse of the man who was to determine their future. He had taken the trouble almost daily since his nomination in July to talk with individual farmers and with small shopkeepers and workers.

He had looked into the faces of all these people and had read the depression statistics imprinted in bold figures in their eyes. In many he had seen actual hunger; in many more he had seen deep anxiety that their children were not receiving an adequate education or even enough food. In *all* these faces he had seen fear—stark fear. In those who did have jobs, there was fear of losing them. In those who still held on to their homes or farms, there was fear of foreclosure. In those who had no jobs, there was fear of the coming hunger for their families and themselves. Even in the faces of millionaire industrialists and financiers with whom he conferred he had seen the same signs: fear of whether a continuance of this disaster would mean an end to the system of private property and free enterprise upon which America (and they) had grown and prospered. How long would the people stand for mass starvation, misery and deprivation, while a handful of them still owned great mansions and estates, industrial empires, yachts and all the luxuries of a mode of living suited to the stock market of 1928 rather than to the days of 1932?

There had already been many ominous signs of unrest. During February of 1933, a Senate Committee had been warned by several eminent witnesses that violent days were ahead unless something was done quickly. Whether armed revolution in 1933 from the 'left' or from the 'right' was a real possibility or not—there can be no doubt that the American system of free enterprise and private profit was in grave danger. Everyone knew what had happened in countries abroad in this century, where great masses of humanity had faced these same conditions. It did not require too much imagination or prescience in March 1933, to see the clear beginning of this process in Germany. It had already happened in Italy. Leaders of American industry and finance had come to visit the President-elect; all had tried to impress him with their fears and with the necessity of doing 'something'. But, as Roosevelt said in later years, few, if any, of them had any constructive ideas about what that 'something' should be; and none of them extended any advice for action which might diminish their own privileges and financial powers. There was throughout the entire nation the same all-pervasive fear—whether it was of starvation, or of the loss of a job, or the loss of a yacht.

On 4 March 1933, it was a man whose soul had been deeply seared by watching so many hundreds of thousands of suffering Americans, who pronounced with set jaw, bold tones, and unmistakable determination, the oath of office prescribed by the Constitution.

He stood bareheaded in the raw wind, holding on to the arm of his eldest son, James, until the oath was completed; and then, with the additional support of a cane, turned and made his way a few steps to the speaker's platform—for he could not walk without these props. There, leaning on the lectern for support he could release his son's arm; and he began his famous first Inaugural Address.

What sort of a man was Roosevelt to have attained this position? His birth, parentage and early youth were not the traditional origins of American Presidents. There was no log cabin, no rising at dawn to milk the cows or do the farm chores; he did not have to sell newspapers, or work to help support his family. He did not have to earn his way through college or law school. He was born and brought up in the pleasant, rich, patrician surroundings of an estate in Hyde Park on the banks of the Hudson River of New York State. As a young boy at home, there were private tutors, private governesses on the many trips with his parents abroad; summer vacations at the Roosevelt home in Campobello Island, Canada, on the bay of Funday; education at Groton, one of the most exclusive private schools in the United States; four years at Harvard University where his college friends were also sons of rich men active in the social life at the turn of the century; Columbia University Law School and admission to the New York Bar; and, finally, a position with a highly respected but very conservative law firm in New York City, which counted among its clients some of the richest men and largest corporations in the United States—who were later to come to hate and abuse President Roosevelt with a bitter violence. This was his early life and career. The ordinary economic and social cares and problems of the world seldom, if ever, intruded.

Prof. Richard E. Neustadt, who had a decade of experience in Washington in posts which provided rare opportunities to watch three Presidents in action (including Roosevelt), has well written · 'The White House is no place for amateurs'. Franklin D. Roosevelt, as he delivered his first Inaugural Address, was no amateur. There have been in the White House men of greater learning and scholarship than Roosevelt, with more theoretical knowledge about economics and political science—but none with his vast political experience in practical politics and with professional politicians.

Roosevelt's first political experience was in Albany, New York as a state senator. It gave him two important advantages: on one hand he established a national reputation as a young man willing to stand up— as he did—against the political bosses of the state in an important fight for the election of a United States Senator, and secondly, by constant mingling, for the first time, with members of different backgrounds, of different social and financial classes, of different religions and ethnic origins, he began to broaden his social horizon far beyond the Hudson River Valley.

His next political experience was as an administrator on the national scene for seven and a half years. He was the Assistant Secretary of the Navy during the Presidency of Woodrow Wilson which included all of the First World War. In the Navy he came to know organized labour in the hard way—

by actual personal contacts with the leaders and members of the unions employed in the Navy yards under his supervision. He earned their respect, as twenty years later, he would have their respect, but also their affection and support. It was his boast that in all his seven and a half years of creating the kind of big Navy he wanted, there had not been a single strike.

This was the 'Progressive Era' in the United States, and President Woodrow Wilson was the centre of it—its heart, its mind and its muscle. Roosevelt was part of it too; and it became part of him. He became a fervent Wilsonian Progressive.

Nothing in Roosevelt's life prepared him for the role of Commander-in-Chief in the Second World War as much as his years as Assistant Secretary. They gave him an understanding of naval construction, operations, equipment, and strategy, which would enable him in the war to meet on terms of equality and mutual respect the leaders of the American Army and Navy, and those of Great Britain, and particularly, the former First Lord of the Admiralty, Winston Churchill—that 'former naval person' with whom he was to correspond, confer, plan and act so frequently in the critical years ahead.

Then, in 1920, he had his first experience as a campaigner on a national scale. He was nominated in 1920 for the Vice-Presidency of the United States. It was a hopeless battle—and Roosevelt knew it, but it gave him great political experience and great stature.

He returned to the life of a private citizen; but now in 1920, he was as well known nationally as any Democrat. He knew, and so did the professional Democratic leaders, that at some time he was to be a serious contender for the Presidency—and he was respected and looked to for leadership as such.

Then disaster struck! Infantile paralysis hit him at Campobello on 10 August 1921, at the age of thirty-nine, at a time when he was in perfect health—muscular, active, and full of energy. In two days it had him on his back, unable to move—even to wiggle his toe. Roosevelt came quickly out of his first few days of depression, and was soon making quips about his condition, expecting to get over it shortly. He was removed from Campobello on a stretcher. Two months later, he was still afflicted with temperature and pain; and though not improved, he started the exercises which he would continue the rest of his life.

A disaster like this would have laid a lesser man low, and glad to yield to the temptation to return to the life of a gentleman of ease amid surroundings where he had his roots, and which he loved so much. But not Roosevelt. He was determined to resume his life and interests anew, where he had left off; nor did he abandon his consuming ambition—the White House.

By the end of 1922, though he could not stand without crutches, he was spiritually fully self-reliant and ready to meet anyone on equal terms. He never accepted completely and finally the idea of total defeat in his efforts to regain normal legs. But for the rest of his life, his legs were to be useless without braces.

Some people who knew Roosevelt personally in those days, and many others who did not, have speculated that it was his crippling and painful experience which created 'that quality of soul which makes him a strong help to all those in sorrow or in trouble' and that 'real interest in his fellow-men'—qualities which Roosevelt had attributed to Alfred E. Smith, nominating Smith for the Presidency in 1928. I do not think that that is the entire explanation. I think that the reason began when he was born; it was in the heart and soul of the man. There was also, of course, his early and continued veneration for the older Roosevelt and for his later progressive policies. Then there was his experience with that other great liberal and progressive President, Woodrow Wilson. But neither of these men had the keen sense of social justice that he had. I do believe, however, that his own suffering and pain had intensified his understanding and compassion for others who, through no fault of their own, had been afflicted with bitter experiences.

In 1928 he ran for the Governorship of New York State. This was the year of the Hoover landslide. It engulfed New York as it did many other Democratic states. Smith, the Democratic candidate for the Presidency, was buried in defeat; Roosevelt just barely escaped the same fate by a majority of only 25,000 votes, about a half of one per cent.

On the very first day of his first term as Governor there began to appear the liberal recommendations he would make to the hostile Republican Legislature during the next four years. They drew towards Roosevelt the attention of liberals and progressives in all parts of the country: development of water power and cheap electricity by the state rather than private utility companies, old age pensions, limitation of hours of work for women and children in industry, extension of workmen's compensation laws for all occupational diseases, slum clearance, closer public utility supervision, relief of agriculture—and many others. These are now all regarded as routine, but in the United States of 1929 they constituted a fairly radical programme.

The basic philosophy and social objectives of President Roosevelt's New Deal proposals of 1933 and 1935 can be found in Governor Roosevelt's speeches and messages during the four years before he became President. The details are different, because the proposals in 1933 were framed for national rather than state action, but the concepts are basically the same.

In 1930 Roosevelt ran for re-election as Governor; this time he won by a majority of 725,000 votes. He was the first Democrat in history to carry upstate New York. Overnight, this unprecedented victory made him a strong - if not the leading contender for the Presidential nomination in 1932. During his second term as Governor, he took a step which placed him far in the lead in that race. More important, it was a step forward in his social and political philosophy—which, when he became President, was to revolutionize the role of the federal government for all foreseeable time to come.

On 29 October 1929, Wall Street collapsed in a panic. The Great Hoover Depression began, and became deeper and deeper during the next three years. After waiting in vain through the dreary winter and spring and most of the summer of 1931 for some action or some leadership from Washington, Roosevelt decided to assume leadership himself, and to provide action in the State of New York. He did it in a message he delivered to the Legislature on 28 August 1931—a landmark date in the history of governmental social thinking in the United States. The message also contained a full statement by him of the underlying concept of what was later, during his Presidency, to be called the 'New Deal'.

'In broad terms I assert that modern society, acting through its government, owes the definite obligation to prevent the starvation or the dire want of any of its fellow men and women who try to maintain themselves but cannot . . . To these unfortunate citizens, aid must be extended by government, not as a matter of charity, *but as a matter of social duty*.' (Emphasis added.) If there was such a thing as a Roosevelt Revolution, this was the first shot—and it was heard around the nation.

This doctrine has now become universally prevalent in the United States under Republican Presidents as well as Democrats. As Roosevelt later said, it was only bringing the United States up to long established standards of many countries in Europe. But in 1931 it was revolutionary.

Roosevelt was nominated for the Presidency in 1932 after a bitter fight in which there were three or four strong contenders. Victory came only after he had made a compromise and a deal by which the conservative John N. Garner, in exchange for the votes of his delegates to the Convention, became the Vice-Presidential candidate.

On 4 March 1933, therefore, Roosevelt had already had a wealth of experience in practical politics, in administration of government, and in the executive and legislative processes. He also brought with him to Washington all his great objectives of social justice.

His inaugural address was important and timely:

'I am certain that my fellow Americans expect that on my induction into the Presidency I will address them with a candour and a decision which the present situation of our Nation impels. This is pre-eminently the time to speak the truth, the whole truth, frankly and boldly.

'. . . So first of all, let me assert my firm belief that the only thing we have to fear is fear itself—nameless, unreasoning, unjustified terror which paralyzes needed efforts to convert retreat into advance.

'. . . This Nation calls for action, and action now . . . Our greatest primary task is to put people to work . . . We must act and act quickly.'

If anyone was in doubt about his conception of the Presidency and of its vast powers, or of his determinations to use them all if needed, he soon dispelled it. To the despairing citizens of the United States his self-confident speech was a flood of light in the darkness: 'I shall ask the Congress for the one remaining instrument to meet the crisis—broad Executive power to wage a war against the emergency, as great as the power that would be given to me if we were in fact invaded by a foreign foe.'

Nor did he have any doubt that the American Constitution was broad and flexible enough to warrant the exercise of such drastic powers, even though no war actually existed.

Prof. James McGregor Burns entitled his outstanding biography of the President: *Franklin D. Roosevelt, the Lion and the Fox*. The entire first Inaugural Address was the roar of a lion; there was not a trace of the fox any place in it. It was later that he was to show that he was sometimes one and sometimes the other.

With this single speech Roosevelt accomplished one of the most significant achievements of his Presidency—the banishment of fear, the renewal of the courage and faith of the American people. Within a week, more than half a million letters and telegrams had gone to the White House, expressing faith in him and in his leadership.

Action was what he had promised the American people—action is what they got. On his first two days as President, he called Congress into extra-ordinary session; he closed all the banks by Federal proclamation, and he began to make preparations to reopen those banks which could be safely opened. On 9 March the Congress met. The President sent them his banking message. Accompanying the message was a proposed bill. The bill was passed by Congress practically unseen. It was sent to the White House and signed by the President by 8.30 p.m. of that same day. The whole process from introduction to final signature took less than eight hours. This speed was typical of what was to happen to many more of Roosevelt's recommendations during that session. Some contemporary wag remarked, during this performance of alacrity and compliance by Congress, that Congress was not really voting on legislation, but merely waving at it as it sailed by.

The banking bill was followed by a quick and steady succession of messages to Congress asking for legislation to carry out his pledge of a New Deal. When Congress adjourned after one hundred days of session (now commonly referred to as the 'One Hundred Days'), it had enacted the most extraordinary programme of recovery and reform in American history up to that time.

People who lived through those days could almost physically see the fog lift. The resurgence of faith and hope was more important than the economic statistics of improvement. By the end of 1933 the production index had gone up substantially. But Roosevelt's interest was always predominantly in human beings, and if they felt the improvement, and shared the renewed confidence, this was more important to him than any figures of production or any political or economic theory or dogmas.

The new spirit of confidence was reflected in, and encouraged by, the new mood of the White House. Many who were familiar with the White House during the Hoover days have remarked, and some have written, about the complete change which occurred when the Roosevelts moved in. The Roosevelts were as gregarious as the Hoovers were isolated. The house was filled with laughter of grandchildren; there was a steady, unremitting flow of overnight and weekend visitors from all parts of the world; there was gaiety amidst the serious planning sessions and conferences; there were gala dinners and social functions; there were, above all, newspaper photographs and moving pictures of a smiling, intrepid, and optimistic President. That was one of Roosevelt's ways of imparting to the American people his own confidence in the future. It succeeded—because it had a genuineness which everybody could feel.

If one examines the product of the hundred days more closely, one will find no coordinated plan of action—no master programme. Roosevelt, even before his nomination, had announced his belief in 'bold experimentation'; he was a practical experimenter, and an idealistic pragmatist, rather than a devotee of any political social or economic theory. Some of the bills during the hundred days and their methods of implimentation were actually inconsistent with each other. But consistency of methods did not weigh nearly so strongly with Roosevelt as practical results and consistency of objectives—and there were no inconsistencies in his objectives all during his tenure.

The pragmatism of the New Deal and its reliance on experimentation were based on one definite conviction—that the inequalities and injustices of the American economic system could be cured, or at least ameliorated, by using political techniques. Roosevelt felt that agencies of government could provide 'practical controls over blind economic forces and blindly selfish men', and could help 'to solve for the individual the ever-rising problems of a complex civilization'.

Many of Roosevelt's experiments were failures; that is what experimentation entails. He would be satisfied, he said, if seventy-five per cent of them produced beneficial results. Experimentation depended on one of his distinctive characteristics—receptivity to new and untried methods and ideas. This receptivity led him, his hostile critics say, to experiments with crack-pot ideas like money-tinkering, greenbelt shelters and others. If Roosevelt had lived to write his own memoirs, he would himself have admitted that many of his ideas and methods did turn out to be impractical, and had to be abandoned. But if this receptivity in his make-up is to be condemned because of the occasional failures, should it not at the same time be credited with success in carrying out many other ideas like minimum wages and maximum hours, regulation of securities selling and securities exchanges, improvements in the banking system, all the vast field of social security, the direct relief and work relief for the unemployed, flood control, the Tennessee Valley Authority, the big western dams which reclaimed to agriculture millions of acres of arid land and also provided the power to make the aluminium which we were to need for our 100,000 planes per year?

Also, should not his receptivity be credited for new ideas to produce unconditional surrender, such as the atom bomb, the proximity fuse, and improved radar as well as a host of other new secret weapons, the over-age destroyer deal, lend-lease, the 'shoot-on-sight' order and the priority of Hitler as the first target?

On the international scene, how about the 'Good Neighbour' policy and western hemisphere solidarity, the Four Freedoms, the Atlantic Charter, UNRRA, the World Bank, the Bretton Woods accord—and finally, the United Nations Organization itself?

Roosevelt felt that it was an essential task of a President as a national leader to educate the American people in the problems of their government, in what their government was doing to solve them, and in what it intended to do in the future. 'Government includes,' he said, 'the art of formulating a policy, and using the political technique to attain so much of that policy as will receive general support; persuading, leading, sacrificing, teaching always, because the greatest duty of a statesman is to educate'.

'Educating', 'teaching'—that was 'high politics' in Roosevelt's dictionary, for it meant assuring his leadership of the people. He enjoyed that kind of politics the most; and he was a master at it. He also enjoyed—but to a lesser degree—the other kind of politics—the 'low politics', the politics of pressure, of threats and promises, of the bait of patronage, of intrigue and behind-the-scenes manipulation; and he was master of that too. He relied on both to exercise his leadership with Congress and to get his legislation passed. But he relied more on the first kind of politics to get support from the people—and their votes.

The most useful instruments for this education, in addition to his regular speeches, were his press conferences with reporters, and his radio talks directly to the people. His press conferences had a style completely his own. The general tone of the 1,011 press conferences which he was to hold during his Presidency was set by his very first words to the reporters at the first conference: 'It is very good to see you all. My hope is that these conferences are going to be merely enlarged editions of the kind of very delightful family conferences I have been holding in Albany for the last four years.'

The conferences in Washington, with from 100 to 200 reporters crowding around his office desk, were indeed 'delightful family conferences', enjoyed by most of the reporters nearly as much as by the President. There were informal remarks, quips, asides by him and by the reporters, with the President at times leaning back in his chair laughing, his cigarette holder at a jaunty angle, eyes twinkling, calling reporters by their first names. At the end of his first conference, the hardboiled, cynical and experienced reporters—not generally addicted to enthusiasm—were so delighted with the new atmosphere he had created that they gave him a prolonged ovation. But sometimes in the press conferences there was grimness or firmness or resentment or resolute determination written into his jaw when occasions warranted them, e.g., in discussing the decisions of the Supreme Court striking down essential New Deal legislation, or during the dark days of the war—but never was there any appearance of fear, panic or being lost on his way—forever calm, dignified, imperturbable, and self-confident.

The other instrument which Roosevelt used for educating the public, for maintaining public morale during dark and trying days, for projecting his own image, for building up support for his policies, and for bringing popular influence to bear on the members of Congress, was the 'fireside chat' Although prior Presidents had used the radio to broadcast speeches they were making to live audiences, Roosevelt was the first President to use the radio when not making a public address, for communicating directly with the people of the nation.

I was present at many of these fireside chats, and was always struck by the simplicity, effectiveness and homey atmosphere of it all. For Roosevelt, by his style of speaking and by the simple words he used, was able to create a feeling of intimacy with each of his listeners. It was as if the microphone had been removed, and he was seated in the living-room of the American families. There was no attempt at oratory; in its place were substituted deep sincerity of tone, friendliness, warmth and calmness of voice. In a word, he would 'chat'. As a result of his use of the press conference and the fireside chat, the American public was better informed about their federal government, its problems, its objectives and its philosophies during the twelve years of Roosevelt than ever before.

In Grosvenor Square in London there is a statue of President Roosevelt;

it shows him in a standing position with his leg braces visible, holding a cane. He could not stand, however, in this manner without some additional support. Even with the support it was painful for him to stand for long periods. His torso rested on a padded circle of steel extending down and attached to his shoes. The braces bent at the knees to permit him, with considerable difficulty and mostly by the use of his strong arms and shoulder, to rise and to sit down.

I never heard him make one bitter or resentful remark about the attack of paralysis or the helplessness in which it left him. The first physical thing that struck you on meeting Roosevelt was that huge powerful body without the use of legs. As you got to know him, it was also the first thing you forgot. His little wheel chair,[1] always present in the background, soon became a normal part of the furniture of the room. Wheeling him in to dinner became as routine as offering your arm to your dinner partner. It was something that he himself seemed never to think much about. In fact when he wanted to end a conversation or a visit, he frequently would say: 'Well, I'm sorry, I have to run now!'—and I am sure it never struck him as a strange thing to say, even though he had not been able to walk since 1921.

In the light of his victory over the effects of paralysis and over all the many obstacles he had faced, there is little wonder that he had such self-confidence and self-assurance. There is little wonder that Mrs Roosevelt was able to write after his death: 'I have never heard him say that there was a problem that he thought it was impossible for human beings to solve. He never talked about his doubts. I never knew him to face life or any problem that came up, with fear . . . I have never known a man who gave one a greater sense of security.' The nation needed 'this sense of security' in 1933. It was to need it even more during the disastrous war days of 1942.

This self-confidence came partly from a deep religious faith—which had been imbued in him from childhood at home. It was fortified at Groton by his headmaster. His wife described his religious faith as 'one of the strongest and . . . most simplistic forces within him'; that it was one which made him feel 'guided in great crises by a strength and a wisdom higher than his own'. The great cross-channel invasion of 6 June 1944, and the mighty onslaught against the man who wanted to abolish all religion, were announced by Roosevelt to the American public, not with martial music and a fighting speech, but by a simple prayer of his own composition.

On the day of his death, he was writing a speech to be delivered on Jefferson Day. The last sentence he wrote was: 'The only limit to our realizations of tomorrow [a day of lasting peace] will be our doubts of today. Let us move forward with strong and active faith.' It seems natural that the last word he was to write was the word 'faith'; and the last thought was to abandon all 'doubts' that faith would find a way.

In the 1935 session of Congress, Roosevelt submitted a new programme of legislation—even more liberal, more reforming, more far-reaching than in 1933. The Congress of 1935 was not as complaisant, however, as the Congress of 1933 had been. The economy had been saved; big business and big finance had been saved; there was no longer any fear or panic in the land. So the conservative opposition in Congress became strong and bitter. Hatred of the President as a 'traitor to his own class' on the part of many big financiers and industrialists gave rise to attacks upon him of a ferocity unparalleled since the days of President Andrew Jackson. The strangest part of this phenomenon was that the loudest and most bitter of the Roosevelt-haters were those who had benefitted most from the New Deal measures.

It took months of the most intense and bitter fighting with Congress to get his recommendations passed. When Congress finally adjourned that year, it had enacted as many and as important pieces of legislation as its predecessor in 1933. The legislation of 1933 and 1935 added together comprised nothing less than a complete change in the social and economic climate of America. Some called it the Roosevelt Revolution, but the fundamentals of the American system of free enterprise and private profit were not touched. The system had been reformed –but it had also been preserved.

It has generally come to be recognized in retrospect that these changes, though seemingly abrupt, were in fact, in the words of Henry Steele Commager, the renowned historian, 'no revolution at all, but rather the culmination of half-a-century of historical development'. Perhaps the best evidence that it was not radical in the ordinary meaning of the word, is that neither of the two conservative Presidents who have followed Roosevelt have touched any of it by so much as a comma. On the contrary, each of them has enlarged and expanded some parts of it.

In a letter to the Young Democratic Clubs in 1939, Roosevelt tried to define what he was politically: 'Liberals are those who—unlike the radicals who want to tear everything up by the roots and plant new and untried seeds—desire to use the existing plants of civilization, to select the best of them, to water them and make them grow—not only for the present use of mankind, but also for the use of generations to come. That is why I call myself a liberal.'

Nevertheless the New Deal was not without its critics. The Supreme Court of the United States began in 1935, and continued in 1936, to strike down one New Deal measure after another. Roosevelt would have to do something about that—but he decided not to do anything until after the 1936 elections. In that election, he ran on two essential themes.

First, that as the New Deal spurred recovery (the evidence of which he recited), it insisted on reform at the same time; that it was the New Deal which, by these reforms, 'saved the system of private profit and free enterprise after it had been dragged to the brink of ruin by these same leaders who now try to scare you' [by calling it communism].

Secondly, that 'we have only just begun to fight for the New Deal objectives, in spite of the forces of selfishness and lust for power'. These forces he described as monopolists, speculators, reckless bankers, and class antagonists. 'I should like to have it said of my first Administration that in it these forces . . . met their match. I should like to have it said of my second Administration that in it these forces met their master.' He was indeed fighting mad at those big industrialists whom he had helped through the crisis of 1933, but who now hated and opposed him because of his insistence on reform.

In the 1936 election he obtained the most compelling mandate 'to continue to fight', by the greatest electoral victory in the history of the United States up to that time since President Monroe. Roosevelt won the electoral vote of forty-six states out of forty-eight, and sixty-one per cent of the popular vote.

He had been thinking about what to do about the Supreme Court ever since its decision in May 1935 declaring unconstitutional the National Recovery Act—one of the main props of the 1933 legislation. But, as so often in the future, he never told anyone about the decision he had come to (except those few people working on it) until he announced it publicly in February 1937.

On 5 February 1937, he sprang his great surprise. Over-confident because of his overwhelming victory in the 1936 election, and relying upon the mandate given to him by the people to 'continue to fight', he started his famous battle with the Supreme Court by asking the Congress for legislation to reorganize it.

The legislation he recommended was to add an additional judge to the Court as soon as a judge reached the age of seventy and refused to retire on a full pay pension. Six of the judges were already over seventy. Since the President appoints the judges of the Supreme Court, this would insure enough liberal judges to overturn the reactionary decisions made in 1935 and 1936.

Roosevelt was subjected to a humiliating defeat on this matter. He failed to rally public opinion behind him, and he was defeated in Congress. He was a vindictive man; he never forgave those responsible for this shattering blow to his objectives and to his prestige. The defeat became an encouraging signal for opposition by Congress to all the new measures he proposed in 1937 and 1938. There came one Congressional rejection after another. In vain he appealed to the people by radio for their support; he could not during 1937 and 1938 repeat his former successes.

To add to his problems, there came late in 1937 what was called the 'Roosevelt Recession'. It was caused primarily by a reduction of government spending, in an effort to bring the budget into balance. Roosevelt tried, but could not shake off the recession until he resumed spending in 1938.

The President began in 1938 a most ill-advised and amateurish effort to 'purge' from the Democratic Party some of the conservative Democrats who had been responsible for these defeats. This move was exactly contrary to his traditional policy of never interfering in local elections. He tried to do it by going into the districts of those he had selected to purge, setting up rival liberal Democrats as opponents, and making personal appeals to the people in each district to vote for the liberal candidate. The 'purge' failed— as it was bound to. It was hurriedly improvised and carried on by amateurs, not by the professional politicians. Only extreme bitterness and vindictive-ness can account for this master politician thinking for a moment that he could go to the State of Georgia, for example, and unseat the venerable and esteemed Senator George, who had respresented Georgia for many terms in the Senate to the complete satisfaction of the people of his state.

By the end of 1938 nearly all his prestige resulting from the overwhelming victory in the election of 1936 had slipped away. The Congressional election results in November 1938 showed the effect upon the voters of all the events which had occurred since the sweep of 1936: the Republican seats in the

Senate were increased and the Republican representation in the House was almost doubled.

It is impossible to say what Roosevelt would or could have done during the years 1939 and 1940 to regain his prestige if the threat of war had not reached an ominous intensity during the latter part of 1938. It is almost axiomatic in American political history that a President during his last two years in office (and these would have been Roosevelt's last two years) gradually loses his influence, as the end of his power approaches. It is doubtful whether Roosevelt could have regained his old prestige and mastery of Congress during those two years in ordinary times. But he never really tried. His eyes began instead to turn to Europe and Asia, and he had little time to fight with Congress on domestic issues. He was now looking toward horizons far beyond the boundaries of the United States—to what was to become his second great crisis—war, and its threat to the whole world.

The crisis was more formidable and dangerous even than that of 1933. The crisis of 1933, moreover, had been visible to everyone; it was right in the midst of every American home. But up until the end of 1941, the second crisis was more than 3,000 miles away. So far away that only a small minority of Americans were able even to see it as a danger to the United States. Many of those who did see it, preferred to stick their heads in the sand, and hope that it would go away. Some who saw it, were not too much concerned. To these few, the events of the crises of 1939-41 were the 'wave of the future' for the whole world; they were confident that they could 'do business with Hitler' at any time.

The President's job as a leader of the American people in this second crisis was more difficult than in 1933. First, he had to make Americans see it. Then he had to show them how dangerous it was to them. Finally, he had to persuade them to do all the costly and dangerous things necessary to meet it. He would have to expand the process of 1933-37 which he described as 'taking the whole nation to school on the nation's business' to taking the whole nation to school on the *world's* business.

Roosevelt's foreign policy as announced back in his first Inaugural Address of 1933 was very simple and understandable. It was the policy of the 'Good Neighbour—the neighbour who resolutely respects himself and . . . the right of others—the neighbour who respects his obligations and respects the sanctity of his agreements with a world of neighbours'. The Good Neighbour policy in Latin America was a steady and expanding movement away from the former policies of imperialism by the United States; and it was particularly effective during the war because of the good-will it had created.

But applying the Good Neighbour policy to the rest of the world was a different kind of problem. In 1935 he had been unable to persuade his country to join the World Court. In the same year, the Neutrality Act which Congress passed—and Roosevelt signed—was only a formal statutory recognition of what everyone knew was the isolationism prevalent throughout the United States. It imposed an embargo of arms on all belligerents, no matter which one was the aggressor and which was the victim.

By 1936 Roosevelt was becoming doubtful of continued peace in Europe. In 1937 the pace of war-like events increased. For Roosevelt, 1937 was the year of decision about his own course of action. He made that decision; he was no longer going to continue to remain silent. He was going to try to educate the American people as to what their isolationism might mean to their own security.

On 5 October 1937, he said: 'There is no escape through mere isolation or neutrality . . . The epidemic of world lawlessness is spreading. When an epidemic of physical disease starts to spread, the community approves and joins in a quarantine . . . in order to protect the health of the community against the spread of the disease.'

From the violent, antagonistic public reaction in the United States, Roosevelt realized that he had made a major mistake in timing. He rarely made such mistakes. He had misjudged public opinion; it was not yet ready for even this. 'It's a terrible thing,' he once said to me 'to look over your shoulder when you are trying to lead—and to find no one there'.

Hitler was pushing ahead in his time-table of aggression; Austria, Sudetenland, the dismemberment of Czechoslovakia. What Roosevelt did as he watched the course of events was minimal. He sent several letters to the different nations involved—none of which accomplished anything. It was getting too late for letters.

But he would not let it get too late for America's self-defence! He went into action in 1938. He started to build up American defences—especially in aircraft. Beginning in January 1939, he kept trying to get from Congress the repeal of the embargo provisions of the Neutrality Act. He recognized that an embargo on arms, if war should develop between Britain and Germany, could only help Germany and hurt Britain. In his Annual Message in January, he announced that 'there are many methods short of war of bringing home to aggressor governments the sentiments of our people'. He did not try to define the ambiguous phrase, 'methods short of war'; but the world would soon get his definition—not in words but in action. In 1939 one request after another went to Congress for funds and more funds— billions of dollars for defence construction of all kinds. Congress passed them all. But the Senate rejected his renewed appeals to repeal the embargo. It was influenced in part by a statement of Senator Borah that his information was better than the State Department's, and that it showed that there would positively be no war in Europe in 1939. This Senate refusal had two dire effects: it encouraged Hitler in his aggression; and it encouraged Stalin to make his pact in August with Hitler. Hitler soon began to make his outrageous demands on Poland. Again the President wrote letters—which were again without result. Hitler invaded Poland on 1 September 1939; and the war was on.

Two nights later, Roosevelt was on the air in a fireside chat. I am sure that every American family was listening. That evening I was in a cottage in the Adirondacks with my family. It was in the middle of the forest, on the shore of a calm, placid lake. There were no roads leading to it; access was only by boat across the water. Everything was very peaceful—an atmosphere so incongruous with the war news. There was literally no sound except the quiet lapping of the lake on the rocks on shore; there were no lights visible except one three miles away on the other side of the lake. We listened to the President at our radio on the porch overlooking the peaceful scene. The voice which came to us was just as calm as the mountains, the forest, and the water. There was no trace of panic, or even of extreme urgency. This was Roosevelt's style in the midst of crisis—the style of 1933 and the style of Pearl Harbor Day. He wanted to reassure the American people, not to frighten them, or even to suggest that he was himself frightened. But it was a firm voice; and it showed his deep concern. He expressed determination to use every effort to keep the United States out of the war. But he warned that we could not shrug off the war as none of our business, for 'every word that comes through the air, every ship that sails the seas, every battle that is fought, does affect the American future'.

Finally in November 1939, Congress repealed the embargo, and substituted the 'cash and carry policy' Roosevelt had recommended. Roosevelt now had a free hand. But the years 1940 and 1941 were to provide the ultimate test of his ability to teach the American people and the Congress, before it was too late, how near to them the Nazi and Japanese threats were, to persuade them to approve the drastic steps he was taking 'short of war', and to approve his shipment to Britain—and later, to Russia—of many of the military supplies we had and those we could make, instead of keeping them at home.

During the first half of 1940, the mood of the American people was clear. Roosevelt, writing in July 1941, only five months before Pearl Harbor, described it as an attitude of a 'very interested spectator', although its sympathies were with Britain.

When the 'phony' war of the winter of 1939-40 broke into a massive attack by the Nazis in April 1940, starting in Denmark and Norway, the American people began to get a more realistic picture of their own position. Denmark and Norway had also been neutral countries, determined to maintain their neutrality and to escape the war—much like the attitude and wishful thinking in the United States. So had Holland, Belgium and Luxembourg—all invaded by Hitler in May. Within a few short weeks, Britain stood all alone in the world against the Nazi might. With the fall of France in June, the war was coming closer to America. It soon came even closer; German submarines began to appear in the waters of the Western Hemisphere.

Roosevelt, in the face of this danger, even while he was educating, acted! In June 1940, while British troops were still being evacuated at Dunkirk by the new Prime Minister of Great Britain—Winson Churchill—Roosevelt released and sent to England at Churchill's urgent request, forty-three million dollars worth of surplus or outdated stocks of arms, munitions, and aircraft. He believed that he had succeeded in part at least in his teaching. 'The year 1940,' the President later wrote, 'witnessed a great change in the attitude of the American people'.

In the same year Roosevelt decided to run for a third term of office. He won the election by a majority of about 5,000,000 votes. His electoral vote was 449 from thirty-eight states against Willkie's eighty-two from ten states.

he complexity of the task which now faced Roosevelt in January 1941 was matched only by its urgency. Great Britain was still standing virtually alone against Hitler. All of western Europe, its resources and productive capacity—and part of the Balkans—were in Nazi hands. Hitler was in a position to try the all too-short jump across the channel. He had made plans to do this in 1940, and even preparations. But he had postponed the invasions temporarily; he thought that he should first concentrate on wiping out the Red Army to protect his eastern front from Stalin. Britain had little but her Navy and the superb courage of her air and ground forces with which to turn him back; and it was England alone and her Navy and the ever-narrowing Atlantic Ocean which stood between Hitler and the United States.

From the beginning of 1941, down until the Japanese took matters out of his hands at Pearl Harbor, he had to walk a narrow line between increasing pressures from all sides. In the Atlantic, German submarines were sinking American vessels outside the combat zones faster than it was possible to make them. In the Pacific the Japanese were accelerating their long-planned aggression. All the isolationists were clamouring that Roosevelt do nothing, because 'Britain was already defeated' and no provocation should be tendered to either the Nazis or the Japanese. On the other hand, Stimson, his Secretary of War, and several other leaders in Washington, as the sinkings in the Atlantic increased, were urging him to go before Congress and forthrightly to ask for a declaration of war. The Secretary of State, Hull, was equally persistent in his contrary advice of caution. Hitler, relying on the division among the American people, did not want war with the United States; on the contrary, he had issued orders against direct provocation of the United States. There was no way that formal war with the United States could help him in 1941—especially after his attack on Russia had begun. Roosevelt wanted no war in the Atlantic or the Pacific if it could be avoided—at least until enough productive machinery for war had been built, and the country was better prepared. All these opposing pressures were on him all during 1941; they changed in emphasis from time to time as the complicated events unfolded. On two things, however, Roosevelt was determined—first, he would get the arms to Britain at all costs; and second, that the sinking of individual ships would not push him into war as it had Wilson. Had Roosevelt proposed to Congress the sale of arms to Great Britain on credit or a gift of arms to Britain, or a loan of money, there is no doubt that he would have been roundly defeated—even if Britain's credit of 1941 had been better than it was. No one knew that better than Roosevelt. So he used the skilful device of Lend Lease. By the invention of the homey analogy of lending your neighbour your garden hose to save his burning home, and getting it back again after the fire was put out, he circumvented all the opposition which would come to anything smacking of war loans. As he put it, 'I want to eliminate the dollar sign'.

No one can tell exactly what was in that secretive mind as Roosevelt went through the events of 1941. But far from trying to 'drag us into war' as some critics would later say, he was doing all he could to stay out. He stalled Japan for more than two years just because he wanted no war with her in the Pacific particularly while he was contending with Hitler's submarines in the Atlantic. He had learned early in life from Admiral Mahan the dangers of a two-ocean war.

In 1941 he occupied Iceland and Greenland before Hitler could get there. He kept calling for more and more planes, at first the 'fantastic' number of 50,000 per year—for which he received plenty of derision as having 'a pipe dream'—but which soon rose to the actual manufacture of 100,000 per year.

On 22 June 1941, Great Britain got its first break in its long dark period of war. It was also a great break for the United States; it bought some more of the precious commodity of time. On that day Hitler invaded Russia. Roosevelt again gambled; he decided to send all the aid possible to Russia. In making this decision, he also stepped out ahead of some American military leaders who thought that Russia could not resist Hitler for more than six weeks. Through Hull, he began a long series of negotiations with Japan to reach a settlement about past attacks by Japan in the Pacific. It all took a long time. This style with Japan, while we continued building our war production plants and military strength, worked for two years. It gave the United States time—time to prepare, and time to produce, and time to ship across the Atlantic.

On 7 December 1941, war was forced upon America by Japan. Roosevelt was now the Commander-in-Chief of a nation at war. He was soon to become the leader of the world in the formation of an organization to maintain the peace. These two projects were the pinnacle of Roosevelt's life. All that he had learned of domestic politics, of international relationships, of naval strategy—all of his skilful style of leadership—all of his receptiveness to new ideas (and new weapons)—all of his self-confidence and self-assurance, especially in personal confrontation—with his flexibility and willingness to compromise—all of his arts of persuasion and conciliation as well as his inflexible stubborness when he felt sure he was right—all of his love of human beings living in the dark alleys of the world, exploited and disadvantaged—all of his past thirty years of training in public life seemed to converge into the style which this world statesman was now to adopt in order to try for his objectives of total victory, continued peace, and a new kind of world based on the Four Freedoms and the Atlantic Charter. Japan had finally united the American people; it had at last obliterated the opposition of the isolationist bloc in Congress.

The first fundamental strategic issue was how to divide U.S. resources against the enemies in the Atlantic and the enemy in the Pacific. That decision had really been made in Washington as early as March 1941 in secret talks between British and United States Staffs—the ABC-1 plan—for strategy if the United States got into the war in both oceans. Roosevelt and Churchill confirmed this strategy. They never wavered from it. 'First things first' had always been Roosevelt's aim—and the first things now were Hitler and Mussolini. The President announced that strategy in a speech, saying that the enemy had failed in its intent at Pearl Harbor to 'terrify us to such an extent that we would divert our industrial and military strength to the Pacific area'.

Roosevelt also became the leading spokesman of the world in psycholo-

Day of infamy—Japan's attack on Pearl Harbor. Naval air station in flames

gical warfare—in the important battle of propaganda. Most of his speeches in 1942 were primarily intended for propaganda; and none failed to devote at least some attention to it. In addition to words, he used action. Action spoke louder than words—and in all languages. The greatest of the propaganda exploits in the bleak days of 1942 was Doolittle's bombing raid on Tokyo.

As Commander-in-Chief, a title in which he took great pride, he went further in his conception of Presidential war powers than any President before him, including Lincoln. Perhaps, the best example was his message to Congress on 7 September 1942 asking for legislation authorizing the President 'to stabilize the cost of living, including the prices of all farm commodities', in order to curb inflation during the war. He insisted, as always that there was no distinction between the fighting front and the home front, that they were so intertwined with each other that there was only *one* war front. Therefore, in his message, he boldly and openly stated as leader of the war and as 'Commander-in-Chief' that if 'Congress should fail to act and act adequately [to give him such authority], I shall accept the responsibility, and I will act . . . The President has the powers, under the Constitution and under Congressional Acts, to take measures necessary to avert a disaster which would interfere with the winning of the war.' He even set a deadline; he gave Congress until 1 October 1942 to take action. Congress did act and it acted 'adequately'—and also within the time limit. Roosevelt believed that to carry out his oath of office to 'preserve, protect and defend the Constitution' he not only *could*, but *had to* take any step necessary to save the nation.

He was Commander-in-Chief not only in name—but in fact. Admiral Leahy, the liaison between the President and the Combined Chiefs of Staff (of Britain and the United States), in his book *I Was There* corroborated many others, when he said:

'Planning of the major campaigns was always done in close cooperation with the President. Frequently, we had sessions in his study . . . The policy and broad objectives were stated by the President . . .

'I may have indicated in this summary that the men who made up the Combined Chiefs of Staff were the men who ran the war. This is inaccurate. There were two men at the top who really fought out and finally agreed on the major moves that led to victory. They were Franklin D. Roosevelt and Winston Churchill. They really ran the war. Of course, they had to have some people like us to help them, but we were just artisans building definite patterns of strategy from the rough blueprints handed to us by our respective Commanders-in-Chief.'

I would myself suggest one amendment to this statement. Although Churchill and Roosevelt often 'really fought out' the major moves, they did not always 'finally agree'. When they did not agree, Roosevelt's decision was final.

The Secretary of War, Henry L. Stimson, in his private diary three days after Roosevelt's death said: 'On the whole he has been a superb war President—far more so than any other President in our history. His role has not been merely a negative one. He has pushed for decisions of sound strategy, and carried them through against strong opposition from Churchill, for example, and others.'

Roosevelt was not given to interfering in the conduct of military operations in the way Churchill did. Nevertheless, he did not take the advice of his Chiefs of Staff without question. At times, he disagreed with them, and said so. On at least two recorded occasions, he expressly overruled them. Several times, when Roosevelt insisted on his own strategy, he told Leahy: 'Bill, I'm a pig-headed Dutchman, and I have made up my mind on this'.

For example, on Torch (the invasion of North Africa) which had been suggested by Churchill as an alternative in 1942 for the cross-channel invasion (Overlord), Stimson, Marshall and King were all opposed. It was ordered by Roosevelt nevertheless—and he insisted also on an early deadline for it.

The President could be quite blunt at times with his Chiefs of Staff. For example, in reply to a memorandum from General Marshall on 10 July 1942 recommending that if Churchill continued to oppose Overlord the United States should change its policy of 'Hitler First', and proceed to use all its force against Japan, he wrote in his own hand at Hyde Park the following memo:

'Gen. Marshall:
    Copy to Ad. King and Gen. Arnold. I have carefully read your estimate of Sunday. My first impression is that it is exactly what Germany hoped the United States would do following Pearl Harbor. Secondly, it does not in fact provide use of American troops in fighting, except in a lot of islands whose occupations will not affect the world situation this year or next. Thirdly, it does not help Russia or the Near East.
    Therefore, it is disapproved as of the present.   ROOSEVELT—C-in-C.'

As an administrator, Roosevelt has received a low rating from most of his associates. Some of them considered him a failure in this role.

Henry L. Stimson who had served many years in the Cabinet of several Presidents complained to his diary that . . . 'the President is the poorest administrator I have ever worked under [this even included Taft] in respect to the orderly procedure and routine of his performance'. His additional complaint (and probably the real cause of his distress) was that 'there are a lot of young men in Washington ambitious to increase the work of their agencies . . . who report on their duties directly to the President . . . and have better access to the President than his Cabinet officers have'.

Other Cabinet officers have made the same complaint, and it is true that as an administrator, Roosevelt had a style all his own. It was fascinating to watch it at work and see how much he could accomplish with it. It was completely unorthodox; it violated every rule in the books of public administration. He paid scant attention to many of the procedures which all trained public administrators respect so much, such as job descriptions, channels of command, etc. He was interested in getting men of ideas and imagination around him, and he always wanted new ideas and innovative approaches to reach him personally and not be blocked by people below. The New Deal was essentially a combination of new ideas in government, and his chief interest was in new ideas rather than straight-laced administration. He even liked to create competition and rivalry among different agencies on the same projects. 'A little rivalry is stimulating . . . It keeps everybody going to prove that he is a better fellow than the next man,' he once said.

There were other characteristics of his style of administration which baffled and irritated many of his subordinates. His sense of timing and his patience in waiting for the right time often led to complaints of indecision and even lethargy. Decision-making in the White House always included a decision not to decide—at least for the moment, or the day, or even for the year. Then he would take his usual delight in what he called 'bombshells' of decision, in dramatic surprises.

The head of the Bureau of the Budget, Harold Smith, one of whose functions was to advise the President on administrative matters, was an orthodox, well-trained and experienced administrator, and he, too, was amazed.

In later years after Roosevelt's death and Smith's retirement—when he had the time and the distance from his daily pressures of the hectic administrative activity, to think leisurely about it—Smith told Robert Sherwood, who was then preparing his *Roosevelt and Hopkins*:

'I've been thinking about it ever since. When I worked with Roosevelt—for six years—I thought, as did many others, that he was a very erratic administrator. But now, when I look back, I can really begin to see the size of his programs. They were by far the largest and most complex programs that any President ever put through. People like me who had the responsibility of watching the pennies could only see the five or six or seven per cent of the programs that went wrong through inefficient organization or direction. But now I can see in perspective the ninety-three or four or five per cent that went right—including the winning of the biggest war in history—because of unbelievably skillful organization and direction. Roosevelt must have been one of the greatest geniuses as an administrator that ever lived. What we couldn't appreciate at the time was the fact that he was a real artist in government.'

His style in dealing with Churchill during their Anglo-American war conferences alone, and with Churchill and Stalin in their tri-partite conferences, shifted from time to time depending upon what his own thinking was at the particular moment, on what he thought the other conferees were intent on doing, and what he wanted to get for the United States out of the conference.

On many occasions, he had to be quite abrupt and stubborn with Churchill. Churchill was not easy to convince; after long arguments he would yield one day, only to return a little later to renew the argument with additional vigour. These two men, in their historic, almost unique, partnership in the conduct of the war, and in their joint efforts toward a post-war peace, understood each other very well. For example, Roosevelt, opposed to all types of colonialism, tried to get Churchill to make concessions to the dissidents in India, as Japan, in its course of conquest, was approaching India from the east. But he did not press too hard. He knew that Churchill was determined to try to keep the Empire in the same state as he had found it, and Churchill had frequently said so. He knew also that Churchill was always subject to hostile questions in the House of Commons and probably could not go along with Roosevelt's ideas about colonialism even if he had so wished.

Churchill, on the other hand, understood the limits of Roosevelt's constitutional powers, and that the President always had to keep one eye on the United States Senate as he made military and political decisions during the war. There was, of course, always mutual respect and even mutual affection. Churchill appreciated that he had to rely on the immeasurably greater resources of men and arms which Roosevelt could control; but there was, nevertheless, always the spirit and atmosphere of an equal partnership.

Much of Roosevelt's style in dealing with Stalin was based on two over-riding considerations. The first was one which all the Combined Chiefs of Staff of the United States and Great Britain were continually urging on him—to get Russia into the war against Japan as soon as possible. We must today remember that up to the date of Roosevelt's death, the United States had not yet successfully exploded a nuclear device. It was not until three months after his death and until five months after Yalta, that we knew that we had succeeded in creating an operable atomic bomb. Without being able to rely on, or even confidently predict, any atomic explosions over the cities of Japan, the American Joint Chiefs of Staff advised Roosevelt at Yalta that victory over Japan by unconditional surrender was going to take several years and a million American casualties, but that Russian active participation in the war against Japan would reduce the time and the human cost. While we now know that this estimate was greatly over-pessimistic because of the great damage which had already been done to Japanese shipping and to her ability to import or manufacture necessary war materials, the Joint Chiefs at the time of Yalta made it as a reasonable estimate.

The second consideration in Roosevelt's mind in dealing with Stalin was to make sure that Russia joined in and supported the United Nations Organization. He knew that the organization could never begin to work without the Soviet Union.

The chief disagreements between Churchill and Roosevelt developed over major problems: the cross-channel invasion; the follow-up landings in the south of France; diversionary moves advanced by Churchill in the eastern Mediterranean, and the establishment of spheres of influence after the war. It is impossible to discuss these within the limits of this chapter; but the final resolution of these differences made these two men two of the most important makers of history in the twentieth century.

Not until 1943 was there any beginning of significant victories for the Allies. In that year, Roosevelt started his active planning for many post-war activities. For him the time had arrived to carry out his oft-repeated statement: 'the time to prepare for peace is at the height of war'. These plans were many and varied: The United Nations Organization; free educational help for returning veterans; the preparation of many benefits for wounded veterans; the punishment of the war criminals; the demobilization of men and facilities; the feeding and clothing of the people of devastated Europe by a United Nations Relief and Rehabilitation Administration (UNRRA).

Roosevelt, always remembering the causes of Wilson's inability in 1919-20 to attain his most cherished dream, acted with the caution and circum-spection of the fox, as he eyed the isolationists in the Senate of his own time. For they might have the power also to defeat his own supreme ambition—to make the United States the leader in creating a world-wide peace-keeping agency. He let Hull move ahead first—without any fanfare or much publicity—to lay the plans. Roosevelt was waiting for the proper timing, keeping open, as usual, all his options on the specific form of the organization.

Another major difference between Wilson and Roosevelt was that Roosevelt did not regard the United Nations Organization, for which he was planning and working, as the ultimate one, as Wilson did the League of Nations. He looked upon it rather as a beginning, as a practical recognition of a principle—a kind of interim organization to be improved as time went on. Wilson, he said at a press conference, made the mistake of 'looking too far ahead; he was looking toward the permanent ending of war ... I cannot look any farther ahead to a world that has ended war for more than a limited period—twenty or twenty-five years'. In his Annual Message of 1943 in discussing the proposed organization, he warned that 'Perfectionism, no less than isolationism or imperialism or power politics, may obstruct the paths to international peace'.

The next year 1944, was significant for increasing military and naval victories, advances in planning for the United Nations Organization, and, at home, for the reversion of Roosevelt to the role of a fighting, liberal New Dealer. He started right off in his State of the Union message in January 1944, which Prof. Burns has called the most radical one he ever sent. In it he called for a new bill of economic rights to supplement the old political bill of rights which the Colonies had insisted upon as a condition of ratifying the proposed Constitution and joining the Union. It was a summation in a new form of the old New Deal objectives and philosophy—that the Government had the responsibility of looking after the welfare of its citizens who were willing to work; and to see to it that each citizen, as a matter of right and regardless of creed or race, was entitled to the following enumerated rights: a decent job at pay sufficient to provide adequate food, clothing and recreation, the assurance of a fair cash income for farmers; protection against monopolies; a decent home; adequate medical care; protection from the economic hazards of old age, sickness, unemployment and accidents; and a good education. It should be pointed out that the succeeding Democratic Administrations in the United States—under Presidents Truman, Kennedy and Johnson—continued to pursue the same objectives as newly enunicated in this message. Whether the slogan of their Administration was 'Fair Deal', 'New Frontiers' or 'Great Society', in effect and in purpose they are all synonomous—for they were all re-statements of the New Deal and this economic bill of rights.

In 1944, came President Roosevelt's election for a fourth term. In 1945 came the summit meeting at Yalta. Roosevelt did obtain at Yalta the realization of his chief objective, efforts for which began as early as the Foreign Minister's meeting at Moscow in October 1943, continued at Teheran, and at Dumbarton Oaks—the creation of a post-war peace-keeping organization. At Yalta, agreement was reached on the last remaining difference between him and Stalin on the voting arrangements. The three Powers agreed on calling a meeting of all the United Nations for 25 April 1945 at San Francisco. His great military aim he also realized—the agreement definitely fixing the time of the Russian entry into the war against Japan, viz., 'three months' after V.E. Day.

In addition to these—and to certain reciprocal military agreements for the rest of the war—Yalta was a great success—*on paper*. Stalin saw to it that it was to become a massive failure in *practice*—almost immediately. This was particularly true about the arrangements for the future of Poland and the other liberated areas of Eastern Europe.

Compromises were reached on some issues, and the decisions on some others were deferred. Russia made substantial concessions; so did the other Allies. Stalin had never broken his pledged word to Roosevelt until after Yalta. Roosevelt had gambled on Stalin's good faith twice—once in 1941 when Russia was invaded; and the second time in 1944, when many predicted that as the Nazi troops were pushed out of Russian territory, Stalin would sign a separate peace with Hitler. Both gambles paid off in final victory. He believed that Stalin would again keep his word this time as he always had during the war. When he learned about Stalin's treachery, he got quite tough in his messages to Stalin. The President died too soon for history to ascertain whether his new tough attitude would have made any difference or where it would lead. The day he died, he cabled in reply to a question from Churchill as to what Roosevelt thought he should report to the House of Commons about the difficulties with Stalin: 'I would minimize the general Soviet problem as much as possible because these problems in one form or another seem to arise every day, and most of them straighten out, as in the case of the Berne meeting (referring to the dispute which had arisen about the surrender of the Nazi troops in Italy). *We must be firm, however, and our course thus far has been correct.*' (Emphasis added.) The 'course' was the firm position he and Churchill were taking with Stalin over Poland.

He was puzzled about what Stalin was doing. He was not yet ready to believe that Stalin had practised pure deceit at Yalta. He speculated as to whether the Politbureau had overruled Stalin. The beginning of the break with Stalin had a depressing effect on the President. I have often wondered, as have many others, whether the Cold War would have come as quickly, and with such intensity, had Roosevelt lived through his fourth term. Certainly, whatever gratitude Stalin and the other Russian leaders were capable of feeling would have been extended personally to Roosevelt—as it was not to Truman. Roosevelt's style with Stalin in turn would have also been different from Truman's, I am sure less abrupt, more patient, more understanding of the problems of the Soviet Union, and, above all, more willing to meet Stalin face to face more frequently. The concessions made by Stalin to Roosevelt at Yalta indicate that Roosevelt did retain to the end of that personal confrontation, a certain capacity to influence Stalin— even though Stalin and the Red Army at that time no longer needed American military help. It is doubtful that any American could, after Roosevelt's death, have the activating or even the restraining influences on Stalin that Roosevelt would have had.

However, the relations between the Soviet and the United States were not within the *ex parte* control of either one. It takes two to reach understanding and agreement, but only one to create mistrust and conflict.

At the Yalta Conference. Roosevelt, with Molotov, reviews Soviet troops

As one merely skims over the many thousands of matters—military, domestic, and international—between 1933 and 1945 for which Roosevelt was responsible, one can get some idea of their impact on a man's physical constitution. By September 1944, he had reached the physical state where he had to deliver his speeches in a seated position. But the physical strain, tremendous as it was, was nothing compared to the mental, nervous, and spiritual strain through which he had gone, especially during the last five years, commencing with the invasions of Norway, Denmark, Holland, Belgium and France.

How can you measure the stress upon a man who decides in the pre-Pearl Harbor years that certain steps are essential, who assumes the responsibility for taking them, or for arguing for them night and day—against the opposition and denunciation of so many millions of his countrymen and so many members of Congress?

And when the war finally was forced upon us, who can measure the strain upon a man of all the events from then to April 1945? Who can say what goes on in a man's mind who has personally insisted on American troops going into action in 1942, and then listens on the radio as they land on the North African beaches.

And what about the conscience of a man who had argued with Churchill for two years, demanding the cross-channel invasion of France time and again—instead of the easier, safer, but what Roosevelt's Chief of Staff called ineffective diversionary tactics Churchill preferred in other parts of Europe?

I was with the President on the night of the cross-channel invasion in 1944, and on the following day when he read on the radio the prayer which he had written. I could see in his eyes the deep concern and the terrible sense of responsibility and the religious faith with which he prayed. But never, never, never did I glimpse a trace of fear or panic—any more than I had at the news of Pearl Harbor or of the repeated victories of the Japanese in 1942. For the following few days after D-Day he eagerly read each and every dispatch, and as prospects grew brighter and brighter, the tension lessened—but it had left its mark.

Add to this the tension of a political election campaign in the midst of all of this—a campaign carried on by his opponent in a manner which led him to refer to it as 'the dirtiest in all history'.

How much does a man put of himself into a constant struggle for three years to get started a new peace-keeping security organization—always with the memory of the tragic failure of Wilson, and always under the jaundiced eye of the Senate of the United States?

Ask any experienced lawyer about his nervous tension before and during a trial in which the life or death of just one client is involved. How must Roosevelt's nerves have felt about the trial of wits, and armed power, and horse-trading, and grand global politics during Teheran and Yalta—where, he was convinced, the fate of the entire future world was involved? He carried the conferences off with an apparent nonchalance approaching gaiety; he always sat at the head of the table, conciliating, trading, insisting, yielding, intent on his main objectives but never neglecting the others. It was a trial which left its effects. I know because I came home with him on his cruiser, and saw him each day as he sat on the top deck with his daughter Anna—thinking, wondering, planning. The buoyancy of the recent campaign, the excitement of preparing to go to Yalta had disappeared. In their place was grey fatigue—sheer mental and physical exhaustion. Add all these trials and tribulations up—to say nothing of those which happened on the domestic scene before 1939—and ponder the miracle that this one man could stand it as long as he did.

He died on 12 April 1945. Had he remained conscious longer than he did—after the massive cerebral hemorrhage hit him, he would have had the satisfaction of looking back upon what he had accomplished. How different the United States was in 1945 from the stricken, fearful, impoverished one he had inherited in 1933! The nation he left behind was now the strongest one in the world—economically, spiritually and militarily. Government was no longer run by the great men of finance and industry. America's democracy, its Constitution, its individual liberties, its individual opportunities, its new feeling of social security, its new bill of economic rights as a goal, its bulwarks against recurrence of another similar depression which had been built in by him—all show that, in the words of Prof. Thomas H. Greer: 'the programme which was once called a threat to private enterprise has proved to be a vital preservative. The fibre of America has been strengthened'.

When Roosevelt's death was announced, there was all through the United States and in much of the world, the same kind of public reaction; the same sense of *personal* grief. His unique appeal to all the people of the United States was his ability to make them feel that he was associating himself personally with each one of them in his or her aspiration for something better in life. He did not appear to be operating from the rarefied atmosphere of the White House. He was right down in the sweaty arena with them, side by side making them feel that he and they were all fighting the battle for social justice together.

As a war leader, and as an architect of the structure of peace, he seemed to be expressing in simple terms the unexpressed yearnings of each man, woman and child who wanted to live in a world without war.

How was Roosevelt able to establish this feeling of personal association with people? The answer is difficult. This much is sure: Roosevelt always *thought* in terms of human beings rather than of abstract problems. To him every problem was defined in terms of its effect on people. And since he did think in those terms, it was not extraordinary that the people should come to realize it—to recognize him as an associate in their struggles and hopes.

'All that is within me cries out to go back to my home on the Hudson River,' he had said in 1944 as he consented to run again for the fourth term, feeling that he had no more right to retire and quit than any of the men then marching towards Germany or flying towards Japan. He lies buried now in the rose garden of that home on the Hudson River. His tombstone is a simple one; on it are inscribed only his name and the years of his life.

There should be added to it the words which Sam Rayburn, Speaker of the House and an old political ally of many years, said of him years later: 'He saved the nation, not once, but twice.' And there should be added to that: 'The second time, he also saved the civilization of the world.'

---

[1] The little wheel chair was a small old-fashioned wooden kitchen chair without arm rests, placed on a small wooden platform on wheels. The absence of arm rests made it easier for him to slide from the wheel chair to his office, or dining-room, or study, chair. But when he was wheeled at a rapid pace over to his office from the White House residence, he had to clutch the sides of the seat to hold on. I was always afraid that on curves he would go over—but he never did.

At his death in June 1973 S.R. was at work on a book entitled The Great Operators in the White House: A Study in Comparative Presidential Style, *to be published by Harper and Row of New York. This essay is based on one of the chapters of the book*

De Valera
by Sir John Wheeler-Bennett

Eamon de Valera

14 Oct. 1882 Born. Educated at Blackrock Intermediate College; University College, Dublin; the National University; and Trinity College, Dublin.

1886 Gladstone's first Irish Home Rule bill.

1891 Parnell's downfall.

1893 Gladstone's second Irish Home Rule bill. Foundation of the Gaelic League.

1899 Irish brigade of volunteers fought under Boer banner in South African war.

1904 Taught physics and mathematics at Rockwell College.

1905 Griffith founded Sinn Fein movement.
General election. Campbell-Bannerman formed Liberal ministry.

1908 Enrolled in Leinster College for instruction of school teachers in Gaelic tongue.

1910 Married Janie Flanagan, who later had five sons and two daughters.

Jan. 1910 General election.*

Dec. 1910 General election.*

*As two major parties had almost exactly same number of votes, Prime Minister Asquith was dependent on support of Irish and Labour parties.

Previous page: the revolutionary nationalist. De Valera reviews a march-past of his republican followers

1911 Parliament Act. John Redmond, leader of the Irish party, helped Asquith get it through on condition that a Home Rule bill would be introduced shortly afterwards.

Jan. 1913 Home Rule bill envisaged a parliament for all Ireland, with limited powers, sitting in Dublin.

1913 De Valera a founder member of Irish volunteers.

March 1914 Curragh incident—officers stationed in Co. Kildare said they would rather be dismissed than enforce the Home Rule bill on Ulster.

26 July 1914 Battle of Bachelor's Walk. British soldiers who had intercepted some gunrunning fired into a crowd after being stoned.

July 1914 Buckingham Palace Conference. Leaders of all parties except Sinn Fein had discussions but failed to reach agreement.

24 April 1916 Easter rising.

30 April 1916 De Valera was last commandant to surrender

early May 1916 Commandants of Irish Volunteers and Citizens' Army and signatories of Irish Declaration of Independence were executed, resulting in Irish sympathy with Sinn Fein.

10 May 1916 De Valera sentenced to death, but sentence commuted to penal servitude for life and he was transferred to Dartmoor prison.

6 April 1917 U.S. entry into First World War stimulated British efforts to solve Irish problem.

June 1917 Royal amnesty freed Sinn Fein prisoners held in British jails. De Valera returned to Dublin. De Valera became Sinn Fein M.P. for East Clare.

25 July 1917 Lloyd George convened a conference but, at de Valera's prompting, Sinn Fein refused to attend.

1917 De Valera elected president of Sinn Fein and of Irish Volunteers.

5 April 1918 Lloyd George's Irish convention adopted a scheme for establishment of a parliament for whole of Ireland.

May 1918 De Valera and other leaders imprisoned in Lincoln jail because Sinn Fein activities had become a threat.

Jan. 1919 Dail Eirann—first Irish parliament since 1800—met in Dublin and declared war on the king's government in Ireland. De Valera elected chairman *in absentia*.

Feb. 1919 Michael Collins devised means by which de Valera escaped from jail. He returned to Dublin.

11 June 1919 Visited New York to achieve recognition of the Irish government. Failed to do so, but raised funds.

23 Dec. 1920 Returned secretly to Dublin.

Dec. 1920 Government of Ireland Act made provision for separate parliaments in Dublin and Belfast, and for a joint Council of Ireland.

11 July 1921 Truce formally declared. Lloyd George proposed meeting with de Valera in London.

Dec. 1921 Anglo-Irish treaty. Irish Free State was formed, with dominion status in the British Commonwealth. Ulster had right to opt out if she wished. De Valera repudiated treaty, which had been negotiated by Griffith and Collins.

7 Jan. 1922 De Valera defeated and Dail ratified treaty.

1923 Irish civil war because of clash of concepts. De Valera tried to establish republican government-in-exile in opposition to the Free State.

1926 De Valera founded Fianna Fail party, dedicated to republican principles and abolition of partition.

1931 Statute of Westminster.

1932 Fianna Fail won general election. De Valera was returned as head of the government (Taoiseach) and Minister of External Affairs.

Dec. 1936 King Edward VIII abdicated. De Valera took opportunity to introduce new constitution, removing all reference to Crown and establishing a Republic of Ireland.

22 April 1938 Anglo-Irish agreement settling economic disputes.

Sept. 1939 Outbreak of Second World War. De Valera regarded his country as neutral.

Feb. 1948 General election. De Valera replaced as Taoiseach by John Costello.

1951 De Valera returned to office.

1954 Second Costello ministry.

March 1957 De Valera returned to office.

June 1959 De Valera resigned from active politics to become President of the Republic of Ireland.

June 1973 Resigned as President.

There are some among the history makers of the twentieth century whose names are inextricably commingled with the foundation of their countries: the Union of South Africa recalls inevitably the names of Botha and Smuts. Tómaš Masaryk created Czechoslovakia, albeit with the able assistance of Eduard Beneš. Ignaz Paderewski fathered the re-born Polish State. Eamon de Valera spilled both British and Irish blood to found the Republic of Ireland.

Born in New York on 14 October 1882, the child of an American citizen of Spanish origin, Vivion Juan de Valéra, and his Irish wife, Catherine Coll, who had immigrated to America from Bruree, County Limerick, some three years before, Eamon de Valera[1] possibly owed to his place of birth and the nationality of his father the fact that his career as a patriot and a statesman was not abruptly terminated in April 1916, when most of his fellow Commandants of the Irish Volunteers and the Citizens' Army and all the signatories of the Irish Declaration of Independence were executed by the British Government after the Easter Rising.

Vivion de Valéra is said by some of his son's biographers to have 'descended from one of the noble houses of Spain' and to have himself 'held high rank in the Spanish army'. How or why he found himself an exiled immigrant in New York is not entirely clear, but it is said that he became variously a professional musician, a sculptor, an actor, a teacher of languages, a doctor, a singer and a college professor, and that he was engaged in the sugar trade. He was said to have come to the United States from the Basque country of Spain, from Cuba and from South America.[2] From this welter of assertions, however, one indisputable fact emerges. All sources agree that Vivion de Valéra was a gifted, educated and entertaining individual who, had he been granted better health, might well have excelled in any of the professions which he is said to have followed. Unfortunately he became so ill that three years after his marriage he was compelled to go to Colorado in search of mountain air. He died in Denver in the spring of 1885, leaving his wife, Kate, in straitened circumstances, and forced to go out to work for herself and her baby Eamon.

She met this challenge with characteristic courage and commonsense. Circumstances had separated her from her husband for the last months of his life and now she reluctantly decided to part with her only child, whom she sent home to Ireland in charge of one of her brothers at the tender age of two and a half, there to grow up in Bruree in the care of his grandmother.[3]

Thus, though the future President of Ireland inherited from his father a certain latin cultural and intellectual background, it was, thanks to his mother's self-sacrifice, in Ireland that he grew up from childhood to manhood and to fame.

In the Ireland in which Eamon de Valera grew up, the seeds of later turmoil were already being sown. The Phoenix Park murders of May 1882,[4] though perpetrated just before his birth, still cast a sombre shadow over Anglo-Irish relations; a shadow which was not dispelled by the defeat of Mr Gladstone's first Home Rule Bill of 1886—which gave no satisfaction to the Irish and drove the last of the Whigs into the arms of the Tory Party—nor by the tragedy of Parnell's downfall in 1890. The introduction of Mr Glad-

274

stone's second Home Rule Bill in 1893, which proposed to reduce the number of the Irish Members at Westminster from 103 to 80, who were not to vote on any issue unless expressly confined to Ireland, again pleased nobody. The Irish Party rejected it as a measure designed to keep Ireland in bondage, while the English advocates of Home Rule withheld their support on the grounds that their enthusiasm for Irish self-government was in large part motivated by the desire to get rid of the Irish representatives in the Imperial Parliament altogether.

Within Ireland itself the struggle for power between the Fenian extremists, who favoured unrestricted 'direct action', and the Nationalist parliamentarians, who advocated representational reform by constitutional means, was already in being. During the Anglo-Boer War, an Irish Brigade of volunteers fought under the Boer banner and efforts were made to impede recruiting in Ireland for the British Army. At the beginning of the new century the failure of a scheme for 'financial devolution' for Ireland added further bitterness.

Thus when Eamon de Valera completed his education[5] and reached manhood, the stage was being set for the penultimate tragedy in Anglo-Irish relations, and the young man was ripe and eager to join in the struggle for Irish freedom. His future, he believed, lay in the instruction of youth, and although he had held several part-time teaching posts under the aegis of the teaching order of the Fathers of the Holy Ghost during the period of his post-graduate studies, his first full-time appointment came in 1904: as an instructor in physics and mathematics at Rockwell College, eleven miles from Cashel, in the shadow of the Galtee Mountains.

He was then just twenty-two years old and already there was developing within him that powerful amalgam of romantic mysticism and stern practicality which characterized his whole career. He was a historical student as well as a mathematician, and the story and glory of Ireland, embodied in the Rock of Cashel, with its memories of Brian Boru and King Cormac, set him dreaming; but there was a starker side to his mind which was now opening up new vistas before him. As an historian the young de Valera was a romantic, but in politics he rarely allowed his heart to rule his head. Not for him was the whimsical feyness of the Irish romantic school, of Yeats and Moore and Russell, then finding expression at the Abbey Theatre and in the literary salons of Dublin; this tall, lanky, dark moustached young man (somehow one can not imagine President de Valera as having ever been 'callow') found his intellectual stimulus in his membership of the Gaelic League, which the erudite Protestant scholar, Dr Douglas Hyde, had founded in 1893 for the revival of the Gaelic language and culture, emphasizing the distinction of Irish nationality.

Dr Hyde also founded Leinster College for the instruction of school teachers in the Gaelic tongue. De Valera enrolled there in 1908 and amongst his teachers he met a charming young woman named Janie Flanagan or, as she preferred to be known, Sinéad Ni Fhlannagáin. They were married in 1910 and have lived in great happiness for the last sixty-three years.

In his young political thinking, de Valera was initially a nationalist rather than a republican. Indeed with the eclipse of the Fenian Movement, republicanism no longer figured as a major issue. Self-government and independence of Westminster and Whitehall were the declared objects of the Irish patriots. It was in these early years of the twentieth century that two men, both slightly older than de Valera, were having a decisive influence in Ireland: Padraic Pearse[6], a mystic, a poet, a schoolmaster—and perhaps almost a saint—with a passionate idealism, dedicated to Ireland and her people, and Arthur Griffith[7], a more practical exponent of Irish nationalism, who had founded and edited the *United Irishmen* in 1899 as a political plat-form for the cultural and industrial development of Ireland, and for the political technique of abandoning parliamentary representation in London with the object of restoring full autonomy to Ireland.

The political development of de Valera was still incomplete, although he had moved some way towards republicanism. Mr Lloyd George's 'People's Budget' of 1909, with its resounding political repercussions, resulted in the dissipation of the overwhelming majority in West-minster with which the Liberal Party had been returned in the General Election of 1905. In the elections of January and December 1910, the two major parties were returned with almost exactly the same number of votes, and the Government was therefore dependent for the passage of its legis-lation—and more especially the Parliament Act of 1911—on the support of the Irish and Labour Parties.

In return for this assistance, John Redmond, leader of the Irish Party, exacted from Mr Asquith the promise of a Home Rule Bill as soon as possible after the Parliament Act became law. This pledge was duly honoured by the introduction of legislation on 11 April 1912, but its provisions, though they might be acceptable to the followers of Mr Redmond, were far from com-plying with the demands and aspirations of Sinn Féin. Moreover they con-tained no provision for the exclusion of Ulster. The Home Rule Bill, passed in May 1914, envisaged a Parliament for all Ireland, albeit with only very limited powers, sitting in Dublin.

The results were momentous. Though Mr Redmond accepted the Bill, Sir Edward Carson announced the formation of a Provisional Government in Belfast, in flagrant defiance of Government authority. The loyalty of the British Army was in question, as was demonstrated by the 'Curragh In-cident'.[8] Volunteer armies were in process of formation in Dublin and in Belfast and were equipped by means of gun-running expeditions in both Northern and Southern Ireland. The first blood of what might well have developed into an Irish Civil War was shed on the Dublin Quays at the 'Battle of Bachelor's Walk'.[9] The Buckingham Palace Conference failed to find any basis of agreement.[10] Only the results of the shots fired by Gavrilo Princip at Sarajevo—in Mr Churchill's telling words, 'cut through the clamour of the haggard, squalid, tragic Irish quarrel which threatened to divide the British nation into two hostile camps'.

At this time de Valera was a name unknown to the people of Ireland. A modest and retiring man, he had no aspiration to leadership. He was an enthusiastic early member of the Irish Volunteers in 1913, but refused nomination for the Executive Committee. He also refused membership of the Irish Republican Brotherhood (I.R.B.) at this time. His natural instincts were inimical to secret societies of any kind, which were in any case disapproved of by his Church. It was not until 1915, when the control of the I.R.B. over the Volunteer movement made it difficult to be a member of one without the other, that he pocketed his scruples and took the secret oath, making it clear, however, that he intended to take no part in the activities of the Brotherhood other than those which were necessary for the efficient fulfilment of his duties as an executive officer of the Volunteers.[11]

Within the military organization, de Valera proved himself a proficient and intelligent leader. By 1915 he commanded the 3rd Battalion and was also Adjutant of the Dublin Brigade; by the Easter Rising of April 1916 he was one of the five Commandants of the armed forces in Dublin of the short-lived Irish Republic.

The Easter Rising of 1916 was ill-conceived and ill-prepared. The councils of the Irish Volunteers were divided on the issue of armed revolt and even more so after it was known that the supplies of German arms, which had been arranged for by Sir Roger Casement, would not be forthcoming and that he himself had been arrested on landing from a U-boat on the west coast of Ireland. Little or no effort had been made to prepare the Irish people to support an armed uprising. However the I.R.B. were determined upon direct action and 24 April was designated as the day. But even after the decision to rise in arms had been taken, Eoin MacNeill, the Chief of Staff of the Volunteers, had second thoughts and sought to countermand the orders.[12]

It is possible that, given the confederate circumstances, de Valera would have made an outstanding military commander. Certainly his heart was in it and in after years he would speak with some pride of his achievements during that fateful Easter week. Nor was his pride unjustified. The sector allotted to him was one in the south-east region of the city, including the Botanical Gardens of Trinity College which commanded the junction of Lansdowne Road and Pembroke Road near Balls Bridge; his headquarters were in a dispensary near Boland's Bakery. He so disposed his meagre force of a little over a hundred men as to catch advancing British troops in ambush, and his tactics succeeded exceedingly well. For a week he held British reinforcements at bay and repelled a number of well mounted attacks. He was the last of the Commandants to surrender on 30 April.

It was a grave disappointment to him that the Rising was received with but little enthusiasm and no popular support. It seemed as if their sacrifice had been made in vain, an empty if gallant gesture. 'If only the people had come out with knives and forks,' was his bitter comment after his surrender. Indeed it was the sequel to the Rising and not the Rising itself which converted the events of Easter Week 1916, from the Sinn Féin point of view, from an inglorious failure into a glorious success.

In judging the sequel one must remember that in the spring of 1916 the tide of war against Germany was running unfavourably for Britain and her allies. Ireland had been stripped of troops for service in France, Flanders and the Dardanelles and, in addition, there was reliable intelligence that Germany was prepared to support, by means of arms and equipment, the forces

Overleaf: after the rising, Dublin, 1916. Relatives visit Republican prisoners and (right) children carry wood from the burnt-out General Post Office

of Sinn Féin. In London, therefore, it seemed that the Irish rebels had attempted a stab in the back at a moment of disadvantage to Britain. Popular clamour in England cried aloud for stern measures against the rebel leaders, and it did not seem that the execution of fifteen men was too stern a measure of retribution for a rebellion in arms which had cost the lives of some hundred and twenty officers and men of the British army and police forces.[13] But among the fifteen men executed were the seven signatories of the Irish Declaration of Independence and four of the five Commandants of the rebel forces in Dublin. Moreover they were tried and condemned by special courts sitting in secret and without any provision for means of defence. The death sentences were carried out within a few hours of being passed. There is little doubt that a more adroit handling of the situation might have prevented the forces of Sinn Féin from establishing their vital grip on the sympathies of the Irish people, and Ireland might have achieved self-government within the British Commonwealth of Nations by peaceful means instead of by the tragic and bloody process which lay ahead. As it was, not for the first time in history, a cause was saved from eclipse by the gratuitous provision of martyrs.

On 8 May 1916, Eamon de Valera was sentenced to death. That he did not share the fate of his fellow Commandants was perhaps due partly to the fact, though this has never been confirmed, that he had been born—and still remained—a United States citizen and the American Consul intervened on his behalf, partly to the intercession of John Redmond, George Bernard Shaw and others, and partly to revulsion of public opinion both in America

and in Britain against the continued executions. He was lucky in that his court martial occurred at the end of those tragic days which began with the execution of Padraic Pearse on 3 May and closed with that of James Connolly, the commander of the Citizen Army, on 12 May.[14] De Valera's sentence was commuted to penal servitude for life and he was transferred to Dartmoor Prison. It is characteristic of him that during the brief proceedings of his trial he made no plea for clemency on the grounds of his American citizenship.[15] He comported himself with the courage and composure of a patriot.

British efforts to arrive at a solution of the Irish problem were given a fresh fillip by the entry into the war of the United States on 6 April 1917. Mr Lloyd George was not unaware of the implications which President Wilson's proclaimed doctrine of self-determination had for Anglo-Irish affairs, nor of the not inconsiderable political influence exercised by the Irish-American bloc in American politics. The Prime Minister, therefore, invited representatives of the Irish Nationalist Party, the Southern Unionists, the Ulster counties and of Sinn Féin to meet in a Convention on 25 July 1917 for the purpose of devising an agreed formula for conciliation and self-government. As an earnest of good faith, a Royal Amnesty freed all Sinn Féin prisoners held in British jails so that they might take part in the proceedings.

Released on 17 June, de Valera returned at once to Dublin to find himself a national hero and an acknowledged leader. The fame of the defender of Boland's Bakery had spread abroad, throughout Ireland and even to the United States. The name of de Valera flamed across the Irish skies. Within a

week he had been elected a Sinn Féin M.P. for East Clare, and under his leadership the Sinn Féin party rejected any idea of participation in the Convention. With brutal logic de Valera put the case during his election campaign: 'There are only two courses Irishmen can follow with a certain amount of logic', he told his constituents, 'the Unionists of the North are consistent in their desire to remain part of the British Empire; the only other position is the Sinn Féin position, completely independent and separate from England. How can they have conciliation?'[16]

In this clear-cut, direct statement de Valera not only doomed the Convention pre-natally to failure,[17] he also defined the fundamental political principle from which he never departed as the aim of his endeavours—an undivided Ireland independent of England—though in the course of events he did condone practical compromises. His statement also epitomized the basic problem of Ireland which is still with us. It was a momentous pronouncement both for its percipience and its simplicity.

In the months that followed, de Valera laboured to rebuild the forces of insurrection from the ruins of the Easter Risings and to reconcile the Right and Left wings of his movement. This was no easy task. Devoted though they all were to the cause of independence, the personalities and principles of, for example, Arthur Griffith, the political philosopher and founder of Sinn Féin, Cathal Brugha, the fanatical republican, and Michael Collins, the dare-devil Post Office worker turned guerrilla, were difficult to drive in harness. Yet de Valera succeeded by the very ascendancy of his ability, his wisdom and his personality. In 1917 he was elected President of both Sinn Féin and of the Irish Volunteers, the two most powerful organizations in the movement. In January 1919, the first Irish Parliament since 1800—Dáil Eireann—met in the Mansion House in Dublin and declared war on the King's Government in Ireland. Later he was elected President of the Dáil *in absentia*.

His absence was caused by the fact that in May 1918, the activities of Sinn Féin had become so great a threat to the British authorities and the King's Writ that a number of leaders were re-arrested, including de Valera, in whose papers were discovered elaborately detailed plans for the establishment of an Irish Republic.[18] Incarcerated in Lincoln Jail, he was not destined to be a prisoner for long. Under supremely romantic circumstances he, Henry Boland and Michael Collins devised a daring means of escape and by February 1919 he was back in Dublin—free but 'on the run'.

On his return he found himself head of a government with organized cabinet departments and an army, whose authority extended over most of Ireland and who had appointed diplomatic missions abroad. The First World War had closed with the defeat of Germany. De Valera decided that the crucial issue now for Ireland was to achieve recognition by the United States and by the Peace Conference in Paris. After the Irish claim had been turned down in Paris, he therefore determined to make a personal visit to America, partly to achieve recognition and partly to raise funds for the prosecution of the fight against England. His decision took most of his colleagues by surprise, but he ultimately gained his point and by devious means he reached New York on 11 June.

The American Mission was not an entirely happy experience.[19] Though a personal triumph for de Valera himself and a highly successful fund-raising achievement—over $6 million were raised by 1921 and more promised—his Irish-American sponsors were at variance among themselves, and subsequently with him. He did not achieve his primary object of recognition by the United States Government. He was not received by President Wilson; he was not invited to address Congress; neither of the major political parties endorsed his plea for recognition and only the somewhat obscure political group, the Farmer-Labour Party passed a resolution in its favour.[20] He did, however, emerge from his mission with the title of 'President of the Irish Republic'—to which office he had never been elected,[21] and it was with mixed emotions that he returned secretly to Dublin on 23 December 1920.

The Ireland to which de Valera returned was very different from that which he had left nearly two years before. Both sides were wearying of the struggle. In the ranks of the Irish Republican Army there were signs of exhaustion, both physical and material, while in England there arose a steadily growing weight of public opinion against the continuance of hostilities. Peace feelers were in the air from both sides and signs of hope were apparent in the new Government of Ireland Act, which received the Royal Assent in December 1920, by which provision was made for separate parliaments in Dublin and in Belfast, and for a joint Council of Ireland.[22]

The spring of 1921 seemed to bring with it a breath of hope. Largely through the efforts of the indefatigable and indomitable 'Andy' Cope, acting as Mr Lloyd George's 'under-cover' envoy in Dublin,[23] contacts of various kinds were established and a secret interview was arranged between de Valera and Sir James Craig, the Ulster leader, in May. In opening the Northern Irish Parliament on 22 June, King George V's speech from the throne contained a gesture of peace toward Sinn Féin and an offer of a truce was known to be in the offing. It was all very secret.

The improved atmosphere of Anglo-Irish relations was nearly wrecked by the over-zealous efforts of a detachment of the Royal Worcestershire Regiment who, in the exercise of their current orders and completely unaware of what was at stake, raided a house on the night of 22 June and arrested a man who proved to be de Valera himself. After frantic efforts on the part of Sir John Anderson, the Under-Secretary, and 'Andy' Cope, his release was obtained, and two days later they handed to him the famous letter from Mr Lloyd George proposing a meeting in London. The Anglo-Irish War was—for all intents and purposes—over; the devious period of negotiation had begun.[24]

The course of the correspondence, and afterwards of the negotiations which terminated some six months later in the signature of the Anglo-Irish Treaty, has been brilliantly described by Lord Longford, in a special study.[25] Sheer intellectual inability as well as dictates of space preclude any attempt by me to compete in any way nor indeed to do anything but epitomize the points at issue between Mr de Valera and his followers and opponents on the one hand, and the British on the other.

From first to last de Valera stood adamant on two basic principles: there must be an Irish Republic and there must be a United Ireland. Mr Lloyd George, as he told the Cabinet, rejected the idea of a Republic as impossible, being inconsistent with the Monarchy. Mr de Valera did not admit the inconsistency.[26] Thus was first propounded the doctrine of 'External Association' to which de Valera adhered throughout, which he later successfully introduced and which now forms a vitally important element in the formula on which the present Commonwealth of Nations is based—alas without the Republic of Ireland! As for partition, he abominated the idea and never ceased to hold it against successive British Governments, nor to use it as a weapon in future negotiations.

As against this definite view of de Valera, there was the 'Hungarian Solution' favoured by Arthur Griffith. From the founding of Sinn Féin he had drawn a parallel between the status of Hungary in the Austro-Hungarian Empire as defined in the Dual Monarchy of 1867, and the future position of Ireland within the British Empire. In return for an independent Irish Parliament with control over its own finances etc., he was prepared to recognize the King as Sovereign of Ireland, to take an oath of allegiance and even, as a last and unpalatable resort, accept the severance of Ulster from the parliamentary authority of Dublin.

It was against this clash of concepts of Irish independence that the Anglo-Irish negotiations were conducted, which permeated the historic debate in the Dáil on the ratification of the Treaty ('The Big Talk') with rancour and bitterness and misunderstanding, and which finally precipitated the Irish Civil War of 1922, sundering the bonds of brotherhood and comradeship and costing the new Irish state some of its most precious lives, which it could ill afford to lose in leadership. [27]

The Treaty which Griffith and Collins brought back from London to Dublin in December 1921 partook far more of the 'Hungarian Solution' than of 'External Association'. Under its provisions there was born the Irish Free State, a member of the British Commonwealth in equal status with Canada and Australia. The Irish Republic had been exchanged for Dominion Status, which entailed the Oath of Allegiance to the King and, moreover, Ulster was accorded the right to opt out of the Irish Free State if she so desired. In addition, Britain retained the right to maintain naval bases at certain Irish ports.

One of the more fascinating 'ifs' of modern history is the speculation as to what would have happened if de Valera had headed the Irish delegation in the treaty negotiations. Would he have succumbed to the amalgam of guile and threats which Lloyd George employed in dealing with Griffith and Collins? Would he have taken his stand upon the Rock of the Republic— with the possibility of 'External Association' as a bargaining point—and called the bluff of the British Prime Minister and his colleagues?[28] Would he or they have made the final choice of the resumption of hostilities in the event of a breakdown in the negotiations? And would the peoples of Britain and Ireland have tolerated such a return to the arbitrament of force and bloodshed? These are conjectures which are impossible of solution but nevertheless worthy of consideration, for they add up to the great and overall reflection—could or would the Irish Civil War have been avoided?

In effect, of course, the current of events went the other way. First in Cabinet and later in the historic debate in the session of the Dáil which sat in the University College, Dublin, there was a bitter and abrasive conflict of ideas. De Valera and his supporters repudiated the Treaty as constituting an act of surrender and even of treason. All that Sinn Féin stood for, all that they had fought for as comrades throughout the bloody brutal struggle of the Anglo-Irish war, had been bartered away in London in exchange for Dominion Status under the British Crown. To these charges Griffith and Collins and their friends replied that the basic principle of independent self-government for Ireland had been retained and achieved. In order to allow this overriding aim of Irish nationalism, was it worth while to cling to names and formulas and outworn shibboleths?

From 14 December 1921 to 7 January 1922 the battle raged in the Dáil[29] until at last de Valera met defeat. By sixty-four votes to fifty-seven, the House agreed to approve the Treaty. De Valera resigned and Arthur Griffith took his place. There followed that saddest of conflicts—civil war. Almost over night men who had been comrades-in-arms for years sought to slaughter one another. De Valera attempted to set up a republican government in opposition to the Free State. The Irish Army was torn by mutiny and sedition. Ireland was delivered over again to bloodshed but it was now brother against brother.

This was the nadir of de Valera's political career. President of the Irish Republic, yet rebel in arms within his own country, he took an active part in an insurrection against the Treaty, culminating in his own arrest after being wounded in the leg at a public meeting. The will of the majority of the people of Ireland was against him. He no longer spoke for Ireland.

A lesser man might well have bowed beneath the weight of defeat and disappeared from public life. Not so de Valera. By 1926 he had decided upon his future line of policy. He would no longer oppose the Irish State by force of arms, but would follow the way of constitutional and parliamentary government. Other than that he abandoned nothing. His programme entailed the substitution of 'External Association' for 'Dominion Status', the establishment of the Republic of Ireland and—though this was a more tenuous aim, though none the less firmly held—the abolition of partition and the creation of a United Ireland. He was prepared to bide his time but he founded his own party, Fianna Fáil, dedicated to republican principles, and in the following year he re-entered the Dáil as Leader of the Opposition. By 1932, Fianne Fáil had won a general election and de Valera was returned as Head of the Government and Minister of External Affairs, a position which he continued to hold until 1948.

In December 1936 King Edward VIII abdicated, an act which, under the provisions of the Statute of Westminster (1931), had to be ratified by each of the governments of the King's Dominions. This was de Valera's great opportunity. He did not ask the Dáil to register approval or dissent on the Act of Abdication but he introduced two Bills of his own which were passed by comfortable majorities; first containing large amendments to the constitution and the other an External Relations Bill. In 1937 he brought in his new constitution. The new instruments of government established a Republic of Ireland, removed all reference to the Crown in relation to domestic affairs but provided for its continued use in external relations. Irish diplomatic representatives, for example, were still accredited in the King's name and bore his Letters of Credence, though henceforward these were to be written exclusively in Irish. 'External Association' had become a reality. The constitutional pundits were confounded. That which Mr Lloyd George had in 1921 rejected as being 'inconsistent with the Monarchy' was now in being. It was a triumph of no mean proportion.[30]

There were further triumphs in store. Mr Neville Chamberlain was about to embark upon that policy of appeasement which was later to end in such lamentable circumstances at Munich. Mr de Valera was a willing beneficiary. In negotiations which continued in London from January to April 1938 he succeeded in achieving an outstanding diplomatic success. By the Anglo-Irish Agreement of 22 April, the financial and economic disputes which had bedevilled relations between the two countries since 1932 were settled very much in Eire's favour and, what was considerably more important, the British Government returned to Eire the Treaty Ports and the rights for their use which had been accorded under Article 7 of the Treaty of 1921.[31]

With one exception, de Valera had now virtually destroyed the structure of the Anglo-Irish relationship built upon the original Treaty and had substituted one of his own. The exception was the fact of Partition. His dream of a United Ireland was still quick within him and he never failed to raise it in season and out of season. To him it remained an act of faith; to successive British governments it was a permanent Banquo's Ghost at any meeting with Irish representatives. It was to play its part in the history of the Second World War.

Of all the Commonwealth Prime Ministers at the outbreak of the war, de Valera's task was perhaps the easiest of all. While other governments wrestled with the problem of automatic support for the United Kingdom's declaration of war on Germany, the people of Ireland regarded themselves as 'automatically neutral'. All parties in the Dáil were virtually unanimous on this point and had de Valera himself felt otherwise and had attempted to sway his countrymen towards war, he would have failed, even to the extent of having a civil war on his hands. For Ireland at this juncture, with characteristic paradox, would rather fight than go to war.[32]

But de Valera did nothing of the sort. He shared his people's aversion to becoming involved in a world war and was ready to defend Ireland's neutrality against all threat or pressure. He successfully maintained this status against the blandishments of Mr Churchill, President Roosevelt and Adolf Hitler. There was only one condition on which he would seek to gain support for the abandonment of neutrality and that, as he explained in June of 1940 to Malcolm MacDonald, Churchill's special envoy and an old friend, was the abandonment by Britain of Partition. Once this had been accomplished, a United Ireland would consider a declaration of war on Germany and he did not regard the possibility of such a declaration as unreasonable but Malcolm MacDonald assured him that such a proposition was 'unrealistic'.[33]

De Valera's sixteen years of premiership came to an end with the General Election of February 1948 when he was replaced as Taoiseach by John Costello, as leader of a coalition of the Fine Gael Labour, farmers, and a new Republican party. There followed a reaction against the policy of 'External Association', which he had persistently followed since July 1921. The Costello Government repealed the External Relations Act, severing all connection with Britain on 18 April 1949. Here indeed was irony. Just nine days later, the Commonwealth Declaration of 27 April made it possible for independent republics, which hitherto had been parts of the British Empire and Commonwealth, to remain within the Commonwealth, of which they recognized the British Sovereign as Head. This was a progression of de Valera's original concept of 'External Association' and he may thus be said, by inference, to be a progenitor of the Third British Commonwealth.[34]

De Valera returned to office in 1951 and again in 1957, and displayed a continued imaginative grasp of policy and affairs. Though he made no attempt to undo the work of John Costello in 1949, one believes that he would never have originated this policy. His belief in the principle of 'External Association' remained unshakable. Age, however, was beginning to tell upon him—he was seventy-five when he became Taoiseach for the last time—and his eyesight was rapidly failing. In 1959 he resigned from active politics to become President of the Republic of Ireland, an office from which he retired in the summer of 1973 at the age of ninety.

'His [de Valera's] greatness is confined within certain limits,' Malcolm MacDonald has written, 'At times he played a distinct part in the Commonwealth and wider affairs, but he is not an international giant, only a national one—a great Irishman who has made a unique contribution to the liberty of his fellow-countrymen.'[35] This analytical judgement is probably correct. He is a world figure only in an indirect sense, and yet he has left his mark on the twentieth century in that he is the architect of his country, and a conceptual progenitor of the Commonwealth as we know it today.

He is difficult of definition; a strange amalgam of dark mysticism, realpolitik and statesmanship. When one is in his presence his eyes, though sightless, seem nevertheless to penetrate to one's very soul and there is the tragedy of all Ireland in his voice. One instinctively feels that here is greatness: an indomitable courage, a great wisdom, a strength of spirit which has survived triumph and disaster and has remained transcendent.

---

[1] Though registered at birth in the records of the city of New York under the Christian name of 'George', when christened some six weeks later at the Church of St Agnes, it was under the name of 'Edward'. In later life he always used the Irish form of this name, 'Eamon'.

[2] The Earl of Longford and Thomas O'Neill, *Eamon de Valera* (London, 1970); Mary C. Bromage, *De Valera and the March of a Nation* (London, 1956); Denis Gwynn, *De Valera* (New York, 1933); David T. Dwane, *Eamon de Valera* (Dublin, 1922); M. J. MacManus, *Eamon de Valera* (Dublin, 1947); Seán O'Faoláin, *De Valera* (London, 1939).

[3] Kate de Valéra remained in the United States until her death in 1932. She moved from New York City upstate to Rochester, where she married Charles Wheelright, an Englishman and a Protestant, by whom she had two children, a daughter who died in childhood and a son who became a priest and entered the Redemptionist order.

[4]On 6 May 1882 the newly appointed Lord Lieutenant of Ireland, Lord Frederick Cavendish, and his Chief Secretary, Mr Thomas Burke, were murdered in Phoenix Park in broad daylight by members of an organization called the 'Invincibles', a break-away from the Fenian movement.

[5]De Valera's education began at the National School of Bruree and thence by way of the Christian Brothers' School at Rathluirc, Co. Cork, Blackrock Intermediate College, to Blackrock University College. He received his B.A. at the Royal University of Ireland. He later pursued his post-graduate work at the National University and at Trinity College, Dublin.

[6]Louis N. Le Roux, *Life of Patrick H. Pearse* (Dublin, n.d.); Hedley McCoy, *Padraic Pearse* (Cork, 1966).

[7]Seán Ó Lúing, *Art Ó Gríofa* (Dublin, 1953), in Irish; Padraic Colum, *Arthur Griffith* (Dublin, 1959).

[8]In March 1914, Brigadier Hubert Gough and fifty-seven other officers of the 3rd Cavalry Brigade, stationed at the Curragh camp in Co. Kildare, declared that they would rather accept dismissal from the Army than obey orders to enforce the provisions of the Home Rule Bill upon Ulster. See Sir James Fergusson, *The Curragh Incident* (London, 1964); A.P. Ryan, *Mutiny at the Curragh* (London, 1956).

[9]On 26 July 1914, men of the King's Own Scottish Borderers, who had intercepted a gun-running expedition on behalf of the Irish Volunteers at Howth, marching back to Dublin, encountered on the quays a crowd which greeted them with jeers and then with stones. A number of troops were injured and (whether with or without a definite order has never been established) they fired into the crowd, killing two men and a woman and wounding thirty-two others.

[10]On 21 July 1914, King George V took the initiative of summoning to Buckingham Palace, Mr Asquith and Mr Lloyd George representing the Government, Lord Lansdowne and Mr Bonar Law the Opposition, Mr John Redmond and Mr John Dillon the Irish Nationalists and Sir Edward Carson and Captain James Craig the Ulster Unionists. (The Sinn Féin Party, it will be noted, were not represented, or indeed invited.) Mr Speaker Lowther presided. The conference sat until 24 July when it dispersed, 'being unable to agree either in principle or in detail'.

[11]Longford and O'Neill, *Eamon de Valera*, p. 25.

[12]P.S. O'Hegarty, *The Victory of Sinn Féin* (Dublin, 1924) p. 18.

[13]103 British officers and other ranks were killed in the Easter Rising, 357 were wounded and 9 were reported missing: of the Royal Irish Constabulary, 14 officers and constables were killed and 23 wounded; 3 members of the Dublin Metropolitan Police were killed and 3 wounded. The complete Irish casualty list was computed at 450 killed, including civilians, and 264 wounded.

[14]James Connolly, a leader of the Irish Labour Party and founder of the Citizens' Army, had been badly wounded in the leg during the defence of the Post Office in the Easter Rising. Being unable to walk he was carried on a stretcher to the place of execution and there tied to a chair. C. Desmond Greaves, *The Life and Times of James Connolly* (London, 1961).

[15]In the course of his American Mission in 1919-20, de Valera was asked if he was an American citizen. He replied, 'I am an Irish citizen . . . I ceased to be an American when I became a soldier of the Irish Republic'. Mary C. Bromage, *De Valera and the March of a Nation*, p. 92.

[16]*The Irish Times*, 6 July 1917.

[17]The Irish Convention met in Dublin on 25 July and its discussions dragged on without much result until the following spring, doomed to failure by the boycott of Sinn Féin. On 15 March 1918 it rejected a resolution to exclude Ulster from the jurisdiction of an Irish Parliament, whereupon the Orangemen withdrew. On 5 April the Convention finally adopted a scheme for the establishment of a Parliament for the whole of Ireland. See *Report of the Proceedings of the Irish Convention* (Cmd. 9019 of 1918); R.B. McDowell, *The Irish Convention 1917-1918* (London,

[18]*Documents Relative to the Sinn Féin Movement* (Cmd. 1108 of 1921).

[19]See Patrick McCortan, *With de Valera in America* (Dublin, 1932); K. O'Doherty, *Assignment— America* (New York, 1957).

[20] The Convention of the American Federation of Labour adopted a resolution recognizing the Irish Republic on 17 June 1919.

[21] When asked on the eve of his first American press conference in Philadelphia what he would say as 'President of the Irish Republic', de Valera replied that he was not 'President' only Chairman of the Dáil. To this one of his Irish-American hosts retorted that it was 'all the same thing' and that 'we had already made him President of the Republic in the minds of the American people'. Later de Valera issued a statement that, 'From today I am in America as the official Head of the Irish Republic, established by the will of the Irish people, in accordance with the principle of self-determination.' But his Philadelphia host had been right; he was 'President de Valera' from then on. (Denis Gwynn, *De Valera*, p. 88.)

[22] For an account of the peace feelers of 1920-21, see Sir John Wheeler-Bennett, *John Anderson, Viscount Waverley* (London, 1962) pp. 69-82.

[23] Mr Alfred ('Andy') Cope was nominally Assistant Under-Secretary of Dublin Castle. He later received the K.C.B. for his part in the Anglo-Irish negotiations.

[24] The Truce was formally declared to be in operation as from noon on 11 July 1921.

[25] In *Peace by Ordeal* (London, revised edition, 1962) and in *Eamon de Valera*, pp. 127-170. See also Dáil Eireann, *Official Correspondence Relating to Peace Negotiations, June-September 1921* (Dublin, October 1921), and Frank Gallagher, *The Anglo-Irish Treaty* (London, 1965) and Tom Jones, *Whitehall Diary*, 'Ireland 1918-1925' (Oxford, 1971), vol. III.

[26] Extract from Cabinet Record quoted by Longford and O'Neill in *Eamon de Valera*, p. 138.

[27] The Irish Civil War cost the lives among leaders of both sides, of Michael Collins, Cathal Brugha, Harry Boland and Erskine Childers. Arthur Griffith died suddenly in August 1922, and Kevin O'Higgins was assassinated by gunmen on his way to Mass in 1927.

[28] The British delegation to the Anglo-Irish Conference was composed, in addition to Mr Lloyd George, of Mr Austen Chamberlain, Lord Birkenhead, Mr Winston Churchill, Sir Laming Worthing-Evans, Sir Hamar Greenwood and Sir Gordon Hewart. The Irish representatives, in addition to Arthur Griffith, were Michael Collins, Robert Barton, Edward Duggan and Gavan Duffy, with Erskine Childers and John Chartres as secretaries.

[29] *Debate in Dáil Eireann on the Treaty between Great Britain and Ireland signed in London on the 6 December, 1921* (Dublin, 1922).

[30] The new republican constitution was endorsed by a plebiscite on 1 July 1937 and came into force on 6 December. The Imperial Conference of 1937, with perhaps more wisdom than logic, agreed to accept the somewhat unusual situation thus created, as constituting no fundamental change in Eire's relationship to the Commonwealth and this attitude was formally enunciated as the policy of His Majesty's Government in the United Kingdom, on 30 December 1937.

[31] At the final meeting of the Conference at No. 10 Downing Street on 25 April, Mr Chamberlain handed to Mr de Valera the field glasses which had been taken from him by a Captain Hintzer after his surrender and arrest at Boland's Mill almost exactly twenty-two years earlier.

[32] The problem, therefore, which had so vexed the constitutional lawyers and interpreters of the Statute of Westminster (1931), as to whether the King could be at war through the act of certain of his governments and neutral through the action of others, and whether a part of the Commonwealth so declaring itself neutral could remain within the fold, was accorded pragmatic solution. There were, however, complications. When the Irish Minister in Berlin died in the course of the war, a successor could not be appointed because, under the External Relations Act, his credentials had to be signed by the King, and the King could not accredit a diplomatic representative to a state with which he was at war. In consequence Eire was compelled to be represented by a *chargé d'affaires* till the end of the war.

[33] Rt Hon. Malcolm MacDonald, O.M., *Titans and Others* (London, 1972) p. 84.

[34] Sir John Wheeler-Bennett, *King George VI, His Life and Reign* (London, 1953) pp. 729-731.

[35] MacDonald, *Titans and Others*, p. 86.

Attlee
by Patrick Gordon Walker

PATRICK GORDON WALKER (b. 1907) attended Wellington College and Christ Church, Oxford, where he later became Student and History Tutor from 1931 until the outbreak of the Second World War, during which he served with the European Services of the B.B.C. In the General Election of 1945 he was returned to Parliament as a Labour member for Smethwick which he retained until 1965 when he lost his seat, but was elected as member for Leyton in the following year, a seat which he still retains. In Mr Attlee's second administration he was Secretary of State for Commonwealth Relations (1950-51) and was Foreign Secretary for a brief period in Mr Wilson's first government. He returned as Secretary for Education and Science during 1967-68, when he resigned. His published works include *The Commonwealth* (1960) and *The Cabinet* (1970).

Clement Attlee

3 Jan. 1883 Born. Educated at Haileybury and University College, Oxford.

1906 Called to the bar by the Inner Temple.

1910 Active in social work. Secretary, Toynbee Hall.

1911 Lecturer on Trade Unionism at Ruskin College, Oxford.

1913-23 Lecturer on social sciences and administration at the London School of Economics.

1914-18 Served during the war in the South Lancashire Regiment and Tank Corps: Gallipoli, Mesopotamia (wounded), and France. Achieved rank of major.

1919 First Labour mayor of Stepney.

1922 Married Violet Helen Miller, who later had one son and three daughters.

Nov. 1922 Elected Labour M.P. for Limehouse division of Stepney. He held this seat until Feb. 1950 when, following constituency reorganization, he became M.P. for West Walthamstow until 1955.

1922-4 Parliamentary Private Secretary to Ramsay MacDonald, leader of the Labour opposition.

Jan. 1924 Under-secretary of State for War in first Labour government, headed by MacDonald.

Nov. 1924 General election. Labour party defeated.

1927 Visited India as Labour member of the Simon Commission, appointed to investigate criticisms of the Imperial regime in India.

1930-31 Chancellor of the Duchy of Lancaster in the Labour government of Ramsay MacDonald which had taken office after the 1929 general election.

1931-35 Went into opposition with most of Labour party when MacDonald formed National Government with

Previous pages: Attlee triumphant during 'Labour Landslide' of 1945

Conservatives. Became deputy leader of Labour opposition under George Lansbury.

1935-40 Leader of the Opposition, Lansbury having resigned after being criticized for his pacifist attitude.

1940-42 Lord President of the Council and Deputy Prime Minister in the coalition government led by Winston Churchill after the resignation of Neville Chamberlain.

1942-43 Secretary of State for Dominion Affairs after Japanese invasion of South East Asia in Dec. 1941 had created a crisis for British Empire in Far East.

July 1945 General election victory for Labour party. Attlee became Prime Minister.

July 1945 Attended three-power Potsdam conference near Berlin to discuss treatment of Germany and settlement of post-war Europe with Stalin and Truman.

1946 Repeal of Trade Disputes Act of 1927.

1946 Bank of England Act.*
Cable and Wireless Act.*
Civil Aviation Act.*
Coal Industry Nationalisation Act.*

1947 Electricity Act.*
Gas Act.*
Transport Act.*

1949 Iron and Steel Act.*

*Nationalization of credit, power and transport.

1946 National Insurance Act.**
National Health Service.**

1947 Part-implementation of 1944 act reforming education.**

1946 and 1949 Housing Acts, encouraging council-house building.**
**the Welfare State.

1947 Independence of India, Ceylon, and Burma.

1947 Marshall Plan for American aid to Europe welcomed by Attlee's government.

May 1948 British forces withdraw from Palestine. Creation of independent state of Israel.

1948 Soviet pressure on western Europe culminating in Berlin blockade and western airlift.

1949 Attlee's government committed Britain to NATO defence agreement.

1950 Korean War. Attlee committed Britain to U.N. defence of South Korea.

Feb. 1950 General election. Labour majority reduced to ten, which made it difficult to conduct business.

Sept. 1951 Attlee dissolved Parliament. Conservatives won general election. Churchill Prime Minister.

April 1955 Attlee led Labour party in general election. Conservative victory.

Dec. 1955 Attlee resigned and was created first Earl Attlee.

8 Oct. 1967 Died.

The Rt. Hon. C. R. Attlee OM. CH.

YOU CAN TRUST MR. ATTLEE

Clement Attlee was much underrated as a Prime Minister both by his opponents and by his more impatient supporters. Like Truman he succeeded a great, articulate and flamboyant war leader: like Truman—as time goes by—he will be increasingly seen to have possessed qualities more apt than those of his predecessor to the intricate, puzzling, unremitting challenge of post-war problems at home and abroad.

Attlee's task was more testing than Truman's, for he had to face a decline in British influence while the President was able to take upon himself the obligations of an unrivalled and self-confident power in the world.

Again like Truman, no one could have foretold from Attlee's characteristics and previous career that he would come to the highest office in the land. He lacked both the thrust of personal ambition and the demagogic arts of leadership. No memorable phrase fixes him in the public memory.

When he got to the top, his long, devoted, obscure apprenticeship stood him in excellent stead—simply because he was always content to do well the various tasks that fell to him.

Born on 3 January 1883, the fourth of eight children of Henry Attlee, solicitor, Attlee grew up in a middle-class home and had a conventional education at Haileybury and University College Oxford. He tood second class honours in History and was called to the Bar by the Inner Temple in 1906.

One source of Attlee's inner strength was his sense of history. His shelves were filled with works of serious historical study including many of the latest date: these he assiduously read right through his Prime Ministership.

Born and bred a Conservative, Attlee soon—though not by any dramatic conversion—became a Socialist, as the result of his association with the Webbs, partly of his self-chosen experience in the East End of London. He joined the Fabian Society and the London School Board, and became Secretary of Toynbee Hall. At this time he and a younger brother lived in a workman's house in Poplar. For a time he took work in the docks. In 1911 he became a lecturer on Trade Unionism at Ruskin College. Two years later he was lecturing at the London School of Economics on social science and administration. No other Prime Minister—indeed very few middle-class socialists—learned so intimately about the life and problems of the working class of his day. The first-hand experience gave him a pragmatic, non-doctrinaire approach to politics: indeed, underneath his convinced socialism he never lost a certain conservative cast of mind.

Attlee had a gallant war record. Within a few weeks of the outbreak of war, at the age of thirty-one, he joined the Inns of Court O.T.C. He served as an officer in Gallipoli. In 1916 he served in Mesopotamia, where he was severely wounded. In 1918 he was in France until the Autumn when he was discharged owing to sickness, with the rank of Major.

On his return to civil life he resumed his lectureship at the L.S.E. Soon he was immersed in active local politics. His experience, education and quiet staunchness marked him out at a time when representatives of Labour Councils in London tended to lack administrative training. In 1919 the Labour majority on Stepney Council invited him as an outsider to become Mayor. He was chosen as Chairman of an association of Labour Mayors, formed to deal with high unemployment in the East End. He led a delegation of Labour Mayors on foot to Downing Street.

In 1922 Attlee was elected M.P. for Limehouse, a seat which he held continuously until the redistribution of 1948, whereafter he sat for West Walthamstow.

Attlee was one of a number of professional and middle-class members whom the 1922 election brought into a Parliamentary Labour Party that had until then been dominated by trade unionists: a transformation that proceeded during the whole of Attlee's political life and helped to bring him forward as a man acceptable to both wings.

Ramsay MacDonald was elected leader of the Labour Opposition in place of Clynes, and appointed Attlee as one of his Private Parliamentary Secretaries. On Baldwin's defeat after his sudden dissolution of Parliament at the end of 1923, MacDonald became Prime Minister of a minority government and made Attlee Under-Secretary of State for War.

Again in opposition in 1924, Attlee continued to discharge unspectacular, but arduous, tasks for the party: he was chosen as front bench spokesman on the Electricity Bill and the Rating and Valuation Bill.

Parliamentary work left him diminishing time for local government and he severed his connection with it on becoming the Labour Member of the Simon Commission to India in 1927. Not ambition or even thought of high office, but the capacity for quiet and persistent industry turned his two years' stint in India into the most significant period of his apprenticeship. Years after, when wrestling with the question of Indian independence, he could recall at will the most complex details of the population, divisions, and problems of the major provinces of the sub-continent.

It appeared at first that his membership of the Simon Commission, by removing him from the centre of politics, had damaged his political prospects. He missed the 1929 election, though he was returned again for Limehouse. For several months he held no office in MacDonald's second minority administration. In the spring of 1930 a vacancy was created by Mosley's resignation. Attlee succeeded him as Chancellor of the Duchy of Lancaster, with the task of helping the Prime Minister with the Imperial Conference that met in London in 1930, and of co-operating with Addison on agricultural policy. The following year he became Postmaster General, the lowest full Ministerial post outside the Cabinet.

He was taken unawares by the economic and Cabinet crisis of 1931. Although he was a close associate of MacDonald, he hesitated not a moment in aligning himself with the majority of the party and went into opposition to MacDonald's National Government.

The subsequent election, which reduced the membership of the Labour Party in the House of Commons to fifty-two, proved to be Attlee's decisive stroke of luck. Lansbury was the only Cabinet Minister to survive and Attlee the next most senior Minister: Lansbury was elected leader with Attlee as his deputy. This seemed a caretaker job since there was a number of admittedly bigger and senior men in the wings. Perhaps the most important of these was Herbert Morrison, who had lost his seat. The depleted leadership involved Attlee in frequent front-bench speeches on a wide range of topics.

Attlee's luck held when, in 1935, only three weeks before an election that would bring back into the House some of Labour's established leaders, Lansbury's pacifism led to a ferocious attack upon him by Bevin at the Party Conference and his resignation as leader. As deputy leader Attlee was Lansbury's natural successor and he found himself, almost at a moment's notice, leading the party in the election, which was a relative success, raising Labour representation to 154.

In the contest for the leadership following the election, Attlee had the great advantage of being the incumbent. He was challenged by Morrison and Greenwood and carried the day after a second ballot. He remained leader in opposition and office for an unbroken twenty years—a record never before or since approached.

Attlee's first period as party leader was difficult and he gave the appearance of hesitation and weakness. He had displaced Lansbury because the latter was felt to be incapable of handling the increasing menace of the dictators. The challenge rapidly mounted. Italy completed its conquest of Abyssinia: Germany denounced the Treaty of Locarno: Germany, Italy and Russia played a sinister part in the Spanish Civil War. The League of Nations showed itself increasingly impotent.

Attlee's own views stiffened but he felt that he must take account of the strong pacifist wing in the Parliamentary Labour Party. He vacillated and temporized, seeking a way out by devious compromise. He began to voice doubts whether collective security—Labour's and his own panacea for all international problems—could survive: but he continued to lead the Parliamentary Party in divisions against the Defence Estimates, whilst increasingly emphasizing that this was not so much against defence as against the Government's mistaken foreign policy.

This equivocation was increasingly attacked by Dalton and others in the privacy of meetings of the Parliamentary Labour Party, almost certainly in accord with Attlee's inner thoughts. But he felt unable to go against the views of a substantial majority of the party. Thus he supported the resolution of the 1936 Annual Conference in favour of non-intervention in Spain; refused in the same year to back the Government's recruiting campaign; and on the eve of the war spoke and voted against conscription in the House.

After the fall of Austria, opinion in the party, partly under the influence of the shift of emphasis in Attlee's speeches, began to swing against the dictators. A new and sharper note appeared in Attlee's words. If, he asked, the bastions of liberty fell one by one, could Britain survive? When Chamberlain defined his policy towards Czechoslovakia, Attlee spoke out forthrightly and with unusual emotion—we could not barter our freedom and we could not accept a peace of slavery. He regarded Munich as no more than an armistice and a resounding victory for Hitler. Indeed he was driven to deny that Labour wanted war: on one occasion he was met in his constituency by demonstrators shouting in chorus—'We want peace: Attlee wants war.'

Attlee was learning the arts of leadership and the methods he applied as Prime Minister—somewhat inglorious, but effective. By the outbreak of war he had carried an undivided party into support of the Government.

The military disasters of the spring of 1940 was a turning point not only in the fortunes of the nation, but of Attlee himself. He spurned Chamberlain's offer to join his administration, but agreed to serve under Churchill. The Labour Party Conference happened to be meeting at this moment and overwhelmingly endorsed this decision.

Attlee was now the undisputed leader of the second party in the State and a major member of the War Cabinet, as Lord President and, two years later, as Deputy Prime Minister. As always, he gave self-effacing service, concentrating on the job in hand with quiet, confident, well-informed and cool judgement. Bevin, who equally but less accommodatingly subordinated himself to Churchill's leadership, appeared the bigger and more prominent man of the two: but he acquired an immense admiration for Attlee. He not only referred to him affectionately as the 'little man' but also—as he once told me—regarded him as the Campbell Bannerman of the Labour Party— the only man who could hold its disparate elements together.

Attlee's versatility and reliability led to his appointment in 1942 as Secretary of State for Dominion Affairs at a time when Japanese advances in South East Asia caused deep anxiety in Australia and New Zealand. Their confidence that they were worthily represented in the highest British councils helped to steady them.

Sixteen months later Attlee again became Lord President, this time with responsibility for the co-ordination of home policy. By November 1943 he was able to tell Parliament that part of the reconstruction programme was already in legislative draft.

Ten days after victory in Europe, in May 1945, Churchill wrote to Attlee proposing that the coalition should stay in being until victory over Japan. Attlee himself and some other Labour Ministers were inclined to favour this suggestion: but he bowed to the strong objections of the National Executive Committee (which also turned down Churchill's proposal for a referendum on this single issue).

The Labour Ministers left the Cabinet: Churchill called an immediate election. During the campaign Attlee out-argued Churchill in correspondence and on the radio and won a surprising and overwhelming victory.

At the age of sixty-two he became Prime Minister with a majority of near 100. In the first hours after electoral victory he displayed a new capacity to move rapidly, ruthlessly and with authority. Laski and Morrison suggested that a meeting of the Parliamentary Labour Party should be held to elect a leader, as usual at the beginning of each session. This was a moot question: how far was a leader with a majority in Parliament—something Labour had never before possessed—different from a leader of a minority government or of the opposition? Attlee, urged on by Bevin, settled the matter by going straight to the Palace and accepting office as Prime Minister. He equally ignored a certain support in the Party for adopting the Australian system of choosing Ministers by party ballot: he appointed his Ministers in the traditional way.

Attlee left his imprint upon the shape and function of the Cabinet. He took

295

Overleaf: Attlee's cabinet, 1945. On his right: Bevin; on his left: Morrison

over and reorganized the structure of war-time Cabinet Committees, thus setting up for the first time in peace such a Committee system. Also for the first time he left a number of full Ministers outside the Cabinet.

All these precedents have since been accepted as a matter of course.

Attlee's role and method as Prime Minister were more complex than is commonly assumed. They depended in part on his character and in part on the fact that during his first administration he was not the biggest or most dynamic man in the Cabinet. His position depended upon a triangle of forces formed by Bevin, Cripps and Morrison, each of whom preferred Attlee as leader to either of the other two. Attlee was therefore sustained by a kind of tense equilibrium beneath him.

Perhaps because of this stance, he had a strong sense of hierarchy in the Cabinet. Top Ministers were treated with deference. He could be sharp and waspish with Ministers below this rank. I recall how once, after an overlong harangue (something Attlee much disliked) by one Minister, Attle's sole comment was, 'Secretary of State you've got the sow by the wrong lug.' With junior Ministers, summoned to the Cabinet for a specific item, he was sometimes abrupt to the point of brutality.

None the less Attlee always respected the Cabinet, if necessary adjusting his own views to an emerging consensus. It is not true, as has been alleged, that he alone decided to make the hydrogen bomb. The decision was taken by a Cabinet Committee, composed of leading Ministers and on which I served as Commonwealth Secretary since the Woomera range in Australia was involved. A paper embodying the conclusions of the Committee was put

before the Cabinet. But Attlee did not conceal from the Committee his view that there were certain highly secret matters, such as this one and security, that should not be disclosed unnecessarily to the whole Cabinet.

Attlee depended most of all upon Bevin, who had a strong independent base in the Trade Union movement; whose loyalty to the Prime Minister was unquestioning and whose powerful character Attlee respected, admired and stood somewhat in awe of.

Once, when I was Commonwealth Secretary, I was summoned to Number Ten and found Attlee alone. He told me that Bevin was soon due and that he wanted to discuss a matter concerning the United States and certain Commonwealth countries. He said he wanted to take a strong line against a policy that was being urged upon us by America. Bevin then arrived and, slumping heavily into his chair, started straight away—'Clem, we must stand by America in this.' Attlee without hesitation agreed.

When he felt sure of himself Attlee could assume decisive leadership—as, for instance, over India. His greatest act of courage was the diversion of several hundred tons of wheat to save Germany from imminent starvation, at the price of imposing bread rationing in peace time.

Attlee sometimes fell very low in public and party esteem. In 1947, when his stock stood perhaps at its lowest, Dalton and Cripps made a concerted effort to displace him. Morrison refused to commit himself. When the conspirators approached Bevin—their candidate for the succession—he at once told Attlee. Sure of Bevin's support, Attlee took the conspiracy in his stride, never referring to it and keeping the plotters in office. A few months

later Attlee's repute had risen again to unassailable heights.

Attlee was an aloof man, hard to get on to personal terms with. Perhaps Bevin was the only one with whom he unbent: but I am not at all sure even of that.

Twice I managed briefly to break through his reserves. Late one night, when we had finished some business in the Cabinet room, he took me to his library and we spent an hour discussing his books and a family diary of which he was proud. On another occasion, also late at night, Attlee said that hardly any permanent head of a department had been at a public school. He handed me a *Who's Who* and himself went through the *Civil Service List*. He was quite right.

On the day following these intimacies things were just as before: no barriers were down. Even when I was a Cabinet Minister, if Attlee sent for me I always went with something of the apprehension of a summons to the housemaster's study.

Attlee was a quick and economical worker. He spent no time on what he regarded as unimportant. He paid little attention to newspapers and on some days never read them at all. If one went to Number Ten, even late at night, the papers were sometimes still in their pristine folds of breakfast time—all save *The Times*, disturbed enough only for the solution of the crossword. During a campaign run by the *Daily Mirror* with the slogan 'Attlee must go', the intended victim was perhaps the only man in the country unaware of the attacks upon him. The evening papers he read during his frequent visits to the Tea Room in the House, mainly frequented by Labour members: during the summer he always turned first to the cricket scores.

Official papers and telegrams he studied with care. Once he sent for me to question me about a small but critical detail in a telegram from Mountbatten: fortunately I could prove that I had acted on Cabinet instructions. Like most busy people, he had time to spare. If a Minister asked to see him, he had rarely to wait more than an hour or two and was frequently seen at once.

Attlee's new authority as Prime Minister enabled him to handle the Parliamentary Party with greater ease and confidence. He and Bevin frequently overrode the Left Wing. But Attlee, more than some Prime Ministers, was ready to recognize the limits imposed upon him by his followers. In 1947 he told the Party that the Government had decided to introduce an eighteenth-month period of conscription: the proposal was carried against substantial opposition. Soon after, seventy-two Labour M.P.s voted against the Conscription Bill and many abstained. Thereupon the Minister of Defence announced to the party meeting that the Cabinet had resolved to reduce conscription to twelve months.

During his term of office Attlee was scarcely ever free from crisis, at home and abroad. Demobilization and redeployment of labour was carried through with exemplary smoothness. But almost at once a severe and intractable balance of payments crisis arose. This was the compound result of the liquidation of Britain's overseas assets during the war; the building up of vast sterling balances owed to India and other countries; Truman's sudden

298

The winter of 1947: hardships and shortages. Alan Sullivan waits for his brother who is queueing for coal

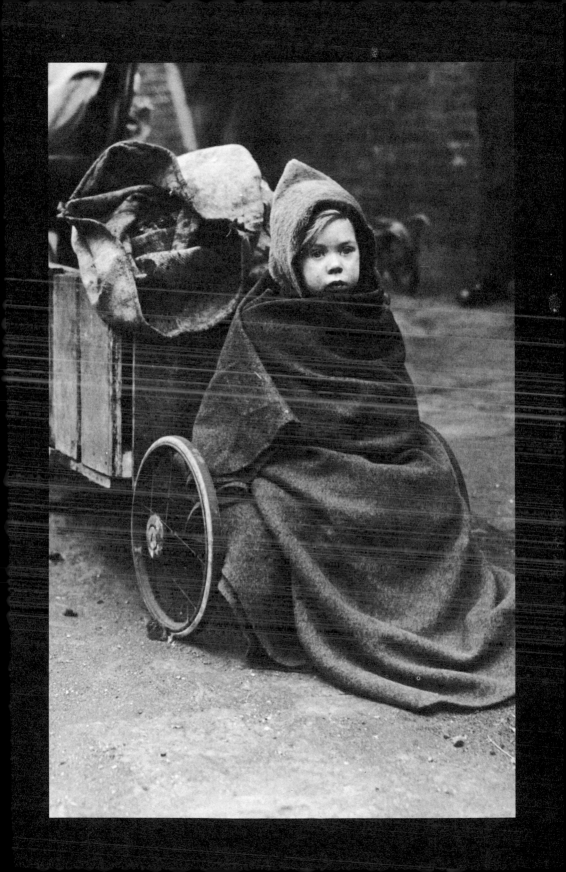

cancellation of Lease-Lend; America's insistence on the premature restoration of free exchange-rates and the rapid erosion, due to inflation, of the American loan designed to finance this operation.

In February 1947 excessively cold weather led to a breakdown of rail transport and a fuel crisis that shut down for some weeks almost the whole of industry.

A policy of austerity was introduced, associated primarily with Cripps, but which Attlee wholly supported and often expounded. Rationing became even stricter than during the war. The hoardings were plastered with the stark slogan *Work or Want*. Both the policy and the terms in which it was cast, gave a drabness to the whole period of Attlee's administrations.

It was against this sombre backdrop that Attlee made decisions that altered the whole course of British history.

To his sole credit must be attributed the transformation of Empire into Commonwealth. The policy was carried further by later Governments, but he took the vital and decisive first steps. Had India not led the way, probably all newly independent countries would have taken the Burma road to the severance of all links with the existing Commonwealth. This was indeed India's first intention when it declared itself a republic in the self-same terms as Burma.

Attlee quickly came to the conclusion that India's independence was inevitable. It was primarily his own decision to dismiss Wavell and appoint Mountbatten as Governor General. He hoped to hand power over to a united country. As India's internal divisions led to deadlock, he grew increasingly impatient. His attitude towards India was always ambivalent. He knew and admired many of its leaders: but he also felt a certain contempt for what he regarded as their loquacious irresponsibility. It was in order to concentrate their minds that he fixed a term for independence and then shortened it.

Attlee was ready if necessary to accept quietly India's, Pakistan's, and Ceylon's secession from the Commonwealth—as he had accepted Burma's. It was his simple and pragmatic approach to this problem that largely solved it. As a matter of course and without any flourish he invited the three Asian Prime Ministers to join their colleagues in a regular meeting in London before they had decided whether or not to continue their membership. Their attitude changed when they found that the Commonwealth consisted of truly independent nations, in no way subordinate to Britain.

Next arose the problem of fitting India as a republic into a monarchial Commonwealth. Long and detailed discussions ensued in the Cabinet and in Cabinet Committees. Many solutions were canvassed, some of which would certainly have driven India out of the Commonwealth. I was at this time Under-Secretary of State at the Commonwealth Office and played a certain part in these transactions, which from time to time brought me into close contact with Attlee. I think I was the first to propose in written memoranda the line that was finally adopted. I also suggested the despatch of envoys to all Commonwealth capitals to prepare for the vital Prime Ministers' meeting, and was myself sent to Delhi, Karachi and Colombo.

The Declaration of London of April 1949 is perhaps the most important of all Commonwealth documents. It simply declared that India, on becoming a Republic, wished to remain in the Commonwealth and that all the other members accepted this.

But for Attlee this formula would not have been proposed. It was another great precedent set by him and it has proved flexible enough to turn the Commonwealth into one of realms and republics, recognizing the Queen as its Head.

Bevin was less sure than Attlee about keeping India in the Commonwealth, but deferred to him. In other fields of overseas policy Bevin tended to take the lead: but was fully supported by the Prime Minister. In effect they worked as one.

The retreat from imperialism went on with the withdrawal from Egypt, the surrender of the Palestine mandate, the repudiation by Iraq of a treaty just concluded and the handing over to the United States of responsibility for the turmoil in Greece and Turkey. These necessary policies probably offended the still instinctive pride of the British people. The ambivalent and as it turned out mistaken attitude towards Europe met with greater popular approval.

The British Government realized sooner than the Americans the menace of Soviet imperialism. Bevin leapt at Marshall's hint of generous aid to the whole of Western Europe. Marshall Aid came just in time to save France and Italy from communism and to enable Britain to play a decisive part in European defence. Bevin and Attlee by the Brussels Treaty and by whole hearted participation in NATO committed the country to a military role that it had never before assumed in peacetime. Towards the end of 1948 Stalin's siege of Berlin was frustrated by the airlift in which Britain fully participated and which led to the first post-war reverse for Russia. In March 1949 Attlee himself flew to Berlin to see the airlift in action.

Though participating in an unprecedented way in the affairs of Europe, Attlee and Bevin felt ill at ease about the federalist movement on the Continent. As leaders of the only European nation that had not been defeated or occupied they were out of sympathy with the mood across the Channel. They were ready and eager to share in inter-governmental co-operation of the type of O.E.C.D. and the E.P.U. But they used their influence to ensure that the Council of Europe should have only consultative functions and be subordinate to a Council of Ministers.

The critical decision concerned the setting up of the Iron and Steel community—the first step towards the Treaty of Rome. The British rejection of an invitation to enter discussions was as much the result of perhaps deliberately clumsy French diplomacy as of British reluctance. The Cabinet informed Schuman of its readiness to discuss supra-nationalism, but was met by an ultimatum that an undertaking to accept supra-nationalism ahead of consultations must be given in a few hours. This affronted the Cabinet and convinced it that the French did not want Britain's presence.

In the midst of these constant distractions and crises overseas, Attlee supervised the massive legislation programme needed to get through major measures of nationalization and the establishment of the most comprehensive system of social security in the world.

It was as well in a period of such turmoil and radical readjustment that Britain was presided over by a Prime Minister with such surefooted realism and calmness of mind.

With the economy (helped by Marshall Aid) apparently on the way to recovery, Labour entered the general election of February 1950 full of confidence in public gratitude, especially for social security. The cutting of its majority to ten was a traumatic shock.

For a variety of reasons, Attlee lost the touch and assurance of his first administration. The whole balance of the Cabinet was disturbed by the departure of Cripps in October 1950, and of Bevin in March 1951, in both cases due to mortal illness. Attlee was no longer sustained by the tension of a triumvirate below him.

Morrison, the survivor of this triumvirate, became Foreign Secretary, but never had good personal relations with Attlee. Gaitskell, the new Chancellor, belonged to the younger generation of the party. Attlee did not succeed in re-establishing the intimacy between a Prime Minister and his Foreign Secretary and Chancellor upon which a stable and effective Cabinet depends.

The pressure on a now less-assured Prime Minister continued unremittingly. In July 1950 North Korea suddenly invaded the South. Attlee without hesitation supported Truman's despatch of United States forces and himself sent a British brigade. But the prolonged campaign led to a world shortage of commodities and turned the terms of trade heavily against Britain. Precarious economic recovery was converted into a balance of payments crisis.

Shortly before this America, in a sudden flurry of alarm about assumed Soviet intentions, suddenly demanded a sharp increase of defence expenditure. One of Bevin's last acts as Foreign Secretary was to push acceptance of this demand through the Cabinet after all too rapid and ill-prepared discussion. As it turned out, it proved impossible to spend all the money allotted.

None the less Gaitskell's subsequent Budget had to accommodate the outlay decided upon. In part as a symbol, but primarily in an attempt to check the open-ended cost of the National Health Service, he imposed a charge on spectacles and false teeth. This led to a grave split in the Cabinet and the resignation in April 1951 of Bevin and Wilson: both of whom widened the argument to one of defence expenditure. Attlee was absent through illness during this crisis; but he kept in close touch and presided over the resignation Cabinet. I was a participant in these affairs and I saw no reason to think that Attlee could have headed off the resignations even had he been in good health throughout.

Within a month the Abadan crisis broke and lasted throughout the remainder of Attlee's term of office. Morrison and Shinwell inclined to favour a military response but Attlee and the bulk of the Cabinet felt that Britain, here too, had to come to terms with nationalism. The closing of the Abadan refinery led to a rapid increase in dollar expenditure for oil and worsened the balance of payments. The reserves began to run down.

The Government was further weakened by its small majority and by clinging to rationing to the mounting discontent of an impatient public.

In October 1951 Attlee unexpectedly dissolved Parliament. He had never believed that a majority of ten was sufficient. Moreover, as he told me, he felt that he could not expose the King, who was about to visit Australia and New Zealand, to the possibility of a fall of the Government during his absence. This seemed to me an inadequate reason for a dissolution, as I pointed out to Attlee. Later I discovered that Morrison and Shinwell, who were in Canada, had likewise protested.

This dissolution was a major error of judgement, due in part to a failure of nerve. Had Attlee held on till the autumn he would have benefited from the swing in the terms of trade in Britain's favour.

Labour lost nineteen seats and control passed to Churchill.

Once again in Opposition, Attlee—perhaps exhausted by eleven continuous years of high office—and plagued by organized faction in the Parliamentary Party—assumed almost the attitude of a detached observer. He again led the party in the 1955 election—for the last time driven by his wife in a motor-car tour throughout the country.

Labour never entered an election with so little confidence and the Conservatives increased their majority to sixty.

The internal party disputes continued, now sharpened by a struggle for succession to the leadership. A number of his former Cabinet colleagues several times met Attlee and begged him to resign in order to give way to Morrison. Attlee stubbornly stayed on till December 1955, in the hope, as was widely believed, of allowing Morrison's age to turn against him. Attlee warmly welcomed Gaitskell's election as leader.

On retirement Attlee at once accepted an earldom. He travelled widely, including visits as leader of a Labour Party delegation to Russia and China. He made a number of exhausting lecture tours to America. He increasingly identified himself with the cause of world government. He strongly supported Gaitskell in the critical dispute over unilateral nuclear disarmament.

In his dry and brief autobiography *As it Happened* he wrote a fitting epitaph for himself: 'Up to the present I have been a very happy and fortunate man in having lived so long in the greatest country in the world, in having a happy family life and in having been given the opportunity of serving in a state of life to which I had never expected to be called.'

I think Attlee's standing as a Prime Minister will steadily rise, though he will never be classed amongst the three or four greatest. He left the world a better place than he found it. In a period of stress and temptation and of advancing tyranny he handed on the torch of democracy to his successors.

It is to Attlee, more than to any other post-war Prime Minister, that is due the disproportionate role that a Britain with diminished power can still play in the world.

Mussolini
by Sir Colin Coote

SIR COLIN COOTE (b. 1893) was educated at Rugby and Balliol, and after leaving Oxford, where he took his degree in Greats, he enlisted in the Army in 1914. He served in the infantry throughout the war, being wounded in 1917, and severely gassed in 1918. He was awarded a D.S.O. on the field after being one of only thirty survivors of his Company of the Gloucesters in July 1918.

He was elected, *in absentia*, in 1917 in the Isle of Ely, as a Lloyd George Liberal at the age of twenty-four, but continued to serve at the Front until the Armistice. He lost his seat in the election of 1922 following the collapse of the Lloyd George Coalition.

He was appointed as correspondent of *The Times* in Rome from 1922-25. He subsequently served on *The Times* in many foreign missions and as a principal leader-writer, but fell out of favour owing to his opposition to appeasement. This led to his change over to *The Daily Telegraph and Morning Post* of which he was Deputy Editor (1942-50) and Managing Editor from 1950-64. He was awarded the Legion of Honour in 1958; and a knighthood in 1962.

Amongst his many publications are a biography of his closest friend, the Rt Hon Walter Elliot, entitled *A Companion of Honour* (1965); an anthology (with P. D. Bunyan) of Sir Winston Churchill's speeches and writings (*Sir Winston Churchill—a Self-Portrait*) in 1954; his own Memoirs (*Editorial*) in 1965; and a history of *The Other Club* in 1971.

Benito Mussolini

29 July 1883	Born. Educated at Salesian Fathers' school in Faenza and lay school in Forlimpopoli.
1902	Expelled from Switzerland for engaging in revolutionary propaganda.
1904	Performed obligatory military service.
1908	Became editor of socialist paper in Austrian city of Trento. Was expelled from Austria.
1910	Founded weekly journal in Forli.
1911	Italian leader Giolitti embarked on Libyan war, thus losing much socialist support.
1911-12	Spent five months in prison for fomenting riots in Forli.
July 1912	Attended national congress of Partito Socialista italiana at Reggio Emilia. Helped to eject moderates from party and revolutionary socialists gained control. Became editor of Milan daily *Avanti*.
1914	Outbreak of First World War. Was dismissed from editorship by P.S.I. for his pro-war views.
Aug. 1915	Called up and spent 18 months on active duty. Wounded during firing practice.
1919	Broad system of proportional representation adopted for election. Two parties emerged triumphant— P.S.L. and *Popolari*.

Previous page: the March on Rome. For the final stage Mussolini changed into a morning suit and his followers into full-dress uniforms

23 March 1919	Mussolini formally inaugurated fascism in Milan—he attacked both the establishment and the socialists.
Sept. 1919	Nationalist poet D'Annunzio seized Fiume in Adriatic, a port which Italy hoped to get in post-war settlement. Mussolini supported him in his paper *Il Popoli d'Italia* D'Annunzio was later shelled out by Prime Minister Giolitti.
1920	Massive unemployment. Sit-in strikes at factories in northern Italy. Mussolini organized armed squads to destroy political and economic organizations of socialists.
15 May 1921	Mussolini and 35 other Fascists elected to parliament.
Nov. 1921	At congress of Rome, Fascism was organized into a *Partito Nazionale Fascista*.
1 Aug. 1922	General strike, which was broken by Fascist armed squads.
Oct. 1922	The concentration of armed squads and the march on Rome. Cabinet, headed by Facta, proclaimed state of emergency. Facta resigned and King Victor Emmanuel III asked Mussolini to form new cabinet.
12 Jan. 1923	Created Fascist Grand Council, whose members he appointed.
10 June 1924	Murder of Matteotti, leading member of Socialist party.
3 Jan. 1925	Mussolini established full dictatorship.
2 Oct. 1925	Palazzo Vidoni pact between industrialists' association (Confindustria) and Fascist syndicates. This neutralized traditional trade unions.
24 Dec. 1925	Law increasing power of head of government, giving him full executive responsibility.
31 Jan. 1926	Decrees given power of laws.
3 April 1926	Right to strike abolished; collective contracts reserved for fascist syndicates.
25 Nov. 1926	Law for defence of the state. Special tribunal for political crimes created.
21 Dec. 1927	Exchange rate fixed at 'quota 90', in order to keep up international value of lira.
11 Feb. 1929	Lateran pacts and Concordat with Vatican, which instituted new status for Church and repealed anti-clerical legislation—a compromise with Fascism.
23 Jan. 1933	Creation of *Istituto per la Ricostruzione Industriale*.
1933	Draining of Pontine marshes, which added 200,000 acres to Italy's arable land.
10 Nov. 1934	Council of Corporations inaugurated in Rome.
5 Oct. 1935	Italian invasion of Abyssinia, defying economic sanctions imposed by League of Nations.
7 Dec. 1935	Hoare-Laval pact which offered Mussolini two-thirds of Abyssinia if he remained anti-German.
July 1936	Italian troops fought for Franco in Spanish civil war.
21 Oct. 1936	Rome-Berlin 'Axis'—secret protocol pledging co-operation on a variety of questions.
March 1938	Mussolini obliged to accept German annexation of Austria.
14 July 1938	Publication of *Manifesto della Razza*. First laws against Jews.
19 Jan. 1939	Creation of *Camera dei Fasci e della Corporazione*, which replaced parliament.
7 April 1939	Italian invasion of Albania.
22 May 1939	Pact of Steel: aggressive military alliance between Italy and Germany.
10 June 1940	Italy entered Second World War. Campaign against France in Alps.
Oct. 1940	Italy invaded Greece—unsuccessful, so Germans took over campaign.
May 1941	Italy lost Abyssinia.
Feb. 1943	Ciano, Grandi, and Bottai were dismissed from Ministries by Mussolini, and became focus for opposition.
March 1943	Series of strikes in Turin and Milan.
25 July 1943	Grand Council of Fascism voted Mussolini out of power. Badoglio ministry took over. Mussolini imprisoned but later rescued by German parachutists.
8 Sept. 1943	Armistice. Nazis took over Italy. King and ministers fled south to take refuge with Allies.
23 Sept. 1943	Mussolini announced creation of fascist socialist republic (Republic do Salo).
28 April 1945	Mussolini executed by partisans.

A reader's first question may well be whether Benito Mussolini deserves any place at all in this gallery of the eminent. 'Fascist' has become a dirty word, though there is no reason in logic or in fact why it should be dirtier than 'Communist'. Personally I do not desire to put him on a pedestal. Five years in Rome at the outset of his attainment of power were enough to erase many illusions, particularly about most of his Fascist associates who smelt more of Chicago in the time of Capone than of classical Rome. But he did have twenty-three years in power, of which about seventeen were years passed in an odour of intermittent and widely if not universally unchallenged efficiency. Thereafter he sagged steadily towards a scrofulous end.

It will be shown later in this essay that his decline and decay were not wholly his own fault. Before they began John Gunter, who wrote, in association with a fellow American journalist, Knickerbocker, that brilliant inter-war assessment called *Inside Europe*, defined him as 'the most formidable combination of turncoat, ruffian, and man of genius in history'. This is a case of damning with strong praise. He had really only two characteristics in common with Napoleon. The first was a dreadful accent in French and the second an indecipherable signature. But if it is ludicrous to give him a political halo, it is also unfair to give him only a noose.

Mussolini began, like Lloyd George, in humble surroundings. Like Lloyd George he slid upwards very easily; had an admirably long-suffering wife, and a long succession of mistresses, including one 'steady' who was a rather finer character than her lover. He was a magnificent orator; and had a talent for engendering admiration rather than trust. Their ends were very different in kind, but perhaps not so different psychologically. Mussolini after five years of what F.W. Deakin calls a 'Brutal Alliance' with Hitler (who was as uncongenial to him as any barbarian ever was to a Roman) died, in the same way as Cola di Rienzi, and was hung by his heels in a square in Milan like a chunk of meat in a butcher's shop; and Lloyd George after his fall from power in 1922 had nearly a generation in the wilderness with precious little manna but a lot of sand-storms and mirages. It is arguable whether the violent or the long-drawn-out demise was the more bitter.

That highly talented cad Gabriele D'Annunzio wrote 'What we want is a blacksmith to cut free the eagle from the Roman Shield'. He was, no doubt, thinking of himself; but the reader was at once reminded of Mussolini who was the son of a blacksmith with opinions as red as his own furnace; and there is no reason to believe that young Benito did not genuinely inherit some of them. His father called him 'Benito' after the Mexican thug who had executed the unhappy Emperor Maximilian in 1865, and thus punctured the reputation of Napoleon III. There was a tradition of revolutionary fervour in the image of Mazzini and Garibaldi—whose portrait hung over the bed of Mussolini senior. And this fervour had a material foundation. The Italian peasantry were desperately poor. In the region of Predappio, his birthplace in the Romagna, conditions could be bad enough, but elsewhere, particularly in the Abruzzi, the poverty was unimaginable. Mussolini himself found a wage of twelve shillings a week in Gualtieri, and under threepence an hour in Switzerland, relative wealth. It is a mistake to suppose that revolutions are always started by the lowest layer of the downtrodden. The most notable—the French Revolution—was led and inspired by the lesser bourgeoisie with a leavening of the noblesse. And the Fascist Revolution was a revolution *against* a proletarian revolution.

It must be remembered that the Italians had suffered horribly in the First World War, both physically and morally. They had endured eleven Battles of the Isonzo, each a miniature Somme, and some of them more like an enlargement. The strength of the British and French armies was the wealth of officer material, which however wastefully squandered, was always there to share the trials of the rank and file. In Italy, very broadly speaking, there were only two classes, the aristocracy and the proletariat. The aristocracy, always few in numbers, was speedily decimated and irreplaceable. An army can, at a pinch, dispense with field-marshals but not with platoon commanders. It is slanderous to jeer at the Italian Army whom I have myself seen putting up with ordeals such as other more vaunted armies would not have tolerated. But they were not well led.

After the 1918 Armistice nobody was more harsh towards the Italian soldiers than their own countrymen. Officers and men in uniform were assaulted in the streets and stripped of their badges of rank and decorations. Mussolini was particularly sensitive to jeers at the Army. The events of his adolescence and early manhood have been over-dramatized; but he was a tiger among the Socialist wolves in the Romagna in 1910; he got into trouble in Switzerland where he had taken refuge when the Romagna became too hot for him; he protested violently enough against Italy's rape of Tripoli in 1911 to be imprisoned; and up to the eve of Italy's entry into the Great War, he had been urging in his own rag of a newspaper that Italy must not be dragged into a capitalist quarrel, using all the usual jargon of those 'too proud to fight'.

Then suddenly the tone changed, and curiously enough it changed simultaneously with a *pourboire* of 15,000 francs from an official of the French Embassy; and of further funds from another source sufficient to start an interventionist paper.

Dog does not eat dog, and a journalist must admit that he was pretty good at writing. The admission comes the more readily because his change of heart, when he was called up in due course, carried his legs into the front line, where he spent some months in a Bersaglieri battalion without disgrace until he got a 'beautiful Blighty' (as we used to call a disabling wound), not, I fear, in an assault but in bomb practice. Later commentators made the most of this episode, and the number of people who claimed to have carried the wounded hero to hospital reached several hundreds. But, like so many survivors of the First World War, he always looked back with nostalgic emotion to his battlefield experience. And the Bainsizza plateau was no scene of 'phoney' war. The Italians were striking for Trieste, and the way there was so bloody that one of those jovially macabre songs, which emerged from the infantry of all armies, ran:

Il General' Cadorna ha scritto alla regina
'Si vuole Lei Trieste, comprate cartolina.'

(The C-in-C wrote to the Queen 'If you want Trieste buy a picture postcard of it'.)

So when, after the war, a yapping and biting ferocity was exhaled by the Left upon soldiers and ex-soldiers, Mussolini resolved to give as good as they got, and started forming a version of the Black and Tans, which were then meeting terrorism with terrorism in Ireland. The Fascisti, so called after the fasces, or bundle of rods, carried by the Roman lictors, brought one new weapon into the armament of terrorism—castor oil. The administration of half a pint to recalcitrants was original and effective, since it fulfilled the best canon in politics of making opponents both uncomfortable and ludicrous.

Perhaps the red rash which spread over Italy was itself a little ludicrous— at least there was a comic touch about some essentially nasty events. The famous 'take-over by the workers' of factories in Turin and elsewhere in 1920 no more resembled a volcanic eruption than our General Strike in 1926. An American owner of a factory, quoted by Professor Salvemini[1] says: 'The workers were simple enough to believe . . . they had started a world revolution. At our place they did no malicious damage . . . They tried to run the factory instead. During their theatricals, I went out to play golf every day. Though I crossed the factory district in my car, I was not molested.'

Of course neither 1920 in Italy nor 1926 in Britain was all fun. In Italy 200 people were killed and 500,000 involved in troubles more lethal than those in Turin. In Britain there were 10,000 cases of alleged intimidation. Nevertheless, statistics for the post-war years show that the redness of Italy was becoming distinctly pink before Mussolini took any notable hand in the matter. Industrial unrest in all countries, which had fought to 'make a land fit for heroes to live in' was tremendous so soon as those countries turned out to be lands fit for unemployed to rot in. It was little worse in Italy than in Britain—the 1920 figures of days lost by strikes are Italy 30½ million, Great Britain 26½ million. And according to the Italian Statistical Annual the nominal value of savings increased by over 30 per cent between 1919 and 1920 and was at least steady in real value. In the same years the production of cars of all kinds increased from about 34,500 to nearly 49,000. Lastly the yield of taxation, according to Signor Bachi's *Italian Economy in 1921*, increased from 15,207 million lire in 1919/20 to 18,820 million lire in 1920/21—again roughly keeping pace with inflation. Indeed the crushing burden of post-war taxation had probably about as much to do with the difficulties of industry as any Red inundations.

Of course in the famous definition of lies, statistics are the third and the worst category. None of the above figures can conceal that for the first two post-war years a patriot was as dirty a word to a rather hippie-like coagulation of Italian Leftists as 'aristo' to the Jacobins in 1789. On balance the lies of the legend probably beat the lies of the mathematics by at least a short head.

But if the Revolution was withering, Mussolini hastened the process by fertilizing the counter-revolution. There were five Prime Ministers between 1919 and 1922, all of the 'wait and see' variety and all but one extremely

310

myopic themselves. The exception was Giolitti. He too expected that if the 'Bolsheviks' were given enough rope, they would hang themselves; but he could act too. He shelled D'Annunzio out of Fiume; and the poet, having conveniently forgotten his oath to die rather than surrender, was thereafter reduced to the status of a clown.

Mussolini inherited from him the leadership of the counter-revolution, and when Giolitti tried to use him as the Government's tool against terrorism, he bit with relish the hand that fed him. The Fascist squadristi were clandestinely armed by the War Ministry and their operations were masked and protected by Government forces. Giolitti greatly increased the Carabinieri and formed a new body called the Royal Guard. But their rôle was to stand on the sidelines and see that no referee interfered with the Fascist goal-scorers. In other words Mussolini was allowed to do what the Government ought to have done themselves.

As blind as Bourbons to the lessons of history, the Leftists formed a so-called 'Alliance of Labour' and announced a General Strike for 1 August 1922. It lasted precisely two days— one fifth of our General Strike in 1926 and five times more fatuous. The Report of the State Railways for 1922/23 affirms that only 60,000 out of 229,000 railwaymen—supposed to be the reddest of the Reds, struck at all. All that the strike really did was to give the Fascists an excuse—endorsed by the inaction of the Government to crush the Opposition in the provinces and prepare to supplant the Government itself in Rome. Their plans were further eased by a split of the Socialist ranks into two almost equal parts—the one moderate, the other 'intransigent'.

The central feature of the legend—the March on Rome has now been reached. It is not the least bedizened part of the story. Some of the more enthralled commentators described it as an irresistible migration of tens of thousands of dedicated patriots of all classes. The dedication was certainly there, but the numbers were not, and the March was far from irresistible. Indeed General Badoglio who was in the news both when the curtain rose on Fascism and when it fell twenty-three years later, opined that 'a few minutes of shooting' would have dispersed that 'rabble.' Precedents, such as Napoleon's 'whiff of grapeshot' which scattered the Jacobin mob, suggest that he was right. And indeed the Prime Minister, Signor Facta, who had no lavish reserve of resolution, was of the same opinion. He presented to the King a decree establishing Martial Law; but after twenty-four hours wobbling, Victor Emmanuel refused to sign. A few months later, members of his entourage, who ought to have known, told me that he had been convinced the Army would not fire on the marchers. I wonder. The Bavarians certainly fired on the marchers in Munich headed by Ludendorff and Hitler. A Punjabi regiment fired on the rioters at Amritsar at the order of General Dyer. Ney, it is true, did not fire on Napoleon, en route from Elba to Paris. The abstention cost him his life after Waterloo; but would you have fired on the Little Corporal?

Whatever the answer, the Army would not fire without the King's order; and when Mussolini arrived by train, he came as Prime Minister designate. A case can be made for saying that, however less than glorious the March on Rome and to Office had been, it was better to make Mussolini Prime

Minister than to save Facta's face. With some exceptions the post-war Italian Parliaments had deserved the same sort of contempt as De Gaulle expressed for the later Parliaments of the Fourth Republic in France. No country can be happy under governments without guts.

Mussolini's trouble was that few, if any, of his leading henchmen had any experience of government, and only a handful had had any of Parliament. As Churchill once said, there is only one thing worse than fighting with allies, and that is fighting without them. Mussolini therefore tried to make peace with the Socialists; but the local Fascists did not at all like this change of tune, and the attempt had to be abandoned. The more palatable Nationalists readily coalesced; and I have always thought that their Ministers (such as Federzoni and de Stefani) in the Government were better than most of their Fascist colleagues who tended to be theatrical posturers.

Only too often responsibility does not change characters. Addicts to violence can seldom be cured, and their addiction tends to increase in proportion as their victims become more defenceless. It was only one step from a beaten Parliament to a puppet Parliament; and only one more from a censored press to the suppression of freedom in both the spoken and the written word. Thugs martyred the brave Amendola, Editor of *Il Mondo*, ejected the objective Albertini brothers from control of the *Corriere della Sera*; and finally murdered the heroic critic of Fascist tyranny and corruption, Matteotti.

This last outrage must be described at some length, because it came quite close to nipping the Fascist regime in the bud. Matteotti was the Socialist scion of a family of rich landowners who, in spite of all obstacles, had secured election to Parliament. In appearance, sincerity, oratory, personal charm, and eruptivity, he resembled our own Michael Foot, with a cooler and less cranky mind. In May 1924, he delivered in the Chamber a rasping and unanswerable exposure of Fascist rigging of the elections, which he and many of his audience, including myself, considered tantamount to signing his own death warrant. I remember watching the effect on Mussolini. A pose of contemptuous indifference gradually disintegrated into a grimace of black fury. So might the countenance of Henry II have changed as he studied the latest 'insolence' of Thomas à Becket. And the result was precisely the same. Hangers-on at Henry's Court heard the King ask, 'Who will rid me of this turbulent Priest?' Some of Mussolini's gutter snipes heard him snarl, 'If you were not a bunch of cowards, you would never have allowed that creature to make such a speech.'

But unlike Henry, Mussolini could not evade vicarious responsibility by public penance. He had to lie his way out of it by pretending to order a hectic search for the victim's body, and to feel a punitive anger towards officials who had allowed so filthy a murder to take place. The whole gang escaped with trivial and token punishments, but Mussolini himself did not. From that time onwards he was a prisoner of the 'hawks' in the sense that what started as a potentially supple Reformist Movement became a politically arthritic dictatorship. He had formed the militia which brought him to power; now he was himself in its power. It had become a para-military Praetorian Guard, carefully immunized from criticism. Indeed its critics

312

were bluntly warned by Mussolini himself with the snarl 'Who touches the Militia shall touch lead'.

In the main debate on the Matteotti affair, old Giolitti, the 'Fox of Piedmont', asked Mussolini not to treat the Italian people 'as though they did not deserve liberty'. That is exactly what he slid into doing. It is highly risky to generalize about nations. But, broadly speaking, the old Romans were a cold, cruel, ruthless, and highly efficient people, whose main quality was 'gravitas', an almost untranslatable word, meaning something like possessing the poise and aura of a first-class headmaster. The Italians were none of these things. Supremely talented artistically, they rather enjoyed the trappings of Black Shirts, banner waving, salutes and so on, but nobody could make them into an imperial race. Several of his cronies told me off the record that in expansive moments Mussolini used to complain about the quality of the material with which he had to work. Italians believed in a United Italy. But they did not believe in becoming a World Power—if it cost a lot in blood and treasure; still less in dying for Germany—the 'brutto Tedesco' of their history.

Mussolini made a strenuous and consistent effort to thrust greatness upon them. When an Italian General on the Albanian Boundary Commission was murdered the Greek island of Corfu was shelled by the Italian Navy with that disregard for danger which we can all display when there isn't any. This variant of the 'Jenkins' Ear' episode came off quite well. But it was a circus turn, and long-term policy required something less gimmicky. Mussolini started with the children—who are to a quite remarkable extent the key to the hearts of Italian parents. Schoolboys were dressed up in a version of the blackshirt uniform and brigaded into a parody of the Boy Scouts, called the Ballilla. The advance in the status of the Blackshirt Militia has already been noted. He rearmed the regular Services, but this, oddly enough, caused one of his worst material errors. For the weapons with which the Services were so copiously endowed turned out to be perfected too soon. They were good enough to beat the largely unequipped Ethiopians; but they did not save the 'volunteers' sent to fight for Franco in the Spanish Civil War from a series of almost ludicrous defeats, and by the time Italy entered a much more serious affair on Hitler's side in 1940 nearly all the planes and tanks and even some of the impressive looking ships were out of date. By 1939, Mussolini was earnestly reminding Hitler that Italy would not be ready for war for another three years; and he was not pleased when the Führer jumped the gun.

But all Mussolini's efforts in other fields were not vain in either sense of the word. In the vexed and vexatious field of industrial relations he introduced a system called the 'Corporative State'. The governing body was an ostensibly elected but in fact nominated 'Chamber of Fascists and Corporations' charged with drawing up regulations for running the economic life of the country. It was provided that, after ten years, a National Referendum should approve or disapprove of the system. Since nobody except the Fascists could be elected at all, and a Fascist Minister could veto any decision of the Chamber, it is clear that F. W. Deakin was correct in declaring that the 'structure became in effect an exclusive field of Party patronage, corruption, and control'.[2]

Nevertheless not every feature of it was fatuous or worse. On technical and professional matters delegates to the Chamber did the best they could for the electors—sometimes it might be thought, too much. For example, after the Second World War, if a British newspaper engaged an Italian journalist, sacking him was, *mutatis mutandis*, about as difficult and expensive as getting to the moon. And one feature of this Fascist structure found favour with Mr Wilson's Socialist Government. This was the Institute for Industrial Reorganization which helped to finance a large variety of industrial enterprises. It still survives.

Nor can it be denied that Mussolini did much for agriculture. By 1933, the Pontine Marshes had been drained, and nearly 200,000 acres added to Italy's supply of arable land. He made an economic blunder in preferring the prestige operation of growing wheat, of which there was a world glut; but he did double the tonnage of wheat grown in Italy. Early in this campaign a friend of mine happened to be visiting some farms near Florence, and complimented one small farmer on a magnificent field of wheat. 'Yes,' he said, 'it is easy to see we have a strong Government.'

Among Mussolini's achievements, it would be unjust to omit his Concordat with the Vatican which ended fifty years of bitterness between the Crown and the Pope. For some time Pius XI had considered him as a predecessor had viewed the great Napoleon—a mixture of *tragediante* and *commediante*; but at that time Popes were not judged only by Stalin's criterion ('The Pope? How Many Divisions has he?'); and dictators in basically Roman Catholic countries preferred Charlemagne to Lenin as a model. It was said that Arnaldo, Mussolini's brother, was the author of the deal. However that may be, Bonito got the credit—not wholly undeservedly. For he had swiftly become the white-haired boy of the Court, which had, in the background, shored up his shaken spirit in the Matteotti affair; and therefore the Vatican knew he could deliver the goods. The marriage enshrined in the Concordat of 1929 was preceded by a fascinating period of flirtation. On his side, Mussolini recanted from his arrival in Rome in 1922 his savage anti-clericalism. On the Pope's side a couple of years later, Pius XI wrecked the Catholic Partito Popolare under Don Sturzo, which had been the second largest in the 1921 Assembly, by forbidding priests to belong to any political party. This neutralized the potentially strongest opposition to the Fascists, and caused Mussolini to escape without any Vatican reproof for the rape of Abyssinia in 1935.

What is a stone cold certainty is that Mussolini himself gave tremendous encouragement to archaeology, and promoted many of the vestiges of classical Rome from slums to impressive national monuments. You may think that the *remplaçant* of D'Annunzio could do no less. But this characteristic happens to appeal to me who would prefer a Dead Sea Scroll to Harold Wilson's complete memoirs any day of the week. I trust that my sense of historical values is not thereby warped. In any case, I am quite sure that much better judges, such as Professor Boni, a principal excavator of the Foro Romano; or Dr Ashby and Mrs Strong of the British Institute; or

315

Overleaf: Mussolini's victims. The primitive soldiers of Ethiopia

Monsieur Franz Cumont, the great authority on Mithraism, would agree that his patronage of archaeology deserves at least a mention on the credit side of Mussolini's account.

How then did it happen that a fly, with so many interludes of sanity could have become mad enough to walk into the parlour of the Nazi spider? The answer is that Ramsay MacDonald in his dotage was the worst Prime Minister, and Sir John Simon, at any time, was the worst Foreign Secretary with whom we have ever been afflicted—and that is no mean achievement when one recalls other combinations. At the Stresa Conference this egregious couple failed even to mention the well-known fact that Mussolini was preparing to avenge the disaster of Adowa, where a generation earlier an Italian Army had been wiped out by Menelik's hordes, by assailing Abyssinia. The Conference had been called in 1935, when Hitler was giving proof that he had written *Mein Kampf* in dead earnest, to devise means of containing the Nazi monster. Mussolini had contained it from raping Austria after the murder of Dolfuss in the previous July; and there is no doubt that he expected a commitment to continue preserving Austria to be rewarded by a free hand elsewhere. In diplomacy, even more than in other fields, 'silence gives consent'. When therefore the assault began, Mussolini was outraged by the declaration of Simon's successor, Sir Samuel Hoare, at Geneva that 'The League stands and my country stands with it, for resolute resistance to all forms of aggression.' Poor Mussolini! He could not know that this fervid oration was destined to prove complete bunkum, partly because Pierre Laval, then Prime Minister of France, was not going to strangle Fascist Italy to make Germany king; but also because our Baldwin was quite correct in saying that effective sanctions mean war; and war he was not going to have, even though it would have been an easy war to win.

The result was that Mussolini won his war twice—once materially in the

field, and once again psychologically thanks to the Hoare-Laval agreement which was about the poorest attempt at face-saving since—well, since D'Annunzio erected a monument in his garden to the 'victory' of Caporetto. Mussolini retained a loss of friendship and of respect for Britain which was not restored by the lifting of sanctions. Though he had prevented a Nazi Anschluss with Austria in 1934 after the murder of Dolfuss by mobilizing several Divisions on the Brenner, he was given a push towards Hitler by the Spanish Civil War in which both the newly revived Luftwaffe had some useful bombing practice on behalf of Franco, and Italian 'volunteers' were transported in large numbers to fight on the same side. The Spanish Republicans, aided by the International Brigade, inflicted upon them a highly disagreeable defeat, nor did Mussolini's attempt at a submarine blockade turn the chapter into a glorious one. But both France and Britain were so clearly suffering from the dithers, that Mussolini became convinced that in any trial of strength theirs could not be the winning side. To one so fundamentally a pragmatist the winning side was the right side. So he made no move when Hitler carried out the rape of Austria—an inactivity far from masterly since, though it earned the Führer's sincere gratitude, it also completely reversed the former roles of pupil and master.

Of all the hurryings and scurryings of the British appeasers none was more fatuous than the attempt to bring Mussolini back to our side. When Neville Chamberlain succeeded in getting rid of Eden from the Foreign Office, Mussolini considered that to be a triumph for himself because Eden, as the supposed child of the League of Nations, was deeply unpopular in Italy, and his thinly disguised dismissal therefore meant that Mussolini was the Duce of Downing Street! To any one who knew his character that was the end of any hope that he would break with Hitler. Indeed, when Sir Percy Loraine was appointed our Ambassador in Rome, and was good enough to talk to me about the prospects, I told him, to his obvious disbelief, that he would encounter contemptuous hostility from the Duce, but genuine friendliness from Ciano, his son-in-law. This assessment is borne out by Ciano's diaries; and by Ciano's ultimate fate! There *was* a pro-British party in Italy. Dino Grandi was a loyal Ambassador in London, but a genuinely brave critic of the Axis in Rome; and a far-sighted patriotism caused him to risk his neck by challenging Mussolini's authority in the Fascist Grand Council with a motion which took all but a rump of Italy out of the war in 1944. But Mussolini, an eye-witness of the shame of Munich and a front-seat spectator of the collapse of the French Army, was hardly to be blamed for betting on a German victory in June 1940. That is the weakness of a dictator. If you lose a bet of that kind you cannot quietly retire and wait for another chance. You are sunk.

Unlike Hitler, there is little evidence that Mussolini, though he did appoint himself, like most dictators, Supreme Commander of the Armed Forces, fancied himself as a strategist. If he had, he would never have declared war with his military equipment insufficient and obsolescent and his few competent commanders such as Badoglio and Graziani convinced that they could win nothing against anything more than token resistance. Graziani very nearly had a victory in North Africa in the early days, when with numerically larger forces he was inching forward towards the Egyptian frontier. But Wavell's few thousand soldiers who 'knew what they were doing and loved what they knew', ended that dream and turned once and for all the Italians into a German liability. For one brief moment in 1942 Mussolini saw himself entering Alexandria by Rommel's side; but that was a mirage. Thereafter the Germans found the Italians more and more useless as Allies, and more and more dangerous as 'resistants' after the war had reached the Italian mainland. The Italians had known all about 'underground' resistance for centuries—*furbo* which means 'sly' is a flattering epithet—and they were pretty good at it.

One wonders what were Mussolini's sensations as everything collapsed around him—an experience rather like that of Daedalus and Icarus when the wax that moulded Icarus's wings on to his shoulders melted in the heat of the sun and he was sent tumbling to perdition. There are few records of more than trite ejaculations. He had one really theatrical, and one really romantic experience—the first when German parachutists rescued him from the mountain prison whither Badoglio and the King had sent him after his fall; the second in the unbreakable devotion of a young girl, Claretta Petacci. But everything suggests that he lived in rancorous ignominy, like a moulting vulture, pecking at the few corpses of critics, including that of his own son-in-law, which he could make or reach.

The end was a shattering horror. All coherent thought save that of escape to Germany had ceased. The Duce declined to a poor wretch disguised as a wounded partisan, cowering in the corner of a German lorry. The vehicle was intercepted by a party of partisans and Mussolini was detected. This party had no designs on his life. But the Communist section of the partisans were determined to execute him, and a certain Audisio, known as Colonel Valerio, discovered the farmhouse where Mussolini and the Petacci were hidden. He took them a few hundred yards and murdered the pair of them by the road-side. All accounts agree that the girl died bravely attempting to shield her lover. I wish there was similar unanimity about his own conduct. Some attempt has been made to show that he merely asked the assassins to shoot him in the breast. But alas, an older and more probable version recounts that as Valerio approached him, a feeble and stuttering protest—*'Ma! Ma! Signor Colonello!'*—greeted the arrival of death.

Well, do you think he ranks among the eminent? According to the great Napoleon, to qualify for this category, one must have luck. This he had for a long time; but who knows whether he deserved it? For my part, I shall escape into the verdict pronounced in a fifteenth-century lyric by a rascally French genius, which makes the blood run cold and is appropriately entitled the *'Ballade des Pendus'*.

> *Hommes ici, n'usez de mocquerie*
> *Mais priez Dieu que tout nous veult absouldre.*

[1] *The Fascist Dictatorship* (London, 1928).

[2] *The Brutal Alliance* (Weidenfeld and Nicolson, 1962).

Truman
by Francis Heller

FRANCIS HELLER, born in Vienna in 1917, emigrated to the United States in 1938 and became a naturalized citizen. He graduated from the Schotten Gymnasium in 1935 and on arrival in America attended the University of Virginia where he obtained a Doctorate of Jurisprudence and also of Philosophy. After the conclusion of the Second World War, during which he served in the Pacific theatre of operations, he taught in the fields of Government and Political Science first at William and Mary College, Virginia and later at the University of Kansas, where he eventually served in various administrative posts including that of Vice-Chancellor for Academic Affairs. He now holds the Roy A. Roberts Professorship in Law and Political Science.

It was during these years at the University of Kansas that Dr Heller became acquainted with President Harry S. Truman, with whom he was closely associated in the writing of the President's memoirs. In his introduction the President expresses his gratitude to Dr Heller for 'the invaluable service he rendered'. Dr Heller was appointed to the Board of Directors of the Harry S. Truman Library · Institute in 1958, becoming its Vice-President in 1963.

Harry S. Truman

8 May 1884	Born. Educated at Independence High School, Missouri. Worked on father's farm and in a bank.
1905	Joined National Guard.
1917-18	When U.S. entered war, Truman joined army and saw active service in France as a captain.
Nov. 1918	End of First World War.
June 1919	Married Bess Wallace, who later had one daughter. Set up a haberdashery in Kansas City.
1922	Failure of this venture after trade recession in 1921. Was appointed overseer for highways for Jackson county by T. J. Prendergast, influential in Kansas City Democratic machine.
1922-24	With Prendergast's support, he became county judge for Jackson county. He studied law in Kansas City night school.
1934	Was elected a senator. In senate became known as able investigator and cross-examiner.
1938	Prendergast's association broke up when he was imprisoned for tax evasion.
1941	Truman re-elected senator. He introduced resolution for creation of senate committee to act as 'watchdog' of U.S. rearmament programme, and then became chairman of the committee.
1944	Democratic convention—Truman was nominated as F. D. Roosevelt's vice-presidential candidate.
12 April 1945	Roosevelt died and Truman succeeded to presidency.

Previous page: a delighted Truman after his election triumph brandishes one of the most famous pieces of journalistic misstatement in American history.

322

8 May 1945 Truman announced surrender of Germany.

July 1945 He authorized dropping of atomic bomb on Japan. Met Churchill and Stalin at Potsdam to discuss peace settlement.

Aug. 1945 Japan capitulated.

6 Sept. 1945 'Fair Deal' programme introduced. But conservative elements blocked its enactment and eventually Truman had to abandon most of it.

Aug. 1946 Politico-economic crisis when railway brotherhood strike threatened national transportation.

Sept. 1946 Truman asked for resignation of H. A. Wallace as secretary of commerce because he undermined U.S. position *vis-à-vis* U.S.S.R. at Paris peace conference.

Feb. 1947 British government's notice that it could no longer supply military and economic aid to Greece and Turkey, which U.S.S.R. sought to bring into its orbit. Truman announced he would undertake this responsibility, to stop spread of communism in Balkans—the 'Truman Doctrine'.

June 1947 Secretary of State Marshall proposed vast U.S. financial aid to restore Europe's shattered economy (the Marshall Plan).

Nov. 1948 Presidential election won by Truman after his 'whistle-stop' campaign.

1949 Accusations by Senator J. R. McCarthy that the administration had 'communists' within it (because withdrawal of U.S. aid to nationalists in China was proposed). Truman set up federal loyalty board to weed out subversives among government employees.

April 1949 Establishment of NATO to protect Western security.

June 1950 Communist Republic of North Korea attacked South Korea. Truman committed U.S. forces, commanded by General MacArthur, to South Korean assistance. The U.N. called for other countries to assist.

Nov. 1950 Most of Korea was under U.N. control. But Chinese communists reinforced North Koreans. Truman placed U.S. on semi-war basis.

Dec. 1950 Truman proclaimed national emergency and organized virtual wartime cabinet. Began shift from civilian to military production to make U.S. and its allies capable of resisting attack from U.S.S.R.

Dec. 1950 NATO approved appointment of General Eisenhower as organizer of a NATO army.

April 1951 Truman removed General MacArthur as commander of U.S. and U.N. forces in Far East on grounds that his tactical plan would have transformed a local conflict into possible global war.

1950-51 Congressional revelations of corruption and maladministration in several executive agencies, notably the bureau of internal revenue, the Reconstruction Finance corporation, and the department of justice. Truman discharged many high government and political officials.

March 1952 Truman announced he would not stand for presidency again.

April 1952 Truman seized steel industry in order to avoid strike. Supreme Court ruled this unconstitutional.

Nov. 1952 Eisenhower elected President.

1955-56 Truman published his memoirs.

26 Dec. 1972 Died.

It was a spring day in 1953 in Kansas City, Missouri. As the noon hour came around, the towering office buildings in the heart of the city's business district began to disgorge the daily flood of clerks and executives on their way to lunch. Among those passing through the doors of the Federal Reserve Bank building at the corner of Grand Avenue and 10th Street was a group of three men moving along in obviously animated conversation. They looked to be in their late fifties or early sixties and nothing about them set them off in the noonday crowd. Yet passers-by stopped to look, and here and there one could hear a querying 'That *is* him, isn't it?' As the three turned east on 10th Street, a barber waved at the trio from his shop; a man walked up to the man in the middle, shook his hand and said, 'Good to have you back in town, Harry!'

One block to the east, the three men walked into the restaurant of the Hotel Pickwick. Although it was not one of the leading hotels of the city (it adjoined and merged into the bus terminal), the Pickwick enjoyed good patronage at lunch; its roast beef sandwiches were justly renowned. The *maître d'hôtel* met the trio at the door and escorted them to a reserved table. At the next table four men rose and came over to shake hands. 'Mr President, welcome home,' one said, while the others introduced themselves. A waitress appeared to take orders, but before she could do so, other guests in the restaurant were crowded around to shake hands with Harry Truman. Another waitress had passed the word to the kitchen staff and white-hatted cooks and aproned dishwashers soon began to mingle with the men in business suits who wanted to greet the man who until a few weeks ago had been the President of the United States.

Harry S. Truman never ate lunch that day. It was his first attempt to mingle with the public as a private citizen; he learned that, once having been President, he could never again be an ordinary citizen. Nineteen years later, walking along the corridor of a local hospital to which he was temporarily confined, other patients would hail him in much the same manner. It never quite ceased to amaze him.

For Truman thought of himself primarily as a citizen who, being called to do his duty, did it as best he knew how. Yes, he had held the highest office in the land, but he continued to view that office almost with awe. Characteristically, he insisted that the museum which is part of the library holding his papers should focus its displays not on him but on the Office of the President. Characteristically also, when he agreed to have some of his post-presidential speeches and lectures published in book form, he asked that the book be titled 'Mr Citizen'. Until illness confined him to his home, he would take particular pride and pleasure in brief appearances before groups of school children visiting the Truman Library when, without fail, he would finish his remarks with the admonition to the young people to cherish and to use the privileges given to them as citizens of the United States.

Truman saw himself, first and foremost, as what he believed a good citizen should be. The world may have seen him as a statesman, conferring with Churchill and Stalin, proclaiming the bold ventures of aid to Greece and Turkey, of Point Four, of North Atlantic unity; political sophisticates in Kansas City might recall, with unconcealed disapproval, that his rise in politics was owed to the 'machine' of 'Boss' Pendergast. Harry Truman saw his career in terms so uncomplicated that political pundits might be unwilling to credit them fully. Truman, however, was consistent throughout his public life: he did what he did because he believed it to be right.

In recent years, so-called 'revisionist' historians have turned their attention to the Truman era in American history and many of them have produced reassessments comparable to the book review that deplores that the author did not write a different book.

Truman is both impatient with and tolerant of the critics. He would grant, especially to those too young to have lived through the period themselves as adults, the right to be critical but he could get testy with those who would not credit his own explanations as honest and candid. Thus, as he was engaged in the preparation of his memoirs, a professional historian had been brought in to assist him; when, six months later, I was asked to take this gentleman's place, one of my first queries was to find out where he had gone wrong. The explanation given me provided an excellent introduction to Truman's thinking: the professor simply refused to accept Truman's statement to him that he, Truman, had seen the employment of the atomic bomb solely in terms of weaponry and not of ethics; Truman had grown weary of the repetition of the question. To him, the matter had been uncomplicated then—it was the quickest means to bring the war to an end—and it had remained uncomplicated

Truman's memoirs are full of explanations which the revisionists reject. Though few persons have had the opportunity to discuss the recent historical writings with him, it stands to reason that he is not upset by the wave of new critics. For one, as a long practising politician he would expect it. His statement that 'if you can't stand the heat, stay out of the kitchen' has become an oft-quoted truism. For another, Truman had always been a devoted reader of history and had come to appreciate the relativity of historical judgement.

He made this point to me, again with telling simplicity, shortly after the first volume of his memoirs had come off the press in late 1955. He was then still occupying the office suite in the Federal Reserve Bank building, in one room of which I had worked while the memoirs were being prepared. I found this room filled literally from wall to wall with stacks of copies of the book. Rose Conway, his long-time devoted secretary, explained that people from all over the United States had been sending the former President their copies of the Memoirs with requests that he return them with his autograph. She was concerned, she added, because so few of the senders had provided return postage; at fourteen cents apiece (not counting wrapping costs) it would cost Mr Truman over a hundred dollars to do the requested favours!

By that time, Mr Truman had come out of his office and invited me to join him there. Quite naturally, I commented on the accumulation of books I had just seen. Truman said he could not quite understand why people were seeking his autograph; indeed, he was still surprised at the number of books that had been sold in the few short weeks since publication. He repeated a sentiment I had heard him express several times before: 'All I wanted to do was to put it down on paper for history!' He was, he knew, no Winston Churchill when it came to writing; so why this interest in his memoirs?

Overleaf: at the Potsdam conference the 'provincial' American politician showed Churchill and Stalin his true mettle

I ventured to suggest that for most Americans the years since the Second World War had been years filled with national and international drama and that there would be many who—regardless of whether or not they had approved of all that he, Truman, had done as President—would want to know what these events looked like from the vantage point of the man who had had to make the crucial decisions.

Truman's response revealed that he understood the dynamics of historical forces. (To appreciate this statement, one needs to recall that in the final year of the Truman administration scandal involving gifts of mink coats and deep freezers had touched some of his close associates; Truman's appointment secretary was even then serving a prison sentence growing out of these revelations.) 'If,' he said after a pause, 'it turns out that I was right in ordering the atomic bomb dropped on Hiroshima, and that I was right in proclaiming the Greek-Turkish Aid Doctrine and initiating the Marshall Plan, in resisting the Berlin blockade, and most importantly in ordering the resistance in Korea—if these were decisions that history will say were right because they turned out to have the right consequences, then people aren't going to spend many chapters writing about deep freezers and mink coats. But if it

turns out—God protect us—that all these things were wrong, then people are going to take every small thing that can be criticized and make a rope out of it for me.'

A critic would readily point out that there is a contradiction in this, essentially relativist, view of historical judgement and the frequent invocation of history as a source of certain knowledge that is to be found at frequent intervals in his recollection of his presidential years. History had always been his favourite reading and he evidently had a flair for the retention of dates and facts. On the other hand, speculations about the nature of history or the problems of historiography were of little interest to him. He accepted the traditional mainstream of history as authoritative and, quite plainly, drew from it for support and reassurance.

The magnificent isolation of the American Presidency makes it, of course, almost essential for the man who occupies the office to place himself in the context of 'the judgement of history'. It is, quite possibly, the major balancing element he can use in the face of the unrelenting pressures of the job. Not surprisingly, allusions to the judgement of history run through the public utterances of virtually all the Presidents (e.g. Lincoln: 'The world will very

little note nor long remember . . .'; F.D.R.'s 'day that shall live in infamy', to cite only the best known). Not only was Truman no exception, but he came to the tasks of the Presidency feeling that history was a mainstay of his intellectual resources. Not only those who knew him as Senator and President attest to this preoccupation, but so do his family and friends and associates from earlier years.

A major thrust of the kind of historical books which the young Harry Truman had so avidly perused was what some scholars have described as the concept of 'Manifest Destiny', the notion that America had a predestined role to fulfill. If, in its earlier manifestations, this idea had served to justify continental expansion, by the late decades of the nineteenth century it had assumed the ideological qualities which Woodrow Wilson would later express in his Fourteen Points. Truman, by his own description, grew up as what would later be described a 'Wilsonian Democrat'. He believed that America had a mission, a responsibility which it could not shirk. He volunteered for service in the First World War because he believed that it was right to do so; thirty years later he would propose a concept of world-wide aid for much the same reasons.

T he First World War marked a watershed in the life of Harry Truman. Biographies of historical personages normally devote much time to the early years and, typically, the record of early achievement. But a *Who's Who* sketch of Harry S. Truman contains next to nothing on the first thirty-three years of his life. The first event noted usually is 'Commanded Battery D, 129th Field Artillery in First World War'. Truman himself never failed to highlight the importance he attached to this experience and gave it visible expression when he had the surviving members of the unit brought to Washington to take a place of honour in the ceremonies on Inauguration Day, 1949.

Interestingly enough, some of the persons who admiringly pointed to the importance of the PT-109 experience in the life of John F. Kennedy would speak disdainfully of Truman's pride in Battery D. In part, this may have been due to the dramatic qualities of Kennedy's exploits as against the unspectacular service typical of the ground forces; in part, it may be attributable to the fact that the National Guard was never seen in a glamour role among the military organizations of the United States.

Truman had first joined the National Guard in 1905, at the age of twenty-one. 'There were,' he reports in his memoirs, 'about sixty men in the organization, and most of them were very fine fellows who worked in banks and stores around town and who would go out to a rented armoury once a week and pay a quarter for the privilege of drilling'. Truman himself worked in a bank, as a book-keeper at the modest salary of sixty dollars a month. He was, in many ways, typical of the men who joined the Guard: they were clerks, journeymen, professional apprentices—a cross-section of the lower middle class. (An exception to this generalization were a few militia units on the Eastern seaboard where historic tradition provided high social status.)

Although the militia tradition has deep roots in the United States (witness its specific confirmation in the Bill of Rights, Amendment II), the inadequacy of a volunteer force of part-time citizen-soldiers, as an instrument of national defence had been demonstrated time and again, most recently in the Spanish-American war. As it had after each such experience with the militia, Congress sought to remedy the situation by legislation. Thus the act of 1903 for the first time provided that the 'organized militia', i.e. the National Guard, would receive arms and equipment from the army for training. More importantly, it stipulated that a National Guard unit, to qualify for support from the national government, had to hold twenty-five drill or target practice sessions a year and participate in a five-day encampment each summer. In practice, however, both equipment and money were slow in coming and National Guard training continued at a rather low level. Training sessions tended to be overshadowed by the socializing that traditionally followed. The fact that the Guard elected its officers and non-commissioned officers tended to reinforce the social aspects of Guard activity.

It was not until 1916 that the officers elected by Guard units were required to pass qualifying tests and meet criteria of physical fitness. This change, coming as it did on the eve of America's entry into the First World War, probably did little to change the character of the Guard until mobilization put the new scheme to the test. Many National Guard officers proved deficient on one ground or the other; Harry S. Truman did very well indeed.

Apparently all his previous Guard activity had been of a kind to qualify him as a sergeant. When his fellow-soldiers elected him a first lieutenant, he had, in his own words, 'a tremendous amount of work to do'. Army records show that he did it exceedingly well. By the time his unit reached the front lines in France in July 1918, he was a captain and in command of Battery D. By the time he returned to civilian life in 1919, his ability to provide leadership had stood the test.

The years immediately after the war included some setbacks which were to receive frequent mention by critics and opponents in later years, most notably the financial failure of the menswear store in 1922. What should attract more attention is the contrast in career orientation between the pre-war and the post-war years. Before the military service period, Harry Truman is a bank clerk, then tends the family farm, embarks on a few, generally unsuccessful, ventures in business; he is a faithful member of the Masons as he is of the National Guard, but in all he is follower rather than leader. After the war he not only accepts, but to a degree seeks, the opportunity to serve the public and readily assumes proffered responsibility. He retains a reserve commission in the army and becomes one of the organizers of the Reserve Officers Association. He begins to move quickly through the advanced degrees of Masonry and is Deputy Grand Master of Missouri by 1924. He runs for public office and serves as one of three members of his county's governing board. His rise into the political arena is at least partly due to the fact that the veterans of Battery D are a ready nucleus of a personal following.

Survivors of that First World War organization have, understandably, been queried about the roots of this loyalty. Their responses vary, of course, considerably but what they have in common might be summarized thus: We came to know Harry Truman as a man of common touch and uncommon dependability; if he told us he would do something, we knew that it would be done; as one of them put it, 'he always gave more than he asked'.

In his years in the White House, Truman would often be criticized because of the preferment he allegedly gave to 'cronies', and 'cronyism in the White House' was a favourite target of the opposition. At the extreme, it was charged that the recognition of the state of Israel was due to the intervention of the President's erstwhile partner in the ill-fated menswear venture, Eddie Jacobson. Anecdotes about the President's willingness to 'help a friend' were being circulated by friend and foe alike.

At the same time, Truman tended to be chary of demands on him, especially if they were couched in terms of obligations owed. He had enjoyed strong support from organized labour when he ran for re-election as senator in 1940, but he reacted with immediate resentment when a high-ranking labour leader, invoking this record of support, sought to influence his decision on the naming of a new Chief Justice in 1946. There is no question that he owed his first success in the political arena to the 'machine' of the Pendergasts; but when it was suggested to him that he should, in return as it were, award some lucrative road construction contracts to the Pendergasts and their friends, he flatly said 'no'. He would give—but he would not be dictated to. Tom Pendergast later was found guilty of income tax evasion and went to prison; but Truman knew him as a friend and—though it scandalized the sophisticates—attended his funeral.

The examples could easily be multiplied. What they confirm is that Truman took a remarkably uncomplicated view of personal relationships in politics. If you conducted yourself as a friend, he regarded you as a friend. There was no reason why people on opposite sides of the political fence could not be friends (his first appointment to the Supreme Court was a Republican friend from his days in the Senate, Harold Hitz Burton of Ohio). You could be friends and disagree totally on political issues. But you could not be friends with someone who maligned the character of his opponents to gain political preferment. Joseph R. McCarthy of Wisconsin was such a person in Truman's eyes and he would never speak well of him. He believed likewise that Richard M. Nixon had violated the canons of propriety in his campaigns for, first, the House of Representatives and, then, the Senate, and thus he viewed him with deep misgivings.

As a product of the 'game of politics' in the United States, Truman viewed politics as a contest rather than a conflict. To be sure, as a life-long Democrat his mental set favoured the 'little man', but there is little in the record of his public (or private) utterances that could be described as of ideological cast. There are numerous indications that he was uncomfortable around people of dogmatic views, be they conservatives, socialists, or liberals. The admiration he held for Franklin Roosevelt was for F.D.R. the pragmatist far more than it was for the proponent of the New Deal. His relationships to any number of fellow-Senators from both sides of the aisle, both before and after he succeeded to the Presidency, fit the same pattern; he appreciated parliamentary workmanship, but, more or less vaguely, suspected ideological rigidity.

This disdain for the dogmatic should not be misunderstood. Truman had (and has) principles and set great store by them. But it is only fair to him to say that his faith was (and is) an affirmation, without many complexities, of the virtues of the society that had nurtured him. In that sense, Truman was always conservative.

But inherent in these virtues was also the spirit of openness that characterized America's Western frontier. The visitor who enters the main portal of the Truman Library in Independence, Missouri, faces a floor-to-ceiling mural by Thomas Hart Benton depicting 'The Opening of the West'; the theme had been Mr Truman's personal choice. Historians may (and do) argue about the character of the 'frontier spirit' but there is little doubt that it was a reality to those of Truman's generation. In the years of his public schooling, much of what lay west of his home town was still underpopulated or even unpopulated. Oklahoma—the north-east corner of which touches the south-west corner of Missouri—was still legally Indian Territory; Kansas, a mere ten miles west of the home-town of Independence, actively recruited settlers for its 'wide open spaces' in England and on the continent. This was country where status counted little and achievement received ready recognition. It was also a setting in which the harshness of conditions imposed a premium on co-operation. Men were judged here on what they could and would do and differences in ancestry, religion or wealth were of secondary importance.

There is much in Truman's record that reflects this attitude that characterized his childhood environment. To be sure, Independence was (and is) a community of Southern perspectives. But its geographic location had traditionally given a westward orientation to its thinking and Truman embodied this blend. This was, for instance, evident in his attitude on racial discrimination. It was during his Presidency that the first steps were taken, most of them by Presidential order, towards the dismantling of the barriers of racial segregation; yet in his retirement years Mr Truman was occasionally quoted in veins suggesting that he thought the Negro push towards equality had gone too far. What his attitude really was may have been best expressed by a rather brusque reply I heard him give to a student questioner: 'Young man, I want every American to have all the rights the Constitution gives him, but I will be the one who decides who eats at my dinner table'. As a person, he was saying, I want to judge other persons on a one-to-one basis; society should not compel me otherwise, but neither should it encumber any person with disabilities unrelated to his personal worth.

This emphasis upon personal worth permeates the record of his relationships in public life. There probably were no two people for whom Harry Truman had higher regard than General Marshall and Dean Acheson. Whenever he referred to either of them, in public or in private, it was always in terms of superlatives. Here were two men who commanded his unqualified admiration. They were, as he saw them, men who had given of themselves without stint, men who held no rancour and who measured others by their deeds and not by their words.

Though he admired both and for much the same reasons, there was a

331

Overleaf: a terrible decision. Hiroshima—explosion and aftermath

marked difference in Truman's relationships to these men. George Catlett Marshall was always 'the General'. It was not my privilege to see the two men together, but others have related (some with noticeable disapproval in their voices) that Truman always displayed something akin to deference in his conversations with Marshall. Certain it is—because we have Truman's own word for it—that the President had the utmost respect for the General. But Marshall is, of course, one of the few major figures of the forties who commanded virtually universal respect and whose reputation has barely suffered even at the hands of the most critical revisionist historians. Truman's unwavering regard for him is, therefore, hardly conclusive proof for the proposition advanced by some critics that Truman, the First World War captain, was overawed by the Second World War generals. In fact, awe may be one emotion that Truman rarely experienced toward others.

If anyone might occasionally have evoked feelings of awe in Harry Truman, it is more likely that Dean Acheson may have done so. Acheson's exceptional memory certainly impressed Truman deeply and he said so on more than one occasion. In turn, the Secretary of State often remarked on the President's ability to recall things he had read and to assimilate readily what had been put in writing for his perusal. But far beyond this mutual respect, Truman and Acheson had a genuine liking for each other. They were, in many ways, an incongruous pair: Acheson tall, erect, always impeccably groomed, the image of the aristocrat to the manner born—Truman by contrast almost the epitome of the middle-class American from the Midwest. Yet no one could be in the presence of these two men without sensing that here was a bond of friendship that far transcended official relationships or even just extended collaboration. Truman and Acheson, it was quite apparent, believed in each other as human beings, as two people who, however different their backgrounds, had arrived at common perceptions of human nature and society.

It may also be that Truman and Acheson agreed so easily because they shared complementary views of their respective roles. Truman's perception of the decision-making responsibility of the President has, of course, often been quoted in the capsule version of the sign on his desk, 'The buck stops here'. Acheson's views have not been given the same pithy coinage but his speeches and writings after he left public office make it quite clear that 'responsibility' was the keyword in his thinking about the Presidency.

Yet it is, of course, common knowledge that there were many—perhaps more in the United States than in other countries—who saw Harry Truman in a very different light. Liberal intellectuals in particular had difficulty identifying with the man from Missouri whose speech and manner readily reflected the fact that he was not—as so many of them were—a product of one of the elite colleges on the east coast. Conservative businessmen were deeply suspicious of the populist heritage evident in the President's views on social and economic issues. In later years it would be said—not entirely in jest—that the difference between Eisenhower, who grew up in a small town in Kansas, and Truman, with his roots in a small town in Missouri, was that Eisenhower had taken up golf while Truman continued to get his exercise by walking.

In the face of these detractions, in the face of almost universal expectations that he would be turned out by the voters, the American people returned Harry Truman to the White House in the 1948 election. The whys and the wherefores of his victory, surprising as it was to apparently everyone but him, have been the subject of numerous books and articles and will undoubtedly continue to be of vexing interest to political historians. In the present context it may be appropriate to note whence the vote for Truman had come. It was avowedly not the vote of wealth nor of the intelligentsia. It was not the vote of the white Southerners, so long the mainstay of Democratic politics. It was, rather, the vote of people like Harry Truman himself, people from small farms, people with small businesses, people from small beginnings for whom America as the land of opportunity was an article of faith.

Sidney Hyman, an experienced journalist who can qualify as a 'President-watcher' of long standing, devoted a large part of his book *The American President* to the thesis that a successful President is one who appears at a given point in time to personify the inarticulated aspirations of the American people. It would seem—at least—arguable that in November 1948 Harry S. Truman thus found himself embodying what 'the little man' projected for his country and for himself. For many others, his success served as an affirmation of a belief in the American political system and its popular base.

Between 1949 and 1952 Truman's popularity was clearly in decline. The reasons were many and complex. He elected—probably wisely—not to seek another term in office and returned to live among his friends in Independence and Kansas City. But not only did he find that a former President never returns to the status of an ordinary citizen; he also soon found that, in retirement, his stature as a President came to receive increasing approval. His willingness to shoulder the responsibility of decision-making emerged as a critical contribution to the Presidential office, specific decisions of his making were seen as enduring and basic to the nation's course. Whether, in his own words, 'it turns out that I was right' is a matter that still awaits the judgement of history. Revisionist historians would urge a negative answer but one could argue that they are writing from a perspective Truman was denied, a knowledge of alternatives enlarged by hindsight.

In his nearly eight years as President of the United States of America Harry S. Truman faced a succession of problems and crises without precedent. His approach was always direct, his objective uncomplicated. He saw himself as a citizen who had been called to serve his country. He viewed his office with unqualified respect while as a person he retained much of the basic traits he had drawn from his early environment. He observed once that he hoped he would be found deserving of a tombstone inscription allegedly seen in a cemetery in a town on the Western frontier: 'Here lies N.N.—he tried his damnedest.' To anyone who knew or knows Harry Truman, there can be little doubt that he offered as an epitaph what he had clearly always viewed as his motto.

The text of Dr Heller's essay was completed and had already been received by the editors before Mr Truman's death on 26 December 1972. Publishing schedules dictated its inclusion in the original form, retaining the present tense as it had appeared in the original manuscript

Hitler
by William Shirer

WILLIAM SHIRER, born in Chicago in 1904, graduated from Coe College, Cedar Rapids, Iowa, in 1925 and at once joined the staff of the Paris edition of the *Chicago Tribune*, for whose Chicago edition he later worked as a foreign correspondent in the major capitals of Europe and in the Near East and India. He forsook newspaper work for radio journalism in 1937 when he became continental representative in Europe for the Columbia Broadcasting System. As journalist, commentator and writer his name and voice became known throughout the world. Among his published works, which include three novels, are *Berlin Diary* (1941), *End of a Berlin Diary* (1947), *The Rise and Fall of the Third Reich* (1961) and *The Collapse of the Third Republic* (1970).

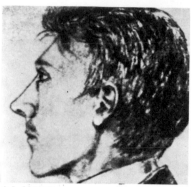

Adolf Hitler

20 April 1889	Born in Austria. Educated at Linz Realschule, and school at Steyr.
1907-13	Worked as casual labourer and freelance art student in Vienna.
1913	Left Vienna for München.
1914-18	Joined German army and served on Western Front. Only achieved rank of corporal but won Iron Cross First Class.
1919	Revolutionary disturbances in München. Hitler employed by army as anti-revolutionary propagandist among troops. Joined Drexler's German Workers' Party (D.A.P.).
1920	D.A.P. changed its name to National Socialist German Workers' Party (Nazis).
1921	Hitler became effective leader of Nazi party, which had brown-shirted strong-arm squads (S.A.).
8 Nov. 1923	Beer Hall *Putsch* in München— unsuccessful attempt by Hitler to overthrow Republican government. Hitler arrested.
1924	Hitler sentenced to five years' imprisonment and party dissolved. Became hero among racialist anti-republican groups. Wrote first volume of *Mein Kampf*.
20 Dec. 1924	Released from prison.
1925	*Mein Kampf* published.
1930	Nazi party, rebuilt by Hitler, made important election gains. Became second largest party in *Reichstag*.
31 July 1932	*Reichstag* election. Nazis became largest party.
6 Nov. 1932	*Reichstag* election. Nazis lost 34 seats.
30 Jan. 1933	Hitler named Chancellor by President Hindenbürg.
27 Feb. 1933	*Reichstag* fire.
23 March 1933	Enabling act by which *Reichstag* abdicated its legislative powers and transferred them to Hitler.
2 May 1933	Trade unions were suppressed.
14 July 1933	Hitler made Germany a one-party state.

Previous page: the brilliant party boss. Hitler in 1931 at a Nazi rally.

30 June 1934 Murder of Roehm and main S.A. leaders, who were obstacle to Hitler's dictatorship.

2 Aug. 1934 Death of President Hindenbürg. Hitler abolished office of President.

March 1935 Started to establish large army, defying terms of treaty after World War I.

1935 Began to construct formidable navy.

7 March 1936 Reoccupied demilitarized zone of Rhineland. Britain and France protested.

4 Feb. 1938 Hitler took over personal command of all armed forces. Ribbentrop appointed Foreign Minister.

11 March 1938 Annexed Austria. Czechoslovakia was now surrounded.

29 Sept. 1938 Chamberlain (Britain), Daladier (France), Mussolini (Italy) and Hitler met at Münich and ceded the Sudetenland in Czechoslovakia to Germany.

March 1939 Hitler marched into and annexed the rest of Czechoslovakia.

23 Aug. 1939 German-Soviet non-aggression pact.

1 Sept. 1939 Hitler attacked Poland.

3 Sept. 1939 Britain and France, honouring treaty obligations to Poland, entered war against Germany.

9 April 1940 Germany invaded Denmark and Norway.

10 May 1940 Germany invaded Belgium, Holland and Luxembourg.

10 June 1940 Italy declared war on Britain and France.

22 June 1940 Franco-German armistice.

1940-1 Battle of Britain between British and German air forces.

22 June 1941 Hitler turned east and invaded Soviet Union.

7/8 Dec. 1941 U.S.A. entered war after Japanese attack on Pearl Harbor.

Dec. 41/ Jan. 1942 German army forced back in Soviet Union.

Summer 1942 Germany army advanced again in Soviet Union.

Oct. 1942 General Rommel was attacked at El Alamein by British Eighth Army under Montgomery and had to fall back.

Nov. 1942 Battle of Stalingrad. German army forced to retreat.

Spring 1943 Anglo-American army under Eisenhower destroyed last Italo-German force in Africa.

6 June 1944 Allied invasion of France.

20 July 1944 Plot against Hitler's life by army officers.

Jan. 1945 Russian troops reached R. Oder, 100 miles from Berlin.

25 April 1945 British and American armies from west and Russians from east met up at R. Elbe, 75 miles south of Berlin.

28 April 1945 Russian troops in Berlin.

29 April 1945 Hitler married Eva Braun.

30 April 1945 Hitler and Eva Braun committed suicide with poison.

Considering his early life as a vagabond in Vienna, where by his own account he acquired a view of life that remained unaltered to the end[1], the achievements of Adolf Hitler constitute one of the most astonishing and disturbing chapters in the modern history of Germany.

From the gutter Hitler manoeuvered his way to the dictatorship of a great nation, made a revolution that convulsed Germany and won the enthusiastic approval of most of its citizens, founded the Third Reich and ruled it with an iron hand, slaughtered five million Jews and an equal number of Slavs in cold blood, conquered a large part of the European continent, and in the end, after raising his country to such dizzy heights, brought it crashing down in utter ruin.

'It is one of the great examples,' as Friedrich Meinecke, the German historian, has said, 'of the singular and incalculable power of personality in historical life'.

Hitler was twenty-four when he left Vienna for Germany in the spring of 1913, mainly to escape the draft, which he had evaded for three years. He had failed at everything he had attempted: at getting an education, at becoming an architect or an artist, even at finding a means to earn a steady, modest living. In his last years in the glittering capital of the dying Austro-Hungarian Empire, he had lived for a time as a tramp, sleeping out on park benches during the summer, in flop-houses for the homeless in the winter, finally settling in a shabby Hostel for Men where he could share a cubicle at night and use a small, ill-lit reading room during the day.

In these unpromising circumstances Hitler acquired, from a scattered reading of the newspapers, pamphlets and books, a smattering of knowledge of history and current politics which provided the 'granite foundation' of his warped view of life and politics. The ideas were half-baked. They were shared by a good many young nationalist-minded Austro-Germans growing up in the capital of the polyglot Habsburg Empire in the early years of the twentieth century, who resented the mounting power in the Monarchy of the non-German minorities: Hungarians, Slavs and the once-persecuted Jews, who together made up a majority of the population. Down and out though he was, lower in means and stature than an honest working man, Hitler also professed to fear the increasing political, economic and social demands of the proletariat, which he thought was being misled by the newly-formed, free trade unions and the Social-Democrat Party. Very quickly he developed a pathological hatred of Jews, Slavs, unions, socialists, liberals, democracy—of all and everything he thought stood in the way of German domination.

From his observations—for he took no part in politics—he absorbed one political lesson that was to serve him well in later years. He saw from the achievements of Karl Lueger's powerful Christian-Social movement that to have clout—at elections and in the streets—a political party had to have the support of the masses and that this could only be won by understanding their social and economic problems, and their prejudices, by hammering at them with demagogic propaganda and oratory, by patient organization from the precinct level up and, above all, by winning support, as Lueger had done, from at least some of the entrenched institutions of the nation: the Church, the Army, the bureaucracy, the world of business and finance. It was a lesson that Hitler never forgot.

By the time he left Vienna, two-fifths of his life, as it turned out, already had been lived, the last five years of it as a drifting, shiftless derelict, and his situation in Munich as he reached twenty-five in the spring of 1914 had not improved. He was friendless, jobless, homeless and, as he said, nameless. He had opted for Germany, he later explained, because that was where, 'since my childhood my secret desires and secret love had drawn me'. No man who went off to war in the German Army that August of 1914, as Hitler, a volunteer, did, would seem to have had less chance of making a name for himself in the German Reich—if he survived the battlefield. He was not even a German citizen.

Adolf Hitler was born on 20 April 1889, in the little Austrian town of Braunau am Inn, across the border from Bavaria. He was the third son of the third marriage of an Austrian customs official who had been born an illegitimate child and who for the first thirty-nine years of his life bore his mother's name, Schicklgruber. Five years after the birth of this child, named Alois, Maria Anna Schicklgruber married Johann Georg Hiedler, a wandering miller, who never legitimized the boy—perhaps because it was not his. Several years after the death of the couple, Johann Georg's brother, Johann von Nepomuk Hiedler, who had brought the boy up, appeared with three relatives before the parish priest at Döellersheim, swore that Georg was the father, and persuaded the priest to alter the original birth certificate to make the thirty-nine-year-old Alois legitimate. This was quite illegal, since under Austrian law a man could not be officially recognized as father after his death. But it was lucky for the future Nazi *Fuehrer*. It is difficult to imagine the frenzied German masses acclaiming a leader with 'Heil Schicklgruber!'. Alois changed the spelling of his name from 'Hiedler' to 'Hitler'.

Actually Adolf Hitler, who later would make documentary proof of one's Aryan ancestry through the grandparents a condition for citizenship in the Third Reich, never knew who his grandfather was. Hans Frank, the Nazi Minister of Justice, whom Hitler once asked to look into the matter, found some evidence that he was a Jew², but it was not conclusive. Probably some of Adolf Hitler's forebears were Czechs, who for centuries mingled with the Austro-Germans in the Waldviertel district in Lower Austria on the border of Bohemia. The Czech name 'Hidlar' or 'Hidlarček' was not uncommon in the region. And the grandfather of Hitler's mother, the man who also brought up his father, bore the Christian name of the Czech national saint, Johann von Nepomuk. Among the many ironies in this strange man's life is that he may have been descended, in part, from the two peoples he hated and wrought such vengeance against: the Jews and the Czechs.

H itler served throughout the First World War in the front line as a dispatch runner, participating in several major battles, being wounded twice and receiving two Iron Crosses for bravery, the second, the 'First Class' Cross, seldom being awarded to a common soldier in the old Imperial Army. Like millions of other Germans, Hitler came out of the war unable to accept the defeat and determined to believe in the shoddy myth that the disaster to the Fatherland had been caused by a 'stab in the back' from the Jews, socialists, trade-unionists and democratic politicians. 'Miserable and degenerate criminals!' he called them. To destroy them, he said, 'I decided to go into politics'. Though it did not seem so at the time, for such an unknown, uneducated ex-soldier, without any political experience whatsoever, it was, as it turned out, a momentous decision—not only for Hitler, but for Germany, Europe, and the world.

Barely four years later, Hitler made his first bid for political power. In the post-war chaos of defeat, revolution, hunger, unemployment, inflation and the collapse of the currency, with a whole uprooted society in dissolution, Hitler, without roots himself, had found his opportunity. Joining an obscure political group in the autumn of 1919 called the German Workers' Party, with less than a hundred members who gathered irregularly in the back room of run-down Munich beer taverns, he soon took it over and began to build it into a rapidly growing political force in Bavaria. He showed at once a talent for party organization and a genius for propaganda and rabble-rousing oratory. Thousands began to flock to hear him speak and were moved to hysteria by his eloquence. Realizing the need of a flag which would appeal to the imagination of the masses and express the aims of the party, he adopted the ancient swastika cross and designed the banner of the black *hakenkreuz* on a white disque set in a red background. From the beginning it aroused a strange, mystical feeling in many Germans, who saw in it a symbol of a righteous cause.

In the spring of 1920, the Party's name was changed to the National Socialist German Workers' Party. This too was a stroke of genius, for it promised to bring together the two strongest ideological faiths in Germany: nationalism and socialism. A year later Hitler's strong-arm squads, originally formed to protect his own meetings and break up those of others, were formally organized as the *Sturm Abteilung* or *S.A.* These were the Nazi brown-shirts who would terrorize the streets of Germany for more than a decade. By the summer of 1921, Hitler had made himself the undisputed leader of the Party, with dictatorial powers and the title of *Fuehrer*.

His immediate subordinates were a motley lot. Captain Ernst Röehm, a bull-necked, scar-faced professional soldier, a tough, brawling, ruthless, driving man, and a homosexual, had joined the Party before Hitler. He proved especially valuable to the *Fuehrer* in organizing the *S.A.* and in providing contacts with the Army. Dietrich Eckart, a drunken, amiable, mediocre poet and playwright, also predated Hitler in the Party and in the first years served as somewhat of a mentor to the leader: polishing his language and his uncouth manners and introducing him to certain wealthy Munich families whom he induced to contribute to the Party and to Hitler's living expenses. Others who were attracted to Hitler and became his aides were Herman Goering, a swashbuckling hero of the German Air Force; Rudolf Hess, a brooding but mindless student who introduced Hitler to Karl Haushofer, the geopolitician; and Alfred Rosenberg, a wooden-headed Balt who had been educated as an architect at Moscow and who for some reason Hitler made the 'philosopher' of the Party. Among the lesser fry was an assortment of ex-convicts, butchers, horse-traders, blackmailers and derelict ex-soldiers, unable to adjust to peacetime. Hitler would later admit that some of them were scoundrels and perverts but that at the time he needed such roughnecks to get the Party going. 'Fundamentally,' he once conceded, 'they were just overgrown children'. But they were among the men who helped Hitler ride to power and who were at his side on the evening of 8 November 1923, and on the following morning when he attempted to carry out his 'Beer Hall' putsch in Munich.

It ended in a fiasco because Hitler overreached himself, as he was to do towards the end of his meteoric career—victim of the age-old sin the Greeks called *hubris*. His Nazi movement did not have the power to take over in Bavaria, much less, as he had planned, in Germany. The putsch, comical in retrospect, began in a beer hall when Hitler, brandishing a pistol and firing a shot at the ceiling, took charge of a meeting being addressed by the triumvirate which ruled Bavaria, and proclaimed himself head of a new provisional German government, with General Erich Ludendorff, the bitterly frustrated hero of the war, as Commander of the new German Army. It ended quickly the next morning in a narrow Munich street when a handful of police fired on a column of 3,000 ragged Storm Troopers led by Hitler and Ludendorff, killing sixteen of them and wounding several more, forcing the Nazi leader to scurry to safety. Tried for treason, he was sentenced to five years in prison and his Party was dissolved. Hitler seemed utterly discredited, a joke to many, and his flashy political career at an end. As it turned out, his career had just been launched. For Hitler, whose intelligence and resilience were always underestimated by his opponents, wisely drew the proper conclusions from his failure.

Brooding in his comfortable room in the Landsberg prison, the fallen leader took stock of himself and his movement, recognized his mistakes and plotted a new course for the future, which he felt sure would bring him to his goal. He realized that he could never come to power through force alone: the Republic's army and police had too many guns, as had been shown in Munich. He would have to win the support of some of the existing power structures in the state, above all the Army, and the conservative industrial interests, which dominated the nation's economy and much of its politics. This was a lesson, as we have seen, that he had first learned in Vienna, where he had noted with admiration how Karl Lueger's Christian Social Party won the backing of the sources of power. It would be necessary to play the Republic's own game of democracy, even, he said, 'if we have to hold our noses', by electing Nazis to the Reichstag. Above all, he would have to build up a massive political organization throughout Germany, making it a shadow-state ready to assume power when the opportunity came. The Nazi Party, confined to Bavaria, had not been large nor ripe enough in 1923 to really take over the state. He began to see, as he later said, that the failure of his putsch was, 'perhaps the greatest piece of good fortune in my life.'

'Fate meant well with us. It did not permit an action to succeed which . . . would in the end have inevitably crashed as a result of the movement's inner immaturity and its deficient organizational and intellectual foundation . . . We recognized that it is not enough to overthrow the old State but that the new State must previously have been built up (by the party) and be ready to take over.'

343

Overleaf: 1938, Hitler addressing enthusiastic crowds in Vienna after incorporating Austria into the Reich

Released from prison at Christmas 1924, after serving nine months of his five-year term, Hitler set out boldly to rebuild just such a party. The months of imprisonment, far from discouraging him, had charged him with a new, fanatical faith in his destiny.

His thoughts had been deepened and clarified by the writing of the first volume of a book, *Mein Kampf*, which would become the Bible of the Nazi world. Though largely ignored for many years by Germans and foreigners alike, it is a remarkable book. For in it, amongst heaps of verbose rubbish, Hitler set down with brutal clarity a blue print of how he intended to attain power and what he meant to do with it in a world which, as he saw it, was a jungle where force was the law and the strong triumphed over—or eliminated—the weak.

It is all in the book, first published in 1925: the crude Darwinism of his beliefs, the violently anti-Semitic racism, the bland assertion of the superiority of the Aryans, especially the Germans, of the right of Germany to more *lebensraum* in the East at the expense of Russia, the necessity to humble the arch-enemy, France, and the aim to destroy democracy and liberalism at home and to replace it with a totalitarian dictatorship with himself as the supreme leader. It was not Hitler's fault that few in Germany, and even fewer abroad, paid any attention to his book—until it was too late. For ultimately he did exactly what he said he would do.

Over the next eight years, between 1925-33, Adolf Hitler, despite many disappointments and setbacks, rebuilt the Nazi Party into the largest and most formidable political movement in Germany. Still, by the beginning of 1933 it had been unable to win over the majority of voters. In the national elections of 31 July 1932, it had won nearly fourteen million votes and 230 seats in the Reichstag, making it by far the largest party in Germany. Though this electoral triumph represented a gain of seven million votes in two years and a gain of nearly thirteen million in four years, it still left Hitler with only 37 per cent of the vote. In new elections four months later, on 6 November, the Party had faltered, losing two million votes and thirty-four seats in the Reichstag. The Nazi tide was ebbing. The Party itself was financially bankrupt. Not long afterwards the German Chancellor, General von Schleicher, assured the visiting Austrian Minister of Justice, Kurt von Schuschnigg, that 'Herr Hitler was no longer a problem; his movement was a thing of the past'.

Hitler was in truth desperate. Realizing that he could never win a parliamentary majority and come to power normally, he set about to gain it by other means. By secret deals with the industrial magnates, with the conservative politicians led by an empty-minded intriguer, Franz von Papen, and with the men around the President, the aged, senile Field Marshal von Hindenburg, and with the approval of the Army, Hitler was named Chancellor by the President on the morning of 30 January 1933. By way of the back door, by means of shabby political deals with the old-school reactionaries he privately detested, the former tramp from Vienna, the once-discredited leader of the comic-opera 'Beer Hall' putsch, the sworn revolutionary and racist, became Chancellor of the great nation.

The Hohenzollern Empire had been built on the armed triumphs of

Prussia; the German Republic on the defeat by the Allies after a great war. But the Third Reich owed nothing to the fortunes of war or to foreign influence. It was inaugurated in peacetime, by the Germans themselves.

Hitler was not dictator yet. He had only three Nazis, including himself, in the cabinet of eleven. The conservatives, led by Papen as Vice-Chancellor and the woolly-headed industrialist and press-lord, Alfred Hugenberg, as Minister of both Economy and Agriculture, had the rest—eight against three. They thought, as they said, that they had the obstreperous Nazi chief in their pockets and that they could use his hold over the masses, which they themselves lacked, to further their own aims—a return to an authoritarian state with no democratic nonsense and perhaps, eventually, to the Imperial Monarchy. Hitler, whom they considered a little too vulgar for their tastes, could then be dropped.

But the Nazi *Fuehrer* was much too shrewd for them. Within six months he had eliminated them and their political party—along with all the other political parties except his own. On 14 July 1933, he decreed, 'The National Socialist German Workers' Party constitutes the only political power in Germany'. The one-party totalitarian state had been achieved with scarcely a whimper of opposition or defiance. Months before, in March, he had forced the Reichstag to abdicate its legislative powers and transfer them to him. A fortnight after its demise, Hitler had by decree abolished the separate powers of the historic states, thus for the first time in German history unifying the Reich by destroying its age-old federal character. On 2 May 1933, the day after they had been allowed—indeed, encouraged—to celebrate the traditional May Day of labour, the trade unions, which had been the bulwark of the Republic, were suppressed without difficulty, without even a strike. When Hitler addressed the rubber-stamp Reichstag on 30 January 1934, the first anniversary of his becoming Chancellor, he could look back to a year of achievement without parallel in German history. He had liquidated the Republic, its democracy and its institutions, and had acquired more power than Bismarck or any other Chancellor ever had; and he had done it overnight, so to speak, and with the greatest of ease. 'It is no victory,' Oswald Spengler, the disillusioned author of *The Decline of the West*, commented acidly, 'for the enemies were lacking'.

As his second year of office began, there remained only three obstacles to his becoming absolute dictator: the S.A., two million strong, led by his close friend, Röehm, which was clamouring for 'a second revolution' and for the right to take over the Army; the Army itself, which was loyal to President Hindenburg and whose generals were alarmed by the threat of the S.A. and a little sickened by its rowdy excesses; and the aged Field Marshal himself, who as President still retained the ultimate political power in the State—he could dismiss Hitler any time and was believed to be inclined to do so unless the Chancellor curbed the S.A.—and held great prestige in the nation.

Röehm and the main S.A. leaders were quickly eliminated in the blood purge of 30 June 1934. Hitler simply massacred them. The Army, rid of its rival, was relieved, and publicly approved the bloody deed though two of its generals, Schleicher, the former Chancellor, and von Bredow, were murdered by the Nazis during the purge. Hitler had honoured his promise to make the *Wehrmacht* the sole bearer of arms in Germany.

The seemingly indestructible Hindenburg died on 2 August 1934, in his eighty-seventh year. The Constitution made it mandatory to call an election to choose his successor. But what was the Constitution to Adolf Hitler? He simply abolished the office of President and took over its prerogatives under a new title: *Fuehrer* of the nation. Before the body of the old soldier was cold, he exacted from all officers and men of the armed forces an oath of allegiance to himself. Adolf Hitler was now the undisputed dictator of the Third Reich—the Army, the Government, the people in his hands. He was forty-five years old.

I saw a good deal of him at the Nazi Party Rally at Nuremberg that September of 1934, when he had just completed his conquest of Germany. He was understandably in a jubilant mood. His hold over the masses seemed greater than ever as he orated day after day. His self-confidence was immense and he beamed with pleasure as he listened to one of his henchmen read his proclamation that, 'The German form of life is definitely determined for the next thousand years'. It was to be a thousand-year Reich.

Having determined that, having carried out and completed his domestic revolution so easily and so quickly, the dictator was now free to pursue the foreign-policy goals for the new Germany which he had outlined with such clarity in *Mein Kampf*: to rearm and rebuild the armed forces and then to use them—and the dynamic force which he had aroused in the people—for conquest.

At first he went from one success to another. On 16 March 1935, he defied the military clauses of the Versailles Treaty, which limited the German Army to 100,000 volunteers, by establishing conscription for a new force of half a million. Britain and France protested, but took no action. A few months later Hitler induced Britain to sign, behind the back of her then allies, France and Italy, and in further defiance of the Peace Treaty, an agreement allowing Germany to build a Navy which though limited in tonnage to 35 per cent of British naval strength actually gave Germany a formidable fleet: five battleships, superior in tonnage and armament to anything the British or French had, twenty-one cruisers, sixty-four destroyers and as many submarines as Britain possessed. Enough would be built by the time the war started to cause Britain disastrous losses.

The next spring, on 7 March 1936, Hitler reoccupied the demilitarized zone of the Rhineland. Again Britain and France protested, but that was all. The *Fuehrer* had got away with an amazing bluff. As he later admitted, had even the French marched, the bluff would have been called and Nazi Germany suffered an inglorious defeat that might have brought down the thousand-year Reich. 'A retreat on our part,' the *Fuehrer* later conceded, 'would have spelled collapse. If the French had marched, we would have had to withdraw with our tails between our legs, for the military resources at our disposal would have been wholly inadequate for even a moderate resistance.' But Hitler was sure the French would not march and that the British would also do nothing. He had sized up their weaknesses as cannily as he had those of his opponents in Germany. This was the last chance of the Western democracies to stop Hitler without waging a major war. They let the chance slip by. The dictator drew his own conclusions.

When Hitler addressed the Reichstag on 30 January 1937, he outlined with justifiable pride the achievements of his first four years in office. He had abolished unemployment, stimulated a business boom, torn up the Versailles Treaty, begun to build up and arm a powerful Army, Navy, and Air Force and reoccupied the Rhineland. He had also kept his promise to keep the peace. 'The time of so-called surprises,' he told the Reichstag, 'has been ended'. In fact, there were no major surprises that year. It was a time of consolidation and of further preparations for later conquests; and for a fateful decision. This came on 5 November 1937, when Hitler called in his senior generals and Foreign Minister and told them bluntly that the die was cast, that they must prepare Germany to go to war in the East and, if necessary, in the West, in the very near future—'at the latest by 1943-45', but most probably sooner.

The top generals were stunned; not on moral grounds but simply because they calculated that Germany was not yet strong enough to win a European war, and would not be for many years, if ever. They protested. But Hitler acted. On 4 February 1938, he cashiered the Army Commander, General Freiherr Werner von Fritsch, and sixteen senior generals, taking over himself personal command of all the armed forces. He fired Neurath as Foreign Minister and replaced him with the fatuous Ribbentrop. He got rid of Papen and some of the old non-Nazi career diplomats. He was free at last of the old-school conservative generals and of the likes of Neurath and Papen, who, though they had helped him come to power—indeed had made it possible—had never, he felt, quite accepted him and never fully comprehended his Nazi revolution and its ambitious goals. They submitted, as everyone else in Hitler's path had done. For five years up to this winter evening the Army had possessed the physical power to overthrow Hitler, and some of its commanding generals had been inclined to do so—especially when General von Fritsch was framed by Hitler, Goering and Himmler on false charges of homosexuality a few weeks before and sent on leave. But they shrank back from so drastic an action, and now they were out on the street, with no power. Fritsch, who for a moment after his fall talked with some of his generals about a military putsch, later explained their plight to the deposed Ambassador von Hassell, who noted it in his diary:

'This man—Hitler—is Germany's destiny for good or evil. If he goes over the abyss— which Fritsch believes he will—he will drag us all down with him. There is nothing we can do.'

Hitler, believing fanatically in that destiny, now began to edge toward the abyss, though it was not discernable to him, or to anyone else—how could it be when his boldness brought a further series of glittering successes? On the night of 11 March 1938, he marched his troops into his native Austria and annexed it as a province of the Greater German Reich. To no surprise of Hitler, the Western Allies again did nothing. He now had democratic Czechoslovakia, which he hated, where he wanted. With the conquest of Austria, German troops surrounded it on three sides. It was obvious that it would be next on Hitler's schedule.

By threatening to attack the Czechs, the *Fuehrer* frightened Prime Minister Chamberlain and Premier Daladier into coming to Munich, where on the night of 29 September 1938, they joined Hitler and Mussolini in ceding the Sudetenland in Czechoslovakia to Germany, leaving the Czech nation truncated and defenceless. So far, Chamberlain had gone along with Hitler's bloodless conquests in the interests of what he thought was peace. But the scales fell from his eyes shortly after 15 March 1939, when Hitler, after browbeating the Czech President into surrender in a nightmarish scene in the Chancellory in Berlin, sent his troops into what was left of Czechoslovakia and annexed it as a 'protectorate' of Germany.

By this time, anyone who was not blind, as Chamberlain had been for so long, could easily determine Hitler's schedule. Poland was bound to be next on his list. Once embarked on his path of conquest, Hitler, like almost all conquerors in history, could not stop himself. He realized, as the confidential notes of his secret utterances make clear, that as a result of Chamberlain's hasty guarantee to Warsaw on 31 March, and of France's treaty obligations to the Poles, an attack on Poland might land Germany in a world war. It was a risk he was willing—even eager—to take. On one condition, though—that he could keep the hated Bolshevik power out of it until he had destroyed Poland and humbled the West. Then it would be Russia's turn.

It seemed inconceivable in the West that fateful summer of 1939, as the war clouds darkened, that Hitler could dupe the Soviet Union, the arch-enemy of Nazi Germany, and a country which Hitler had damned as evil incarnate all the days of his political life, into agreeing to stay out of a German war against Poland and the West. But this was again to underestimate the political genius of the *Fuehrer*, his boldness under pressure, his willingness to strike a temporary bargain with the Devil to achieve his immediate ends. In return for Russia's staying out of the war he offered the Soviet dictator a tempting bait—one the Western Allies, who themselves were half-heartedly dickering with the Russians in Moscow, could not, or would not, match: a large chunk of Polish territory and a free hand to gobble up the former Tsarist provinces in the Baltic. Stalin, as blind to Hitler's long-term ends as Chamberlain had been, took the bait.

To the consternation of the West and the bewilderment of the German people—and no doubt of the Russian people—a 'non-aggression' pact between Germany and the Soviet Union was signed in the Kremlin late in the night of 23 August 1939. Hitler had got what he wanted. Each power undertook not to go to war with the other. The price the Nazi chief paid was set down in a secret protocol, the terms of which did not become known until after the war. Poland once again was to be partitioned between the two powers. Russia was given a free hand to regain its former provinces in the Baltic and Bessarabia in Rumania. Hitler freed by Stalin from the old German nightmare of a two-front war, could now begin hostilities. A week later, on 1 September 1939, he attacked Poland. Two days later, honouring their treaty obligations to Poland, Great Britain and France entered the war against Germany. The Second World War had begun. Russia, honouring *its* treaty commitments, stayed out.

The career of Adolf Hitler as war lord now began. Again his initial successes were stupendous. He conquered Poland in three weeks, added peaceful, unarmed Denmark and Norway to his victims in the following spring, and in May and June 1940, overran Holland, Belgium and France. By the beginning of summer, Hitler was being heralded as a military genius, the greatest of German conquerors, and indeed by his bold strategy, sense of timing and constant pressure on the generals to press ahead, he deserved much of the credit for the astounding victories. His armies now occupied most of Europe, from the North Cape to the Pyrenees, from the English channel to the River Bug in Eastern Poland. On 10 June, when the conquest of the West was all but over, Mussolini, like a jackal, had taken Italy into the war on Hitler's side to try to get in on the spoils.

And then, for the first time, Hitler faltered. He did not know, nor did his generals and admirals, how to get his victorious army across the narrow English channel to invade England, which now stood alone and, except for its Air Force, virtually defenceless, the bulk of its army and armament having been lost in the Battle of France. That autumn the war lord assembled a powerful army and thousands of nondescript barges and boats—he had neglected to build landing craft—on the channel coast of France and Belgium for the onslaught on England. The shipping and the war vessels to protect it were inadequate, Hitler hesitated. He set several dates for D-Day and then postponed them. Finally, he ordered Goering's *Luftwaffe* first to clear Britain's fighter planes from the skies. When this proved impossible— the Battle of Britain was his first setback after a year of glittering triumphs —he abandoned the attack and turned to the East, as he had always intended.

On 22 June 1941, the day Napoleon had crossed the Nieman in 1812 on his way to Moscow, and in violation of still another treaty. Hitler attacked Russia on a thousand-mile front from the Baltic to the Black Sea with the largest army, air and tank force Germany had ever assembled. The Red Army, caught by surprise despite the repeated warnings given to Stalin by London and Washington, was at first overwhelmed, hundreds of thousands of troops being quickly encircled and captured. Three and a half months later, on 3 October, Hitler rushed back to Berlin to proclaim 'without any reservation' that the Soviet Union 'had been struck down and will never rise again'.

True, his armies had rapidly overrun the Ukraine, Russia's breadbasket, arrived at the outskirts of Leningrad and were driving in a final push on Moscow, which seemed largely undefended. It looked even to Western military analysts as though the Soviet Union was finished. But Hitler, falling victim to overconfidence, which was to prove his Nemesis, was counting his chickens before they were hatched. Early in December, in the bitter cold and snow which had helped to defeat Napoleon, General Georgi Zhukov, fell on the German armies before Moscow with a force of a hundred divisions, which Hitler had not suspected existed. The Germans were forced to retreat—for the first time in the war. Tens of thousands of Hitler's best troops perished in the snow, and thousands of guns and tanks were lost.[3] 'The myth of the invincibility of the German army,' General Franz Halder, Chief of the General Staff, noted sadly, 'was broken'. The myth of Adolf Hitler as military genius too.

351

Overleaf: nemesis. U.S. bombs rain down on Berlin, 1944

Count Ciano, the Italian Foreign Minister, and Josef Goebbels, the Nazi Minister of Propaganda, who saw Hitler early in the spring, noted that his hair had turned 'quite grey'. 'He truly worries me,' Goebbels noted in his diary. 'He told me he had had to fight off severe attacks of giddiness.' Deterioration in the war lord's health—and nerves and mind—had begun.

Still, with his iron will apparently undiminished, he did not give up. Stirred by the news of Japan's attack on Pearl Harbour, 7 December 1941, he had been rash enough to hurry back to Berlin on 9 December, three days after his armies in Russia started reeling back from Zhukov's counter-offensive, and two days later, to please his Japanese ally, he declared war on the United States, thus adding, after Russia, that potentially formidable power to his enemies, which six months before had consisted only of besieged Britain. He now faced, by his own volition, the very coalition of powers (minus France) which had brought Germany down in the First World War, though there is no hint in his secret conversations that he realized the consequences of this—he who until a year ago had been so uncanny in assessing the balance of power in the world. Now he had turned it against him.

Oblivious to that stark fact, he hastened back to headquarters to direct the stemming of the Soviet counter-offensive. For a time in January 1942, it appeared that his retreating armies might disintegrate and perish in the Russian snows, as had Napoleon's Grand Army just 130 years before. Later, many of his generals would reluctantly credit the *Fuehrer*'s granite will and fanatical determination with finally halting the Russian drive by the end of February. Day after day he ordered his weary, frozen troops to stand and fight—and die. He cashiered a number of commanding field marshals, including Rundstedt, sacked General Guderian, the founder and brilliant leader of the *Panzerkorps*, and ousted the army chief, Brauchitsch—all for sanctioning withdrawals in defiance of his orders to stand fast. He took over direct command of the Army himself. He wheedled fifty-two fresh divisions from his Rumanian, Hungarian, Italian, Slovak and Spanish allies for a new offensive he already envisaged as soon as the snows melted and the roads were dry. He rebuilt and refitted his own shattered armies; and as another summer, 1942, came, he struck again, this time on the southern flank of Russia with the aim of obtaining the oil fields of the Caucasus. 'If I do not get this oil,' he told his generals, 'then I must end the war'. He did not get it, though he came close, and this new failure, coupled with another, in North Africa, spelled his eventual doom.

Once again that summer a great victory seemed within his grasp. By the end of August the Sixth Army had reached the Volga just north of Stalingrad, cutting that lifeline so crucial to the Russians. Farther south, a great Panzer force in the Caucasus was within fifty miles of the main Soviet oil centre around Grozny and a bare hundred miles from the Caspian Sea. Once more Hitler convinced himself that the Russians were 'finished' and talked with General Halder of pushing on with part of his victorious forces through Iran to the Persian Gulf and eventually linking up with the Japanese in India. But such talk was unrealistic—it marked a growing megalomania in the war lord—and when Halder and some of the field marshals told him that he was overreaching himself and that the Russians were not only not finished but about to attack his over-exposed flanks, he sacked them.⁴

But that did not hold back the Russians. On 19 November 1942, in the midst of a great blizzard and sub-zero temperatures, thirteen Soviet armies, backed by thousands of tanks, guns and planes, attacked the German, Rumanian and Italian armies north, west, and south of Stalingrad, broke through their fronts, and forced them into precipitous retreat. The generals urged Hitler to permit the Sixth Army to withdraw from Stalingrad while there was still time, but he forbade it. 'I won't leave the Volga!' he shouted at his chief of staff. The Sixth Army was left to its fate as the rest of the forces retreated rapidly westwards. These retreats in turn threatened to leave the German armies in the Caucasus cut off, as was the Sixth Army at Stalingrad. Reluctantly Hitler agreed to their withdrawal. The vision of getting the Russian oil fields, so essential for his further prosecution of the war—and so essential for Russia's survival—vanished. On the last day of January 1943, the remnants of the Sixth Army surrendered at Stalingrad. 'It was,' wrote a German military historian, 'the greatest defeat that a German army had ever undergone'.

But that was not all. Disaster had also come to Hitler's armies in North Africa. One of his great favourites, General Erwin Rommel, commander of the *Afrika Korps*, after driving the British back to within sixty-five miles of Alexandria and the Nile early in the summer of 1942, was attacked at El Alamein on 23 October, by the greatly strengthened British Eighth Army under a new and resourceful commander, General Montgomery. Within a month, Rommel was forced to fall back 700 miles, his vaunted *Afrika Korps* shattered. Then another blow hit Hitler's no longer invincible troops. An Anglo-American army under General Eisenhower landed in Morocco and Algeria on 8 November, and by the following spring had joined up with Montgomery's Eighth Army to destroy the last Italo-German force in Africa which Hitler, at the last moment, foolishly had reinforced with a quarter of a million troops. More Germans were captured in the German surrender in Tunisia than at Stalingrad.

In the snows of Stalingrad and in the burning sands of North Africa the war had reached a fateful turning point. Though not ended, it was lost for Germany. The Third Reich—and its fanatical leader—were doomed.

We now come to the last chapter, the last two years, of Hitler's life. How amazing it is to the historian—as it must be to the reader—that after all that had happened and would shortly happen as the Allied armies closed in on Germany and Anglo-American bombers flattened its great cities and industrial plants, Adolf Hitler, failing though he was in body and mind, could, by the force of his iron will and his mysterious charisma, retain his absolute control over the Army and the people, forcing them to continue to do his bidding until millions more Germans had been killed or wounded and the Fatherland laid waste!

The end was inevitable. Yet Hitler fought desperately and resourcefully for two years to stave it off, rallying his armies to halt temporarily here and there the Russians in the East and in the West the Anglo-American armies, which had landed in Normandy on 6 June 1944 and by autumn reached the western frontier of Germany; and successfully urging his war-weary, bombed-out people to further sacrifice by continual assurances that, despite all the setbacks and hardships, Germany would triumph in the end. The confidence of the mass of German people in their still charismatic *Fuehrer*, who had led them on such a foolish venture at such terrible cost, remained undiminished. There was no sign of revolt.

A few army officers, mostly retired, whose consciences did lead them finally to rebel—though not until they realized the war was lost—attempted to kill Hitler in July 1944 and take over the stricken country. But they bungled the job and were slain by the dictator—along with thousands of other officers and civilians whom Hitler suspected were lacking in complete loyalty to him. 'This time,' Hitler stormed, 'the criminals will be given short shrift. No military tribunals. We'll haul them before the People's Court. No long speeches from them. The court will act with lightning speed. And two hours after the sentence it will be carried out. By hanging—without mercy.'

He was as good as his word. According to one official figure, 4,980 officers and civilians were executed. The generals still at their posts did not condemn this savage revenge on their fellow-officers and fellow-countrymen. Hitler's hold on them was absolute.

How could this be? The generals knew where he was leading them—and the nation. They knew from personal experience that Hitler was becoming an irresponsible, raving maniac. General Guderian, restored to favour and made Chief of the General Staff, has told of how the *Fuehrer*, on receipt of the news in January 1945, that the Russians had reached the Oder, only a hundred miles from Berlin, turned on him. 'He stood in front of me shaking his fists, so that my good Chief of Staff, Thomale, felt constrained to seize me by the skirt of my jacket and pull me backward lest I be the victim of physical assault.'

A few days later, while the two were conferring about the worsening situation on the Russian front, Hitler was at him again.

'His fists raised, his cheeks flushed with rage, his whole body trembling, the man stood there in front of me, beside himself with fury and having lost all self-control. At each outburst Hitler would stride up and down the carpet edge, then suddenly stop before me and hurl his next accusation in my face. He was almost screaming, his eyes seemed to pop out of his head and the veins stood out in his temples.'

Yet neither the Chief of the General Staff nor his fellow generals still in command thought of getting rid of the mad war lord, though they had the power to do so. Guderian tells us why:

'The great proportion of the German people still believed in Adolf Hitler and would have been convinced that with his death the assassin had removed the only man who might still be able to bring the war to a favourable conclusion.'

It was in this maniacal state of mind, so graphically described by Guderian, that Adolf Hitler made one of the last momentous—and barbarous—decisions of his life. On 19 March 1945, he decreed that all remaining industry, transportation and communication installations were to be destroyed along with all stores of food, clothing and oil. Germany was to be made one vast wasteland. When Albert Speer, Minister of Armaments, protested that this would deprive the German people of the means to continue living, the *Fuehrer* replied:

'If the war is lost, the nation will perish . . . There is no necessity to take into consideration the basis which the people will need to continue a most primitive existence. On the contrary, it will be better to destroy these things ourselves . . . Those who remain are only the inferior ones, for the good ones have been killed.'

Adolf Hitler, his own personal fate sealed, was not interested in the continued existence of the German people, for whom he had always professed such boundless love. Though many fanatical Nazi leaders and some officers, in total obedience to the last, tried to carry out the war lord's senseless order, Speer and his friends in the Army were able to sabotage it. Only when all was lost, did they dare to defy—for the first time—their leader's criminal edicts.

As spring came in 1945, the end approached for the Army, the Third Reich and its leader. The British and American armies from the West, the Russians from the East, now converged on the heart of Germany, linking up on 25 April at the Elbe, seventy-five miles south of Berlin. The Red Army was already at its outskirts. Hitler was cut off in the capital.

In his last days on earth, the once arrogant master of Germany and of most of Europe had become a hollow shell of his former self. Aides who remained with him have described how he went to pieces, hysterically cursing the Army for its 'treason' in not relieving Berlin, issuing idiotic orders to armies that no longer existed to counter-attack, wildly waving road maps that were fast disintegrating from the sweat of his hands and pointing to blotched spots to show where the Russians could still be stopped if the Germans would only fight. When an S.S. officer in charge of the Prisoners of War Office conferred with him in the Chancellery bunker, which had now become his headquarters and home, on 23 April·

'He suddenly shrieked: "Everyone has deceived me! No one has told me the truth! The Armed forces have lied to me!" . . . He went on and on in a loud voice. Then his face went purple. I thought he was going to have a stroke.'

He almost did—a few moments later when word came in (false, as it turned out) that revolt had broken out in his native Austria and adopted Bavaria.

'His hand was shaking, his leg was shaking and his head was shaking, and he kept saying: "Shoot them all! Shoot them all!"'

The time had come for Hitler to shoot himself, and for the woman who was about to become his bride to join him in death. On 28 April Russian troops approached the Potsdamerplatz, but a block away. Sometime between 1 a.m. and 3 a.m. the next morning Hitler married his colourless mistress, Eva Braun, and afterwards entertained his aides at a macabre wedding breakfast at which champagne toasts were offered to the bridal couple. Thirty-six hours later, after word had come that the bunker could not hold out more than a day or two, the great *Fuehrer* of the Third Reich shot himself, and his bride swallowed poison. It was 3.30 p.m., 30 April 1945, ten days after Adolf Hitler's fifty-sixth birthday, and twelve years and three months to a day since he had become Chancellor and founded the 'thousand-year' Third Reich. It would survive him by only a week.

Before dying, Hitler had hastily written his Last Will and Testament and dictated a final message to General Keitel, Chief of the High Command. They are illuminating documents. They show that the man who had ruled Germany with an iron hand for more than twelve years, and most of Europe, for four, had learned nothing from his experiences; not even his reverses and shattering final failure had taught him anything. Indeed, in the last hours of his life he reverted to the young man he had been in his vagabond years in Vienna and in the early rowdy beer hall period in Munich; blaming the Jews for all the ills of the world and for his fall, and exhorting his successors to carry on the fight for Nazism and its 'glorious' principles. In his Testament and in his farewell message to Keitel he put responsibility for the defeat on— after the Jews—the generals and especially on the General Staff—'it cannot be compared to the General Staff of the First World War. Its achievements were far behind those of the fighting front'. So, the great victories had been due to him, the defeats and final failure to the generals, to their 'disloyalty and betrayal'.

And then the parting valediction—the last recorded words of the mad genius's life—which again showed how little he had learned since he first put them down in *Mein Kampf*. 'The aim must still be,' he admonished Keitel with his dying breath, 'to win territory in the East for the German people.'

All the millions of German dead, all the millions of German homes crushed under the bombs, even the destruction of the German Reich had not convinced him that the robbing of the lands of the Slavic peoples to the East was—morals aside—a futile Teutonic dream.

The conquering German war lord, who had come so close to achieving his barbarous aims, died deflated—he helped to deflate himself. Yet he has left a considerable imprint on history, evil as it is. From nothing he rose to be the ruler of a great country and people, designed a revolution and carried it out, built up the mightiest war machine Europe had yet seen, conquered and enslaved most of the continent and from the first to the last held the acclaim and the loyal support of supposedly one of the most civilized and Christian people in Europe, whom he deprived of their personal freedom, and who never seemed to mind that or mind the horrors he inflicted on so many of their fellow human beings.

Yet there is a terrifying gap between the man, who in his person was so petty and vulgar and ignorant and brutish and hysterical, and the catastrophic magnitude of what he wrought, that continues to baffle the historians and especially one like myself, who watched him for years at first hand. There is little logical connection between the person and his achievements.

Adolf Hitler, though, cannot be dismissed as a charlatan or a lucky crackpot. Despite all his flaws, there was considerable substance in him. As we have seen, he had an unusual intellect, a soaring imagination, a will of granite, a sense of history, and, until drunk with power he faltered at the end, a genius in sensing the weaknesses of his opponents and for timing his bold moves to take advantage of them. He was the greatest of twentieth-century propagandists. No other man of our time had quite his genius for communicating with the masses—at least the German masses—by the spoken word (especially after he could reach them by radio), for swaying them as he wished and shaping them to his own ambitious purposes. One could see it work, but not understand how, for the secret of human communication remains largely a mystery, as does the secret of charisma, which Hitler had in such large measure for so many Germans.

It is true that he found in the German people, as a mysterious Providence and centuries of experience had moulded them, a natural instrument which he was able to use for his own ends. But without Adolf Hitler there almost certainly would never have been a Third Reich, and mankind would have been spared much agony, including that of the Second World War and the massacre of the Jews. Hitler founded that Reich, shaped it, gave it its terrifying power and maintained it as long as he lived. With his death, it ceased to exist.

He had a fatal flaw, one that has doomed almost all the world's conquerors—Napoleon, for instance, to whom Hitler may with some reason be compared. Like Bonaparte, he overreached himself. Like him, once embarked on conquest he could not stop, no matter how the odds against him grew. It is a very old flaw in the great, and the consequences are predictable. Power corrupts, to revert to Lord Acton's phrase, hackneyed as it may sound today, though it remains one of the few truths we know about man. Absolute power corrupts absolutely. The strange life of Adolf Hitler is but another example.

---

[1] 'In this period there took shape within me a world picture and a philosophy which became the granite foundation of all my acts. In addition to what I then created, I had to learn little; and I have had to alter nothing.'— Hitler in *Mein Kampf*, on his Vienna days.

[2] Hans Frank, *Im Angesicht des Galgens.*

[3] German casualties in Russia up to the end of February 1942, when the retreat ended and the front was stabilized, were one million, or thirty per cent of all troops. Of these, 200,000 were killed, 725,000 wounded and 46,000 missing. Casualties from frostbite were 116,627.

[4] When a staff officer attempted to read an Intelligence report to that effect, says Halder, 'Hitler flew at him with clenched fists and foam in the corners of his mouth and forbade him to read any more of such "idiotic twaddle".'

De Gaulle
by Lord Gladwyn

LORD GLADWYN (b. 1900 as Gladwyn Jebb) was educated at Eton and Magdalen College, Oxford (where he got a First in History), and then entered the Diplomatic Service in 1924 to establish himself in the thirty-six years of his career as one of the outstanding members of his profession. Having served in Tehran and Rome and in the Foreign Office, he was appointed Head of the Reconstruction Department charged with the manifold and arduous tasks of post-war planning. In this capacity he attended all the major conferences of the Second World War and was Executive Secretary of the Preparatory Commission of the United Nations, acting as Secretary-General during the First Assembly. He succeeded Sir Alexander Cadogan as U.K. Representative to the United Nations in 1950 and four years later was appointed H.M. Ambassador to France. Created a hereditary peer before his retirement at the end of 1960, he is now the Deputy Leader of the Liberal Party in the House of Lords and a member of the British Parliamentary Delegation to the Assemblies of the Council of Europe and W.E.U. For the last ten years he has been the champion of British participation in the European Community and is the author of various historical and diplomatic studies, among them *The European Idea* (1967) and *Europe after de Gaulle* (1970). He published his Memoirs in 1972.

Charles de Gaulle

22 Nov. 1890	Born. Educated at École Militaire, St Cyr.
1913	Joined 33rd Infantry Regiment and fought in early campaigns in World War I.
March 1916	Wounded at Battle of Verdun and taken prisoner for rest of war.
1921	Lecturer at École Militaire, St Cyr.
1927	Served at Trier in army occupying Rhineland.
1932	Published *Le Fil de l'Epée*.*
1934	Published *Vers l'Armée de Métier*.*

*pleaded for mechanized professional army and suggested strategic plan.

1939	Upon outbreak of Second World War commanded brigade of tanks attached to 5th Army in Alsace.
6 June 1940	New premier, Paul Reynaud, appointed him Under-Secretary of State for War.
18 June 1940	After Petain, Reynaud's successor, sought an armistice, de Gaulle broadcast strong appeal to French to continue to fight. He became leader of the Free French.
Aug. 1944	Liberation of metropolitan France. De Gaulle returned to Paris in triumph.
Sept. 1944	Formation of provisional government. Two constituent assemblies were elected to draft new constitution.
Oct. 1946	De Gaulle disapproved of new constitution, which was parliamentary in character. When it was accepted by referendum, he retired.

Previous page: de Gaulle in Africa in 1958, acknowledging cheers in Brazzaville

April 1947 De Gaulle formed Rassemblement du Peuple Français (R.P.F.) to campaign against weak parliamentary system.

1953 As this political party had lost ground, it was disbanded. De Gaulle retired into private life.

May 1958 Army leaders in Algeria defied government in Paris and France was threatened with civil war.

June 1958 Pledging himself to solve Algerian problem, de Gaulle was returned to office.

Sept. 1958 New constitution in which Assembly could be dissolved at President's will and had no real ability to censure the government.

Dec. 1958 Elected President of the Fifth Republic.

Feb. 1960 France became a nuclear power by exploding its first atomic bomb.

May 1960 Summit meeting in Paris broke up in dispute over violations of Soviet airspace by U.S. reconnaissance planes. De Gaulle now wanted to establish the E.E.C. as a political entity under French leadership.

1960 Practically all former French colonies became independent.

Nov. 1961 British negotiate for membership of E.E.C. This would destroy de Gaulle's plans, so he looked to Germany for an ally. Thus:

July 1962 State visit of German Chancellor, Adenauer, to France. Speeches proclaimed Franco-German reconciliation and intention to organize political unity in Europe.

March 1962 Ceasefire agreement signed with Algerian provisional government ending seven-year war.

April 1962 Referendum-voters approved peace accord, but great hostility to it from right-wing and traditional parties.

Oct. 1962 Therefore de Gaulle proposed to revise constitution and held referendum on the subject. Only a moderate success.

Nov. 1962 But subsequent elections a triumph for de Gaulle, whose party gained absolute majority in National Assembly.

Dec. 1962 Conference with Harold Macmillan at Rambouillet about British entry to E.E.C.

Jan. 1963 Press conference at which de Gaulle vetoed British entry.

Jan. 1963 Franco-German treaty. But, later, German parliament approved a preamble which contradicted what treaty stood for.

Jan. 1964 Disillusioned with Germany, de Gaulle turned to Third World; he recognized Communist China and advocated neutralization of South-East Asia.

July 1965 De Gaulle tried to destroy supra-national element in E.E.C. France boycotted the Common Market.

Dec. 1965 De Gaulle won presidential election.

July 1966 French withdrawal from N.A.T.O.

June/ July 1966 De Gaulle visited U.S.S.R. to propose co-operation over a settlement of the German problem.

May 1967 Vetoed second British effort to enter E.E.C.

June 1967 Condemnation of Israel.*

Nov. 1967 Appeal to Quebec nationalists.*

*alarmed the French nation

April 1969 Referendum on constitutional reform. When France refused to support de Gaulle, he resigned.

9 Nov. 1970 Died.

On a November afternoon of 1970, in the bleak countryside of his own election, Death, which he so often faced with open eyes, by stealth laid his icy hand on President de Gaulle. As far back as 1957 he was, as he says in his Memoirs, 'feeling the approach of the eternal cold'. Dead, his powerful and sombre spirit will continue to brood over and to influence the land he loved. For this great man there can be no conventional praise or blame. Physically and mentally he was outsize. Except for Winston Churchill, and possibly Mao Tse-Tung, he was the most impressive political figure of our generation. No one devoted to the accomplishment of a political end, namely the promotion of what he believed to be the interests of his country, more authority, intelligence, craft, courage, vision and indeed earthy common-sense. He was a completely dedicated man.

I well remember our first meeting in June 1940. A few days previously the General had delivered his famous B.B.C. broadcast (*'l'Appel'*) to the French nation. A slightly alarmed Government insisted that his next major broadcast, to be delivered at 8.30 p.m. on 26 June, should be vetted by the Foreign Office. (We must remember that it was not until 28 June that he was even recognized as the Leader of the Free French.) Seven o'clock and still no script. My chief, Sir Alexander Cadogan, went off leaving me with strict instructions. Shortly after, it arrived. I found it brilliant, but it did violate several of my rules. Making the minimum changes and even so taking a very considerable risk, I rushed round to the Rubens Hotel, only to be told that the General had not yet finished his dinner. Just before eight he emerged, clearly in a bad temper, and gazing down on me said: *'Qui êtes-vous?'* I explained that I was a mere subordinate, but that owing to the late arrival of the text it had fallen to me to propose certain *'légères modifications'*. *'Donnez-les moi!'* Awful pause. *'Je les trouve ridicules,'* said the General. *'Parfaitement ri-di-cules.'* I felt bound to point out that it was now five past eight, that the delay was not my fault and that, not to put too fine a point on it, if he could not accept the *'modifications'* he would not be able to broadcast. The ultimatum succeeded. One of the General's main characteristics was that if there was absolutely nothing to be done about something he did not kick against the pricks. Like the elephant, he advanced in a straight line through the jungle crushing everything that came along until confronted by the baobab tree, when he executed a détour. *'Eh bien,'* he said, *'j'accepte, c'est ridicule, mais j'accepte.'* And so he did, even (reluctantly) agreeing that I should accompany him to the studio. Sitting behind him, I shall never forget how, trembling with emotion, he started off, *'Monsieur le Maréchal, par les ondes, au-dessus de la mer, c'est un soldat français qui vous parle'*. Ah! That was magnificent. For the remainder of the war I was, in spite of his often impossible behaviour, a strong Gaullist and an even more convinced opponent of Marshal Pétain.

How can one best sum up the prodigious figure who has left us? That he had dreadful faults no one could possibly deny. He was vindictive, arrogant, proud, unscrupulous, self-centred, rather merciless and, in a queer way, out of date. He may have called himself a Christian: certainly he was a conforming churchman. It may even be that he genuinely accepted Catholic doctrine. But he could hardly be said to have given proof in his life of elementary Christian virtues. He had no humility, little compassion, and he by no means loved his neighbour as himself. Indeed he had not very much love to spare for anybody, more especially the human race. Men, he thought, were nearly always actuated by base motives. Like Walpole, he tended to assume that every man has his price. His sense of humour was considerable but what he found most funny was the misfortunes of his friends.

Nor was he a warm personality. He could hardly ever unbend. He had indeed little conception of what ordinary people were thinking or feeling. They only interested him as a mass, to which he made an extraordinary appeal. To this extent, and with the notable exception of his devotion to his family and particularly to his mentally retarded daughter, he may be said to have been positively inhumane—if super-human is not perhaps a better word. For even his total physical courage had a rather disconcerting side. What could one make of a man whose only words of consolation to his poor wife, after they had been missed by inches at point-blank range by a hundred bullets, were reported to have been *'Mais voyons, ma chère Yvonne, ils tirent comme des cochons'* ('Really, my dear Yvonne, their shooting is beneath contempt')? But even his worst enemies (and he had many) never compared him to ruthless dictators such as Ivan the Terrible, or Genghis Khan, or Stalin; to the operatic Mussolini; least of all to the appalling Hitler. De Gaulle was a civilized man. Save when he wanted to be rude, his manners were beautiful. He had read widely and well. As a young man he composed a long epic poem. He was a French intellectual, and accepted as such. Not perhaps in the same class, from a strictly literary point of view, as Bossuet or Chateaubriand or Péguy, on whom he modelled his style, but not greatly inferior to them as a writer of French prose. In other words, he ranked among the best trained intelligences of the world. But he was something more.

The fact was that he was possessed by an all-consuming and uncontrollable passion, transcending all other cravings, for France. It was a love-affair with an abstraction which took the physical form of 'mingling' whenever possible with a crowd of loyal supporters. 'All the sentimental side of my nature', he tells us himself, 'inclines me to picture France as a sort of fairy-tale princess or as a madonna in a fresco for whom some wonderful and exceptional future is in store. I instinctively feel that Providence has decreed that she must either be completely successful or utterly un-successful'. For France, 'mediocrity' he continues, is an 'absurd anomaly'. France is only herself if she is in the front rank. Only 'vast enterprises' can control the centrifugal forces of this anarchic nation. 'In short, as I see it, France cannot be France without grandeur.' In this, the first verse of the first chapter of the Gospel according to de Gaulle, as it were, all is said. It will be observed that in the General's view it would actually be preferable for France to find her soul 'resisting' some alien occupation than to enjoy the middle-class economic triumphs of another good King Louis Philippe. For France, heroism is the thing.

His romantic affair had rather extraordinary consequences. It ac-counted in the first instance for de Gaulle's success as an unknown rebellious brigadier-general in forcing first a rather reluctant Britain and then a very reluctant America to recognize him as the real representative of France. But since he was sincerely convinced that he, and only he was, mystically, France herself, this difficulty in taking him at his own valuation resulted in his later tending to lump what he called *'les anglo-saxons'* together as something alien and potentially hostile. This tendency was fostered by his St Cyr education which emphasized the constant efforts of Britain to frustrate the policy of her nearest neighbour. To this school of thought, undeniably widespread in France itself, Fashoda was a much livelier memory than the Entente Cordiale and the shared sacrifices of the First World War. His relations with Winston Churchill during the war were öften thundery—did not the P.M. say that the greatest cross he had to bear was that of Lorraine?—but for him, and other British leaders, such as Anthony Eden and Harold Macmillan, de Gaulle had a high regard. The commonly held idea that he bore a tremendous grudge against the British nation as the result of his war experiences was not true. Rather the reverse. But his scurvy treatment at the hands of President Roosevelt and Cordell Hull did induce a positive dislike of America—though not of individual Americans with some of whom he got on very well.

De Gaulle was also persuaded, possibly rightly, that if he had had his way in the thirties the Second World War would never have happened and therefore that no French dependence on any outside state would have been necessary at all. His whole philosophy of the offensive, to say nothing of the rôle of a leader, was latent in *Le fil de l'Epée* (published in 1932), and in 1934 he worked out a detailed strategical plan in *Vers l'armée de métier*. A forward French military policy, based on a *'corps d'élite'*, namely a striking force of at least six armoured divisions with the necessary air support, which he then recommended, would have meant that the Germans could never have attacked France's allies in the East without losing the Ruhr and the Rhineland. Nor incidentally could they ever have re-occupied the latter in 1936. With such an arm the French, in alliance with the Russians, might have ruled Europe: and then Paris, rather than London or New York, could have been the capital of the world. It was paradoxical that de Gaulle's plan, adopted by the German Generalstab, and brilliantly executed by Guderian, was primarily responsible for the complete collapse of France. Nobody could say that this was in any way the responsibility of the General.

So when on that historic afternoon of 26 August 1944, he marched down the Champs Elysées at the head of the Conseil National de la Résistance in the presence of two million wildly cheering Parisians (and not an 'Anglo-Saxon' soldier of any kind to be seen) he already knew what he wanted. Out of the ruin of his liberated land he would forge by his own tremendous will a new nation, confident, purposeful, the obvious leader of some Western European Confederation, no doubt, as often as not, associated with the 'Anglo-Saxons' but in independent relationship with the Russians and in friendly touch with a 'liberated' French Empire which would continue to look to Paris for encouragement and support.

The chances of achieving this would, he thought, be enhanced by the acute tension between Russia and America. This might be the basis, as he candidly revealed in the last Volume of his Memoirs, published at the end

366

A proud moment. De Gaulle leads a parade through newly liberated Paris, November 1944

of 1959, for a 'vast plan' to assure [French] security in Western Europe by removing any threat from the Reich: to collaborate with both West and East, if necessary contracting alliances with one side or the other, without ever placing France in a dependent position: to transform the French Union into a free Association: to group together, from the political, economic and strategic points of view the states bordering on the Rhine, the Alps and the Pyrenees [i.e., presumably, France, Germany, the Low Countries, Austria, Switzerland, Italy and Spain, but not, on the face of it, the United Kingdom or Scandinavia] to make this organization one of the three World Powers and even perhaps one day an 'arbiter' between the rival camps of the Russians and the Anglo-Saxons.

This, then, was the heady vision that swam before his eyes. It seems that he really thought in 1944 that it was a possibility, and this in spite of the fact that Stalin, who seemed at that moment to be thinking far more in terms of Anglo-Soviet-American co-operation, did not respond to the feelers which the General put out during his visit to Moscow in December of that year. But admittedly, it would only be possible on one condition. France, by agreeing to drastic reforms of her political structure, must prove herself worthy of the task. The old *système* must obviously disappear. In its place there must be a strong executive, 'democratic' in that it might derive its main support from plebiscites, but only to a minor degree dependent on an Assembly composed of a number of warring factions whose feuds, as he saw it, had resulted in France's having no lasting Government, and consequently no consistent policy since the days, at least, of Clemenceau. Strong Government was necessary for the ungovernable Gauls. The new Assembly must be purely consultative or all the old weaknesses would reappear. We know what happened. De Gaulle lost his battle with the parties. The Constitution finally adopted in December 1946 was entirely parliamentary in character. Short of organizing a coup d'état and governing as a Dictator—which he would not do—there was no way out save retiring gracefully. He retired. But he probably believed at that time that it would not be long before the inevitable weaknesses of the *système* resulted in the nation's again appealing to the man who had, as he believed, preserved her essential being, or, as he would have preferred to say, her soul.

In so thinking he was both wrong and right. Many of the French Parliamentarians were excellent and able men. The corps of officials was undoubtedly first-class. For many years the Fourth Republic did, on the whole, pretty well. Nearly all the reforms which were to blossom in the Fifth Republic were prepared by the Fourth. The voluntary exile of Colombey-les-deux-Églises, though he kept in touch with events, became more and more gloomy and remote. When, after having taken over the Paris Embassy, I conversed with him for the second time in January 1957, that is to say after his eleven years in the wilderness, he even seemed to be bordering on despair. Before the *redressement* of France, in which he still believed, could take place 'de Gaulle' he announced to me dramatically, with tears in his eyes, 'would be dead'. But eventually he was justified. The stresses and strains of 'decolonization', in Indo-China first and then, more critically, in Algeria, were too severe for the Fourth Republic. As I believe, rather to his own surprise, he was swept back into office in June 1958.

Now he really had it all his own way. The new constitution was exactly to his liking. The Assembly which had in practice no real ability even to censure the Government, thereby repudiating its policy, and which could be dissolved at the President's will, became gradually less and less significant. This was deplorable, but, as he had always prophesied, a strong Government which had every prospect of enduring, at any rate for some years, enormously increased the wealth and greatly reinforced the economy of France.

It was this feeling of political security that enabled him to proceed with hardly any criticism to his first major operation—the liberation of the component parts of the old French Union. Algeria took twice as long to settle as he had supposed, but even that ulcer was removed. This process, protracted though it was, was one of the most brilliant operations of the General's career. To have gained power by putting himself at the head of rebellious generals and settlers who were demanding an *'Algérie française'* and then to have gradually adopted, and finally imposed, the totally opposite policy of an *'Algérie algérienne'*, was an example of political manipulation and, if you will, downright deceit, rarely equalled in history. No doubt he even deceived himself, for the eventual settlement was clearly far removed from what he had had in mind originally. No wonder that the General incurred the undying hostility of the French right wing, insufficiently versed, it must be assumed, in the fundamental principles of Machiavelli.

Then, for foreign policy generally, there was already in being a brand new and potentially wonderful tool—the European Economic Community. Again, not exactly what he would have desired himself, but what a chance for France! Here was clearly a chance of moving towards the execution of the 'vast plan'. Bring back the troops from Algeria; transform Western Germany into an associated and subservient vassal; disregard the Italians and the Belgians; isolate the Dutch; develop France's nuclear potential; deal directly with the Russians. But first he must prepare the way and remove, if possible, any apprehensions on the part of the Anglo-Saxons, to whom he had caused appeasing messages to be sent, through intermediaries, in the critical days of May 1958.

It is with this background that we must approach the famous 'memorandum' of July 1958, which suggested the reform of NATO by the creation of what was in fact a 'Political Standing Group' of the U.S.A., the U.K., and France. Had it been accepted, even in principle, the General would certainly have set about organizing his Western European Confederation under French leadership straightaway because his 'special position' would have given him the requisite prestige. But the Anglo-Saxons, to his disgust, would hear nothing of it. So the Germans must first be brought into a new relationship with France and to that extent taken out of a predominantly 'Anglo-Saxon' orientation. With incomparable *maîtrise* de Gaulle bent the aged and susceptible German Chancellor to his will. The operation was at the expense of his relationship with Russia, of course, but that could be patched up later. Anyway, standing up to the Russians on Berlin would not, as he saw it, result in war. The abortive summit meeting of 1960 was to confirm the rightness of this view. The immediate thing was to make it

369

apparent that he was the Germans' only loyal friend. Once the E.E.C. was firmly established as a political entity—under French leadership—then France would be a great power in her own right, in every respect the equal of the U.K., quite possibly, her superior. To clinch this it would be necessary for her also to build up a nuclear capability at least comparable to that of Britain. But, given all this, how best to handle the British?

It was a real problem, perhaps the greatest he ever had to face. On the one hand he could not, nor did he ever, deny that Britain was a European Power, less directly involved in Europe, no doubt, than France because of the Channel, but nevertheless for historical, if not for geographical reasons, part of the whole European order— 'l'Europe', as he once said in one of his more majestic moments, 'et sa fille, l'Amérique'. If she had powerful outside connections also, well, so had France—as he was never tired of suggesting. On the other hand it was evident, whatever he might say to the contrary, that Britain's outside connections were more important than France's: there was the Commonwealth which was much more significant, as being largely based on blood and sentiment than the old 'Union Française'; and there was the famous 'special relationship' with America which, however it might be interpreted, was something which (he believed) Britain had and France probably could never have. How therefore could Britain in practice fit into his 'imposing European Confederation' which he had already publicly announced (in 1960) as being the object of his policy?

I myself asked him this shortly before I left Paris in September 1960. I could understand, though I could not approve, his action in bringing to an end the negotiations for a Free Trade Area. But did he, or did he not, propose that my country should be a member of his Confederation? What would happen supposing one day she actually applied for membership of the E.E.C.? The General never minded a straight question. 'Monsieur l'Ambassadeur,' he replied, 'in my opinion I do not think that you can possibly do such a thing now. You have your Commonwealth; you have your great system of Imperial Preferences. This is not a thing which you can lightly abandon. If I were you, I would never willingly consent to this.' But after some further argument he eventually said 'Well, as a matter of fact, I think you will one day have to apply for membership; but what I believe is that you will not be able to do so for a considerable time to come.' Obviously what he wanted was to put off the day when England would have to apply for membership of the E.E.C. until he had actually established his Confederation, under French leadership, and until it was apparent that the U.K. would not be entering as the head of the Commonwealth or the agent of the Pentagon, but rather as a poor relation who would be finally, and even prodigally received, her 'outside' influence having disappeared, as an ordinary European state into the European fold.

It was therefore a shock to him when, barely a year after our conversation, H.M.G., in a brilliant and daring initiative, did precisely what he had said they could not do for a long period to come. Once Britain was inside his potential Confederation, what would happen to his 'vast plan'? If one thing was certain, it was that a Britain which retained her Commonwealth connection, her economic strength, and her independent nuclear deterrent would never agree to the 'Third Force' and implicitly neutralist connotations of this plan which the General's mysterious phrase 'Europe from the Atlantic to the Urals' had invested with even more sinister implications. She might—she said she would—agree to some form of European political union: but she would certainly use her considerable influence in the direction of seeing to it that the whole contraption, whatever it might in practice turn out to be, remained firmly within the orbit of the Western Alliance. Besides, what chance would there be in such circumstances of maintaining the physical dominance of France? On the other hand there was clear enthusiasm for British membership of the E.E.C. (provided she accepted the economic disciplines and the political implications of the Treaty of Rome) in all the countries of the Six, even in his own. Unless the elephant was to encounter the baobab tree, delaying action was obviously necessary. But France alone could not prevent the entry of Britain into the Community. An ally was essential. The aged Adenauer must once again be rallied to the cause as he had been at the end of 1958 to repulse the first effort of the U.K. to get into Europe on the basis of the Free Trade Area scheme. The great manoeuvre worked.

All through the long negotiations which began in October 1961 the Germans, firmly restrained by the Chancellor, were only permitted to give moderate support to the British case; all this time the General's special project for a Franco German alliance was gradually promoted. De Gaulle's visit to Germany was a personal triumph. Adenauer was subsequently received in France as no foreign statesman had ever been received before. The German and the French Armies paraded together on the fields of Champagne: together the two leaders knelt before the High Altar of Rheims Cathedral. Internationally, the Treaty would secure the General's rear. Internally, while the referendum of October 1962 had only been a moderate success, the ensuing elections were a triumph. For the first time a single party—his own—had achieved a majority in the French Parliament. De Gaulle was clearly at the height of his power and was clearly now able to strike. But was it inevitable that he would strike? Opinions differ.

Many of those most competent to judge believe that the decision to break was probably taken before the Conference between the General and Harold Macmillan at Rambouillet in December 1962, but after the visit to Paris of Hugh Gaitskell at the end of November, the subsequent Bermuda agreement between the P.M. and President Kennedy being only a convenient excuse for action. It is possible that up till about that time the General did not exclude the possibility that Britain was sufficiently 'advanced' to accept the necessary political obligations in Europe, namely the constitution of a European Political Authority which, while remaining technically within the Western Alliance, would be completely autonomous in the sense of not necessarily, in the long run, having to look to America for support. Here was the crux. How far, if at all, could Britain subscribe to any real 'Third Force' conception? Would her presence in the European fold really tend to drown it—as he suggested in his famous Press Conference of 14 January 1963—in some vague 'Atlantic Community'? But if he excluded Britain by his own positive action would it not be flouting his own repeated declarations that of course Britain could join if she accepted the Treaty of Rome, to say nothing of his famous utterances at Oxford in November 1941 to the effect that after the war the first necessity would be some form of Franco-British union? And could he even hold the Six together if he publicly administered a rebuff to 'l'Angleterre'? He must have reflected deeply before he acted. *'Ah, Dieu, l'étrange peine . . .'* Nevertheless the first veto was his greatest mistake and the beginning of his downfall.

Not that the chances for the 'vast plan' were ever very great, and it is even arguable that he never really expected to achieve anything very concrete, the plan being simply a framework in which he could manoeuvre, always keeping 'free hands' for France. In any case, the first check to the project, in so far as it was a project, came when the German Parliament approved a Preamble to the Franco-German Treaty that virtually contradicted everything that the Treaty stood for. De Gaulle then tried to assert his policy by mobilizing the 'Third World' under the leadership of France; by making a great and partially successful effort to destroy the supra-national element in the E.E.C. in 1965; by withdrawing from NATO in 1966; and by what, as he probably hoped, was to be the supreme gesture of visiting the Soviet Union at the end of that year and fruitlessly suggesting that the Russians should agree to work out some German settlement with the French over the heads of the United States of America.

But by then he had shot his bolt. It is true that at the end of 1967 he still had enough strength, though at the cost of alienating his German allies even further, to veto the second and possibly more determined effort of Britain to enter the Common Market. Internationally, however, his reputation was on the wane. Both his appeal to the Quebec nationalists and his condemnation of Israel alarmed the French nation more than anything else. 'Après-Gaullism' became the favourite subject of conversation in Paris and it is probable that ways and means would have been found of returning him to grass in Colombey-les-deux-Églises had it not been for the extraordinary 'events' on the tenth anniversary of his accession to power. Less than a year later, the General had himself taken the road back to Colombey, the nation having denied him, in the referendum of April 1969, the support to which he thought he was entitled.

All power corrupts, and genius is to madness near allied. The General's career did not altogether disprove these gloomy dicta. Fairly early on many French intellectuals came to the conclusion that, apart from his absolute belief in himself as a Leader, he had no political convictions of any kind and only did whatever was best suited to confound his enemies—and indeed his friends—at any given moment in time. Many consequently regarded him as a cunning and sinister Lucifer against whom the democratic hosts of heaven could only with difficulty prevail. I think this judgement would be exaggerated. De Gaulle was not diabolical and he was in an odd way redeemed by his perfectly genuine love-affair with France. He never consciously said 'Evil, be thou my good'. He just assumed that everything he did must be good if only for the fact that it was he (France) that did it. But though not wicked, he was nevertheless overwhelming and

374

overweening, a kind of Nietschean Superman 'on the other side of good and evil'. With us, I suppose only Cromwell had such an effect on his compatriots and contemporaries. Even Churchill was a less extraordinary man.

However prodigious, political leaders are nevertheless human and, therefore, fallible. Undoubtedly the General's chief failing—and in the long run it was disastrous—was to cast his country for a role which was beyond her power. Great though the French nation undoubtedly is, its relative importance in the world is far less than it was under Louis XIV or even than it was in 1939. What chiefly characterizes the French is their sense of 'measure'. It is arguable that a kind of Bonapartism is the natural expression of the French political genius and that this, therefore, may continue. But on the whole it seems probable—and all democrats must hold it to be desirable— that after a heroic period they will abandon the pursuit of grandeur and revert to a more normal role as a great co-operative member of Western Society, sharing the leadership of the new Europe which we hope to see established not only with Britain but with Germany and Italy as well. De Gaulle's great achievement was to bring his countrymen out of their sense of 'inferiority' based on defeat and occupation, and notably out of any sense of inferiority as regards 'l'Angleterre'. It is on that rather than on his 'vast plan' that his reputation will surely rest, along with Charlemagne and Saint Louis and the Maid of Orleans, in the legendary annals of Gaul.

In my speech at the enormous banquet at the Elysée which he gave my wife and me when we left the Embassy, I quoted the tremendous words of Chateaubriand. *'Rien n'est plus vain que la gloire à moins qu'elle n'ait fait vivre l'amitié, qu'elle n'ait été utile à la vertu, secourable au malheur'.* Like other great rulers of France, against whom he can indeed be measured, the General's path of glory led but to the grave. Like them, the good that he did will not altogether be buried with his bones. Let the British and the French, now that the reign of him who restored French confidence and belief in France's destiny is over, combine, as equals, in the construction of that Europe which, within the Western Alliance, cannot be formed without the presence of both. That would be the best tribute of all to the vanished giant.

Kenyatta

by
Malcolm MacDona

MALCOLM MACDONALD (b. 1901), son of the first Socialist Prime Minister of Britain, having been educated at Bedales School and the Queen's College, Oxford, embarked on a meteoric political career. A member of Parliament at twenty-eight, he remained in the House of Commons for sixteen years. He was a junior Minister in Mr Ramsay MacDonald's National Government at the age of thirty and entered the Cabinet in the Baldwin National Government formed in 1935 when still in his thirties. He was Secretary of State for the Colonies and for Dominions Affairs from 1931 to 1940, and then for a brief period Minister of Health in Mr Churchill's war-time Government. Thereafter his public service lay in the Dominions and Commonwealth, encompassing a variety of appointments which few men have achieved. These included U.K. High Commissioner in Canada (1941-46); Governor-General of the Malayan Union and Singapore (1946-48); U.K. Commissioner-General in South East Asia (1948-55); U.K. High Commissioner in India (1955-60); Governor, later Governor-General, and later still U.K. High Commissioner in Kenya (1963-65); and Special Representative of the U.K. in Africa (1966-69) —a truly remarkable career. On his retirement he was appointed to the Order of Merit. Among his varied works are *People and Places* (1969) and *Titans and Others* (1972).

Jomo Kenyatta

approx. 1893	Born.
1909	Attended Church of Scotland mission school.
1913	Indian National Congress formed in East Africa to complain that Indians had no representation on the Legislative Council.
1916	Went to live in Nairobi.
1919	Origin of East African Association in which Harry Thuku was prominent.
1920	Founding of the Kikuyu Association to press for redress of grievances, such as alienation of land to white immigrants.
1921	Harry Thuku was Secretary of radical Young Kikuyu Association concerned with land and labour grievances.
March 1922	Harry Thuku arrested—led to disturbances.
1924	Kikuyu Central Association (K.C.A.), successor to Young Kikuyu Association, was formed. Kenyatta joined.
1928	Kenyatta became K.C.A. secretary.
Feb. 1929	K.C.A. sent Kenyatta to London to put claims for better educational, economic, and political conditions to British Government.
Aug. 1929	Kenyatta visited U.S.S.R.
1930	Harry Thuku returned from deportation. Controversy in Kenya over female circumcision. Some schools were

Previous page: prisoner of the British, 1952. Kenyatta leaves court where he is being tried as Mau Mau suspect

closed, which led to demand for independent Kikuyu schools.

Sept. 1930 Kenyatta returned to Kenya.

May 1931 Kenyatta and colleague arrived in England as representatives of K.C.A. to present its views to Parliamentary Joint Committee on Closer Union in East Africa. Committee agreed to hear them. Kenyatta did not return to Kenya for fifteen years.

1932/3 Travelled in U.S.S.R.

1932 Gave evidence before Kenya Land Commission (Carter Commission) which decided that the Kikuyu had been illegally deprived of 100 sq. miles.

1933-36 Worked in Dept. of African Phonetics at University College, London, and taught Kikuyu at School of Oriental and African Studies.

1935 Kikuyu Provincial Association founded by Harry Thuku.

1936 Kenyatta went to London School of Economics to take diploma in anthropology under Professor Malinowski.

1938 Published *Facing Mount Kenya,* a study of the Kikuyu people.

1939 Peter Koinange returned from from America and Britain and founded Githunguri Teachers' Training College.

1940 K.C.A. declared an illegal society.

1941 Leaders of K.C.A. detained.

1943 Twelve K.C.A. leaders released from detention.

1944 Nomination of Eliud Mathu, first African member to Legislative Council.

Oct. 1944 Kenya African Study Union inaugurated to press for more land.

1945 Secret K.C.A. meetings.

Feb. 1946 K.A.S.U. renamed Kenya African Union (K.A.U.)

Sept. 1946 Kenyatta returned to Kenya.

June 1947 Kenyatta elected President of K.A.U. He advocated unqualified independence for Kenyans.

1949 Secret oathing began (to bind people to work against government), inspired by group of extremists, the 'Forty Group'. New movement came to be known as 'Mau Mau'.

Aug. 1950 Mau Mau declared an illegal society.

May 1952 Chief Waruhiu, loyal to colonial government, assassinated.

Oct. 1952 State of emergency proclaimed. Kenyatta arrested and later sentenced to seven years' imprisonment.

1956 Mau Mau rebellion ended.

March 1957 Lyttleton Plan—Africans allowed to

vote on restricted franchise, and eight Africans were elected.

1958 Lennox-Boyd constitution, giving Africans six more elected members.

1959 Kenyatta moved into less rigorous detention.

1960 Lancaster House conference promised outright majority rule in foreseeable future. Africans were promised a majority of elected members. Demands for Kenyatta's release.

1961 General election, fought by two African parties: Kenya African National Union (KANU) and Kenya African Democratic Union (KADU). KANU won most African constituencies.

Aug. 1961 Kenyatta released.

Jan. 1962 Became member of Legislative Council.

April 1962 Became a minister.

June 1963 General election, won by KANU

Dec. 1963 Kenya obtained independence.

Dec. 1964 Kenya declared a republic with Kenyatta president. KADU voluntarily dissolved.

The exact year of Jomo Kenyatta's birth is uncertain. Sometime in the early or middle 1890s he came into the world in a small hut in southern Kikuyuland where his father owned land. Traditional tribal life continued undisturbed there as it had done for centuries. Yet only about twenty miles away the recent arrival of white men heralded great changes to come.

During his childhood Kenyatta imbibed the ancient lore of the Kikuyus, first as a baby strapped on his mother's back whilst she did her farm work, then as an infant listening to his parents' teaching of the legends and customs which guided their tribe's conduct, and later as a lad herding the family's sheep and goats. His father died when he was still a boy, and he passed into the care of an unaffectionate uncle. He was devoted to his mother; but a few years later she too died. So he became an orphan. His childhood was prematurely over, and the cool relations with his uncle made him feel lonely.

He heard tales of a different world which was starting to appear alongside an extraordinary, monstrous iron serpent called a railway which queer white men, helped by brown coolie labour, had created nearby. His grandfather happened to live there, having migrated several years earlier with a group of Kikuyus seeking new land. Young teenage Kenyatta decided to join him, and walked to that strange region. It was the first demonstration of an independence and venturesomeness which were to abide with him throughout life.

His grandfather was a tribal magician whose workings of charms often guided the local community's actions. Now a decrepit old fellow, he welcomed his grandson's help in carrying around his load of equipment. So the youngster added knowledge of a medicine-man's craft to what he already knew about other hallowed customs which governed the Kikuyus' way of life. They became deep-rooted in his make-up, and continued to affect his outlook profoundly long after he moved into societies that sowed many different notions in him. His pride in being a Kikuyu, and his respect for much of their historic culture, are essential parts of his character.

But his eager, youthful desire to learn about the white man's magic, which could evidently produce astonishing novel advantages, made him take another unusual step. In 1909 by his own will he became one of the first pupils at a Church of Scotland mission school in the neighbourhood. Staying as a boarder there, he ceased to live in tribal conditions herding sheep and goats, and instead washed dishes and cooked in addition to learning reading, writing, arithmetic and the Christian faith. Some of his classmates attended the school against their parents' wishes; so a small group of a new generation of Kikuyu began to grow, partly separated from their ancestral way of life and entering a more modern, Westernized type of society. Nevertheless, Kenyatta's break with traditional African existence was only partial. During his school years he underwent a tribal initiation ceremony as well as being baptized as a Christian. He became part of two different worlds.

At school he showed himself an intelligent, lively and likeable youth; but—though a sincere Christian—he was not always ready to conform to the missionaries' discipline. Probably he felt he had gained all he could from life at their institution. The wider, changeful world into which his generation was growing beckoned nearby in a fascinating pioneer town called Nairobi. The administrative capital of Britain's East African Protectorate, it had a mixed population of white government officials and settlers, brown Asian traders and artisans, and detribalized blacks who had left their rural homes to earn money in urban employment. From 1916 onwards Kenyatta did various jobs in its neighbourhood, and during one of them lived in humble circumstances in the city itself. He welcomed this partly because he wished to continue his education: after each day's work he attended an evening class.

A difficult political situation was developing in Kenya, arising from conflicting interests among its different racial communities. After the First World War the number of white settlers was considerably increased by the granting of farms on easy terms to British ex-servicemen; and their most influential leaders (who sat as members of the Governor's advisory council) were demanding an end to colonial rule and the establishment of a self-governing Kenya ruled by themselves. The Indians, who composed a much larger part of the population, agitated for equal rights with the whites, whilst the Africans' chiefs began to press for a redress of grievances which their people suffered, such as the alienation of areas of their land to white immigrants, forced labour on those newcomers' farms, and other complaints. The African requests were made in friendly ways by the Kikuyu Association, founded in 1920 by tribal elders with missionary help. When the Indians' pleas for equal rights with the whites were rejected, their shrewd political leaders adopted the tactic of supporting also the black population's demands, and in 1921 they helped the younger, more radical natives to form a rival political body named the East African Association. Its head was a Kikuyu called Harry Thuku. Eloquent and eager, he stirred up an emotional agitation in Kikuyuland which annoyed the conservative chiefs, and prompted them to seek government aid against him. In 1922 he was arrested. African workers in Nairobi went on strike, and a partly inquisitive and partly angry crowd gathered outside the police quarters where Thuku was detained. The police opened fire on them, and many people were killed. The East African Association broke up, and Thuku remained in detention without trial for many years. But a spark of African political fervour had been lit which would later flicker into flame.

Shortly after Thuku's arrest Kenyatta started a job in the service of Nairobi's municipal council. Its pay improved his material circumstances. He built a modest house for himself and his wife, bought rather smart clothes, and acquired a bicycle. He had taken no part in the political movement stirring among his fellow tribesmen, although many of his school-educated contemporaries had. He remained more interested in other activities. His reputation in Nairobi began to grow as a jocular, intelligent and exuberant lover of a gay life.

At some parties he met young Kikuyus concerned with public affairs. In conversations he naturally agreed with their views on current problems such as their tribe's desire to recover alienated land. Discontent about this

381

and other grievances was spreading, and the unresponsive attitude of the government made even some of the traditional chiefs begin to agree with the more outspoken attitude of the new generation of political thinkers. In the mid-1920s a fresh organization to propagate their cause called the Kikuyu Central Association was formed. Its officers sought Kenyatta's help in translating into English letters which they sent to government authorities. He did this for money, and still showed no particular political interest. Gradually, however, he became more involved. The K.C.A. leaders appreciated his capacities, and in 1928 they persuaded him to become the Association's secretary.

One of its aims was to spread its influence throughout Kikuyuland in order to reduce earlier regional divisions and encourage tribal unity. To help him in promoting this purpose Kenyatta was given a motor-bicycle on which he rode widely, forming many branches of the K.C.A. His novel 'piki-piki' vehicle as well as his genial personality excited enthusiasm wherever he went. He was hail-fellow-well-met with everyone, and became a popular figure.

But he acted cautiously, partly fearing that if he provoked hostility among the Colonial officials they would lock him up in detention, as they had done to Thuku. Another reason was his and his colleagues' moderation in their outlook on public affairs. They wished to forward their cause by loyal cooperation with the British government, and indeed with friendliness towards the white and brown residents in their shared homeland. In those days they entertained no thought of suggesting an end to Colonial rule.

Nevertheless, their rising concern at the Africans' unfair treatment made them determined to press firmly as well as peacefully the natives' claims to better economic, educational and political conditions. A mood of criticism of colonialism which was gradually spreading among populations in dependant countries all round the world communicated itself to peoples in various countries across the 'Dark Continent'. And since the Governor and his officials in Nairobi seemed unsympathetic to their case, the K.C.A. decided to send a representative to put it directly to the authorities in London. Early in 1929 Kenyatta arrived there to do so.

Naturally his experiences in a modern Western country were in many ways a revelation to an African who had never before left his native land, and inevitably they caused significant developments in his thinking. For nine months government officials in Whitehall (not to mention Ministers) sent no written reply to a reasoned petition which he submitted on behalf of the K.C.A. to the Secretary of State for the Colonies, and they showed equal reluctance to invite him for a talk with them. He sat around impatiently. Whilst thus frustrated he met many other people for friendly discussions about African affairs in general and the Kenyan problem in particular. Among them were West African intellectuals who were demanding complete self-rule for their countrymen, members of the Labour Party who advocated a steady advance to independence for all Colonial peoples, and ex-Kenyan officials and missionaries who opposed the Nairobi administration's favouritism towards white settlers. Before long Communist agents approached Kenyatta, and he accepted an invitation to travel at their expense in several countries in Europe, including Russia. From his point of view this was mainly for sight-seeing and self-education purposes, but they of course hoped to gain Kenyatta's support for their plans to stimulate world-wide revolution.

His visit to Moscow was made without prior information to any British friends, and it aroused suspicion about his motives in some official and unofficial circles in Britain and Kenya. After his return to England viciously worded anti-Colonial interviews with him were published in Communist papers, and critics promptly dubbed him a Communist. He denied the charge, asserting that the language attributed to him was much more extreme than he had used, and that it was printed without his knowledge. Certainly speeches that he made and letters that he wrote for publication later were much more moderate.

Whatever the explanation may be, there is no doubt that his associations with all sorts of political left-wingers in Britain and elsewhere during those first travels outside Kenya caused significant developments in his personality as well as his opinions. He became more dedicated to political work. Probably he felt persuaded that the right ultimate aim for the Kenyans was self-government, although the African majority should work in friendly co-operation with the white and brown minorities in their common homeland. Perhaps he acquired not only an ambition but also a sense of destiny that he was to be their pre eminent leader. Certainly some of his British friends observed that the hitherto rather immature, inexperienced and sometimes ineffective African had become a self-confident and impressively capable, as well as more cosmopolitan, character. They were critical of some of his conduct in private life, but believed he was now a public man of importance who should be treated with respect.

The Governor and his advisers in Nairobi took a very different view. They thought him a seditious fellow who represented no important Kikuyu opinion. In their judgement the old conservative chiefs were the Africans' truly representative leaders, whose position the British authorities should not undermine by contacts with upstarts like Kenyatta. That was why the Whitehall officials refrained from seeing him for almost a year. Only when a Labour Government came into office did a junior Minister in the Colonial Office have a friendly talk and exchange correspondence with him. The new government adopted a wise policy based on their recognition of the inevitability of change in the Colonial situation in Africa as well as elsewhere. For a while a rift between the views of the authorities in London and Nairobi developed.

The Governor introduced repressive measures to curb modern-style democratic political activities by Africans. For instance, no meetings could be held among them without official permission. Partly because Kenyatta feared he might be arrested if he returned to Kenya, he delayed his departure; but late in 1930 he returned there. His prestige was now high among his compatriots because of his stay in Britain and acquaintance with important people there. They looked increasingly to him for a lead.

The British government appointed a Parliamentary Committee to consider a proposal for union between Uganda, Kenya and Tanganyika; and they announced the names of one African representative from each of those lands who were invited to London to give evidence before it. The Kenyan was an elderly Kikuyu chief. The K.C.A. requested that other spokesmen should also be invited, but the proposal was refused. They decided nevertheless to send two representatives to express their views before the Committee; and in May 1931 Kenyatta and a colleague arrived in London. As things turned out, he did not return to Kenya for fifteen years.

The Parliamentary Committee refused to see him or his companion; so that purpose of his visit to England got baulked. But he acted energetically in other fields, propagating the Kenyan Africans' case in discussions at gatherings representing various sections of British public opinion. He talked, too, with many visitors from overseas, including Mahatma Gandhi who was in London attending the historic Round Table Conference on India. And he pursued another of his aims: always eager to improve his education, he studied for several months (at an English friend's expense) in a Quaker college. When the Parliamentary Committee published its report, it recommended among other things the appointment of a special commision to investigate the question of native land rights in Kenya—a proposal which the K.C.A. had long advocated. Kenyatta wrote a comprehensive memorandum for presentation to the commission; and later he himself gave verbal evidence before its chairman in London.

Among people of various shades of political opinion with whom he kept in touch were negro Communists who showed interest in the Kenyan problem. Suddenly, in August 1932, he accompanied some of them to Germany, and in the winter moved to Russia. For several months he stayed there (again at no cost to himself), partly travelling to see agricultural developments in backward regions, but mostly attending a revolutionary training course in Moscow.

In the summer of 1933 he re-appeared in England. He wished to return to Kenya, but learned that his colleague from Nairobi had pocketed their travelling expenses, and departed. Stranded with no financial resources of his own, he was compelled to rely for help on various sources.

He now felt convinced that the right ultimate solution to the Kenyan question was a complete end to colonialism and the establishment of an independent nation with democratic majority rule. In this he had moved ahead of current opinion among most of his fellow tribesmen. Deciding on reflection that the attitude of the Nairobi authorities would allow no secure place for him in Kenya at present, he resolved to continue fruitful activities in Britain. During the next few years he taught Swahili to students, assisted in a university phonetics department, studied in the British Museum reading room, acted a part in one of Alexander Korda's films, attended Professor Malinowski's course in anthropology, and wrote his book *Facing Mount Kenya* which described traditional Kikuyu culture. And all the time he continued his advocacy of the Africans' political cause in lectures, letters written to newspapers, and public speeches.

At numerous gatherings he met other adult students from various parts

384

of Africa, and they discussed the current problems of their peoples. They developed a Pan-African outlook. His was the only Kenyan voice raised among others from Africa, Asia, the Caribbean and elsewhere in the anti-Imperialist campaign which gathered momentum in the late 1930s. When Britain declared war against the threat of Nazi dictatorship throughout Europe, he and they argued that the British people who were fighting to maintain their freedom against alien rule should be equally favourable to liberty for the dependent peoples in their Empire.

During most of the war he worked as a farm labourer in Sussex; but he was also engaged as a lecturer to army education classes and other adult audiences. Being a Kikuyu accustomed to polygamy, he married an English wife. He was happy, and yet partially frustrated. His main concern remained the struggle for his fellow countrymen's freedom; but in Kenya the K.C.A. was now banned, its leaders were detained, and his contacts with them got broken. He felt home-sick. He remarked to a friend, 'I feel like a general separated by 5,000 miles from his troops'.

When the allies won the war in Europe and the Labour Party won the 1945 election in Britain the prospect of colonial peoples progressing to independence brightened. Africans from various countries stepped up their agitation, seeking in every possible way to influence British parliamentary and public opinion. Prominent among them were Nkrumah from Ghana and Kenyatta from Kenya.

Towards the end of 1946 Kenyatta decided that the time was opportune for him to return to Kenya. The war had caused significant developments in political opinion among its natives. Many young men from various tribes, for instance, had served with armed forces overseas, come in contact with Asians, Americans, Europeans and others with liberal views on racial questions, and grown resentful at the discrimination shown against them in official and unofficial white circles in their own homeland. On their return they determined to strive for their rights as the equals of other races, and this resolve was strengthened by the continuing attitude of most of the white settlers, who still pressed for an independent Konya ruled by themselves.

Kenyatta's fame as a champion of independence for the blacks had grown steadily in Nairobi, and when he arrived there he received a tumultuous hero's welcome. Slight differences between the outlooks of traditional tribal chiefs and the detribalized political leaders still lingered. Kenyatta's past associated him with the latter group, and he realized that if he was to achieve authority as a truly national leader he must establish close relations with the others too. This was helped when he married as his third wife—the second having stayed in England—a daughter of the most respected Kikuyu elder, Chief Koinange. And he showed himself an unchanging member of the tribe by farming on ancestral land near his birthplace. At the same time he played active parts in promoting modern schooling for youngsters throughout Kikuyuland, and in organizing a fresh nationalist movement among not only the Kikuyu but also other tribes.

A body called the Kenya African Union had been formed two years earlier to support the first, solitary black African representative appointed to the Legislative Council. Kenyatta was now elected its president. Although already in his fifties, none of the younger aspirants disputed his right to be their unchallenged leader. Not only his prestige but also his personality made him pre-eminent. His leonine, bearded face, brilliant qualities as 'a showman to his finger-tips', and witty as well as serious eloquence, aroused popular enthusiasm wherever he addressed mass meetings throughout the country. Yet his speeches did not seek to win support by irresponsible mob oratory; he spoke realistically more than emotionally, and often criticized his African audiences for their faults. He advocated unqualified independence for the Kenyans, but urged that the black natives should attain it by peaceful, constitutional means in friendly co-operation with their white and brown fellow countrymen.

His immense popularity with his own people, however, made him the chief object of hostility from most of the white settlers. They sought to persuade the government that he was a treacherous influence who should be banished from the scene. Their bitter antagonism grew as the difficult political situation produced a new movement among the Kikuyu called 'Mau Mau'. It was definitely anti-white, advocated violence as the means for the blacks to attain their ends, and reinstituted traditional Kikuyu oath-taking in attempts to enforce massive support. Kenyatta opposed them in public speeches—but the white settlers alleged that he secretly aided them. Conditions deteriorated as Mau Mau bands began to commit murders, first of Kikuyu opponents and then of white farmers. In October 1952 the government declared a state of emergency, and Kenyatta and other K.A.U. personalities were at once arrested. He was flown with a few of them to a remote spot in Kenya's desert northland.

At their subsequent trial Kenyatta maintained that he had consistently opposed Mau Mau, and that the charge of complicity in its activities was baseless. But, although experts who searched the masses of papers seized from his home found nothing to incriminate him, the authorities were determined to convict him. They produced a witness whose verbal evidence was accepted by the judge against that of several witnesses to the contrary. Kenyatta and his colleagues were condemned to seven years' imprisonment with hard labour. Some years later the prosecution witness confessed that his evidence had been false, having been invented in return for a promise by the Attorney General's department of both financial and educational help.

The conditions in which the prisoners were confined during the next years were in some ways cruel; but Kenyatta did not allow them to break his spirit or alter his views. He continued to argue with his fellow convicts that their political aims should be achieved by peaceful means, in friendly co-operation with the local white residents.

When his term of imprisonment ended in 1959 he was moved to a slightly less unpleasant region further south, and for the first time since his trial his African wife (the third, for his second had died sometime before his imprisonment) could be with him. He was also allowed to receive a few visitors, but otherwise remained severely restricted. In the meantime events elsewhere in the old British Empire had moved in directions which would inevitably lead to ultimate self-government in Kenya. Not only the Indians, Pakistanis and other peoples in Asia, but also the Egyptians, Sudanese and Ghanaians in Africa had gained independence. In Kenya itself slower constitutional advances had gradually increased black African representation in the legislature. Then, in 1960, the Lancaster House conference in London, arranged by the Conservative government, accepted a policy which promised outright majority rule to its peoples in the foreseeable future.

On their return to Nairobi from that conference rival African leaders formed two mutually opposed political parties to woo the voters in an impending general election. They were divided mainly on tribal grounds, one (the Kenya African National Union, or KANU) being supported mostly by the major Kikuyu and Luo tribes, and the other (the Kenya African Democratic Union, or KADU) by lesser tribes who feared domination by those two. During Kenyatta's long years of imprisonment the colonial government had tried first to discredit him completely and then to make his name forgotten among his fellow countrymen. To some extent they succeeded in rousing suspicion against him, especially among non-Kikuyu tribes. But other native circles still admired him, and they now demanded his release so that he could become their active leader. The Governor rejected the plea, striving to stimulate further hostility against him by declaring him 'a leader to darkness and death'

In the general election the KANU party won a majority of African constituencies. Its members repeated their request that Kenyatta should be freed, and refused to enter the government when the Governor again resisted. The KADU party joined the Council of Ministers with liberal white settlers, as well as official support. But the development of events inside and outside Kenya made it increasingly impossible for the authorities to maintain their opposition to the famous Kenyatta's release; and in August 1961 he returned as a free man to his home near Nairobi. He received a cheering, singing and dancing welcome from vast enthusiastic crowds.

In earlier talks with visitors during his detention he had refrained from giving support to either political party, urging that all the tribes should co-operate in one party to give unity to the new nation when it attained independence. After his release he gathered the rival leaders together in an attempt to achieve this aim. He failed, and later agreed to be the president of KANU.

Events moved fast. In January 1962 he became a member of the Legislative Council, and in April was sworn in as a Minister in a coalition administration in which the two parties did co-operate. During the next year they negotiated an agreement with the British Government and among themselves on a constitution for an independent Kenya. As soon as accord on it was reached the parties split apart again to fight another election. KANU won the contest, and in June 1963 KADU went into parliamentary opposition whilst Kenyatta became the Prime Minister of a KANU Cabinet exercising government in the nation's internal affairs. In December, Kenya graduated to complete independence, and twelve months later declared itself a republic with Kenyatta as President.

Throughout the decade since mid-1963 he has exerted supreme personal authority in fact as well as name in a government which has included other remarkably able Ministers. At the age of slightly more or slightly less than eighty—depending on the exact year of his birth—he still does so. Nor has he asserted it only over members of his original K A N U party. From the moment when he became Prime Minister his persuasive, dynamic, and masterful personality increased its influence also among opposition members of Parliament. His pleas that the various tribes should forget past rivalries and co-operate in building a united nation attracted them, and when he showed that he intended to practice what he preached by distributing important public offices to many non-Kikuyus and non-Luos, he won them over. A few days before Kenya became a republic K A D U voluntarily dissolved, most of its supporters joined K A N U, and his new government contained representatives of all the tribes. I do not suggest that he is wholly free from prejudice in favour of his own Kikuyus. Although he has given an immense share of influence in national affairs to others, several of the most vitally important positions belong to his fellow tribesmen— partly because they are often in any case the ablest local Africans. Nor do I suggest that old inter-tribal strains have disappeared into thin air. This cannot happen quickly, and they still lurk beneath the surface. But Kenyatta has made what may prove a decisive contribution to the Kenyans' progress from being a group of divided, often quarrelling tribes to becoming a cohesive modern nation.

When he became Prime Minister he stimulated another cause close to his heart. He acted boldly and generously to create not only a multi-tribal but also a multi-racial nation. Already both K A N U and K A D U included white and brown as well as black politicians among their members, for some leaders of the minority communities were adapting themselves wisely to the 'wind of change' blowing through Africa, which was bound to bring majority rule to Kenya in due course. Yet emotional African nationalism could well have ended co-operation in high affairs like government with the previously often oppressive minority races after the black majority actually attained independence. Kenyatta not only checked any such inclination, but encouraged even more friendliness. For example, he made a white farmer a Minister in his cabinet, appointed several others—including men who had been among his most bitter critics in the past—to various important national posts, and assured all the settlers that they were welcome to stay in Kenya so long as they were loyal to the new nation. Shortly afterwards he made his famous speech to an audience of white farmers in which he said, 'There is no society of angels, whether it is white, brown or black. We are all human beings, and as such we are bound to make mistakes. If I have done a wrong to you, it is for you to forgive me; and if you have done something wrong to me, it is for me to forgive you. The Africans cannot say the Europeans have done all the wrong; and the Europeans cannot say the Africans have done all the wrong. You have something to forget, just as I have. Many of you are just as Kenyan as myself.' And of his imprisonment he added, 'This has been worrying many of you; but let me tell you Jomo Kenyatta has no intention of retaliating or looking backwards. We are going to forget the past, and look

388

forward to the future. I have suffered imprisonment and detention: but that is gone, and I am not going to remember it. Let us join hands and work for the benefit of Kenya.'

Magnanimity is perhaps the rarest quality of statesmanship. It has never been more nobly shown than by Kenyatta. As a result many white residents who had resolved to leave Kenya as soon as majority rule dawned have continued to live contentedly there ever since. Kenyatta's government has treated with similar amity Asians who were ready to be loyal citizens of independent Kenya.

Kenyatta would be the first to admit that he has his weaknesses as well as strengths. Alongside a streak of pride in him at being a historic leader of his people lies a sense of humility because he knows that he is a mere man with his share of human faults. In many matters he has shown superlative wisdom, but in others he has made mistakes. There is no room in this short biographical sketch to analyse comprehensively the lights and shades in his character. I shall only comment on one matter which indicates some of them.

After his visits to Russia many people thought he had become at least Communist inclined. I doubt whether he ever did. Probably two main reasons prompted him to go to Moscow. First, all his expenses were paid, and he was ready to exploit for his own benefit any such generosity from whatever source it came. Eager to improve his knowledge of the world by seeing fresh parts of it, he was willing to give benefactors an impression that he agreed with them about current problems if that were necessary to achieve his purpose. There were times in his younger years when, as a result, he appeared to be all things to all men. Second, at the time of his Russian visits he was still a comparative novice in political affairs. He was feeling his way, studying various ideas, and gradually forming his own views. His desire was to serve his people, but he was not yet certain what would be the best way for them to achieve their aims. He must explore every alternative, and the Russian revolutionaries might be able to teach him something. My guess is that on examination he rejected their notions. For one thing, he was not primarily concerned with class, but with race. He wished to uplift his fellow countrymen not because they were workers, but because they were Africans. Proud of his Kikuyu heritage, he believed the black tribesmen were fundamentally the equals of human beings of any other colour, and he wished them to be so recognized by all the white, brown and other races. And just as he was not interested in Marxist class war, so also he did not want racial war. There may have been moments when he wondered whether racialist white men among the administrators and settlers in Kenya would allow the blacks to gain their rights by peaceful means. At some periods his language was bitter. Indeed, he sometimes warned that if constitutional methods were not permitted to succeed, violence would inevitably break out—from which everyone, including his own people, would suffer. He therefore always hoped that peaceful means would succeed. It seems clear, for example, that he never agreed with the Mau Mau way of doing things. One reason for my expressing this view is that I know from my personal association with him since the beginning of 1963 that he is blessed with not only a very wise head but also a very warm heart. He is full of kindness, and hates cruelty.

I do not suggest that he is a prim pacifist who would never in any circumstances resort to physical violence. If circumstances arose in which he thought it the only means of achieving a vital end, I believe he would support it. He may sometimes have condoned it. I admit that occasionally I have seen not only a mischievous look—for he is often full of fun—but a flash of wickedness in his eyes. There may well be a touch of a devil as well as a chunk of an angel in this fascinating, lovable and great man.

He never proposed that the Africans should push the white men out of their their country. Believing earnestly that blacks, white, browns and others are all brothers, he always intended that the independent Kenya of his dreams should be a land where everyone of various races and creeds lived as friends together, the majority community treating the minorities with absolute fairness as fellow citizens. One could quote many words spoken by him to that effect at significant moments through the last fifty years— and his deeds during the last ten confirm his absolute sincerity.

In these times of many difficult and delicate inter-racial problems peoples all round the world could learn a lot from his humanity.

The author would like to thank Mr Jeremy Murray-Brown for kindly letting him read a proof copy of his admirable biography of Jomo Kenyatta before it was published.

Mao
by CP Fitzgerald

C. P. FITZGERALD (b. 1902) was educated at Clifton College and the School of Oriental and African Studies. Between 1923 and 1939 he lived, with short intervals, in China, mainly in Peking but also in Wuhan and Nanking, and, in the last three years, at Tali, Yunnan Province. He was awarded a Leverhulme Fellowship. After war service in London, he returned as the British Council Representative to north China. In 1951 he was appointed Professor of Far Eastern History at the Australian National University, Canberra, and continued to visit China and south-east Asia. He was made Professor Emeritus on his retirement in 1969.

Professor FitzGerald has written numerous books and articles on China, including, *China: a Short Cultural History* (1962 and 1965); *The Birth of Communist China* (1964); *The Chinese View of Their Place in the World* (1969); *Barbarian Reds: the Origin of the Chair in China* (1965).

Mao Tsetung

26 Dec. 1893	Born in Shaoshan village, Hunan province.
1900	Peking occupied by allied troops after Boxer rebellion.
1910	Went to Tungshan Primary School in Hsiang-hsiang.
1911	Went to Ch'angsha to attend Middle School. Embraced republicanism and joined revolutionary army.
22 Oct. 1911	Revolution in Ch'angsha against imperial regime (Manchu).
1912	Demobilized and admitted into Hunan First Middle School. Became acquainted with west European books. Ch'ing dynasty came to an end with abdication of the last Emperor. Now military-type government of 'Warlords'.
1913	Entered Teachers' Training School.
1917	China participated in World War I on side of Allies. Attempt to restore Ch'ing dynasty. War in Mao's home province of Hunan. Russian Revolution and advance of Bolshevik regime into eastern Siberia, contiguous to China.
April 1918	Mao graduated. He and friends formed New Citizens' Society.
Sept. 1918	Went to Peking to work as assistant in Peking University library, where he became well-acquainted with doctrines of Marxism. Met Li Ta-chao, best of early Chinese Communist theorists.
March 1919	Taught in primary school on Ch'angsha.
May 1919	May 4th Movement. Chou En Lai and others founded socialist groups.
March 1920	Chinese Communist youth group started in Paris. One of founder-members was Chou En Lai.

Previous page: fifty-five Chinese girls produced this silk-embroidered tapestry for Chairman Mao

Sept. 1920 Mao organized Communist groups in Ch'angsha and Shanghai. Other Communist groups started elsewhere.

July 1921 Mao attended First Congress of Chinese Communist Party in Shanghai.

Oct. 1921 Became Secretary of Hunan Committee of C.C.P. and married Yang K'ai-hui.

Nov. 1922 Elected Chairman of Association of Trade Unions of Hunan.

Jan. 1923 U.S.S.R. supplied Nationalist Party (Kuomintang) with arms and money to set up a government in Canton.

Jan. 1924 Mao elected a member of Central Executive Committee of Kuomintang, which did not wish to unite with Communists, but would admit individual members.

May 1925 May 30th Movement: anti-foreign and nationalist agitation.

Aug. 1925 Mao editor of *Political Weekly*.

July 1926 Chiang Kai-Shek ordered mobilization of Kuomintang troops, who had been trained by Russian advisers. Seized whole Yangtze valley.

1927 Communist Party in Shanghai organized uprising which seized control of Chinese-ruled part of city.

April 1927 Clash between Chiang Kai-Shek's men—who opposed leftward trend of the revolution—and Communists. Communists were massacred.

1 Aug. 1927 A division of the army under Communist officers raised Red Flag at Nanchung and proclaimed itself the Red Army.

Aug. 1927 Mao led Autumn Harvest Uprising to raise countryside to Communist side. Was captured by Nationalist soldiers but escaped. Joined Red Army's retreat into mountains.

1930 Mao's wife Yang K'ai-hui executed by Kuomintang. Mao married Ho Tzu-chen.

Oct. 1930 Mao took Chian and created Kiangsi Provincial Soviet Government.

1932-4 Kuomintang campaigns against Communists.

Oct. 1934 Communist armies were forced back 7,000 miles into west China—the Long March.

Jan. 1935 On Long March, at small town of Tsunyi Mao was elected Chairman of Communist Party.

Dec. 1936 The Red capital was moved to Yenan —a challenge to Nationalist regime in Nanking.

July 1937 Japanese attack in north China. Japanese occupied nearly half the country until 1945.

1939 Mao married Lan-p'ing.

1937-45 During war Communist Party applied own system of government in areas it won back from Japanese.

1945 Japanese surrender. Danger of civil war between Communists and Nationalists. U.S. sent General George Marshall to China as mediator.

1947 Civil war began.

Nov. 1948 Manchurian campaign in which Nationalists defeated by Communists.

Dec. 1948 Communist siege of Peking.

April 1949 Peace negotiations between Communists and Nationalists failed. Communists took Nanking.

May 1949 Communists took Shanghai and Wuhan.

1 Oct. 1949 Mao proclaimed Peoples' Republic of China. Remnants of Nationalist forces had withdrawn to Taiwan island.

Dec. 1949 Mao visited Stalin in U.S.S.R.

1955-6 Higher Stage Co-operative land reform abolished individual tenure.

1958-9 Creation of Land Communes.

1958 'Great Leap Forward' aimed at equalling steel production of Britain in fifteen years. Emnity developed between Mao and Khrushchev.

1959 Opposition to Mao's Commune programme and to quarrel with U.S.S.R.

1959-65 Cultural Revolution—to create a nation dedicated to service of the revolution. Agents were Red Guards, students of 14-20 years of age.

1960 U.S.S.R. withdrew experts from China.

1964 China exploded her first nuclear device.

1970 Communist government of China won recognition in U.N.

1972 President Nixon of U.S. visited China.

Many of the great prime movers in revolution and political change in the past two centuries have been men who were not identified by birth with the countries which later formed the scene of their careers; Napoleon, the Corsican, Hitler the Austrian, Stalin the Georgian, did not devote their lives to their native lands, but rather to the greater expansion of the more powerful states which had incorporated their own home countries. Mao Tsetung, on the contrary, is pure Chinese, coming from a central region of China which was perhaps one of the least open to the foreign influences and political pressures of outside powers. Although, as a Marxist, Mao professes faith in world wide revolution, his active career has been within China and directed to aims concerned with the reconstruction and modernization of Chinese society in all its aspects. This concentration on Chinese interests has ended in the virtual division of the Communist world between the 'Old Communists' who follow Moscow and the 'Maoists' who accept the leadership of Mao and the primacy of his ideas, or 'Thoughts'. Mao himself would not see the distinction in these terms. For him, the Russians and their supporters are 'revisionists', who have strayed from the true revolutionary path, taken the 'capitalist-bourgeois road' which must end in the betrayal of the revolutionary cause. On the other hand he and his followers would believe that this is a dead-end road, from which later leaders will turn back, guided by the pure light of Mao's doctrines as practised in China.

There is much in Mao's personal history and character to explain this outlook. His education was entirely in China, and the foreign learning he acquired was wholly through the medium of Chinese interpretation. He speaks no foreign language. His early education was in the classical tradition of the old empire, under which he was born. His knowledge of the works of Marx and other Communist writers came to him only through such very partial translations into Chinese as had been made in the early decades of this century when he joined with a handful of others to found the Chinese Communist Party. He had never left China until his first journey to Moscow late in 1949 to sign the Sino-Soviet Treaty of alliance after his party had triumphed in the civil war and set up the Chinese Peoples' Republic. Deeply read in Chinese history, much of his writing reflects the traditions of Chinese statecraft re-interpreted to put the People, rather than an Emperor, as the source of sovereignty and power; but power is still exercised to uphold an all embracing orthodoxy, translated in political terms as a single centralized state which claims ideological conformity as well as obedience to its laws and authority. Mao Tsetung, in fact, is essentially a Chinese. The thrust of his new ideology is more potent than a time-worn Confucianism could be, his authority more far reaching and complete than the most powerful emperors of the past could achieve with the limited technology of their epoch.

The scale of his achievement would have appeared improbable to the last degree to men of his youth and early manhood. China, to natives and foreigners alike, appeared to be the most conservative human society; the past was venerated, the present deplored, the future seen with little hope. True, the Chinese people were admired for their past artistic creativity, their endurance and industry; but admiration for their fortitude in adversity shaded into contempt for their passive acceptance of corrupt, inefficient and archaic rulers, their tolerance of a social system which had long outlived its origins and its capacity for adaptation. To revive China, renew her strength, assert her ancient power and make her once more the model and teacher of her world was the aim of all the reformers and revolutionaries from the last quarter of the nineteenth century down to our own times. Their methods differed, their ideas were sometimes contradictory, but their purpose was identical. One key to Mao's success was that he built upon this concealed unity of purpose recognized throughout the educated class, and sensed by those who lacked learning. The second key to success was the understanding of the social needs of his people, and a just appreciation of how their support could be won. Mao has always, it would seem from boyhood, admired the folk heroes of popular Chinese literature; the heroic opponents of corrupt and evil rulers, the just men driven into outlawry by tyranny, who defend the poor and take revenge upon the oppressors. These were the books which the young Mao read, books which the Manchu Dynasty frowned upon, and half-heartedly tried to suppress. But Mao saw the flaw in the careers of these heroes. Sooner or later, beguiled, or won over by the clemency of the ruling class under a more enlightened despot, they abandon their opposition, accept pardon for themselves and their followers and enjoy a happy old age—within the system.

In truth the great peasant rebels of the past had no ideology of their own; they sought to capture the system and make it work more justly, not to overthrow it and substitute a wholly new pattern of society. Mao can be seen as the latest and greatest of the long line of peasant rebel leaders, stretching back for upwards of two thousand years; he is also without doubt the first to inspire his movement with a new objective, not to capture and enjoy the flesh pots of the old system of power, but to destroy them for ever and substitute the direct rule of the People themselves, operating through the instrument of their creation, which was the Communist Party of China. When, in the 1960s, Mao came to doubt whether this instrument was not itself becoming rusted and corrupted, he turned upon it and virtually destroyed it; to reconstruct it in a form which he hopes will be proof, for a time, against further deterioration. But he has clear-sightedly declared that renovation new Cultural Revolutions—will be needed in the future. Whether his successors will have the ability or the dedication to follow this prescription cannot be forseen.

If the real motivation of Mao Tsetung's career was the renovation of Chinese society, it may be asked why is he a Communist? Or more precisely, is he a Communist because the message of Marx has a world-wide significance for him; or because Communism happened to be, at the time when Mao was seeking an ideology which could revive Chinese society, the latest of the many Western systems which had become known in China, and the one which seemed to be least esteemed by the rulers of what Mao and his fellow countrymen all agreed to be the imperialist aggressor powers? 'The enemy of mine enemy is my friend.' It was axiomatic to men of Mao's generation, however nationalist their sentiments, that viable political and social ideas must derive from the West. Not because they were foreign, but because they were modern; Chinese experience was no longer seen as relevant, China had never produced a real alternative to absolute monarchy, even if scholars knew that the character of the monarchy had changed with the centuries. The changes were not sufficient for the modern age of active involvement in the international jungle of predatory beasts. Useless to claim that all the ruler of China needed was virtue, and the barbarians would come in reverence to his throne.

Mao became a Communist after he had studied other Western systems, had seen the collapse and failure of the attempt to establish parliamentary democracy, and recognized that superficial changes such as arbitrary Presidents in place of hereditary Emperors did nothing to alleviate the burdens of the mass of the people or revitalize society. The Communist system appeared to him, as to many of his contemporaries in China, better; firstly because it was anti-imperialist and promised a way in which China could be freed from foreign pressure; secondly because it seemed to offer a more thorough and complete social transformation, not merely a political solution which left the real social problems untouched. The weakness of the original anti-Manchu revolution of 1912 had been that its leaders had total faith in political changes, a Republic for the Monarchy; and no knowledge of and no programme for the basic questions of social inequalities, the archaic land tenure system, nor the stagnant economy.

Great revolutionary leaders rarely derive from the poorest of the poor. In China only one of the dynastic founders had such an origin, and very many years passed before he was strong enough to dream of a throne. Mao was not a 'poor peasant', the category most honoured today, meaning men who had either no land of their own, and worked for hire, or held such minute plots that they had to seek outside work to keep their families alive. Mao was, by modern ratings, from a 'middle' or even a 'rich peasant' family. His family home in Shaoshan village, Hunan province, is today a national monument and attests the status of the family. It is no hovel, but a well built and reasonably commodious farm house. Mao was sent to school, at an old fashioned classical-learning school, although he did farm work in holidays and spare time. His father employed labour on the farm, all characteristics of the upper segment of peasant farmers, and far above the desperate poverty and hardships of the real poor. These facts are not denied nor concealed; the great virtue seen in Mao is that he did not become a supporter of his mildly exploiting class, but the champion of the dispossessed, the architect of a new society. The elder Mao was a typical traditional Chinese *pater familias*, severe, authoritarian, ultra-conservative. Mao's mother was a devout Buddhist. It was not from family influence that the young Mao Tsetung acquired revolutionary ideas.

These were introduced to him through the medium of his later education. At the age of twenty, after a brief period in the revolutionary army formed at the time of the overthrow of the Manchu dynasty, Mao decided to become a teacher, and entered, in 1913, the First Teacher's Training School in Ch'angsha, the provincial capital of Hunan. It was to prove a decisive move. Hunan, and Ch'angsha its chief city, have long enjoyed a double reputation, for producing fine scholars and ardent warriors. Ch'angsha alone, under the leadership of its scholar gentry, withstood the Taiping Rebellion in the sixties of the last century, and it was from Hunan that the Chinese army which finally conquered the Taipings was recruited, led by the same men, in the service of the almost helpless dynasty.

Hunan, in northern Chinese eyes, is a southern province; but to the Cantonese of the far south, it is the north. It lies just south of the Yangtze River, and can be seen as the very heart of China. In speech it falls within the wide range of what was called 'Mandarin' (now Standard Speech) even if the Hunan accent is strange to many northern ears. As the site of an ancient kingdom, Chu, which long opposed the northern powers of ancient China, it has always remained somewhat distrustful of northern rule, self reliant, proud of its scholarly record and of its military history. Significantly not only Mao but the majority of the top leaders of the Communist Party came from Hunan, or neighbouring districts in adjoining provinces. Hunan, and Ch'angsha, was thus a centre of learning, but not only of the old classical learning. Modern revolutionary ideas were active, the schools were seed-beds of these movements; the armed forces had been early won to the revolutionary cause. Nevertheless, the scholar gentry still dominated society, being more concerned with the survival of their class, its outlook and its traditional role, than with the fate of any alien dynasty. In Hunan, as in most of the centre and south of China the revolution of 1912 was primarily the overthrow of the northern, alien Manchus, not the social change which the younger generation were beginning to seek.

Already as a young student Mao joined wholeheartedly in this search. He began to contribute articles to the local papers which were highly critical of the old culture and its customs. It was in these years, in 1915, that 'Ch'ing Nien' ('La Jeunesse') the most famous critical journal of the age began to appear in Peking. Its contributors numbering almost all those celebrated in Chinese literature, political thought, and revolutionary leadership in subsequent years. At Teacher's Training School Mao Tsetung also met and studied under men who had been to Europe, read and spoke foreign languages, and opened to him a wider world of Western learning. These men were also liberals, or moderate revolutionaries, deeply concerned with the fallen status of China. When Mao Tsetung graduated in 1918 he obtained a very minor post in the Library of Peking University. That institution, already the leader in China, was the centre of the movements of thought and reform for the whole country. Reform of the written language to make it accessible to the masses of illiterate people, reform above all of the corrupt and lamentable government, now in the hands of military despots ('the Warlords'), and also of the whole structure of society. To Western observers who did not read Chinese the condition of the country had never seemed more hopeless, decadent, and deplorable. But behind this decaying façade was a most active intellectual ferment embracing almost the entire younger generation, dedicated to revolution of a more thorough type, although far from unanimous on methods or even on ends. This society had just been stirred to even more passionate dispute and concern by two events; the Russian Revolution, and the advance of the Bolshevik regime into eastern Siberia, contiguous to China itself; and the decision of the Versailles peace makers to allot the former German leased territory and railway in Shantung province to Japan, and not to return it to China; even though China had been a participant on the allied side since 1917. In 1919, a year after Mao arrived in Peking, the concurrence in this decision by the corrupt central government led to major student riots in Peking, supported by faculty members and by the general public, which sparked off the 'May Fourth 1919 Movement'—now recognized as one of the major developments in the Chinese Revolution. Mao himself has said 'The May Fourth Movement came into being at the call of the Russian Revolution of Lenin'. At that time the Chinese Communist Party did not exist.

Mao met in Peking two scholars of the university who were among the founders of that Party, two years later: Li Ta-chao and Ch'en Tu-hsiu. The former is now regarded as the best theorist of the early Chinese Communists, until his death in 1927 at the hands of the reactionary Warlord government of the day. Ch'en became the first General Secretary of the Chinese Communist Party, but was later discarded. By 1921 Mao had left his Peking job, had travelled south, and was one of the eleven (or by some accounts thirteen) who met clandestinely in Shanghai to found the Chinese Communist Party. A branch founded almost simultaneously among the Chinese students in Paris soon amalgamated. One of its founder members was Chou En-lai. Many of the original members are dead; some changed sides in later life; but Mao and Chou have from that time onward never ceased to occupy ever more important positions in the Chinese Communist Movement, and today are the leaders of their nation.

Dr Sun Yat-sen, leader of the old revolutionary anti-Manchu party, now renamed Nationalist Party (Kuomintang), was at this time also living in Shanghai, out of power. Within a year he had met Adolf Joffe, emissary of the new Soviet Union government, and concluded with him agreements by which the U.S.S.R. supplied him with arms, munitions and money so that he could re-establish himself in Canton, setting up a government which he asserted to be the only legitimate heir of the Republic. The Western powers would not grant Dr Sun this status, but continued to deal with the Warlord regime in Peking, under its constantly displaced leadership. The Nationalist Party, while affirming that it did not consider China a suitable country for a Communist system, admitted the individual members of the Chinese Communist Party as members of the Nationalist Party, while eschewing union between the two organizations. On these terms Mao soon went to Canton where he conducted an agency devoted to stirring up agitation in the rural areas into which it was hoped the new Nationalist Army would advance on its road to Peking and power. The headquarters of this institution, now also a national monument, were lodged in the former Confucian Temple, a venerable building thus preserved for posterity.

One of the main turning points in modern Chinese history was now at hand. One year after the death of Dr Sun Yat-sen in 1925 (a year which had also been marked by violent and intense national feeling aroused by a foreign Settlement police shooting in Shanghai), the army of the

Canton government, re-equipped and trained by Russian advisers and led by officers, some of whom, like their Commander, Chiang Kai-shek, had trained in Russia, took the offensive. The Warlords of the provinces, like the Warlord in power in Peking, had all lost 'face' in Chinese eyes from their supine inability to assert China's rights, or manifest any overt patriotism in the tense months of nationwide anti-foreign and nationalist agitation from 30 May to the end of 1925, and later. They were divided by rivalries and jealousies; their men had no interest in fighting for them, no sound training, and very poor equipment. Consequently they went down like ninepins before the relatively weak thrust of the Canton government's forces. By the end of the campaigning season, November 1926, the Nationalist armies had seized the whole Yangtze valley down to Nanking. Early in the spring of 1927 when the advance was resumed, the Chinese Communist Party in Shanghai organized an uprising which seized control of the Chinese ruled part of that city. One of the organizers was Chou En-lai. Mao Tsetung was then back in his native Hunan, organizing rural agitation in support of the campaign, but also laying the foundations for a more Communist orientated movement which he hoped would later take control of the Revolution.

This was indeed the crux; the rich bankers and merchants of Shanghai were sincerely Nationalist, opposed to the corrupt and tyrannous Warlords; but they were not Communists, nor supporters of social revolution. Chiang Kai-shek, who had connections with these classes also opposed the leftward trend of the Revolution, particularly manifest in the government itself, which had moved north from Canton to Wuhan, the great triple city of the middle Yangtze (Wuchang, Hankow, Hanyang). In April 1927, after Chiang's regulars had arrived at Shanghai, there occurred the inevitable clash. Chiang attacked, disarmed, and massacred the Communists and their supporters in Shanghai. This 'blood-bath' was never forgotten, and vengeance for it exacted twenty-two years later. Before long, setting up a right wing Nationalist regime in Nanking, Chiang obtained the submission of the former government in Wuhan. The Communists were expelled from the Nationalist Party, their leaders proscribed. On 1 August 1927 a division of the Army under Communist officers raised the Red Flag at Nanchang, in Kiangsi province, and proclaimed itself the Red Army. It was commanded by Chu Teh, the ultimate architect of Communist victory in 1949, and one of its junior officers was Lin Piao. From this day the Red Army, later renamed Peoples' Liberation Army, fought first the Nationalists then the Japanese, and once more the Nationalists until final victory in 1949.

Mao Tsetung, in Hunan, had been organizing the 'Autumn Harvest Uprising' designed to raise the countryside to the Communist side in the burgeoning civil war. The activities of the Communist Party, which was still tolerated in Wuhan, and its attempts (under Stalin's orders) to continue co-operation with the Nationalist regime in Wuhan led to many obscure events at this time. It is probable that Mao was dismissed from his post by the appeasing leadership; it has been alleged that he was expelled from the Party. Documents are lost, memories are discreet; it may be many years before the real history of those tense days is known. It is at least clear that in late 1927 Mao was 'on the run' in Hunan, was once captured by Nationalist

401

soldiery, but was not recognized, and thus escaped. He fled with a few followers to the wild mountain borders of Kiangsi and Hunan provinces, the ancient bandit stronghold of Chikang-shan. There a short time later he was joined by the battered remnants of Chu Teh's Red Army, which had failed to seize and hold several large southern cities, a plan laid down by the Russian advisers. Virtually fugitives, Chu Teh led his men to the same wild refuge in the mountains. Yet from this meeting, and the steady reorganization of armed forces and political action to win peasant support, the later power of the Chinese Communist Party derived. No one at the time even knew of the event, or would have known of those concerned in it either. It was some time before Chiang Kai-shek and the Nationalist regime realized that the embers were still burning, and rising in a new flame.

Chiang had had other preoccupations; the conquest of the North; and then the beginning of Japanese intervention in Manchuria (1931). When he realised that the Communist strength was reviving and spreading in south China, he endeavoured to crush it with overwhelming force. In the years between 1932 and 1934 five 'bandit extermination campaigns' were launched against the Communist area, which had grown to comprise a large part of the province of Kiangsi. The first four, although engaging the main strength of the government armies, in the end numbering nearly 500,000 men, were all repulsed, and with heavy losses to the attackers. The fifth campaign, mounted with a close blockade, on the advice of Chiang's German military advisers, forced the Communist armies to break out on the famous Long March. Taking a full year, and traversing some 7,000 miles in the far interior of West China, this finally brought them to a secure haven in the north-west, in Shensi province near the city of Yenan (1935).

During this period of intense warfare the rise of Mao Tsetung to leadership occurred, not without checks and opposition. The Shanghai Central Committee, living 'underground' in the Foreign Settlement, and still controlled by the Moscow returned student leadership favoured by Stalin, proved itself ineffective and divisive in leadership. In constant danger of discovery it finally migrated, secretly, to the Kiangsi stronghold, and for a time constituted the effective supreme leadership there. There were certainly disputes, disagreements on policy, and probably on personalities during this time; much of the detailed history is still unrevealed, and controversial. Mao himself has attributed the final need to abandon the area to the errors committed in tactics and strategy—and he does not acknowledge that these were his errors, but clearly attributes them to the former Shanghai leaders. This view seems to have prevailed, for at the small town of Tsunyi, in Kueichow province, on the Long March in early 1935, Mao was elected Chairman of the Chinese Communist Party, a post which he has held from that day to the present time, thirty-eight years.

As unchallenged leader he conducted the Long March to a successful conclusion, although at great cost, and became, in Yenan, the head of a government which more and more posed a real challenge to the Nationalist regime in Nanking.

The Yenan period, as it is usually called, constitutes the time when on the one hand the Japanese invasion changed the military and political situation, ultimately in favour of the Communist Party; and also the period when Mao wrote most of his best known works on revolutionary purpose, methods and strategies. Politically it was his most constructive period, when the guidelines for a future Communist government were laid down. It would seem that Mao himself now never really doubted that ultimate victory would be his. In late 1936, the Nationalist army which Chiang was about to launch upon Yenan in another 'extermination campaign', mutinied at Sian, and took Chiang himself prisoner. The mutineers, led by their commanding general, Chang Hsueh-liang, son of the former Manchurian Warlord, demanded an end to civil war and national unity against the imminent Japanese invasion. Chiang, aided by the mediation of the Communists, Chou En-lai being their emissary, was compelled to agree, or face execution. A truce was called, and the two sides, in apparent amity, prepared for the war with Japan. This was provoked by a Japanese attack in north China on 7 July 1937.

The war which followed, leading to a Japanese occupation of nearly half the country, the passive resistance in the west of the Nationalists entrenched beyond the impassable Yangtze gorges, and the active guerilla campaigns of the Communist armies within the occupied area, lasted until the Japanese surrender in 1945. It transformed the Chinese world. The small and harried Communist Party and army of 1935 now controlled some ninety million people, in North China; it had a large battle-trained army, and an immense militia raised from the peasantry of every village. It had won the confidence of the masses in the so-called Occupied Areas, and applied its own legislation and system of government in the expanding 'Liberated Areas' won back from the Japanese. It was a formidable rival to the corrupt, inefficient and depressed armies of the central government, now once more established in Nanking. The obvious danger of civil war induced the U.S. government to send General George Marshall to China as a mediator. His sincere efforts failed in the face of profound mutual distrust between Communists and Nationalists aggravated by many local clashes, and the memory of the treacherous attack carried out by Nationalist forces upon the Communist Fourth Army in the midst of the war, in 1941. Negotiations broke down: open civil war began in early 1947. It soon became obvious that in spite of ephemeral advances in non-strategic areas, the Nationalist side was failing in its main objective, to establish control of and communication with Manchuria, which the Russians, having ejected the Japanese, had in turn evacuated. The second objective was to restore communications between the Yangtze valley and North China, which had been cut, passing through Communist held 'Liberated Areas'. By 1948 the defeat of the Nationalists in both campaigns was certain. Late in that year their forces, totally routed near Mukden, surrendered in Manchuria; and in the last months of 1948 the great battle of Huai Hai (Huai River and Lung Hai railway) north of Nanking, in which more than a million men were engaged on the two sides, ended in the complete destruction of the Nationalist army. The Communists advanced to the banks of the Yangtze, opposite Nanking. The first months of spring 1949 saw the end of the Nationalist regime. Nanking and Shanghai fell with little resistance. The southern provinces followed, the West surrendered. By 1 October 1949, the date on which the Peoples' Republic of China was proclaimed in Peking, the remnants of the Nationalist forces had withdrawn to Taiwan island. After twenty-two years of warfare, against odds which appeared at first impossible, Mao Tsetung and the Communist Party had come to full power in China.

In one matter the Chinese Communists had failed; the negotiations in late 1948 and early 1949 to bring about an agreed surrender of the Nationalists, which would have created a government dominated by the Communists, but still the same legal recognized government of China, broke down. Consequently the Communists now ruled by right of conquest. Chiang called his regime in Taiwan the government of China, and the U.S. continued for many years to recognize it as such. The government of China in Peking had a long journey before it, until world wide recognition and China's seat in the U.N. were won in 1970.

The first task which faced the new government over which Mao presided was the restoration of communications and the revival of the economy. All railways had been disrupted, in many cases destroyed over long sections. Fantastic inflation had brought the Nationalist currency from the value (nominal) of four *yuan* to the U.S. dollar in August 1948 to over four million to the dollar by the end of that year. When the Communists began the siege of Peking on 12 December 1948 the population threw away the old currency. One might walk along main streets littered with high denomination notes: the people of Peking, and the defending Nationalist army, reverted to the open use of the old silver dollar, prohibited and illegal for many years, but now brought out of hiding places. Less than a year after the establishment of the Communist regime the inflation had been brought to an end, and the *yuan* stabilized at the value it has since retained. It had been predicted, that without railway communication with the northern coal fields, and with the naval blockade still maintained by the Nationalists from Taiwan, Shanghai in the winter of 1949-50 would freeze, and all industry would cease: but before the winter came the new government had restored the railway to adequate use and by strict priority brought sufficient coal to the largest city in China. Shanghai and other large eastern coastal cities had been fed by wheat and rice imported from abroad in the last years of Nationalist rule. This source being now cut off, the new regime supplied the region with grain and rice from the western province of Ssuchuan, always a surplus region, by bringing the rice down the Yangtze, for over a thousand miles, by river steamer and barges. The work of restoration, not specifically a Communist policy, but simply salvage, was carried out with astonishing speed and efficiency. It undoubtedly was a major factor in winning the support of the mass of the Chinese people.

Yet there was, by implication, a Communist aspect to this achievement. Economic factors, gain, or loss, were not taken into any account in ordering priorities. The government decided everything, gave orders, supervised their implementation; and if they reckoned the cost, did not reveal any figures to the public.

At a very early stage the first characteristic Communist policy to be inaugurated was land reform. This was not collectivization, for which the peasants were not yet ready, but distribution of all land to those who worked it, in shares as equal as topography would permit. Landlords, if exonerated from charges of oppression, and willing to work, also received their small share of their former property. At the same time the prosecution of tyrannical or oppressive landlords before Peoples' Courts, proceeded all over the country, and a large number, it is not clear what the real total was, were sentenced, more often to prison than to death. This policy was defended on two grounds. Firstly the people themselves were associated with the overthrow of the old social system and thus implicated in the government's policy. They could not claim to have been passive spectators, nor could it be said that prosecutions came only from a distant and impersonal bureaucracy. There were many acquittals. Secondly the institution of peoples' courts probably, perhaps certainly, forestalled what might have become a nation wide *jacquerie* in which much rougher justice, if any at all, would have been meted out to a class which had earned so much hatred from the peasantry.

'Land to the tiller', the slogan of the Republican Sun Yat-sen, was not a truly Communist policy. It was soon followed by the organization of co-operative teams which began to direct what should be sown and whose land should be used, while making the operation of agriculture a community task. This in turn was followed by the 'lower stage of co-operative farming', in which the whole production of the village was planned and the work carried out by the Co-operative, but the peasant still retained individual title to his land. In 1955-56 the Higher Stage Co-operatives abolished individual tenure, removed all land marks, and established a system by which the former landowner became a member of the co-operative, receiving his proportionate share of its earnings in return for his labour. Basically, this is still the system which prevails; the creation of the Communes in 1958-59 having merely combined co-operatives into larger units, at first centrally directed from the Commune headquarters; later when this proved too cumbersome and inefficient, once more subdivided for work purposes into teams more closely identified with individual villages. It is known that Mao has personally given much of his attention to the land policy: the Commune was claimed as his own contribution; although, on the spot, some Commune leaders did not appear to know this, and stated that the system had evolved in their area during the Japanese occupation. It is consonant with Mao's often expressed view that the people themselves should initiate changes and give birth to new policies, which the Party should implement, but not impose.

The reform of commerce and business in the great cities, the reduction of private enterprise to a minor place, and the institution of the 'state-private' system by which the state owns and decides policy, while the former capitalists act as directors and managers—at a reward limited to five per cent—evolved at much the same time, also by stages; but with much more direct governmental or Party intervention, and not with the same degree of support which land policy has obtained. The conversion of the great industrial and commercial city of Shanghai to the new policy was certainly not achieved without stress and tension. It is also in Shanghai that the left extremists of the Cultural Revolution found their warmest support and power base. Shanghai presented an ambivalent aspect to the new regime. On the one hand it had been the stronghold of the still very small capitalist system and class in China; on the other it was the major concentration of an industrial proletariat, long harshly oppressed, and deprived of freedom to organize. Under these circumstances both the harshness of the conversion to socialist programmes and the strength of left extremism in Shanghai are explicable.

An important aspect of the policy Mao has followed in economic development have been the changes in the direction given to industrial development. Heavy industry was at first encouraged and promoted, with impressive results which have transformed many ancient cities, particularly in North China, into modern centres of steel-making and other industry. But the 'Great Leap Forward' of 1958 aimed at equalling the steel production of the United Kingdom in fifteen years, did not reach this goal: and combined with the over-optimistic expectations from the first Commune programme, two years of exceptional drought, and the developing feud with Soviet Russia, resulted in a serious economic set-back. The political consequences of this seem, now that some information appeared during the Cultural Revolution, to have been serious, and may have been the origin of the disputes which later exploded in the Cultural Revolution. The economic effects were also serious, but China was able to recover from these within a few years. The intensification of the quarrel with Russia remained a permanent feature. The Russian withdrawal of experts and blue prints in 1960 was seen by the Chinese as a hostile act, which they do not forgive, although they claim it proved a benefit in the end by forcing them to do for themselves what had been dependent on Russian assistance. It is certainly true that one presumed objective of the Russian action, the halting of the Chinese nuclear fission programme, failed to attain that purpose. China exploded her first nuclear device four years later, in 1964, and has continued along the path of nuclear armament rather faster than Western observers at first expected.

The dispute with Russia, steadily growing more acute, began, at least in public, after the denunciation of Stalin's policies by Khrushchev in 1956. The Chinese were not forewarned of the intention to make this famous speech. They have continued to resent this treatment, and in the stream of polemics directed against the Soviet government and leadership the literary style of Mao Tsetung, earthy and salty, can easily be recognized. It became known that in 1958, at the time of the Off Shore Islands crisis and Khrushchev's visit to President Eisenhower at Camp David, bitter personal enmity developed between Mao and Khrushchev. In later years the quarrel originally predominantly ideological, came to focus on territorial claims and accusations of domination on the one side, and of subverting the unity of the Communist world on the other. An outside observer might well think both charges justified. It is certain that relations, good or bad, with Russia dominate Chinese foreign policy, and other developments and initiatives are to be understood in relation to this central preoccupation. Whether Mao Tsetung himself is a prime factor in the dispute is open to doubt; it would seem as probable that he reflects the widespread feelings of the Chinese people on the question.

406

With Lin Piao (right), at a Peking rally, 1966. Overleaf: men and girls in militia exercises

Yet Mao Tsetung is the unquestioned leader of the regime. Its policies are his, and so are the achievements. Yet after some years, from 1950 to 1959, during which there appeared no rifts in the leadership, it has now been revealed that a serious and lasting difference arose in 1959 following upon the programme of land reform which brought the Commune system into being; and also the increasing aggravation of the Sino-Soviet dispute. An opposition to the Commune programme, and to the quarrel with Russia, developed around the personality of the War Minister, P'eng Te-huai. At the Plenum meeting of the Party in the hill resort of Lushan, Mao was able to rally support and have P'eng put out of office; but he in turn was forced to yield the office of Chairman of the Government— Head of State—although he retained the more significant post of Chairman of the Communist Party. At the time the truth was concealed, but it is now

known that this move, which put Liu Shao-ch'i into the office of Chairman of the Government, represented a real challenge to Mao, and amounted to a partial defeat.

The hidden struggle continued for the next six years; slowly Mao, using the army and its new War Minister, Lin Piao, as his main power base, began to prepare his counter attack. This, as is now well known, took the form of the Great Proletarian Cultural Revolution—one of the most extraordinary political operations of our time, and in some ways unique. The purpose of the Cultural Revolution was two-fold; to drive out of power the leaders who did not share Mao's views, and who had opposed him in various ways since 1959. The second aim was to create among the Chinese people a nation dedicated to the selfless service of the Revolution, eschewing personal gain, career rewards, and most material comforts also. The instruments for the attainment of these aims were the Red Guards, adolescent students from fourteen to twenty years old, the discontented generation which found the promises of the new society too often reserved for the fortunate privileged few.

How far Mao succeeded in these aims is still controversial. He certainly destroyed the existing Communist Party, his own creation; drove out the leaders who had opposed him, conserving only the few most loyal (among them Chou En-lai—the grand survivor). He has now set out to rebuild the Party purified of its 'revisionist' elements. The Red Guards served their turn, grew faction-ridden, became a nuisance and a menace to public order, and were then disbanded and dispersed. These achievements, politically speaking, are of a high order. In the battlefield of contending factions and sections of the Party Mao remained the clear, decisive victor. In the wider aim of re-constructing the Chinese society, ridding it of the old traits, and instilling a new and fundamentally changed ideology, it is perhaps too soon to judge. Many inequalities have been removed; many privileges eliminated. The Cultural Revolution was so called because Mao judged that whereas the political revolution, by which the Communist Party came to power, had been achieved in 1949, and the economic revolution, particularly on the land, completed by the Commune system after 1958, there still remained a cultural revolution to be won, which would change the traditions and the artistic taste of the Chinese as completely as the other revolutions had changed their government and livelihood. It was also intended to change the charac-ter of the Chinese people, and remove all selfish motivation from their psychology.

These are high sights; the argument that many have aimed at these things in the past, and only a very few had even the smallest measure of success, would not deter Mao Tsetung. They lacked the right ideology, their Thought was not so analytic and thorough as his own. He has said that his purpose cannot be achieved by one Cultural Revolution; many more, at intervals roughly equivalent to one generation will be needed. He will not live to lead them; but he hopes that the first one has trained a generation which will provide this leadership. Mao Tsetung, at seventy-nine, is still alive and as healthy as a man of his age can expect to be. It is too soon to write the obituary of a man of such infinite flexibility.

Kennedy

by Arthur Schlesinger

ARTHUR SCHLESINGER (b. 1917), the son of a distinguished historian, has himself had a brilliant academic career. Having graduated from Harvard, *summa cum laude* in 1938, he spent a year at Peterhouse, Cambridge before returning to Harvard to teach in the history department. His war service was first with the Office of War Information and later with the Office of Strategic Services. In 1946 he was again at Harvard, retiring in 1961 with the rank of full professor, to serve with President John F. Kennedy as Special Assistant. Since 1966 he has been Schweitzer Professor of the Humanities at the City University of New York.

Professor Schlesinger's major work has lain in the field of modern American history, to which he has made outstanding contribution, notably *The Age of Roosevelt*, in three volumes (1956-60) and *A Thousand Days, John F. Kennedy in the White House* (1965). He twice received a Pulitzer Prize—for history in 1945 and for biography twenty years later—and has also been awarded the Gold Medal for History by the National Institute of Arts and Letters (1967).

John Fitzgerald Kennedy

29 May 1917 Born in Brookline, Massachusetts. Educated at Canterbury School, New Milford, and Choate, Wallingford. Entered Princeton but transferred to Harvard.

1940 Graduated from Harvard. Published *Why England Slept*. Attended Stanford University graduate school of business.

1941 When U.S. entered Second World War, Kennedy enlisted in navy. Served in Pacific where he incurred back injury which plagued him for rest of life.

1946 Elected as Democrat from Massachusetts to House of Representatives. Supported President Truman's New Deal social welfare policies.

Nov. 1952 Defeated Republican Henry Cabot Lodge in elections for Senate.

Sept. 1953 Married Jacqueline Bouvier, who later had a son and a daughter.

1954-55 Hospitalized for surgery on his back.

1956 Published *Profiles in Courage*, which got Pulitzer Prize in following year.
Democratic convention. Kennedy made unsuccessful bid for vice-presidential nomination under Adlai Stevenson.

1957 Called for independence of Algeria. Supported civil rights bill which would authorize federal government to enforce racial desegregation of all-white schools.

1960 Secured nomination as Democratic party candidate for Presidency. Ran against Richard Nixon and was elected President. Inaugural speech dealt almost exclusively with foreign affairs—he perceived Cold War as power conflict.

Previous page: at a news conference, 1962

Dec. 1960	Brother, Robert, became Attorney-General.
March 1961	Establishment of Peace Corps, to show Third World value of American democracy.
April 1961	Agreed to attempted invasion of Cuba by anti-Castro exiles. Result was Bay of Pigs fiasco which ended in total failure.
May 1961	Announced U.S. aim of landing man on moon before end of decade.
June 1961	Met Krushchev in Vienna. Soviet leader threatened status of western powers in Berlin. He agreed to Kennedy's plan for neutralization of Laos.
1961	Counter-insurgency schools were set up (to deal with Soviet attempts to exploit insurgencies in Third World). U.S. long-range missile force increased.
Aug. 1961	East Germans erected Berlin wall to stop refugee flow to West.
Sept. 1961	U.S.S.R. resumed nuclear testing.
1961	Kennedy agreed in effect to trade neutralization of Laos for increased U.S. aid to government of South Vietnam. U.S. commitment escalated.
July 1962	Laid down plan for phased withdrawal from Vietnam of U.S. forces by end 1965.
Oct. 1962	Soviet nuclear build-up in Cuba. This made medium-range Soviet missiles effective against American targets. Kennedy instituted naval blockade of Cuba and threatened invasion. The bases were dismantled.
Oct. 1962	Sent federal troops into Oxford, Mississippi, to protect admission of a black student to the university.
June 1963	Triumphal visit to Europe, including West Berlin.
July 1963	London, Washington, and Moscow agreed on text of a nuclear test-ban treaty.
Aug. 1963	Martin Luther King's civil rights march to Washington.
1963	Kennedy introduced civil rights legislation which was passed after his death.
Nov. 1963	Diem, South Vietnamese President, was murdered.
22 Nov. 1963	Assassinated in Dallas, Texas.

L ittle is more inconstant than the reputations of American Presidents or more predictable than a decline, often brief, in such reputation in the period of ten to twenty years after the President's death. When I was an undergraduate in the 1930s, Theodore Roosevelt (d. 1919) was regarded as a blustering adolescent and Woodrow Wilson (d. 1924) as a wrong-headed fanatic. T. Roosevelt and Wilson shares have subsequently recovered on the historical exchange. We are always in a zone of imperfect visibility so far as the past just over our shoulder is concerned. It is as if we swim in the hollow of the historical wave; not until we reach the crest of the next wave can we look back and see clearly what went on before. (I used this simile in 1957 in the foreword to volume I of *The Age of Roosevelt* to explain the diminished reputation of Franklin Roosevelt a dozen years after his death. F. Roosevelt shares have subsequently recovered too.)

There are evident reasons for this historiographical rhythm. After great men die, passion and partisanship give way to detached historical judgement, exercised at a distance, informed by the knowledge of consequences and inevitably disillusioned because the 'solutions' contrived by great men always break down. Less admirably, there may be the Aristides effect—envy and resentment toward leaders who have enjoyed popular affection, an egalitarian determination to cut towering men down to size, even a desire for posthumous vengence. Moreover, as Emerson said, 'Every hero becomes a bore at last'. Whether for sound or sorry reasons revisionism seems inescapable.

It is a decade since John Kennedy was murdered in Dallas, and the predictable process is well under way. Only the other day an English historian, a Marxist but generally a serious scholar, referred to 'that most dangerous and megalomaniac of Administrations—the late John Kennedy's'.[1] One doubts that this will be the ultimate verdict. Still it is only an extreme statement of views urged not infrequently these days from the hollow of the wave. In offering another view, I must, as one who served in the Kennedy White House, declare an interest. It is not my purpose, however, to defend the Kennedy Presidency. Rather, as an historian, I must assess the past as best I can.

J ohn Fitzgerald Kennedy was born in Brookline, Massachusetts, on 29 May 1917. His father was Joseph P. Kennedy, a businessman who became immensely rich through corporate speculations and re-organizations in the 1920s and went on to serve in the 1930s as the first chairman of Franklin Roosevelt's Securities and Exchange Commission, and later as Roosevelt's Ambassador to London. The Kennedys were a large, spirited, and closely-knit family. As wealthy Catholics of Irish origin, they were in an ambiguous social position. The old barriers against the Irish began to fall after the First World War, and money could assure entrée in many places. But Massachusetts society continued to exclude the Irish, even when they were as charming and as rich as the Kennedys. Joe Kennedy consequently moved his family to an affluent suburb of New York City when John Kennedy was nine years old.

He sent his sons to Protestant preparatory schools and then to Harvard

414

(where he had gone himself). But he remained proudly Irish, Catholic, and Democratic. A friend and supporter of Franklin Roosevelt's till the Second World War, Joe Kennedy knew the world of money-making too well to be impressed by it, forbade the discussion of business at the family table and instructed his children that their duty lay in some form of public service. No doubt he hoped to be the father of the first Catholic President. This was not a dishonourable ambition. He wished too many things for his children to stultify them by insisting they adopt his own increasingly conservative views.

John Kennedy, the second son, graduated from Harvard in 1940. His honours essay, a study of British appeasement, was published under the title *Why England Slept*—a brash play on the title of Churchill's *While England Slept*. When war reached America, young Kennedy enlisted in the Navy and served heroically as a PT-boat commander in the Pacific. After the war he briefly contemplated journalism as a career, then turned to politics, winning election as a Democrat from Massachusetts to the House of Representatives in 1946 and to the Senate in 1952. In 1953 he married Jacqueline Bouvier, a girl of luminous beauty, also of sensitivity and expectation. In 1954-55, he nearly died from the complications following surgery on his back. While recuperating he wrote a series of biographical essays on American politicians who had stood by principle at the risk of career. A resulting book, *Profiles in Courage*, received the Pulitzer Prize in 1957.

Critics now suggested that Kennedy had not shown much courage himself when he had evaded the McCarthy issue in the Senate. Mrs Franklin Roosevelt, who had come to dislike Joe Kennedy for his pre-war isolationism and who mistrusted Catholics anyway, described young Kennedy as 'someone who understands what courage is and admires it but has not quite the independence to have it' (she later changed her mind). In private John Kennedy had no use for Joe McCarthy; and he was in fact receiving last rites in the hospital in the period when the Senate finally censured McCarthy. On the other hand, his Irish constituency in Massachusetts relished McCarthy's anti-communist demagoguery. Nor did Kennedy himself then see McCarthyism as his sort of issue (indeed, with a few splendid exceptions, his fellow senators showed little enthusiasm about taking McCarthy on). Kennedy's liberalism at that time applied mainly to social and economic questions, on which he was reliable and effective. He was most daring in the field of foreign affairs, where he emerged as an outspoken critic of French colonialism in Indo-China and North Africa. A bold speech of 1957 calling for the independence of Algeria much irritated the American foreign policy establishment, including fellow Democrats like Dean Acheson and even Adlai Stevenson. In general, he was something of a loner in the Senate, holding himself a bit apart from his colleagues, on and off the floor. He was richer than the rest, had a more beautiful wife, was better educated and better read, more reserved and more ambitious.

He made a short and unsuccessful fight for the vice presidential nomination at the Democratic convention in 1956. Soon thereafter he began to lay plans to take the presidential nomination in 1960. Conventional politicians held his youth, his religion and his independence against him; but these

416

could be assets too. In the primary contests of 1960, coolly managed by his younger brother Robert, John Kennedy began to emerge as a fresh and distinctive personality. A series of television debates in the autumn displayed him to advantage against Richard Nixon, the smarmy Republican candidate; a session with Protestant ministers in Texas disposed of the religious issue; and his appeal to 'get the country moving again' struck a national nerve after eight years of quiescence under Eisenhower. 'We stand today,' he had said when he accepted the nomination, 'on the edge of a new frontier—the frontier of the 1960s, a frontier of unknown opportunities and paths, a frontier of unfulfilled hopes and threats . . . The times demand invention, innovation, imagination, decision. I am asking each of you to be new pioneers on that new frontier.'

The *persona* was fresh and distinctive; it also had elements of mystery. Norman Mailer saw in Kennedy 'the wisdom of a man who senses death within him and gambles that he can cure it by risking his life.' The only question Mailer said, was whether the nation would be 'brave enough to enlist the romantic dream of itself . . . vote for the image of the mirror of its unconscious.' This was the question perhaps that frightened the country when, in the few days before the vote, there was a strange ebbing away of Kennedy's support—as if the electorate began to think that the adventure of Kennedy might be too much, that it had better fall back to the safe and familiar Nixon. In the end he barely won, with 49.7 per cent of the popular vote as against 49.5 per cent for Nixon, a margin of 119,000 in a total vote of 69 million. The margin in the electoral college—303 to 219—was more decisive.

Kennedy was not only the youngest man and the first Roman Catholic elected to the Presidency; he was also the first American President born in the twentieth century. As he put it in his inaugural address, he was one of 'a new generation of Americans—born in this century, tempered in war, disciplined by a hard and bitter peace'. His private self-description—an 'idealist without illusions'—suggested the combination of high purpose with the ironic, often self-mocking, tone that was characteristic of the war generation and that, distilled in Kennedy, came to be known as the Kennedy style. (When someone asked him how he became a war hero, he said, 'It was involuntary. They sank my boat'.)

He brought to the White House a well-defined view of the Presidency. 'The history of this nation—in its brightest and its bleakest pages—,' he said in a speech early in 1960, 'has been written largely in terms of the different views our Presidents have had of the Presidency itself . . . The American people in 1960 have an imperative right to know what the man bidding for the Presidency thinks about the place he is bidding for, whether he is aware of and willing to use the powerful resources of that office; whether his model will be Taft or Roosevelt, Wilson or Harding.'

Kennedy's models were Roosevelt and Wilson. His rejection of the Whig theory of the Presidency, of which his immediate predecessor had been so dogged an exponent, was reinforced by his own activism of temperament and mind. When he discussed a problem, he always wanted to know what could be done about it. Inaction was often painful. At the same time, he was far from incautious; 'prudent' was a favourite adjective; and he did not see great

o

point in picking fights he could not win. He was a gifted politician but also hoped, in the manner of the Roosevelts and Wilson, to release impulses of idealism he believed had been repressed during the Eisenhower quiescence. He attracted and sought out intellectuals and academics, who entered his administration in unprecedented numbers.

His inaugural address struck a high tone, though it was much affected by a more than usually bellicose speech delivered a fortnight earlier by N.S. Khrushchev, chairman of the Soviet Council of Ministers. The Russian leader, in what seemed a menacingly euphoric mood, had forecast the irresistible triumph of communism, especially—in the passages that most alarmed Washington—through Soviet support for 'national-liberation wars' in the Third World. Citing Vietnam, Algeria, and Cuba as promising examples, Khrushchev named Asia, Africa, and Latin America as 'the most important centres of revolutionary struggle against imperialism'.

In retrospect it seems probable that Khrushchev's belligerence was meant less as a provocation to the United States than as an element in a complex manoeuvre aimed at China. For he also seized the opportunity to reaffirm his rejection of nuclear war and his belief in 'peaceful coexistence'. These were positions unacceptable to the Chinese; and, by insisting on them in an otherwise truculent context, Khrushchev may have been trying to persuade his comrades in China and elsewhere that nuclear coexistence was not incompatible with the aggressive support of revolution in the Third World. Perhaps he thought that his militancy would head off the Chinese, while his softer words would reassure the west. Inevitably Peking and Washington each believed only the passages written for the other. Certainly no one in Washington recognized the extent of Russian-Chinese differences; nor, recalling Khrushchev as the man who banged his shoe on a U.N. desk during Harold Macmillan's speech at the General Assembly, did many conceive him as a notably subtle man. So Washington missed his subtleties, if indeed they were there, and heard only boasts and threats.

Reading the speech as a deliberate challenge, Kennedy in response devoted his inaugural almost exclusively to foreign affairs. It was, he hyperbolically declared, an 'hour of maximum danger'. He added, in grandiloquent language, 'Let every nation know, whether it wishes us well or ill, that we shall pay any price, bear any burden, meet any hardship, support any friend, oppose any foe, in order to assure the survival and the success of liberty'. He concluded: 'And so, my fellow Americans, ask not what your country can do for you: Ask what you can do for your country'.

Such rhetoric came easily enough: Kennedy was a child of the Cold War. But he lacked the ideological passions of the Dulles years and perceived the Cold War not as a religious but as a power conflict. Communism was for him not a creed of changeless, irrevocable wickedness (in *Profiles in Courage* he had quoted Lincoln: 'There are few things wholly evil or wholly good') but an historical phenomenon produced by historical circumstance and subject to historical modulation. Moreover, he had no doubt that nuclear war would mean the end of civilization. So his inaugural address also condemned the arms race, asked to 'bring the absolute power to destroy other nations under the absolute control of all nations', observed that 'civility is

418

not a sign of weakness' and declared: 'Let us never negotiate out of fear. But let us never fear to negotiate'.

The mingling of themes suggests the ways in which Kennedy was a transitional figure in American foreign policy. Despite his inaugural extravagance, he had an acute sense of the limitations of American power. In November 1961, under attack from Senator Barry Goldwater and the radical right on the ground that he was pursuing a 'no-win' policy instead of striving, like all right-minded Americans, for 'total victory' over communism, Kennedy asked his fellow citizens to 'face the fact that the United States is neither omnipotent nor omniscient—that we are only six per cent of the world's population—that we cannot impose our will upon the other ninety-four per cent of mankind—that we cannot right every wrong or reverse each adversity—and that therefore there cannot be an American solution to every world problem'.

This was his more fundamental and abiding belief. He had no illusions about the feasibility of a *pax America*. But, if he did not think there could be an American solution to every world problem, he did not think there could be a Russian solution either. His broad idea, which he proposed to Khrushchev in a meeting in Vienna in June 1961, was that each super-power should abstain from initiatives that, by upsetting the rough balance into which the post-war world had settled, might invite miscalculation and compel reaction by the other. Beyond this, his vision was of what he called a 'world of diversity'—a world of nations various in institutions and creeds, 'where, within a framework of international co-operation, every country can solve its own problems according to its own traditions and ideals'. In his view, the 'revolution of national independence' was the source and guarantee of the world of diversity. Communism could be one element in this pluralistic world, but diversity, he argued, was ultimately incompatible with the Communist belief that all societies went through the same stages and all roads had a single destination. 'The great currents of history', he said, 'are carrying the world away from the monolithic toward the pluralist idea—away from communism and toward national independence and freedom'. In his American University speech of June 1963 he summed up his policy in a conscious revision of Wilson's famous line: 'If we cannot end now our differences, at least we can help make the world safe for diversity'.

Given the nuclear stalemate, Kennedy agreed with Khrushchev that the Third World had become the immediate battleground. Abandoning the 'for-us-or-against-us' policy of the Eisenhower years, he repudiated Dulles's aphorism that neutralism was 'immoral' and made clear the new administration's sympathy with states struggling for nationhood outside the framework of the Cold War. He did this with particular success in Africa. In South East Asia he reversed the Eisenhower policy of building a 'bastion of the west' in the swamps of Laos and instead sought neutralization. In Latin America the Alliance for Progress asserted the necessity for structural change if economic aid were to be effective. 'Those who make peaceful revolution impossible,' Kennedy told the Latin American oligarchs, 'will make violent revolution inevitable'. The foreign-assistance programme in general underwent revision so that an increasing share of aid went to modernize economies rather than to build armies. The Peace Corps, an undertaking especially close to Kennedy's heart, channelled the idealism of individual Americans into face-to-face co-operation with students and peasants of underdeveloped countries.

His purpose was to persuade the Third World that democratic methods offered assurance of development and independence. But there remained the problem of protecting the modernization process, at once disruptive and agonizingly slow, against Communist intrusion—a problem presumably all the more urgent because of Khrushchev's enthusiasm for national-liberation wars. The American view was that, the nuclear stand-off having reduced the threat of general war, the great danger to world peace would come if local crises in the Third World led on to direct Soviet-American confrontation.

To prevent this, it seemed essential to persuade Moscow that the national-liberation-war technique would not work. A basic shift in American defence doctrine, wrought by Secretary of Defence Robert McNamara, had already replaced the Eisenhower-Dulles strategy of massive nuclear retaliation by the strategy of flexible response—that is, by the diversification of military force so that the level of deterrence could be precisely graduated to meet the level of threat. This shift was designed to enable the west to respond to Soviet aggression in Europe by other means than nuclear war; but it also produced a variety of conventional forces that could be used locally elsewhere in the world.

President Eisenhower, greatly affected by the Korean experience, had shown consistent reluctance to commit regular troops abroad (though, on leaving office, he counselled Kennedy that the preservation of Laos from communism was so essential that he should be willing, if necessary, 'to intervene unilaterally'). Instead, the Eisenhower administration had developed the Central Intelligence Agency as the instrument of American intervention. Under Eisenhower the C.I.A. mounted a series of ambitious clandestine operations, helping to overthrow governments regarded as Communist or pro-Communist in Iran (1953) and Guatemala (1954), failing to do so in Indonesia (1958), helping to install supposedly pro-western governments in Egypt (1954) and Laos (1959), organizing an expedition of Cuban refugees against the Castro regime (1960).

Another of Eisenhower's parting admonitions to Kennedy was that this last project 'be continued and accelerated', emphasizing that it was 'the policy of this government' to aid the anti-Castro forces 'to the utmost'. Kennedy mistakenly accepted this advice, perhaps fearing the domestic political outcry that would follow the disbandment of an exile army his revered predecessor had organized. When the expedition went down to defeat at the Bay of Pigs in April 1961, Kennedy resisted pressure from the military for escalation. Instead of sending in the Marines, he cut his losses and accepted full responsibility for the disaster. He thereafter exhibited severely qualified confidence in the judgement of the Joint Chiefs of Staff and the C.I.A.

But he felt more than ever the need to develop new ways of dealing with Soviet attempts to exploit insurgencies in the Third World. The answer now appeared to lie in the new thesis of 'counter-insurgency'. With Kennedy's personal encouragement, counter-insurgency doctrine was propounded, counter-insurgency schools were set up, and elite counter-guerrilla units, like the Green Berets, were established. As Kennedy conceived it, counter-insurgency would operate within a context of social reform in the manner of Magsaysay's successful campaign against the Hukbalahaps in the Philippines. But the political component did not take root; and the counter-insurgency mystique primarily nourished the belief in the American capacity and right to intervene in foreign lands. It brought out the worst in the over-confident activism of the New Frontier: the faith that American energy and technology could solve everything; the 'when in doubt, do something' approach to policy; the officious pragmatism that could quickly degenerate into cynical manipulation.

At the same time, Kennedy also increased the American long-range missile force. The missile build-up of 1961, as some in the administration felt at the time and most felt later, was another over-reaction to the Khrushchev speech. It was more than American security required; it ended the hope of freezing the rival missile forces at lower levels; and it sent the wrong message to Moscow, no doubt leading Khrushchev to feel that, for his own security and prestige, he had to increase Soviet military strength. For whatever reason, Khrushchev stormed ahead. At Vienna perhaps misled by the Bay of Pigs into seeing Kennedy as irresolute, he brusquely rejected the proposal of a global stand-still (except in Laos, where he agreed to neutralization) and adopted a tough, even bullying, tone. Germany remained the critical issue for Moscow, the more so because of the rising flow of refugees from East Germany into West Berlin. Khrushchev told Kennedy that by the end of the year he would conclude with East Germany a peace treaty that would extinguish western occupation and access rights in West Berlin. Kennedy replied that so drastic an alteration in the world balance was unacceptable; Khrushchev himself would not accept a comparable shift in favour of the west. Khrushchev said that, if America wanted war over Berlin, there was nothing he could do about it; he was going to sign the treaty by 31 December. When the two men parted, Kennedy said, 'It will be a cold winter'.

On his return to Washington, Kennedy requested a further increase in the defence budget and called out 150,000 reservists. At the same time, he declared his readiness to work out arrangements to meet Russia's security interests in Western Europe. On 13 August 1961, the East Germans erected the Berlin Wall, thereby stopping the refugee flow. Khrushchev continued to deliver bellicose speeches, and in September the Soviet Union resumed nuclear testing in the atmosphere—the first nation to do so since 1958; but the Soviet leader postponed his treaty deadline in October; and the Berlin crisis, for a moment so frightening, subsided.

Khrushchev had by no means abandoned his interest in Berlin. Blocked by Kennedy's firm response to his direct move, he evidently decided to turn the American flank. In the summer of 1962 he began to prepare for the installation in Cuba of bases for nuclear missiles targeted against the United States—an unprecedented action for the Russians, who had never before placed their missiles in another country. If successful, the operation would

SAM S

1 CRATE

1 BEAGLE

17 CRATES

3 FUSELAGES

NLARGEMENT

422

not only protect Cuba from American invasion—the objective later alleged by Khrushchev (though this could have been more simply achieved by stationing Soviet troops on the island)—but would give Russia a potent bargaining counter when it chose to re-open the Berlin question. Moreover, by making medium-range Soviet missiles effective against American targets, it would double Soviet nuclear first-strike capacity and do so without major additional strain on the Soviet budget. It would deal America a staggering political blow by showing the Soviet capacity to penetrate the American sphere of influence with impunity. And it would strengthen the Russian hand within the Communist world against the ever more exasperating Chinese by proving Moscow capable of bold action in the cause of Communist revolution.

Washington had not objected to the Russian supply of conventional weapons to Cuba; but Kennedy warned Khrushchev that if there were evidence of 'significant offensive capability . . . the gravest issues would arise'. Khrushchev repeatedly denied both publicly and privately that he had any such intention. Nor did Washington consider such recklessness likely. Then on 14 October 1962, an American U-2 over-flight found conclusive evidence that Khrushchev had lied and that a Soviet nuclear build-up was well under way ninety miles off the American coast.

For a grim week, Kennedy, meeting in total secrecy with a small group of advisers, pondered his course. The attempted nuclearization of Cuba was, in his view, 'a deliberately provocative and unjustified change in the *status quo*'. If the United States were to accept so gross an intrusion into what the Russians, always themselves so preternaturally sensitive to spheres of interest, had previously respected as the American zone, this would, he feared, persuade both Khrushchev and the western allies that the Soviet Union could get away with almost anything and would embolden Khrushchev to further acts that would make the Third World War inescapable. Rejecting proposals from the Joint Chiefs of Staff that the missile bases be taken out by surprise air attack, Kennedy instead brilliantly used a naval quarantine and the threat of invasion to force the dismantling of the bases and the removal of the missiles. In exchange, he agreed not to invade Cuba, which (apart from the missiles) he had no intention of doing anyway, and he also said he would remove American missiles from Turkey, a removal which he had, in fact, ordered some months before the crisis.

For thirteen excruciating days, the world had trembled on the abyss of war. Kennedy now hoped he had made to Khrushchev the point he had tried to make in Vienna—that neither side should tamper carelessly with the complex and explosive international equilibrium. In this hope he renewed his quest, begun in 1961, for a treaty banning nuclear testing. In his notable speech at an American University in June 1963 he called on Americans as well as Russians to re-think the Cold War; 'our attitude is as essential as theirs'. Both sides, he said, were 'caught up in a vicious and dangerous cycle in which suspicion on one side breeds suspicion on the other, and new weapons beget counterweapons'. Khrushchev, who later described this as 'the greatest speech by any American President since Roosevelt', now expressed readiness to receive an Anglo-American mission. In July Washing-

423

Aerial photo confirming presence of Russian missiles on Cuba

ton, London and Moscow agreed on the text of a treaty. The quick ratification of the test ban by the Senate, following the warm reception given to the American University speech with its quiet rejection of the clichés of the Cold War, showed the revolution Kennedy had wrought in American attitudes towards the Soviet Union. In the autumn of 1963 he even began secret explorations through the United Nations looking toward the normalization of relations with Cuba.

In the meantime, however, the theory that stopping national-liberation wars was the key to peace had drawn America into increasing trouble in Indo-China. In the early 1950s, the National Security Council had reached the singular conclusion that 'the loss of Indo-China would be critical to the security of the U.S.', and for twenty years thereafter no President questioned this appraisal. In 1961, struggling to reverse the Eisenhower policy on Laos and confronted by much resistance in the national security bureaucracy, Kennedy agreed in effect to trade the neutralization of Laos for increased American aid to the government of South Vietnam, where 250,000 government troops faced 15,000 Viet Cong guerrillas and the military situation appeared manageable. This manageability was an illusion. The situation grew worse; and, though Kennedy rejected recommendations that he commit American combat units and air power, he did send in military 'advisers' assigned to South Vietnamese units, plus Green Berets, helicopter pilots and C.I.A. spooks.

In the spring of 1963 Buddhist protests against the Saigon regime belatedly showed Kennedy that the problem was as much political as military. He now tried, without success, to persuade Ngo Dinh Diem, the South Vietnamese President, to reform his regime. When Diem persisted in policies of reaction and repression, a group of dissident South Vietnamese generals, with the knowledge of the Americans, organized a coup against him and, without American knowledge, murdered him.

Kennedy never fully clarified his views on Vietnam. On the one hand, he accepted a version of the domino theory. 'For us to withdraw,' he said in July 1963, '. . . would mean a collapse not only of South Vietnam but of South East Asia'. On the other hand, he hated to commit American troops to the Asian mainland and laid down in July 1962 a plan for the phased withdrawal of American forces by the end of 1965—a plan that remained national policy till four months after his death. Though he gradually increased the number of American advisers—there were 16,300 American troops in Vietnam at the end of 1963—only seventy-three Americans were killed in combat during his Presidency.

While regarding the United States as 'overcommitted' in South East Asia, Kennedy also felt that, the commitment having been made, America could not let South Vietnam fall cheaply to the Communists. How far he would have gone to prevent this outcome no one can know. His memory of the French experience had convinced him that too large an infusion of white soldiers would only unite Vietnamese nationalism against the alien presence; and he had proven in Laos, at the Bay of Pigs and during the Cuban missile crisis his capacity to refuse escalation. 'In the final analysis,' he said in September 1963 of the people of South Vietnam, 'it is their war. They are the ones who have to win it or lose it. We can help them, we can give them equipment, we can send our men out there as advisers, but they have to win it, the people of Vietnam.' When his successor began to call it 'our war', the change was more than semantic.

I n domestic affairs Kennedy's effort to redeem his campaign promise of 'getting America moving again' was complicated by the extreme narrowness of his 1960 victory and by the strength of the conservative coalition between Republicans and Southern Democrats in the House of Representatives (where his party actually had twenty fewer members in 1961 than in 1959). Brooding over his congressional dilemmas, he used to quote Jefferson: 'Great innovations should not be forced on slender majorities.' And, though Kennedy had served for fourteen years in the Congress, he was never in his bones a Capitol Hill man—a fact that, perceived as it was at both ends of Pennsylvania Avenue, further inhibited his efforts at congressional persuasion.[2]

Yet, in spite of obstacles, he compiled a fairly extensive legislative record. And, as the first Keynesian President, he steadily pursued an expansionist economic policy. This policy, carried further by a tax reduction bill introduced in his administration and passed after his death, helped produce the longest peacetime period of sustained growth in American history. Again the congressional situation created problems. Privately Kennedy would have preferred to keep taxes up and to stimulate the economy by increased social spending, especially for the war against poverty that he planned as a central feature of his 1964 programme; but, given the congressional line-up, the only way he could get legislative support for the stimulus the economy required was by lowering taxes.

In the area of civil rights, the congressional situation required him to concentrate at first on executive rather than legislative action. He took immediate steps to end segregation in inter-state transportation and to secure the right of Negroes to vote. In October 1962 he sent federal troops into Oxford, Mississippi, to protect the admission of a black student to the University of Mississippi. For a time he underestimated the intensity of the black revolution. Then outrages against Martin Luther King in Birmingham, Alabama, in April 1963 caused a surge of national indignation. In June, pronouncing racial justice 'a moral issue . . . as old as the scriptures and . . . as clear as the American Constitution', Kennedy opened up a new fight to commit the nation to the proposition 'that race has no place in American life or law'. Sweeping civil rights legislation introduced that year was also passed after his death.

In the White House Kennedy's directness and openness of mind, his faith in reason and his compassionate vision of American life helped break the intellectual as well as the political crust that had settled over America in the fifties. He communicated not only an insistence on personal excellence but a skepticism about conventional ideas and institutions. His message was that the old Cold War was played out, that America had vital ties of sympathy and interest with the emerging world, that at home the American way of life was in poor shape, that the nation was neglectful of its young and its

425

Overleaf: moments after the assassination. The presidential car speeds to hospital with secret service agent standing on back. Afterwards: the funeral

old and callous toward its poor people and its non-white minorities, that its cities and schools and landscapes were a mess, that national motives were tending toward meanness and materialism. His own high standards for his country encouraged an immense discharge of critical energy throughout American society.

His very *persona*, as Mailer saw before his election, had a liberating effect. He gave people the belief that things could be done, and that public policy must be determined by open and reasoned discussion. For a moment he made politics seem in truth (in a phrase he cherished from John Buchan's *Pilgrim's Way*) 'the greatest and most honourable adventure'. He was greatly admired and trusted in the black community, and he was the first President since Roosevelt who had anything to say to the young. With his more radical younger brother, Robert Kennedy, the intimate partner in the great decisions (after the Bay of Pigs) of his administration, he produced a dynastic image of concern and courage.

Not only his purposes but, in the much abused word of the time, his 'style'— that combination of intellectuality and toughness, of satiric wit and steely determination, of personal openness and political skill—seemed to unfold new vistas. The age of adventure was renewed for a nation that thought it had long since relinquished adventure as an episode of the past; the future suddenly seemed a challenge, not a threat. Felicitously it was Kennedy who said in May 1961 that the United States 'should commit itself to achieving the goal, before this decade is out, of landing a man on the moon and returning him safely to earth'.

Certainly the instinct for activism and adventure could lead to jingoism, victory-at-any-cost and Vietnams. But Kennedy was personally saved from excess by his very considerable intelligence and his strong commitment to reason. He was by nature a conciliator, always hopeful that differences could be rationally worked out, whether with Khrushchev, the President of United States Steel or the Governors of Mississippi and Alabama. He acted according to the maxim of Liddell Hart he had quoted in a 1960 book review: 'Never corner an opponent, and always assist him to save his face. Put yourself in his shoes—so as to see things through his eyes. Avoid self-righteousness like the devil—nothing is so self-blinding.'

He was saved from excess too by irony. He knew both the limits of national power and the frustrations of human striving. 'There is always an inequity in life,' he said at one press conference. 'Some men are killed in a war and some men are wounded and some men never leave the country . . . Life is unfair.' But, while he perceived the cruelty of life, he never permitted this perception to sever the nerve of action or to shatter his hope for measureable improvements in the human condition. He was strengthened by a complex view of history and humanity in which the comic and the tragic visions mingled in delicate proportions.

He had his share of human frailty—and did not conceal it from himself. He made mistakes—and was often quick to avow them. He could be wilful, impatient and, on occasion, arbitrary. And his actual achievements in office were limited—ironic for a man who valued other Presidents less for their intangible influence than for their tangible accomplishment. But, as he visibly grew in strength and clarity of purpose, the promise of his Presidency came to seem almost unlimited. His murder in Dallas, Texas, on 22 November 1963, sent a wave of incredulity, shame and grief not only across the United States but around the planet.

The bullets cut off Kennedy's life when his potentialities were displayed but not fulfilled. A thousand day Presidency was not so very long. It was as if Lincoln had been killed six months after Gettysburg, or Roosevelt at the end of 1935. No one knows where Kennedy might have taken the country —whether the renaissance he seemed to promise was gold or glister. One does know that with his death something came to an end in American life. In the later days of pessimism and violence, Americans, if asked when things began to go wrong with the republic, generally answered: at Dallas in November 1963. At the same time, for all the cruel brevity of his Presidency, Kennedy's mettle, verve and gallantry remained a vital force in his own country; perhaps in the world.

---

[1] Eric Hobsbawm in *The Listener*, 18 May 1972.

[2] The contrast between Kennedy and his successor underlines the importance of the congressional arithmetic. Lyndon Johnson *was* a Capitol Hill man; he rejoiced in the game of congressional cajolery, bargaining and arm-twisting. Few Presidents have enjoyed Johnson's relations and resources in dealing with Congress. But too much should not be attributed to parliamentary sorcery which was really due to political mathematics. The reason for Johnson's remarkable record of legislative accomplishment in 1965-66 was the philanthropy of the Republicans in running Barry Goldwater for President in 1964—a philanthropy that bestowed on the Democrats an extra 37 seats in the House of Representatives, nearly all from the north. The 1964 election made Johnson the first Democratic President since Roosevelt before 1938 with a working progressive majority in the House. When Johnson lost 48 Democratic House seats in 1966, he found himself, despite unremitting efforts at congressional persuasion, in the same condition of stalemate that had thwarted every Democratic President since 1938. Had the sequence been different, had Johnson been elected to the Presidency in 1960 with Kennedy as his Vice President, and had Johnson then offered the 87th Congress the same legislative programme actually offered by Kennedy, the probability is that he would have had no more success than Kennedy—perhaps even less because he appealed less effectively to public opinion. And, if Johnson had died in 1963 and Kennedy had beaten Goldwater by a large margin in 1964, then Kennedy would have had those extra votes in the House of Representatives, and political pundits would doubtless have contrasted his cool management of the Congress with the frenetic and bumbling efforts of his predecessor. In the end, arithmetic is decisive.

Nasser
by Sir Harold Beeley

SIR HAROLD BEELEY (b. 1909) came down from the Queen's College, Oxford, in 1930 with a first-class degree in Modern History and for the next nine years he taught at Sheffield, London, Oxford and Leicester. At the outbreak of the Second World War he became a member of the Foreign Office Research Department and as such attended the United Nations Conference at San Francisco in 1945 and served as Secretary to the Anglo-American Committee of Enquiry on Palestine in 1946. In the same year he became a career member of the Foreign Service and, after a brief period as Counsellor at Copenhagen, became an expert in Middle Eastern affairs. He was Counsellor at the Embassy in Iraq and at Washington; Assistant Under-Secretary in the Foreign Office; Ambassador (briefly) in Saudi Arabia; Deputy U.K. Representative to the United Nations; U.K. Representative to the Geneva Disarmament Conference and, for two periods, Ambassador in Cairo. On his retirement in 1969 Sir Harold returned to his early academic calling and was appointed Special Lecturer in History at Queen Mary College, London, a post which he still holds. He was awarded a C.B.E. in 1946 and a K.C.M.G. in 1961.

Gamal Abd-al Nasser

15 Jan. 1918	Born. Educated at secondary school in Cairo.
1936	For short time was student of law at Cairo university.
1937	When Military Academy opened to sons of unprivileged families, Nasser enrolled.
1942	Was appointed a lecturer.
1945	Officers formed secret organization around Nasser dedicated to cause of Egyptian nationalism.
1948	Saw active service in Palestine during Arab-Jewish war. Humiliating defeat by Israelis which exposed incompetence of Egyptian government.
1949	Nasser back in Cairo as instructor at Staff College. His group became more organized and was named the 'Society of Free Officers'.
Oct. 1951	Wafdist government denounced treaty under which British forces occupied Canal Zone. Subsequent guerilla activity in Zone.
25 Jan. 1952	British counter-action in Ismailia in which Egyptian auxiliary police were killed.
26 Jan. 1952	Protest march and riots in Cairo. Some British and other foreign residents murdered. King dismissed Nahas Pasha's Wafd government.
23 July 1952	The Free Officers seized general headquarters, radio station and key buildings in Cairo. Nasser, Anwar Sadat, and General Neguib were the prominent leaders, dedicated to ending British occupation, purging and strengthening army and abolition of 'feudalism'.

Previous page: Nasser in 1954, two years before Suez. Already a power in the Middle East and being likened by some British to Hitler

26 July 1952 King Farouk made to abdicate. The Free Officers installed as prime minister Ali Maher, with a civilian cabinet.

Sept. 1952 Ali Maher and civilian politicians dismissed because of opposition to Free Officers' plan to limit individual owners to holding 200 acres of land. General Neguib became prime minister, Nasser deputy prime minister and minister of the interior.

Jan. 1953 Politicians arrested, parties dissolved, constitution abolished. Neguib presided over Revolutionary Command Council (R.C.C.).

1954 Nasser supplanted Neguib as president of R.C.C.

Nov. 1954 Neguib was removed as President of the Republic.

1954 Anglo-Egyptian settlement that all British forces would be withdrawn by June 1956.

Feb. 1955 Treaty between Iraq and Turkey— basis of Baghdad Pact in which Iraq sought protection of West. Nasser objected, thus re-establishing his position with the nationalists and gaining a point in contest between Cairo and Baghdad for influence in Syria, Jordan and Lebanon.

28 Feb. 1955 Israeli attack on Egyptian military post near Gaza. Nasser intensified efforts to re-equip armed forces— turned to U.S.S.R.

Sept. 1955 Egyptian agreement with Czechoslovakia for supply of arms.

1955 Nasser led Egyptian delegation to Afro-Asian conference in Bandung— became Arab spokesman for non-alignment.

July 1956 U.S. and Britain withdrew offer to finance Aswan dam after Nasser established diplomatic relations with Peking.

26 July 1956 Nasser retaliated by nationalizing Suez Canal Company. Britain and France decided to liberate canal by force.

Aug. 1956 Israelis overran Sinai. Anglo-French expedition was halted near Port Said by American pressure on London.

March 1957 Israelis completed evacuation from Sinai.

1957 The Liberation Rally was replaced by the National Union—a link between the leadership and the people.

1958 Syrian-Egyptian union which led to creation of first United Arab Republic (U.A.R.), of which Nasser was president.

By 1961 Virtually the whole of industry, mining and foreign commerce had been brought under state ownership or control.

1961 Property of 850 'reactionary' families sequestrated. All foreign-owned agricultural land was nationalized and a decree was issued restricting maximum landholding to 100 acres.

Sept. 1961 Federation with Syria, which Yemen had joined, collapsed.

1962 National Union was replaced by Arab Socialist Union.

Sept. 1962 Officers' coup against Imam of Yemen partly misfired—Nasser was asked for help. He sent air and ground forces: war lasted five years.

Feb. 1963 Military coup in Iraq.

March 1963 Military coup in Syria.

April 1963 Second U.A.R. federation formed.

1964 Nasser entertained Krushchev at celebrations to mark completion of first stage of Aswan dam.

1965-66 Zakaria Mohieddin was Prime Minister.

7 April 1967 Israeli fighters shot down six Syrian planes.

May 1967 Nasser moved troops into Sinai and demanded withdrawal of U.N. posts (stationed there after 1956 incident). Nasser announced blockade of Israel.

5 June 1967 Israel attacked Egypt. Sinai was quickly overrun and Israelis established themselves on east bank of Suez canal.

9 June 1967 Nasser announced resignation from presidency. But popular opinion forced him to change mind.

1968 University students' unrest.

1969 Revolutions in Sudan and Libya. Nasser's first heart attack.

27 Sept. 1970 Conference in Cairo to terminate conflict between King Hussein of Jordan and Palestine guerrillas.

28 Sept. 1970 Nasser died from heart attack.

Egypt has the natural isolation of an island. On none of her land frontiers does she have a settled population, and apart from the coast road to Libya she has no easy surface communication with her neighbours. Although it is sand and not water that separates her from them, the social and political effects have been much the same. There has been and still is a school of thought in Egypt which has wished to take advantage of this circumstance to pursue purely Egyptian interests, with only secondary reference to the problems of the surrounding Arab countries. The Egyptian revolution could conceivably have taken this course. But although Gamal Abdul Nasser himself was until 1952 exclusively absorbed by Egypt's problems, it was scarcely possible thereafter for him to renounce the role Egypt was expected to play in Arab politics. Already in 1954 there appeared a book to which he gave his name, though the style suggests he did not write it, and which expressed his ideas and ambitions. In *The Philosophy of the Revolution*, Egypt is depicted as the point at which three worlds converge—of Islam, of the Arabs and of Africa—and as being summoned to fulfil a wider destiny.

This was his tragedy. He acquired a stature in Arab and Afro-Asian politics with which the strength of his Egyptian base was not commensurate, and in trying to play the part to which he was called both by his own reflections and by the expectations of Arab opinion he imposed burdens on Egypt which largely frustrated the intentions with which he had originally come into power.

Gamal Abdul Nasser was born in Beni Mor on 15 January 1918. His father was a post office clerk, and his mother was the daughter of a coal merchant. Both families came from the peasantry of Upper Egypt, and Nasser's father had spent the first fifteen years of his life in his native village, a few miles from Assiut. Both father and grandfather were typical of the movement from village to town in search of the better conditions of life offered by minor government service or petty commerce. Life was extremely frugal still, but its horizons were wide enough for Gamal to be given a secondary education and even to enrol briefly as a student of law at Cairo University.

From these early years he retained the taste for a simple and conventional way of life, an aversion to luxury and a suspicion of rich people and rich nations, in short an instinctive and distrustful puritanism. This was probably reinforced when he was eight by emotional shock at the death of his mother, to whom he was deeply attached, and later at his father's re-marriage.

He was not a successful student, partly because he was already distracted by political issues and drawn into the student demonstrations endemic in Egypt in the 1930s. But as he entered the University in the autumn of 1936 an unforseen alternative career was opened to him. For at that time the government of Nahas Pasha was removing the restrictions which had hitherto excluded the sons of unprivileged families from the Military Academy. This was an unconscious but decisive step in the preparation of the revolution of 1952. Not only Nasser himself but also most of those who were to be his closest companions in planning and launching the military coup were among the Academy entries of 1937 and 1938. As they worked their way into positions of influence and authority, so for the first time would it be possible to use the army, traditional shield of the established order, as a revolutionary force.

The preparation took fifteen years. During this time Nasser graduated from the Military Academy, passed through a normal series of assignments, saw active service in Palestine in 1948 and was subsequently appointed an instructor at the Staff College. He read widely and was especially drawn to the heroic personalities and episodes of modern European history. Two novels which left a deep impression on him were *A Tale of Two Cities* and *The Scarlet Pimpernel*.

He was the central figure in a group of young officers, meeting one another as the chances of the service permitted, discussing their discontents and their hopes, contemplating imprecise plans for revolutionary action. They were oppressed by the condition of Egypt—the limitations placed on the country's freedom of action by the Treaty with Britain, its undignified role in the Second World War, the humiliation of defeat by the Israelis in 1948, the corruption and complacency in high places. As General Neguib, the senior officer who accepted the titular leadership of their movement, was to write later: 'We seized power because we could no longer endure the humiliations to which we, along with the rest of the Egyptian people, were being subjected'. It was a revolution of disgust and an assertion of dignity.

Nasser's principal role in this period was to hold the group together and to dissuade its more ardent spirits (including his eventual successor as President, Anwar Sadat) from actions which he considered as premature and condemned to failure. Probably his influence also contributed to the fact that no member of the group was absorbed into the more broadly based and more overt radical movements which were active in Egypt at this time. The desire to prevent the erosion of their movement by the pull of conflicting ideologies helps to explain why the officers never tried to agree on a detailed programme to be carried out after their seizure of power. The revolution was regarded almost as an end in itself.

It was brought nearer by external events. The first Arab-Jewish war, that of 1948, was important not because the situation in Palestine had much influence on the revolutionary current in Egypt but because it exposed the incompetence of the Egyptian Government and the higher military command and led to accusations that the inadequate and often defective equipment of the troops was a consequence of negligence and corruption. The conversations which Nasser had during the negotiation of a truce with his Israeli opposite number, Captain Mordechai Cohen, showed what were his priorities at that time. 'The subject Gamal Abdul Nasser invariably discussed with me whenever we met,' Cohen wrote later, 'was our struggle against the British, the way we organized our secret resistance movement against them and the way we succeeded in mobilizing world opinion on our side against them'.

It was in the year following the defeat in Palestine that Nasser, now back in Cairo at the Staff College, transformed his group into a more tightly-knit organization to which was given the name of the 'Society of Free

Officers'. They gave themselves five years to prepare for action. That it came about in half that time was due to events they could not control. In October 1951 the Wafdist Government denounced the Treaty under which British forces occupied the Canal Zone. This was followed by guerrilla activity in the Zone, and on 25 January 1952 a British counter-action in Ismailia resulted in the deaths of between forty and fifty Egyptian auxiliary police. On the following day, 'Black Saturday', a protest march of the auxiliary police in Cairo was followed by riots in which many buildings particularly associated with the British community were set on fire and a number of British and other foreign residents murdered. The responsibility for allowing the disorder to continue from early morning until mid-afternoon, when at last the army started to clear the streets, must be shared by the King and the Wafd. Each was manoeuvring to discredit the other, and it was the Wafd that lost. In dismissing Nahas Pasha's Government, however, the King deprived his regime of the one barrier which the Free Officers would have hesitated to attack.

As their preparations accelerated they inevitably became more conspicuous. The final choice of a date for their coup was determined in the knowledge that the King and the military authorities were preparing to move against them. On the night of 22-23 July units under the command of Free Officers seized the general headquarters, radio station and other key buildings in Cairo. At seven o'clock in the morning Anwar Sadat broadcast a proclamation in the name of General Neguib, announcing little more than a purge of the army and calling for the maintenance of order. The King was in Alexandria; it was not until the 26th that he was made to abdicate and allowed to leave the country. Some of the officers had wanted his execution, but Neguib and Nasser prevailed against them. 'We cannot,' Nasser said in a message from Cairo to the officers in Alexandria, 'execute Farouk without a trial. Neither can we afford to keep him in jail and preoccupy ourselves with the rights and wrongs of his case at the risk of neglecting the other purposes of the revolution.'

What were 'the other purposes of the revolution'? As defined in July 1952 they were confined to the termination of the British occupation, the purging and strengthening of the army and the abolition of 'feudalism'. New systems of government or of social organization were no part of their programme. They installed as Prime Minister Ali Maher, a leading politician of the previous regime, with a civilian Cabinet, and they appear to have assumed that the parliamentary system would be resumed after a brief interval. (The question did not arise immediately, as Farouk had dissolved his last Parliament shortly before the revolution.)

There was however one reform which they insisted on effecting without delay. This was the division of the large landed estates. No less than sixty-five per cent of Egypt's severely limited area of cultivable land was held by six per cent of the landowners. It was a system which aggravated the poverty of Egypt's overcrowded villages, starved industry and commerce of investment capital, preserved a feudal structure of society and constituted a basis of power which could have threatened a reversal of the revolution. Drawing on reform projects which had been in circulation for some years, the Free Officers decided on a limit of 200 acres for the holding of any individual owner, with an additional 100 for his dependents. In the light of experience and the growing pressure of population these limits were later considered to be too generous, and the maximum of 200 acres was reduced to 100 and eventually to 50. In 1952, however, the original proposal was too radical for Ali Maher and the civilian politicians. He was dismissed in September and replaced as Prime Minister by General Neguib.

This was the parting of the ways between the new leaders and the old. The dream of co-operation with the political parties and elections for a new Parliament now faded rapidly in Nasser's mind. Many politicians were arrested, the parties were dissolved, the constitution was abolished and elections were postponed for three years. By January 1953 the new men were clearly in exclusive control. Their central institution was the former free officers' executive committee, now known as the Revolutionary Command Council and presided over by Neguib. It attempted to provide itself with a popular basis by the first of the three attempts which were made in Nasser's lifetime to organize a single party—this time the Liberation Rally.

The leadership was not free from internal dissension. Neguib, more deeply influenced than the younger men by the habits of the previous regime and a less ardent revolutionary, continued to hope for the establishment of a reformed but traditional civilian government and for the return of the army to its professional duties. Eventually, in the spring of 1954, Nasser decided that Neguib, like Ali Maher, must be removed. His method was unusual. He drafted and secured the agreement of the R.C.C. to issue a proclamation announcing their adoption of Neguib's policy in its most extreme form: the restoration of political parties, elections to a constituent assembly within three months and the immediate surrender of the R.C.C.'s powers to this assembly. The result was to provoke demonstrations, organized by the Liberation Rally and backed by strikes, demanding the withdrawal of the proposals and the continuance of the revolution. The proclamation was withdrawn. Neguib retained the Presidency of the Republic (until he was deposed in November) but gave way to Nasser in the seat of effective power, the Presidency of the R.C.C. Not for the last time, Nasser had attained his objective by appearing to turn his back on it.

While Nasser was concentrating power in his own hands he was also working for the primary aim of the revolution, the ending of the British military presence which had lasted for seventy years. The removal of the monarchy with its historical claim to the Sudan made an Anglo-Egyptian settlement easier. It was reached in 1954, with an agreement that all British forces would be withdrawn by June 1956. The base, however, could be re-occupied if during the seven following years there should be an armed attack on any State member of the Arab collective security pact or on Turkey.

Nationalist opinion, in Egypt and in other Arab countries, was critical of this agreement. True, the British were leaving at last; but they had exacted a price which meant that Egypt was still tied to the Western alliance system. The revolt against the West had not reached its logical conclusion. It seemed indeed that the new regime was prepared to accept a measure of continuity

437

Overleaf: Suez. British press reports and (inset): British troops frisk Arabs in Port Said

with the foreign policy of its predecessors, and while loosening Egypt's ties with Britain to remain within the Western field of influence. The United States was the foreign Power on which the greatest hopes were placed in the first phase of the revolution.

This phase of Nasser's foreign policy came to an abrupt end in 1955, the decisive year for the determination of his future course. In February a treaty was concluded between Iraq and Turkey which became the basis of the Baghdad Pact to which Britain quickly adhered and with which the United States became associated. Somewhat paradoxically in the light of the terms of his own agreement with Britain, Nasser took strong exception to the Iraqi move. In so doing he helped to re-establish his own position with the intransigent nationalists, and to contrast himself in their eyes with the

CALL-UP PLANS
Three Navy
MOTHBALL
FLEET
ALERTED

THE Suez crisis is moving to a climax. Military and economic plans announced in London and Washington last night face Nasser with mounting pressure.

1. Britain is ready to call up 20,000 Class A Reservists, mostly fully trained Regulars and Korea veterans.

2. Three Royal Navy aircraft-carriers, with crack jet fighters, and a 10,000-ton cruiser are under sailing orders to take the call-up troops to the Mediterranean. Other ships may be taken out of mothballs. Earl Mountbatten, First Sea Lord, has postponed his visit to the Mediterranean and is remaining in London.

Sealed orders have been issued to captains of all naval vessels in Cyprus waters. They include the cruiser Jamaica, the carrier Eagle, and the fast minelayer Manxman.

Mr. Selwyn Lloyd, Foreign Secretary, told M.P.s that Britain's attitude is : " We mean business."

3. Mr. Dulles, U.S. Secretary of State, arrives in London today to join the three-Power talks. His visit, made at the request of President Eisenhower, who has been in direct touch with Sir Anthony Eden, means the Commons debate on Suez, due tonight, is postponed until tomorrow.

4. The United States "froze" all Suez Canal Company and Egyptian Government assets in America. Britain and France have already done this.

Prime Minister of Iraq, Nuri el-Said, the only contemporary Arab leader who was his match in political skill and force of character. Nasser was justified in the sense that his concessions to the British negotiators were given reluctantly whereas Nuri was positively seeking the protection of the West. But he was also conscious that he was gaining a major point in the contest between Cairo and Baghdad for influence in Syria, Jordan and Lebanon.

Four days after the Turco-Iraqi treaty, on 28 February, came another event impelling Nasser towards a preoccupation with pan-Arab politics. On that day David Ben Gurion signalized his return to office as Israel's Minister of Defence by launching an attack on an Egyptian military post near Gaza, which left forty Egyptian dead and many wounded. Since one of the aims of the revolution had been to strengthen the army, this was a humiliating

---

...aps some of the conse-... Eden's ...reaks the

States to use violence to secure their interests.

force of world opinion was great enough to influence Moscow.

Then Israel crossed the Egyptian

imperils every this message ha the blood of he

N CRISIS FO

Gaitskell demands an answer today

HOW will Sir Anthony Eden escape from the growing dilemma he is in as world opinion gathers to condemn the war he has started in Egypt?

Pressure by the Labour Party yesterday forced the Government to agree to a meeting of the House of Commons today, the first time Parliament has met on a Saturday since 1949.

Mr. Butler promised that the Prime Minister will be available to make a statement at noon. Sir Anthony will speak on BBC television and radio at o'clock tonight. Mr. Gaitskell may reply to him tomorrow night.

The world condemns

Can he, in view of the condemnation of world opinion and the mounting dignation in Britain, go on with the war in Egypt?

By 64 votes to five the General Assembly of the United Nations yesterday lered an immediate cease-fire and the recall of troops.

"Do you not realise," Mr. Gaitskell asked the Premier yesterday, "that t is a resolution which the Government, in all honour, is bound to ept?" Sir Anthony pleaded for time. He had not read the United Nations speeches. Later, when Mr. Butler had announced that the House would meet today, Mr. Gaitskell

FIVE MO

L TO

reverse. It led Nasser to intensify his effort to re-equip the armed forces; and when help was refused by the Western governments except on conditions which he found unacceptable, and which included a change in his attitude to the Baghdad Pact, he turned for the first time to the Soviet Union. In September he was able to announce to a cheering crowd an agreement with Czechoslovakia for the supply of arms.

The year 1955 also saw Nasser's first personal appearance on the international scene, leading the Egyptian delegation to the Afro-Asian conference in Bandung. Here he found himself in close contact with Nehru, whom he had already met and who was to influence him (though less profoundly than Tito) and with Chou En-lai, whom he came greatly to admire. He was accepted as the Arab spokesman for non-alignment, in opposition to the Foreign Minister of Iraq, and established his position as one of the doctrine's leading adherents.

Nasser's first move to the East did not prevent the American and British Governments from agreeing to participate in the financing of Egypt's major economic project, the High Dam at Assuan. But as evidence accumulated of further commitments to purchase arms from the Eastern bloc, and especially after Nasser established diplomatic relations with Peking, John Foster Dulles decided—with the concurrence of the British Government—that the offer should be withdrawn. The decision was announced in terms which took little account of Egyptian sensibility, still less of Nasser's, stressing as it did the weakness of Egypt's economy. To restore national pride had been the basic aim of the revolution, and an affront to it invariably left Nasser angry and with an impulse to retaliate. He did so on this occasion by nationalizing the Suez Canal Company, thus precipitating the crisis which raised him to the zenith of his career.

It is difficult in retrospect to understand the intensity of the emotions released in London and Paris by the nationalization of the company controlling the Suez Canal. The British Government lived in the shadow of Churchill and were hypnotized by the myth of Munich; Nasser was portrayed as another Hitler or Mussolini, bent on the destruction of vital British interests. The French similarly exaggerated the importance of Egyptian support for the Algerian rebellion. Together they decided to liberate the Canal by force, and to do it in association with the Israelis, who set themselves' the more realistic aims of ejecting the Egyptians from the Gaza strip and securing control over the seaway through the Gulf of Aqaba.

In the event the Israelis overran Sinai but the Anglo-French expedition was halted twenty-five miles south of Port Said, essentially by American pressure on London. All French and British forces were withdrawn by the end of the year, while the Israelis under further pressure from Washington finally completed their evacuation of the Sinai peninsula in March 1957. What had seemed an overwhelming threat was dispersed. Nasser emerged from the crisis with enhanced confidence and authority. The military weakness shown in the Sinai campaign was forgotten. His judgement and handling of political forces were vindicated, he had frustrated the hostile purposes of two major European Powers and of Israel, he was the hero of the Arab world.

The experiences of the long conspiratorial apprenticeship and of four eventful years in power had shaped and hardened the personality with which the world was to become familiar. His height, his massive build, his un-hurried movements, his habitual calm, all contributed to an immediate impression of assurance and authority. He spoke English fluently, received most of his foreign visitors alone, with neither interpreter nor secretary, and displayed a confident mastery of the subjects under discussion. He worked indefatigably and had retained the habit of reading; he kept English and American newspapers at his bedside, observing that he read them for the sport and the crime as well as for the politics. He had an insatiable appetite for detail. But the detail he found most absorbing was that con-tained in the intelligence reports which flowed steadily across his desk. He appeared to have more faith in information deviously obtained than in direct and open sources, to the detriment of his judgement of events and people.

He was inclined to trust men who shared his own history of underground conspiracy or who were engaged in some form of intelligence activity rather than those who thought in broader political terms. By his methods of rule he tended to de-politicize the government of Egypt. Even in the inner circle of his original companions, who were very gradually and never completely dispersed, political talent was not encouraged. One of the group, Zakaria Mohieddin, was an impressively effective Prime Minister for eleven months in 1965-66, but was not given a second opportunity.

Nasser's Egypt was a police-ridden society in which the expression of dissenting political opinion, in private as well as in public, was severely limited. Certainly Nasser was conscious of the need for some institutional link between the leadership and the people, if only to provide a channel through which he could be informed of the state of public opinion and through which his decisions could be transmitted and explained. The Liberation Rally was replaced by the National Union in 1957, and this in turn by the Arab Socialist Union five years later. Neither of the first two developed any spontaneous life. The third attempt was less unsuccessful because its establishment was associated with a complex of socialist measures and it had therefore a more definite ideological content.

It was not until after his return from Bandung that Nasser began to speak in terms of socialism. The first major impetus towards a socialist economy was given by the Egyptianization of British and French interests in 1956. Other measures followed until in 1961 virtually the whole of industry, mining and foreign commerce was brought under State ownership or control. At the same time private shareholdings and incomes generally were subjected to the same kind of limitation as had already been imposed on the ownership of agricultural land. Once again there were political as well as economic and social motives, and later in the same year the property of 850 'reactionary' families was sequestered as a further precaution against counter-revolution.

Most of those who suffered from these measures had contacts abroad, and their grievances influenced the international image of revolutionary Egypt. Less has been heard of the positive aspects of the regime's social policy and its beneficiaries. The mass of Egyptians continue to live in extreme poverty, and many measures directed at raising the standard of living are blunted by the high rate of population growth. (The population of Egypt has increased by sixty per cent since the revolution.) Probably the revolution's most important social achievement has been the provision of basic amenities in the villages—more schools, easier access to medical services, piped water—together with the rationalization of peasant micro-farming by centrally guided co-operatives. The urban workers benefited similarly from improved services, and also from minimum wage legislation which was easier to enforce in the towns than in the countryside. The attempt to establish tolerable social conditions for an increasing proportion of the workers and peasants was a constant aim, and despite Nasser's political preoccupations he never underestimated the importance of this task or lost his awareness of the poor man's daily problems. The strength of his hold on the common people, his enduring personal ascendancy, owed much to their feeling that he had not altogether ceased to be one of them.

During these middle years of his rule, Nasser was increasingly concerned with Arab affairs beyond the borders of Egypt. His triumph in 1956 had raised his prestige throughout the Arab world to a height far beyond that of any other modern Arab leader. In the eyes of the Arab peoples he was a symbol of national resurgence, social modernization, defiance of the 'imperialists', rejection of Israel and above all Arab self-respect. Through Cairo's powerful radio system he could exert his influence directly on public opinion and oblige Governments to seek his endorsement. It was a position of unique authority, but at the same time it made him a prisoner. For in order not to forfeit his reputation and the power it gave him he accepted responsibilities which were beyond the strength of Egypt and which finally led Egypt to disaster.

The first of these prestige-induced blunders was the union with Syria. Nasser did not want it, but when at the beginning of 1958 political and military leaders from Damascus insisted that he alone could save Syria from becoming a satellite of Russia or the West, he saw no alternative to accepting the challenge and creating the United Arab Republic. It lasted for three and a half years, and broke up because the Egyptians who exercised authority in Syria tended instinctively to treat the country as a colony. The secessionist coup in September 1961 was, Nasser said shortly afterwards, 'one of the bitterest moments of my life'. Until his death Egypt retained the title of the United Arab Republic, thus avoiding the humiliation of accepting a simple return to the *status quo ante* and emphasizing her continued readiness to accept union with other Arab States. Characteristically Nasser told me at this time that he had always felt uneasy when he was obliged to take decisions relating to Syria because he could not, as he could in Egyptian affairs, visualize exactly what his verdict would mean in practice.

Within a year of the Syrian secession Nasser was confronted with another test of his pan-Arab credentials. In September 1962 an officers' coup against the Imam of the Yemen partially misfired. The Imam escaped from his capital to the territory of loyal tribes and appealed for help to Saudi Arabia. The revolutionaries turned to Nasser for support, and once again he faced the fact that a refusal could do incalculable damage to his image and therefore his authority in the Arab world. He sent some air force units in the first instance, but was obliged to follow them with ground forces and was gradually drawn into a deeper and deeper involvement. The civil war lasted for five years, and at its height the Egyptian expeditionary force is believed to have numbered 70,000. Nasser ruefully described the situation as 'my Vietnam', and he was still committed there when the third Arab-Israel war broke out in June 1967.

Once more Nasser was obeying the Arab imperative. The crisis of 1967 developed out of incidents on Israel's frontiers with Jordan and Syria, reaching a climax on 7 April when Israeli fighters shot down six Syrian planes and flew over Damascus before returning home. A Jordanian newspaper summarized the widespread criticism of Egypt's passivity in this period. 'What has Cairo done,' it asked, 'in the face of this flagrant air aggression on Damascus, the Syrian capital?' Egypt, it was said, was sheltering behind the United Nations Emergency Force which had been stationed in Sinai in the aftermath of the war of 1956.

In May Nasser moved troops into Sinai and demanded the withdrawal of the U.N. posts from the frontier. The Secretary-General decided that he had no alternative but to comply with the host country's wishes. In principle this was correct, but it has been reasonably argued that it was not necessary to act so precipitately and that it was almost perverse of U Thant to insist that if U.N.E.F. left the frontier it must be withdrawn altogether. This meant that no attempt was made to prevent or delay the return to Egyptian control of the fortified post of Sharm al-Shaikh which commanded the Straits of Tiran and from which Israel's maritime communications east of Suez could therefore be severed. With Sharm al-Shaikh in his hands again, Nasser was faced yet again with the same question: as the leader of the Arabs, what was he expected to do? He announced a blockade of Israel. It was, he observed, 'one of the things our Arab brothers had always insisted on'. It was also Israel's *casus belli*.

The evidence for Nasser's state of mind at this time is not altogether conclusive. It seems certain on the one hand that he had no intention of attacking Israel, but on the other that he realized he was running the risk of provoking an Israeli offensive. Probably he was deluded by his own mythical version of the events of 1956 into believing that without the support of powerful allies Israel would hesitate to initiate hostilities, and that if she did the fighting would be stopped by the United Nations before too much damage was done. At any rate he was prepared to co-operate with the United States in the search for a peaceful resolution of the crisis; emissaries sent urgently to Cairo by President Johnson obtained his agreement that Zakaria Mohieddin would arrive in Washington on 7 June to pursue this negotiation.

Was it the news of this agreement, reached on 2 June, that precipitated the Israeli Government's decision, taken late on the following day, to launch their attack on the 5th? It seems highly probable.

In the early hours of the 5th Nasser's air force was almost totally destroyed on the ground. The destruction of his army, left without defence against attack from the air in the arid wastes of Sinai, followed inevitably and swiftly. The Security Council did play its anticipated part in calling for a cease-fire, but by that time the whole of Sinai was overrun and the Israelis were established on the eastern bank of the Canal.

Faced with total defeat, Nasser had to confront his people. He spoke to them, on television and radio, on the evening of the 9th, accepting responsibility for the disaster and announcing that he was resigning the Presidency in favour of Zakaria Mohieddin. The effect of this speech was dramatic. People who had been listening in their houses or in the cafés poured on to the streets in thousands and began to make their way towards Nasser's residence, demanding that he reverse his decision. A Minister trying to reach him was mistaken for Mohieddin and manhandled by the crowd. On the following morning Nasser went to the National Assembly and withdrew his resignation.

Recalling his tactics in the dispute with Neguib thirteen years before, many observers concluded that the resignation was a manoeuvre and that Nasser never doubted its outcome. The facts that he neither consulted Mohieddin before making the announcement nor permitted him to broadcast his refusal of the Presidency lend credence to this view. It is also clear that district leaders of the A.S.U. played a part in organizing the demonstration. On the other hand the organized groups were swamped by the much larger spontaneous demonstration, and Nasser could not have been certain that this would happen. The people of Cairo had renewed his mandate; whatever his responsibility might be for the situation in which they found themselves, his leadership seemed more than ever indispensable.

National defeat was followed by private sorrow. Nasser's closest friend before and after the revolution was Abdul Hakim Amer, who had been directly and uninterruptedly responsible for the armed forces since 1953. Dismissed after the six-day war, he allowed himself to be involved in a military conspiracy, was arrested and committed suicide.

There were other symptoms of unrest after the defeat, principally among the university students in 1968 (the year of world-wide student revolt). But in the main the regime was remarkably stable in adversity, and its prestige remained high in the Arab countries. The revolutions of 1969 in the Sudan and Libya followed the Egyptian pattern, and their leaders turned to Cairo for support and guidance.

Nevertheless the situation was evidently critical, and it led Nasser to concentrate power still further in his own hands; successively he took over the positions of Prime Minister and Secretary-General of the A.S.U., thereby hastening his death. It was in 1968 that his health began to give rise to anxiety, and in the following year he had a first heart attack. Both Russian and Egyptian doctors urged him to reduce his working hours and lead a more relaxed life, but it was not in his nature to do so.

The military situation after the cease fire, continuing Israeli occupation of a part of the national territory and the need to replace the vast quantities of arms destroyed or captured obliged Nasser to draw closer to the Soviet Union. And when continued sporadic fighting along the Canal led to Israeli raids into the interior of Egypt, the Russians assumed a measure of res-

ponsibility for the country's air defences. The trend towards closer association with the Soviet Union had continued since 1955, Russian aid being
given not only in the military field but also for economic development and
in particular for the High Dam where it was able to exploit the Western
refusal. At the same time Nasser had remained committed to the ideology
of non-alignment, and at the United Nations General Assembly of 1960 had
taken his place with Nehru and Tito as one of the leaders of the third world.
Now in 1968 he bitterly disappointed Tito by remaining silent when the
Russians invaded Czechoslovakia.

Nevertheless, though his ability to manoeuvre was diminishing, Nasser
never lost his determination to avoid any irrevocable commitment to either
East or West. His overriding aim in the last years was the recovery of the
occupied territory, and he knew that there was no immediate possibility
of this except through American influence. Less than five months before
his death he addressed an appeal to President Nixon: 'Despite all that has
happened we have not closed the door finally with the U.S.A.' Everything
would depend on the American attitude to Israel 'I inform President Nixon
that we have reached a decisive moment in Arab-American relations—either
we will be estranged forever or there will be a new, serious and definite
start.' The tone is desperate, but it is not that of a committed Soviet satellite.

On 27 September 1970 Nasser acted for the last time as an arbiter of Arab
affairs, presiding over a conference held in Cairo to terminate the conflict
between King Hussein of Jordan and the Palestinian guerrillas. On the
following day, after saying goodbye at the airport to one of his guests, he
suffered the heart attack which killed him within a few hours. It was Anwar
Sadat, who had been the first to tell the Egyptian people of the revolution
eighteen years before, who told them now that Nasser was dead. The funeral
was attended by Heads of State, Heads of Government and high-ranking
representatives from many Governments, but the procession in which they
were to walk never took place. The dense crowds, swollen by tens of thousands from outside the city, broke through the barriers and pressed in on
the cortege. As in June 1967, the people claimed him for their own.

Dr Dekmejian's book, *Egypt under Nasir*, contains the judgement
that 'among the charismatic leaders of the neutralist bloc who
emerged after World War Two, Nasir was perhaps the most successful
in re-ordering the social-political life of his country'. His achievement might have been greater if less of his attention had been diverted into
other fields and if he had given a higher priority to slowing down the growth
of population. He succeeded nevertheless in reducing inequality and therefore increasing social stability, and in accelerating the movement towards
a modern economy. The accompanying destruction of the diverse and
sophisticated if corrupt political life of Farouk's Egypt entailed both loss
and gain. For the politically minded middle class it meant a loss of freedom,
but at the same time the working masses gained a new sense of participation
in public affairs. The nation became more conscious of itself, and Egypt
acquired a greater significance in Middle Eastern and in world politics than
it had previously possessed.

Index

INDEX

PHOTO ACKNOWLEDGEMENTS

Mary Evans Picture Library, 10

Popperfoto, 11, 75, 90, 104, 125, 150, 278, 288-9, 336-7, 338, 379

Radio Times Hulton Picture Library, 26-7, 34-5, 114, 117, 138-9, 140, 272, 299

Keystone, 36, 98, 102-3, 108, 122-3, 175, 191, 197, 198, 219, 296-7, 304-5, 306, 307, 313, 316-7, 352-3, 363, 370, 376-7, 393-4, 395, 407, 408-9, 413, 415, 422, 427, 430-1

Associated Press, 45, 238-9, 241
Camera Press, 55, 56, 66-7, 68-9
Conway Picture Library, 57, 105, 115, 124, 141, 152-3, 154, 160, 172-3, 174, 204, 214, 215, 240, 266-7, 270-1, 290, 320-1, 322, 323, 326-7, 330-1, 360-1, 362, 367, 371, 378, 389, 411, 412, 415, 426-7, 432, 433

Mansell Collection, 66, 67, 226-7

Topix, 76

BPC/IWM, 82-3
Fox Photos, 88-9
Conway/Evening Standard, 91
John Hillelson/Eric Salomon, 91
Novosti, 130, 131, 232-3, 233
National Army Museum, 144, 145
Syndication International, 164-5
United Press International, 212-3, 344-5, 415
Press Association, 279